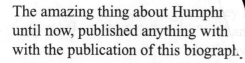

The amazing thing about Humphrey Bogart's early life is that no one has, until now, published anything with any meat in it. All of that changed with the publication of this biography by Darwin Porter.
—*Joseph Mosbach*

In 1980, Darwin Porter inherited a vast but disorganized archive that had been compiled over a period of 50 years by eyewitnesses to the Jazz-Age shenanigans of Humphrey Bogart. Enriching it with information from players who either loved or hated Bogart (or both), Porter has distilled this treasure trove of historic data into one blockbuster of a Hollywood read.
—*Danforth Prince*

Darwin Porter reveals the full story of what was really under that trench coat.
—*Use-It*

Read about all the stuff that Bogie never told Lauren Bacall.
—*Outrage*

This biography is required reading for studies about Hollywood during the 1930s.
—*Lothian*

Porter's bio emerges as a brilliant, insightful portrait of Bogie, using material never published about him before. It gives a glitzy overview of Hollywood when its future legends were getting drunk, banging each other in odd couplings, switchhitting, ruining their lives and those of others, and creating the personalities that still intrigue us decades later.
—*What's New in Biography*

There's more life and erotic adventure in *The Secret Life of Humphrey Bogart* than in a shelf of other movie-star biographies.
—*X-TRA!*

This is the stuff of gossipy legend. A detailed, fascinating portrait of the years in Bogie's life before he became really famous—his pre-*Casablanca,* pre-Bacall, pre-*African Queen* years.
—*La Noche*

A volcanic and unflinching portrait of a complex, provocative, fascinating man caught with his jockey shorts down.
—*La Movida*

At last! A biography of what Bogie was doing as a young man. Many of his cult followers only know him from *Casablanca* and the 'Bogie and Baby' years with Lauren Bacall. This never-before-told story reveals that America's favorite actor actually had a past, set with intensity against the backdrop of Broadway and Hollywood during the Jazz Age.
—*George S. Mills*

Unexpected revelations about the screen's greatest star.
—*Cruiser*

In this riveting bio of the young, hot and horny Bogie, Porter defangs the myths.
—*Hinnerk*

There is no finer behind-the-scenes depiction of Hollywood during the debut of the Talkies. Darwin Porter carves a razor-sharp portrait of a time and place that gay director George Cukor defined as "our *Belle Époque.*"
—*Queer Biz*

In this, the first of an ongoing series about Humphrey Bogart, Darwin Porter uses the life of the most celebrated movie star of the 20th century as a vehicle for an eyewitness account of Broadway and Hollywood during Prohibition. It reveals a behind-the-scenes look at Bogie himself—a man whose early life has, until now, been shrouded in mystery.
—*Between the Covers*

An awesome piece of research and reportage drawn from the murky depths of the secret closets of Hollywood.
—*James Stafford*

Even for confirmed heterosexuals, Hollywood was ever so gay back in its Golden Age, as this riveting bio reveals. I loved every page.

—Kathryn Cobb

This epitome of American *machismo*, Humphrey Bogart has been hidden behind the shadows of his image. This extraordinary biography unmasks the man behind the myth.

—Siegessaule

This is not just a biography of Bogie during his young and promiscuous 20s and 30s. It's an evocative portrait of the Hollywood stars of the early Talkies. They're here: Spencer Tracy, Bette Davis, Joan Crawford, Tallulah Bankhead, and about 45 others whose activities off the screen were a hell of a lot more interesting than the movie characters they portrayed.

—Fab Magazine

The mystery and glamour of the Golden Age of Hollywood lives again in this extraordinary tale of Bogie and his women. Like the good biographer he is, Darwin Porter makes Bogie and the other players of his era live again.

—Time Out for Books

The Secret Life of Humphrey Bogart pumps flesh and blood—as well as love, jealousy, hatred, blackmail, intrigue, and violence—into our understanding of the Golden Age.

—Gab

Humphrey Bogart was voted the Top Star of the 20th Century. Was he really a tough guy, or a "cream puff" as Judy Garland later referred to him in private?

—Sortie

The Gods bestow their gifts at random, and They decided to give Bogie equal doses of good and bad luck. He paid a terrible price when They decreed that he was to die early of cancer. But, as compensation, They granted him immortality. Darwin Porter in this masterly biography provides the greatest insight yet of the young man, Humphrey Bogart, before he became "Bogie" the legend.

—Books Today

A juicy saga of this film icon's love affairs.
—*Esther Phillips*

This is the most definitive—and most shocking—tale about the secret life of Humphrey Bogart ever written. Bogie had a lot to be secretive about. —*Joan Blourer*

Bogart was no hero, and he belted a few women in his day. And he was known to run from a fight. But what a hell of a guy he was! Darwin Porter tells everything.
—*Nat og Dag*

Steamy reading, pulling no punches, *The Secret Life of Humphrey Bogart* describes the romantic trysts of the private man. Every chapter is loaded with new insights into Bogie.
—*Advance Reviews*

This biography covers Bogart's early years on Broadway and in Hollywood. No wonder Bogie in later life never wanted to talk about it.
—*Angles*

This is the provocative story of young Bogart's odyssey at the advent of talking pictures. It's based on heretofore unpublished memoirs, letters, diaries, and personal interviews from the women—and the men—who loved him. There are also revelations from colleagues, ex-friends, and jilted lovers who wanted him to burn in hell.
—*Stanford Bylines*

The Secret Life of
Humphrey Bogart
The Early Years
(1899-1931)

Darwin Porter

The Georgia Literary Associaition
75 Saint Marks Place
Staten Island, NY 10301
www.GeorgiaLit.com

Humphrey Bogart
1899-1957

ALSO BY DARWIN PORTER:

Hollywood's Silent Closet
Midnight in Savannah
Butterflies in Heat
Razzle-Dazzle
Blood Moon
Rhinestone Country
Marika
Venus
And many of the ***Frommer Guides*** to Europe, The Caribbean, and parts
of North America

The Secret Life of Humphrey Bogart:
The Early Years (1899-1931)

Copyright 2003, The Georgia Literary Association
First Edition published in the summer of 2003

ISBN 0-9668030-5-1

See our website at www.GeorgiaLit.com
Contact us at GeorgiaLit@aol.com

Photos courtesy of Photofest, New York City (PhotofestNYC.com)
and other sources
Cover art by SylvesterQ.com

MEMORIA

More than 20 years ago, I made a promise to fulfill the dream of two men, Kenneth MacKenna (1899-1962), and my long-term life partner Stanley Mills Haggart (1910-1980). The dream of these very close friends, who had lived together during an eighteen-month period in the 1930s, involved writing a biography of Humphrey Bogart.

They originally envisioned it in the 1930s, after Bogie's success in *The Petrified Forest*. By 1946, when Bogart was firmly established as a star, Stanley had already compiled an impressive roster of notes which he continued to amplify, based on dialogues with participants in the Bogart myth, for the next thirty years.

In 1980, dying of cancer in a New York City hospital, Stanley asked me to finish the book that he had begun researching nearly a half-century before. Among the material he left me were eleven cardboard boxes of data.

The core of this book, therefore, derives from the treasure trove of information gathered and recorded by Stanley during his collaboration with Kenneth. It was supplemented with interviews and with information gathered personally by me. Like a tapestry, it incorporates memories and nostalgia from a wide spectrum of sources, some of them hostile to Bogart, some of them raptly enamored with his memory. It is as accurate and factual an account as I can provide based on material that was experienced and/or collected by other people, in some cases long before I was born, and filtered through progressive recitations and repetitions. This acknowledgement is meant to honor them.

During their time together in Hollywood, Kenneth MacKenna was Bogie's only confidant. Always friends, but sometimes rivals, Bogie and Kenneth both married, in 1928 and 1938, respectively, the same woman, Broadway stage actress Mary Philips. For the copious anecdotes that Kenneth related to Stanley, as recorded in the early drafts of this biography, we're profoundly grateful. Kenneth's dialogues with Stanley about Kenneth's former wife, Kay Francis, were especially startling, as were the stories Bogie told Kenneth about his friend, Spencer Tracy.

Stanley Haggart's mother, Maria Jane Haggart, worked in the office of Broadway showman and theatrical entrepreneur, William Brady Sr., and became friends with his daughter, Alice Brady, and his second wife, Grace George, both famous actresses of their day. For her sometimes enraptured recitation of anecdotes about the Broadway stage in the 20s, and Bogart's role within it. I am deeply grateful to Maria Jane. She was also a friend of Humphrey's parents, Maud and Belmont Bogart, occasionally visiting them at their summer home on the shoreline of Canandaigua Lake in western New York State.

Both Kenneth MacKenna and Stanley Haggart were privileged to know, rather intimately, Bill Brady Jr., Bogie's boyhood friend, and Stuart Rose, Bogart's brother-in-law through Bogart's sister, Frances. Both of these men provided generous information about Bogie's teen years, and about Bogie in his twenties.

Stanley was also friends with three of Bogie's wives: Helen Menken, Mary Philips, and Mayo Methot. Likewise, Stanley interviewed many of the people who went to school with Bogie and who served with him during his brief but unhappy stint in the U.S. Navy during the closing days of World War I.

Stanley's data, and later anecdotes he relayed to me orally, were particularly revealing about Bogie's involvement with Edmund Lowe and his wife, Lilyan Tashman, and about the sometimes peculiar habits and priorities of George O'Brien and Charles Farrell. Stanley was intimately involved with all four stars.

Much of the data that's relayed in this biography about Howard Hughes originated with Randolph Scott. Scott had been Stanley Haggart's close friend and roommate before Scott broke off his relationship with Stanley and moved in with Cary Grant. But during his time with Stanley, Scott was relentlessly forthcoming with information about Hollywood insiders, relaying anecdotes about both Hughes and another of his lovers, Gary Cooper. Scott never dreamed that his revelations would eventually appear in print, but in consideration of the light they shed on some of America's cultural icons, we respectfully acknowledge his role in the compilation of this book. In fairness to Scott, it must be said that he would have been horrified to learn that some of his revelations had been printed.

Other information in this biography emerged from my own talks and associations with stars of the theater and screen during the decades I devoted to collecting and compiling insiderish information about their lives. I spent long, boozy evenings with Joan Crawford, Tallulah Bankhead, Bette Davis, and dozens of lesser icons. I'm especially grateful to Joan Blondell, who lived in my house in New York City during the summer of 1974. During our time together, she relayed enough material to fill many volumes about Warner Brothers and the intimate lives of its stars during the 1930s. She was particularly revealing about Glenda Farrell, her best friend.

There are countless others to thank, including Eric Linden, one of Stanley's best friends. Philippe de Lacy was particularly helpful, especially with insights into Mary Pickford, as was James Kirkwood, Jr., co-author of *A Chorus Line*. Jay Garon, the literary agent for John Grisham, supplied much information about director George Cukor during the year and a half he lived with the director.

I am especially grateful to the legendary Mercedes de Acosta, whom I met late in her life. Sometimes I saw her three times a week at her apartment in New York City, when she'd talk for hours about her life, including the parts she didn't reveal in her autobiography, *Here Lies the Heart*. She was especially helpful in providing information about Greta Garbo, Marlene Dietrich, Helen Menken, and many, many others.

Gratitude is extended to the memory of George Raft. Stanley and I met him in London at the Colony Club, when he was 71 years old, and when we were composing copy for an early edition of *The Frommer Guides*. Later, we renewed our dialogues with him in Los Angeles. He provided rich and nuanced insights into Bogie, especially as regards Bogie's interchanges with Molly O'Day, Howard Hughes, Gary Cooper, Texas Guinan, Mae West, and Billie Dove. He also relayed till-then unknown secrets about his life with a then-undiscovered Rudolph Valentino when they were both gigolos in New York City, sometimes simultaneously servicing the same clients.

Others who contributed their recollections to this biography included Mae West in interviews conducted in her Los Angeles apartment; Louise Brooks during some exceptionally candid conversations in Rochester, New York; Shirley Booth, who appeared on stage with Bogie in *Hell's Bells,* and Ruth Gordon, who had an affair with Bogie during their joint appearance in *Saturday's Children.* Ms. Gordon was especially frank in her insights about her onetime friend, Spencer Tracy.

A very special thank you is extended to the aristocratic-looking actress Eleanor Boardman, who once allowed me to invade her San Bernardino home for a long weekend. The "most outspoken woman in Hollywood" was particularly vivid in describing an almost pornographic scene involving Bogart at a "farewell-to-Hollywood" party thrown for him by Lilyan Tashman.

Especially helpful was the dearly beloved John Springer, deceased in November of 2001, the most extraordinary and sought-after Hollywood press agent of the 20th century. Clients who considered him their friend (and for whom he sometimes went way, way beyond the demands of his job description) included Bette Davis, Joan Crawford, Myrna Loy, Mary Pickford, Lana Turner, Ginger Rogers, Marlene Dietrich, Grace Kelly, Rosalind Russell, Gary Cooper, Henry Fonda, Robert Mitchum, Montgomery Clift, David Selznick, Samuel Goldwyn, and, lest we forget, Walt Disney. Although in public Springer never revealed the secrets of the stars, he had a lot to say about them in private.

To all these people (may they rest in peace), and to many others not mentioned here, I am profoundly grateful.

Darwin Porter
New York City, 2003

The author dedicates this book to Danforth Prince

About the Author:

Darwin Porter, one of the most prolific writers in publishing today, has keenly observed the Hollywood scene since he worked as an entertainment columnist for *The Miami Herald* at the tender age of 20.

He specializes in sagas, many of them brutal, all of them artful, showcasing some aspect of the social history of America during the 20th century. Many of his insights draw upon extensive interviews with eyewitnesses to events, relationships, and imbroglios that Hollywood publicists worked hard to suppress. His writing is not for the prudish, the squeamish, or the fainthearted. His observations about Hollywood tend to be ballsy, edgy, satirical, and charming, But despite their sensationalism, they're grounded in fact. In many cases, they've never been revealed to the general public before, making them valuable to librarians, archivists, scholars, and latterday fans.

Recent works by Darwin Porter have included *Hollywood's Silent Closet,* which a London-based critic defined as "a brilliant primer" for the *Who's Who* of early filmmaking. Based on interviews with eyewitnesses during the final years of their lives, *Hollywood's Silent Closet* presents a steamy but accurate portrait, set between 1919 and 1926, of the gossipy world of pre-Talkie Hollywood, which had a lot to be silent about, and where many of the sins were never depicted on the screen. Porter is also the author of *Rhinestone Country,* a gritty exploration of the country-western music industry and closeted lives south of the Mason-Dixon line, and *Blood Moon,* an "artfully brutal" novel about power, money, sex, love, religion, and obsession. One Nashville-based critic described it as "an IMAX spectacle about the power of male beauty, with red-hot icons, a breathless climax, and erotica akin to Anaïs Nin on Viagra with a bump of meth."

Aside from his writing about Hollywood and the entertainment industry, Porter is the highly visible co-author of more than 800 editions of the **Frommer Travel Guides** to destinations that include most of Europe, the Caribbean, the Carolinas, and Georgia. When not traveling, which is rare, he lives in New York City.

The Georgia Literary Association

is a private enterprise that's devoted to the production and distribution of provocative and stimulating entertainment for worldly, sexually sophisticated 21st-century readers. We specialize in biographies, info-novels, social satires, and potboilers about the history of the Arts in America, with a special emphasis on the history and backlot intrigues of the Entertainment Industry.

We were established in Washington, Georgia, in 1997, by professional journalists with links to *The New York Times* and *The Miami Herald*. For many years, about 80% of our day-to-day activities have involved writing, researching and updating annual or bi-annual editions of many of *The Frommer Guides,* North America's most comprehensive and most widely read travel guides. Our long-term involvement with Frommer has been fruitful, fulfilling, and productive, for the most part focusing on the travel scenes in Europe, The Caribbean, Georgia, and The Carolinas.

We pride ourselves on linking literary craftsmanship with popular, mass-market tastes. But because of their nonstandard themes and preconceptions, some of our books might not be endorsed by larger, more conservative publishing companies, including many located in the Deep South.

But despite our irreverence, we retain a profound respect for the distinguished literary history (and the sometimes tormented social history) of Georgia. Some of our titles have reflected the ironies and irrationalities of that state and its distinctive blend of love, loyalty, betrayal, repression, wounded pride, and hatred. But as our company has evolved, we've moved away from exclusively Southern issues into broader terrain.

Today, our primary ambition revolves around literary treatments of information that's derived from living eyewitnesses, many of them now in their 70s and 80s, about the history of Hollywood. And as their tales are compiled into commercially viable biographies and "info-novels," we're confronting increasing numbers of older eyewitnesses who seem passionate about transmitting their observations, experiences, and gossip—some of it salacious, most of it fascinating—to new generations of Americans.

We're proud to bring this unusual biography of Humphrey Bogart—the best on the market today—to your attention. Thanks for your interest. We wish you good fortune and joy in the pursuit of your reading.

Sincere best wishes,
The Georgia Literary Association (www.GeorgiaLit.com)

The Georgia Literary Association: Bringing you the kind of entertainment you wouldn't necessarily expect from the Deep South.

Chapter One

It was an idyllic setting, a picture postcard of Victorian life that still thrived in America before its last vestiges were swept away by the coming of the Great War.

Ever since the final summer of the nineteenth century, handsome Dr. Belmont DeForest Bogart, and his successful artist wife, Maud, with her frizzy red hair and strong jaw, had come to a manicured spot on the shoreline of Lake Canandaigua in New York State's Finger Lakes to relax and go sailing on his deluxe yacht, *Comrade*, moored just two hundred feet from their gingerbread-decorated, two-floor Victorian manse.

A local brewer, Jonathan Mulhouse, had built the house in 1871 for his rotund wife and their equally hefty brood of six very fat children. Although Mulhouse himself looked like a lean and mean Abraham Lincoln, his children resembled his blubber wife more than they did himself. The Mulhouse family was the scandal of Seneca Point. The children were ridiculed for their weight and for a physical deformity inherited from Mrs. Mulhouse. None of the brood had a neck. Locals called them the "no-neck Mulhouses." This genetic flaw also didn't come from Mr. Mulhouse, who had one of the longest necks east of the Mississippi.

The ridiculous appearance of the Mulhouses was not the only subject of local gossip. Rumor had it Mrs. Mulhouse allowed all her children to drink beer from her husband's brewery even though they were underage.

It had been with a sigh of relief that neighbors learned in 1899 that a New York doctor and his wife had taken over the Mulhouse home. "To judge from the size of Mr. Bogart's yacht moored on the lake, I think they are rich New Yorkers," the Mayor, Frank Schmidt, proudly announced at a private dinner of the Chamber of Commerce. "From what I hear, the Bogarts are a most respectable family."

The arrival of the Bogarts at Canandaigua and their departure every Labor Day was considered a news event to be reported in *The Canandaigua Gazette*.

On a particularly lovely summer afternoon in July 5, 1913, the spire of the tower room of the Bogart home still stood proudly after the Fourth of July fireworks. The lawns sweeping down to the lake were immaculately trimmed.

The crops were at full bloom in the adjoining farmlands, and cows grazed in the surrounding pasturelands. Even the woods seemed quiet except for a young farmhand sneaking into the darkest part of the forest with one of the local wives whose husband was in New York on a business trip. From his bedroom window, the teenage son, Humphrey, nicknamed, "Hump," looked out at the weeping willows that fluttered in the wind so gracefully that their movements seemed to be

1

the work of a choreographer.

When Maud had first seen the fluttery willows and a bubbling brook running alongside their property, she'd dubbed their new home "Willow Brook." She set about to furnish it with crystal, tapestries, classical statues, precious china, antiques, and Oriental carpets.

The Bogarts' neighbors were invariably from Boston or New York, and they'd come to Seneca Point, a rich community directly south of Canandaigua, to escape from the blistering summer heat of those two cities. Wealthy businessmen hobnobbed with bankers, newspaper columnists, presidents of colleges, and even a well-cared-for clergyman who was said to drink five bottles of wine a day.

It was at Seneca Point that young Hump first met two men called the Warner Brothers. They were not the brothers who built a powerful Hollywood studio that would bring Hump his greatest fame, when he was no longer called "Hump" but "Bogie." These Warner Brothers, Henry and David, designed and constructed steamboats, including some showboats that sailed up and down the Mississippi.

Even more fascinating were another pair of brothers, Frank and Arthur Hamlin, who lived next door to the Bogarts. Their father was the local banker. Ever since Hump rescued Arthur from the lake when the youngster fell off the dock, the Hamlins had told Hump he could consider "our house your second home."

Although Hump enjoyed playing games with the boys, he mostly liked coming over to visit their mother, Mary Hamlin, in the afternoons where she gave him rich pastries and told him of her life in the theater.

She wrote religious dramas which played across the country. It wasn't Hump's type of drama but he loved listening to her stories about life in the theater. She knew all the great actors of her day and confided the most intimate stories about their personal lives.

"It's a world of make-believe," she told Hump. "You can lose yourself in the world of the theater." Mary urged Hump and his playmates to launch an impromptu theater at the lakeshore near the bandstand, setting up their own summer playhouse.

Until meeting Mary, Hump had never considered being an actor. When it was first suggested to him, he told Mary that it wasn't his kind of thing. "Father wants me to be a surgeon, but I'd rather be a sailor."

In time, breaking from religious dramas, Mary Hamlin would write *Alexander Hamilton*, a play that became a hit on Broadway. Warner Brothers, Hump's future studio, purchased the rights to it and filmed it in 1931. The movie became one of the most successful talkies of that time.

In his bedroom, a noise distracted Hump, who went to look out the rear of his window, from which he had a good view of the carriage road that ran over a one-lane stone-built bridge at the rear of their manse.

Their cook was receiving a load of fresh produce from a local farmer. From a horse-pulled carriage, he could see the unloading of the largest, ripest beefsteak tomatoes he'd ever seen, along with peaches, potatoes, carrots, and grapes so fresh that the aroma of the vineyard rose to his second-floor open window. Maud always insisted that she get "only the best" of the local bounty before it was shipped off to the stifling city markets of New York City or Philadelphia.

Seneca Point in those days was a staunchly Republican enclave even though only that summer, a young Democrat, Franklin Delano Roosevelt, had arrived, ostensibly on what he'd told his cronies was a "hunting expedition." The daughters of the prosperous families of Seneca Point were said to have produced the loveliest single concentration of "female pulchritude" this side of Broadway. Roosevelt became enamored of one young belle, Beth Ferguson, whom he invited every afternoon to the lake for swimming. It was while showing off his prowess as a swimmer that Roosevelt had been stricken with a stomach cramp. When Beth saw his right arm go up into the air and then her boyfriend go under, she thought he was playing another one of his many tricks on her. Since meeting her, he'd always chided her for being so gullible. At first she'd thought that he was only pretending to be drowning. When he didn't surface for a while, she grew panicky and screamed for help.

The family of Dwight St. Davids was having a picnic nearby along the shores of the lake. Beth screamed to them to rescue Roosevelt. Their youngest son, Peter, was home for the holidays from Princeton. Sensing what was wrong, Peter, an expert swimmer, dived into the cold lake and swam toward Roosevelt. Peter went underwater and emerged with Roosevelt gasping for air. Peter brought the body ashore and called for his other family members to help him carry the body to the nearby Bogart home.

When Dr. Belmont Bogart came out onto his front verandah, he encountered what he thought was a dead victim of drowning. He rushed to give the young man medical attention.

The commotion attracted the rest of the Bogart family. Hump, Maud, and the two daughters, Catherine and Frances, also came out onto the porch. They looked in horror as Belmont seemingly brought life back to the victim. When young Roosevelt was breathing properly once again, Belmont ordered that he be taken upstairs and put in Hump's bed.

Laid to rest on the soft bed upstairs, Roosevelt fell into a deep coma-like sleep. Belmont ordered Hump to stay in the room with the recovering victim in case he should experience a turn for the worse. "Make sure that he's breathing all right," Belmont said before heading downstairs to join Maud.

Hump resented spending the rest of the afternoon and evening guarding Roosevelt. A surly Irish maid arrived with a tray of food for his supper. She plopped down the tray telling him, "Eat it if you don't want to starve."

"I don't like turnips," Hump protested.

"Then throw the bloody things out the window," the maid said before going out and slamming the door.

With those turnips still uneaten on his plate, Hump had fallen asleep somewhere during the middle of the night. Before nodding off, he'd checked on

Roosevelt. The young man was snoring loudly.

The following morning, it had been Roosevelt who awakened Hump. The doctor and Maud had departed on a shopping expedition, and had left Hump to have breakfast alone with Roosevelt after the doctor had examined him and had pronounced him fit.

Roosevelt appeared to be in his late twenties or even early thirties. It had been over the breakfast table where Hump finally got his favorite dish—ham and eggs—that he'd begun to learn who their mysterious guest was.

Even though innocent at the time, Hump soon realized that Roosevelt, who had quickly become "Franklin" to him, was not supposed to be at Seneca Point but had told his wife, Eleanor, that he was in Philadelphia on business. "Being an attorney allows me to go out of town on occasion," Franklin said, "and seize the opportunity."

"Are you related to Theodore Roosevelt?" Hump asked.

"Actually, he's my fifth cousin," Roosevelt said, "but we're not particularly close. In fact, I married one of my cousins, Eleanor. A fine woman but a bit plain. Perhaps you'll meet her one day. If you do, please keep my visit to Seneca Point a secret."

Hump promised that he would.

After thanking Hump for the hospitality and leaving a note for Dr. Bogart, whom he claimed "saved my life," Franklin departed, planning to return to New York City. He told Hump he was heading for Washington where he was going to become Assistant Secretary of the Navy. "Cousin Theodore held that post before moving on to become governor of New York and later president of the United States. Who knows? I might follow his trail." Before leaving, Franklin said, "Since we share a dark secret, young man, I want to invite you to come and visit me in Washington when you grow up a bit more. Washington may not have as many beautiful young girls as Seneca Point, but I'm sure to find a suitable debutante for you."

"That's a promise I'll hold you to," Hump said before shaking the young politician's hand.

"This is not good-bye," Franklin said. "It's just a temporary farewell until we meet again. Hopefully, under far better circumstances."

The strange visit of Franklin Roosevelt to Seneca Point had been the highlight of Hump's summer there. Otherwise, he found the days long, lazy, and slow. He craved action and wasn't getting any excitement from anywhere except from books. He loved to read.

Back in his upstairs bedroom following a big lunch, he felt bloated. He liked to lie down after eating to digest his food.

Maud always preferred to go with his father to sit on their large front verandah overlooking the lake. Over the lunch table, Hump had gotten mad at the mean family cook. Although the meal had consisted of two roasts, and a selection of seven fresh vegetables from the field, there was no ham on the table. He

4

always complained when he saw no ham.

Going downstairs for a glass of cold water, Hump looked out through the French doors onto the porch where his parents were resting in a large swing. He wondered if he'd ever grow to be as tall as his father, all six feet of him with shoulders so broad he could have been a football player. Even on the hottest days, Belmont never appeared outside the house unless he was dressed in a heavy suit of dark blue wool along with a white shirt and a stiff collar. He always ordered the maid to "make my collars extra stiff."

Almost as tall as her husband, Maud was an Edwardian beauty. She invariably wore only mauve, lavender, or gray—mostly graceful silks that seemed to flow in the wind, or else heavily starched cotton dresses that were immaculately tailored. She had thirty pairs of high-heeled, high-button shoes, always with a lavender ribbon. The tiny shoes were like those of a little girl's. Almost daily, Maud commented on her size two and a half feet. "They're so tiny I don't know how they carry me around. Some six-year-old girls have feet larger than mine."

Remarks such as that always brought a compliment from Belmont. "In China I hear they bind women's feet to make them as small, tender, and beautiful as yours. I don't dare get you near a Chinaman because he'd kidnap you for his harem and make love to your feet all night."

Returning with his cold water to take upstairs, where he was reading Joseph Conrad's *The Nigger of the Narcissus*, Hump paused once again to look out at the bucolic scene of his parents sitting in the swing on their verandah on this perfect summer day.

From his black leather satchel, Belmont removed a syringe. Maud was wearing a long-sleeved dress in soft tones of mauve with gray accessories. She unbuttoned the pearl buttons on her left arm and rolled up her sleeve. With his wife's forearm exposed in all its porcelain beauty, Belmont very gently inserted a needle into her arm. She closed her eyes and leaned back in the swing as if enjoying a respite from the hot summer afternoon by a cooling breeze blowing in from the lake.

After having injected his wife, Belmont removed his jacket and rolled up the sleeve of his white shirt. He then injected the needle into his own arm.

Hump had seen enough. He didn't know exactly what was happening, only that his parents were injecting morphine into their arms. Morphine, he'd heard, was to be injected only into sick people. His parents weren't sick. They'd never looked better and healthier.

Placing the glass of water on a nearby antique, Hump quietly tiptoed upstairs. He didn't want his parents to know he'd been spying on them in a secret moment.

Back in his bedroom, he was deeply disturbed by that scene he'd just witnessed on the porch. He picked up his book and tried to resume reading it on his bed.

Somehow he knew that what his father was doing was not right, but he didn't exactly understand why it was wrong. From the safety of his bedroom, he tried to

5

think this out rationally. His father was a surgeon and a leading heart and lung specialist, earning $20,000 a year, so Hump figured his father must have a valid reason to shoot morphine into himself and into Maud.

An awful reality dawned. His parents weren't healthy at all. They were sick and that's why they needed the morphine, perhaps to prevent some incurable illness.

He dropped his Conrad book to the floor and sat up in his bed. This idyllic summer home, and their grand life in New York City would surely come to an end if his parents died. Who would raise him and his sisters?

A paralyzing fear swept over him. He had to find out what was the matter with them.

His world as he'd known it was now in jeopardy.

***

Two days after Hump had seen his father shooting morphine into his mother's arm and his own arm, he went to Maud's studio and knocked on her door. When working, she'd left instructions not to disturb her for any reason, "even if someone is dying." Showing her displeasure, she threw open the door. "What is it?"

"I saw the needles going into your arms," he blurted out.

She pulled him inside. "You're to tell no one, especially your sisters. Certainly none of the neighbors."

"If you're sick, I want to know," he protested.

Very patiently Maud sat him down and told him that three years before he was born, his father had been in a dreadful accident after he'd earned his degree at Columbia University's College of Physicians and Surgeons.

"Your father was an intern being driven in a horse-drawn ambulance going at top speed. The vehicle accidentally overturned when it hit an enormous pothole. Belmont fell out of the ambulance onto the cobblestones. The ambulance turned over on him, breaking five of his ribs and his left leg. The leg was not set properly. It had to be broken again and reset by more competent surgeons. Ever since that day, your father's health has declined, and he constantly suffers unbearable pain. He doesn't want you children to know the extent of his pain. He puts up a brave front for all of us."

"I'm sorry to hear that," Hump said. "That tells me a lot about father. But what's the matter with you? Why do you need morphine?"

"I don't suffer as much as Belmont does, but I have this skin disease. The words won't mean anything to you. It's called erysipelas, a streptococcal inflammation. That means fiery hot, red skin that burns me so badly at times it's like putting my skin on a hot stove. Sometimes when I'm in here retreating from the world, it's because I can't show my face. Either my left or right eye will close completely. A whole side of my face will burst into flames. The condition will even spread to my breasts. Morphine is the only thing to cure it. Belmont thinks that the condition is so severe, the pain so unbearable, that I will be driven crazy if I don't take drugs."

"But won't morphine turn you and father into drug addicts?"

Enraged, Maud grabbed the back of Hump's stiff shirt and ushered him toward the door. As he stepped into the hallway, she said, "Don't you ever come into my studio again." She slammed the door in his face.

Humiliated, Hump rushed down the hall, colliding into one of the Irish maids, Jane Byrne, "Watch where in the hell you're going, you little shit," she cried out at him. She used the word "shit" all the time.

All the servants called him "the little shit," never Humphrey. It was "the little shit" this, or "the little shit" that. For the rest of his life, Hump would refuse to allow the word "shit" to be uttered in his presence.

He didn't understand why Maud always recruited from the lowest class of Irish servants, each of whom received $3.50 a week in pay. They had vile tempers, horrible manners, and terrible language. Without provocation, a servant would suddenly strike either him or one of his sisters. Complaints about the behavior of the staff to his parents went unheeded. They didn't seem to care.

When Hump had told Maud that the male servant, Liam Mangam, had taken off his leather belt and had beaten him severely, she'd said, "I'm sure he wouldn't have done that if you'd been behaving properly."

After Maud had ushered him from her studio, Hump wanted to run away or at least escape from their summer house for the rest of the day.

He stood in the living room, not certain where to go. Over the fireplace mantle Maud had hung a baby picture he hated. It was an idealized portrait she'd painted of him in 1900 when he was only one year old.

Known as the "Maud Humphrey Baby," the portrait had been reproduced across the country, becoming the most famous baby picture in the nation. It later appeared on the label of the best-selling brand of baby food of its day, Mellins Baby Food.

Later in life, the man then known as "Bogie" would say, "There was a period in American history when you couldn't pick up a God damn magazine without seeing my cute little kisser in it."

Maud was a true Victorian illustrator, who believed that babies should be cherubic, their faces round, their cheeks evoking chipmunks. If they also had ruby-red lips, a long white starched dress, curly blond ringlets, large trusting eyes, and a frilly collar, so much the better.

On a wall overlooking the dining room table hung another Maud portrait of him when he was two years old. He was as chubby cheeked as ever but his slickly combed hair was revealed, no more baby bonnet. He looked like Little Lord Fauntleroy in side-buttoned overalls with rolled-up cuffs and a billowing white shirt, again stiffly starched.

Hump was determined that, if not today, maybe tomorrow, he was going to grow up to be a man and not some powder puff.

***

Later, on the same day he'd been banished from Maud's summer studio, Hump wandered alone around the tranquil lake. Except for the turmoil going on in his own home, the setting looked like the fantasy life his Dutch ancestors had sought when they'd come over to help settle New York.

Hump always felt that it could be a dreamy life for all of the Bogarts if only his parents were different. They were cold and distant and never gave him the love he needed, not even a kiss on the cheek or a warm embrace.

Even though they were his parents, Hump didn't know all that much about them, since they rarely mentioned their own childhoods. Both parents traced their lineage to Europe as far back as the early 16th century. Members of royalty were included among both Dr. Bogart's ancestors and those of Maud.

Decades later, one royal link would be leaked to the press. It was reported at the wedding of Lady Diana Spencer to Britain's Prince Charles, that his new princess was the seventh cousin of Humphrey Bogart on his mother's side.

Dr. Bogart's father, Adam Watkins Bogart, had run an inn for summer visitors to the Finger Lakes. Arriving from Holland in the 17th century, his family had farmed in Brooklyn, which until the 20th century had a "Bogart Avenue" in their memory. In 1853 the family moved to the Finger Lakes.

At Canandaigua, Adam had run a tough tavern, with a jailhouse in the basement. It was called Franklin House, and it was the only inn in Canandaigua, attracting men who smoked cheap stogies and wore muddy boots reeking of manure.

The woman he'd married, Julia, was considerably better off financially than Adam. After marriage, he moved with her to Jefferson House in the village of Watkins on Lake Seneca. There they ran a small three-story hotel with more than a dozen rooms to rent. It was here they gave birth to their first born, pretentiously naming him Cornelius Edward Bogart. Cornelius was killed at the age of six when he attempted to slide down the banister of stairs that led into the lobby of Jefferson House. He fell on his head on the black and white checkerboard Tuscan tile and died instantly.

Their second son, Belmont DeForest Bogart, was born in 1866, a year after the death of his brother. Julia was to live only two years after the birth of her second son. She developed a "mysterious" illness and lay in bed for five months, suffering. In her will, she left all her money to Belmont, and none to her husband, Adam.

In 1871, Adam sued her estate, eventually winning control of the money and his son. Julia had asked that Belmont be taken away from his father and placed in the care of either of her sisters.

After her death, Adam never remarried. Using Julia's money, he grew rich when he created a method of lithographing on tin plates, a technique later used

8

extensively in advertisements.

Maud had been born about a year before her husband on March 30, 1865, the daughter of a rich shoe manufacturer, John Perkins Humphrey, in Rochester, New York.

Her family was wealthy enough to finance her artistic career, sending her to the Art Students' League in New York from 1886 to 1894 and later to the Académie Julian in Paris where she'd studied with James McNeill Whistler. There were rumors that she'd had an affair with the fabled American painter, who was in his 50s when he first met Maud. Throughout her life, Maud never confirmed nor denied the rumor, saying, "It's for damn sure I didn't pose for *Whistler's Mother.*"

It was in Paris that she'd painted her first nude. The model was the well-built former prizefighter, Rodolphe Julian, who frequently modeled in the nude at the Académie he'd founded. Some of the art students jokingly said that Rodolphe had founded the art school only so he could "show off his ample assets" before the art classes, as he'd often confess that he himself "knew nothing about art. I know what I like—and that's that."

Even though aging when Maud had met him, Rodolphe still kept his body as neat and trim as that of an Olympic athlete. In those days, only male artists were allowed to paint male nudes. Most art schools didn't even encourage female painters and, if they allowed them entrance, did not let them paint nude models either male or female.

At his Académie, Rodolphe changed all that. It was said that many young women signed up for his classes just to see what a man looked like in the nude. Many women at the time saw a naked man for the first time on their wedding night, with virtually no prior knowledge of the male anatomy.

"After looking at Rodolphe, and painting him, it's probably inevitable that we'll be disappointed with our husbands," Maud confided to a fellow art student, Mary Fielding, from Charleston, South Carolina.

Maud was known for her razor-tongued wit, and she found a perfect match in the equally sharp-tongued Belmont. Each could take the other down with biting sarcasm. Both of them passed this dubious characteristic onto their son, Humphrey.

Bogie's future director, John Huston, said the actor was known throughout his life for needling people, or "sticking in the saber," as Huston put it.

What his parents didn't pass on to their son was their political conservatism. Belmont was a Republican and a Presbyterian, Maud a Tory and an Episcopalian. Humphrey would grow up to become a liberal Democrat.

Born on Christmas Day, 1899, "a Christmas gift to his parents," as later reported by publicists at Warner Brothers, Humphrey DeForest Bogart came into the world at Sloane's Hospital in New York, weighing eight pounds and seven ounces. He'd been born six days before the end of the 19th century, and in later life always referred to himself as a "man of the last century."

He'd had an elongated foreskin, and his doctor father had recommended circumcision. Maud had been adamantly opposed, claiming that "was a barbaric

Jewish custom."

Until he'd gone into the Navy at the end of World War I, Humphrey had lived with this extended foreskin. After his military service, when he ran into his former classmate, Doug Storer, at a tavern, he confided, "I had a doctor trim it a bit, but he left enough for me to still have fun."

Belmont himself in 1901 delivered his second child, a girl named Frances Bogart. Because she was chubby as an infant, Hump nicknamed her "Fat." When she grew up and lost her excess weight, she was called Pat. Two years later, another sister, Catherine, was born.

In his early years Maud and Belmont had big plans and high hopes for Hump. Belmont, dining at Luchow's, his favorite German restaurant on 14th Street in New York, boasted that his adolescent son would one day go to Yale and become a world-famous surgeon. "My wife says Columbia, but I definitely see the boy as a Yale man."

Hump's one and only attempt at performing surgery had ended in disaster when he'd attempted it when he was eight years old. His sister Catherine had developed a large boil with a pus-filled head. She begged her brother to puncture it, since Belmont was away on a hunting trip. Retreiving his father's first-aid kit, with its scalpel, needles, and cotton, he attempted to lance the boil with a needle. When it didn't work, he used his pocket knife. Immediately, a mixture of pus and blood shot with high velocity into his face. His screaming sister had to be rushed to the nearest hospital before she bled to death.

One afternoon, about a month later, Hump found Maud terribly depressed, revealing that she'd learned some "very bad news." She told him that she'd visited an itinerant fortune teller who was passing through the Finger Lakes that summer. "Your son will grow up to enjoy fabulous wealth and will know many loves," the gypsy had told her. "But both of your daughters are destined for tragic lives."

***

Hump was heartbroken to learn that Maud and Belmont had placed Willow Brook up for sale in August of 1913. If a buyer could be found, their summer home and their days at the lake would be over. Maud promised the children a summer cottage on Fire Island for the coming year.

She'd taken a position as an illustrator on the magazine, *Delineator*, and needed to be close to New York, the magazine's base of operations. "The pay is fabulous," she told Hump. "Fifty-thousand dollars a year."

Walking down by the lake, Hump recalled his happiest times here when Belmont took him sailing on his champion yacht, *Comrade*. It was on that very lake that Belmont had taught Hump how to sail, a passion his son would enjoy until the day of his death.

In time, Belmont purchased a one-cylinder motor boat, which Hump had called

Desire, and he went out, putt-putting around the lake all by himself. In later life, Bogie would tell friends that sailing on the lake by himself was "the only time in my life I've ever felt free."

His sister, Pat, later told friends that her brother went through a typical adolescent period when he developed crushes on males. "It was just a period," Pat said, "and in no time at all he grew out of it. He certainly didn't grow up to be a homosexual, as many of his leading ladies can testify."

That summer Hump made Belmont the focus of his attention. Belmont was tall and good looking, a strong man and avid hunter, a real outdoors type, everything that Hump wanted to be, but wasn't. When his father would invite him sailing, Hump was thrilled to have Belmont to himself and not have to share him with family or patients.

When Belmont first met his neighbor, Mrs. Harry Lansing, he no longer invited Hump sailing. Although a bit hefty, Mrs. Lansing was extremely beautiful to Belmont. He pursued the married woman when Maud wasn't present. Her husband, Harry, the son of a railroad tycoon, was never at home. Rumors were that he was an alcoholic. When not drinking, he was said to chase after other women.

Sometimes Belmont would announce to his family that he was taking Hump sailing with him. But when they got to the lake, Mrs. Lansing would be waiting for the doctor. Belmont always gave Hump money to spend in town while he sailed away with Mrs. Lansing.

Out there alone on the lake, Belmont was surely making love to Mrs. Lansing, or so Hump suspected. They'd be gone for hours. Instead of going to town, Hump would often wait for him beside the pier, no matter how long it took.

Perhaps Maud learned that summer of her husband's affair, or maybe she didn't. All Hump knew was that during those final days on the lake, before they returned to the city, Maud moved out of the master bedroom she shared with her husband and took a smaller bedroom on the top floor.

"I'm still going to be married to your father," she told Hump, "but one phase of our relationship is definitely over. You'll have no more brothers or sisters."

That bitter rejection by his father was eased when Hump was introduced to Mrs. Lansing's daughter, Grace. Hump felt that she was the most beautiful girl he'd ever seen, even more stunning than Franklin Roosevelt's young mistress.

They'd met when Mary Hamlin had organized the resort's young people into the Seneca Point Players. Over his protests, she'd named Hump the producer and director and had cast him as the lead in the players' first production, *Sunset in the Old West*. Mary had cast the Lansing daughter, Grace, as Hump's romantic female lead.

Before leaving for Seneca Point that summer, Hump had met a patient of his father's, William Brady Sr., a handsome showman and promoter and the son of Irish immigrants. Living next door, Brady had called on Belmont, claiming that "my cook has given me ptomaine poisoning."

Hump had also been in his father's office that day, and had found Brady a fascinating man. He regaled Hump with stories of his former life when he'd gone from shoeshine boy to newsboy, from stage manager to actor, and from comedian to play director. "Now I'm a producer," Brady said. "I also manage boxers, none of whom know how to throw a punch. That is, except for two winners, both heavy-weight title holders, Jim Corbett and Jim Jeffries. I have luck with boxers named Jim."

Before Brady had been called into Belmont's office, the producer turned to Hump. "I have a son about your age, William Brady Jr. I'll introduce you to him. I'm sure you'll hit it off real swell."

Hump had to go to Seneca Point for the summer, but he eagerly looked forward to seeing young Brady when he came back to New York. Hump was in dire need of a male best friend.

When Brady Sr. learned that a local theater troupe was being formed at Seneca Point, he sent some discarded Broadway costumes to the Bogart family. Brady had just closed down a show on Broadway, *The Girl of the Golden West*, and he had plenty of outfits to spare, including chaps, boots, and western garb.

Hump tried on a ten-gallon hat that practically drowned his head, but he wore it in his first play anyway. He played the star, a role that depicted him as a "good man gone wrong." He'd become a gun slinging bandit—that is, until he met the heroine of the play who "sets him on the straight and narrow path once again."

Grace, the female lead, won his heart in the play and also won his heart in real life. The audience around the bandstand peacefully watched this farce. They'd paid five cents each for tickets, plus another one penny for a glass of cold lemonade.

Throughout the rehearsals, thoughts of Grace had consumed Hump. The day after the play closed, he bribed one of the Irish maids to pack a picnic lunch for him. He'd invited Grace to go hiking in the nearby woods, and she'd accepted.

After their picnic on a blanket, he leaned over and kissed her. Decades later, Grace said she kissed him back, even though she'd never let a boy kiss her before. "He was handsome and charming, and I genuinely liked him. But he got carried away when I kissed him. He wanted to go farther."

As a summer rain fell across the meadow, Hump jumped up and begged her to strip off her clothing with him. Even though she remained fully dressed, he pulled off his trousers, shirts, and underwear and danced around her in the nude, urging her to take off her clothes too. "I'd never seen a boy's penis before," Grace said, much less one erect, and I was terrified. I started running across the slippery meadow heading for home, leaving him standing nude with his erection on the wet blanket."

He later told his friend, Peter St. Davids, "I'm not much of a lover, I guess. I got the gal at the end of that stupid play, but not in real life."

Later when Grace Lansing had become Mrs. Gerald Lambert of Princeton, New Jersey and Palm Beach, Florida, she became friends with Bogie's first wife,

12

Helen Menken, telling her of that summer on the lake with Humphrey. "I always regretted we didn't fool around that day," Grace said, "especially when he became a world famous screen actor. I could have claimed to be Humphrey Bogart's first love. But, alas, it was not to be."

***

With no buyer found for Willow Brook, the Bogarts returned to New York City where Belmont resumed his practice, and Maud took up her job as an illustrator for the magazine, *Delineator*, a position she would hold for twenty years. The sole purpose of the magazine was to sell dress-sewing patterns manufactured by its parent company, the Butterick Pattern Company, in an era when many women sewed their own clothing at home.

The magazine was one of the first to publish pictures of females in nightgowns, bathing suits, and underwear. Mainly it featured women appearing in fashionable clothing. Its backers hoped that America's women readers would fall in love with the illustration, then go out and purchase the Butterick dress pattern.

In spite of its focus on sewing patterns, the magazine also had pages devoted to serious fiction. Its editor was the novelist Theodore Dreiser, who printed pieces by such famous journalists as H.L. Mencken. Maud was especially proud of the magazine because it published articles about her favorite cause, women's suffrage.

One afternoon Hump's mother invited her boss, Theodore Dreiser, and the famously caustic visiting writer from Baltimore, H.L. Mencken, back to her townhouse for afternoon tea. Both men were ostensibly there to meet the "Maud Humphrey baby," even though Hump was a growing adolescent at that time.

The Bogart sisters were not at home. Hump dressed himself formally, as requested by Maud. He eagerly awaited his introduction to both men, even though he wasn't quite sure who they were. Maud had talked at length about their status as "literary lions."

Dreiser was the first to enter the house, firmly shaking Hump's hand. "My, oh my," he said, "how that baby did grow. They're still publishing Maud's portrait of you as an adorable baby, though. You're easily as famous as the Arrow Collar Man or the Schweppes Commander."

Dreiser had not yet written his masterpiece, *An American Tragedy* which wasn't penned until 1925, but *Sister Carrie*, written in 1900 when Hump was one year old, had already been broadly distributed throughout the country. Dreiser had brought an autographed copy as a gift for the boy. "Maud claims you read one novel a week. Try mine. I must warn you, though. Even my publisher tried to suppress this book."

With perfect manners, Hump accepted it with genuine gratitude. It would be the first of many autographed books that writers would present to him as tokens of their esteem. They'd eventually include men as diverse as Ernest Hemingway

13

and Truman Capote.

At that point, H.L. Mencken arrived, with Maud on his arm, both of them having overheard the friendly exchange between Hump and Dreiser. Bombastically turning to Dreiser, Mencken said, "Your publisher didn't want to suppress *Sister Carrie* because it was racy; he wanted to suppress it because its style is so weak. There are lines in that novel that simply don't work, like 'he worked in a truly swell saloon.' Calling a saloon 'truly swell' sounds inarticulate and unsavvy, and sometimes I wonder how you got away with it. I could go on and on, citing other examples."

Averting his gaze from Dreiser's angry eyes, Mencken extended his hand to Hump. "Hello, I'm H.L. Mencken." Hump stammered his hellos.

Ignoring Mencken, Dreiser returned to his dialogue with Hump. "Please overlook the occasional unevenness in my style. I'm interested in bigger game, especially the expression of broader ideas. I write as a means of proving that history does not dominate a man, but that it's actually an expression of mankind at its most creative. It is man who creates history, not history that creates men."

Taking off his coat, Mencken acerbically shot back. "Is that what we do?" he asked Dreiser. He turned back to Hump. "Be careful—reading *Sister Carrie* will stunt your growth."

Smiling grimly at the insults, but holding his tongue, Dreiser got up, supposedly to pee. Maud showed him down the corridor to the toilet. Mencken sat down next to Hump on the sofa. "It was my reading of *Huckleberry Finn* at the age of nine that changed my life. It was, in fact, the most stupendous awakening of my entire life. It turned me into a bookworm and eventually a writer. Do you want to be a writer?"

"Father wants me to study medicine and follow in his footsteps."

"Become anything but a shyster lawyer," Mencken said. "I detest lawyers, especially Jewish lawyers. They are the worst."

Hump silently noted that Mencken shared Maud's anti-Semitism.

"After you've read the important books, go out and learn from life itself, taking all the worldly wisdom you can glean from the saloon keeper, the cop on the block, even the midwife, or especially the midwife if she performs a few abortions on the side. I figured being a newspaper reporter was the best way to meet people from all walks of life. After my first story, a five-line report about a horse thief, was published in the Baltimore *Morning Herald*, I was committed to journalism from that day forward."

At that point, Maud came back into the living room with Dreiser, who looked over at Mencken. "Why don't you move to New York and leave that hick town of Baltimore behind you?"

"New York is but a third-rate Babylon," Mencken said. "I prefer the frowzier charms of Baltimore. Even that immense protein factory known as Chesapeake Bay."

Dreiser had to excuse himself again to go up to Maud's studio to look over some of her latest sketches.

Humphrey chose that moment to invite Mencken up on the roof to look at his pigeon coop. "Maud finds these birds disgusting and unsanitary. When I came down with pneumonia, she blamed the pigeons."

Mencken didn't much like pigeons either. But he was entranced with the view of the New York skyline from the Bogart roof. The bracing air delighted him, and seemed to spark some crazed ambition within him. Hump suspected that he'd had a few whiskies before arriving at the Bogart house.

Mencken waved his arms in the air and seemed to be speaking to the world at large, and not specifically to Hump. "I want to be the native American Voltaire," Mencken said. "I see myself as the enemy of all Puritans. I will become a heretic within academia—a one-man demolition crew of Victorian morality."

Later, Maud called them for tea in her little garden in back, although Hump suspected that both of these men would have preferred whiskey.

Over tea, Mencken continued to lecture Dreiser, albeit more diplomatically. "There is only one way to make money publishing books. You can write about only four subjects. First, murder stories. Second, novels in which the beautiful heroine is forcibly overcome by the handsome hero. Third, books about spiritualism, occultism and such claptrap. Fourth, any book devoted to Abraham Lincoln."

"Speaking of Lincoln," Dreiser said, "Someone recently submitted an essay for publication in my magazine. It's written by Theodore Ward, a historian, and based on extensive research. It's an exposé of the sex life of Abraham Lincoln, but I fear I cannot publish it, although it's a hell of an interesting article."

"Is it too controversial?" Maud asked.

"That it is," Dreiser said. "It maintains that Lincoln was a homosexual and had a five-year love affair with another man."

"I don't think that article will ever be published," Maud said.

"Maybe in fifty years the public will be ready for it," Mencken said.

As Maud was pouring tea for Dreiser, a large butterly flew from a flower bush, winging by her head. Dropping her tea pot, she screamed as if ten rapists had surrounded her. She ran into the living room and up the steps leading to her studio.

Both Dreiser and Mencken looked to Hump for some explanation of this erratic behavior.

"All her life she's been terrified of butterflies," Hump said.

***

It wasn't only Dreiser and Mencken who wanted to meet the Maud Humphrey Baby. The stigma of having posed for that picture followed Hump throughout of his school days. He'd been mocked and ridiculed when he'd entered Delancy School, which he'd attended to the fifth grade. He still hadn't shaken the curse when, at the age of thirteen, he enrolled in Trinity School, which was housed in a sandstone building at 91ˢᵗ Street between Columbus and Amsterdam Avenues. An Episcopal institutional "for the training of young gentlemen," it was the oldest continuously operating school in the country.

Doug Storer, a classmate, recalled that virtually every day after school, a gang of bullies waited for Hump, calling him "sissy" or chanting, "rock-a-bye baby."

The confrontation sometimes led to Hump arriving home with a bloody lip and, on more than one occasion, a black eye.

At school, Hump had turned out to be a poor student, excelling in nothing, and with particularly low marks in German. Since Belmont, a classically educated descendant of the original Dutch burghers of New York, spoke fluent German, he had demanded that his son learn the language too.

Hump's grades in other classes were almost as bad. As the months went by, it became apparent to Belmont and Maud that their son would not follow in his father's footsteps as a surgeon.

"He'll be lucky if he graduates from high school," Belmont told Maud. To compound matters, Hump developed scarlet fever and had to repeat the eleventh grade.

Although Belmont had been a notable athlete, Hump did not willingly participate in organized sports unless he was forced to as part of the school curriculum. He told classmate Storer that he especially disliked wrestling. "I loathe such close contact with other guys. There's one fucking guy who gets a hard-on every time he pins me down on the mat. I can feel the God damn thing pressing up against me."

Storer remembers that there was a debate among some of the girls over whether Hump was "handsome" or "just good looking." His classmate recalls that, "His appearance was always neat. I never saw him when he wasn't well-groomed. He had a slim figure with very dark eyes and jet-black hair that was always plastered down to his head with some kind of cream. He showed up every day in a dark blue wool serge suit with a vest and a stiffly starched white shirt with detachable collars held on by gold-plated brass buttons. His black shoes were always highly polished. His ties were never garish but always in some somber color like navy blue or berry brown, the stuff bankers wore at the time."

In winter he'd appear in a Chesterfield overcoat with a velvet collar.

The author, Eric Hodgins, remembers that "Bogart always wore a black derby hat, rain or shine. It set him apart from the other boys. Many a time he would get that hat knocked off his head. But he always picked it up, dusted it off, put it back on his head, and went on his way."

Hump told Storer that he didn't want to get out of bed sometimes, knowing that at three o'clock that afternoon a gang was waiting to taunt him. He was not a fighter and had never taken on one of the neighborhood toughs in combat. If Hump defended himself at all, it was to raise his hands to protect his face.

One cold January afternoon, the toughest guy on the block plowed his steel-knuckled fist into Hump's face, breaking his nose. He'd run all the way to his father's office at 245 West 103rd Street. The office on the second floor of the family brownstone was covered in a thick moss green carpet with beautiful mahogany paneling rescued from a townhouse in Chelsea which had been demolished. It was one of the few houses in the neighborhood that had a telephone, a necessity because Hump's father was a doctor. Belmont had tended to his son's nose, making emergency repairs before taking him to the hospital. All the way to the clinic, Belmont had chided Hump for not defending himself better. "When I was your age, I could beat up any boy in my hometown. Maud's making a sissy of you. I hate the name Humphrey she gave you. That's a sissy name."

Even as Hump had moved into his teenage years, Maud had continued to dictate his dress. At formal school dances, she'd demanded that he wear white kid gloves and black patent leather pumps. "I was like a God damn teenage dandy," Bogie later told his favorite director, John Huston.

***

One afternoon Maud called her teenage son into her studio and revealed to him some of the male nudes that she'd painted in Paris. He was shocked because until then, he had known only her scenes of Victorian innocence.

For reasons not known to him at the time, she'd tried to explain to him when male nudity was acceptable and when it was not.

"When a man is nude and aroused, and is showing himself off, that is not acceptable," she informed her son. "But when a man in a flaccid state is posing nude for an art class, that is acceptable. The men and women painting him have no actual interest in his sex. They view the body as a whole, as an object from which they can make an artistic statement. It's the same when your father sees a nude man or woman in his office. He has them strip to examine them in detail. But as a doctor, he has the same disinterest in the nude body that an artist does while painting a nude in his studio. This is called sexless nudity."

After that rather detailed and pedantic explanation, Maud invited Hump to accompany her that afternoon to her art classes.

At the Artists and Models Studio on West 28th Street, Maud had been temporarily teaching classes to young illustrators who wanted to become working commercial artists like herself. Since she was widely known as a Victorian illustrator portraying an idealized fantasy life of home and hearth, she'd been an odd choice to teach classes with nude models, although her background in Paris had prepared her for such an assignment.

When she arrived with Hump at the studio, she still hadn't told him why he was here. It turned out that Maud had been filling in during a sick leave of Duane Edwards, the regular teacher. To an increasing degree, Maud had been leaving the house on mysterious errands. Hump had heard her talking over the phone several times with someone named "Duane," and he'd suspected that Maud was having an affair now that she was no longer sleeping in the same bed with his father.

In a back dressing room, Maud told her son, "Remember what I said about nude modeling. There is nothing about the nude male body that we have to be ashamed of. Our regular model is not here today. He's just a young boy who models for classes. The class has painted mature models, both female and male, in the nude. This week we are painting young boys. I want you to model nude and fill in for our regular model who is sick."

Horrified at his mother's suggestion, Hump wanted to bolt from the building. Except for a medical examination, he'd never pulled off his clothes before any-one, and certainly not in front of women. Since he had no real basis for compari-sons, and hadn't seen any pictures, he had not been certain just how he measured up with other boys his age.

He'd always been curious about other male genitalia, but when he'd been at a latrine with other boys, he'd always looked away, afraid to be caught gazing at them. He'd feared that because of his reputation as a sissy, all he would need was to be spotted glancing at the genitals of other boys. He'd never showered with other boys and had never seen his father in the nude either.

When he revolted at the idea of the posing session, Maud taunted him. "Don't tell me you're afraid to take off your clothes in front of artists. Are you ashamed of the way you're developed? You don't have to be."

As he looked at her, he began to think that he hated her. Defiantly, he began to peel off his clothes. Before he'd taken his trousers down, she turned and walked away.

A school custodian came into his dressing room, finding Hump standing there looking pathetically naked. He handed him a white robe, telling him to wear it out into the studio. "When you go up on the platform in front of the class, drop your robe and sit naturally on the stool I put there."

Years later, Bogie recalled how he'd come into the studio so embarrassed that he didn't dare look at anybody. He was red-faced but he did as he was told and dropped his robe, going at once to a large stool in the center of the platform. There he had braced himself for a long sketching session, crossing his legs.

The custodian came out and pried his legs apart, exposing Hump's genitalia to the painters. His heart was beating so fiercely at that point that Hump didn't much care what happened next. His only thought was that Maud was there, along with the others, looking at her son in all his shame.

As the artists painted, Hump tried to think of anything except what was actu-ally happening in the studio.

The session ended exactly at noon. Hump put on his robe and retreated to the rear where the custodian brought roast beef sandwiches for the artists. He'd offered one to Hump. Because he was hungry, he accepted, only wishing that it had been a ham sandwich.

Maud remained in the studio evaluating the nude drawings of her son. At one o'clock, Hump was summoned back to the platform. The second time wasn't as traumatic for him. He still refused to make eye contact with any of the painters in the room, not even knowing whether they were men or women.

He was called back for a final session at three o'clock, and at exactly four o'clock, the day's work ended.

Fully dressed, he waited outside on the street for Maud. When she appeared, he was embarrassed to look into her face. "Now that wasn't so bad," she said. "You're to come back with me four more days this week. The good news is that you're going to get fifty dollars for your work. Imagine that. Fifty dollars, the most money you've ever seen at one time in your life."

She told him that he'd have to go home alone, as she had to visit a sick friend. She was obviously going to meet her new friend, Duane.

Hump stood watching Maud go up the street to her next rendezvous. A militant suffragette, she passed out pamphlets as she made her way along the crowded boulevard, calling on passers-by to give the vote to the women of America.

***

His parents names appeared regularly in *Dua's New York Blue Book* since 1907, but Belmont constantly attacked his wife for "trying to climb the social ladder." The son of a saloon keeper, he couldn't care less about the opinions of New York society.

Every night at their New York home, their arguments were virtually the same. "When you're not social climbing, you're driven by your career like some God damn maniac," he'd shout at her when drunk.

Matching him drink for drink, Maud always stood up to him. She constantly reminded him that her profession brought in more than twice as much money as his did.

She claimed that she was known among the very upper crust of New York society, and enjoyed a national reputation as an illustrator, whereas he "consorted with river rats."

Instead of accepting invitations into some of the finest homes of New York's Upper East Side, Belmont preferred the company of saloon keepers, mechanics, janitors, and truck drivers. He'd frequent the taverns of blue-collar laborers, preferring those saloons along New York's waterfront where he'd find "men of the sea." If he'd had enough to drink, he'd invite sailors back to his home to spend a night or even a weekend.

That had led to some of Maud's most brutal fights with her husband. "These bums aren't coming into my living room," she'd shout at her husband in front of the Bogart children. She'd demand that the doctor take his newly acquired sailor friend up to the fourth-floor bedroom, which was usually assigned to a servant. "You can sleep up there with him," she'd said. "Don't come to my bed tonight."

19

That had seemed like a strange remark to Hump, because Belmont, at least to his knowledge, hadn't entered Maud's bed in years.

Maud had also insisted that this "waterfront trash" eat in the kitchen with the Irish servants. To defy her, Belmont would also take his meals in the kitchen with the object of that evening's fascination.

Usually, a "river rat" would visit the Bogart home only once. Belmont's interest in these uneducated specimens he would pick up rarely lasted more than two or three days.

The exception had been a handsome, ruggedly masculine, and well-built "man of the sea," Lars Schmidt. Depending on what day of the week you asked him, Lars claimed to be Norwegian, Swedish, or Danish, and during one particularly frank dialogue, German.

Because he spoke six languages, had incredible good looks, and always dressed nicely, Maud had at first been attracted to his charm and personality. Even Hump had been fascinated with Lars. He'd entertain the boy with tales of all the shipwrecks he'd survived. The most fascinating adventure, as he'd related, was when his merchant ship had almost collided with another in the middle of the Atlantic. This ghost ship had seemingly come out of nowhere, appearing mysteriously in the fog.

"It was definitely a Swedish man-of-war from the 17th century," Lars had claimed. "Our crew could actually see seventeen sailors standing on deck as the ship passed us by. They were as lifelike as you are sitting across from me. We were awestruck as we watched the vessel drift away into the dawn. I've never seen anything like that before or since."

Whenever Lars came to the port of New York, he always arrived unannounced at the Bogart home. His parents' explosion over Lars had come one hot, blistering August day as the entire city was melting down under a record-breaking heat wave.

It was so hot that when Lars had to walk outside of his bedroom to go to the bathroom on the second floor, he'd wandered down the stairs stark naked. One of the Bogart daughters, Frances, had seen him nude in the hall and had run to her mother in her studio to report on this.

Maud had been furious and had climbed to the top floor to see what was going on. The door to the bedroom where her husband had slept the night before with Lars was wide open. She'd looked inside and found Lars in the middle of the bed playing with himself. He'd invited her in to join him.

She'd screamed and had run downstairs.

That night when Belmont came home after a day's work at the local hospital, she confronted him. "Lars is not a man," she shouted in front of the children and the servants. "He's a freak of nature. That is no penis that belongs on a man. A horse maybe. Frances will be ruined for life having seen such a thing. For all that poor girl knows, all men are built like that. Because of this, she'll never marry, and if she does, she'll be afraid to go to bed with her husband."

20

That night had led to a Bogart family drinking marathon and more violent arguments. Maud threatened that, "If Lars darkens this door again, I'm packing up, moving out, and taking the children with me."

Despite the enormous pressure, that drunken night didn't end Belmont's friendship with Lars. Whenever the sailor came to New York, the doctor packed a suitcase and checked into the Hotel Marseilles with Lars. A then-fashionable address, it lay across the street from the Bogart home.

Like any hotel, it operated like a world unto itself. The beer kings, the Rheingold brothers, called it home, as did Sara Delano Roosevelt, mother of Franklin.

When Mrs. Roosevelt learned of Belmont's rescue of her son during the nearly fatal drowning incident at the lake, she sent a servant across the street with an invitation for Dr. and Mrs. Bogart and their young son, Humphrey. She may not have known about the existence of the two Bogart sisters.

As Maud rarely accepted any social invitation and attended almost no parties, she tore up the invitation without telling her husband. Maud was offended by the politics of Theodore Roosevelt and didn't want to seek any more intimate contact with the Roosevelts after she'd reluctantly sheltered Franklin for one night at her summer home.

When Lars had some time off from sailing, he would go with Belmont on a train to Canada. Up there at an address never revealed to his family, the doctor and Lars would stay at a rustic hunting lodge owned by Belmont. Sometimes for weeks at a time, Belmont would neglect his medical practice, coming back to New York only when his supply of morphine had run out.

On one particularly long trip, Maud had talked to Hump. "There are men like your father who don't have natural instincts. He'd rather be socializing with riff-raff than in a good clean bed with his own wife. We stay together but only for the sake of you children. In time you'll understand what a loveless marriage is. Perhaps you'll even have one or two of your own."

***

At one school dance during his early teen years, Hump asked Leonore Strunsky—nicknamed Lee—to be his date. It was the beginning of a friendship that would last for the rest of his life, because Lee in time would become famously married to another Bogie friend, the lyricist Ira Gershwin.

At the dance, just before Lee excused herself to go to the ladies' room, she'd asked for a glass of punch. While he was getting it for her, two older students in their senior year had deliberately bumped into Hump. "Still dressing like a girl?" one of them had taunted him.

Instead of trying to defend himself, Hump had escaped and fled to his school locker. Once there, he'd removed the Daisy Air Rifle his father had given him six weeks before. Belmont was a superb wing shot, and he wanted to pass his skill on to his son.

Running outside of the school hall, he'd taken the rifle and aimed it at all the red lanterns lighting up the night. He hit every one of them before the school custodian had found him, chasing him from the grounds.

He'd later walked in Central Park arm in arm with Lee, rather proud of his accomplishment. He'd known he couldn't take the boys on in combat, but in some way had felt he'd gotten revenge.

On a bench in Central Park, they'd indulged in some heavy necking. Lee not only let him kiss her, but told him that, "It'll feel much better if you stick your tongue in my mouth."

He'd done just that. She didn't object when he reached inside her dress and felt the firmness of her breasts. But she did not let him do any exploring below her beltline. "That's only for when we're married," Lee told him.

When he'd gotten home, after kissing Lee good night, he felt like a real man.

The moment he walked into the Bogart's living room, he knew that something was wrong. His father was there waiting for him, and he'd been drinking heavily. Maybe the doctor had also been drugged.

The principal from the school had already contacted Belmont about the lantern shoot-out. Coming up to his son, his father seemed to tower above his teenage boy.

Without warning, Belmont delivered several chopping blows to his son's face, loosening two front teeth and smashing his upper lip repeatedly until part of it was torn from the boy's face.

As he'd stood back, realizing the damage he'd done, the doctor seemed to sober up. Maud rushed into the room. Seeing her son, she screamed before turning to confront her husband. "You touch him again, and so help me God I'll kill you."

When the male servant, Liam Mangam, came up from the rear, having been aroused from his bed with one of the Irish maids, Belmont ordered him to carry Hump upstairs to his office.

Once there, the doctor sewed up his son's lip, but he was too drunk to do an adequate job. He ordered Mangam to summon a cabbie to take them to the nearest hospital.

In the aftermath of the injury, Hump's upper lip never healed properly. As every close-up in nearly every movie house in the world later revealed, Bogie's upper lip throughout his adult life bore the scar of that awful night. His lip was to remain partly paralyzed, giving him a slight lisp.

After surgery on his lip for the second time in five hours, Hump had been told that he'd have to go to the family dentist in the morning to replace those two missing front teeth.

The attending doctor at the hospital, John Kells, also gave the teenage boy a thorough physical examination. He recorded that he was 5 feet, 9 inches, weighed 110 pounds, had brown eyes, a fair complexion and light brown hair, his chest measuring 33 inches.

Belmont reported to Kells that his son had had a severe case of the mumps two years ago and that they had "fallen." That most often led to a temporary enlargement of the testicles, followed by a massive shrinkage to a withered pea.

Dr. Kells examined Hump's testicles, finding that he'd escaped from this curse relatively intact, although noting a swelling of the spermatic vein on the left side of the boy's scrotum. Both doctors agreed that this was a "congenital condition" and would probably not affect Hump's ability to father children at some point in the future.

At midnight, Hump, accompanied by a chastised Belmont and Mangam, was released from the hospital to return to the dismal life at 103rd Street.

During his first week home, Hump made one trip to the dentist, accompanied by one of the Irish maids. The dentist replaced Hump's two front teeth. Hump insisted on having his teeth in place before "my best gal," Lee Strunsky came to visit him at the family brownstone.

Having never had a girl friend before, Hump was excited when Lee called to tell him that she was coming over at three that afternoon.

Maud ushered Lee upstairs to Hump's bedroom, where he was convalescing. From the look on his mother's face, Hump knew that Maud disapproved of this visit.

It wasn't until an hour later, after Lee had gone, that Maud stormed into his bedroom. "Don't you ever invite that stinking little tramp into my house again," she yelled at her son.

"She's a very respectable girl, and very nice," Hump protested.

"She's a slimy Jew," Maud charged. "I don't want a son of mine going out with a Jewess. These money-changers are the anti-Christ. They have no appreciation of the finer things of life. They're all about greed and chicanery. They are the bottom-feeders of life."

"Jews are just as good as anybody else," Hump said. "No better, no worse."

"You're a moronic fool if you think that," Maud said, her temper flaring. "If you ever again invite a Jew into my house, boy or girl, I will personally shut the door in their face. Is that understood, young man?" She turned and left the room, leaving Hump in total bewilderment. Since he didn't plan to give Lee up, he'd sneak away and see her in private.

Maybe, when he finished school, he might even ask Lee to marry him. That would really piss off Maud.

As Hump saw it, there was one major problem in their courtship. Lee wanted to wait until they were married before doing it.

Hump decided the time for seduction was at hand. In the days ahead, he was going to figure out a way to charm the bloomers off that pretty girl.

The way he saw it, a Jewish pussy could be just as hot as a Gentile one. Maybe even more so. Time would attest to the accuracy of that perception.

Chapter Two

In ways that anticipated the plots of some of the movies he'd eventually make in the 1930s for Warner Brothers, Hump did not get the girl in the final reel. He never knew exactly what happened to his budding relationship with Lee, but it ended almost as suddenly as it had begun.

All Hump found out later was that Maud had placed a telephone call to Lee. He never knew what his mother had said to his young girl friend, but Lee never saw him until decades later, and he did not press her for the answer.

Hump even went to her house, but a servant informed him that Lee was not at home, even though he suspected that she was upstairs hiding in her bedroom.

Hump would meet Lee later in life as a political ally and friend. He always referred to her as "my first girl friend," even in front of her husband, Ira Gershwin.

A new friend had come into Hump's life that made him forget all about Lee. William Brady Jr. was the son of the showman and promoter, William Brady Sr., whom Hump had met when this entrepreneur was a patient at his father's office. Brady Sr. had promised an introduction to his son, who was Hump's age, and in spite of the producer's busy schedule, he remembered and set it up.

The moment he arrived at the Brady house and met Bill Jr., Hump almost overnight transferred his crush on Belmont to Bill. Bill was a handsome, precocious young man, filled with facile charm and a manly grace. He'd grown up in a world of famous names in both boxing and the theater, and he had a sophistication that Hump envied.

Many young girls were captivated by this dashing man, but once Bill met Hump Bill had no more time for the females in his life. The two young boys became fast friends. Soon after they met, they pledged loyalty to each other and a devoted friendship "for the rest of our lives."

When Hump was finally invited into the Brady home for chocolate milk and cookies, he was dazzled by the opulence of the parlor. Although Maud decorated her house elegantly, it didn't have the ostentation of the Brady home, which some guests had described as "a Victorian stage set."

Not only was Bill's father famous, but so were his mother and step-sister. Hump was especially intrigued by Bill's mother, Grace George, a bigtime star of her day who had appeared in many of her husband's films or Broadway productions.

A darling of Broadway's theater critics, George had gone from triumph after theatrical triumph that included appearances in George Bernard Shaw's *Major Barbara,* as well as *Divorçons, The School for Scandal,* and *Kind Lady.* She was also a major talent scout for her husband, encouraging him to offer breaks to such newcomers as Helen Hayes in *What Every Woman Knows*. She also picked out the then-relatively-unknown Douglas Fairbanks, Sr., from a cast of hopefuls, persuading her husband to cast him opposite her in *Clothes,* even though "he's not good-looking."

The daughter from Brady's first marriage, born in 1892, was Alice Brady, a rising star in her own right. Seven years older than Hump, beautiful, and educated during a period of her life in a convent in New Jersey, she captivated Hump with her talent and charm. She had abandoned a budding career as a singer in grand opera, preferring instead a career as a Broadway actress. She had been appearing on Broadway since her debut as an ingénue in *The Balkan Princess* in 1911. Having made a name for herself in several Gilbert and Sullivan revivals, she had been in dozens of her father's silent films shot for World, his film company. She'd first appeared on screen in 1914 in a flick called *As Ye Sow*. When Hump met her, she'd just filmed *The Gilded Cage*.

The first time Hump appeared in her living room, Grace George was polite but distant, and soon excused herself to go and read a script sent over by her husband. Alice remained behind to have a cup of tea, but it quickly became obvious that she was not smitten with Bill's young friend the way Hump seemed to be with her.

As she recalled years later, "He was just too young for me when we first met. But when Humphrey came back from the Navy, he'd matured a lot. I became very interested in him despite the difference in our ages."

Brady Sr. always gave his son all the free passes he wanted to Broadway shows, both his own productions and those of his rivals. Bill's father had dreams of becoming a theatrical producer as well known and successful as David Belasco.

Paying a nickel fare, Hump and Bill rode to 42nd Street on the rickety Broadway trolley, headed for a vaudeville show at the Palace Theater. Hump had never been to a performance at a major Broadway theater before, and he was immediately captivated by the bright lights and bustle. The show they were headed for was noteworthy in that it included, on the same bill, both Sarah Bernhardt, the greatest dramatic actress of her day, and the comic actor, juggler, and drunk, W.C. Fields.

Decades later, Mae West, co-starring with Fields in *My Little Chickadee*, and herself a Broadway star at the time of Hump's introduction to the theater, dismissed the claim that "The Divine Sarah" and Fields appeared on the same bill. "I'm sure Madame Bernhardt has other things to do than appear on stage with a low-rent, drunken comedian," West claimed. "If Fields thinks Bernhardt was there, he'd had too many drinks, as usual."

But despite Mae West's denials, Bogie maintained through the rest of his life that he'd seen Bernhardt on the same playbill with Fields.

When Bernhardt was rolled onto the stage in a wheelchair, Hump was shocked.

He'd expected to see some tall and statuesque figure of glamour and intrigue. Instead he saw a pale and very frail hospital patient in her 70s, with frizzy red hair. In an accident in France, she'd slipped and had fallen, breaking her leg. Gangrene had set in, and her doctors had to amputate her leg. For her first U.S. performance, she had turned that tragedy into an advantage. Wearing a *poilu* (the uniform French soldiers wore at the time), she'd appeared in New York playing a French soldier who had lost a leg. She'd held a battered flag in her hand while standing unsupported on her still-remaining good leg. Hollow cheeked and colorless, she emphasized her deadly whiteness with a dense coat of chalk-colored *poudre-de-riz* on her face. Looking like a consumptive wraith, she evoked the mummy of an Egyptian Pharaoh.

But when Bernhardt spoke lines from Dumas *fils' La Dame aux Camélias*, her beautiful voice radiated magic. Even from her wheelchair, she moved her body with the lashing grace of a panther.

Spellbound, Hump sat with Bill throughout the performance in a state of rapture. At the end, Bernhardt received a standing ovation that lasted ten minutes. Of her *voix d'or*, the writer, Maurice Baring, rhapsodized, calling her sound, "A symphony of golden flutes and muted strings, a silver dawn lit by lambent lightnings, soft stars and a clear-cut crescent moon."

After that day, Hump became addicted to the theater the way an addict is to heroin. He couldn't get enough of Broadway shows.

Back home that night, Hump poured out his enthusiasm for the world of the Bradys and his love of the theater. Maud was not impressed. "Not only are they in show business, they are Jews." Hump didn't care.

***

As days drifted into weeks, Bill Brady was becoming more possessive of Hump, who no longer planned his own life but allowed his best friend to do it for him. At plays or at the cinema, Bill took to holding Hump's hand. Hump never objected to this and enjoyed the camaraderie. Even when Bill put his arm around him and walked along the streets of Manhattan or Brooklyn, Hump did not object. A lot of schoolboys in those days did that.

The word "homosexual" was just coming into vogue in avant-garde circles, but in the minds of most people, if such a thing existed at all, it was never spoken about. Many indulgent parents, especially those as sophisticated as Belmont and Maud, assumed that a young boy went through periods of infatuation with another boy his own age. Even if extreme affection was displayed, it was taken for granted that this was just a "stage" a young man went through before meeting the girl of his dreams and settling down.

In spite of the domestic horror surrounding the shooting incident at school, and the subsequent injury to his lip, Hump had not lost interest in his Daisy Air Rifle. Nor had it been taken away from him by his father. The future actor, who would one day become a famous icon in a trench coat carrying a gun, spent hours in his room dismantling his gun and reassembling it.

He even carried it in the leg of his trousers and took it with him whenever he went with Bill to the theater. After a show let out, they would find nearly deserted streets where no cop could be seen, then shoot out the globes of gas lamps before scampering off into the darkness of an alleyway to hide if anyone tried to chase after them.

One late summer afternoon, Hump tired of his air rifle and wanted something more lethal. Before going over to Bill's house, Hump went into the basement of the Bogart home and removed a .22 caliber pistol from his father's collection which he kept there.

Bill had been given tickets to see a performance that evening by Alla Nazimova. This Russian-born stage actress and silent film star was famous for her interpretations of works by the Norwegian playwright Henrik Ibsen. Hump was anxious to see her in the flesh, having read much press on her at Brady Sr.'s theatrical offices. It could not have been imagined by Hump at the time that he would one day live at the Garden of Allah in Hollywood which, as "the Garden of Alla," had been Nazimova's home before it was turned into a hotel and colony of bungalows.

But it wasn't a work by Ibsen that Nazimova was performing that night. She was starring in *Bella Donna*, a frothy lust-and-revenge melodrama. Hump would have preferred a more classical introduction to her repertoire. After all, this was the electrifying actress who had brought Chekhov and Stanislavsky to the American theater.

Hump found the diminutive star "shatteringly powerful" and marveled at her "foreign sophistication." This exotic actress would, in fact, pave the way for the likes of silent screen vamp Pola Negri and, in time, Greta Garbo and Marlene Dietrich. In just a few years Nazimova would select Rudolph Valentino as her co-star in the film *Camille* before stealing his wife, the stunningly beautiful Natacha Rambova, as part of a well-publicized and notorious lesbian tryst.

After seeing *Bella Donna*, Bill and Hump headed for a Broadway diner for a plate of ham and eggs for Hump and a hamburger for Bill. His friend told Hump, "Don't go falling for Nazimova. She likes to have sex with women—not men."

This was the first knowledge Hump had of lesbianism, although he would in the 30s and 40s appear with more lesbian stars than any other leading male actor in Hollywood.

He'd heard that boys fooled around together, and had late at night wondered if his own father might have some sort of "unnatural attachment" to the sailor riff-raff he brought to their home. Like Queen Victoria, he'd never given lesbianism a thought.

Bill claimed that Nazimova had fallen in love with his mother, Grace George, and had ardently pursued her, sending her roses every day, even expensive gifts, until Nazimova had tired of Grace's lack of response. By then, Nazimova had moved on, having fallen in love with another actress, Eva Le Gallienne.

Later, Bill promised to invite Hump up to his bedroom where he claimed he would show him some "dirty French postcards" he'd stolen from his father's files. Hump eagerly accepted that invitation. He'd never seen a picture of a man and a woman having sex together.

After a snack Bill asked Hump to go with him to Coney Island to ride the ferris wheel. Later the boys planned to shoot out some more bright lights.

On the fast-spinning wheel, something went wrong. The pistol Hump had concealed in his trousers blasted off. The bullet missed his chest, which could have killed him, but blasted into his right wrist. At first Bill thought that Hump was screaming at the thrill of the ride until Hump held up his wrist in agony as the blood gushed out.

Nothing could be done until the end of the ride. Knowing they would have to seek help from the police, Bill took the gun from Hump and tossed it into the night.

At the end of the ride, the manager saw that young Hump had been injured and immediately called the police. Hump, with Bill in attendance, was rushed to the hospital where a doctor discovered that it was a bullet wound. Until then, the police believed that somehow he'd been cut, perhaps by one of the moving parts on the Ferris wheel.

Hump lied to the police and to the doctor, claiming that during the ride a sniper had shot at them, missing Bill but hitting him. The police bought that unlikely story.

When the police drove Hump back home to Manhattan that night, Maud and Belmont were in the foyer waiting for him. After thanking the cops for their assistance, an angry Belmont didn't strike his son in the face this time. What he did do was to forbid him to carry guns any more. He said that he'd gone to his son's room and removed the beloved Daisy Air Rifle.

"It's time to ship you off to the Phillips Academy at Andover to prepare you for Yale," Belmont said.

"And I absolutely forbid you to see that Brady boy again," Maud said. "You were a good boy until you took up with the likes of that Jew."

"I'll go to the academy," Hump said to his parents. "But there's no way in hell I'll give up my friendship with the Bradys." He stormed upstairs to his bedroom, slamming the door behind him.

***

With a bandaged wrist, Hump accepted Bill's invitation to visit his bedroom at the Brady house to view a collection of pornographic French postcards. They had been collected by his father on a visit to Paris and smuggled through U.S. Customs, as was the way in those days of heavy censorship.

Today, in an era when pre-adolescents routinely watch porno on television, it's difficult to imagine the effect back then of a "dirty picture" on young boys at the height of their sexual potency.

Hump was fascinated by the sepia-toned photographs, one showing a young man with a large erection standing up while two bare-breasted women kneeled to service him. Another depicted the same man bedding one of the women. Yet another pictured him plunging down on a woman in the act of cunnilingus.

Bill became so excited by the pictures that he whipped out his penis and began masturbating, urging Hump to do the same. Reluctantly Hump pulled out his penis and he too masturbated.

Within a few minutes, Bill became more intrigued with Hump's penis than the postcards. "You're bigger than me," he told Hump. "And you're not circumcised like I am."

"You're Jewish," Hump said.

When Bill reached to play with him, Hump did not object but let his friend masturbate him, although he turned down the offer to play with Bill's own penis. After Hump reached a climax, he told Bill he didn't want to turn him down. "But there's absolutely no way I can jerk you off."

"Why not?" Bill asked.

"You've got no foreskin," Hump said. "How can you do it?"

"Us circumcized guys have to manage," Bill said. "It's harder for us to get off than it is for you Gentiles."

After putting the postcards back into their folder, Bill asked Hump to kiss him since he hadn't touched him during their sex together.

Hump agreed, providing Bill would swear not to tell anybody. "It's okay," Bill told him. "I've done this to other guys. All the guys at school do it."

Hump kissed him back. As he was to recall years later to his friend, Truman Capote, "It wasn't at all bad. It felt kinda nice. I didn't think anybody in the world loved me at the time, and it was good to know that Bill did. At first I kissed him because I felt I owed him a favor. After we kissed, I liked it a lot. It was the beginning of many kisses we'd exchange over the years. Our relationship never developed much beyond that. Kissing and playing with each other was as far as I was willing to go. I knew Bill wanted to do some of the things in those pictures, but I could never bring myself to it. I loved the guy, though."

***

The marriage between Phillips Academy at Andover, Massachusetts, some twenty miles north of Boston, and Humphrey Bogart was doomed from the beginning, when he arrived there a week late for classes during an unseasonably cool September in 1917. Founded by Calvinists during the American Revolution, it was the finest prep school in the country. One of its stated purposes was to guard young men "against the first dawnings of depraved nature."

The Academy could name-drop like no other school, having historical ties

30

with John Hancock, Paul Revere, John Adams (its fourth principal), George Washington (who gave an address there), and, in time, Judge Oliver Wendell Holmes and, much later, President George Bush Sr.

Belmont had graduated with the class of 1888, having excelled in baseball and football. He'd written his former schoolmate, Alfred Stearns, now headmaster, asking him to admit his son in spite of his poor grades at Trinity.

On the train to Andover, Hump read *Stove at Yale*, Owen Johnson's popular novel which painted a romanticized version of what college life was really like. To Hump, the novel read like a saccharine-laced fantasy. He'd also bought a newspaper that morning, as he always read the frontpage news carefully. The United States had entered the war on the side of the Allies on April 6, 1917. Before leaving New York, Belmont had told him that many of the students at Andover, along with some faculty members, had temporarily resigned or left the Academy to join the forces on the Western Front in Europe, battling the Kaiser's armies.

Assigned a spartan-looking cell, Number Five, at Taylor Hall, Hump felt that his steel cot evoked a prison cell. Up to now, he'd lived in grand comfort.

Next to Hump's room was the bathroom, shared by twelve other young men on the floor. A previous occupant of Hump's cell must have had an interest in boys taking a shower, because he'd carved a hole about the size of a baseball between Hump's room and the shower.

Hump discovered that hole in the wall on his second day there when he went to remove the reproduction of an antique map of Massachusetts. Looking through the hole, he could have a perfect view of the genitalia of the young men showering. Fortunately, no one was in the shower room when he peeked in, or else he would have been embarrassed.

Lonely and sad to be away from Bill and the bright lights of Broadway, the seventeen-year-old Hump found himself facing a Puritan regime that was launched at 7:30 every morning at chapel.

Classes were boring and he wanted to drop out of Phillips Academy after the first semester until he met schoolmate Floyd Furlow, who also lived in Manhattan. The son of the president of Otis Elevator Company, Floyd was a fun-loving guy full of wicked humor.

Although only eighteen years of age, Floyd claimed to have had ten affairs with women, three of whom were married to some of his father's best friends. He also stashed away booze in his room and would invite his "favorites" on the floor to come and join him.

Floyd and his friends seemed to know much about the world. All of them had been to Europe and one of them, Philip Burton, had once been taken to Africa on a safari with his father.

Hump couldn't match these adventures, as he'd never been taken even to Canada on one of Belmont's hunting trips.

Frederick Boyce, the stern headmaster of Hump's dormitory, was also a phys-

31

ics teacher. With his white mop of hair, he stuck his eagle's beak into everybody's business. Boyce was known for raining hell and damnation onto anyone who violated house rules.

With his wife, Betty, and their three children, Boyce lived on the dormitory's main floor so he could observe the coming and going of all "my boys." Students were forbidden to use the entrance in the rear.

The only boy on the floor who Hump disliked intensely was a nerd who wore thick wire-rimmed glasses, Charles Yardley Chittick. Chittick wanted to study law at either Harvard or Yale. Hump suspected that he was a spy, reporting every infraction to Boyce.

Charles had the single cell directly opposite Hump's. Whenever they would meet in the hallway, neither spoke to each other. If they encountered each other in the shower room, Hump would turn his back to Charlie and conceal his genitals.

Charles had told Floyd that he considered Hump a spoiled brat, secretly resenting that Hump was invited to Floyd's drinking parties and that he was excluded. Both Floyd and Hump referred to Charles as "a bookworm."

Hump eagerly awaited the Christmas vacation when he could return to Manhattan and take in some Broadway entertainment and resume his friendship with Bill.

Ten days before Hump's anticipated return to New York, Dr. Stearns had written Belmont a bad report. "Your son appears bored in class, his mind dreaming dreams of God only knows what. He is indifferent to the school curriculum. He doesn't participate in sports or any school activities. He doesn't even try to maintain a respectable gentleman's C average. Although we are allowing him to return after the holidays, I must withdraw all off-campus privileges. He will be confined to his room, the library, the dining room, and his classrooms. Despite your earlier assurances to the contrary, I fear that your son is definitely not Andover material. Unless he improves in the upcoming semester, I fear for the continuation of his academic career."

That Christmas, a few days before his eighteenth birthday, Hump was certain of only one thing: he didn't want to be a surgeon like his father, and he didn't want to go to Yale or Harvard.

Home from Andover for the holidays, Hump endured the criticism of his parents and listened to how disappointed they were over his academic record. He promised them he'd buckle down during the second term and make them proud of him, although secretly he had no intention of changing any of his behavior at the academy. None of the teachers inspired him, and their boring recitations of dates and historical events conveyed no drama for him.

On the first night of his return, Hump couldn't wait for the end of his reunion with his parents, so he could sneak out of the house to see Bill Brady. While at the Phillips Academy, Bill had written him almost daily, and Hump had answered every letter. At times Bill's letters were all that kept Hump from wanting to commit suicide.

At the Brady home, Hump was welcomed more lovingly by this Jewish family than by his own dysfunctional and coldhearted parents. Brady Sr. seemed genuinely interested in him, and Grace George and Alice Brady filled him in on all the news of their latest theatrical successes. Hump was particularly intrigued by the silent screen flickers Alice was making, although Grace George considered the movies a passing fancy and not worthy of the attention of a serious actor.

Once alone with Hump in his upstairs bedroom, Bill hugged Hump in a tender embrace and kissed him on the lips. "You're still my best buddy or did you mate with some other person up at Andover?"

"I'm still your best friend," Hump said. "For always. I'm pretty much a loner at school."

In spite of this pledge of devotion, Bill regaled Hump with tales of his recent sexual exploits. Hump was surprised that Bill had never mentioned this in any of his letters. "I met this girl," Bill said. "Priscilla Davenport. I know. A real dumb name. But she was terrific. She let me get into her bloomers any time I wanted. Those secret sessions you and I had together were just kid's stuff. I got the real thing and it was terrific."

"I can't match your record," Hump said. "I pursued a few gals at Andover but nothing happened. A harmless date here and there. Maybe a kiss. Nothing heavy. I'd like to meet this gal of yours."

"Too late for that," Bill said. "She moved to California with her family. Her dad's in the movie business. He thinks Hollywood will one day be the center of films. My dad knows a lot more about flickers than Priscilla's old man. Dad says the heart of the film colony will still be New York and New Jersey."

Hump had mixed feelings about Bill's relationship with Priscilla. He was both happy about his friend's scoring with a woman, yet jealous at the same time. For some reason he resented Bill's intimacy with someone else.

Those feelings of resentment disappeared later that afternoon when Alice Brady introduced Hump to her new beau.

Only slightly younger than Hump, Stuart Rose was the best-looking and most dashing teenager Hump had ever met. In his case, Alice didn't seem to mind that Stuart was younger than herself. She'd treated Hump like a kid, but related to the even younger Stuart like a man of the world.

Precocious for his age, Stuart was a cavalryman in the U.S. Army and was home on leave. The Rose family lived on Riverside Drive, only a ten-minute walk from the Bogart home.

Alice had met Stuart when he'd come backstage to congratulate her for her appearance in the revival of *Little Women*, in which she played Meg, a role she'd first performed on Broadway in 1912.

"Since that first meeting, we've seen each other every day," she told Hump, as she took Stuart's hand and gazed into his eyes.

Caught up as they were in the theatrical productions of Brady, Sr., each member of the Brady family was preoccupied with his newest film, *Love Eternal*, being produced on a sound stage in Queens. Even the dignified Grace George, despite her oft-expressed disdain for "the flickers," was about to appear in her husband's movie, having agreed at the last minute to replace the film's original star, actress Beatrice Lane, who had suddenly fallen ill with pneumonia. Grace was co-starring in the movie with her stepdaughter, Alice Brady, who played the role of the naïve *ingénue,* and young Bill was working as the assistant director to his father.

One evening, when every member of the Brady family was caught up in some aspect of the film's production, Stuart Rose found himself alone for the evening. Finding himself in the same position, Hump immediately invited him to dinner at Luchow's, the long-established German restaurant on 14th Street so beloved by his father, Belmont.

Throughout the evening, Hump became enthralled with Stuart, who entertained him with stories of his life as a cavalryman. "Women really go for a man in uniform."

Hump was amazed that a teenager even younger than himself had had so many exploits with women. Hump always remembered his introduction to Stuart as "one of the most memorable evenings of my life. With Bill I felt like I was a boy talking to another boy. With Stuart, I felt we were talking man to man. My blossoming friendship with him became a rite of passage into manhood."

When Bill called the next day to invite Hump to a Broadway play, Hump had to turn him down. He'd already accepted an invitation for horseback riding with Stuart, who had a lot of free time because Alice "was shooting some stupid movie during the day and appearing as Meg in *Little Women* at night."

Bill seemed disappointed that Hump had made a "new best friend" so suddenly. Nonetheless, to show what a good sport he was, he invited both Stuart and Hump to a Broadway musical to which his father had given him free tickets. But during the performance, Bill felt a little left out and neglected, as Hump devoted all his attention to Stuart, exaggerating his hell-raising days at Andover and his conquests of campus beauties.

Shortly before Stuart had to report back to military service, he came to the Bogart home to retrieve Hump for another afternoon of horseback riding.

Frances (Pat) Bogart was in the living room, and Hump introduced the good-looking Army man to his sister. Frances was almost the same height as her brother and had a shapely figure even then. When Stuart learned that she didn't have an escort for the school dance the following night, he volunteered his services.

Stuart was so captivated with Frances that he asked Hump if he could postpone their horseback ride for another time. He invited Frances to go for a stroll with him in Central Park.

After Hump returned to Andover, Frances wrote to him from St. Mary's School in Peekskill, New York, where she informed him that she received a letter from Stuart almost every day. Hump wrote several letters to Stuart himself, but only a brief postcard every now and then came in reply.

Before his departure for Phillips Academy, he hadn't even bothered to call Bill to tell him good-bye and to thank him for his hospitality. But confronted anew with the loneliness of Andover, Hump started writing Bill again. Hump's temporarily deserted friend responded with enthusiastic letters, and their friendship resumed with only slightly less intensity than before.

***

After his third week back at Andover, Hump's dormitory maniacally celebrated the end of a winning football game. Even the stern headmaster, Boyce, temporarily relaxed his iron-fisted rules and allowed the young men to celebrate the school's victory. Having no interest in sports, Hump had stayed in his room trying to study, hoping for some passing grades.

Some of the men on Hump's floor had slipped beer upstairs and were having a wild party, running up and down the corridor. When this party overflowed into the shower room, it appeared that some of the men were pouring beer over the heads of the others, as they showered.

Anxious to see what was going on, Hump turned off the lamp in his room, removed the antique map, and peered through the hole in the wall at the naked boys in the shower.

That was a big mistake. Somehow Charles Yardley Chittick, even without his horn-rimmed glasses, happened to notice a hole in the wall to the shower room. He detected someone spying on them.

Poking his fingers through the hole in the wall, Chittick encountered the framed map, which had fallen back into position as Hump had jumped back. The wire holding the map came unhooked, the print falling to the floor, its glass frame breaking. Terrified at having been caught peeking, Hump concealed himself in the corner of the darkened room.

"We've got a live one, guys," Chittick yelled to the other boys. "Bogart's spying on our dicks."

As Hump cringed in his darkened room, he heard catcalls and cries of "Sissy, sissy." One of the young men shouted inside the hole, "Look at mine if you want to see a big dick. I'll let you be my gal, Nancy boy."

The next day, humiliated, Hump darted in and out of his classes, hoping not to encounter any of his dorm mates. When he returned to his dormitory, Boyce was waiting for him and asked him to step inside the library. There Boyce appeared to be under reasonable control but his eyes avoided Hump's when he spoke. "Many young men go through certain periods of adjustment in their lives," Boyce said, like a professor giving a physics lecture. "These are natural things. It doesn't mean that these same boys can't grow up to become responsible citizens and loving fathers with a good wife and healthy children. I think you'll grow out of your present behavior. It will take time, though. In the meantime, you're confined to your room after classes let out for the day. You're to leave this building only to go to the dining hall. As for your new room assignment, there is a small one right next to my apartment. It used to belong to a janitor who worked here. You're to take that room. I've had your stuff moved downstairs. Your room upstairs will be assigned to someone else next term. Needless to say, that hole carved in the wall will be sealed up. I'll write Dr. Bogart and bill him for damages. To spare you, I won't tell him why you damaged the wall."

"But I didn't..." Hump stammered in protest but soon realized that it was useless. He'd already been tried and convicted.

After the shower incident, the other young men in Hump's dormitory avoided him, all except one, Floyd Furlow. Catching up with Hump after class one day, Floyd told him that he didn't believe all the stories being spread. "If anyone's a fucking sissy, it's Chittick himself. I wouldn't take a shower with him."

Over a cup of coffee and a hamburger at a local café, Floyd told Hump that the only way he could salvage his reputation at the Phillips Academy was to have an affair. "I've been seeing this older woman regularly. Her name's Medora Falkenstein, and she loves young men. She even likes to do nude drawings of them. I can set up a meeting. When the guys learn you're seeing Medora, they'll forget all about Chittick's dumb gossip."

At first Hump had raised a number of protests, including that he was confined to his room after class. "I'm not even supposed to be here right now," Hump said, looking around the café. "I'll tell Boyce I was studying at the library."

"The Boyce family is sound asleep by ten o'clock every night," Floyd said. "All the guys know that. Your new room is on the ground floor. All you have to do is open your window and slip out after the Boyces are snoring."

Slipping out the next night, Hump was shaking a bit as he knocked on the door of Medora Falkenstein. He was a bit disappointed when she answered the door. A shade past forty, she was garishly made up and wore an artist's smock. He wasn't certain what her body looked like under that ill-fitting garment. But even if he wasn't immediately smitten with her, Medora was enthralled with Hump.

She invited him in and gave him a large glass of Scotch. She also filled him with compliments about "what a beauty you are, far more so than Floyd, although I love that boy dearly."

Hump later told Floyd that he fully expected to get laid that afternoon, and had wanted to get it over with, so he could slip back into the dormitory, letting Floyd spread the word the next day of his conquest.

Medora had her own ideas about sex and how she liked it. On his third drink, when Hump's head was reeling, she showed him nude sketches she'd done of several boys on the campus, especially three of Floyd himself. She claimed that she'd moved to Andover just to be close to campus and "its never-ending supply of good-looking men."

"Who buys this stuff?" Hump asked her.

"I deal exclusively with a private art dealer in Boston," she said. "He has clients all over the country."

"You mean women buy this?" Hump asked.

"Heavens no," she said. "Men who like to be discreet. They pay top prices to see nude sketches of some of the country's most beautiful young men in their prime. Perhaps you'll pose for me one day."

"I couldn't do that," Hump said, no doubt thinking of the time he'd posed nude for Maud's art class.

"There's a hundred dollars in it for you," she said.

He was amazed at being offered that amount of money. It sounded like a fantastic sum. "I'll think about it."

"You don't have something you're ashamed of?" Medora asked, reaching to unbutton Hump's fly. With deft fingers, she removed his penis. "My, oh my, what a big boy you are. Much bigger than Floyd and he's not bad." Before Hump truly comprehended what was happening, Medora skinned back the cap of his penis and descended on him, as he immediately hardened.

In later life Bogie would tell friends that Medora got him addicted to blow-jobs. "She was the first person who ever gave me one, and she was also the best. A suction pump. She never allowed herself to be penetrated so she had developed her technique of the blow-job to absolute perfection since that was her only thing." Medora would masturbate herself as she performed fellatio on young men from Phillips Academy who ventured into her studio.

Afternoon visits to Medora became a ritual for Hump, who would go and see her right after his last class of the day. He managed to convince Boyce that he was spending the time in the academy library.

Eventually, since she always plied him with "hooch," as she called it, she didn't have much trouble persuading Hump to pose nude for her. After all, he didn't have anything to hide from her prying eyes that she hadn't seen in intimate close-up. Even buck-naked, he was completely relaxed in her studio, unlike his time in front of Maud's class when he'd been so nervous that he felt he'd shrunk a lot.

That was not his problem with Medora. Sometimes her sketching of him was interrupted when he'd get hard. She'd abandon her drawing and fellate him.

His sessions with Medora continued for nearly a month until one Saturday she invited him to come over around eleven in the evening. "My time with you is too brief. I want to make a night of it. Give you an around-the-world. It drives the boys crazy."

He wasn't certain what an around the world meant, but was intrigued at the prospect. That night a heavy snowstorm descended on Andover, and, anticipating his visit, Hump borrowed a pair of skis from the school athletic room and stored them in his tiny bedroom.

When the Boyces seemed to be deep into their nightmares and snores, he raised his window and slipped out of the dorm, attaching his skis and gliding his way to Medora's studio.

That night there were no nude sketches. Hump quickly learned that Medora's talented tongue could not only tame a hardened penis, but knew how to explore every crevice of a male body. The next day he reported in astonishment to Floyd that "the bitch even sucked my asshole."

Regrettably when returning to the dormitory in the pre-dawn hours, Hump was greeted by Boyce who caught him trying to sneak back into his window with the skis. The two men wrestled in the snow. Boyce's coat was ripped, his head injured.

The next morning, Headmaster Stearns called Hump into his office, informing him that he was expelled and was to check out of the dormitory that day, taking the train back to New York. "You are not worthy of the Academy," Stearns told him. "I predict you'll be a miserable failure in life, and have so informed Dr. Bogart."

By three o'clock on that snowy day in 1918, Hump had told Floyd good-bye and was on the train to Boston where he'd catch a larger train bound for New York.

Fearing the wrath of his parents, he decided that before he reached Manhattan he would take charge of his own life. He was going to make some bold career move and announce it the moment he came into the Bogart living room.

Before the train neared the outskirts of New York, Hump had made up his mind. The United States had already joined with the Allies to fight Germany in World War I. He'd join the fray.

Beginning tomorrow morning he was going to enlist in the U.S. Navy and would write his friend, Franklin D. Roosevelt, of his decision. The date was May 28, 1918.

***

If his parents had been cold and distant when he joined the Navy in the closing weeks of World War I, the Brady family was just the opposite. Brady Sr., Alice, Grace, and especially Bill Jr. were saddened to see him go. Each family member, promising to be on shore to welcome him home whenever his discharge might eventually arrive, had hugged and kissed him.

At the Bogart home, Maud would surely have dismissed such a farewell "as cheap theatrics common among Jews." She had given Hump a handshake, as had Belmont. His sisters, Frances and Catherine, had each kissed his cheek and wished him a safe return.

On June 19, 1918, a doctor at the Brooklyn Naval Base found that Hump was free of both syphilis and gonorrhea. In the event of Hump's death while overseas, he was told that his father would collect $35.90 per month for six months.

If he thought life was regimented at Andover, Hump was hardly prepared for the severe discipline of basic training which began July 2 at the Pelham Park Reserve in New York.

By November 9, about four months later, he was pronounced fit for duty and assigned to the USS *Leviathan,* a transport ship with a trio of gigantic funnels and zebra-like camouflage stripes. He came aboard as a helmsman, but even before the ship sailed from Hoboken, New Jersey, news reached the crew of the armistice. Germany had surrendered on November 11, 1918, and World War I was at an end.

There was still a job for the crew of the *Leviathan,* however. Ironically, it had originally been commissioned as the *Vaterland* and assigned to transport the Kaiser's forces. However, when the United States and Germany declared war, the *Vaterland* was in Hoboken and was seized by the United States Treasury Department. After some repairs and alterations, it was rechristened the *Leviathan.* Capable of carrying 14,500 men, it was the largest transport ship in the U.S. Navy.

Although he'd never seen active duty, Seaman No.1123062 put on his sailor's dress uniform with its knotted cravat and white puttees for a victory parade in Brooklyn. The next morning he sailed for Liverpool.

The vessel had been assigned for the next six months to haul U.S. servicemen back from France and England. En route to England, a junior officer, Robert Browne, demanded that Hump carry away some coffee cups and dirty dishes that had been left on deck by the officers. "Not my detail," Hump informed Browne. The officer kicked him in the face, bloodying his nose. "When an officer speaks to you and issues a command, you obey orders, boy."

"Yes, sir," Hump answered. There is no further record of Hump showing insubordination to an officer. Quickly learning that the U.S. Navy was not a democracy, he was a dutiful sailor until his term of duty came to an end.

All those stories, many made up by Bogie himself or his biographers, about the action he saw in World War I were inspired more by the bottle than real life. Bogie was a lot tougher on screen in his trench coat, carrying a gun, than he was in his Navy bell bottoms. Before heading overseas, he was widely quoted as proclaiming, "I'm not afraid of death."

He had no reason to be. The naval historian, Richard Wright, in a report filed with the State Department, wrote, "No troopship coming to the coast of France or England by an American escort was successfully attacked. The U.S. Navy transported two-million troops without losing a single man."

That didn't mean that Hump was freed of all the horrors of war. He was forever scarred by what he'd witnessed when returning soldiers were brought aboard his vessel. The young and the healthy came back from the battlefields "without a scratch." But other, sadder men had lost legs or arms on the battlefields of Eastern France. Some soldiers who'd been the victim of mustard gas were permanently wrecked. "When I saw the suffering of these men, and even though I was just a teenager, the terror of war struck my heart," Bogie was later to say. "War no longer seemed the grand adventure it had when I first sailed."

In later years, it was widely publicized that Bogie had received the famous injury to his upper lip when the *Leviathan* came under German shelling. That was just a fanciful tale conjured up in Hollywood long after the war was over, the U-boat menace itself something for the history pages. In later years, Bogie was embarrassed by his lack of action in World War I, and often invented stories to impress his cronies.

Over the years, Bogie also took particular delight in describing shore leave when he'd take the train from whichever French port where the *Leviathan* had docked, heading for Paris and "all those French dames." Bogie described in detail to John Huston and others how he visited the city's famous *maisons de tolerance*--a graceful term for "whorehouse." Bogie later claimed that he'd spent an entire week at one bordello on the Left Bank, venturing out only for meals. "Everything I learned about sex I learned in that house with about a dozen French-speaking prostitutes including some from Siam and Africa."

The biggest problem with that story is that the crew of the *Leviathan* was never granted shore leave to visit Paris during Hump's entire tour of duty aboard the vessel. He did, however, dock in Southampton, England, and visited the Red Lion Pub which staged drag acts so popular with the English.

Bogie never liked to talk about the most dramatic event of his military career. In February of 1919, he was transferred from the *Leviathan* to the USS *Santa Olivia*, which would be sailing from Hoboken, New Jersey, to Brest, France.

Fearing he wouldn't get laid for at least six weeks, he'd gone to The Gilded Cage, a notorious bar in Hoboken that catered to lonely sailors, relieving them of their money and their misery with "some of the most beautiful girls in Jersey."

The bar was run by a German-born lesbian, "Isak Smith," who claimed to be Swedish because of anti-German sentiment in the United States at the time. Apparently her real name was Isak but she changed her last name to Smith because it sounded American. Isak was said to have "auditioned" all the girls who worked in her bar before turning them loose to hustle sailors.

The Gilded Cage was famous for pushing drinks. Each working girl got a commission for every glass of overpriced booze she pushed onto a sailor. By the time many sailors reached a prostitute's bed, they were too drunk to perform although they were charged ten dollars anyway.

Hump had one-hundred dollars in his pocket, and he'd demanded the best-looking woman in the bar. When he left with a beautiful boozy blonde for a room in a nearby hotel, he was falling down drunk.

He had to report to duty at five that morning. As he later remembered it, his new-found girl friend had agreed to wake him up in time. The next morning her clock revealed that it was ten o'clock. The *Olivia* had sailed at seven that morning.

Putting on his trousers, Hump rushed to Naval Headquarters in Hoboken where he turned himself in. He was officially placed in the brig and fed a diet of only bread and water.

Branded a deserter, he very cleverly decided to call in a favor from none other than Franklin Roosevelt, then assistant secretary of the Navy. He wrote Roosevelt,

40

recalling their meeting and their night together at Seneca Point. True to his word and eager to return a kindness, Roosevelt intervened and got Hump's offense changed from deserter to "absent without leave."

Because of Roosevelt's intervention, Hump—despite his status as a deserter—received an honorable discharge at the Brooklyn Naval Yard on June 18, 1919, with a ranking as seaman second class--not the rank of quartermaster that he had hoped for. All that he had to show for his time in the service was twelve dollars in his pocket and a Victory Medal--an award that was routinely given to every serviceman who had completed a term of duty in the Armed Forces.

At the Bogart home on his first evening back, he found the atmosphere even chillier than when he'd left. His sisters were away at school, and all Maud could manage was another handshake. Belmont was away working as a ship's doctor on a cruise to Florida.

"We can't help you at all," Maud told Hump. Their rich life with a house full of servants was over. "There is no more money, only debts." He learned that the summer home at Seneca Point had finally been sold, the profit having gone to pay off mounting debts. Belmont had invested the family money in a get-rich-quick scheme in Michigan timberland and had lost every penny.

Because of his severe drug abuse, his once-flourishing medical practice had fallen off severely as patients drifted away. That's why he took assignments as a ship's doctor aboard cruises for long periods of time.

Wandering alone on the streets of New York, Hump found himself in the same situation as many returning veterans. He was out of work, relatively uneducated, and not qualified for most professions.

He longed for that overdue reunion with the Bradys, knowing that loving and supportive family might help him decide what to do with his life. He especially missed Bill. But all of the Bradys, including Grace and Alice, were out of town touring with a roadshow.

Hump wrote Bill in Philadelphia. "Hurry back to New York and be my best pal once again. I miss you something awful. My life's a waste. I'm a failure."

***

In desperation and out of cash, Hump tried to find a job. He was hired to work in the mail department of the National Biscuit Company for $25 a week. After a month, and after showing up late for work four times in only two weeks, he was fired. An entire month went by before he found a job with the Pennsylvania Tug and Literage Company, where he was hired to trace shipments reported lost. Part of this job involved inspecting tugboats. Hump had distorted his Navy service record, and had claimed during his job interview that he was qualified as a boat inspector, which he wasn't. After sending in a number of reports that his boss called "nonsensical," Hump was fired.

Out of work and unable to find another job, Hump asked Belmont for help.

Belmont's ill-fated investments were handled by the Wall Street firm of S.W. Strauss & Co. Belmont's longtime friend and investment broker, Wilbur Jenkins, was a vice president of the company. After Belmont appealed to Jenkins, the company hired Hump as a "runner" for $30 a week. He was charged with delivering securities and stock certificates to brokerage houses and banks.

When Bill Jr. returned to New York, Hump told him that he "was going to start out like Horatio Alger and work my way up to becoming president one day." Although Hump hated the runner's job, he held onto the position because he needed the money to party with his friends. The post-war era had arrived, and Hump expressed his desire "to become a Jazz Age baby."

As much as he hated his temporary jobs, Hump loved the rediscovery of his old friend. Although both men actively pursued girls, Hump and Bill Brady seemed more bonded than ever. Their boy/boy sexual flirtation with each other was about to enter a new phase. Although Hump was still considered very good looking in an unconventional way, Bill had grown into a remarkably handsome man, eagerly pursued by both girls and older women.

The dashing Stuart Rose had returned from military duty and had resumed his friendships with both Hump and Bill. He spent most of his time dating Frances. When Frances was at school, Stuart joined Bill and Hump on their jaunts to the Playhouse, a theater that William Brady Sr. operated on West 48th Street.

Sometimes, Stuart invited Hump and Bill to one of his equestrian classes at the Squadron A. Armory. Originally Hump had been afraid of horses but he trusted Stuart and responded to his teaching. Stuart pronounced him the best pupil he'd ever had.

Bill was much more interested in "the theater and girls," although he still joined in on the rides. On Sunday rides in Central Park, they would sometimes be joined by John Cromwell, the director.

The only problem was that Maud insisted on dressing Hump in fashionable riding gear that she'd seen in English sporting magazines. Hump stood out as a bit of a dandy and terribly overdressed.

It was a time for making new friends and going to social gatherings in Greenwich Village. Bill and Hump learned to love parties in the village where they felt a part of bohemian life for the first time. If given a chance, Hump would sing at these parties. Hump had made another friend, Kenneth Mielziner, who was an actor using the name "Kenneth MacKenna." Although he could not have known it at the time, Kenneth was to become one of Bogie's closest confidants during his first attempt at a film career in Hollywood. Kenneth shared a brownstone on Waverly Place in Greenwich Village with his brother, "Jo" Mielziner, who was slated for future fame as one of America's leading stage designers.

Kenneth later recalled that he and Hump "liked the same type of woman," although the breed was never specified, since Kenneth's taste ranged from blondes to redheads, from tall, skinny girls to shorter, more fully rounded ones. "When I was through with a girl, I would pass her on to Hump. My attention span with women was short at the time, and I quickly became bored. I picked up girls with greater ease than Hump who was still a bit shy around the fairer sex. He was all too eager to date my discards."

By 1938 the situation would reverse itself when Kenneth married one of Bogie's "discards," his second wife, Mary Philips.

Hump was finding it harder and harder to report to work as a runner on Wall Street. Nights were for frequenting speakeasies, listening to jazz, smoking, drinking bootleg hooch, and chasing after pretty women. Stuart remained faithful to Frances, but partly because of their promiscuity, Kenneth, Hump, John Cromwell and Bill nicknamed themselves "the pussy posse."

If a woman had a choice of these men, she usually opted for Bill Jr., since he possessed great charm and personality. If a girl couldn't get Bill, she settled for one of the other young men. Perhaps because he was smaller and less dynamic around women, Hump was often the last to get picked for a date.

For a very brief time, a young actor, James Cagney, joined the pussy posse. Hump and Bill felt uncomfortable around Cagney but Kenneth insisted on inviting him. Unlike Hump's "sissy" upbringing, Cagney, a man of the streets, had joined gangs as a kid and had learned to use his fists. He was the tough city kid, actually living the role that Hump would play at Warner Brothers when he often vied for the same parts that Cagney garnered, or else co-starred with him. Cagney told Hump that he could not make up his mind: he wanted to be either a song-and-dance man or else a farmer.

Although Cagney exuded masculinity, when he first met Hump he was appearing as a "showgal" in a revival of a production called *Every Sailor*. Originally conceived as a morale-booster for members of the Navy far from home, its cast included many recently discharged sailors. As in the original, all the female parts were played by men. When one of the cast members got sick, a friend introduced Cagney to the producer, Phil Dunning, who hired him on the spot, providing he'd appear in drag.

"Listen, for $35 a week, I'll come out nude if they want me to," Cagney told Hump. Cagney claimed that he looked great as a gal, especially when he painted his mouth in scarlet red in a "sort of beesting," like screen goddess Mae Murray. Hump couldn't believe that Cagney could transform himself into a gorgeous dame. Cagney said that he'd show up for their next night on the town in full drag. "The men will flock around me like moths to the flame."

Indeed Cagney showed up two nights later dressed as a woman, and the pussy posse was stunned. Bill claimed that he would have asked Cagney for a date if he didn't know he had a dick under that gown.

Cagney demonstrated his skill as a vamp by capturing the attention of the handsomest man at the speakeasy. On a dare Cagney disappeared two hours later with a young Wall Street broker. What happened later that night remains unknown. Cagney never told the pussy posse how the evening ended, and in his authorized biography, *James Cagney*, he makes no mention of having known Hump in their early days.

The next morning, hung over from an all-night party, Hump showed up late for work and was severely chastised by his boss on Wall Street. He was given documents to deliver to a firm ten blocks away. On the way there, he recalled having a splitting headache. Deep into his hangover, and barely able to continue down the block, he opted for breakfast at a coffee shop, hoping that would cure his pain. Shortly thereafter, three blocks from the scene of his ham and eggs breakfast, he realized with horror that he'd left the valuable documents in a brief-case perched on the coffee shop's coat rack. He hurried back, only to discover that the briefcase had been stolen.

"Knowing I was going to get fired when I returned to the office, I decided not to go back," Hump later recalled.

On an impulse and having given it no thought beforehand, he rode the sub-way to the theatrical offices of William Brady, Sr. Hump felt that he should have checked with Bill before asking his father for a job but there was no time for that.

William Sr. welcomed Hump into his office as Hump had remained a family favorite. Telling the elder showman of his plight, Hump found him most sympathetic. "I just happen to have an opening," Brady said. "As an office boy. The pay's $35 a week."

Hump eagerly took the job and was thrilled to be making that much money in 1920. "As you know, sir, Bill and I both love the theater. To be a part of it in some way would make me very happy."

"Cut out all of this I-love-the-theater crap," Brady said. "The Broadway stage is just fine, and I guess it'll go on forever. But the future of mass entertainment lies in the flickers. From now on, I'm a movie producer."

***

Hump found his new job as an office boy exciting, as he would relate to an attractive brunette, Ruth Rankin, who he was dating at the time. He'd given her a handsome picture of himself in his full dress Navy uniform, and she kept the photograph by her bedside, which was always there to greet him during his frequent visits to that much-used bed.

Although Hump humped frequently, he confessed to Bill that, "I don't really love her." Bill chided him, "You don't have to love a gal to fuck her."

After working for Brady for only a month, Hump was promoted to production manager of the Brady film studio at Fort Lee, New Jersey, his pay raised to $50 a week. His duties included renting props and paying off the actors in cash.

When Brady Sr. saw the first rushes of a film, *Life*, that he'd commissioned, he fired the director, Travers Vale, and assigned Hump to take over the job.

Knowing nothing about acting or directing, Hump found a beret and a pair of black boots in the wardrobe department and showed up the next day, thinking himself a budding Erich von Stroheim or Cecil B. DeMille. The stars of the film

44

were Arline Pretty, Nita Naldi, and Rod La Rocque.

When Bill Brady Jr. visited the set on the second day of Hump's tenure as director, he immediately fell in love with Arline Pretty, launching a hot, torrid affair that lasted exactly three days, until Nita Naldi reported for work. Bill immediately dumped Arline and chased after Naldi. Hump called his friend a "lovesick pup," while denying that he was attracted to Naldi himself. Actually he wanted her and was jealous of Bill for capturing her so soon.

The witty and glamorous Naldi was Hump's first experience with a screen vamp. Ironically, like Alice Brady herself, Naldi had been raised in a convent in New Jersey, where the Mother Superior happened to be her great-aunt. For someone with such a sheltered background, Hump thought Naldi had "street smarts." On the first day of shooting, Naldi informed her young director, "Even though I'm supposed to be a vamp in this pisser of a flick, I don't want to be photographed looking like Theda Bara buried for two-thousand years and just dug up."

After five days of filming, Bill invited Hump to join him after work at a speakeasy in Fort Lee for a private conversation. "I'm in love with Nita and she's in love with herself. I'm having the time of my life, but she says we can't go on unless you get involved."

"What in hell does that mean?" Hump asked.

"She wants you to join us in bed. Otherwise, it's no dice."

"You've got to be kidding," Hump said.

"C'mon," Bill urged. "It's not like we haven't known each other real intimate like. We already know that both of us are made of sugar and spice."

Hump didn't hesitate for long. A few drinks of bootleg gin lowered his inhibitions. He desperately wanted to seduce Naldi. Figuring if this was his only chance, and considering that Bill was such a close friend, he agreed to meet that night in Naldi's hotel room.

For the next ten days, shooting on *Life* slowed down considerably, as Bill, Naldi, and Hump spent as much as two hours a day in her makeshift dressing room. For reasons of her own, Naldi could no longer see either man at night.

She'd later confess to her Hollywood comrade and sometimes lover, Natacha Rambova, the second wife of Rudolph Valentino, that she'd let Bill get on her first before allowing Hump to mount her. "I wouldn't let either of them stay on long. When they started getting too excited, I'd make one get off and the other get on. I'd string this out for a long time before letting them have their well-earned climaxes. No woman in New York was more sexually fulfilled than I was. I learned about multiple orgasms for the first time."

Born Donna Dooley in New York City two years before Hump, Nita Naldi was the first of many screen vamps Hump would seduce. Fresh from the convent, she'd acquired an immediate job as a clothes model at $15 a week before joining the chorus line at the Winter Garden's Century Roof.

Hump might have fallen for Naldi, but the male star of the film, Rod La Rocque, had fallen for his director.

Born in Chicago of an Irish mother and a French father, Rod had played mainly "boy parts," often at a dollar a performance, before Brady Sr. cast him in *Life*. At the time he met Hump, he was living at a local YMCA with another aspiring actor, Ralph Graves. A closeted homosexual, known for his good looks, elegant profile, and--years later--for a real-estate fortune he developed by buying up then-undesirable California real estate, Rod quickly became a factor in young Hump's life. La Rocque had already appeared in a Brady theatrical production, *Up the Ladder*, with Brady's daughter, Alice. The play had bombed, but Brady Sr. was sufficiently impressed with the actor to give him a chance on film.

As Hump tried to direct Rod, the male star of the film had eyes only for Hump and not the camera. Rod even suggested that Hump direct him privately so he'd know how to play his love scenes with Nita Naldi. "I can play Naldi's part and you can be me in the love scenes."

Fellow sailors during his military duty had put the make on Hump, but he'd never been pursued by a homosexual as aggressively as he was chased by La Rocque.

"The fucker even sends me roses and buys me chocolates," Hump confessed to Bill. "Like I'm his best dame or something. He begs me to go out with him. I can't even go take a piss in the latrine but what he follows me, panting away. He begs me to let him suck my dick. I'm too nice a guy to punch him out. Besides, he's the star of my picture, and I don't want to mess up his face."

Hump didn't become La Rocque's lover but offered some good professional advice when the actor came to him to discuss screen billings. "Here is my choice of names," La Rocque said. He'd written down suggestions for screen credit on a piece of paper which he handed to Hump.

Roderick La Rock. Rodney La Rock. Roderick La Rocque. Rodney LaRocque or Rod LaRocque. Hump studied the sheet, then wrote, "None of the above. Make it Rod La Rocque. It's catchy."

When Brady Sr. back in New York saw the first footage of *Life* directed by Hump, he was horrified. In several scenes, the drunken cameraman had actually put Hump into the frame, frantically directing his players. "The fucking director is being photographed directing," Brady screamed out in his office.

The news that came in that day was even worse. Two of *Life's* bit players filmed in a speeding car were supposed to be fighting for control of the steering wheel as the vehicle raced toward a stone wall. Hump had instructed the actors, Betty Furnall and Adolf Brunnen, to wait for a signal from him, at which point they were to swerve the car out of harm's way, avoiding the wall. Hump miscalculated.

When he finally signaled, the car had gone beyond the point of no return. It crashed into the wall, and an ambulance was summoned to take the two victims to a hospital. Although injured, they survived the crash and lived to send Brady their medical bills.

The next day Brady drove over to Fort Lee and personally fired Hump, taking over as director himself.

That same day, Nita Naldi informed both Bill and Hump that she couldn't see them any more. While dancing at the Winter Garden in the chorus, she'd been spotted by none other than John Barrymore. She claimed that he had fallen in love with her and was going to cast her opposite him in his flicker, *Dr. Jekyll and Mr. Hyde.*

Sorry to see her go, Hump and Bill agreed that Naldi would be one of the many chorus girls that The Great Profile would pick up and discard. In this rare instance, however, Barrymore did indeed cast her in the role, and Nita Naldi went on to become one of the reigning screen vamps of the Twenties. Her biggest break came in Cecil B. DeMille's *The Ten Commandments*, where she played the Eurasian temptress, Sally Lung, who contracts leprosy as a "wages-of-sin" payment for her evil ways. Her co-star? None other than Rod La Rocque himself.

Brady Sr. went on to salvage *Life*, eventually selling it to Adolph Zukor for $100,000. After he'd purchased the film, Zukor looked at it carefully, deciding it wasn't worth releasing. He assigned it to storage where it managed to disappear.

When Bogie in later life learned there were no more copies left, he said, "Thank the Devil for that."

***

Out of work, Hump spent the next three weeks writing a scenario for a gory film, *Blood and Death*. He wrote the script at the 21 Club, then one of New York's most famous speakeasies. Thinking that such a costume made him look more like a writer, he wore a tweed jacket and smoked a pipe.

Even though he'd been fired by Brady, Hump showed up at his office with his completed film script. Fearing rejection, Hump was surprised when "Mr. Showman" himself thought the script "could play." He sent it over to a trio of producers he knew, Jesse L. Lasky, Samuel Goldfish (later Goldwyn), and Cecil B. DeMille. All three producers were too busy to read it, and they turned the script over to an office assistant, Walter Wanger. He skimmed it before tossing it into a wastepaper basket.

In later life, when Wanger had become one of Hollywood's biggest producers and Bogie one of its biggest male stars, Wanger always claimed that "Bogart used to write for me."

Wanger went on to produce such classics as Greta Garbo's *Queen Cristina* in 1933, John Ford's *Stagecoach* in 1939, and even the ill-fated *Cleopatra* in 1963, co-starring Elizabeth Taylor and Richard Burton.

Following a night of tabloid scandal in 1951, Bogie visited Wanger in jail. The previous evening in a fit of jealous rage, Wanger had shot a well-known Hollywood agent, Jennings Lang, in the groin. The agent managed the career of the then famous actress, Joan Bennett. "I was aiming for the fucker's balls," Wanger told Bogie, "but I missed." Bogie's reply: "So what in hell was the matter with my screenplay?"

Hump wasn't off the Brady payroll for long. Brady Sr. claimed he had no peace at home, because his wife, Grace George, his daughter, Alice, and his son, Bill, kept urging him to give Hump another chance. Brady rehired Hump at $50 a week and sent him on tour as the stage manager for Grace's play, *The Ruined Lady*.

He toured with Grace for six months in East Coast cities, including Philadelphia and Boston. He did not fall for Grace, who remained faithful to her husband, but she later recalled that he always managed to find a female companion in the seedy hotels her husband had booked them in. Mostly they stayed in fleabags that accepted traveling actors. Many hotels in those days refused to accommodate actors because they gave loud, drunken parties late at night, tore up the furniture, and usually skipped town without paying the bill.

Bogie in later life would view that tour of *The Ruined Lady* as the most sexually liberating period of his life. "Everything I learned about women, I learned then. I'd had sexual experiences with the likes of Nita Naldi and others, but on the road I met all sorts of women—all shapes, sizes, whatever. I learned that some gals will do things to a man that respectable women never do. After that road show, I found a return to New York restrictive."

Co-starring beside Grace was a handsome young actor, Neil Hamilton, playing the *ingénu* lead. Although Hamilton was headed for a big career in Hollywood where he would become one of its most durable actors, Hump as stage manager wasn't impressed with him. He called Hamilton "the stuffed shirt model," because the actor had posed for so many shirt ads in magazines. Hamilton countered by calling Hump "Baby Food." Behind Hump's back, he referred to him as "Baby Shit."

On tour with Hamilton, Hump needled him for "having such a soft job. All you have to do is show up every night, mouth some writer's words, and get your paycheck." Hamilton always protested that there was more to acting than that.

Before sending him out on the road, Brady had insisted that Hump understudy all the male parts in case one of the actors got sick. Before the final performance of *The Ruined Lady*, Hamilton developed the flu and called in to cancel.

The cast assembled that Saturday afternoon for a dry run with Hump as the male lead. He'd memorized all the parts, having heard them week after week. But facing the seats of the empty theater, he was paralyzed and couldn't remember one line of dialogue.

Fortunately for Hump, Grace also developed a fever, perhaps having caught the flu germs from Hamilton during their love scenes. When members of the prospective audience showed up that night, their money was refunded at the box office.

In spite of what Hump would later call "the disaster that never was," the ever-faithful Brady family continued to believe in his acting talent. In May of 1921, Alice Brady offered him a walk-on part in her play, *Drifting*. It was going to have try-outs in Brooklyn in hope of obtaining backers for a Broadway production.

Its director was John Cromwell, Hump's close friend who was also a stage performer himself. In time, he would become one of Hollywood's leading directors, known for turning out such classics as *Of Human Bondage* in 1934, *Algiers* in 1938, *Abe Lincoln in Illinois* in 1940, and *Anna and the King of Siam* in 1946.

For Hump's stage debut in *Drifting* at Brooklyn's Fulton Theater, he invited everyone he knew. Maud chose not to go see her son on stage, still disapproving of his preferred choice of a profession. But the ever-faithful Bill Brady Jr. showed up, bringing with him Belmont and Stuart Rose. Stuart was still dating Frances. Hump's sister had just seen her husband-to-be march in the Memorial Day parade. All three were eager to see Hump on the stage, hoping it would be a triumph for him.

To Stuart's horror, he discovered that Hump was spectacularly miscast in the role of a Japanese butler. Alice played a *femme fatale*, an archetype that would be perfected by Marlene Dietrich in films of the 30s. In later life, Hump called her role "early Sadie Thompson." Kicked out of her home by her Puritan father, Alice's character ended up in Singapore "drifting" into a life of depravity before being rescued by a handsome American soldier who falls in love with her.

Bogie made his brief appearance carrying a tray of pink gin fizzes. Trying to imitate a Japanese accent, he uttered the words, "Drinks for my lady and for her most honored guests." Frances and Stuart slid down in their seats in embarrassment, although Belmont later said that he thought his son "did a right fair job."

After he became a star, Bogie always derided the role as "the dumb Jap butler part," as if anticipating the words of Erich von Stroheim who called his role in *Sunset Boulevard* opposite Gloria Swanson "the dumb butler part." Von Stroheim made the role the greatest butler part of all time, whereas Bogie's stage debut hardly merits a footnote in theatrical history.

Somewhere between the time the tryouts were held and the play's Broadway opening, Hump and the slightly older Alice began a quiet affair, even though she had married James Crane.

"It's a cordial romance," Hump told Bill, who didn't seem at all horrified that his best friend was sexually involved with his married step-sister. As Hump related to Bill, "We talk theater half the night and then get into bed together. Fortunately, Crane is out of town a lot. I get on top of her, do my job, then roll over and go to sleep,"

It wasn't love, but it was sex. Actually it evolved more into friendship than anything else. Until her death, Hump would remain her steadfast friend.

Drifting did make it to Broadway and ran for sixty-three performances, even though Alan Dale, theater critic for the *New York American*, called the play "strangely protuberant." Its Broadway run at an end, Brady sent Alice and Hump on the road with *Drifting*.

Two months into the run of *Drifting,* Alice announced to Hump that she was pregnant and was going to leave the cast. At first he was petrified, thinking that he might be the father. Alice assured him that the father was her husband.

After she bowed out of the show, she never resumed her affair with Hump, later referring to it as "that brief fling that often happens between actors." For Hump, it would become the role model for a future series of involvements with actresses with whom he appeared on stage or in films.

Brady hired a fast-emerging young star of her day, Helen Menken, to replace his daughter. Arriving at the theater, Helen spotted Hump backstage. She told the theater manager, Glenn Wilson, "Daddy, I want a taste of that."

***

A slender, beautiful actress, Helen Menken--because of her temper tantrums--was known as "the Irish Menk" in theatrical circles. She had moppish hair, a sort of auburn red, and her cupid's-bow mouth was just as expressive as her hands, which Richard Schnel, a theater critic, had called "the most expressive on Broadway."

She looked at the world through liquid dark brown eyes that sometimes left the impression that she was misty-eyed. Her face was thin and pale, made even more so by her excessive use of rice powder. She kept her figure because of an extraordinary diet of two boiled eggs a day and perhaps a leaf of lettuce. That dietary advice had been given to her by the stage actress, Nazimova, who recommended it to all aspiring actresses as a guaranteed way of keeping one's figure. Nazimova, as Hump was to learn later, had introduced young Helen to the delights of lesbian love.

When Helen met Hump, she was already an established star, although not yet at the height of her fame. She'd appeared in Victoria Herbert's play, *The Red Mill*, to critical acclaim.

She'd also scored a success in 1918 in *Three Wise Fools*, a play by Austin Strong. Before her steady employment in the theater, she sold women's hats and also did some clothes modeling at department stores. Prospective employers always commented on her "narrow shoulders," preferring, even then, the more broad-shouldered look that in just a few more years would be popularized by Joan Crawford.

Helen had made her theatrical debut at the age of six when she'd walked out nude in a production of *Midsummer Night's Dream*. It is said that the circumstances that surrounded Helen's true-life stage debut at the age of six inspired the creation of the fictional career of the character of Margo Channing in the 1950 film, *All About Eve*, starring Bette Davis.

Poorly educated and born into poverty, Helen had acquired a gloss of sophistication because of all her years in the theater. Born in New York City, she was the oldest of three children. For some reason of her own, Helen was proud to be a direct descendant of John Wilkes Booth.

Hump was intrigued by her upbringing, which she called "my world of silence." Both of her parents were deaf mutes, although Helen had been born with perfect hearing. She learned to communicate with them in sign language. Whenever her parents would get into an argument, one of them would turn off the lights, ending a fight since they could no longer see each other to communicate.

Helen's mother earned $3.50 a week sewing identification badges for business conventions, but her father had never held down a job for very long. Helen herself had come from a rough-and-tumble background of acting in road shows and sleeping in seedy rooms above drunken saloons.

She remembered when one of these fleabag hotels near Trenton, New Jersey, had caught fire. "I climbed down from the second-floor window since the fire was raging up the only stairway. I raced out into the night and was standing out on the highway before I realized I was stark naked. It was twenty degrees that night."

For years she'd supported her family and had even managed to send one of her brothers to college. Helen herself had had only one and a half years of grade school. She didn't enroll in school until she was twelve years old.

Hump disliked Helen on sight. Because of Alice's sudden withdrawal from the play, he had only twenty-four hours to teach her her lines. He might not have liked her personally but was amazed at how fast she learned the script. Before the curtain went up the following night, she was letter perfect.

Unfortunately the play called for a series of eight complicated set changes. Deep into the second act, Hump and the stagehands in their haste had not secured the props. In the middle of Helen's big scene, the wall of a set collapsed on her, burying her in front of the audience. Hump had to pull the curtain before Helen, who had not been hurt, could resume her theatrics.

Helen tried to recoup her dignity but many customers walked out, demanding a refund on their tickets, claiming that they had only purchased them to see Alice Brady.

Enraged, Helen rushed backstage to confront Hump. "You asshole!" she shrieked at him. "You little shit."

Because of the abuse suffered at the hands of Maud's ill-mannered and ill-tempered servants, Hump could not stand being called little shit. He kicked her in the rump, sending her sprawling onto the wooden floor. Jumping up, she aimed her sharply pointed high-heel shoe at his groin, scoring a bull's-eye assault on his testicles. Falling to the floor, he doubled over in pain, which is where she left him as she stalked off to her dressing room.

It was the beginning of a beautiful friendship.

***

Within six weeks Helen was professing her love for Hump. That love was not reciprocated, although he later told his friend Bill that "she's great in the sack." She invited him to come and live with her at her flat at 43 East 25th Street in New

York but only for four nights each week. The other three nights of her week, Helen enjoyed the "wild side" of New York with her newly discovered companion, Tallulah Bankhead.

Tallulah was a gorgeous and outrageous Alabama belle, living at the Algonquin Hotel on $50 a week sent to her by her daddy. Her stated ambition for coming to New York was: (1) to become the biggest Broadway star of all time; (2) to seduce John Barrymore, and (3) to "fuck Ethel Barrymore."

Hump had moved in with Helen without knowing much about her. In the first month or so, she kept him like a "toy boy," not introducing him to her friends or making him part of her glittering Broadway world. It was as if she couldn't decide what role he was going to play in her life.

Day by day Hump learned more about his new girl friend. A high strung, nervous woman with a bizarre (perhaps anorexic) diet and a tendency to drink heavily, she worried and fretted most of the day. She read Broadway news with a certain fury, often bursting into violent rages when a rival actress received a part that she felt she was "destined to play."

Although bitterly resentful of the success of other actresses, she encouraged Hump with his theatrical ambitions. "After all, you're no competition to me, darling. Be an actor out in front of the lights, not some God damn prop man. As a stagehand, you stink." She constantly ribbed Hump for that opening night when the scenery fell on her.

Helen had some peculiarities. Long before the world ever heard of Imelda Marcos, Helen spent a good part of her salary buying expensive shoes, even it if meant going without some of life's essentials. She adored her tiny feet, which to Hump evoked memories of Maud's small feet.

The only difference was that Helen demanded that Hump spend as much time in bed kissing, licking, and biting her feet, as well as sucking her toes, as he did in attacking other parts of her body. Helen would spend hours washing, bathing, and caring for her feet, with endless pedicures. She would fret over the right nail polish to use for her dainty toes.

In spite of her lack of schooling, she spoke perfect English. She said she'd learned to speak properly listening to other actresses on the stage, beginning with the star Annie Russell in *Midsummer Night's Dream*. Helen's voice sounded slightly husky, something like that of the future actress, Barbara Stanwyck, Bogie's 1947 co-star in *The Two Mrs. Carrolls*.

Helen was much the same off-stage as she was on, which was very flamboyant. She called everybody "darling," an appellation soon picked up by her protégée, Tallulah.

Almost overnight, Helen became the toast of Broadway. Austin Strong had "loved" her performance in his play, *Three Wise Fools*, and campaigned for her to be cast as Diane in his latest play, *Seventh Heaven*, which opened on Broadway in 1922 and became an immediate hit.

Hump himself was in the opening night audience and was dazzled at her performance. In the role, she played a street urchin in Paris. Her most memorable scene was when she took a bullwhip, and in her rage and despair, drove her mean sister out of the house.

Before meeting Helen, Hump had dated an aspiring young actress, Katherine Alexander. Briefly smitten with her, Hump pursued Katherine for a week or two. He'd never known anyone who'd been born and reared in Alaska, and was fascinated to learn of her experiences in the cold north. "I can take the chill off you," he promised Katherine. She never gave him a chance to prove that.

When he introduced Katherine to the handsomer, taller, richer, better built, and more successful Bill Brady Jr., Hump's romance with Katherine came to an abrupt end. She fell at once for Bill. Hump showed little jealousy, and even suggested at one point that "we should share her," evoking their brief fling with Nita Naldi.

After the third week, Bill would stand for no more talk like that. He'd fallen madly in love with Katherine, and planned to make her "my exclusive property." Within six weeks of meeting Katherine, Bill invited Hump to be his best man at their wedding. Hump asked Helen to accompany him.

Attending the wedding of Katherine and Bill must have given Helen an idea. Within weeks, she was urging Hump to marry her. She was proposing to him as if he were the prospective bride and she the groom. Hump didn't turn her down but didn't accept her proposal either.

He turned to his friend Bill for advice. "If I marry Helen," he said, "I'll be repeating Maud's pattern with Belmont. Strong woman, the bread earner, supporting weak husband."

"Forget about that," Bill said. "Marry the bitch. She's a friend of all the critics and knows all the big-name producers. She'll advance your career. Trust me on this one. If you scorn Helen, she'll cut off your balls. She's already kicked them. You may never work on Broadway again."

Hump remained uncertain and confused. At Helen's urging, he went to secure a marriage license, which he would carry around in his wallet for the next four years. In an interview on April 5, 1922, Hump told the *New York Times*, "I plan to marry Helen Menken." Because of Helen's prominence as a Broadway star, the paper gave it a headline. Suddenly, all of Broadway became aware of the struggling actor, Humphrey Bogart. He hadn't even married her yet, and already Bill's advice was proving to be true. Almost overnight, producers started offering Hump parts, no doubt with a little urging from Helen herself.

With the *Times* announcing her engagement, Helen no longer had any reason to keep Hump a secret in the closet. Her toy boy (although men weren't called that then) could emerge into the full theatricality of her glittering world. He would meet for the first time Miss Tallulah Bankhead, whom he had confided in Bill was "Helen's other boy friend."

Chapter Three

Instead of being threatened or offended by Helen's sexual involvement with Tallulah, Hump was intrigued. He pointedly asked his friend Bill, "Just what do women do in bed together? I understand the kissing part, but the plumbing doesn't seem quite right."

In detail, the more worldly Bill tried to explain lesbian love and how it worked. Even so, Hump didn't quite get it.

That evening, Bill invited him to Harlem's Red Garter, a notorious nightclub that flourished briefly and illegally in the early 1920s until the police shut it down. Patronized only by male customers, the club specialized in presenting live sex acts on its small stage but only between women performers.

The lesbian black actress, Hattie McDaniel, was said to be a frequent patron of the club and was even rumored to have been a performer. Hattie would go on to greater fame playing Mammy to Scarlett O'Hara in *Gone with the Wind*. As a further irony, she was to become the lover of Tallulah Bankhead, as Tallulah in her declining years would readily admit to her homosexual "cunties," as she called her all-male entourage.

It was a wiser and more experienced Humphrey Bogart, man of the world, who escorted Helen to the 21 Club to meet Tallulah Bankhead.

When Hump was introduced, Tallulah Bankhead's hair looked badly combed, yet it was radiant. Her mouse-brown dress, however, should long ago have been sent to the cleaners. "Forgive my appearance, darling," she said, aping Helen's habit of calling everybody darling. "I've just gone down on John Barrymore and haven't had time to make myself into a lady again."

"You look beautiful," Hump assured her. Actually he didn't know what to make of this Alabama bombshell, although he could understand Helen's fascination with her.

"I must ask a tiny favor," she said. "To catch the streetcar home, I need one tiny, little, small penny as I have only four cents in my purse, hardly enough for the five-cent fare."

"I don't understand why you're always broke," Helen said, ordering an illegal martini from the waiter at 21. "You employ a French maid."

"I know, darling," Tallulah said. "Daddy sends me $50 a week, and I have to give the maid half of that. That means I'm penniless for three days a week."

"Fire the maid," Hump said. "My mother did when the family fortune disappeared."

"Perish the thought, darling," Tallulah said. "No respectable lady could live in New York without a French maid. It's simply not done."

Helen was the more established star, but Tallulah dominated the night. Hump concluded that Tallulah was the "man" in her relationship with Helen, his girl friend the submissive female.

"You must meet my sister, Eugenia," Tallulah said to Hump, reaching over to caress his hand. "She's not a classic beauty like me, but one hell of a woman. Those stories about her being a lesbian are exaggerated. She lives in an apartment next door to Zelda and Scott Fitzgerald. They've been anxious to meet the two of you since the *New York Times* referred to your coupling as a union of two Jazz Age Babies. Scott views himself as the world's expert on Jazz Age babies."

Since Tallulah didn't have any money, Helen invited her to join them for dinner at Sam's Vanity, a popular little restaurant that flourished for three months until its owner, Sam Martin, was fatally shot by his estranged wife.

At table, Tallulah stuffed herself, while claiming that Sam didn't know how to cook Southern fried chicken. After dinner, she made a telephone call and invited Helen and Hump to go with her to visit a British friend. "An absolutely fascinating man," she assured them. "You'll adore him, darling."

She looked over at Hump. "One look at you, and he'll fall madly for you, you handsome devil you. Helen tells me you've got a big one, darling, but I like to check things out for myself. People exaggerate so." She laughed hysterically at her own observation.

In a taxi en route to their destination, Tallulah confessed that she was "passionately involved" with this British gentleman. "John Barrymore for sex, or Ethel if I can get her, but for true love it's Napier George Henry Stuart Alington. You can call him Naps for short. He's the third Baron of Alington."

Even though claiming undying love for this Englishman, Tallulah revealed that Noël Coward had just left New York, returning to London. "During Coward's visit, I was never alone with Naps. That bitch, Noël, used up all of Naps' sexual energy, leaving nothing for me, the selfish bastard." She pulled out a cigarette. Hump tried to light it for her. "I light my own cigarettes, darling." Later she claimed that she'd been unkind in her catty remarks about Coward. "He's actually a God from Mt. Olympus. Both of you must meet him." Ironically Bogie in later life would become a very close friend of Noël Coward's.

As Naps stood at the door of his plushly furnished Victorian apartment, Hump and Helen at last got to meet him. In his mid-20s, he appeared to be a gentle soul, and Hump was surprised that he was Tallulah's type. Under a mop of blond hair, he had a small delicate build. His most sensuous physicality was in his thick lips. He had a nervous habit of constantly licking the roof of his mouth, as if he were tasting honey.

Ushered into the living room, Helen, Hump, and Tallulah were served martinis by an English butler. Spread out on Naps' glass-topped coffee table was a virtual shopping cart of drugs, including not only cocaine, but heroin and also morphine, the substance so beloved by Maud and Belmont Bogart.

The heroin came in little vanity boxes, lined in red silk, evocative of Tiffany jewel boxes. Small hypodermic needles were arranged moonlike around the heroin boxes. For his drug of choice, Hump selected morphine, hoping to understand his parents' infatuation with the drug.

Tallulah claimed that she found morphine boring and chided Hump for not selecting cocaine, which she said was the drug of the moment. Cocaine was enjoying the same type of popularity among New York's jazz babies in the early Twenties as marijuana did among the hippies of the late Sixties. Instead of masquerade balls, "snow balls" were all the rage, and Tallulah said she attended two every week of her life.

The next day when Hump related the drama of the previous night to Bill, Hump was a little vague on details, not that he was holding back information. He honestly claimed he couldn't remember. "That morphine sent me into another world."

All he recalled was that Tallulah and Helen started kissing on the sofa and he watched as their tongues darted inside each other's mouths. "It was like a white girls' show at the Red Garter."

At one point Naps appeared nude in the living room and invited all of them into his bedroom. "Tallulah and Helen took turns kissing me and feeding me their breasts, while I lay naked on the guy's bed. Naps was a real sexual opportunist. When the women had worked me into white heat, he descended like a suction pump and drained me dry."

Somewhere before dawn, Helen and Hump dropped Tallulah off at some mysterious apartment on West 51st Street, and Helen directed the cabbie to head for her own apartment.

Both Hump and Helen had accepted Tallulah's invitation for the following evening, as each was anxious to meet the notorious Fitzgerald couple.

"I guess I got a real introduction to your world," Hump said to Helen in the taxi.

"Darling," Helen said, "Until tonight I didn't think you were sophisticated enough to handle it. You're a city boy but still a bit provincial."

"Perhaps," he said, "but after that Alabama hurricane and that fucking Naps, I was really initiated. It's a night to remember. Better yet, it's a night to forget."

She reached over and kissed his cheek. "It's only the beginning, my love. Our marriage will be perfect. A shared marriage."

"This 'country boy' has never heard of a shared marriage."

"We must not be selfish," Helen said. "You're a gorgeous man and I'm a devastating female. We'll have to share our marriage with others."

"You mean, carry on with others like we did tonight? I could do without that Naps. Never again!"

"There will be others, so many others we can invite into our marriage bed. Variety, that's the only way to guarantee that a marriage will stay vital and not become a bloody bore. We'll ask Zelda and Scott tomorrow night what they think about that."

***

The following evening, Helen had to excuse herself because she was asked at the last minute to meet with a producer about a change of casting in her play.

Hump was the first to arrive at the Algonquin Hotel where he asked the receptionist to call up to Tallulah's room. She claimed that she'd be down in the lobby quicker than it would take "Ethel Barrymore to slap my gorgeous face." Hump had heard that Ms. Barrymore had slapped Tallulah's face when the grand actress had walked into a party and caught Tallulah doing a devastating impression of her.

He was into his second club soda when Tallulah showed up in the lobby in a fur coat borrowed from her much older friend, Estelle Winwood. Hump sat in a corner table. She walked over and kissed him on the lips. "Sorry Helen couldn't make it tonight. I was hoping to be the meat in a sandwich between the two of you."

As Tallulah started to launch into one of her many stories about the men and women pursuing her in New York, she was interrupted by the arrival of Scott and Zelda Fitzgerald, the darlings of the New York tabloids and the embodiment of the Jazz Age. The romantic couple was already deep into a bottle of gin which Scott carried in a pocket of his raccoon coat. In contrast, Zelda wore a thin red woolen coat.

Tallulah jumped up and kissed each of the Fitzgeralds on the lips before introducing them to Hump.

Hump had already read the novel, *This Side of Paradise*, recounting the adventures, romantic and otherwise, of a Princeton man. He'd also read *Flappers and Philosophers*. Standing in front of Scott and Zelda in the flesh, he sensed that they were trying to become public manifestations of the flappers and sheiks he described in his writing.

Shaking Scott's hand, Hump found him rather effeminate. A woman newspaper columnist, Rena Willson, had only recently written a feature story about him that Hump had read. She had claimed that "Scott's face dances between pretty boy and handsome, and his long-lipped mouth virtually cries out for lipstick and belongs more on a girl than a young man."

As Zelda and Tallulah excused themselves to go to the powder room, Scott settled onto the banquette opposite Hump. Watching the women go, he expressed his disappointment that he wouldn't have a chance to meet Helen tonight. "I've seen her latest play and thought she gave a brilliant performance."

"I'll convey that to her," Hump said. "She'll be delighted."

"Before the ladies get back, I've got to ask you something," Scott said. "I read in the papers that you and Helen are getting married. Forgive me, but have you slept with her yet, or are you waiting until the wedding?"

Ever the kidder, Hump startled Scott by looking at him with a deadpan expression and saying, "In all honesty, I can say that I don't recall."

Scott weighed that for a moment then burst into laughter, putting his arm around Hump. "You're my kind of man."

With this trio, Hump hardly could slip in even the smallest observation. Scott, Zelda, and Tallulah had opinions about everything and everybody, and expressed them in such a candid manner as to shock society.

Tallulah went to the reception desk and placed a call upstairs to the room where John Barrymore was temporarily staying. She rushed over to Scott. "I tried to get John to come down and join us, but he's entertaining some lucky gal. He will speak to you on the phone."

As Tallulah and Scott departed, Zelda slid closer to Hump. "Tallulah told me about your party last night with Naps."

"Don't you believe half of what Tallulah says," Hump said, embarrassed at having someone else know about the previous evening.

"She claims you're a most satisfying lover," Zelda said, "and I'm envious. Scott can't satisfy me sexually. His equipment is too small."

Hump had never heard a woman, much less a wife, make such an observation about her husband.

He studied her face carefully. Her dark honey-blonde hair had been given the world's worst permanent. Her skin was pink and white, a delicate porcelain look. She had a sensual and alluring mouth and deep blue eyes that reflected a sparkling deviltry. If she had any imperfection at all, it was her sharp nose that was a bit beaky.

Her method of conservation was strictly biographical. "I'm named for a gypsy woman. It was mama's idea. I was the baby in a family of five, and I grew up to be a real tomboy. I always outrode the men in a foxhunt."

"You don't look like a tomboy to me," Hump said.

"Aren't you a dear?" she said, bending over and kissing him on the nose. "The real reason Scott wants to talk to John Barrymore is that he has a crush on him. Scott's a fairy, you know. I'll prove it." She reached into her purse and produced a photograph, which she said she always carried around to parties.

Staring back at Hump was a stunning looking dame in an off-the-shoulder gown and black high heels.

"It was snapped for The Triangle Club at Princeton," Zelda said. "Scott appeared in a play this way in drag, and his picture was circulated all over campus. He was hailed as the Princeton Play Girl."

"Since there are no women undergraduates at Princeton," Hump said, "men play the female parts. I know this actor, Jimmy Cagney, who launched himself in show business doing drag."

"That may be true, but why was Scott chosen to play the beautiful showgirl?" Zelda asked. "Having met him, don't you detect a decidedly feminine nature to him?"

Before he could answer, Scott and Tallulah returned. Scott seemed thrilled at having talked to The Great Profile himself. That made Zelda jealous. Sensing that, he turned his charm and attention on her, stroking her hand. He told Tallulah and Hump that he had met Zelda at a country club dance when she was only seventeen. "We resembled each other so much that people thought we were brother and sister. She's my soul mate. If I were a woman, I would have been Zelda."

Zelda spoke of their trip to Europe and how much they'd enjoyed it. "We had lunch with the mother of Winston Churchill. We went to Oxford. Everything was so thrilling."

"I liked England," Scott said, "but I utterly detested France. Paris actually made me ill. I think Britain and the United States should have let the Kaiser conquer France. It's an utterly worthless country with no culture."

The waiter kept the quinine water flowing to their table, and Scott kept lacing their drinks with gin. Hump was amazed that Zelda seemed to be encouraging Scott to drink. As Scott was engrossed in conversation with Tallulah, Hump leaned over to Zelda. "If you get him too drunk, he won't be able to write in the morning."

"That's fine with me," she said with a smirk on her face.

"But he's a writer. Writers have to write."

"Are you suggesting that I'm jealous of his work and want to keep him from writing?" she asked. "I have no reason to be jealous. In time I'm going to write fiction myself. The world can judge who is the better novelist."

Drunk and out on the street again, Scott dared them to race toward the theater district. With Hump reluctantly trailing behind, Zelda, Scott, and Tallulah darted down the crowded sidewalk, not caring if they bumped into someone. They were like crazed young things without a care in the world.

Even though he ran to keep up with them, Hump felt that all of them were like some incorrigible undergraduates he'd known at Andover. With the wind blowing through his hair, Scott led them right into the dense traffic along Seventh Avenue. "We'll defy death," he shouted back at them.

Arriving at a popular dance club, Montmarte, plenty of bootleg hooch was on its way. Both Tallulah and Zelda found the patrons "sluggish." Zelda suggested that she and Tallulah take to the dance floor and enliven the joint.

As the orchestra struck up an inappropriate Highland Fling, Zelda whirled around the suddenly emptied dance floor turning cartwheels for the amusement of the crowd. Right on her heels was Tallulah, equally adept at turning cartwheels herself. The only difference between the two performers was that Tallulah had forgotten to put on her bloomers.

At Scott's suggestion, the party moved to the Plaza Hotel. In those days newspaper photographers were always posted in the lobby, hoping to take pictures of celebrities coming and going.

Seeing the cameramen, Scott did a handstand in the lobby, as his picture was snapped. Getting to his feet again, he told Hump, "I'm sure to get my picture in the papers in the morning. I haven't been mentioned for an entire week, so I had to do something."

Zelda suggested to Tallulah that she and Hump join Scott and her in one of their favorite games on the elevator. Once inside the cage, she said that they were to ride up and down. When the door opened to let on new passengers, they were to shock the hotel guests by having Zelda kiss Tallulah on the mouth and Scott kiss Hump on the mouth. Hump didn't much like the idea of the game, but didn't want to live up to Helen's accusation of him as a country boy.

For about fifteen minutes that night, they rode up and down in the elevator with Zelda kissing Tallulah and Scott kissing Hump. And indeed the hotel guests were shocked, many expressing their disapproval with outrageous indignation.

Back in the lobby, one of the photographers approached Scott, telling him that he'd run out of film after the handstand photograph was snapped. He asked Scott to do it again.

"I've got a better idea," Scott said, grabbing Zelda's hand and racing toward the door. Followed by Tallulah and Hump, he ran over to the fountain, dropping his fur coat. "Let's go for a midnight bath," he shouted. "Last one in is an ugly duckling."

Scott jumped into the fountain and began splashing about, as Zelda and then Tallulah followed. Feeling like a fool, Hump jumped in with them as two shutterbugs snapped their pictures for tomorrow's tabloids.

Out of the fountain, cold and dripping wet, Scott raced toward a cab parked in front of the hotel with Zelda trailing him. When she reached it, Zelda turned and kissed both Tallulah and Hump on the lips.

Scott leaned out the window of the cab. "Remember," he said to both Tallulah and Hump. "You two pretty things should know that Oscar Wilde got it right. The only thing worse than being talked about is being forgotten." Zelda jumped in the back seat of the taxi with him, as they headed off into the night.

Still soaked from the fountain, Tallulah screeched for a second cab. "Since Helen and Naps are tied up with other engagements this evening," she said, "I guess that means you're stuck with me as your fuck buddy."

***

Scripts were frequently offered to Hump by Brady Sr. Bill Jr. remained Hump's steadfast friend, and promoted Hump as an actor to his father, despite telling his stepsister, Alice, that Hump "really has no talent." Bill also confessed to her that the only reason he hyped roles for Hump was that he wanted him to have a weekly paycheck. "I'm tired of always picking up the bill at speakeasies."

Brady Sr. had revived *Up the Ladder*, a four-act play presented at The Playhouse on March 6, 1922. Originally, George Le Guere played the part of Stanley Grant. After a respectable run, when Le Guere opted to move on to other venues, Bill talked his father into giving the role to Hump. The play starred Nannette

Comstock and George Farren. The original production had featured Rod La Rocque, who still wrote Hump letters, claiming that, "I'm mad about the boy," predating the Noël Coward lyrics.

Hump had seen Farren on the screen in 1917 when he appeared in *The Cinderella Man*. During rehearsals Farren was always forgetting his lines. "No wonder," Hump later told Bill. "He was born before the Civil War."

It was during his appearance in *Up the Ladder* that Hump befriended the actor, Paul Kelly, who was also appearing in the play, but in a minor role.

Hump formed a strong bond with him, and was impressed with Paul's background. He'd been performing on stage since he was seven years old, and had started making films at the age of eight out at Flatbush's Vitagraph Studios. His biggest role was in Booth Tarkington's *Penrod*, opposite a young Helen Hayes. Kelly would go on to become a Broadway star and a major supporting player in Hollywood films of the 30s, 40s, and 50s.

His life was to be marred with scandal in 1927 when the press dubbed him "Killer Kelly." This 180-pounder, a tough six-footer with the build of a football player, known for his red hair and Irish temper, had been dating "hot stuff," Dorothy Mackaye, married to a wiry song-and-dance man, Ray Raymond. On one drunken night, Kelly and Raymond fought bitterly over Dorothy's affections. Two days later Raymond died because of blows to his head. Kelly was charged with manslaughter and convicted, serving 25 months in the infamous San Quentin prison. Judged an accomplice, Dorothy herself was also briefly imprisoned, but would get out of jail and go on to marry Kelly in 1931, a bond that lasted until her death in 1940 in an automobile accident.

When *Up the Ladder* closed, a play called *Swifty* followed. Brady Sr. offered Hump the role of the juvenile lead, Tom Proctor, described by playwrights John Peter Toohey and W.C. Percival as "a young sprig of the aristocracy." John Cromwell, a member of Hump's "pussy posse," was signed on as the director.

The male star was Hale Hamilton, not the more famous Neil Hamilton as many biographers have reported. Throughout their professional lives, the two actors were often confused because of their name similarity. Hump had worked with Neil Hamilton during the ill-fated production of *The Ruined Lady* with Grace George.

The female lead in *Up the Ladder* was played by Frances Howard, and Hump was immediately attracted to her. A flapper, Frances was hailed as one of the great beauties of Broadway. She'd already appeared in *The Intimate Stranger*, starring Alfred Lunt and Billie Burke. Burke was the wife of Florenz Ziegfeld at the time and had actively boosted Frances' career, even trying to get the young actress signed by the Samuel Goldwyn office in New York. When Goldwyn in Hollywood saw the screen test, he said, "Why did you waste your time and my money this way?"

Frances was slender and well-proportioned with big dark eyes. Her features were so exquisitely chiseled, Hump called her a "fragile doll." Under bobbed raven-colored hair, she had a true peaches-and-cream complexion.

In spite of her strict Catholic upbringing, her years in show business had toughened her. Bill was the first to have an affair with her, calling her a "sexual predator in bed." When Hump pressed him for more details, he said, "You'll have to find that out for yourself."

Frances told Hump that she'd learned "all there was to know about men" when at the age of fifteen she toured with her sister, Connie, in an act billed as "The Howard Sisters." In between stage jobs, Frances doubled as both a fashion model and a chorus girl.

Hump was eager to fill in those three lonely nights a week when Helen was out with Tallulah and a pack of actresses called "the girls." Without telling Frances that he was engaged to Helen Menken, he actively pursued Frances who kept turning him down.

Rehearsals on *Swifty* were going poorly. Brady Sr. himself wasn't pleased with Cromwell's direction, and had virtually taken over as "co-director." Brady placed himself in the back seat of the theater. During rehearsals, every time Hump uttered a line, Brady would shout, "What? Louder! Louder!" Handicapped by his lisp, Hump was mumbling some of his lines.

Growing increasingly despondent with what he saw on the stage, Brady brought in Ring Lardner as play doctor to save *Swifty*. But even such a writing talent could not do the job.

In his role in the play as a "young sprig of the aristocracy," Hump was said to have "deflowered" a girl in an Adirondack cabin and then deserted her.

In the play, Hump made his first appearance with a gun, a pose that would eventually become legendary for him. He was directed to rush toward Hale Hamilton, shouting, "I'll kill you! I'll kill you! I'll kill you!"

Moving down to a front row seat for the final rehearsal, Brady had ordered Hump to repeat his big moment in the play a total of twenty times.

When Brady ordered Hump to do the scene yet another time, Hump was exhausted and near tears. Consumed with rage, he gave the role his all. When he'd finished, he looked over the pit at Brady in the front row. The showman was asleep or at least feigning sleep.

Screaming in rage, Hump ran off the stage and tried to attack Brady, but was restrained by both Hale and Bill Jr. The men took Hump into an alley and cooled him down, Bill offering a cigarette and Hale producing some brandy from a hip flash.

Opening night could proceed. What a disaster it was. Hale and Frances were trained professionals, and did the best they could. But Hump's mouth became so dry he disappeared from the stage to get a glass of water, leaving Hale to "vamp till ready." Hale at that point didn't know if Hump would come back on stage or not. Finally, he did and the play proceeded to its dull ending, receiving very weak and only scattered applause.

The only blessing that came out of that night was that Hale wanted to go to a party and not accompany Frances back to her hotel room as she'd requested. Remembering that Hump had been repeatedly asking her out for a date, she agreed to go to the 21 Club with him. She told him, "I hope your performance later in the evening will be better than what you did on stage."

After midnight, Frances invited him back to her hotel room, where he discovered what his friend Bill had already learned. Frances might look like a fragile doll but in bed she was a steel magnolia. "She taught me a trick or two," Hump told Bill Jr. the next day.

When Hump woke up the following morning, Frances was already getting dressed. "You're good," she said. "Almost as good as Bill. But last night was our one and only time."

"What's the matter?" Hump asked. "Last night I had you crying out for more."

"Occasionally I do it for fun," she said, messing with her hair. "I waste few favors on struggling actors, especially bad struggling actors. I'll never get ahead fucking the penniless. I'm determined to go to Hollywood where I'm gonna marry some bigtime producer or director. He'll not only make me a star but I'll become the wife of a millionaire."

To Hump, Frances' ambitions sounded like just so much morning after pillow talk. That's why he was eventually astonished to read on April 23, 1925 that Frances had married her "dream man" in Jersey City.

She had found the perfect role for herself, a part that she would play for almost fifty years. She'd persuaded Samuel Goldwyn to marry her.

Years later, Bogie chided Goldwyn, "I broke Frances in for you. You should be grateful. If it hadn't been for me, Frances wouldn't know what an uncut cock tastes like." Goldwyn threatened to give Bogie yet another scar on his lip if he didn't shut his mouth.

After a night of riding Frances, Hump realized that the sex had been hot, but that there was virtually no chance of any long-term relationship. When he arrived at the Bogart home the morning after, Maud was waiting with the newspapers and his reviews.

Alexander Woollcott, the leading theater critic of his day, had been referred to by Noël Coward as a "caged cobra." Harpo Marx, noting Woollcott's plump, owl-face and his acid tongue, joked publicly that he looked like "something that had gotten loose from a Macy's Thanksgiving Parade."

Woollcott wrote of *Swifty*: "The young man who embodied the aforesaid sprig was what might mercifully be described as inadequate." Bogie would carry around Woollcott's review in his wallet for the rest of his life.

Only Helen Menken urged him to keep trying to become a successful Broadway actor. One day she altered that vision of his future profession. "I've decided you should be on the silver screen."

***

Until Kenneth Anger published *Hollywood Babylon* in 1975, the average member of the public was not aware of the rumors that had persisted for years about D.W. Griffith's virginal-looking Gish sisters, Lillian and Dorothy. According to the rumors, they not only had lesbian tendencies, but they often slept with each other. That is, when they couldn't find a beautiful partner like actress Mildred Harris, married to Charlie Chaplin.

Anger obviously never talked to Humphrey Bogart, who could have supplied far more information. Helen Menken was always vague, even to her husband-to-be, about how she had met Lillian Gish. Tallulah later claimed that she was the one who introduced Helen to Lillian Gish, presenting Helen as "my discard" in the lobby of the Hotel Algonquin.

Discard or not, Helen seemed to mesmerize Miss Gish, who suggested that "a beauty like yourself should also appear in flickers. You'd look lovely in close-ups." Coming from Lillian Gish, the Griffith star who invented close-ups, that was high praise indeed.

Helen later confided in Hump that lesbian sex with Lillian was "birdlike," without ever explaining exactly what that meant.

In one of the few times that Hump flew into a jealous rage, it was over Lillian Gish. He threatened to break up with Helen if she didn't stop seeing the star. Helen placated Hump by telling him that she had secured a screen test for him in Lillian's upcoming film, *The White Sister*.

The film script of *The White Sister* was written by F. Marion Crawford and Walter Hackett. It had opened in September 27, 1909 at Daly's Theatre in New York, having only a short run before it closed November 6. Lillian and Henry King hoped to resurrect this tired vehicle, as indeed they would one day as a film.

Two days later in a barnlike studio in Astoria, Queens, Hump was introduced to the already legendary Lillian Gish, who told him that in her upcoming film she hoped to capture a "spiritual fragility."

Hump remembered that she maintained several quirky "little conceits," which included referring to her Canadian friend as Gladys Smith, even though Gladys was known to the world at large as Mary Pickford. "Griffith used to pay Dorothy and me five dollars a day," Lillian said. "Henry King and I hope to pay you considerably more."

Henry King, the director, introduced himself to Hump just before his screen test and explained in rough outline the plot for *The White Sister*. Lillian was to play Angela Chiaromonte, the daughter of a rich Italian count killed in a fall from his horse. Lillian is cheated out of her estate by her older half-sister and is thrown into poverty. She's saved by her engagement to a dashing officer, Captain Giovanni Severini, but he is captured by Arabs in an expedition to Africa. She dedicates her life to her lover's memory by becoming a nun. She's not aware that her lover has escaped and returned to Italy. The climax takes place against a backdrop of the eruption of Mount Vesuvius.

"Just my kind of part," Hump told King, who apparently did not catch the sarcasm in the actor's voice. Hump thought the script ridiculous but agreed to film the final close-up with Lillian minus the volcanic eruption.

He never saw the screen test but felt that he was very wooden with Lillian. "We had all the screen chemistry of yesterday's bathwater." To Hump's surprise, both King and Lillian complimented him on his performance, claiming that they felt he had "real screen presence."

Hump was asked to stay at the studio until after lunch. King was considering asking him to film one more segment of *The White Sister*, depicting when the captain first meets the woman who will become the love of his life.

When Hump returned from lunch, another actor was waiting in the reception room. An Englishman named Ronald Colman was eight years older than Hump. He appeared suave and debonair with a soft cultured voice that contrasted with Hump's lisp. Hump, thinking the role was his, was upset to learn that Colman was also testing for the part. He not only "spoke pretty," as Hump later recalled, "but he was also God damn good looking." Colman, in fact, would in a decade be voted "the handsomest man on the screen." Both King and Lillian had seen Colman appearing in a Ruth Chatterton play and had been impressed with his performance.

Hump and Colman were interrupted when King came into the studio. With Colman's permission, King penciled in a mustache on the clean-shaven actor, a tonsorial touch that would remain with the star for the rest of his life.

Even before the more polished Colman went before the cameras, Hump knew that the British actor had the part. He suspected that King and Lillian had tested him only as a favor to Helen. King called Colman into the studio and dismissed Hump, claiming it wasn't necessary to stick around for that second scene.

Colman not only won the part of the tragic soldier hero in *The White Sister*, he went on to become one of Hollywood's greatest film stars, pioneering a band of "gentleman heroes" on the screen. As Hump went from one "dumb comedy to another," he watched Colman's meteoric rise to film fame.

For the rest of his life, Bogie would refer to Colman as "that limey bum," blaming the British actor for sabotaging Hump's own screen career in silent pictures.

***

One evening Bill Brady Jr. invited Hump to the opening night of his father's 1923 Broadway production, *The Mad Honeymoon*. They sat next to George M. Cohan.

At the time, any aspiring actor was in awe of George M. Cohan, "the man who owned Broadway." The song-and-dance man of all song-and-dance men, Cohan was celebrated for his hit song, "Over There," for which Franklin Roosevelt would one day award him the congressional Medal of Honor. Cohan would go on to write such hits as "Give My Regards to Broadway," "You're a Grand Old Flag," and "I'm a Yankee Doodle Dandy." Ironically, Hump's future film rival at Warner Brothers, James Cagney, would win an Academy Award for his impersonation of Cohan in the 1943 film hit, *Yankee Doodle Dandy.*

Fifteen minutes into *The Mad Honeymoon*, both Bill and Hump knew that the show would be a disaster. The only saving grace of the play was when a teenage actress, Mayo Methot, walked onstage as the maid. She had only five lines of dialogue, but brought momentary life to the dying play.

In their front row seats, Hump remembered being intrigued by her cupid's-bow mouth and mass of blonde curls inspired by the MGM screen goddess, Mae Murray. Mayo had big, soulful eyes that looked out across the stage lights, seeming to make direct contact with the audience.

When the curtain went down, Cohan had nothing to say about the play. It received only scattered applause and was lambasted the next morning by all the leading critics of the day.

With his sharp eye for good theater, Cohan said nothing to Bill about his father's opening night disaster, but asked to be taken backstage to meet the maid. "I have just discovered the next Lillian Gish."

Hump was surprised, thinking that a comparison to Mae Murray—not Gish—would have been more apt.

When word spread that Cohan had come backstage, the stars of the play expected that Mr. Showman had come to greet them. They were startled at having been ignored. Cohan sought out Mayo and told her that she was terrific in the role. Mayo reached over with her cupid's bow mouth and kissed Cohan right on his lips.

She shook hands with Bill and Hump but her eyes remained focused on Cohan. That very night he offered her the role of Leola Lane opposite him in his new production, *The Song and Dance Man.* Without even knowing what the role entailed, she accepted on the spot.

Hump remembered Mayo as a cute little blonde, and Bill and he would liked to have dated her, even though Bill was married and Hump engaged. It was obvious that Cohan had seen her first and had a lot more to offer her.

Years later, Mayo recalled her first meeting with Cohan "which changed my life." She also recollected meeting Bill Brady Jr., the son of the producer of *The Mad Honeymoon.* She had "no memory whatsoever" of being introduced to Humphrey Bogart. She later told an interviewer, "If someone had told me then that I would one day become the third Mrs. Bogart, I would have fallen on my cute ass."

***

Hump went back to working as a stage manager for Brady Sr. At night he frequented the speakeasies, spending every dollar he made. Sometimes Helen accompanied him, and often he was joined by Bill and his new wife, the always competent but never exciting actress, Katherine Alexander, who was forging ahead with her career playing wronged wives, society snobs, and respectable women. John Barrymore was in hot pursuit of her, but she claimed she was still faithful to Bill.

Sometimes the director, John Cromwell, would also join the crowd as it made its way from such mob joints in Harlem as the Cotton Club over to Connie's Inn. When they had more money, Hump's party showed up at The Dover Club.

With Stuart Rose, Hump continued to go horseback riding in Central Park. Stuart and Hump also took up ice skating, usually with Hump's sister, Frances. Stuart and Frances were still "an item," as they called it.

Smoking his Andover pipe, Hump went sailing off Long Island whenever he was free from Broadway. He was seen frequently at Mayfair, an actors club, when he wasn't at Lambs Club, another hangout for actors. Often he took Helen dancing at the Ritz-Carlton Hotel, and the 21 Club remained his favorite watering hole. He was also becoming known for his expert chess playing.

When a year went by and Hump wasn't offered another role, he felt his career as an actor had come to an end. Unexpectedly, Rosalie Stewart, a producer, sent him a script, *Meet the Wife*, a comedy starring Mary Boland and Clifton Webb. Hump was offered the role of a young, fresh-faced reporter, Gregory Brown, in this three-act comedy by Lynn Starling, up-and-coming playwright of her day.

Mary Boland was already an established stage star when Hump first met her. Born in Philadelphia in 1880, she'd begun her career at the age of fifteen, following the death of her actor father, W.A. Boland. Hump had seen her film debut in 1914, *The Edge of the Abyss*. She'd become a star in 1919 playing the stately scatterbrain, Mrs. Wheeler, in Booth Tarkington's *Clarence* opposite Alfred Lunt.

From the first day they met, Hump was fascinated by the male co-star of *Meet the Wife*. Clifton Webb and Bogie would become friends and remain so for the rest of their lives together. They were an odd couple. Webb was an immaculate dresser and had impeccable manners, but this young dancer turned actor was known along Broadway as "Miss Priss." Born in Indianapolis in 1891, he changed his name from Webb Parmallee Hollenbeck to Clifton Webb. Hump both affectionately and jokingly called him Parmallee.

Known as "the Irritable Bachelor," Clifton even then was a notorious homosexual, specializing in seducing young juvenile leads who appeared with him. The still handsome Hump became his chief target during rehearsals for *Meet the Wife*. Hump felt as ardently pursued by Clifton as he had been by Rod La Rocque when he'd directed that actor in the film, *Life*.

One night at a Harlem night spot, Hump decided to confront Clifton. "I'm not going to become your boy, and if you come on to me again I'll punch you out," Hump told him. "But I will be your friend. I like you a hell of a lot. I don't take it up the ass."

"Don't worry, my dear fellow," Clifton said. "I'm a famous bottom." Clifton bent over the table and affectionately kissed Hump on the nose. Somehow this impulsive act endeared Clifton all the more to Hump. Never again did seduction rear its head.

Clifton Webb marked the beginning of a series of friendships—not love relationships—that Bogie would have with homosexuals, including the closeted Spencer Tracy and the not-so-closeted Noël Coward and Truman Capote.

Meet the Wife opened at New York's Klaw Theater and would run for 232 performances, with Hump drawing a weekly paycheck of $150, which he spent immediately. A critic for *The New York World* gave Hump the first good notice of his career, referring to the role he played as that of "a handsome and nicely mannered reporter, which is refreshing."

Two nights before the play closed, Hump had been up all night partying in the hot spots of Harlem. When he showed up the next day to perform in *Meet the Wife*, he was hung over and had had no sleep.

On stage during a pivotal scene, he forgot his lines and stood looking glazed against the scenery. Mary Boland was forced to frantically ad lib and even had to feed him some of his lines, hoping he would pick up the rhythm of the play. When the curtain was pulled, she walked backstage and slapped his face real hard. "I'll see to it that you never work again on Broadway."

The next night, at the closing performance, he knew all his lines. However, after Act Two, as if determined to sabotage his career, he disappeared into a dive across the street, claiming he was starved and wanted a plate of ham and eggs. Somehow he completely forgot that he had to stick around to deliver four lines in Act Three.

When he did remember, he raced toward the theater door, just in time to hear the applause as the curtain went down. The stage manager, Bert French, who was also producing the play with Rosalie Stewart, slugged Hump, who struck back, hitting French in the nose just as Mary Boland and Clifton Webb were taking their final bows.

Chiming in with Mary Boland, French also threatened to end Hump's Broadway days. But Hump was heartened that Maud, without Belmont, showed up that night and praised his acting skill. Being Maud, she had to add a warning. "An actor will spend most of his life starving between parts, and you could have done so much more with your life."

His spirits were lifted when an out-of-town reviewer, Peggy Hill, of Atlanta, saw the play and informed her readers that "Humphrey Bogart is more manly and a lot handsomer than Rudolph Valentino. If I had to be carried away to a Sheik's tent in the desert, I'd much rather be in Bogart's arms than prissy Valentino's."

***

Hump couldn't take Mary Boland's threat to destroy his stage career too seriously. His friend, Bill Brady, was producing a Broadway play with a part in it just right for Hump. Once again, when all else failed, he could count on the dependable, reliable, and steadfast Brady family.

Less than one month after *Meet the Wife* closed, Hump was offered his biggest role to date, the meaty part of an aviator in a play, *Nerves*, which was being both directed and produced by Bill Brady Jr. The play had been written by Stephen Vincent Benét and John Farrar, and contained only two acts, unusually short for that day. The first act takes place at a Yale house party where several couples, all on the same night, commit themselves to be engaged. The second act occurs in the officers' mess of a squadron of American aviators based in France during World War I. The wartime experience shatters the nerves of one of the aviators—hence, the title of the play.

The star of the show was the now largely forgotten Marie Curtis, who had just completed a run on Broadway in the play, *Time*. Earlier, her attempts at a career in silent films had bombed after she'd appeared as "Lady Dolly" in *Her Greatest Love*.

She played opposite Paul Kelly, only years before his international notoriety and jail term as a convicted man slaughterer.

Bill angered Hump by casting their longtime friend, Kenneth MacKenna, in the third lead over Hump's own fourth billing. Although they would eventually become bitter rivals over the affections of Mary Philips, Kenneth at the time was still a close friend of Hump's, and a faithful member of the coterie that still referred to itself as "the pussy posse," a group that included John Cromwell and Bill Brady, Jr.

Although not officially a member of the posse, Kenneth's brother, Jo Mielziner, signed on as stage designer. It was during rehearsals for *Nerves* that Hump realized for the first time what an immense talent Jo was. Born in Paris two years after Hump, Jo, like Kenneth, was the son of a Jewish and Irish marriage.

The same year Jo designed the sets for *Nerves*, he also created sets for *The Guardsman*. Written by Ferenc Molnar, it was an early Theatre Guild production that brought Jo to the attentions of the moguls of Broadway.

Before his death in 1976, Jo would go on to design the sets for at least 270 stage and film productions. His most memorable stage work included such classics as *Strange Interlude; Death of a Salesman; Carousel; The King and I; South Pacific; Look Homeward, Angel; Tea and Sympathy, Picnic,* and *The Emperor Jones*.

The young actress Mary Philips was cast as one of the supporting players in *Nerves*. Three years younger than Hump, Mary was born in New London and educated in a convent in New Haven. "In those days," as Bogie later recalled, describing his stage career, "I was always deflowering maidens fresh from some God damn convent." Mary characterized herself as a "staunch New Englander but with Irish wit and temperament." When she first met Hump, she later declared, she detected a strong Puritan streak in him.

She'd made her debut as a chorus girl showing off her bosom and her legs in the *Follies Revue* of 1919. It was what playwright James Kirkwood Jr. decades later in *A Chorus Line* would call a "tits and ass" part.

Mary would go on to appear in such productions as *Two Girls Wanted* and *The Old Soak*, which did good business but would hardly merit a footnote in theatrical histories of the 20s.

She was a honey blonde with penetrating gray-blue eyes. She would often be compared, to her detriment, to the more successful actress, Ina Claire.

By today's standards of beauty, Mary had a long nose. Hump kidded her, calling it "the beak." "Where do you put that nose when you go to kiss a man?" he asked her during rehearsals. "That's for me to know and for you to find out," Mary told him.

Except for that nose, she had the most perfectly formed lips of all of Bogie's future wives. Her hands were her most attractive feature, and critics often wrote that they were "porcelain like and delicate."

Mary was short and rather small. "Just my type," Hump told Kenneth. She was understanding, sympathetic, and attractive but not flashy, as opposed to the more self-centered and narcissistic Helen Menken. And in definite contrast to Hump's mother, Maud, she was supportive of, rather than critical of, men.

Mary's appearance as a fragile doll was deceiving. She was actually a sports-loving outdoor girl who excelled in tennis and golf. Her Irish temper matched that of Helen's.

During rehearsals, Mary infuriated Hump. In his big scene, when he was to be left alone on the stage, Mary walked toward the wings. "That was what she was supposed to do," Bogie later recalled. "But it was the damn way she walked off. I would have to wait until I saw Marilyn Monroe in the 1951 movie, *Niagara*, before I'd see a walk like that again. I confronted her back stage and accused her of upstaging me. That seemed to piss her off. She slapped my face and told me that she'd walk any way she damn well pleased, and there wasn't anything I could do about it. I wanted to punch her out. I'd hit ladies before and would again. But somehow that slap turned me on. I felt I could really fall for this gal."

The more he worked with Mary, the more intrigued Hump became. Mary told him that she could hold her liquor better than he did. Back then, Hump always said, "I don't trust women who don't drink. They'll betray you every time."

Kenneth was also growing increasingly intrigued by Mary. He even warned Hump to "lay off Mary. She's gonna become my gal, and besides you're engaged to Helen."

"Helen knows I see women on the side," Hump said. "Fuck you, asshole. Helen herself sees women on the side. Maybe I'll take Mary back to Helen's apartment. We could share her."

Kenneth punched him in the mouth. Before a major fight could break out, Bill Brady, Jr. separated the two actors. "You're like two fucking roosters fighting over the prize hen in the barnyard. Don't you guys know there are more than enough women on Broadway to go around? There are at least three showgals for every single male since at least half the men in the theater are fairies. Enjoy! Enjoy! As for Mary, I've taken director's privilege. She got hired on the casting couch. For the duration of the play, she's my private piece and don't tell Katherine."

Both Kenneth and Hump were shocked to learn that Mary was having an affair with Bill. At the Hotsy Totsy that night, Kenneth and Hump repaired their friendship over several tall gin fizzes. "Let's don't let a woman come between us," Kenneth said. "If Bill is fucking Mary, that makes her a slut. We can pick up any slut we want in this club in five minutes. Wanta bet?"

Hump didn't take him up on the bet, knowing that what Kenneth said was true. Midnight found the two men, along with "two sluts," checking into the Hotel Baltimore. They seduced the women on the same double bed, switching partners around two o'clock. Instead of picking up the prostitutes, the two men could have gone to a crystal ball-gazer who might have told them that Hump would marry Mary Philips in 1928 and that Kenneth would marry the same woman in 1938.

Years later, Mary would rank the sexual performances of the three leading members of the pussy posse in this order: Number one, Bill Brady Jr. "because of his incredible technique"; number two, Kenneth MacKenna because "of the sincerity in his eyes when he got on top of you," and, number three, Humphrey Bogart "because he always had a far and distant look in his eyes when he was making love to you, enough so that you always suspected that his mind was somewhere else."

Both Hump and Kenneth feared that Bill was jeopardizing his marriage to Katherine Alexander by going out to the speakeasies every night with Mary. "Never fear," Bill assured them. "Katherine specializes in wronged wife parts. I'm just giving her first-hand experience so she'll be a better actress."

One night Bill called Hump to tell him that he'd just bailed Mary out of jail. They had been caught staggering drunk from the speakeasy, Hotsy Totsy. When a cop tried to arrest Mary, she bit his finger down to the bone. She was hauled off to the pokey. Bill had had far more to drink than Mary, but he was not arrested. Brady Sr. posted a five-hundred dollar bail, securing her release.

Nerves opened at the Comedy Theater on September 1, 1924, a date that roughly coincided with the opening of *What Price Glory?*. *Glory* became the biggest hit of any play addressing the issues of World War I, and audiences and critics alike flocked to it instead of *Nerves*. *Nerves* would run for only sixteen performances, as critics ridiculed it and audiences stayed away in droves. Brady, Sr. denounced his son for producing such a flop.

Ironically, Hump received respectable reviews for his role in the play, enough--in Mary's opinion--to give him a "swelled head." Even Hump's nemesis, the critic, Alexander Woollcott, who'd denounced him as the "inadequate sprig" wrote, "Those words are hereby eaten."

Another prominent critic of the day was Heywood Broun, a well-known sports writer and columnist for New York newspapers, and also a leading member of the

Socialist Party until he was expelled in 1933. Broun found Hump's performance "most effective." Hump couldn't help but be delighted when Broun faulted co-actor Kenneth's performance, claiming that the actor "suffers from trying too hard to make a feeble play take on the breath of life."

At the play's closing, Helen was preparing to take her own Broadway success, *Seventh Heaven*, to Los Angeles, leaving Hump at her apartment. Before departing, she told Hump that she would marry him but was too busy to fit a wedding into her schedule. "I'm at the height of my stardom," she told him, "and I can't let a little thing like marriage stand in my way. Some stars like Bernhardt will last forever. In my case, I fear I will burn terribly bright, then flicker out." Unlike Hump, she spoke in highly dramatic terms, unusual for a person with so little formal education.

As Helen boarded the train to Los Angeles, going via Chicago, she told Hump that he didn't necessarily have to be lonely when she was away in spite of their engagement. She gave him the telephone number of "a young and very beautiful actress that I've been dating. Call her. She's very amusing. She and I are going nowhere fast in our relationship. Women, I fear, are mere playthings for her. She really prefers men. Besides no one can replace Tallulah—that whore—in my life."

Bidding Helen good-bye, Hump returned to the empty apartment. After three hours and drunk on gin, he dialed the number of Helen's actress friend. He was determined to find out the degree to which this mystery woman liked men.

On the other end of the line, a haunting, dramatic voice picked up the receiver. "Hello, this is Louise Brooks. Who's this?"

***

After one night, Hump was so mesmerized by Louise Brooks that he told Bill Brady that he wanted to break off his engagement with Helen and propose to "Brooksie" instead. He claimed that she was the best sex he'd ever had with any woman. "She's one earthy broad," Hump said. "We did things I've never even heard of before."

Bill was disdainful of Louise. "She's nothing but a teenage prostitute. She's shacked up with that high roller, A.C. Blumenthal, who's taking over for Ziegfeld. Brooks is a real casting-couch climber. I also hear she's a lesbian."

On their first date together, Hump showed up at her hotel dressed for dinner, as she'd accepted his invitation to go to a supper club. When she opened the door to her room, she wore a sheer white nightgown with nothing on underneath it. "Come on in, handsome," she said, reaching for his hand. "We'll have room service send us a hamburger. That way, we'll have more time in the sack, as I have to get up early in the morning."

Hump was immediately taken with this "Kansas sunflower," a former Ziegfeld Follies dancer who'd also appeared in George White's Scandals. Her raven-black hair was radiant, and she'd styled it in a way that had already led to her reputation as "the girl in the black helmet." Closely cropped into an exaggerated page-boy, her hair indeed looked like she was wearing a helmet.

As she invited him in and offered him some whiskey, he felt that he was encountering the Jazz Age flapper supreme, perhaps someone not real but a creation of F. Scott Fitzgerald.

"Helen tells me you're not rich but I agreed to see you anyway," Louise said. "I have this friend, Peggy Fears, who dances in the Follies. She has a strict rule about dating, 'No ice, no dice.' She thinks I should go out only with rich stage-door Johnnies. But I also like to get fucked, and these old guys are too worn out for my tastes. That's why I turn to guys like you. Trinkets are nice but getting plowed for fun is one of the joys of life, and I want it all."

"I hope I won't disappoint," Hump said.

"I'm sure you won't," Louise said. "Helen has already given me a critique. I asked Helen if you were a redhead. She assured me you were brunette."

"What have you got against redheaded men?"

"I absolutely refuse to go to bed with them," she said. "Based on my experience, I have found that their pricks are always tiny and even misshapen, usually bent to the left and most unappetizing."

"You've lost me there," he said, downing the rest of his whiskey. "I've never done a survey."

"Take my word for it," she said, going over to him and kissing him on the lips as he sat in her sole armchair. When she finally broke away, she said, "You have the most beautiful lips I've ever seen on any man."

"Thanks."

"You've got this little scar on your upper lip. It adds character to your face. I especially like this quilted piece that hangs down in a tiny scallop." She ran her tongue along it. "It's an imperfection I find terribly appealing."

"Hell," he said, drawing back slightly, not at all comfortable with the conversation. "I should have it surgically removed."

"I disapprove of surgically removing skin from men," she said. "I hope you're not circumcised because I delight in men with foreskins."

"I'm all there," he said, as she reached to fondle him.

"I like the feel of it," she said. "You see I'm a basket-watcher. That's why I spend a lot of time at the ballet watching men in form-fitting leotards. I hate most men's trousers. Except for a few sailors who wear tight pants, they're usually far too baggy."

"You're some gal," he said, "I never heard a woman talk like you."

"Don't get me wrong," Louise said. "An average size prick can offer some satisfaction to a woman but they always leave one unfulfilled. There are three things I like done to me, and only a big prick can do the job."

"Just three?" he said.

"That's right. Unless you can conjure up something new." She rose from his

74

lap, removing her nightgown to stand nude in front of him. "Audition time." With her head she motioned to her empty double bed.

As Hump would later relate to Bill, "It was the wildest ride I've ever had in my life. If Brooksie had a hole somewhere, she wanted it plugged."

When she finally rose from the bed, she went into her bathroom, leaving the door open. He heard what sounded like a cow's piss, followed by a loud fart. Although Tallulah Bankhead would become notorious for "taking a tinkle" in front of such illustrious guests as Eleanor Roosevelt, Louise Brooks was the first woman Hump had ever known who had no shame about what she did in the bathroom.

Coming back into the bedroom, she noted the surprise on his face. "We've got to be very French about these matters," she said. "After all, Queen Victoria is dead."

She called room service for hamburgers. "After that roll in the hay, you deserve a big juicy one."

Over burgers, she told him that she'd seen the second performance of *Nerves*, having been given a ticket by Helen. She congratulated him on his "well-projected baritone and good diction," not mentioning his lisp.

He thanked her and walked over to the cabinet to pour both of them another whiskey.

"I guess Helen has told you that I also go to bed with women," Louise said.

"I've heard rumors," he said.

"They're true, but I'm not a lesbian. I occasionally sleep with women like Tallulah Bankhead and Helen herself, but only as a means of understanding female love. It's not what I most enjoy, although there's the most delicious sensation when a woman goes down on you. Lesbians are great because attacking a pussy with their tongue is their big thing. They are much better at it than men. Don't you agree?"

"I have no basis for comparison," he said.

"I'm not a nymphomaniac like some people claim," she said. "I prefer to characterize myself as a connoisseur of heterosexual men. Actually, I'm even fonder of homosexual men. After all those months with the Denishawn dance troupe I learned that homosexual men make better lovers than heterosexual men. Don't you agree?"

"Again, I have no basis for comparison," he said.

"Mainly I hang out with lesbians to feed my vanity," she said. "Sometimes a rich stage-door Johnny will ask Peggy Fears and me to stage an exhibition before he fucks both of us. I'll agree to it if the rent's coming due."

He took her back to bed for another round, although she complained then of his "missionary position."

After he'd finished and she'd paid another call on the bathroom, she wanted to tell him about her wild night with Tallulah. "She likes sailors, and sometimes she gets carried away and invites too many back to her hotel. I often have to go over there and help her out with the servicemen. It's a patriotic duty for me."

Every story that seemed to come out of her head intrigued him. He was later to say, "I had never met a woman like Louise Brooks, and I wasn't ever going to do so again."

"Last night Tallulah and I both confessed to each other that we had never gone to bed with a black man before," she said. "Tallulah had heard that all of them have big pricks. However, the homosexual dancers I've appeared with tell me that it is not true—just a myth. A lot of black dick is small. Speaking of dick, Tallulah and I hit it lucky on our first shared experience. We were at this speak-easy where we met this jazz musician, Roger Verlaine, from New Orleans. We singled him out for a *menage à trois*. He was a brute of a man, and he wanted to become the heavyweight boxing champion of the world. Or at least that's what he said. When we got him back to her hotel, and we got naked with him and got him excited, Tallulah actually measured it. It came to a towering ten inches. She later told me that she'd once met a sailor, famous along the New York waterfront, who had a twelve-inch prick. I didn't know pricks came that big. Since then, of course, I've learned differently. Nonetheless a woman or a gay male has to wait a long time to find a man with a foot-long prick. Some women and some gay boys go through their entire lives without enjoying such a massive intrusion of their bodies."

"I'm sorry that some of us let you down," Hump said.

"Not you," she said. "You're very well endowed without being some freak of nature. After that session with you in bed, I can tell that you're deservedly confident of your performance."

"I don't have insecurities about my manhood," he said. "The work I do on stage is what frightens me. Helen is always bringing her theatrical friends to see me perform, and I'm always playing some dumb juvenile part."

"I predict you'll become a big star one day," she said. "I will too. Just wait and see."

She went over to her closet and removed a red dress. "I've got this fabulous idea," she said. "Get dressed. I want you to walk along Broadway with me. We'll look at all the names up in lights and imagine that one day the names of Louise Brooks and Humphrey Bogart will be up there for all the world to see."

As he was reaching for his trousers, she challenged him. "Eddie Goulding told me that all actresses should be compared to a flower. I can't decide what flower to be? You decide for me."

He looked her over carefully from her tiny feet to her helmet hairdo. "An exotic black orchid."

***

Like many actors of the 20s, including Gary Cooper, Hump went through a period where he tried to model himself after America's reigning heartthrob of the screen, Rudolph Valentino, who had electrified audiences, especially women, with his performances in *The Four Horsemen of the Apocalypse* and *The Sheik.*

Although the men did not really look alike, Broadway writers often cited the physical resemblance between Valentino and Hump. Typical of the comments was an interview written by Elita Miller Lenz in 1924. "Humphrey Bogart is one of the few young actors along Broadway that can be classed as a Valentino type in color, which should help much in the matter of future popularity."

Just for fun, Helen Menken acquired a Sheik costume for Hump, which he wore to a masquerade ball at the Plaza Hotel. Helen herself appeared disguised as Agnes Ayres, who had starred opposite Valentino in *The Sheik.* Their photograph ended up in the New York papers.

Helen had even gone so far as to purchase pink silk underwear for Hump, after reading in a fan magazine that Natacha Rambova, Valentino's second wife, insisted that he appear "only in pink bloomers."

Whenever Hump pulled off his trousers in the bedroom of many a chorus girl, his partner for the evening often laughed at his "pink powder puff" underwear. However, when Hump slipped off what he called "those sissy drawers," the laughter stopped as he went about his sexual maneuvering for the evening.

As 1924 drew to a close, producer and playwrite Barry Connors offered Hump the role of the male lead in a three-act comedy directed by John Hayden. The play was *Hell's Bells*, and it starred two women, the established Broadway actress, Olive May, and also Shirley Booth making her debut at the dawn of a stage and film career that would bring her international fame.

Connors described Jimmy Todhunter, the character Hump would play, as "a regular fellow of twenty-seven, well-educated, ambitious, self-reliant, and industrious." The role would launch Hump into a series of juvenile parts, each of which required the standard costume for an *ingénu* of that era--white duck trousers and a blue blazer. Each of these early roles was radically more wholesome than some of the gangster and tough guy roles (among them Duke Mantee, Sam Spade, Charlie Allnut, and Captain Queeg) that Hump would later play. But at least in the 1920s, Hump became known for playing characters that Alexander Woollcott referred to as "young sprigs."

Hell's Bells would hardly be remembered except for one immortal line, which Hump delivered and which would forever haunt him, becoming part of the national vocabulary.

The director, Hayden, needed a device to move some actors off the stage to make way for a scene that focused only on his two leading actresses, Shirley Booth and Olive Mae. He devised a setup whereby Hump appeared on stage carrying a tennis racquet. Surveying the male actors, he asked of them, "Tennis anyone?" Even today, *Casablanca's* Rick is ridiculed for playing such a toothsome juvenile with such a jejune image.

Although admitting that he had at one time or another delivered some of the most ridiculous lines ever written for the Broadway stage, Hump in later life repeatedly denied that he had come on stage and said, "Tennis, anyone?" in *Hell's Bells* or any other play. Hump claimed the line was, "It's forty-love outside. Anyone care to watch?"

Clifton Webb, who had become a close friend and who was actively involved on Broadway at the time, agreed with Bogie, claiming that the expression was not in vogue at the time.

However, Richard Watts Jr., longtime theater critic for *The New York Post*, claimed that he reviewed the opening night of *Hell's Bells* and that indeed Bogart did say that line. "I made a note of it but didn't publish it in my review."

When an attempt at a revival of the play was made in 1934 for a road show tour, Hayden's original script was discovered. The line about it being "forty-love outside" was indeed in the script as Bogie later claimed. But before opening night, Hayden had crossed over the line and written, "Tennis anyone?"

In later life Bogie often spoke bitterly of his early career on the stage. "With my hair slicked back, I'd appear in white flannels with pale blue knit sweaters, always carrying a tennis racquet. Those early parts made me feel silly and girlish. The god damn director would have me come out modeling the latest pinch-back sports coat with pansy neck cloths and a swishy new hairdo."

The star of *Hell's Bells*, Olive May, had been appearing on Broadway since Hump was one year old, introducing herself to audiences in *The Surprises of Love* on January 22, 1900.

During rehearsals Hump met and became briefly attached to Shirley Booth, who was one year older than he was. Those who know her today only as the irrepressible maid on the television series, *Hazel*, which ran from 1961 to 1966, may not understand the physical allure that Shirley had during her youth. In 1925 she was a lovely, gracious, and even beautiful woman. Born Thelma Booth Ford in New York City, she had had an even more miserable childhood than Hump. Her mother, Virginia Wright, was terminally ill, and her father, business executive, Albert J. Ford, was a brutal, stern father. Over her father's objections and at the age of fourteen, Shirley dropped out of school, determined to be an actress on stage.

Interviewed years later at her saltbox house in North Chatham, Massachusetts, she was reluctant to talk about her involvement with Bogie.

"I wouldn't call our first meeting an affair, more like a weekend together," she said. "He was a real gentleman, very polite and respectful of women, although I'd heard that he had a run-in or two with the star, Olive May. We were two frightened kids trying to make our way on Broadway, and we sensed a soulmate in each other, and perhaps turned to each other for a little comfort. I don't have much to say about that. On the few occasions we talked later in life, we both sympathized with each other about how long it took each of us to become a star."

Hell's Bells opened at the Wallack Theatre on the night of January 26, 1925. It was a flop, running for only fifteen performances. The only consolation for Hump was a claim by Alan Dale, critic for *The New York American*, that "Bogart gorgeously acted his role."

"I don't know how it happened," Bogie later said. "Maybe it was because I'd appeared in three comedies on Broadway, *Swifty, Meet the Wife*, and *Hell's Bells*. All of a sudden I was typecast as a comedy actor on stage. The next few years would offer me nothing but a series of three-act comedies, most of them not funny."

***

Helen was a friend of Alexander Woollcott, the powerful New York theater critic who had found Hump's "sprig" so inadequate on stage. She felt that Hump's career would be advanced if he actually met some of the critics who would one day review his future plays.

He escorted her to a speakeasy, Tony's, which was patronized by hard-drinking actors and writers. There Hump met the owner, Tony Soma, who loved artists and who welcomed him with great enthusiasm. That welcome would continue for years even when Hump went as long as three months without paying his large and forever mounting bar tabs.

Tony's was the kind of watering hole where Dorothy Parker and Robert Benchley would go with Scott and Zelda Fitzgerald to celebrate Jack Dempsey's four-round victory over Georges Carpentier. When Hump first saw all the celebrated patrons of Tony's, he felt that it was another branch of the famous Algonquin Roundtable. One by one he met all of them.

He was first introduced to Robert Sherwood, who would one day write *The Petrified Forest* which would be Bogie's last stage play, and also his best, and would be made into a film with Bogie and Bette Davis that would become the biggest break of his movie career.

Helen decided she had "to work the room." Before she had finished making the rounds, she introduced Hump to the newspaper reporter, Mark Hellinger, who invited him for a drink at the bar. Even though he couldn't afford it in those days, Mark was known for picking up everyone's bar tabs. Hump and Mark liked each other at once, having no inkling, of course, what important roles they would play in each other's future life.

Tony Soma put his arm around Hump and invited him to frequent his bar and "make it your favorite. You're always welcome here. In return, I want you to marry that Helen. She's one good-looking woman, and I'm afraid some man is going to snare her if you don't tie the knot."

"I'll think about it," Hump said. He didn't take Tony up on his urging to marry Helen, but he showed up at Tony's the following night without his bride-to-be. He'd invited Bill Brady and Stuart Rose instead. Hump's sister, Frances, had been invited but was feeling ill.

After only two nights, Hump became a regular at Tony's, often dropping in alone and continuing to meet and talk to some of the fabulous personalities of New York in the 1920s. He encountered Mark Hellinger often, and the reporter kept promising to take him on the town but never did.

Hump's most memorable and embarrassing night was when he showed up at Tony's with Stuart Rose. Both men had been drinking heavily and continued to do so after arriving at the speakeasy. Tony kept the drinks flowing to Hump and his friend, even though Hump had already accumulated a three-hundred dollar bar tab.

Seated next to them was what Hump called a "table of pansies." Five effeminate-looking men had formed their own roundtable. The waiter told Hump that they were appearing in a drag revue in Greenwich Village. "Hedda Hoopskirt," the star of the revue, kept waving her wrists at Hump and blowing kisses at him. But it was the much handsomer and more masculine Stuart who attracted the attention of the rest of the table. When Stuart got up to go to the men's room, there was practically a stampede. Only Hedda remained, blinking his eyes at Hump.

When Stuart came back to the table, he told Hump, "Have you ever tried to take a piss with three guys staring at your dick?"

Hump and Stuart were distracted by the arrival of boxing champion Gentleman Jim Corbett, and his beautiful date for the evening. Before committing himself more firmly to Broadway, William Brady Sr. had managed the early boxing career of this famous sports figure.

The sports world still talked about that night in New Orleans on September 7, 1892 when Corbett in the first championship fight ever to use padded gloves knocked out the reigning champ, John L. Sullivan, winning the title in the 21st round.

Corbett had spent the rest of his life making appearances, often in Broadway shows. His fancy dress had earned him the nickname of "the Beau Brummel of New York." He appeared at Tony's in a long black Chesterfield coat with a velvet collar, a derby hat, a starched stiff white shirt with emerald-colored tie, a gleaming diamond stickpin, dove-gray fawn gloves, an ivory white silk scarf, and his characteristic gray spats. In one of those ironic twists that ran through Bogie's life, the story of Corbett would in 1942 be depicted on the screen by Errol Flynn, Bogie's friend and fellow contract player at Warner Brothers.

Corbett stood six feet two, weighing more than two-hundred pounds. Originally called "Handsome Jim" and later "Pompadour Jim," he had settled on "Gentleman Jim."

It took Stuart and Hump a moment to realize that that was no lady Corbett was escorting. His date was Julian Eltinge, the world's most famous female impersonator. The actor had lived at the Los Angeles Athletic Club for a year with Charlie Chaplin, during which point they'd had a torrid affair, which was no secret to Hollywood insiders. Julian had also seduced Rudolph Valentino in his pre-Sheik days and had offered him a small part in a flicker Julian had made in Los Angeles.

Having a brief drink with Hump and Stuart, Tony told them that Gentleman

Jim "has this thing for transvestites. Mark Hellinger and Walter Winchell know about it but they like Jim and never make references to his dates in the press. It's his private thing and everyone at my bar indulges him. The only problem is, drag queens walk around with a sore ass for a week or more after Jim plows 'em." Tony excused himself, claiming he had to go home early.

After three more drinks, Hump and Stuart were growing increasingly annoyed by Hedda's table, especially when the impersonators started talking in loud voices about how they'd like to get plowed by Stuart's dick, which they had seen in the urinal. "Let's take them out," Hump said. "Tony's gone and there are just too many pansies growing in this garden tonight."

Sucking in their guts, both men got up on wobbly feet and accosted Hedda's table, grabbing two of the men to toss them on the street.

Seeing what was happening, the "father of modern boxing," agile and jack-rabbit quick, jumped up from his table, excusing himself from Julian. He went over and grabbed Hump and Stuart by the back of their necks. He banged their heads together so hard it almost cracked their skulls.

With Hump on his left arm and Stuart on the right, he carried both men up the steps and tossed them onto the rainy street.

Six months went by before Hump dared enter Tony's again. When he did, he always sent a friend ahead of him to see if Gentleman Jim was among the patrons with his "date" for the night.

***

When the newspaper reporter, Mark Hellinger, finally got around to inviting Hump for that night on the town, he made up for lost time. Mark's world, then known as "gay Broadway," was comprised of a square mile of real estate between 40th and 50th streets, bounded by 6th and 8th Avenue. If it wasn't the world's most glamorous mile, it was the most exciting, a district of dime-a-dance joints, speakeasies, chop-suey outlets, cabarets, theaters, movie houses, plush apartments for kept women, panhandlers, Minsky's Burlesque, the Palace theater, and even Spinrad's Barbershop.

The barbershop was pointed out to Hump by Mark who suggested he should go in there tomorrow and ask for George. "If you're going to be a big Broadway star, you've got to get your hair cut right," Mark said. He also promised Hump to introduce him to his tailor. "The Jimmy Walker cut is the way to go." Hump had heard about the political aspirations of this fancy dresser, whose career had included stints as a Broadway actor. He was also a talented musician, having written such songs as "Will You Love Me in December As You Do in May?" Rising through the ranks of Tammany Hall, Jimmy Walker was entering the mayor's race.

Mark Hellinger was on a first-name basis with Jack Dempsey, Clarence Darrow, Theodore Dreiser, Ethel Barrymore, Florenz Ziegfeld, W.C. Fields, Eddie

Cantor, Jeanne Eagles, Bobby Jones, and even Eleanora Duse and Aimee Semple McPherson. He spent his nights in some of New York's five-thousand speakeasies devoted to drinking "Staten Island or New Jersey champagne" at $35 a bottle or unreliable Bahamian Scotch at $20 a fifth.

On his rounds Mark was accompanied by another reporter, columnist Walter Winchell. Hellinger eventually evolved into the world's first Broadway reporter, Winchell the first of the Broadway gossip columnists. The two men were seen together practically every night of the week, so much so that they were rumored to be lovers.

Disdaining Winchell's show biz gossip, Mark preferred the heart-rendering sob story, filled with laughter and tears, with an O'Henry ending. Mark called his reporting "short stories about the people of Broadway," ranging from the long-legged Ziegfeld girls to the Irish immigrant cop on the block with a nightstick, to the little Sicilian hood who dreamed that he might one day take over Al Capone's crime empire.

Mark had invited Hump to El Fey club, run by bootlegger Larry Fay. (The club was named after him but spelled slightly differently.) Rumor had it that Fay didn't know how to spell his name. The club's hostess was the fabulous Texas Guinan, whose own club had recently been closed by the police for selling bootleg hooch.

Hump was eager to meet Texas Guinan, a name known all over Broadway. The flamboyant show-biz personality and actress was born in Texas in 1884 as Mary Louise Cecilia Guinan. The robust Irish lass grew up on a small ranch near Waco where she became an accomplished horseback rider and roper. She went from there into live Wild West dramas, and in time ended up in the chorus line in such Chicago comedies as *The Gay Musician*.

In Hollywood, cast as the gun-girl heroine in a silent screen western, *The Wildcat* in 1917, this pistol-packing, barrel-riding queen of the West became America's first movie cowgirl long before the likes of Dale Evans. She went on to appear as a gunslinger in *The Gun Woman* of 1918 and *Little Miss Deputy* in 1919 before being lured by the aura of New York in the Roaring Twenties.

When Hump entered the bar with Mark, Texas Guinan called out, "Hello, suckers! Come on in and leave your wallet on the bar." On meeting her, Hump liked her free-wheeling, devil-may-care aura. "I'm hanging out at Larry's dump," she said, "because the cops have padlocked my place. I don't have to worry about an automobile ride in New York. Taxpayers foot the bill. Unfortunately, my free ride from the city is always to jail. I've fucked Jimmy Walker six times. He owes me plenty of favors. When he becomes mayor, the cops will get off my back except when they come around to fuck me in the ass."

"You're my kind of gal," Hump said to Texas as Mark lost himself in the bowels of the club.

"I've got some special entertainment planned for you tonight in more ways than one," Texas said.

She ordered Hump a drink, although she always denied that alcohol was sold in her speakeasies. When his drink was served, she told Hump where Fay had stolen the booze. "The other night some of Fay's hoods armed themselves with pistols, sawed-off shotguns, and Tommy guns," she said. "They piled into a large boat and sailed ten miles out to sea where they hijacked a French freighter like a team of God damn pirates. They made off with five-hundred cases of whiskey, wine, champagne, and brandy. Fay didn't go out on the raid himself. He was waiting on shore and paid a measly one-hundred bucks for the whole thing. He'll make thousands off the stuff, especially when my brother, Tommy, waters it down at the bar."

Surveying the club, she said, "I'm not doing too bad. When I was a movie star in Hollywood, I earned fifty dollars a week—those asshole cheats out there. Before the year is out in New York, I expect to earn $700,000."

As the night progressed, she told him that a producer was here tonight, considering casting her in the appropriately titled Broadway review *Padlocks of 1925*. It took a while for the revue to be produced, and the title had to be changed to *Padlocks of 1927*.

"I'm gonna die young," Texas told him. "But I'm gonna have a hell of a lot of fun along the way. What about you, Bogart?"

"I'm gonna die young too but I'm gonna have more fun than you," he said.

"I'll race you to the finish line, sucker," she said before getting up to announce the star act of the evening.

In another one of the strange coincidences in Hump's life, the act being introduced by Texas that night at El Fey was a dance routine by George Raft.

This was the same George Raft that would become the legendary Broadway dancer, the Hollywood tough guy, the gambler, and Don Juan himself with a life-long courtship with the underworld. Hump had read in Winchell's column that Raft had taught the Charleston to Edward, Prince of Wales, later King Edward VIII, and later, the Duke of Windsor.

In his early reviews, Hump was called the Valentino of Broadway. But in Hollywood it was George Raft who'd be billed as Paramount's "replacement" for the long-dead Valentino.

To Hump's regret in the 30s, Warner brothers eventually signed Raft to a stable of cinema tough guys that included Edward G. Robinson and James Cagney. Hump would often find that whenever he was competing for a choice film role, Raft got the part instead.

All of that was to change in the early Forties when Raft started turning down motion pictures, the parts going to Bogie. One of those films was *Casablanca*.

***

Future movie stardom was hardly on Hump's mind as he sat mesmerized, watching Raft dance to an audience of patrons consisting of millionaires and bluebloods mingling with nattily dressed hoodlums.

After introducing Raft, the brassy, shoot-'em-up gal, Texas herself, rejoined Hump at table. "Raft is the weirdest, maddest dancer you've ever seen," Texas said in her tough, deep voice. She quickly waved at a couple entering to see Raft dance. "Fuck, I'm starting to attract the literati." Hump recognized Robert Sherwood escorting Dorothy Parker.

"Raft mesmerizes my customers," Texas said. "All eyes shine on Raft as he whirls faster and faster. Every night he stops the show. He's taking in a thousand big ones a week."

Hump didn't need this running dance critique from Texas. He watched in fascination as Raft performed his mongrel dance, called "the Peabody." It was a fantastic speed dance with all kinds of interpolations, a choreography strangely known as "cake-eating." The dance was filled with dozens of twists, turns, and jerks.

The owner of the club, Fay, joined Texas and Hump at table. It was obvious that he'd been quarreling with Texas. Texas was attracting an upper-crust crowd of the Whitneys, the Vanderbilts, and the Astors, whereas Fay was inviting his hoodlum friends from Brooklyn. There was no place with such a mixed clientele in all of New York. An aristocrat like Vincent Astor could be spotted at the bar drinking with five gun-toting and trigger-happy desperados.

Hump was equally fascinated by Raft's incredible speed dance and by Fay himself. Bootlegger Fay looked like a tough hood from Brooklyn, perhaps an unruly labor organizer, more than the owner of a swank night club. Hump later claimed that he used Fay as his role model when he first had to impersonate a gangster in films.

After his performance, Texas brought Raft over to the table to meet Hump. "Here's the actor who's gonna marry Helen Menken." And although they were later to become bitter rivals for the same film roles, Hump liked Raft at once. The young dancer was actually the character that latter-day film fans thought Bogie was, even though his background and character were almost the complete opposite of Raft's.

Raft had slicked down his black hair with what appeared to be a whole jar of Vaseline, a hairstyle that had become known as the patent-leather look. Unlike the baggy suits of the day, he wore tight, form-fitting trousers and jackets, along with three diamond rings, one on his pinkie.

He spoke with such brutal honesty and candor about who he was and what he did that Hump was mildly surprised that he'd been so confessional to a stranger. "Listen, unless you're going to fuck Texas tonight, I can get you a hot date," Raft said. "I'll give you the phone number of this go-to-hell pussy, Grayce Mulrooney. She's my wife."

At first Hump thought that Raft was joking until he realized that the dancer was perfectly serious.

"She's alone every night." Raft pointed to a cute little brunette dancing in the chorus line. "That's Ruby Keeler, She's only fourteen and working for Texas and Fay illegally. I'm going to go for her tonight. I'm gonna make the big play. Sometimes I fuck young."

Two men in their twenties passed by their table en route to the men's room. In their tuxedos, each one looked like a twin of Rudolph Valentino. "Everybody's trying to get in on the Valentino act," Raft said contemptuously. "I've even read that about you."

"I don't think I'm going to become another Valentino," Hump said. "We're too different. Besides, I don't look that good in Arab drag."

Raft laughed. "There's talk that I'll be the screen's next Valentino, although it seems like Roman Novarro has beat me out. I know Rudy very well. We once shared a room together when we were going through rough days back in our taxi-dancing times, long before America knew what a Sheik was."

"I heard he was a gigolo," Hump said.

"You might call it that," Raft said, downing a whiskey. "We were both gigolos, hiring ourselves out on the dance floor for a buck. Often we went home with our partners. Old broads used to request me more than they did Rudy. Once or twice Rudy and I fucked an old bitch in the same bed. Back then women called me Blacksnake, for reasons I won't go into. Rudy and I had a good hustling business going until that pansy Sheik fell in love with me. He's a real fairy. He used to beg me all the time to let him suck my big dick. Once or twice when I was drunk I threw him a mercy fuck. We're still friends but I had to break up our business because he became some lovesick little schoolgal. I figured one of those lez wives he married can take care of him. Or, better yet, I'm sure Ramon Novarro will open up his ass to Rudy any time he wants. Rudy's first wife, Jean Acker, keeps writing me to go on the road with her in a dance act, imitating the act that Natacha Rambova and Rudy toured in. Acker wants the billing to read, 'Mrs. Rudolph Valentino and George Raft.' No way. I'm gonna be a star without any help from the Valentino name."

Texas introduced a young comedian, Milton Berle, as the next act. Hump excused himself to go to the men's room. Raft reached over and took his wrist. "I'd better go piss with you. That way you'll be safe."

"What in hell does that mean?" Hump asked.

"Texas and Fay let me run the pissoir concession here," Raft said, getting up. "When one of the customers is totally polluted and goes to take a piss, one of my boys in the men's room picks his pocket. I taught my boys all they know. I'm an expert pickpocket myself." He reached into his jacket and retrieved Hump's wallet. "When Texas yells, 'Hello, sucker,' she really means it."

In the men's room, Raft nodded to his boys as he stood at the latrine pissing with Hump. A quick pecker-check revealed to Hump that he and Raft looked about equally matched in the male equipment department.

Back at the table where more drinks were served, Raft told Hump that after work, and while still dressed in his tuxedo, he ran beer convoys. "I work not just for Fay but for Dutch Schultz and 'Legs' Diamond," Raft said. "Mostly I work for a guy called Big Frenchy. Sometimes we make heists when we raid our competition's booze being trucked into New York. You might think I'm a fantastic dancer, but I'm even better as a truck driver. I can cut corners on two wheels. Turn a truck on a dime and hold the fucker steady going eighty miles an hour, all the time ducking some trigger-happy fool."

Raft wasn't making this up, although it sounded like a script for one of the films both men would later make at Warner Brothers. Raft also wasn't lying about his driving skills. Because of his expertise learned on illegal booze heists in New York in the Twenties, he would one day save Bogie's life when the brakes gave out on a truck Raft was driving on the set of a film.

Texas returned to the table to warn Raft that she was about to introduce him for his second show of the evening. When Raft excused himself, Texas told Hump that since he had seen Raft dance, she had more entertainment planned for him. "But for the grand finale, you're coming to bed with me," Texas said, leaning over to kiss his lips.

One of the waiters ushered Hump into one of the backrooms filled with a blue haze because of the heavy smoking of the other male patrons. When the film went on, Hump could understand why these were called blue movies. The star of tonight's porn movie was a dancer who'd been a hit in stag movies and a star at private smokers before going on to Hollywood.

As the actress on film danced the Charleston in the nude, the cameraman told Hump her name was Lucille LeSueur.

Fast forward: It is 1954, and Hump, the "king of Hollywood," is escorting the "queen of Hollywood" to the Academy Awards ceremony.

More than a decade after Louis B. Mayer had kicked Hump's date for the evening off the MGM lot, she'd bounced back to regain her throne as queen, although not for long.

With a mink stole draped across her shoulder and around her wrinkled neck, Bogie was taking out Joan Crawford, once known as Lucille LeSueur.

***

The Broadway season was ripe for Bogie's women-to-be in 1925, carrying through the spring of 1926. Wife-to-be number one, Helen Menken, was appearing in *Makropoulos Secret*. Wife number two, Mary Philips, was a star in *The Wisdom Tooth*, and wife number three, Mayo Methot, was appearing in *Alias the Deacon*. Wife number four? The one-year old Betty Bacall was in her Bronx nursery dirtying her diapers.

The actress, Mary Boland, had threatened to destroy Hump's stage career because of his unprofessional conduct when he'd appeared with her in *Meet the Wife*. When no suitable young actor could be found for her new three-act comedy, she reluctantly said, "Okay, get Bogart."

Cradle Snatchers was written by Norma Mitchell and Russell Medcraft and directed by Sam Forrest. It was a raucous and bawdy farce about three society women who sneak away with three handsome college men hired as gigolos. The plot thickens when the husbands show up at the same hideaway, thinking that it's a high-class bordello.

It was well-cast, especially with the enormously comical actress Edna May Oliver in a co-starring role. Hump played a minor role, that of Jose Vallejo. Also appearing in a minor role was another actor, Raymond Guion, whom Hump befriended.

Like Rod La Rocque, Raymond wasn't pleased with his name. After several drunken talks in speakeasies, he won Hump's approval for his new stage name. As Gene Raymond, Broadway's so-called "nearly perfect juvenile" would go on to be a successful film career as a handsome, blond-haired actor with a well-toned body.

Gene Raymond's greatest fame came on June 16, 1937 when he married MGM's golden singing sensation, Jeanette MacDonald. Much of the movie-going public was disappointed to learn of the marriage. Movie polls showed that the majority of American women wanted MacDonald to marry her frequent co-star, singer/actor Nelson Eddy, with whom she'd appeared in such films as *Naughty Marietta, Rose Marie,* and *Maytime.* What the public didn't know at the time was that Nelson Eddy was gay.

Discreet in California, Eddy was frequently seen in New York at the gay baths and at gay watering holes. His recording of "Stouthearted Men" from *New Moon* became a gay cult favorite in the 1950s, and remains in the standard repertoire of gay men's choruses. Composer lyricist Jerry Herman officially "outed" Eddy in his song, "Nelson."

Back in 1925, both Raymond and Hump thought they'd found steady employment in *Cradle Snatchers.* Woollcott found Hump's performance "competent," but a visiting theater critic from Chicago, Amy Leslie, was more enthusiastic. She claimed Bogart was "as handsome as Valentino and as graceful as any of our best romantic actors." Opening on September 7, 1925, at the Music Box, *Cradle Snatchers* would run for 332 performances, the hit of the season.

For Hump, the highlight of the play's run was the night Louise Brooks showed up with her new boy friend, Charlie Chaplin. Hump's only regret was that no one in the audience actually watched the play that night, as all eyes were focused on Charlie Chaplin. He was, after all, the most famous man on earth. As one stagehand claimed, "I don't know who the president of the United States is, but I sure know who The Little Tramp is."

Louise had taken Charlie to see Helen perform that previous evening, and had even gone with the film star backstage to meet Helen. Louise later claimed that Charlie and she were bitterly disappointed in Helen's performance both on and off the stage. "It's the same show whether the curtain is up or whether she's in her dressing room taking off her makeup," Louise said. "She's so histrionic, so t-h-e-a-t-e-r. Her white, thin face is always ecstatically lifted up to her vision of the Drama. I never heard her talk about anything except the art of the theater. She ignored me and was trying to impress Charlie. It didn't work. He couldn't wait to escape from her clutches."

Like an awestruck fan, Hump was delighted to meet Charlie after his performance and even more pleased when Louise invited him to join Charlie, her sometimes girl friend, Peggy Fears, and herself for a tour of some East Side speakeasies. The Little Tramp had developed a fondness for gypsy musicians newly arrived from Budapest. At the final speakeasy visit of the night, Charlie sat enraptured listening to a wild Hungarian violinist, Bela Varga, with an Albert Einstein coiffure, playing nostalgic music left over from the collapse of the Austro-Hungarian Empire.

Invited back to Charlie's suite, the entertainment continued as Charlie did his impressions, the most brilliant being that of John Barrymore reciting the most famous soliloquy of *Hamlet* as he picked his nose. He then rushed into his bedroom and emerged in quick drag, impersonating Isadora Duncan dancing barefoot in a storm of toilet paper. His most comedic impression was left for last—that of how Lillian Gish would achieve orgasm if she ever went to bed with anyone but her sister, Dorothy.

Tired of performing, Charlie offered Louise and Peggy Fears five-hundred dollars if they would strip naked and perform lesbian love on the sofa in front of his eager eyes. Without hesitation, both women stripped down and got on the sofa, where Charlie, only twelve inches from the scene, played director. The performance must have excited him, as he disappeared inside the bedroom and emerged later totally nude.

Hump was shocked to see that Charlie had coated his monstrous erection with iodine. He proceeded to chase both Peggy and Louise around the living room, finally capturing Louise. As he disappeared inside his bedroom with her, shutting the door behind him, he invited Hump to enjoy Peggy Fears for the night.

After they'd gone, Peggy plopped down on the sofa. "Okay, big boy, show time! Strip down for action. Louise has already told me about you. For a change, I'm gonna lay you for free."

*****

Four years after taking out the marriage license—it was still valid—Humphrey Bogart wed Helen Menken on May 20, 1926. The wedding took place at Helen's apartment at 52 Gramercy Place.

Hump selected his brother-in-law, Stuart Rose, as his best man. He'd wed Hump's sister Frances two years before. Many of Helen's friends, a regular *Who's Who in the Theater*, showed up. Some one-hundred and thirty guests crammed into the apartment.

Hump invited the Bradys, including Jr. and Sr., Grace George, and Alice Brady.

His fellow pussy posse member, Kenneth MacKenna, was also a guest, as was Maud Bogart. Hump's father was at sea at the time.

Stuart was later to recall that the ceremony "was macabre, almost obscene." John Kent, a pastor at St. Ann's Church for Deaf Mutes, conducted the ceremony. He was deaf himself and had been asked to perform the marriage because both of Helen's parents, who were attending the wedding, were also deaf.

Unlike Helen's parents, the reverend had learned to read the service in a kind of warped guttural speech, a sing-song way of talking evocative of Helen Keller. Kent both spoke the words of the ceremony and performed in sign language.

The pastor couldn't hear Hump's "I do," although Helen delivered her "I do" in sign language. After the ceremony, Helen rushed over to Mary Boland where she gushed, "I've been so frightfully busy on Broadway and other stages, I just haven't found time to marry in all these four years, even though Humphrey urged me to do so every day."

When newsmen showed up with photographers, Helen became unstrung. She burst into hysterics. As Louise Brooks would later satirically observe, "For Helen, that wasn't hard to do. She did that every night on stage whether the part called for it or not."

Maud Bogart, Frances, and Helen's mother helped the just-married actress to her bedroom. One of the guests, Dr. Nathan Blomenthal, was summoned to sedate her. Hump did not bother to go into the bedroom to check on the condition of his new bride.

When they'd gone, he turned to Bill Jr. and Stuart. "I think I've made a dreadful mistake."

Chapter Four

The marriage with Helen Menken began with violence. There was no honeymoon, other than a dinner at Luchow's and a night alone in the apartment. Helen had a fat Cocker Spaniel named "Sam." She insisted on feeding the dog caviar, claiming, "It's his favorite food."

Hump countered that the mutt only ate caviar because there was nothing else in his bowl. Awaking early after their first night as a married couple, Hump went and got the dog a bowl of chopped meat. The animal was in the act of gobbling down the red meat when Helen came into the kitchen. She screamed at her new husband for feeding the dog hamburger and claimed it would give him worms. The fight accelerated until she slapped him severely.

Enraged, he punched her in the face and sent her sprawling on the floor. She couldn't appear on the street for two weeks, and Hump spent the time as a houseguest of Bill Jr. and Katherine Alexander.

When Hump and Helen finally spoke, it was by telephone, when she called to tell him that she was going to appear in a play called *The Captive*.

"What's the plot?" he asked sarcastically. "Do you get kidnapped by African cannibals?"

"Nothing like that," she said. "It's a play about lesbianism."

"Type casting," he kidded her.

"If that God damn drag queen, Mae West, can play a nymphomaniac in some shitty play called *Sex*, then I can play a lesbian in *The Captive*—and if you and the public don't like it, you can all go fuck yourselves." She slammed down the phone.

True to her word, Helen began rehearsals for what would be one of the most controversial plays in the history of Broadway of the 1920s. Deciding to make up with Helen, Hump attended rehearsals.

At the theater, he met the actor, Basil Rathbone, who was seven years older than him. Rathbone had been born in Johannesburg, South Africa, where his family had to flee to escape the Boers because Rathbone's father, Edgar Philip Rathbone, a mining engineer, had been accused of being a British spy.

He had married Ouida Bergère in April of 1926. His union with this scriptwriter would last until Rathbone's death in 1967, although he told Hump that, "You are and I are destined to love many different women." When he said that, he, of course, was perfectly aware of Hump's marriage to Helen. He also told Hump that, "Helen has told me that she has had many real experiences as a lesbian, so she feels perfectly qualified in the role. When we open, though, I fear the revenge of the bluenoses, who are perfectly capable of tarring us, feathering us, and riding us out of town on a rail."

***

"Hello, sucker," were the words greeting Hump after he was awakened by the blaring sound of a ringing phone. Hung over and with a splitting headache, he had staggered toward the phone, thinking it might be Helen calling from Philadelphia which she'd visited as part of one of her mysterious and frequent trips out of town. At the sound of that voice, he knew at once it was Texas Guinan.

"Come to El Fey tonight," she said. "I'll reserve you a ringside table. You can sit next to Raft. Some really big names will be at the club tonight, like Valentino. He's been showing up here every night. Raft will do his dance, of course, but I've got other acts."

With the prospect of a hot evening, Hump accepted. "What about us?" he asked. "Want to get together later? My wife's out of town, and I'm between engagements."

"Why not?" Texas said. "You throw one of the best fucks in town, and I'm ready for a repeat performance."

Hump went through his day obsessed with Valentino, the actor to whom he was most frequently compared in the press. He'd seen all of the Sheik's movies and saw little, if any resemblance. In contrast, George Raft did resemble Valentino, only because he carefully modeled himself after his former taxi dancer companion, especially in his patent-leather, slicked-back black hair look.

That night at El Fey, Raft's act wasn't scheduled until midnight, so Hump welcomed the chance to renew his friendship with this fascinating, if slightly dangerous, new friend. Raft was sitting and talking at the ringside table with Texas.

She immediately got up and kissed Hump on the lips. "Both of you guys are such great lovers," she said, looking first at Raft and then at Hump. "I can't decide which one to choose tonight. I'd love to take you both on at once, the way Valentino and Georgie used to do back in their gigolo days."

As Hump sat down and was served a whiskey, Raft seemed angered at Texas' remark. "This one," he said, his eyes flashing at Texas, "still treats me like El Fey's dancing male whore. She's always demanding that I fuck whichever society broad takes a fancy to me. I prefer to do my own picking and choosing, and I like young gals from the five-and-dime a lot more than the rich, fat assed broads who come here."

"Blacksnake is good for my business," Texas said. "A broad, if it's her lucky night, can not only watch him perform the most fascinating dance in New York, but she'll get to learn later why Georgie here is called Blacksnake."

After that tantalizing bit of information, Texas excused herself to go backstage

92

to talk to one of the performers. "Catch you later, Hump," she said. "God, what an appropriate nickname."

No sooner had Texas departed than one of Raft's guests arrived at table, trailed by two hoodlums. "Hi, ladykiller," he said to Raft, warmly embracing him. Hump was introduced to Arthur Flegenheimer, better known as "Dutch Schultz." He sat down at table, looking at his bodyguards. "It's better for my health to travel with some protection," he said to Hump.

"Georgie," Schultz said. "I was fucking that little teenage broad, Ruby Keeler, that you fixed me up with last night. The bitch said she'd rather fuck you than me 'cause your dick's twice as long. I should have belted her."

"All of us are made different," Raft said diplomatically. "We have different talents."

"I wish I had your talent for fucking, Georgie," Schultz said. "You must do something special. It's always been hard for me to make a woman scream out in passion. That is, until last year when I learned to get the screams I want. I put a gun to a broad's God damn head. I threaten to blow her fucking brains out if she doesn't holler in passion. That sure gets to 'em every time."

Raft and Schultz laughed at that. Fearing it was true, Hump managed a smile. Raft dealt with gangsters on a daily basis. To Hump, it was a new and altogether frightening experience. "Maud didn't raise no gangster," Hump once said to Bill Brady Jr.

Schultz turned once again to Hump. "Georgie here is making big bucks by capitalizing off this fantasy women have about Valentino," Schultz said. "Most women can't get a taste of Valentino's overrated dick, so they turn to Georgie as a substitute."

Hump noted anger flashing across Raft's face, although the dancer had no choice but to take Schultz's insults.

"All of us guys know that Valentino is nothing but a dago fairy," Schultz said. "But he's big box office. When Georgie does the Latin tango, women in the audience swoon. They imagine Valentino. They cream in their bloomers."

Suddenly, Raft rose to his feet. At first Hump thought he was going to strike Schultz but it was to welcome two new guests to his table. Schultz stayed glued to his seat but Hump rose for an awkward encounter with the man who had so thoroughly trounced him that night in Tony's speakeasy, Gentleman Jim Corbett, who was bearing on his arm the voluptuous comedienne, Mae West. Both of them immediately recognized Hump.

Turning to Hump, West said, "Glad to see ya, big boy…how's that pretty little wife of yours? When ya see her, tell her that I can't help it if people want to see a goddess like me having sex, in a play called *Sex*, instead of having a bunch of lesbians talking about pussy all night. After all, I'm an institution—something like the Statue of Liberty, in this case in a missionary position."

"Helen's okay," Hump assured her, smiling despite himself. "She's just a bit jealous."

Gentleman Jim shook Hump's hand. "Sorry I had to crack your skull at Tony's but you asked for it, and I can't have you insulting the ladies—after all, some of them are my friends."

"I heard about that fight," West chimed in. "Don't pick on the pansies. They're some of my biggest fans. I hear one of them does Mae West better than I do. Speaking of Mae West imitators, here comes one now."

It was Texas herself striding over to Raft's table to greet her famous, newly arrived guests.

Draped in feathers, diamonds, and furs, West was attracting a lot of attention from the other patrons. "I'm auditioning Gentleman Jim tonight and considering making him part of my act. You'll have to come over to Newark to see us. I'll be appearing with Minnie Palmer's *Four Marx Brothers*."

Later, when Raft once again escorted Hump to the men's urinal, passing his pickpocket boys, Raft whispered to Hump. "Mae could be in the company of the president of the United States. But if a boxer with a crooked nose, cauliflower ears, and the IQ of a well-hung ape shows up, she'll dump the prez and go for the fighter."

As Hump was to learn later, Raft was absolutely right. Gentleman Jim, even though twice her age at the time, must have passed his audition, as West and the Champ began a torrid affair. West went on to make other conquests among the fighters of her era, including Max Baer, Gentleman Jim's successor as world heavyweight champion, and then moved on to Joe Louis, the young black heavyweight.

As West would reveal years later in her Los Angeles apartment, "Joe was the first time I ever crossed the color line. I wanted to find out if it's true what they say about black men. Joe was hung pretty well, but no more so than one of my boys, Steve Cochran. Talk about an appropriate last name. He should spell Cochran with a 'k'"

In time, West would bestow her charms on fighters other than heavyweights. After bedding one more heavyweight, Jack Dempsey, she teamed up with the Filipino, Speedy Dado, the world's bantamweight champion, who was widely celebrated at the time throughout California. And years later, when West was a bit long in the tooth, she maintained a long-running affair with a world-class "featherweight," Albert "Chalky" Wright, title-holder from 1942 to 1944.

Texas soon reappeared at table with Rudolph Valentino. Even Mae West quieted down, perhaps because she knew she couldn't compete with the Sheik. She did, however, invite him to become part of her act. "When Mae West and Rudy Valentino tango together across the stage, tickets will be selling for fifty bucks each," she said.

Valentino was seated between Hump and Raft. He turned to Hump. "I keep reading in the papers that you're the new Valentino." He glanced affectionately over at Raft, then ran his fingers along the dancer's cheek, and winked at him.

Hump was surprised that Valentino would act in such an effeminate manner in public. "I don't think you look like me at all," Valentino said to Hump. "You're beautiful. But you're definitely not Latin."

"I don't know why these tabloid writers compare us to one another," Hump said, slightly embarrassed. "We're not the same type, and, unlike you boys, I don't dance."

"Georgie and I got our start as taxi-dancers," Valentino said.

"Yeah," Raft said. "But you got jealous every time I went home with a broad. You wanted me for yourself, you fucker."

"There's only one Blacksnake," he said, reaching to feel Raft's arm. He turned to Hump again. "Did I ever tell you why Georgie is called Blacksnake?"

"No, but I keep hearing that that's his nickname," Hump said.

"I'll tell you about it some other time," Valentino said. "after I get to know you better." He seemed to study Hump's face for a moment. "I think your best feature is your lips. In spite of that imperfection, they're very beautiful lips, very kissable. I like the way you always keep them wet."

"I don't go that route," Hump said. Valentino's come-on had made him feel very awkward. He'd been shocked at the Sheik's appearance. He looked hollow, gaunt, and pale. He often touched his abdomen, as his face winced in pain.

"I am so lonely tonight," Valentino said. "All the women in the world and half the men desire me, but I have no one."

"I thought you were carrying on with the vamp, Pola Negri?" Hump said.

"I detest that Polish bitch," Valentino said. "Besides, she's a lesbian. All I need to do is to marry my third lesbian. It would be too much. Jean Acker and Natacha Rambova were enough for one lifetime."

When Valentino once again touched his stomach and winced with pain, Raft suggested that he should see a doctor.

"I abhor doctors," Valentino said vehemently. "Natacha was warned in a vision. A visit to a doctor, she predicted, will lead to my death."

Conversations stopped when the lights shone on Texas, who was introducing the first entertainer of the evening, an East Indian fakir, Rahmin Bey. He was said to be able to pierce his arm and not bleed. After demonstrating this amazing feat to the audience by lancing his arm without drawing blood, he called for volunteers from the audience.

Hump was surprised that Valentino was the first to volunteer. When he removed his jacket and rolled up the sleeve of his dress shirt, the women in the audience swooned at the sight of his muscled arm. After promising Valentino that he wouldn't bleed, Bey pierced the Sheik's arm with a small knife. Blood gushed out of the wound, as some women in the audience screamed.

On a signal from Shultz, his two gunmen rushed to the stage and hustled Valentino off and into a dressing room.

At first, members of the audience sat in stunned silence, perhaps thinking that all of this was part of the evening's entertainment. The fakir, Bey, looked stunned, his face revealing his shock as if to say that an incident like this had never happened to him before.

Finally, when the audience saw two stagehands rounding up Bey's show business props, and they heard Texas Guinan screaming from backstage, they realized that Bey had actually injured their Sheik. Their shock turned to anger. As Bey was hustled offstage, glassware and bottles were tossed after him. There was loud booing from the floor. One man yelled, "He's a God damn faker all right."

A prominent New York doctor, Vincent C. Sherman, was in the audience that night with the playgirl and gold-digger, Peggy Hopkins Joyce. Texas summoned him backstage and asked everyone to leave the dressing room while the doctor attended to Valentino.

After about an hour, the doctor came out of the dressing room and went over to Raft, who was standing backstage with Hump. "His injury will be okay," Sherman said, "but there are other problems. My advice is that you check him into a hospital at once. He's calling for you."

Raft asked Hump to go with him to the dressing room. His arm bandaged, Valentino was having a drink from a bottle of hooch. "Gentlemen," he said, "the Sheik of Araby is spending the weekend at this lonely old mansion on Long Island. I want both of you to come out there with me. I'm afraid to be there by myself."

Within the hour, Hump found himself in the back seat of a long black limousine that looked like some funeral hearse. He definitely felt like an uninvited third party. It was obvious from the beginning that Valentino wanted to be alone with Raft, hoping to recapture some younger, even happier, time. Several times en route to the mansion, Valentino clutched his stomach, as Raft continued to urge him to order the limousine back to New York and to a hospital.

"I'll be fine," Valentino said, "just a little indigestion. Texas is a rotten cook."

Arriving at a large, ghostly looking house, Hump felt even more isolated, as Valentino directed none of the conversation to him. Hump didn't know who owned this mansion. He'd heard rumors that Valentino had some long-ago connection to a German baron, with whom he'd lived in New York in his pre-flicker days. The baron was said to have fallen in love with him and also to have blackmail evidence that Valentino had been involved in a murder. Because of what he knew about Valentino, the baron was able to summon him at will, seemingly whenever he wanted. Valentino only said that he was expecting "a friend from Europe" to arrive at the mansion on Monday.

After a drink in the library, Hump excused himself as a servant showed him the way upstairs to his bedroom. Intuitively, he suspected that Raft and Valentino didn't really want an audience, although he would have been tantalized to hear about their past life together.

Somewhere in the middle of the night, perhaps around three o'clock, Hump heard loud moaning from Valentino's bedroom. Thinking he should see what was the matter, he opened the door slightly and peered out just in time to see Raft in his red silk pajamas go into Valentino's bedroom.

When Hump woke up the next morning, he decided to take the train back to New York. He didn't want to stay at the mansion any more. As he walked by Raft's bedroom, he noticed that the door was open. He looked inside and called out to Raft but there was no answer. At first he was tempted to knock on Valentino's bedroom door, thinking Raft might still be there. Deciding against it, he went downstairs, wrote a note thanking Valentino for his hospitality, and quietly left the mansion heading for the train station.

That Monday morning, August 23, 1926, Hump was walking along Sixth Avenue when he was greeted with a banner headline in the *Daily Mirror*.

VALENTINO DYING.

***

When *The Captive* starring Helen Menken, opened on September 29, 1926, it shocked and disgusted Broadway audiences. Only Mae West, in her play *Sex*, was generating more newspaper publicity. Unlike Helen, West was enjoying the publicity and notoriety surrounding *Sex*. She was virtually rewriting the script every night, coming up with new and different *double entendres*. Eighty percent of her audience was male, and many of them were returning for a second, third, or even fourth viewing. Because West played it with different nuances and with different scripts and different ad libs every night, it was as if the audience was seeing a different play every time.

As West tried to lure more women into her audiences, Helen Menken wanted more males to attend *The Captive*. Her audiences were nearly eighty percent female. Lesbians from as far away as London and San Francisco flocked to see *The Captive*, the first play on Broadway to deal with the subject of female homosexuality.

New York's district attorney, Joab Banton, was coming under increasing pressure from John Sumner's Society for the Prevention of Vice. Banton made frequent statements to the press, claiming that Broadway wasn't going to become as scandal-ridden as Hollywood. He cited the murder in Hollywood of the director, William Desmond Taylor, and the scandal involving the trial of screen comedian, Fatty Arbuckle, accused of raping actress Virginia Rappé, causing her death.

Banton found no support from New York's playboy mayor, Jimmy Walker. Walker had attended both plays and claimed he liked them very much. "They're not family entertainment," Walker said, "but there's nothing wrong with having plays for mature audiences." Involved in a torrid affair with his mistress, Betty Compton, Walker was hardly a champion of morality.

When Walker departed for Havana in February of 1927 for a vacation, the acting mayor, Joseph B. McKee—known as "Holy Joe"—seized his opportunity to punish Broadway. He ordered Banton to "banish nudity and obscenity" from the Broadway stage.

An order went out on February 5 to have plainclothesmen from the vice squad monitor the productions of both *The Captive* and *Sex*. On February 9, Holy Joe had his evidence, and he issued orders to have the casts of both plays arrested and charged with offending public morals.

Basil Rathbone and Helen were in the middle of their play's second act when armed policemen stormed directly onto the stage and arrested both of them, along with the rest of the cast. The entire troupe was herded into a Black Maria (an armored paddy wagon used at the time for rounding up, among others, drunks and vagrants) waiting outside the theater. To her shock and surprise, Helen encountered Mae West and the entire cast of *Sex* within the same Black Maria.

Both casts were boiling mad. Each production had been jealous of the other play for the publicity and audiences it was generating. Suddenly, being herded together like cattle and thrown into the smelly, hot *Black Maria* for a bouncy ride to the police station had the effect of lighting a fuse.

Arguments broke out between the two casts. Mae West felt that she had to defend "my boys," and Helen took it upon herself to champion the cause of the cast of *The Captive*. "We're at least normal," West announced to Helen. "I'm not the one who's up on stage appearing nightly as a sexual deviate. From what I hear, you not only play a lesbian, you *are* a lesbian. I'm told your marriage to Bogart is just a sham. George Raft said your lisping husband is a faggot and your marriage just for show."

Unable to withstand such verbal assault, the already infuriated Helen moved toward West, grabbing her by her blonde hair. It was a wig. As the hairpiece fell to the floor, Helen stomped on it. West's own hair was matted down with a protective veil. Fearing she'd have to face newspaper photographers at the jail, West shoved Helen, sending her sprawling down onto the floor of the Black Maria, as West picked up her wig and began to make emergency repairs to it.

Rathbone graciously lifted Helen from the floor and dusted her off. Helen at this point was furious enough with West to attack her again, but Rathbone restrained her. "I hear you're not a real woman at all," Helen shouted at West. "I hear you're a female impersonator. That piece of crap you wrote, *Drag*, is based on your own secret life as a drag queen. Guys who've gone to bed with you claim you're a man. And even worse, a man with a little tiny dick!"

"You ugly bitch," West screamed. "If I could get to you, I'd tear every dyed hair out of your ugly head."

At the Jefferson Market Women's Prison, both Helen and Mae West were booked. Hump arrived and rushed to Helen, taking her in his arms. With him were two attorneys from Charles Frohman Productions, Inc.

Before the night was out, the attorneys for *The Captive* had worked out an agreement with the district attorney's office. Helen and the rest of the cast and the producers would accept a proposal of "implied immunity" if they would withdraw *The Captive* from the Broadway stage.

West chose to go the opposite route, preferring to continue with her play *Sex*. Her attorneys would get an injunction from the Supreme Court, barring police shutdown until a trial was held.

The trial itself became a fashion parade for West, who appeared in a different, outrageous, and gorgeous gown for every court appearance. She often wore black satin, some outfits with bugle beads, others with georgette tops. West eventually was convicted for producing *Sex* and sentenced to a ten-day jail term and a fine of $500. She would serve only eight days of her sentence at Welfare Island, getting off for good behavior.

Alone with Hump, Helen remained in seclusion at her apartment, refusing to see anyone and turning down all interviews. In desperation, Hump called Bill Jr. "You know how high strung she is. The arrest has done her in. She's having a nervous breakdown, and I don't know what to do."

"For Christ's sake, call Belmont," Bill advised. "He can shoot her up with morphine, and everything will be okay."

***

When she'd recovered, Helen secured an audition for Hump with the noted director, Guthrie McClintic, to test for the three-act comedy, *Saturday's Children* by Maxwell Anderson. Ironically, Hump knew that the part of Rims O'Neil was up for grabs because he'd already been called by Pussy Posse cohort and the play's set designer, Jo Mielziner. Originally the actor, Roger Pryor, had created the role but he dropped out of the competition after being hospitalized for bleeding ulcers.

McClintic liked Hump's audition and gave him the part. He had only hours to learn the role. Back at Helen's apartment she stayed up all night rehearsing him.

The star of the play, Ruth Hammond, virtually ignored Hump. All she'd said to him backstage was, "Mary Boland has already warned me about you." He thought that Hammond was unprofessional because she upstaged all the other actors.

Hump did not get along with the male star of the comedy either. The Hoosier actor, Richard Barbee, like F. Scott Fitzgerald, had gone to Princeton. Hump felt that Barbee too closely modeled himself after one of Fitzgerald's fictional characters and was not particularly convincing on stage. .

Hump struck out with the stars of the play, but was befriended by two members of the supporting cast, Ruth Gordon and Beulah Bondi, both of whom would go on to become celebrated in the theater and in films.

If Hump was known as a kidder and a needler, he met his match when the director introduced him to Ruth Gordon, playing a minor role in *Saturday's Children*. Three years older than Hump, she was witty and urbane, known for making such remarks as, "The rich have no friends. They merely know a lot of people."

Despite her ribbings, he was immediately attracted to this daughter of a ship's captain. Their affair, launched the week after their initial meeting, lasted about as long as his romance with Shirley Booth. Gordon later said, "It was over before it even began. I think we had sex. But who remembers so far back, and what difference would it make if I did remember? He's got Betty now, and I've got Garson."

At the time she met Hump, Ruth Gordon didn't have playwright, Garson Kanin, sixteen years her junior. She was married to actor Gregory Kelly, who would die in 1927.

Before heading for a prolonged run in Chicago, *Saturday's Children* would last for 310 performances on Broadway at the Booth Theatre. The play was not all that Hump was headed for, as his short-term marriage to Helen was rapidly coming to its predictable end.

Newspapers were still comparing Hump's look to that of Valentino, but actually he more closely resembled the newspaper columnist, Ed Sullivan. This journalist wrote a Broadway gossip column for the *Daily News*. A rock-faced Irishman with a hot temper, Sullivan also had a painful shyness and a disdain for phonies.

Sullivan would later achieve international fame on CBS's variety program, *Toast of the Town* (1948-55), later called *The Ed Sullivan Show* (1955-71). The show became a national institution, introducing to American audiences such talents as Elvis Presley (Sullivan refused to allow cameramen to photograph him below the hips) and later the sensational appearance of the Beatles.

As he made his rounds across the scope of the Broadway speakeasies, Hump often had gossips come over to him, giving him hot tips for his column tomorrow. Since Hump liked to put people on, he never revealed to them that he was an actor, not the newspaper journalist, Ed Sullivan, whom he closely resembled. With a perverted and not altogether kind sense of humor, Hump would often confide some very indiscreet gossip to these strangers. That gossip in most cases got back to its target. Sullivan in the late Twenties found himself in a number of feuds with show biz personalities, never knowing the reason why.

One night Hump wandered alone into the Mayfair Supper Club, since some of New York's prettiest and most available showgirls frequented the place. He was free to go on the town because Helen was in Boston. She claimed it was on business, but Hump suspected that it was an off-the-record sexual tryst.

At a red leather banquette and at the best table in the club, New York's handsome and newly elected mayor, Jimmy Walker, was in the company of two long-legged showgirls, one blonde, one a redhead.

Walker was a dapper dresser, though not as flamboyant in attire as Gentleman Jim. Unlike the champ who preferred to date drag queens, Walker preferred Ziegfeld showgirls when he was not occupied with his mistress.

"Hi, Ed," the mayor called out to Hump. "Loved your column today. C'mon over."

Hump thought that his ultimate coup would be to allow New York's mayor to mistake him for Ed Sullivan. He came over to the mayor's table and was introduced to the two bimbos of the evening. Hump joined the party not only for dinner but for a round of drinking. Even though booze was prohibited, Walker always said that that law didn't apply to New York's mayor or his guests.

Still impersonating Sullivan, Hump entertained the mayor and his guests with racy stories about Broadway personalities, gossip so hot it couldn't be printed in his column.

Later he joined the mayor heading for the men's room and pissed beside him at one of the club's porcelain urinals. The men did the obligatory pecker-checking, which caused the well-hung mayor to whisper, "Looks like you can take on one of the gals tonight as well as I can." Shaking himself dry, Walker said, "I had planned to sneak away with both of them. But I've had a bad day. I've got a hell of a meeting tomorrow at City Hall. Some farthole is accusing me of being on the take. So please, my good boy, Ed, take one of the bitches off my hands for the night."

"I'd be happy to oblige your Lordship," Hump said.

Back at table, Hump had assumed that the mayor would select the blonde over the redhead, because Walker was well known for liking blondes. Surprisingly, he chose the stripper, Rhonda Miles, who billed her act—for some strange reason— as "Ringworm." Into her second bottle of Staten Island champagne, Rhonda giggled. "When I first met Jimmy, he told me he only went for blonde fluff. I went and got myself dyed down there, and Jimmy is anxious to see the results. Tomorrow he's gonna pay to have my whole head dyed blonde."

Since he was ordered to do so by the mayor himself, Hump disappeared into the evening with the blonde stripper, who billed herself as Mabel Norman, perhaps in the hope that her audience would equate her stage name with the famous silent screen comedienne, Mabel Normand.

Without ever knowing why, Ed Sullivan found himself uncharacteristically thought of as a stud in the weeks ahead. Mabel Norman, thinking Hump was Ed, had given Hump's performance in bed a rave review.

Sullivan never found out the reason for his sudden popularity with Broadway showgirls.

**

Producer John Turek's decision in 1927 to revive that tired old chestnut, a three-act farce, *Baby Mine*, was a move he'd regret. Turek had seen *Saturday's Children*, and had been impressed with Hump's performance, considering him ideal for the role of the straight-laced juvenile husband, Alfred Hardy, in Margaret Mayo's successful play, which had run for 287 performances when it had originally opened back in 1910.

It was a great year on Broadway and Turek faced stiff competition from other shows, notably Sydney Howard's oedipal melodrama, *The Silver Cord*; Philip Barry's witty *Paris Bound*, and Eugene O'Neill's innovative *The Great God Brown*.

That 320-pound mass of blubber, Roscoe (Fatty) Arbuckle had signed to star as Jimmy Jenks in *Baby Mine*. The screen comedian had arrived in New York hoping for a comeback, following his acquittal on charges of raping and killing Virginia Rappé in a San Francisco hotel suite several years previously.

His once flourishing multi-million-dollar screen career was at an end, as his movies were boycotted in spite of his acquittal. In three trials for manslaughter, all the witnesses and even the district attorney had lied, frequently changing their stories. The first two juries could not reach a verdict but the third acquitted Arbuckle.

From their first meeting, Hump was antagonistic toward Arbuckle. Hump told Turek, "Frankly, I think whale blubber killed that slut, Virginia Rappé. But even sluts deserve to live. I heard Arbuckle is impotent. Can't get a rise out of his little dickie. That's probably why he had to use a milk bottle."

At first rumors were spread that Arbuckle had raped Rappé with a jagged piece of ice. Later the rumor was changed, the jagged ice story giving way to a milk bottle. The bottle was said to have ruptured Rappé's bladder, causing her eventual death.

On the first day of rehearsals, and to show his contempt, Hump asked the stage manager to deliver an empty milk bottle to Arbuckle's dressing room. Hump had penned a note and attached it to the bottle: "Either call me in to handle your next piece of tail or use this on her."

After that, the fat comedian never spoke to Hump throughout the short duration of the play, except on stage when he had to.

Although Hump detested the star of *Baby Mine*, he told Bill Brady Jr. that he had fallen "madly in love" with the young actress playing the juvenile female lead in the show. She was the very lovely Lee Patrick, a smallish young woman with fair hair, which she wore bobbed like a flapper. Most directors found her face "kind instead of sexy."

Still very young, Lee Patrick had not developed the persona of the brash, sassy blonde she would play in many of her upcoming sixty-five films. She is remembered today for playing the ditsy Henrietta Topper in the Topper television series. She also appeared in a number of film classics, playing second fiddle to legendary screen goddesses such as Bette Davis in the 1942 *Now, Voyager*; the 1945 *Mildred Pierce* with Joan Crawford, and the 1948 *The Snake Pit* with Olivia de Havilland. Ironically, one of her most remembered roles was as Effie Perrine, the secretary and confidante in the 1941 *The Maltese Falcon* opposite none other than Bogie himself.

Hump found that his role of a priggish young husband in *Baby Mine* was silly and not convincing. Miss Patrick played the role of his wife, an addictive flirt who maneuvers her way into a lunch alone with Hump's best friend. When he learns of this "transgression," Hump's character walks out on his wife. As part of the intricately contrived plot, Patrick "rents" three babies for an afternoon and, in a dramatic presentation, claims to Hump that all of them belong to her. Finally,

Hump learns the truth about these ridiculous episodes, interprets them as minor but adorable quirks of his flirtatious wife's personality, and agrees to let her return to his home and hearth.

Hump's very Victorian role lacked style, grace, and humor, and he was forced to deliver such lines as, "My wife had the effrontery, the bad taste, the idiocy to lunch in a public restaurant with that blackguard." The blackguard referred to was supposed to be Hump's best friend in the play.

Throughout the early rehearsals Hump avidly pursued Patrick, giving her candies and flowers. She repeatedly turned down his overtures until the second week when she agreed to have dinner with him at The 21 Club. After a few drinks, he propositioned her and she turned him down once again. Finally, she said, "I'll go to bed with you on one condition."

"And that is?" he asked.

"That you'll marry me. I know you're already married to Helen. But everybody on Broadway knows it's not a real marriage. The reason I insist on marriage is that I long ago decided that when I go to bed with a man, it's going to be forever."

Startled, Hump almost left her alone in 21 and fled into the night until his hormones won the battle. He took her back to a hotel room where he seduced her "in the missionary position," as he later confided to Bill Brady Jr. "None of that Louise Brooks kinky stuff—not with a virgin."

After they'd had sex, Patrick cried for what was left of the night. In between sobs, she told Hump that she had fallen in love with him and that there would never be another man in her life but him.

The next day at rehearsals, she confided to him that she had disliked the sex intensely and that it had hurt her. "A friend of mine told me yesterday that the first time always hurts, but it gets better the second and third time until a woman starts to enjoy it."

Hump told her that was true, and round two and round three—each played out in the same hotel bed—soon followed. But by the time the play opened, he was already losing interest in Patrick. As he confided to Brady, "It's too much like fucking a nun."

Baby Mine opened on the night of June 7, and the house was packed. Hump felt that audiences were more interested in seeing Arbuckle in the flesh than they were in going to their play. At the close of the final curtain on opening night, Arbuckle appeared before the audience, pleading with them not to believe all the bad press he'd received. He urged them to return again to his play and to bring their friends and relatives.

When Hump from the wings saw the fat comedian shedding tears in front of the audience, he found the act "pathetic." Audiences dwindled during the following nights, and Turek closed the show after only twelve performances.

Hump not only left the play at Chanin's Forty-Sixth Street Playhouse, he also told Patrick that their relationship was over. In her dressing room, she broke down and cried, threatening suicide. He didn't take that threat seriously.

Patrick went on to prove her claim that at heart she was a one-man woman and was "the true blue type." In time she met the writer, Thomas Wood, and married him, a union lasting for forty-five years.

***

After the closing of *Baby Mine*, Hump was out of work for only a week. A sudden call from Chicago and he was asked to get on the next train leaving New York. An actor had taken ill, and the producers wanted Hump to repeat his role in *Saturday's Children* in which he'd appeared with Ruth Hammond and had had that brief affair with actress Ruth Gordon.

Out of work and glad to get another role, Hump agreed to go to Chicago and take over the part. At her apartment, he asked Helen if she'd go with him to Chicago since she, too, was out of work. She flatly refused, claiming she was negotiating to reprise her role in *Seventh Heaven* on the London stage.

Already in London and a sensation over there, Tallulah had written to assure Helen that, "The audiences will adore you, darling. Perhaps you won't create the hysteria I do when I appear in my fancy lingerie, but you'll go over just swell."

Helen's refusal to go to Chicago led to the biggest fight yet between the Bogarts, signaling the final deterioration of their shaky marriage.

"Me, go to Chicago?" Helen shouted at him. "I'm an actress, not a housewife, God damn you if you haven't noticed that. A real actress, not some dumb little actor playing silly walk-ons with a tennis racquet for the mindless. Why in hell do you think I would want to sit in some fleabag Chicago hotel waiting for you to come home at night when the curtain goes down? Why indeed when I could be the toast of London?"

"Say it like it is," Hump yelled back at her. "What you mean is, you'd rather be licking Tallulah's pussy than getting fucked by me."

"You bastard!" She picked up a vase of flowers and hurled it at him, narrowly missing his face.

"You fucking dyke," he yelled at her, as she picked up another object, a silver platter her mother had given her. Before she could hurl this metal missile at him, he grabbed her wrist and forced her to drop it. As a final goodbye, he punched her hard in the face, scoring a bull's eye. The impact was so forceful that he injured his own hand. She fell to the floor as he stormed out of the apartment.

That night in a speakeasy, he told Bill Brady Jr., "I hit her harder than I've ever hit anyone before. At the moment I struck her, I hated all women. I hated the power they've had over me. When I plowed my fist into her face, I was striking back at all women. Even Maud who made me pose nude in that art class. I was hitting every woman who has ever attacked me."

"Maybe you're not the marrying kind," Bill said.

"Maybe I'm not." He looked at Bill, knowing that he had cheated on his wife as many times as Hump had. "You can play the game. Lie to your wife. But I want to be free of any woman. That way I can't be accused of infidelity."

Over a few more drinks, Bill agreed with his friend that a Menken/Bogart divorce was inevitable. "You were completely mismatched," Bill said. "Besides, Helen doesn't need a husband. She needs a string of young and admiring actresses around her, some of whom she will seduce."

"You're right," Hump agreed. "If she'd wanted a real man in her life, she would have stuck it out with me even though I'm not perfect."

Bill's wife, Katherine Alexander, was out of town for the weekend, and he invited Hump to spend the night with him until he was ready to catch the train for Chicago in the morning.

As they undressed for bed, Bill impulsively kissed Hump on the lips and held him real tight in an embrace that lasted for what seemed like two minutes. Bill was shaking uncontrollably. Finally, he broke away. "It should have been the two of us against the wind. In a different world where men aren't expected to marry, it would have been too. Just you and me, two men who love each other."

"That's great, old buddy," Hump said, embarrassed and dismissive of this kind of talk. "Only catch is, we're not homosexual. We like girls and plenty of them. Right?"

"Right," Bill said weakly, crawling in bed with Hump and turning over on his side, his back to his friend.

Five hours later at Grand Central Station, Bill had a strange, forlorn look on his face as he embraced Hump in a goodbye. Hump would remember that hangdog expression all the way to Chicago as he rode the rails.

Her face badly swollen, Helen was treated at a clinic in mid-Manhattan. Taking a taxi back to her apartment, she tried to conceal her large black eye from the doorman. She could make no more appearances until her wound healed.

Before signing the contract to go to London to appear in *Seventh Heaven*, she filed for divorce, waiving alimony but demanding that Hump return $2,500 which he'd borrowed from her and had never repaid.

She lied to reporters, claiming that she had been willing to give up her career and "make a real home" for Hump, but had suffered nothing but mental and physical abuse from him. "Sometimes he'd be gone for days at a time, and I never knew where he was or with whom. To him his stage career meant everything. A wife meant nothing to him other than a sometimes convenience."

She found that the press was sympathetic to her fantasies. If anybody valued her stage career more than her home life, it was Helen Menken herself. She officially charged Hump with "desertion, cruelty, and abuse."

His upcoming divorce was splashed all over the New York newspapers because the names of Helen Menken and, to a lesser extent, Humphrey Bogart, were well known on Broadway. In Chicago neither actor was known.

Fearing that Helen had permanently damaged his professional reputation, Hump wrote Bill Brady Jr. "All this crap that Helen has been tossing at me in the press is going to smell up my career on Broadway. I fear there will be no roles waiting for me when I come back. I'll be blacklisted."

Bill wrote back that Hump need not worry. "What are friends for?" he asked in a letter. "Between Dad, Alice, or me, a job will be waiting for you on Broadway. We'll see to that."

To forget Helen and the divorce mess swirling around him, Hump drank even more heavily than before—and that was a lot. After the curtain went down every night, he headed for the speakeasies of Chicago. He'd never realized it before, but Chicago seemed to have as many good-looking and available chorus girls as New York.

After the first week of making the rounds, he wrote Bill of his conquests. "So far, I've been having auditions nightly. On some occasions, two or three auditions a night. Want to know what I've concluded? There is not one single virgin in Chicago. If I find one, I'll take care of that problem."

***

When Hump returned from Chicago, he continued to make the rounds of the speakeasies with Bill Brady and Kenneth MacKenna. MacKenna wasn't playing around very much, as he was steadily dating that cute little blonde, Mary Philips, who had appeared with Hump and him in *Nerves*.

Married or not, Bill seemed to be free every night after the show to join Hump in a tour of the speakeasies, hitting clubs like Hotsy-Totsy, Chez Flo, the Bandbox, and the Clamhouse.

Hump was staring thirty in the face, and in between booze and chorus girls, he expressed fears about his future to Bill. "How long can I go on playing juveniles? Already I'm getting a little long in the tooth for the roles I'm cast into, some of which would be more suited to a nineteen-year old."

"You need a real meaty part," Bill said, "and I'm sorry I haven't been able to offer you one."

"I'm grateful for the work you've given me," Hump said. "Don't get me wrong. But I need something juicier."

"Have you considered films?" Bill asked.

"What could I play?" Hump asked. "Scarface? This fucking lip of mine would look great blown up on the silver screen."

"Get it operated on," Bill advised. "You'll never remove the scar but you could get rid of that scallop."

"Maybe you're right," he said. "I'll talk to my dad about it. After all, he was the one who gave it to me."

When Hump visited his parents the following day, he found them separated. He hadn't seen either Maud or Belmont for several months, nor had he called them. Belmont had become increasingly addicted to morphine, and had lost their elegant town house because of bad investments. He was forced to move into a small apartment in the East 40s.

106

Facing failing health and a declining medical practice, Belmont still went out on call as a ship's doctor. When not at sea, he spent most of his time in bed. Maud lived in an apartment next door, and money from her art work supported not only her but took care of most of Belmont's ever-growing number of bills.

Hump was saddened to see both parents in severe decline after having known such prestige and prosperity when they were listed in *Dau's New York Blue Book*.

Hump called on Maud first. Her face was drawn into bitter lines, and she looked dissipated and filled with despair. "I go next door and cook his breakfast every morning. I also go over and see that he has a decent dinner—that is, when I can get him to eat anything. He has these attacks at times, and I have to hire nurses for him, paying out money I can ill afford."

"What kind of attacks?" Hump asked.

"Attacks," she said, dismissing the question. "You always want to know everything."

"Are you guys going to get a divorce?" he asked.

"I have no intention of doing that," she said. "But your father's getting too weak to travel on ships any more. I fear he's going to be bedridden for the few years that remain to him."

"Are you still taking morphine too?" he asked.

"Why don't you go see your father and let me alone this morning?" she said. "I have a job. Not a well-paying assignment but a job, and I need to devote all my time to it—not to your questions."

"I love you," he protested. "I want to know."

"Do I interfere in your life?" she asked, her fury reflected in her stern face. "Did I ask you why you married a lesbian? Why you lay out drunk every night in speakeasies, picking up floozies like your father used to bring home sailor riffraff from the wharves? Do I interrogate you about why you continue in an illicit friendship with the Jew, Bill Brady? The stories spread about him. I can't believe that my son has slept in the same bed with that one."

"Bill is my friend, and he's going to stay my friend. There's nothing wrong with our relationship."

"Please leave," she said. "Just leave. My nerves are shattered."

Next door Hump found Belmont in unusually good spirits, or else he was putting on a brave show for his son. The doctor carefully avoided talk of his failed marriage, his declining career, and his reduced circumstances in life. Unlike Maud, Belmont seemed eager to hear about his son's many "triumphs" in the theater, and Hump exaggerated his achievements and praise.

"The one thing I can't understand," Belmont said, "is why you're always compared to Valentino when there's a write-up about you in the press. I just don't see the resemblance. Besides, he's long dead."

"I don't get it either," Hump said. "There are worse comparisons, though. At least they don't think I look like that rapist, Fatty Arbuckle."

Hump told him that Bill Brady Jr. had suggested a possible career for him in films. He was hesitant to bring up his lip disfigurement since Belmont was to blame for that.

Without ever excusing what he'd done to his son, Belmont said, "I can't remove the scar, but I can do minor surgery and get rid of that scallop. After all, when you become a big-time movie star, and the camera moves in for a close-up, you don't need all that extra skin blown up to giant size on the silver screen. I'll operate this morning."

"You mean, right now?" Hump asked, wondering if Belmont was in any condition to operate on him and fearing that the surgery might lead to greater disfigurement.

"I didn't raise a sissy for a son," Belmont said, rising slowly from his bed. "Go into my clinic down the hall and take off your shirt. We might as well get this over with if you're planning to go to Hollywood one day. Since Valentino died early in life, and no other actor has replaced him, it might as well be my son, Humphrey Bogart. But you'll have to come up with a less sissy name than Humphrey for the marquee."

***

Taking Bill's challenge of going to Hollywood seriously, Hump went alone to see *The Jazz Singer*, that partially talking picture starring Al Jolson. The word reaching New York was that in a year or two recorded human voices would be heard in all future films. Since many stars in Hollywood had awful voices, there was going to be a demand for Broadway actors trained in speaking parts.

Hump still had his slight lisp, but at least he no longer had that scallop on his lip thanks to Belmont who had given it to him in the first place.

The Jazz Singer had been running for several months before Hump got around to seeing it, and he was impressed, trying to imagine his face on the silver screen. He'd also heard that the pay out in Hollywood was much better than it was in the New York theater.

After seeing the film, he went two blocks down the street to a theater where the actress, Mary Halliday, was appearing in a play. In October 26, 1925, Helen had taken him to the opening of Halliday's play, *Easy Come, Easy Go*, and he'd liked the actress and wanted to call on her and wish her luck. He had learned that actresses like Mary Boland or Grace George might occasionally recommend him for future roles in their plays, so he felt it was important to keep in touch with some of the many theatrical celebrities he'd met through Helen.

Backstage on the way to see Halliday, he encountered another Mary. Mary Philips, the actress with whom he'd appeared with his "second best friend," Kenneth MacKenna, in the 1924 play, *Nerves*. He'd all but forgotten Mary, but remembered that he'd objected to the sexy way that she'd walked offstage, upstaging his best scene in the play.

To his surprise, Hump saw Kenneth emerging from the men's room, walking

108

toward them. He came up to Mary and kissed her on the mouth, possessively putting his arm around her as if to signal his fellow Pussy Posse member to back off in case he had any designs on Mary.

After the actors paid their respects to Halliday, Hump invited Mary and Kenneth to join him for "drinks, fun, and maybe a little dinner" at Sardi's.

Over drinks, Mary told Hump how sorry she was to learn of the breakup of his marriage to Helen. "Frankly," Mary said, after a few drinks, "I was surprised she wanted to marry any man. The rumor along Broadway was that you and Helen kept a scoreboard every week to see how many young actresses each of you could seduce. In spite of your reputation as a ladies' man, I was told that Helen beats you virtually every weekend."

Instead of making him boil, Hump laughed and ordered another drink. What Mary had just said to him was what he might have said to someone. It seemed she liked to kid and needle people as much as he did.

Kenneth remained aloof from their conversation. The more they drank and the more fun they seemed to be having, the more Kenneth resented it. He reminded Hump several times that he and Mary were seriously considering marriage. Although Kenneth could drink as much as Hump could, he ordered only bottled club soda. "Someone's got to keep a clear head. Otherwise the two of you will never find your way home."

When Kenneth got up to go to the men's room, Mary slipped Hump her phone number and gave him a kiss on the cheek. "Mae West is always telling stage-door johnnies to come up and see her some time. I can't think of a better way to say it."

"Invitation accepted." Then, as he was to tell Bill Brady Jr., Mary did something that shocked him. She reached under the table and placed her delicate hand in his crotch, fondling him.

"You sure have Kenneth beat by a country mile."

Kenneth was so anxious to return to table that he came back into the dining room still zipping up. Mary discreetly removed her hand from Hump's crotch. She was giving him a hard-on.

Mary had come a long way since her days in that New Haven convent. Hump was determined to seduce Mary, even though he knew that his friend, Bill Brady, and obviously Kenneth had sampled the honeypot long before he'd get a taste.

In the weeks ahead, Hump got to know Mary very well. She visited him three or four times a week at his apartment. Since she was unofficially engaged to Kenneth, she didn't want to be seen at any of the Broadway dives with Hump. Sometimes she would arrive a bit disheveled at Hump's apartment, and he knew that she'd just risen from Kenneth's bed. "It's sloppy seconds for me again today," he'd kid her.

Although she didn't have the professional stature of Helen Menken, Mary Philips was an established Broadway star when she met Hump. From that very first night at Sardi's, Hump realized that, especially when a total of five fans stopped by their table to ask for her autograph. Although they were established actors on Broadway, neither Hump nor Kenneth attracted autograph seekers.

Hump later told Bill that he wasn't even considering marriage, "and if I do it will to be a Roaming in the Gloaming type. And if I marry anybody it will be Mary Philips. New England and Irish, the perfect combination for me."

"If you do marry Mary, I can vouch that your future wife's not bad in the sack. That's one hot little number."

That provocative remark didn't make Hump mad because he already knew of the affair Bill had had with Mary. He sipped his drink and cast a steely glance at Bill. "Your wife's not bad in the sack either. Dear Katherine. I did have to teach her a few tricks, though."

***

"Kenneth has officially proposed," Mary Philips said one morning when rising from Hump's bed after a night of passionate lovemaking, the best ever for him. "He's even bought the ring."

"Did you accept?" Hump asked, rubbing sleep from his eyes.

"I've asked him to give me a month to make up my mind." Completely nude, she towered over Hump who remained in bed. "At the end of the month, if I don't have an official proposal of marriage—engagement ring and everything—from one Humphrey Bogart, I'm marrying Kenneth." With that remark, she turned and walked toward his bathroom to repair the damages of the night.

The next few days were agonizing ones for Hump. At speakeasies, he had long, drunken talks with Bill about what he should do. "For God's sake, marry her," Bill advised.

"What about Kenneth?" Hump asked. "He is one of my best friends. I think if I take Mary from him, it will break his heart."

"There are a lot of beautiful women on Broadway that will mend Kenneth's heart," Bill said. "He's one handsome guy. Most women think he's far better looking than we are. He's wildly popular with the gals. A month after your marriage, he will have forgotten all about Mary."

The next night at Tony's, it was painful for Hump to listen to Kenneth's plans for his future life with Mary. "We're not even married yet, and already we're having fights."

"What kind of fights?" Hump asked, more than curious.

"Stuart thinks I'm Hollywood material, and I'm planning to go to the coast."

Hump's brother-in-law, Stuart Rose, had become the East Coast story editor for the Fox Film Corporation.

"When do you think you'll go?" Hump asked.

"As soon as Mary and I get married. I'm taking her to LA with me. A woman's place is beside her husband wherever he goes. Mary believes that the theater is the only true calling for an actor. She thinks movies are for ridiculous types like the late Valentino or that daffy blonde, Mae Murray. Or larger-than-life types like

110

Gloria Swanson or Erich von Stroheim."

"You've got a problem, guy," Hump said. "Don't get Mary's Irish up. That's one determined broad."

"So she thinks," Kenneth said. "I'm more stubborn than she is. Within two years, I predict, I'm going to become the biggest male star in motion pictures. When I come home at night, Mary's going to have a pot of Irish stew bubbling on the stove and my slippers waiting at the door."

"Dream on," Hump said, realizing how little Kenneth understood Mary's fierce determination to succeed on the stage.

Exactly one day before Hump's marriage proposal deadline with Mary ran out, he asked her to become his second wife. Remembering his four-year engagement to Helen, he told her he wanted to get married as soon as they could get a license and a minister.

Mary accepted and kissed him long, hard, and passionately. Even so, he was in for a surprise. It would be the beginning of many surprises in their years together. "I want to go and sleep with Kenneth tonight," she said. "A night of grand love-making. I feel I owe him that."

"Fuck that!" Hump protested. "You'll do nothing of the sort. You're my broad now. I've staked my claim."

"What do you think I am?" she asked. "Some Broadway cow you own in your stable? A big tit bovine you've branded with a hot iron? When I agreed to marry you, I didn't say I'd swear off other men. No marriage can work unless a husband and wife are free to have sex with others."

Echoes of his recently failed marital arrangement with Helen resounded in his head. Did all Broadway actresses believe in an open marriage? Not wanting to repeat the mistakes he'd made with Helen, he turned on Mary. "What crap!" he yelled at her. "Many married couples are faithful to each other. Have you ever heard of the vow, forsaking all others?"

"I suppose the next thing you'll throw at me is the perfect marriage of your parents. It was idyllic all right just so long as Belmont could cruise the waterfront and bring home sailors. Or that Maud could have a discreet affair or two on the side. You told me that yourself."

"My own parents are hardly an example I would want to follow," he said.

"What about your marriage to Menken?" she demanded to know. "Everybody up and down Broadway knows that the two of you slept with everything that had two legs and could spread them."

"My marriage with Helen failed," he said. "I don't want that to happen to us!"

"Maybe there's going to be no God damn marriage," she said. "What are you, some fucking Puritan? I'm not going to agree to marry you unless you let me continue to sleep with Kenneth. And maybe some other good-looking guys I meet. My only promise to you is that these guys will always be actors. That way, we'll keep it in our Broadway family."

"That is the sickest talk I've ever heard," he said, turning from her in disgust.

"Yeah," she said, confronting him. "But it sounds healthy to me. A lot healthier than those three-ways you and Helen had with Tallulah Bankhead. That cozy arrangement had all of Broadway talking. I've heard that you've even had three-ways with Scott and Zelda Fitzgerald."

"That's a God damn lie."

"You were seen kissing Fitzgerald in the elevator of the Plaza Hotel."

"That was just some drunken game we were playing that night," he said.

"When I fuck Kenneth tonight, I'll make sure we're drunk and that it's all a game," she said defiantly. "I don't care what you say. I'm going to do what I God damn please." She stormed out of his living room, heading for the door.

"Forget I ever proposed to a whore like you," he shouted to her departing back. Even when stalking out of the apartment, she still had that same sexy walk she'd used on the stage in *Nerves*. "I wouldn't marry you if you were the last blonde slut on Broadway, which you aren't. Your type is a dime a dozen."

Her answer to that was the loudest slamming of a door he'd ever heard.

***

It was in Hartford, Connecticut on April 3, 1928, that the minor Broadway actor, Humphrey Bogart, aged 28, married Miss Mary Philips, the Broadway star. Whatever differences they had, they had momentarily suppressed them. They'd hardly worked them out.

Arriving two hours before the wedding, Kenneth had gone into seclusion with Mary, pleading with her to, "Marry me, not Hump." Mary had wavered back and forth between the two men, deciding first on Kenneth, then on Hump. Years later, she would sigh and say, "I was really pissed off. Why can't a woman have two husbands? I wanted to marry both of them."

In time, she would.

Kissing Kenneth good-bye and telling him to leave Hartford, Mary turned down his proposal of marriage. She held out a promise to him. "When I get back to New York, I'll still be your wife, but only on certain nights of the week."

Bill Brady Jr. was Hump's best man. The wedding was to take place at the home of Mary's mother, Anne, at 24 Hopkins Street, an apartment in a building across from the old Hartford Public High School.

Only ten minutes before the wedding, Hump told Bill, "I'm a fool to go through with this marriage. It has all the earmarks of a disaster—just like my marriage to Helen. History is repeating itself. She'll probably throw Kenneth a mercy fuck a few minutes before she walks in here to say 'I do.'"

"Maybe the line should be changed to, 'I just did,'" Bill said, joking with Hump and hoping to cheer him up.

After a tearful embrace, Mary finally appeared in front of the justice of the peace, her guilty eyes avoiding Hump's. The couple exchanged marriage vows, even a promise to forsake all others, although Hump knew that was a meaningless promise.

After the ceremony, when he'd put a ring on Mary's finger and kissed her, Hump stood in front of a bowl of punch with the justice of the peace. "We know what a fine star Miss Philips is. Or should I say Mrs. Bogart? But what kind of actor are you?"

"They call me a 'white pants Willy,'" he said.

"What does that mean? I'm afraid I'm not familiar with show business terms."

"A handsome but callow young man who is a staple in many drawing-room comedies."

As they were at the train station heading back to New York, Hump and Mary got caught up in a torchlight parade for Hartford's newest mayor, "Batty" Batterson, who'd just been narrowly elected despite widespread allegations of vote fraud.

After a one-night stopover in New York, in which Mary was gone for two hours for drinks with Kenneth, they headed for a two-week honeymoon in Atlantic City. "It was the beginning of ten years of deepening misery for me," Bogie in the years to come would say in recalling his New Jersey honeymoon.

When the honeymooners returned to New York, Mary immediately called Kenneth who told her that he was leaving in the morning on a train bound for Los Angeles. He was going to break into the movies and had been promised a "really big part."

Mary kissed Hump good-bye and told him, "I just have to spend this final night with Kenneth. I'm sure you'll understand. After all, I've been with you for two entire weeks."

He wished her a good time. He'd just read in a Broadway column that Helen had returned from her engagement in London. He called her apartment. After receiving her congratulations on his new marriage, he asked her if he could come over and spend the night.

"You're always welcome," she said.

After putting down the receiver, he headed for the shower. He wanted to look handsome and well-groomed for Helen.

That night would mark the beginning of an affair with his first wife that would last for the entire duration of his marriage to his second wife, Mary Philips.

***

The next week Hump went to the theatrical agents, Charles Frohman Productions, and signed on with them, telling them he wanted to break into the movies. As Helen's representative, Frohman had secured lawyers for Helen and gotten her out of trouble when she was arrested for appearing in the lesbian play, *The Captive*. Even so, Hump wasn't very cooperative, but one of the staff members, Sheila Crystal, took a liking to Hump and felt that he might photograph well. She'd already seen two plays in which he'd appeared. She was also aware that

Broadway columnists still compared his looks to the dead actor, Valentino.

Hump left the agency thinking nothing would come of his signing on. In two weeks, Sheila called him. Even without a screen test, she'd secured him the male lead in a two-reeler, *The Dancing Town*. "The star will be Helen Hayes," Sheila said. "That's Helen Hayes with an s, not Helen Haye. Everybody gets those two gals mixed up."

That night on his tour of the speakeasies with Mary, Hump was thrilled at the offer. He was disappointed in Mary's reaction. "Films are just a novelty," she said. "I think in a few years there will be no films. The theater is the only place for an actor. I told Kenneth that, but the fool wouldn't listen. He's dreaming of seeing himself up on that silver screen."

"You've got it ass backwards," he said. "All the big Broadway stars today will be forgotten a hundred years from now. Films like that crap Valentino made will still be shown."

The day he went to meet Helen Hayes, Hump was excited to be working with her. He'd never met her, but another Helen, his first wife, knew her well. Both of them had gone to see Helen Hayes in the Broadway play, *To the Ladies*, in which she'd appeared from 1922 to 1924. She'd had great success in Oliver Goldsmith's ribald 18th-century comedy, *She Stoops to Conquer*, and she'd followed that by playing Cleopatra in George Bernard Shaw's *Caesar and Cleopatra*.

Helen Hayes had married the same year that Hump had wed Mary Philips. Her husband was the very handsome Charles MacArthur, whom Hump knew casually from their long nights spent drinking at Tony's saloon. Hump was surprised that the demure and ever so elegant Helen Hayes would marry a hard-drinking, hard-living playwright like Charles MacArthur, who was having his big Broadway success with his memorable play, *The Front Page*.

When Hump had first met MacArthur, he was having affairs with both Dorothy Parker and Ned Sheldon, the playwright with whom he had collaborated on the 1926 play, *Lulu Belle*. Hump knew that MacArthur swung both ways, but he didn't know if Miss Hayes knew that, and it wasn't his job to tell her. Bill Brady Jr. always claimed that, "MacArthur will drop his trousers for anybody, male or female, if he's drunk enough." Like his own marriage, Hump didn't give the Hayes/MacArthur union much of a chance.

Helen Hayes was hardly the First Lady of the American Theater the day Hump met her at a studio in Queens. But she was every bit a lady. She was so tiny she made him feel tall. If modern generations have an image of Helen at all, it is of a grandmotherly looking woman with gray hair. But when Hump met her, Helen was "the serpent of the Nile," and she'd appeared in a number of flapper roles, although he felt that she was "too pure" to have real sex appeal.

Over coffee and waiting for the cameras to be set up, Helen confessed that she was planning to accompany her husband to Hollywood where he wanted to become a screenwriter for Metro-Goldwyn-Mayer. "Now that the flickers have learned to talk, maybe I'll consider a film career as well. Heaven only knows, I'm no sex pot who can do bathtub scenes like Gloria Swanson."

"I think you're a very sexy lady, and within the hour I expect to be making mad, passionate love to you."

"Heavens," she said, "I'm flattered. You're very handsome, not as much so as my Charles, but a very good-looking man. I'm faithful to my husband, though, even if he isn't to me."

Apparently, she already knew about her husband's extramarital affairs. "I wasn't making a proposition," Hump said. "I've read the script. It calls for us to make mad, passionate love."

"Oh, I see." She looked embarrassed. "It's in the script?"

"I suggest we at least do some heavy kissing before the cameras are turned on us," he suggested. "After all, if you and I are going to become movie stars, we don't want to appear like limp dish rags when we embrace on screen."

"You're probably right," she said. "Lillian Gish has always warned me that the camera--unlike the stage--picks up every facial nuance."

His lips already moist, he wetted them again as he went over to her in her dressing room and took her in his arms. He gently pressed his mouth down on hers. At first she resisted but soon gave in, reaching to put her small arms around him.

The kissing scene was going so well that he inserted his tongue ever so gently into her mouth, not knowing what she'd think of this French kissing. He seemed to be getting to her because she sucked his tongue lovingly as if enjoying the taste.

Although it was hardly called for in the script, he placed his hand on her thigh and started moving to the North Pole. He'd never know what might have happened because suddenly there was a rude knock on the door. The director wanted both of them on the set.

Hump would later recall that their love-making on the silver screen never matched their warm-up in Helen's dressing room.

Regrettably, there are no known copies of this two-reeler today, which starred two of the most famous actors of the 20th century, Helen Hayes and Humphrey Bogart.

***

"I'm impotent." Hump walked with Stuart Rose along a serene lake near Fairfield, Connecticut where Mary and he were renting a house next to his brother-in-law and his sister, Frances.

"It'll pass," Stuart assured him. "Just give it time."

He took hold of Stuart's arm and confronted him. "Has it ever happened to you and Frances?"

"Can't say that it has, but it happens to a lot of men," Stuart said. "More than they'll tell you. My own father was impotent for two years before he got it back again."

"If only Mary didn't make it worse," Hump said. "When I can't get it up, she mocks me and ridicules me. I should never have married her."

Stuart looked deeply into Hump's eyes. "What's the real problem?"

"It's the kind of marriage we have," Hump said. "I think she's still in love with Kenneth. She sleeps around and tells me about it. She says that what she can't get at home she finds somewhere else. She claims most men don't have my problem."

"Where's Mary now?" Stuart asked.

"She's gone back to New York," Hump said. "We'll probably get a divorce. My reputation will be ruined on Broadway. No gal will want to sleep with me ever again."

The marriage was saved by a three-act comedy, *The Skyrocket*, that was set to open January 11, 1929 at the Lyceum Theatre. It was produced and directed by Guthrie McClintic who had hired Kenneth's brother, Jo Mielziner, as the set designer.

Mary was cast as the star, with Humphrey playing her husband. After reading the script, he told Jo, "It's another one of those sprig parts. But I need work so I'll take it."

It was like a Broadway homecoming for Hump. Guthrie had directed *Saturday's Children* two years earlier, with Jo doing the sets. The script was one of those rags-to-riches-to-rags stories. Couple strikes it rich but money makes them unhappy. They go broke again and find true love and happiness in their poverty.

Hump's role as "Rims" in *Saturday's Children* had been minor, and he hadn't really gotten to know its director as he'd filled in for another actor after the show was blocked. Both Mary and he were eager to work with McClintic.

In their daydreams, Mary and Hump fantasized with each other about becoming the "second Guthrie McClintic and Katharine Cornell." Alexander Woollcott might not have been impressed with Hump's stage "sprig," but he was overwhelmed by Guthrie's wife, Katharine Cornell, calling her "The First Lady of the Theater." Helen Hayes claimed that position for herself as well, as did Lynn Fontanne, Cornell's two chief rivals for glory.

Even without Woollcott's usual hyperbole, Cornell was indisputably the reigning Broadway star of the second quarter of the 20th century. When she'd made her debut in 1921 in *Nice People*, her future husband, then a young casting director, saw her performance and recorded in his notebook. "Interesting. Monotonous. Watch."

By the autumn of that year, he'd married her, forming a theatrical union that lasted forty years until his death in 1961, in spite of the fact that she was a lesbian and he was a homosexual. At the time of his death she abandoned the stage. "I can't go on without Guthrie," she told the press.

When Guthrie told his two stars, Mary and Hump, that his wife was going to visit for the final rehearsal, they were thrilled and were glad to have been warned.

116

Each of them planned to give their best performance during the rehearsal even if it left them drained for opening night.

Guthrie had also told them that Cornell, following such great theatrical successes as W. Somerset Maugham's *The Letter* and Edith Wharton's *The Age of Innocence*, planned to manage her own productions in the future. Mary told Hump that if Cornell were impressed with them, she might hire them for one of her shows.

At the day of the final run-through, Guthrie delayed *The Skyrocket* for one hour, waiting for his wife. Cornell finally showed up. In a beautifully tailored suit, she took a seat in the final row of the theater. Like an imperial grande dame, she signaled her husband that the show could begin.

At the end of the performance, the curtain was pulled shut. When it was opened again, Mary and Hump stepped forward, hoping to hear the applause of Cornell. Guthrie told them that she'd left the theater but had written a note for them. It was addressed to "Mr. and Mrs. Humphrey Bogart."

Dear Aspirant Thespians,

Although you struggled, and I'm sure performed, to the best of your ability, this Skyrocket will never make it to heaven. Actually, the two of you are not to blame. The playwright, Mark Reed, deserves full responsibility. His mother should have smothered him at birth.
All good wishes,

Katharine Cornell.

Somewhere during rehearsals Hump had regained his confidence and his sexual prowess and was once again sleeping with Mary. The attack from Cornell destroyed his confidence once again. On opening night he was jittery and explosive.

To compound his feeling of an impending disaster, Mary chose that horrendously inappropriate moment to confess to an infidelity that had been going on right before his eyes, even though he hadn't seen it.

"I've been having an affair with Jo," she said. "I guess I missed Kenneth now that he's gone Hollywood. They say if a gal goes for one brother, she can go for another. Actually I find Jo better in bed than Kenneth. Brothers don't make love the same way."

Hump wanted to slap her, even belt her a good one, but was told that the curtain was going up. He was understandably nervous on opening night, especially after Mary's revelations. Critics pronounced *Skyrocket* a "showy counterfeit." One called it "spurious." Mr. and Mrs. Humphrey Bogart received only faint praise.

An out-of-town critic, John Davenport, from Hartford, wrote, "It's surprising that the two stars, Mary Philips and Humphrey Bogart, are in fact newlyweds. There is absolutely no chemistry between them on stage at all."

Of all the critics that night, Davenport was the only one who got it right. *Skyrocket* quickly closed, and both Mary and Hump found themselves out of work once again.

His bouts of impotence continued on and off for several months. He told Bill that his marriage was a "sometimes thing." Mary seemed more excited to get a letter from Kenneth in Hollywood than she did in going out to the speakeasies with her new husband. Sometimes she'd disappear for a week at a time and never tell Hump where she'd been or with whom. "When I'm gone, feel free to date other women," she told him.

No other woman interested him. It wasn't that he wanted only Mary. He didn't want any woman. One night when he'd been alone and drinking heavily in his apartment for three days, Bill Brady Jr. arrived unexpectedly, finding Hump unbathed, unshaven, and almost suicidal.

"I finally figured out what's the matter with me," Hump said, heading to the kitchen to pour himself another drink. "I've decided I'm a homosexual."

"We all go through periods like that," Bill said. "Our own relationship is a perfect example of that."

"It's worse than you think," Hump said. "The other night I was trying to jack off. I willed my mind to think of Mary, but the thing that did it for me—the image that made me pop off—was thinking of what Stuart looked like naked."

"I'm jealous," was all Bill said. "Now come on, big boy, we're going to give you a bath, sober you up a bit, and take you out on the town. Stuart will have to be put on the backburner. You're my date for tonight." Bill winked at him.

As the weeks went by, Hump continued to be filled with loathing of himself and self-doubt about his manhood. It was one of the most morbidly depressing periods of his life, and at times he contemplated suicide. He later told Bill, "I never get beyond the thinking stage of it. I just can't see myself taking a razor to my throat." Bill tried his best to cheer him up and break his mood.

Alone in his apartment on one of the blackest days of his life, Hump saw no future for himself, certainly no career in the theater. His marriage to Mary was rapidly deteriorating, in ways that evoked the earlier collapse of his marriage to Helen.

But ironically, he had resumed seeing Helen again whenever Mary was away. With Helen, he didn't experience impotence, only with Mary. Helen always made him feel like a real man.

One night at a speakeasy, when he'd been battling with Mary, he told her, "On those rare occasions with you when I can get it up—that is, when you're not trying to take a razor to my balls—I feel you're thinking about getting plugged by Kenneth and not by me."

118

"A lady is entitled to her fantasies," Mary had said, rising from her chair and staggering toward the bar to order another drink.

On that dark, rainy afternoon, as he drank alone and grew more despondent in his bleak apartment, the phone rang. Thinking it was Bill, he picked it up to discover Sheila Crystal on the line. His theatrical agent had gotten him another film job.

The great singing star of the Twenties, Ruth Etting, had seen Hump's performance in the short-lived *Skyrocket*, and had told her backers that she thought "Bogart would be ideal as my leading man" in a ten-minute short she'd contracted to film for Warner Brothers' Vitaphone Corporation.

Once again and without ever setting foot in Hollywood, Hump found himself cast in a movie opposite a famous woman star.

***

Like Katharine Cornell, the songbird, Ruth Etting, was late on the first day of rehearsals for their film short. She'd been rehearsing for her upcoming Broadway show, *Whoopee!* She was Hump's favorite recording star, and he always proclaimed that she had a "gorgeous voice." He'd seen many pictures of her in the tabloids and had found her a "great beauty."

Etting lived up to her billing. When she finally did show up, Hump was dazzled by the sultry torch singer known as "America's sweetheart of song." Only two years older than Hump, Etting had been born in Nebraska. But, as he later told Bill Brady, Jr. "She looked like no cow gal I've ever seen." When introduced to him, he shook her gloved hand. She reached over to kiss him gently on the lips. "It's good for me to see you in the flesh and up close," she said, still holding his hand. "I found you very sexy and commanding in *Skyrocket* even if the critics didn't."

He looked into her eyes. He'd later say, "I never saw a woman's eyes dance before I met Ruth. We clicked from the very first. After only an hour together, we were confessing intimate secrets. She even told him that her secret ambition was to design clothing. "I design some of my outfits on Broadway," she said.

Later, when he had to come on to her in the film script, he found that his impotence had been miraculously cured. Fortunately they were seated at a table. Otherwise, the camera might have recorded one of his biggest erections.

Although he wanted to, Hump didn't put the make on Etting the first day. She gave him several opportunities and seemed to actively encourage him. Hump was afraid—not of Etting, but of her husband. She was married to the Chicago gangster, Martin Snyder, nicknamed "The Gimp" because of a lame left leg. He was promoting her singing career by throwing his weight around Broadway, using tactics he'd learned from a life on the streets in Chicago's underworld.

As work on the short film began, Etting confessed that she'd left "The Gimp" and planned to dump him. She also told Hump that she'd had a very brief affair

119

with showman Florenz Ziegfeld when she'd starred in the *Ziegfeld Follies of 1927*, singing Irving Berlin's "Shaking the Blues Away."

When Hump didn't invite her out that night, she asked him to go on tour of the speakeasies. After a few drinks, she confessed that she was having an affair with the young singer, Bing Crosby. "The Gimp" was supposed to be fanatically jealous of Etting but she seemed to be screwing around a lot even when she was living with the gangster.

Shortly before midnight, Etting invited Hump back to her apartment. "I thought you'd never ask," he said.

Once in the apartment, she put on a record of one of her songs. She stood in front of her record player and told him to turn off the lights. Not knowing what was about to happen, he turned off the sole light in the room. "Lights," she called out after less than a minute.

When he turned on the light bulb again, Etting was standing nude in front of her record player. She sang "Love Me Or Leave Me" to him. As she sang, he removed his clothing. At the wrap of her song, he moved toward her, his erection guiding his way.

In one of the many ironies of Hump's life, that was not the last time "Love Me Or Leave Me" would figure into his career. Nearing the end of Bogie's life in 1954, Metro-Goldwyn-Mayer considered him for their upcoming picture, *Love Me Or Leave Me* conceived as a vehicle for Doris Day. The studio felt that Hump would be ideal cast as Etting's gangster lover, "The Gimp." Feeling the film was too much a star part for Day, he turned down the role, which went to James Cagney, his longtime rival for gangster roles at Warner Brothers in the 1930s.

***

As it had with so many other women, his affair with Ruth Etting ended almost before it began. "The Gimp" arrived back in New York and had a reconciliation with Etting. Bill Brady Jr. told Hump that "The Gimp" often assigned hit men "to beat up or kill any man who moves in on his lady love." Even with the dangerous gangster back in her life, Etting placed three more calls, hoping to arrange a private assignation with Hump. He was too afraid to return her calls.

Still sleeping with Mary, he had managed a one-night stand with a beautiful actress who had had a brief walk-on in the Vitaphone short, *Broadway's Like That*, in which he co-starred with Etting. Her name was Joan Blondell and her nickname was "Rosebud." To him, she was a blonde bombshell from Texas, and he'd been captivated by her youthful exuberance, expressive face, and popped-out eyes that seemed to devour whatever man they focused on.

Like Kenneth MacKenna, she was heading for Hollywood to play the third lead in a Warner Brothers picture, *The Office Wife,* which was to star Dorothy Mackaill, Lewis Stone, and Hobart Bosworth, all big names of the era. Hump was impressed that Joan had been given third billing in such a cast line-up. *The*

Office Wife would mark the beginning of a series of "wife vs. secretary" films.

After their one night of passion, Joan seemed to have fallen in love with Hump. She made him promise to "look me up if you ever come to Hollywood." She gave him a phone number where she could be reached in Los Angeles. He wrote it down but didn't expect to ever see her again.

As he said good-bye to Joan when he went down to see her off at Grand Central, little did he know that this would be "the beginning of a beautiful friendship," and that he would one day be co-starring with her in motion pictures. Not only that, their one-night stand would mark the beginning of one of the most enduring and long-running love affairs of his life.

***

Work came in the form of another three-act Broadway comedy, this one a play by Laurence E. Johnson, produced and directed by David Belasco at the Belasco Theatre. *It's a Wise Child* was slated to open on August 6, 1929, starring Helen Lowell, Olga Krolow, Leila Bennett, Mildred McCoy, and George Walcott. No longer a co-star as he was in *The Skyrocket* with Mary, Hump got fifth billing in yet another juvenile part.

In spite of another inane comedy and another juvenile part, Hump got to work with some of the biggest names on Broadway. First, Guthrie McClintic had been his director. Now, he was being directed by David Belasco, called "The Bishop of Broadway." The theater, constructed in 1907, in which their play was to open, was even named after Belasco, who had emerged as one of the most influential men in the entertainment industry at the time. He had seemingly done everything in the theater, including the writing of a smash hit, *The Heart of Maryland*, about the Civil War. He had even selected the name "Mary Pickford" for the film actress who would eventually become "America's sweetheart."

Belasco was known as a star maker, and the roster of famous actors he'd launched included Frances Starr, Ina Claire, Leonore Ulric, and Blanche Bates.

During the first week of rehearsals, Hump had been disappointed that Belasco, as director, spent so little time coaching him in his role of Roger Baldwin, a part he loathed. The comedy concerned a woman who falls for a young bank clerk as played by Hump. Already saddled with an elderly fiancé, she tells him she's pregnant with another man's child. Hump's role was conceived as that of a "transitional beau," and his character was described as "not one of those silly dancing and drinking men" but as "one of the best-looking men you were likely to ever meet, with the profile of a Greek God." In the final act, the beautiful heroine irrationally dismisses Hump as "just a foolish kid" when he tells her that he cares more about his job than he does about her.

Contrary to his usual custom, Hump did not fall for the female star of the show, Helen Lowell. Lowell had been born in New York City in 1866, one year after the Civil War came to an end, so there was a bit of a difference in their ages.

"I too belong to the 19th century," he told her the day they were introduced. Self-conscious about her mounting years, Lowell was not charmed by Bogart. He told fellow actor, George Walcott," I was still dumping in my diapers when she opened in *Quality Street* in 1901."

Not going for the aging star, Helen Lowell, Hump made a play instead for the enchantingly lovely second female lead, Mildred McCoy, considering her "twice as beautiful as Mary." Mildred seemed fascinated with Hump and invited his amorous attention, even though she constantly refused to go out with him.

Word of Hump's flirtation with Mildred must have reached her beau. As rehearsals began one Monday morning, the stage manager came backstage to tell him that Mildred's lover was sitting alone out front. He was none other than Chief Buffalo Child Long Lance, the most famous "Indian" in America. Hump was even wearing a pair of canvas running shoes, "Long Lance Sport Shoes," named after him.

Long Lance was a darling of the tabloids, which exploited his alleged adventures as an athlete. He was said to have been trained by the legendary Jim Thorpe and in addition, he was a war hero. He was also a journalist, biographer, public lecturer, pilot, Indian rights advocate, and was heading to Hollywood to become a movie star. Not only that, he was a boxer, having claimed that he had knocked out Jack Dempsey during a sparring match.

In the glittering world of New York society of the 1920s, hostesses vied in sending out invitations to this so-called full-blooded Blackfoot chief, who had captured the imagination of North America with the story of his life and the plight of downtrodden Indians. As a special dispensation, Woodrow Wilson had even appointed Long Lance to West Point.

Not everybody bought his story. There were rumors that he was not a Cherokee from Oklahoma at all. He'd become such a famous fixture on the American landscape that reporters were investigating rumors about his true identity. Reports were turning up from western North Carolina that Long Lance was descended from African slaves. He was dark skinned but not black skinned so he was able to pass as an Indian. Other rumors suggested that his actual father might have been a tobacco planter from England who had moved to the Winston-Salem area, and conceived Lance with a local woman of color, which would account for Long Lance's skin tone.

Mildred was only the latest of a string of international celebrities with whom he was linked. He had had an affair with Vivian Hart, a celebrated opera singer of her day, and was most famously linked with Anita Baldwin, another tabloid darling. Along with Barbara Hutton and Doris Duke, Anita Baldwin was one of the richest women in the United States, her fortune acquired from her father, "Lucky" Baldwin, who had made millions in his casinos built along the shores of Lake Tahoe.

After the rehearsals, Long Lance went backstage to meet Belasco and other actors. In front of Hump, he kissed Mildred on the lips, asserting his territorial rights. He was an imposing figure towering over Hump. From that day on, Long

Lance attended every rehearsal, always coming backstage to rescue Mildred.

After a few days, Long Lance's hostility toward Hump ended as he'd come to view him as no competition for Mildred's affections. "What would she want with that little runt when she's got me?" he asked Belasco one day, "After all, they don't call me Long Lance for nothing."

Long Lance even invited Hump to join Mildred and him on a round of the city's speakeasies, where Long Lance dominated the conversation with tall tales of his exploits. Hump listened attentively and seemed enthralled, although later telling Belasco that he too believed that Long Lance was an imposter. "An imposter," Hump said, "but a glorious one."

Regardless of his bloodline, he was a magnificent specimen of manhood with a swarthy complexion that could easily look like that of a Croatan Indian.

As he got to know Long Lance better, Hump came to believe that he was indeed black but had assumed the Indian identity to escape the restrictive segregationist policies of the South. Long Lance viewed himself as following in the tradition of what he said was his "remote maternal relative," Kit Carson, and was filled with fascinating tales of his experiences which allegedly ranged from being a rider in a Wild West show to fighting bravely as a Canadian soldier who'd won the Italian War Cross and the French *Croix de guerre*.

One day Long Lance didn't show up for rehearsals, but cornered Hump when he was leaving the theater in the late afternoon. There was a look of desperation on Long Lance's face. Hump went across the street to talk to him. "You can have Mildred," Long Lance said. "She's all yours. In fact, I want you to take her off my hands."

"What's going on here?" Hump asked.

"One of America's most famous women has fallen madly in love with me."

"You mean, Anita Baldwin?"

"Anita and I are through," Long Lance said. "It's someone else. She's big. I can't tell you her name. But I've got to get rid of Mildred. You go after her. Maybe she'll fall for you. If not, she might fuck up this new thing I have going."

Hump said he'd always found Mildred sexy and appealing, and he'd do his best to lure her away from Long Lance.

"You're a swell guy, Bogart," Long Lance said.

That didn't sound like Cherokee talk to Hump. The two men talked for an hour, pledging eternal friendship to each other. Long Lance even promised to make Hump an honorary Cherokee.

Having been dumped by Long Lance, Mildred finally agreed to go out with Hump after the opening night curtain fell on *It's a Wise Child*. They were in a mood to celebrate when they hit Tony's. Many of the critics also descended on Tony's that night, having already filed their reviews of *It's a Wise Child*. Hump was eager to ask them what they had written but knew that that wasn't proper Broadway protocol.

Mildred and Hump waited for the reviews, which were lukewarm. She was disappointed that three reviews only listed her, with no comment about her acting. Alexander Woollcott found Hump playing the role with "more than his usual vigor and sincerity."

Feeling despondent and wanting to be cheered up, Mildred invited Hump back to her hotel room.

The next morning he got one of the worst reviews of his young life. Over coffee downstairs in the breakfast room, Mildred confessed to him. "You and I have no future," she told him. "After enjoying the embrace of Long Lance for many weeks, I find you that inadequate sprig reviewers are always citing."

***

During the run of the play, the Wall Street crash of October, 1929 came tumbling down on the worldwide economy, but miraculously, the play survived the drop-off in business. Many other theaters shut their doors. At first Hump and Mary were unaware of how thoroughly Broadway would eventually be impacted by America's financial crisis. "In bad times, people need to be entertained," Mary told him. "They'll flock to the theater for escapism."

"Yeah," Hump said. "But how in the fuck are they going to afford the tickets?"

Even in the midst of the disaster, Hollywood agents had descended on New York, hoping to find "actors who know how to talk." Out on the West Coast the unattractive voices of many silent-screen greats were assigning them to the dustbin of film history.

Stuart Rose had become good friends with the former Broadway producer, Al Lewis, who ran the New York office for Fox in which Stuart worked. Stuart's job involved reading plays, hoping to find one suitable to be filmed. He managed to persuade Lewis to give his brother-in-law a chance at a screen test. Stuart took Lewis to see *It's a Wise Child*, and Lewis reluctantly agreed, although not impressed with the scar on Hump's upper lip.

Hump didn't think much would come of yet another screen test for him, but he did a ten-minute segment from *The Man Who Came Back*.

When Lewis sent Hump's test to Fox in Hollywood, the studio wired him to sign Bogart for $750 a week. If he did well, an option called for his paycheck to go up to $1,000 a week, a virtual fortune at the beginning of the Depression.

Without checking with Mary, Hump signed with Fox. In their apartment that night, he tried to persuade Mary to drop out of *The Tavern*, a play in which she was starring on Broadway. He asked her to go on the train with him to Los Angeles. She refused, and violently so, leading to one of their biggest fights.

"You want to become a big-time movie star," Mary shouted at him. "Well, I want to become a big-time Broadway star. Bigger than your dyke wife, Helen Menken."

"You're not talented enough to carry the train of Helen's gown on stage," he yelled back at her. "She's a bigger star than you'll ever be. I thought you'd jump at the chance to go to Hollywood. That way you could fuck Kenneth one night, me the next."

She stormed out of their apartment and didn't come back all night. Even if she had returned, Hump wouldn't have been there.

After having farewell drinks with Bill and Stuart at Tony's, Hump called Helen Menken and asked her if he could spend the night with her. She agreed, inviting him to come over right away. With his suitcase already packed, he hugged and kissed both Stuart and Bill good-bye, and took a taxi to Helen's apartment.

Waking up the next morning, he smelled breakfast cooking. Helen was freshly made up and had his favorite bacon and eggs on the table. It was Helen, not Mary, who accompanied him to Grand Central where he caught a train that would take him to Chicago and on to Los Angeles.

On the way to Chicago, drinking heavily, he mixed freely with the passengers, and, like a little boy, even showed some doubters his newly signed contract with Fox. After a few drinks, he told one Kansas City cattleman, who'd never heard of Humphrey Bogart, that those Broadway screen writers were right on the mark. "That silly fop, Valentino, is going to be replaced by me. I'm going to become the biggest movie star Hollywood's ever seen."

When he staggered toward the men's room, he walked into the cramped compartment to discover Long Lance relieving himself. "Bogart," he said, "just the man I want to see." He shook himself dry and with the same unwashed hand reached to shake Hump's paw. "You did the job for Mildred like I asked you to, and now I've got an even bigger assignment."

"Hell, man," Hump said, "I came in here to take a horse piss. I didn't know you were aboard."

"I already found out you were on the train," he said, "and I was planning to corner you as soon as I saw you alone. You've got to save my neck one more time."

"That thing with Mildred didn't work out," Hump said. "I'm afraid I'm not the man you are."

"Nobody is," Long Lance said. "Remember that famous woman I told you about, the one I was dumping Mildred for? She's on this train right now heading for Los Angeles."

"Lucky you," Hump said, standing at the urinal.

"Not so lucky," Long Lance said. "It seems that Anita Baldwin is on the same train. Anita and I have made up. You've got to spend the night in my mistress's compartment, pretending to be her lover, when I'm shacked up with Anita."

"That might be enticing," Hump said. "I'd be your beard. Tell me, is this mystery lady beautiful?"

"She's one of the most beautiful women in America," Long Lance said. "She's seen you on Broadway and considers you the next Valentino."

"If she's got that much good taste," Hump said, "I want to meet her."

"Go to Wagon 6, Compartment C, and knock on the door," Long Lance said.

"She'll be waiting for you. I was so confident that you'd agree to what I wanted that I already cleared it with my ladylove. She agreed to it. Later when I'm with Anita we'll accidentally run into the two of you in the dining car. If you pull this one off for me, I'll owe you a big favor."

"Maybe you're doing me the favor," Hump said.

Long Lance outlined a plan of action with Hump before he headed down the corridor to call at Wagon 6, Compartment C. After a discreet knock on the door, followed by a long delay, the compartment was opened.

As the train rolled across the American landscape, he was invited in. Long Lance might have lied about being an Indian, but he hadn't lied about the occupant of that compartment.

In the fading light of a Midwest afternoon, he gazed upon one of the most famous women in the world, and, yes, one of its most beautiful.

Chapter Five

The sultry Natacha Rambova—sometimes known as "Madam Valentino"—stood back and allowed Hump to enter her cabin. "I'm honored to meet you," he said. "I knew your husband briefly right before he passed on. Wonderful man. Great star."

"I know," she said. "I created him. Without me, there would have been no Valentino." She invited him to sit down.

As the train rolled west, Hump settled in in an attempt to get to know one of Hollywood's most mysterious women. He was confused as to why she was having an affair with Long Lance since her lesbian affairs were known and documented from New York to Hollywood.

"I do not miss Rudy," she said, "because I communicate with him once a week at spiritualist séances. When I gaze into my crystal ball, I see him and can talk to him the way I'm speaking to you now."

"The church would say you were dabbling in things unholy," he said. "Not that I'm much of a spokesman for the church." He felt that he was riding the rails with a nut. He tried to change the subject. "Why are you going to Hollywood?"

"I have various theatrical, literary, and fashion enterprises to pursue there," she said. "I'm also going to set up a circle of spiritualists like I had in New York. Perhaps you'd be interested in joining."

"Perhaps," he said. "You'll have to invite me to one of the meetings."

She looked at him sharply. "And what brings you to Hollywood?"

"I know it's a bit of a joke," he said. "But there are some stupid asses who think I can be the next Valentino."

She said nothing for a long moment. "As if any earthly creature could replace the Great Valentino. You'll never be what he was." Then she paused again for dramatic effect. "Unless I create you the way I created him, and I'm not at all sure I can do that. Maybe it was my destiny to create only one great star in a lifetime."

"I see your point," he said, feeling increasingly sorry that he'd accepted Long Lance's invitation to go to her cabin. He wanted a cigarette until she told him she was allergic to smoke.

As the train rolled on, he studied her closely. She wore a turban, and her legs were covered by an ankle-length black skirt.

In the blaze of a glorious golden light on a dying Midwest afternoon, Natacha Rambova was the most exotic creature he'd ever encountered. When she caught him studying her too intently, she warned him, "If you think the invitation to my cabin involved sexual privileges, you are very mistaken. The real Valentino never penetrated me, and I have no intention of letting one of his many imitators do that either."

"There, there," he said, "At least I know where I stand. You mean, not even Long Lance?"

"There are other ways a woman can satisfy a man," she said, her pretty pink tongue darting out in case he didn't get her point.

"I see," he said, settling back.

"Don't think for one moment that you'll be so rewarded," she said. "Before you came to my compartment, I looked into my crystal ball. I always carry it with me. The spirits told me that our relationship is going to be spiritual, not sexual."

That night, as prearranged, Rambova dressed herself in one of her most exotic creations, an outfit she called "Bird of Paradise," before entering the dining car where she pretended to be meeting Long Lance for the first time. He introduced her to Anita Baldwin who seemed stunned and a bit jealous of Rambova's beauty, costume, jewelry, and charm, although Baldwin could buy and sell her in a flash.

Rambova introduced Hump to both Baldwin and Long Lance, calling him "my latest protégé."

Over the table in the dining car, Rambova warned her companions that because of the Great Depression a revolution in the United States "is unavoidable." She particularly had dire warnings for Baldwin, claiming that because of her great wealth "the American peasants will rise in revolt in the fields and storm the citadels of the very rich to take it all back. After all, the peasant was the one who actually earned the money."

Understandably Baldwin did not like this talk and did not invite either Hump or Rambova to join her for any more gatherings.

Before the train reached California, Long Lance managed to slip into Rambova's compartment for whatever it was that they did together. Hump waited outside smoking a cigarette.

As the train crossed the California border, Rambova brought out her crystal ball. He didn't believe one word of what she predicted as a fortune teller. Amazingly, time would reveal her to be right on target.

"You will fail in Hollywood," she predicted. "In despair, you will leave the West Coast and return to New York where you will know poverty. In time, an amazing breakthrough will occur for you in New York, and you will return to the West Coast once again. You will spin your heels there for many years. Then one day a man who was very close to my husband—I'm not sure who it is—will make a fatal career decision. You will benefit from his lack of judgment. You will at long last become a star. But it will happen late in life for you. Your life will not be long. You will die a painful death. But you will have achieved everlasting stardom like Rudy."

"Thanks a lot," he said nervously. "I don't know if I want to hear this or not….And your friend, Long Lance?" he asked. "What about him?"

She gazed into her crystal ball and said nothing for a long while. "He will meet a tragic end. That end is coming sooner than later."

Without ever getting a blow-job from her, not even a kiss on the cheek, Hump went to sleep that night only a few feet from Rambova. They did not touch.

The next morning, the train pulled into Los Angeles. Photographers rushed to snap pictures of the most famous passengers, clustering around Anita Baldwin, Long Lance, and Rambova. In all the confusion, Hump was ignored until he saw Kenneth MacKenna rushing to embrace him at the station. "Welcome to Hollywood," Kenneth said. "Old buddy, old pal."

Hump embraced him warmly. It was good to see someone from New York.

"My apartment's waiting for you," Kenneth said. "I even washed the toilet seat."

As he was leaving the station, Hump looked back one more time at the celebrities he was leaving behind. From that day forth, the only news he had of either of them was what he read in the tabloids.

While still in Hollywood, Hump read of the death of Long Lance. In 1932 he was found shot dead in the Arcadia, California home of Anita Baldwin. A pistol was by his side. A statement released to the press said that Long Lance, Chief Buffalo Child, had "absented himself from this harsh world by a pistol shot."

Anita Baldwin was in the house that night. Although widely suspected of murdering Long Lance, she was never brought to trial. When American Indians forced the authorities in Arcadia to hold an inquest, Baldwin did not attend, claiming that her doctor had ordered her "to remain away from any further strain and take a complete rest."

She had great power in Arcadia, a town that had been founded by her father, and which had been carved out of his huge estate. At the time of Long Lance's mysterious death, Anita was assessed, and paid, half of the town's annual tax revenue. The Arcadia police, based on virtually no evidence, speedily concluded that "only Long Lance himself could have fired the fatal shot" and quickly dropped the case.

But until he died, Hump always claimed that he believed that Baldwin killed her black lover, "the great Indian impostor."

***

En route in a taxi to Kenneth's apartment, Hump looked for signs of resentment or hostility from Kenneth, finding none. Even though he'd been in love with Mary and had proposed to her first, he seemed to have forgiven Hump for marrying her instead.

Hump was candid with him, admitting that he and Mary were seeing other people and that the marriage had indeed been a mistake. Hump could have let it go at that, but he was the constant provocateur. He confessed Mary's secret to

Kenneth: that she was having an affair with Kenneth's brother, Jo Mielziner. This news seemed to hurt Kenneth, and the moment Hump told his friend that, he regretted the confession.

Even when they got to the apartment, Kenneth didn't say much as he showed Hump around. There wasn't much to see. It was a sparsely furnished one-bedroom apartment—the two men, both lovers of Mary, would be sharing the same bed.

Kenneth was eager to talk about work, not Mary. He said he'd made a film, *Men Without Women*, co-starring Frank Albertson and Paul Page. The 70-minute film depicted the saga of 14 sailors trapped in a sunken submarine with not enough escape gear to go around. It was directed by John Ford.

"That Ford is one tough bastard," Kenneth said. "His first words to me were, 'I run a tight ship. I'm the officer in command and don't forget it!'" He paused to light a cigarette. "I hope you never work with this Ford asshole. He nearly killed all of us."

"I read a book by Hemingway called *Men Without Women,*" Hump said. "It wasn't about a submarine, though."

"Ford shamelessly borrowed the title from Hemingway without crediting him," Kenneth said. "We shot a lot of the picture on Catalina. A lot of homosexuals were in the cast, and they were after this big, tall, handsome guy named Duke Morrison. On location the poor guy couldn't take a shower without three or four guys following him to see the show. Duke was a prop man, operating this air compressor on a yacht that Ford pretended was a submarine. Duke filled in for one of the actors who couldn't swim and made repeated dives in the cold water. He had some bookmaker after his hide and desperately needed the money. I think this Duke Morrison is someone to watch. I think he's going to be big."

After shooting *Men Without Women*, Ford would not work with Duke again for another ten years until he cast him as The Ringo Kid in a film for United Artists, *Stagecoach*. By then Duke Morrison was billing himself as John Wayne.

Eager to share news about his own success in films, Hump told Kenneth that Fox had brought him out as a candidate for the leading role in *The Man Who Came Back*. Kenneth laughed when he heard the news. "You're the fifth actor they've brought out as a candidate for that role in the film. I was the first. None of us is going to get the role. It's going to Charles Farrell, and he's still stuck in the methodologies of the Silent Screen. He can't even talk right."

Hump felt that Kenneth had seemed a little too gleeful in informing him of this, no doubt paying him back for the revelation about Mary having an affair with his brother Jo.

That night after both men had finished off a bottle of Scotch, Hump went to sleep in the very small double bed with Kenneth. He was the first man Hump had ever known who slept in the nude. Kenneth even walked around the apartment nude, and Hump had never seen a man do that before. Except for Maud's nude art classes, he'd grown up with the idea that men kept their clothes on. With both of his wives, he had slept in pajamas. Now he found himself in a cramped Hollywood apartment sleeping with a nude man. Hump didn't wear pajamas but kept his undershorts on.

The next day Hump got up early and reported to work at Fox as a contract player. To his painful regret, he learned that Kenneth was right. Not only was silent screen star Charles Farrell already signed to play the lead in *The Man Who Came Back*, Hump had been assigned the job of giving him diction lessons.

Farrell became a big star just as the screen learned to talk, and he'd been famously teamed with Janet Gaynor, especially in their big hit in the 1927 version of *Seventh Heaven*. Ironically, *Seventh Heaven* had been Helen Menken's most successful play a few years previously.

Only a year younger than Hump, Charles Farrell was the Brad Pitt of his day, and with his well-developed physique, had been doing nude scenes on film back in the silent era. When Hump met the hunk in 1930, Farrell was decades away from his future role as mayor of Palm Springs, a position he was elected to in the late Forties.

Hump had seen the film, *Seventh Heaven*, and felt it was the sappy peak of silent screen romanticism, a gauzy, idyllic romance combined with wholesome vitality. Farrell was wholesome all right, and, in fact, was one of the handsomest actors Hump had ever known. Hump was quickly learning that film actors were required to be more beautiful and photogenic than stage actors.

Even though Hump was forced to work with Charles for six weeks, he took an instant dislike to the star. "I hope you don't teach me your fucking lisp," Farrell said. "You sound like a fairy."

Hump wanted to belt him one, but he feared that Farrell with his athletic physique might flatten him.

On the third day of voice coaching, Farrell became so angry at Hump that he crushed his cigarette out in Hump's palm. Hump winced in pain and rushed into the bathroom to run cold water over his wound. "You fucking conceited bastard," Hump said. "Fox contract or no Fox contract, I'm going to lick you for that."

"I'm sorry," Farrell said. "I didn't mean to do it. I'm mad at Raoul Walsh for making me take diction lessons from some lisping New York actor. But it's not that I mind working with a homosexual. In fact, I actually prefer it."

His hand still stinging from the cigarette burn, Hump came out of the bathroom. "Okay, that's it. You've gone too far. I'm not a homosexual."

"With the lisp, I just assumed," Farrell said.

"Don't assume anything."

"If you want to go outside and duke it out, I must warn you I was state boxing champion in college. I'm pretty good with my fists. Compared to me, you're a runt."

"Okay, okay, don't rub it in," Hump said.

"I'm really sorry," Farrell said. "I don't know what came over me. When I did that cigarette number on you, I wasn't trying to hurt you. I was standing up for all silent-screen actors who are losing their jobs to Broadway thespians." He said the word almost like he was saying lesbian.

"Listen, I need this job, and I want it to work out for me," Hump said. "Let's get on with it. God knows someone should teach you to speak English."

"Just to show there are no hard feelings, I want you to go out with me on my boat this weekend."

"Forget it," Hump said, returning to his diction lessons. That night as he was leaving the studio, he reconsidered Farrell's offer. "If there's one thing I love to do, it's go boating. I've never sailed the Pacific. I'd like to go with you. But if you get wild with that cigarette again, I'll feed you to the sharks."

"It's a deal," Farrell said. "I still feel sorry about that cigarette thing. The third lead, the juvenile role, hasn't been cast yet. I think you'd be ideal. I know you wanted the lead, but third billing in the latest Gaynor/Farrell film ain't bad."

"You'd put in a plug for me?"

"It's a deal." Farrell embraced Hump and told him to meet him at his marina at six o'clock in the morning. He scribbled down the address.

When Hump got back to Kenneth's apartment that night, his actor friend was jubilant. "I just got a call from Raoul Walsh. He's cast me in *The Man Who Came Back* after all."

The news stunned Hump. "You mean Farrell's out of the flick?"

"Not at all," Kenneth said, his face radiant. "I've been cast in the supporting part of the juvenile lead."

***

Out on the boat with Charles Farrell, Hump tried to get over his loss of the third lead to Kenneth. It was to be his first of hundreds of sails on the Pacific, and he felt that the sea would help cure his bitter disappointment. He'd just arrived in Hollywood and already he'd lost two roles, both in the same film.

"I went to bat for you," Farrell said, steering his boat. "But that one-eyed fucker, Raoul 'Asshole' Walsh decided to give it to this pansy actor, Kenneth MacKenna. Do you know him?"

Hump hesitated for a moment before deciding to conceal from Farrell that he not only knew Kenneth but was sleeping in the same bed with him buck-assed naked every night. He wasn't sure if Farrell was calling Kenneth a pansy just as a derogatory remark or if the word was carefully chosen.

"I know who MacKenna is," Hump finally said. "I saw him in *The American Venus* with that Brooks dame."

"Wanta hear the latest Hollywood gossip?" Farrell asked.

Hump nodded that he did, as he wanted to learn everything he could about Kenneth. He figured that his actor friend, at least during the day, was sleeping with someone else other than him.

"It began on that *Venus* picture," Farrell said. "Louise Brooks is a real slut. She found MacKenna and young Doug Fairbanks very attractive and fucked both of them. The star of the picture, Esther Ralston, told me that Brooks, MacKenna, and the Fairbanks kid were having a three-way. It was obvious to everybody on the set, and especially to its director Frank Tuttle. Brooks fled town but Doug Jr. and MacKenna are still at it."

"I had no idea," Hump said, and he was telling the truth. "From what I heard, MacKenna and the Fairbanks boy love the ladies. I've heard tales they're womanizers."

"Show me a womanizer in Hollywood, and I'll show you a faggot," Farrell said. "You're new to the game out here. You'll meet few actors who aren't faggots. If they're not an out-and-out pansy, they're at least bisexual. I can't name one major star in Hollywood who hasn't gone to bed—at least once or twice—with a man. We're actors and we're curious as to what it's like. Even if it isn't our thing, we're mighty curious. Mark my words. You're a good-looking guy. From the way you fill out the crotch of your bathing suit, I see you're packing some meat in there. Here's what I predict: You're going to get hit upon by both women and men in every picture you make. Let's face it: most of the women out here are just former chorus gals. Most of them were hookers before they became stars, and that's true from the biggest of them all. Even Marion Davies and Barbara Stanwyck used to turn tricks in New York."

Farrell was feeding him information so fast he couldn't digest it all at once. Years from that day, Bogie would always claim that it was Farrell who whetted his first taste for Hollywood gossip, an endeavor he'd pursue until the end of his days.

"You're trying to tell me something, aren't you?" Hump asked. "You're telling me that the captain of this here boat likes to get plugged once in a while?"

"More than once in a while," Farrell said. "Every day, if I can find a guy willing to drop his trousers."

"I can't believe this," Hump said. "Charlie Farrell, a faggot? Hell, man, you and Janet Gaynor are America's sweethearts."

"I've got something else to lay on you," Farrell said. "Janet is a lesbian."

"You're putting me on," Hump said. "America's dear, sweet little Janet Gaynor?"

"That little dynamo has had more pussy than the two of us combined," Farrell said. "You'll meet her next week."

"I think she's kind of cute," Hump said. "I'll make a play for her. One night with me and she'll never go back to women."

"Yeah, right." Farrell said, steering his boat toward Catalina. "Dream on."

Over drinks in Catalina at a tavern, Farrell told him how he'd broken into Hollywood, appearing first as an extra in the Lon Chaney version of the silent film, *The Hunchback of Notre-Dame*. "I got the job through one of the stars of that flicker, Norman Kerry. He'd been supporting Valentino for years. The Sheik was a male hustler, you know. When Valentino dumped Kerry, Kerry picked me up one night and promised to help me break into pictures."

After that, Farrell related how one job followed another with him getting a part as an extra in Charlie Chaplin's *A Woman in Paris,* which starred his mistress, Edna Purviance. "From that I went right into Mary Pickford's *Rosita*," Farrell said.

"That's the one in which she starred with Holbrook Blinn," Hump said. "My wife, Mary Philips, and I were with Holbrook when he died. We were horse racing."

"Poor guy," Farrell said. "He was one of the few actors ever to hit Hollywood who was certifiably straight. When I was doing Cecil B. DeMille's *The Ten Commandments*, I met Rod La Rocque and dropped Kerry. Rod took better care of me."

"Fuck, Rod said *I* was the only man for him," Hump said in jest. "I directed his first picture in New York. It was a disaster. I never dreamed he'd go to Hollywood and become such a big star."

"Rod fell for me really big," Farrell said. "He's such a girl. He only pretends to pursue those silly vamps, Pola Negri and Gloria Swanson. The man loves a big dick up his ass. We were together for a while until he met another actor with an even bigger dick than mine, Gary Cooper. Gary will drop his trousers for any man who has money or will help him break into pictures."

Farrell claimed that he'd slept with guys on every movie he made except *Clash of the Wolves.*

"Your luck ran out?" Hump asked.

"No," Farrell said. "I could have fucked with the star but I didn't. He was always humping my leg, though. It was Rin-Tin-Tin."

Back in his boat, a drunken Farrell pointedly asked Hump, "What in the fuck does Walsh tell you is wrong with my voice?"

"He claims it's a high New England voice, okay for a tennis game on Cape Cod but not for the talkies. He wants me to get you to speak in a deeper voice, more manly. You don't want to sound like a squeaky version of John Gilbert."

"Walsh did a sound test with Gaynor and me," Farrell said. "It was a kissing scene. When we saw it with him in the projection room, the fucker went bat-shit. He started screaming about my voice. And even worse, he claimed that when I kiss, I sound like a suction pump. One reason I took you out on this little ride over to Catalina was because I wanted you to teach me how to kiss for the screen without sound effects. As a kisser, and much to Gaynor's horror, I'm a bit of a slurper."

"That doesn't fit my job description," Hump said. "I'll teach you to talk but not to kiss. For that, you'd better call Rod La Rocque."

As the evening wore on, it was amazing how persuasive Farrell could be. Images of bisexuality were dancing through Hump's head. He didn't understand AC/DC, and from what he'd sampled of it, it was not his thing. Still, he was intrigued, realizing that he was sleeping in the same bed with a bisexual every night—Kenneth MacKenna—who was carrying on an affair with one of the

134

handsomest stars in Hollywood, Douglas Fairbanks Jr.

As the liquor flowed, Hump finally broke down and promised, "I'm up for one kiss and that's it. No crotch grabbing and crap like that. I've kissed men before, so I shouldn't hold out on you. One kiss, mind one, and that's it."

"You've found your mate," Farrell said. "Only thing is I'm entitled to one feel. If I find you getting hard, off comes the bathing suit and down I go."

***

The next day on the set Hump encountered for the first time the director of *The Man Who Came Back*, Raoul Walsh, who had voted against casting him as the star of the film. Since Walsh had demoted him to the job of diction teacher to Farrell, he was antsy and uncomfortable about the prospect of meeting the famed director.

The men circled each other like two boxers in a ring waiting to deliver the knockout punch. It was Walsh who eventually moved in for the kill. "I hope you're having luck with that pansy Farrell. I guess he's sucked your cock by now. I heard you two guys went to Catalina together. No man has ever stepped onto Farrell's boat without getting his dick sucked."

"I was drunk," Hump said in a way of mild protest. "I don't remember what happened."

"That's the exact same line Duke Morrison said when I found out that Farrell had sucked him off," Walsh said. "That's what they all say. Farrell's even sucked my dick. Don't worry about it. This is Hollywood. I've always said there are too many faggots out here and not enough good cocksuckers."

Walsh wore a black patch over one eye. When he saw Hump noticing it, he said, "My eye was pecked out by a buzzard in Arizona. I was acting in a flick, *In Old Arizona*. You know I'm an actor don't you?"

"Who could forget you playing John Wilkes Booth in *Birth of a Nation*?" Hump said.

"Warner Baxter replaced me in *Arizona* and went on to win an Academy Award," Walsh said with bitterness. "Those are the breaks, kid. A God damn buzzard changed my life."

Later that day Hump was to learn that the buzzard story was fictional. Walsh felt that it sounded better than what really happened. He was driving his car in Arizona when a jackrabbit crashed through his windshield, a piece of jagged glass cutting deep into his eye. Walsh would wear that patch for the rest of his life.

Walsh's most recent achievement was the casting of Duke Morrison, playing his first leading role and his first speaking part in *The Big Trail*, a remake of the 1923 silent, *The Covered Wagon*. "I've just spent two-million dollars, and we're in the middle of a depression. When I cast Duke, he complained to me that he didn't know how to speak lines. I told the fart all he had to do was sit tall on a horse and point. What a fucker."

135

"I read about the filming in the paper," Hump said. "Seems the entire cast almost drowned in a river crossing when a violent rainstorm came down on them. I heard you kept the cameras rolling."

"Realism," Walsh said. "Tough realism is called for on the screen today. Depression-era audiences want rugged he-men and lots of rough and tough action. It helps them forget about the bank that's about to repossess their homestead. The pink and sappy powder puff style of Valentino is dead and gone. Only a rugged he-man can create a box office success today. I'm talking about a guy like Duke, and I've got my eye on Gary Cooper too, although I hear he's a pansy too, just like that overrated faggot, John Gilbert."

As crude as it was, that bit of dialogue seemed to break the ice between Walsh and Hump. Inviting him for a drink in his private on-set dressing room, Walsh told the struggling young actor that he was a New Yorker too. Born two years before him, Walsh was like no Manhattan man he'd ever known. Walsh had been a sailor, bronco buster, and prizefighter before becoming a director. His "he-man" background had led studios to hire him to direct pictures.

In silents he'd had such big hits as *The Thief of Bagdad* (sic), starring Douglas Fairbanks Sr., *What Price Glory?* with Victor McLaglen and Edmund Lowe, and *Sadie Thompson* with Gloria Swanson.

Fox had recently assigned a major task to Walsh: He'd been told that he was needed to turn some "pansy fops" of the silent screen into "talking heroes" who knew how to fight on camera.

After a few more drinks, Walsh ushered Hump out the door. "Sorry, Bogart, I could have made a star out of you if you didn't have that God damn queenie lisp. I've got nothing against faggots but you're not he-man enough for the screen. We need big guys like Duke Morrison. You're too much of a city slicker. You're also a shrimp. If I need a stand-in for Janet Gaynor, I'll call you."

"You wouldn't buy it if I told you I'm not a faggot?" Hump asked.

Walsh burst into laughter, grabbing Hump in a tight embrace and wet-lipping him. He pulled away. "No way, sweet cheeks. Those are faggot lips if I've seen a set of them before."

"You got me wrong, man," Hump said. "But let it go."

"My advice to you, guy, would be to stay in the closet," Walsh said. "I know you're a queen. But don't let the rest of Hollywood find out. Go out with women. Marry a few. Throw the gossip wolves off your track."

"I'll follow your advice, Mr. Walsh," Hump said, realizing how hopeless it was to convince the director of anything once he'd made up his mind.

As he left the dressing room that day, Hump was bitterly disappointed at Walsh's appraisal of his future on the screen. For one moment that afternoon, he almost wanted to give up and return to New York and Mary. But he decided to stick it out.

He could only have guessed that this unlikely director would eventually make films in which Bogie would star, including *High Sierra* in 1941 that would eventually make the name Humphrey Bogart a household word throughout America.

In spite of all the evidence to the contrary, Walsh went to his grave on December 31, 1980 in Los Angeles, always claiming that "Bogie was the most closeted faggot ever to set foot in Hollywood. I loved the bastard. But I can spot a cocksucker a mile away."

***

A few days later, early in the morning, Kenneth had already gotten up, dressed, and headed for the studio, two hours before he was due to report there. Hump got up and burnt some toast for himself and made some bitter black coffee, which he ate and drank alone. He'd never even mentioned to Kenneth that he'd been under consideration for the juvenile lead that Kenneth would be playing.

Sucking in the California morning air, Hump headed for the studio in a secondhand car he'd recently purchased for $250. He had long ago despaired of ever teaching Farrell how to speak.

When Hump arrived at the Fox lot, he headed at once for Farrell's dressing room where he encountered the female half of "America's sweethearts," Janet Gaynor. She didn't look like any dyke he'd ever known, just the opposite. She was petite and adorable. He remembered the two-reelers Gaynor had made for Hal Roach, which he'd seen in New York several years previously with Bill Brady, Jr.

The eventual winner of history's first Oscar for best actress stood in front of him, shaking his hand. In front of Farrell, he told both of them "how wonderful, how truly wonderful" he'd found them to be in their big hit, *Seventh Heaven*, that launched them as the screen's most romantic duo, despite the sometimes sordid details of their private lives off-screen.

Gaynor's voice was high-pitched and a bit girlish, a trait she shared with her male co-star, Farrell. She was truly a "child-woman," or at least appeared so, and it was obvious why film critics always called her "the Cinderella of today." She stood barely five feet tall, with Farrell hovering behind her at six feet, two inches. Around the Fox lot Gaynor and Farrell were called "Mutt & Jeff."

Before she left, Gaynor on tiptoes gave Hump a gentle kiss on the cheek. "I'm sure you're going to be one of Hollywood's biggest and brightest stars, Mr. Bogart." She looked back toward Farrell. "That is, when you teach Charlie here how to speak like a man. The sound engineers claim that our voices are too similar."

"Shut that cute little Cupid mouth of yours," Farrell warned her, "or I'll tell Bogart what those pretty, kissable lips were doing last night."

Her charming demeanor faded quickly as she flashed anger at Farrell. Her face warned him to shut up.

When she'd gone and the door was shut, Farrell said, "Would you believe Barbara Stanwyck?"

"Is she a dyke too?" Hump asked.

"The biggest in town," Farrell said. "I'm glad you're here early. Before I begin my diction lesson, how about another quickie like the one on the boat?"

"That encounter is our last," Hump said. "I told you I don't go that route."

"You came, didn't you?" Farrell said. "Hell, why am I asking you if you came? You nearly drowned me."

"You swallowed every drop," Hump said. "But that was your last time. They don't call you the slurper for nothing. The straightest man in the world would cum in your mouth when you crank up that suction pump."

A knock on the door, and Hump opened it to find a young messenger boy summoning Farrell to the set one hour before he had been told he was needed. In a loud whisper, the messenger boy leaned his head into the dressing room and said, "Walsh has taken off his black patch today, and that always spells hell for all the actors."

After Farrell parted with a promise to meet Hump for lunch, Hump had nothing to do so he wandered over to Kenneth's dressing room, wishing that it were his and not his friend's. He heard voices coming from the dressing room as if an early morning party were going on. He knocked on the door, which was opened by Janet Gaynor. "Mr. Bogart, come on in," she said. "Kenneth tells me that you and he are roommates. I didn't know that." She eyed him suspiciously as if evaluating Hump in a different light with a new perspective. She turned around to the tall and handsome man standing beside her. "Have you met the charming, the delightful, the gorgeous, the endearing…"

The man stepped forward to introduce himself. "I'm Doug Fairbanks Jr."

Hump was astonished. Maybe Farrell's gossip had some ring of authenticity. Perhaps Doug Fairbanks Jr. and Kenneth were having an affair. Even though they lived together, Kenneth had never told Hump that he knew the young Fairbanks as a friend, which was suspicious in itself.

Hump soon learned that Gaynor's advance billing of Fairbanks was deadly accurate. He was one of the most charming and handsomest actors Hump had ever encountered, true movie star quality. He was also Hollywood royalty, the son of the screen swashbuckler, Douglas Fairbanks Sr., and the stepson of the reigning queen of the silents, Mary Pickford, who had been deeply entrenched as America's sweetheart before Janet Gaynor won that lollipop appellation.

After an hour in Kenneth's dressing room, Hump once again paid his respects to Gaynor, and wished Kenneth luck on the picture that had been denied to him. "I'm heading for some lunch," Fairbanks said. "We could drop in on Mary and Dad at Pickfair, or the tavern across the street."

"The tavern across the street would be more my speed," Hump said. "I'd be too much in awe of your parents to eat."

Over lunch Hump found himself taking delight in Fairbanks' company. The young man seemed educated and full of charm and wit. Kenneth's resemblance to Fairbanks was amazing, except Kenneth was the dime store version, Fairbanks the Tiffany original.

As the talk grew confidential, Hump was tempted to ask him about his relationship with Kenneth but didn't dare be the provocateur, contrary to his usual nature when he might have said, "So Farrell claims you're having an affair with Kenneth..."

Fairbanks hadn't yet acquired the sophistication and discretion he would show in later years when he was to have affairs with everybody from Marlene Dietrich on down. He was more like a young man basking in the glory of his female conquests, and at no point did he even suggest that he might be engaged in any affairs with men.

To hear Fairbanks boast, he was a man strictly for the ladies. "Since you're not a gossip columnist," he said, "I can let you in on some gossip. My latest conquests."

"Let me guess," Hump said. "Louise Brooks."

"Old news." he said. "That fling is over."

"You can carry on and still stay married to Joan Crawford?" Hump asked.

"I'm very discreet," he said. "Joan's none the wiser. You'll love Joan. She's a great gal. I'll introduce you sometime. Perhaps the two of you will make a picture together one day. She's a great actress. You've seen all of her films, of course."

Forever the needler, Hump had held back on revealing to Fairbanks that he was aware of his bisexuality. But he couldn't resist the bait with that remark about Crawford. "I've seen all her films," Hump said, ordering another drink and feeling no pain. If this wet lunch kept up, he would have slurred speech and would be of no help with Farrell's diction. "In fact, I saw her first film as Lucille LeSueur."

"What do you mean?" Fairbanks asked. "What film was that?"

"Don't tell me you don't know," Hump said. "That stag film she made. The one that Texas Guinan used to show at smokers in New York."

Suddenly Fairbanks lost his charming demeanor. Anger and hostility flashed across his beautiful face. "I don't believe that. It must be some other chorus gal you saw. My wife would never make a stag film. If word like that got out, it could destroy her career before it takes off real big like it's going to."

"If you don't believe me, call Texas at her club in New York," Hump said. "She'll tell you all about it."

Fairbanks was growing increasingly agitated. "You've dropped hell on my head. If what you say is true, I've got to get those films and buy up every one of them before they fall into the hands of a blackmailer. God damn, God damn. Just when everything was going so well."

He got up from the table. "I'm going to drive over to my lawyer's." Without saying good-bye, he left the table but turned back, shaking a finger at Hump. "If you're shitting me...." He didn't finish his sentence, heading quickly for the door.

***

At long last Hump was freed from having to give diction lessons to Farrell. Fox gave him his first major film role, a picture called *A Devil with Women*, based on a novel, *Dust and Sun* by Clements Ripley. It was to star Victor McLaglen and Mona Maris.

His brother-in-law, Stuart Rose, was on a train to Hollywood, bringing with him a series of plays and novels from the New York office, with recommendations of each of them as a possible film scenario. Kenneth had invited Stuart to stay at his apartment, with Hump agreeing to sleep on the sofa.

When Hump met Stuart at the railway station in Los Angeles, he was eager for news from New York. Stuart, though seemingly glad to see Hump, was not forthcoming with much information, as if deliberately concealing what he knew about what was going on back east.

Stuart and Frances had not visited the Bogarts in weeks and didn't know how they were doing. He'd not seen Mary Philips either. Since coming to Hollywood, Hump had written his wife only two letters, neither of which was answered.

In a taxi en route to Kenneth's apartment, Hump detected that something had gone seriously wrong in Stuart's marriage to his sister, Frances. It wasn't anything that Stuart specifically said. That he said almost nothing about Frances left the lingering suspicion that the marriage was on the rocks.

Finally, Hump decided to press the issue. "God damn it," he said. "I want to know. How are my sisters?"

Anger flashed across Stuart's face. "Okay, if you must know. Catherine has become a hopeless alcoholic and is sleeping with every guy in town. As for Frances, she grows more mentally unstable every month. The last time I talked to your dad about it, he held out the possibility that we might have to put her in a asylum."

"My God," Hump said.

"I don't want to talk about it now with Kenneth," Stuart said. "It's too painful. Before I go back east, I'll let you know everything. I figured you had enough on your mind trying to launch yourself at Fox."

Once upstairs, Kenneth and Stuart warmly embraced. Each man's face lit up at the sight of the other. Up to that point, Hump never knew that Stuart and Kenneth were any more than casual acquaintances. But they related to each other like two best friends bonded at the hip. There was a lot of touching and feeling. At one point, Stuart gently rubbed Kenneth's cheek. "You get better looking every day, you fucker."

"Look who's talking," Kenneth said. "A handsome and dashing former cavalry officer in the Army. With the trimmest, most well-built figure in Hollywood. You should be playing the Charlie Farrell role instead of him. He thinks he's a male pin-up. But you've got him beat by a New York mile."

As if suddenly aware of Hump in the living room, Stuart turned to Hump. "I bet our boy Kenneth has to fight off the beautiful gals out here in Hollywood."

His eyes downcast, Hump headed for the kitchen to get himself a beer. "Something like that." He wondered if Stuart had any idea that Kenneth was having an affair with Douglas Fairbanks Jr.

He heard the phone ring. When he returned from the kitchen with his beer, Kenneth told him that he had to report back to the set of *The Man Who Came Back* to reshoot a scene.

After he'd dressed, Kenneth again embraced Stuart warmly and agreed to meet back at the apartment later where all three of them would go out on the town.

After Stuart showered and dressed, he came into the kitchen and joined Hump at the table, accepting a can of beer. "The publicity department at Fox called me, and they want to begin your buildup. Since the scar on your lip can't be concealed on screen, we've got to invent a cover-up story."

"I got it." Hump said. "We don't want to implicate Belmont in this."

"No we don't," Stuart said. "The Fox publicist I talked to thinks we can claim that you were injured by a flying wooden splinter from a bursting shell when your naval vessel, *Leviathan*, came under fire from a German U-boat."

"Neat story," Hump said. "If anybody checked, though, I saw no action in the war. The *Leviathan* never came under fire. You're good at embellishing. Can't you come up with a better story, one that can't be checked?"

Stuart excused himself and made some business calls to Fox. When he came back, he said, "I think I've got it. We'll have you stationed in Portsmouth. The Navy had assigned you to take a handcuffed prisoner—let's call him Johnny Ireland—from the naval station to a military prison forty miles away. Ireland, let's say, had been arrested in Boston and charged with desertion. At one point as you're changing trains, let's have Ireland ask you for a cigarette. As you go to light it for him, Ireland raises up his handcuffed hands, smashing you in the face, damaging your lip. We'll then say that Ireland made a run for it. With some skin on your upper lip hanging by a thread, you take out a .45 and shoot the man in his left buttock, grounding him. We'll have some Navy doctor sewing up your lip. Badly."

"That's kinda cute," Hump said. "I like the ring of it. Let's go for it."

That fantasy, conceived by Stuart late one afternoon in a small Hollywood apartment, became, in time, a Hollywood legend.

When Kenneth returned from the studio, and Hump told him the new story of his lip, Kenneth only smiled, "Why not? This is the land of make-believe."

Over dinner, Hump felt like the unwanted guest. Nearly every remark Kenneth made was directed at Stuart. Stuart couldn't seem to take his eyes off Kenneth. Each man continued to compliment the other about how good-looking he was.

The implication was all too clear to Hump. For the first time he began to wonder if his brother-in-law was a homosexual. Did Frances know? So far, from his early impressions, everybody in Hollywood seemed to be bisexual.

That night after they'd made the rounds of two clubs after dinner, all three men returned to the small apartment. Hump stayed in the living room but Kenneth and Stuart retreated to the bedroom where they left the door open. Hump had to go through the bedroom to reach the bathroom. When he needed to take a piss, he passed through the bedroom and couldn't help but notice that both men were jaybird naked. Stuart lay on the bed and Kenneth sat in a chair, as both men listened to Ruth Etting on the radio. Neither man seemed to take notice of his passing through to the toilet.

Around two o'clock that morning, Kenneth and Stuart closed the door but didn't lock it since Hump needed access to the bathroom. The apartment became deadly still. Later, through the thin walls separating the bedroom and the living room, Hump heard noises. They were unmistakable. Kenneth and Stuart were making love.

Shortly before six that morning, Hump got off the sofa and made for the bathroom. When he quietly opened the door and sneaked in, he saw that Kenneth and Stuart were asleep in each other's arms.

All through his day at Fox, he tried to put that image out of his mind. When he came back to the apartment that night, both Kenneth and Stuart invited him to go out with them again for dinner. He politely refused, not wanting a repeat of the previous evening. It was clear to him that the two men wanted to be alone.

When they'd gone, Hump felt a sense of incredible loneliness. He thought he might write Mary another letter, but he decided against that, thinking he should wait until she'd answered one of his.

It was Friday night and all of Hollywood seemed to be having a good time. Mary had said that during their separation he was free to date. So far, he'd met no one.

He then remembered that bouncy blonde bombshell, Joan Blondell, with whom he'd appeared in that Ruth Etting flick, *Broadway's Like That*. He searched through his papers until he found her number.

Feeling a bit shy, he went to the phone. It was probably a useless gesture. A woman as sexy as Joan Blondell probably had guys lining up at her door, especially on a big date night like Friday in Hollywood. "What the hell," he said, deciding to ring her up anyway.

***

"Say hello to Miss Dallas, honey," the expressive face with the pop eyes said to Hump as she pulled up in front of his apartment house to find him already waiting on the sidewalk. "Miss Dallas, Texas, and I've got the pictures to prove it."

"Good to see you out here in Hollywood," Hump said, leaning in to kiss Joan on the lips. "Here we are: Two stars of tomorrow."

142

"Get in, handsome." Her big smile and big blue eyes lured him into the passenger seat of her secondhand 1927 Dodge, with its dented fenders and ripped canvas hood tied down with a rope to keep it from flapping. "As you can see, this ain't no Gloria Swanson limousine," Joan said.

She drove toward Santa Monica where she knew a small and charming Italian restaurant where they could dine quietly. On the way there, he brought her up to date on what was happening—or not happening—to his career at Fox.

With a youthful exuberance lighting up her kewpie doll face, she told him about her own career. "I've been out here long enough to know that Warners has got me pegged as a brassy, gum-chewing, wisecracking blonde floozy. Better that than no work at all."

"I hear that back East a lot of us thespian hacks are out of work," he said. "They call it a depression."

"Jimmy Cagney and me are going to try to make the world forget its troubles," she said. "They signed us both to five-year contracts. He gets the big bills. I get the small change. But it's a job. I'll take any part they want me to play. The only thing I'm fighting is my name change."

"I think Joan Blondell is a great name for a movie star," he said. "What did the Warner friars come up with?"

"Inez Holmes."

He burst into laughter and reached for a cigarette, offering her one.

"Don't laugh too loud," she said. "You don't think Fox is going to let you keep Humphrey, do you? Bogart is okay, but Humphrey. I'm sure they're going to change it to something like Dale or maybe Cary. What about Brad?"

"Hell with that," he said. "It's going to be Humphrey Bogart or nothing. Don't let them rename you Inez Holmes. Warners will take enough from you. Hold onto that name, girl."

Over dinner he got to know her for the first time, as they'd hardly gotten acquainted in New York when they'd made that two-reeler with Ruth Etting. At the time, Hump had eyes only for Etting.

Before the spaghetti was served, he'd learned that her father, Ed Blondell, had been one of the original Katzenjammer Kids. Joan was a true "born in a trunk" show biz woman, reared on vaudeville stages, having made her first appearance at the age of three months when she was brought out before the lights as a "carry-on" in the play, *The Greatest Love.*

"I grew up on the stage," she said. "I've taken more baths in train station toilets than anyone."

"How did you get the nickname, Rosebud?" he asked.

"We toured everywhere," she said. "Ed even took the Blondells to China. My big number was called 'In a Rosebud Garden of Girls.' Since then, only my intimates are allowed to call me Rosebud. But before the night is out, I hope you'll be calling me that."

She leaned over and planted a light kiss on his lips.

"Before this night is over, I hope your rosebud and I are on intimate terms," he said.

"Now, now," she said. "No need to get vulgar. Let's keep it clean."

The waiter arrived with the veal parmigiana just as she was telling him how she came to be teamed with Cagney. Hump had told her that he'd known Cagney in New York. "He was a drag queen appearing in cabaret revues back then," he said.

She seemed startled to hear that, and Hump deliberately didn't tell her how Cagney was offered a drag role.

"That big cheese, George Kelly, spotted Jimmy and me trying out this dance number," she said. "He cast us in *Maggie the Magnificent*. Kelly thought Jimmy looked like a fresh mutt, and I, of course, the blonde hooker with the heart of gold."

"I'm hearing real good things about the two of you," he said, reaching for her hand. "I'm just a little bit jealous."

"I thought you belonged to Ruth Etting when I met you," she said. "God knows how Mary Philips fits into all this?"

"They're in New York, and we're out here," he said, squeezing her hand.

"Anyway," she said, "back to Cagney. Our timing was perfect. We opened *Maggie* on Broadway the same week as the Stock Market crash. After that, we did *Penny Arcade* about the seamy side of Coney Island. Al Jolson came to see it and bought the rights. I'm working in the flick now. They're calling it *Sinners' Holiday*. Jimmy says the title has about as much to do with the plot as it does with Winnie-the-Pooh. Warners didn't think Jimmy and I have big marquee names. So they gave us supporting parts and gave the star roles to Grant Withers and Evelyn Knapp."

"Talk about big names," he said sarcastically.

"Jimmy feels that after teaming with me, he'll never know another day of poverty," she said.

"Hey, gal, all night I've been hearing Jimmy this, Jimmy that," he said. "Are you guys shacking up?"

She hesitated a long moment before answering. "Let's say we're having a romantic liaison."

"Call it what you want but isn't he married to some chorus gal?" he asked.

"To one Frances Willard Vernon Cagney," she said. "He calls her Willie. She keeps him on a short leash. He has to account for every penny, even a three-cent stamp. When we go out together, I have to pick up the check even though he's earning five-hundred bucks a week."

"Well, I'm earning $750 a week at Fox, so I have him beat," he said.

"Rumor has it in more ways than one," she said running a red-nailed finger gently along his cheek.

"You're going to have to check that out for yourself tonight," he said. "Why rely on rumors when you can get some first-hand experience?"

144

After dinner they went for a walk along the Santa Monica pier, noticing the boats rocking from side to side as the water was choppy. He spotted a drunk throwing up over a rail.

"I'm living with Kenneth MacKenna," he said, "and my brother-in-law is in from the east," he said.

"And I'm living with three broads and sharing the rent," she said. "But there are ways."

"What do you mean?" he asked.

"Have you ever tried it in the back seat of a broken down Dodge?"

***

On the Fox lot Hump encountered his director for *A Devil with Women*, Irving Cummings, for the first time. Hump was startled to learn that if *A Devil With Women* became a hit, the studio planned to co-star him in an ongoing series of adventure stories with the film's big-name star, Victor McLaglen. Cummings seemed very excited at this prospect but Hump managed only a faint smile.

The idea of playing second fiddle to McLaglen, or to any other actor, in an ongoing series of B pictures wasn't part of Hump's dream before he came to Hollywood. He found the prospect so dismal, and the plot line so inane, that secretly he hoped that the picture would fail. Ironically, if the film had been successful, its success would probably have typecast Hump into the kind of marginal bit player whose consequences might have haunted him for the rest of his career.

Cummings put his arm around Hump and walked him over to McLaglen's dressing room. "You might as well meet the star of the picture. If my gut instinct is right, you'll appear with him in at least twelve films, and I'll direct every one of them. The McLaglen/Bogart films will be my old-age pension."

When Cummings introduced Hump to the British actor, McLaglen had just emerged dripping wet from the shower. At that point an aide summoned Cummings to the set, leaving Hump standing alone with a jaybird naked McLaglen.

"Fix yourself a whiskey, kid," McLaglen said, reaching for a thick towel. "Pour one for me too, letting it fall from the bottle into the glass like a horse pisses."

Hump poured the actor a drink and said, "I'm happy to be working with you Mr. *Mack-loff-len*."

"That's *Muh-clog-len*," he said. "Since you can't pronounce my name, just call me Victor."

During their two-hour wait before they were due on the set, Hump got acquainted with this famous and rambunctious star who stood six feet, three inches. His hair was jet-black, and he had a twinkle in his blue-gray eyes. Hump became more comfortable after McLaglen put on his drawers, although nude he was an impressive sight.

In those days, whenever McLaglen was introduced to someone, he took delight in drinking with them and talking about the exploits of his private life, which were actually true and not some tall tales invented by the publicity department.

The son of the Right Reverend Andrew McLaglen, a Protestant clergyman in South Africa, the young Victor was the eldest of eight brothers. He tried to fight in the Boer War by joining the Life Guards, but the Reverend McLaglen tracked him down and, drawing on his persuasive powers and his political connections, secured his release.

Heading for Canada, he worked only temporarily on a farm devoted mainly to turnips before running off to become a professional prizefighter. That was followed by a tour in circuses, vaudeville shows, and Wild West shows. In these shows, he was billed as a fighter who would take on all comers in the audience. Any young man who could last three rounds with McLaglen was paid $25. He toured with these shows from America to Australia. In Sydney he fought heavyweight champion Jack Johnson, the champ knocking McLaglen out after six rounds.

When World War I broke out, McLaglen signed up with the Irish Fusiliers and was sent to the Middle East. Eventually he became the Provost Marshal for the city of Baghdad, responsible for the military police.

With his pugnacious nature, he had hoped to resume his boxing career after the war but ended up being cast in the *Call of the Road* in 1920. From that day on, he became a popular leading man in English silents.

By 1924 he'd been lured to Hollywood to appear in *The Beloved Brute*. One role followed another, from *Women and Diamonds*, also in 1924, to *Beau Geste* in 1926. His own glory came to him when he played Captain Flagg in *What Price Glory?* in 1926.

Described as a "British-born Wallace Beery," McLaglen was a two-fisted man of action. Under Raoul Walsh's direction, McLaglen's appearance in the antiwar film was a smash hit at the box office. Audiences delighted in the ribald, gregarious interplay between Flagg and his sergeant, Quirt, as played by Edmund Lowe. Little did Hump know on that first meeting with McLaglen that Raoul Walsh, in about a year, would team McLaglen as Flagg and Edmund Lowe as Sergeant Quirt in a derivative flicker loosely inspired by *What Price Glory?*, *Women of All Nations*.

Hump himself would appear in that movie. No longer viewed as a candidate for a costarring role opposite McLaglen, Hump suffered ninth billing in the screen credits.

. "Do you like women?" McLaglen asked abruptly. "Or, are you one of those Hollywood pansies like George O'Brien and Charles Farrell?"

"I go for the gals," Hump said. "Been married twice."

"Good to hear that," McLaglen said. "I've heard stories about you. If you're telling me the truth and not bullshitting, you're in luck. Our female star, Mona Maris, is the Argentine bombshell. Fox has imported a Buenos Aires tango queen

146

into Hollywood to provide some screen competition for Lupe Velez. That Mexican chili pepper can really heat up the screen when she's not getting plugged with Gary Cooper's ten inches. I heard that he fucked her nine times in one night. Talk about a *Hot-Cha!*"

"Why does that make me lucky?" Hump asked. "I don't get it."

"Mona is Hollywood's top fellator," McLaglen said. "Not as good as Charlie Farrell, but she's got all the other gals beat. She can deep-throat any man. One day she emptied four big loads from me. I'm afraid I'll be too weak to make the movie if you don't help me out."

"You're putting me on," Hump said.

"She'll be here any minute. You'll see what I mean."

As if on cue, Mona Maris barged into the dressing room, not bothering to knock. "Oh, Victor," she said in a heavily accented Spanish voice. "I've missed you so."

"Bullshit," he said, "you don't even like me." He reached into the fly of his underwear and extracted his penis, which was already hardening. "You like this, gal. Admit it."

She smiled before turning to Hump. "I hear you are going to be my love interest in our movie. I'm glad to meet you."

"Glad to meet you too," he said, extending his hand.

She ignored it, pressing her body up against his and descending on his mouth. The moment their lips met, she darted her tongue inside his mouth.

"Do Bogart later," McLaglen called out to her. "Look at this all day sucker I've got for you."

Maris tore herself away from Hump's lips long enough to cast a glance at McLaglen. Her fiery Argentine eyes lit up at the sight of his impressive hard-on. She kissed Hump once more on the lips before moving away. "Excuse me, señor," she said to Hump, "but Victor discovered my special talent before you. There will be time for us later."

As Hump made a retreat from the dressing room, he glanced over his shoulder. McLaglen remained seated in a chair. On her knees, Maris bent over to service him, her pretty head bobbing up and down.

"Catch you guys later," Hump said as he headed out the door and onto the set.

He immediately encountered Robert Edson, one of the supporting players who'd been cast as General Garcia in the film. Edson shook his hand and looked over to McLaglen's dressing room. "Welcome to Hollywood, Bogart," he said.

***

In *A Devil With Women*, McLaglen was cast in the role of Jerry Maxton, a soldier-of-fortune at large in a banana republic in Central America. He played a womanizer, romancing "anything in skirts," especially the fair señorita, Rosita Fernandez, as interpreted by the great fellator, Mona Maris. To judge from all that hot action back in the dressing room, the off-screen romance was also heating up.

In contrast, Hump played a supporting role of the clean-cut but wastrelly rich nephew of the country's wealthiest man.

In the film, McLaglen's job involves ending the reign of terror of the notorious bandito, Morloff, who is terrorizing the countryside. McLaglen falls for a woman gun smuggler. Alone with Hump's character, he's lured into the enemy camp, where the two men narrowly escape a firing squad. Maris's character of Rosita provides a refuge for them. The bandits are enticed inside Maris's hacienda where one by one McLaglen, the former prizefighter, knocks them out in a series of one-punch fights.

At the end of the film, McLaglen is ready to claim Rosita as his girl, but she tells him that her heart belongs to Tom Standish, the role played by Bogart. Hump in his first major film gets the girl in the final reel.

During filming, Mona Maris managed to fellate most of the crew, at least the more rugged and handsome members. McLaglen with his studly meat remained her favorite, although she claimed Hump was a "cutie-pie," an English expression she'd recently learned.

Today it appears amazing that Hump was ever cast in another movie after the release of *A Devil with Women*. A financial and artistic failure with a stupid plot and mismatched actors, it should have ended his career. Fox executives wisely decided not to continue pairing McLaglen with Bogart, abandoning forever the notion of continuing their original idea about the ongoing series of adventure films. Later in life Bogie threatened to buy up all copies of the film and have them destroyed.

The director, Irving Cummings, was particularly brutal to the neophyte film actor. "McLaglen is biting off your balls and chewing them up on screen. You come off like some rich little twerp repeating one of your Broadway 'Tennis, anyone?' parts."

"God damn it, that's what the role calls for," Hump protested.

"We've got to come up with some business to make your character real," Cummings said.

The director probably gave Hump the worst advice he could. A stage actor unaware of how the camera picked up the tiniest facial nuance, Hump set out to match the almost constant ear-to-ear grin of the burly looking, battered, and brutish British actor.

The writer, Robert Sklar, in reviewing the film, said it best: "Bogart plays a coltish fool, tossing his head, slapping his knees, and laughing with his mouth open so wide you can almost see his tonsils. He looks like an actor who is uncomfortable not only with his part, but also with his body. He employs a few stock gestures that he repeats again and again: arms awkwardly held in front of his body; then pushing back his jacket; then fists at the belt; then into his pockets; then back to the belt, arms akimbo. Smiles, arch delivery of lines, more smiles."

Mona Maris with her superb deep-throat technique was taking such good care of Hump on the set that he hardly had enough left for Joan Blondell in the evening. Joan wasn't free every night, only when Cagney could escape from the clutches of his "Willie."

Stuart Rose had left Kenneth MacKenna's apartment and embraces to return to the Fox New York office and his unhappy bed with Frances. Hump sensed that Kenneth wanted him out of the apartment so he could conduct his private life with greater secrecy.

When the apartment next door became available, Hump eagerly signed a lease and set out to buy some secondhand furniture. He didn't want to purchase anything too expensive, because he feared that his days as a Fox movie star were about to come to an end.

Kenneth was supportive, but Hump sensed that his host was relieved to see him go. The third morning after taking the apartment, Hump opened the door to pick up the morning newspaper. Just as he did, he spotted Douglas Fairbanks Jr. leaving Kenneth's flat. Remembering the disastrous ending to their earlier meeting, Hump merely nodded and said, "Good morning," before quickly shutting his door.

Fairbanks appeared slightly embarrassed at having been caught leaving Kenneth's apartment, but handled it with his usual charm and grace.

Hump felt like he was becoming a full-time Hollywood resident when a phone was finally installed in his own name. The first night he had the phone, he called Joan Blondell, only to learn that she was seeing Cagney that night.

"Don't worry," Joan said. "I ran into an old friend of yours from New York. I gave her your number. You definitely won't be lonely tonight."

"Who is it?"

"And spoil the surprise?" Joan said. "Have fun, duckie." She put down the receiver.

About an hour later, the phone rang. With some reluctance, he picked up the receiver.

"This is Barbara Stanwyck," the voice said. "Could this be the one and only Humphrey Bogart?"

"Miss Stanwyck," he stammered, fearing at first someone was pulling a trick on him. "I'm honored that you'd call me."

"Joan gave me your number," Stanwyck said.

"She said you were an old friend of mine," he said. "We've never met. Of course, I'd be honored to take you out."

"Never met!" Stanwyck said, mocking him. "In Brooklyn where I come from, when a man fucks a woman, he's met her."

"You and I..." Hump was totally confused.

"I'm Ruby Stevens," Stanwyck said. "That hot Jazz Baby from the chorus line. You told me I was the greatest fuck of your life."

***

149

No longer the tough-talking little chorus girl from Brooklyn, Ruby Stevens—a.k.a. Barbara Stanwyck—was now a take-charge movie star. Within two hours of Stanwyck's call, Hump found himself dressing for a double date. The supporting cast was to consist of two struggling actors, Kenneth MacKenna and himself. The stars of the evening were Barbara Stanwyck and Kay Francis.

Stanwyck showed up at their apartment house as the driver of her own sleek new car. "I know you struggling actors drive around in junk-heaps, and I have my image to think of," she'd said on the phone.

When Hump opened the door and a stunningly beautiful and elegantly dressed Stanwyck was standing there, he searched for some telltale clue in her face that this ravishing beauty, who was aspiring to become the new queen of Hollywood, was the same chorus girl he'd allegedly bedded. He found none but enjoyed it when she hugged him and kissed him succulently on the lips. He was certain that if he'd ever gone to bed with a dame like this, he would never forget her, but he suspected that Hollywood had drastically changed the image of whatever woman she might have been before.

Dressed in his best suit, a dark blue number, Kenneth had already come over to Hump's apartment to wait for their dates. Hump had ordered him into the kitchen to make drinks for everybody from the only bottle of Scotch he owned, and it was running low.

Kenneth came out of the kitchen with drinks and practically fell into Stanwyck's arms until Hump laid a firm hand on his shoulder. "Lady Babs is my date for tonight," Hump said.

"Barbara, he gets all the women," Kenneth said. "I even tried to marry his wife, Mary Philips."

"I know Mary," Stanwyck said with a certain enthusiasm. "Me and her turned a few tricks together back in New York."

Before either Hump or Kenneth had time to ponder that, Stanwyck gulped down her drink and was urging them out the door. "Kay's waiting in the car," she said, "and that's one pussy who doesn't like to wait for no man." She paused. "Or woman either."

On the way downstairs, Stanwyck claimed she met Hump one night when he'd stumbled drunk from Texas Guinan's place. "I was working the honky-tonk next door."

Something jolted in Hump's brain, but he wasn't certain. He vaguely recalled picking up some thin girl. Unlike the other ladies in the chorus line, she had few curves and her legs were less well-developed than the others. In years to come, no one could accuse Barbara Stanwyck of competing with the gams of Marlene Dietrich or Betty Grable. With her pretty auburn hair and her blue eyes, Hump had been attracted to her but he still didn't remember fucking her.

Although Kay Francis was seated in the back seat when Stanwyck introduced her to Hump and Kenneth, it was only when they arrived at the Cock & Bull for dinner that Hump came to appreciate her beauty. Like Stanwyck, Francis was a stunning-looking woman, tall and brunette. She was the epitome of chic. Compared to Stanwyck, she looked like the movie star, Stanwyck the secretary companion.

When it became obvious that she was the most overdressed woman in the tavern, Francis said, "I have to dress up. My fans expect it of me. Even if they assign me rotten movies in the years ahead, my public, most often women, will flock to my pictures just to see what I'm wearing."

Stanwyck seemed to have developed a deeply entrenched hate-love relationship with Francis and liked to prick her vanity. "Kay wants to become the most ostentatious clothes horse of the Thirties, copy-catting what those two pussies, Pola Negri and Gloria Swanson, did in the Twenties."

"If not *moi*," Francis asked, "who?"

Before the shrimp cocktail arrived, Francis and Kenneth discovered that they had a link through his father, Leo Mielziner. "Your dad and I had an affair in 1922 when he painted my portrait."

Kenneth looked shocked. But in front of Hump, he wanted to appear sophisticated so he quickly masked his surprise. "I've seen that portrait. It's a grand likeness of you. You know, in 1926 he exhibited it at the British Royal Academy."

"Yes, I know," Francis said smugly. "I hear I stole the show."

"As you always do," Stanwyck said, reaching over to caress her hand. "As indeed you're trying to now. You want all the attention devoted to you this evening instead of to me. Don't forget. You're a mere up-and-coming actress. I'm the biggest star in this whole fucking room."

"Oh, Barbara, don't exaggerate," Francis said. "I'm making as many pictures as you are."

Kenneth wanted to steer talk back to his father. "How did you come to pose for him?"

"It's a long story," she said. "Some other night I'll tell you about it. Later I'm going to see if you measure up to your father." She leaned over and kissed him on the lips.

Both Stanwyck and Hump laughed, and Kenneth seemed embarrassed, reflecting his insecurity.

When Francis got up to go to the women's room, as she did once every hour to check her makeup and make emergency repairs, Stanwyck slipped onto the banquette beside Kenneth. At first Hump thought he'd lost his date for the evening. "I deliberately brought Kay here to see you tonight," Stanwyck said to Kenneth. "She's seen a photo of you and found you very attractive. Come on strong with her. Seduce her. Make her fall in love with you."

"Hey," Hump chimed in, "what's this all about?"

"Kay's chasing after me every day," Stanwyck said, "and I've got other fish to fry. She's always trying to rip off my bloomers. I was hoping old Ken boy here could divert her. Kay goes both ways."

"So do I," Kenneth said provocatively, looking directly into Stanwyck's eyes without blinking and then staring steadfastly at Hump. Maybe it was the liquor talking, but Hump was surprised that Kenneth would be so open about his sexuality. Stanwyck had created an atmosphere where one could speak the truth.

"I'm glad you admitted it," she said. "I already knew about it anyway. Word about you and Fairbanks Jr. has spread across town. I'm going to go after that handsome stud myself."

"Put the brake on, gal," Kenneth said. "He belongs to me."

"Like hell he does," Stanwyck said. "He's up for grabs. I hear he's much more attracted to the gals than to pansies. One night after I'd gone down on Joan Crawford, she told me all about it. Who knows Fairbanks better than his moll, Lady Crawford herself."

"Talk about switch-hitters," Hump said. "Crawford and Fairbanks belong together. Instead of musical chairs, they play musical beds."

"Seriously," Kenneth said, feeling threatened by Stanwyck's voracious determination, "lay off Doug. Hollywood has so many other good-looking guys."

"Sorry, Chump," Stanwyck said, "you may have a succulent black hole. But once Doug discovers my tight pussy, he'll be knocking at my door every night begging for more."

Back at table, Francis once again tried to divert attention to herself. "I hope all of you saw me in *Dangerous Curves,"* she said.

No one said anything. Francis indicated mild shock on her face. "I play a vamp. A trapeze artist named Zara. I got to seduce Richard Arlen both on and off the screen. But Clara Bow, playing the circus waif, wins him at the end of the picture."

"I understand you seduced Clara Bow more often than Arlen did," Stanwyck said, as she grew drunker and more provocative. She reminded Hump of himself when he was drinking heavily, which was most of the time.

"Darling," Francis said, chiding Stanwyck. "You keep giving this sweet, handsome man, Kenneth here, the distinct impression that I'm a lesbian." She leaned over and kissed Kenneth on the lips. "As this divine stud is going to find out later, that is definitely not the case."

"Oh, yeah," Stanwyck said, growing more belligerent as she drank. "If I recall, we've bumped pussies a few times."

"Babs," Francis said, "let's not get vulgar. It's unbecoming to a lady."

"Fuck that!" Stanwyck said. "Lady? I'm Ruby Stevens from Brooklyn. I was pinned down and raped by four teenage jerks when I was nine years old. I learned about life the hard way. On my back. Bold and brassy, that's going to be my style in pictures."

Whatever Stanwyck was or was to become, she was definitely a prophet.

All four of them ordered steaks from a handsome blond-haired waiter, who was more beautiful than any of the four stars or would-be stars at the table. With his eyes, he made it clear to each of them that, if asked, he would easily be their bed partner for the night, maybe even in a five-way.

Everybody ordered steaks in various degrees of doneness. Stanwyck gave the most "manly" order. "Just sweep it over the brush fire lightly," she told the waiter.

It was one o'clock before they staggered out of the tavern. Although technically, she was too drunk to drive, Stanwyck took control of the wheels of her car anyway. Without anybody saying anything, it was just assumed that all four of them were heading back to the men's apartment building.

At the door to Kenneth's apartment, Stanwyck kissed both Francis and him on the lips, her succulent pink tongue darting out for each of them.

When they had gone inside, Hump fumbled drunkenly with the key at his own apartment door. "Once again I'm going to get to fuck Ruby Stevens, and I'm drunk as a skunk for the second time."

"When aren't you drunk?" Stanwyck said with a touch of hostility in her voice. She took the key from him and opened the door right away, entering the apartment before he did.

When he staggered inside, she slammed the door and locked it. "Let's get one thing straight, Bogart. I've got to warn you. When I take you to bed, I run the fuck."

***

In Hump's apartment, it was three o'clock in the morning. Stanwyck was right: she ran the fuck. Twice she'd mounted him. Both times he'd lain on his back as she did her gymnastics over him. He wanted more of that kind of loving, although he didn't plan to abandon his missionary position with Joan Blondell.

She stood at his soot-streaked window clad only in a brassière, not bloomers, and looked out into the night, although his view opened onto a brick wall. The room was dark. Propped up in bed, he could only make out the glow of her fiery hot cigarette. She smoked like she acted in movies—with gusto.

Until he would meet Joan Crawford, Stanwyck was the most ambitious actress he'd ever known. It made stars he'd appeared with on Broadway, including Mary Boland and Shirley Booth, look like gentle ladies-in-waiting at the court of some dowager queen.

In some respects, Stanwyck's story was very similar to that of another star, Marilyn Monroe, whom Stanwyck would seduce and briefly fall in love with when they were cast together in *Clash by Night* shot for RKO in 1952.

Stanwyck, like Monroe, had been shunted from one uncaring foster home to another where she was abused, even sexually molested.

As Bogie would say later in life, "Ruby Stevens was one tough, sassy broad but she had class. She was hard-boiled yet soft and vulnerable, a free-spirited woman who took no crap from any man. She was also one of the sexiest women I've ever known."

Yet, even though she'd seduce many men in her life, including William Holden, Robert Wagner, Glenn Ford, and Gary Cooper, Hump suspected that in her heart she was a lesbian. It didn't appear that passion drove her to men. Stanwyck once told him, "I save my real loving, my gentle side, for women. With men, things immediately revolve around power games."

Hump bolted up in bed, "My God, I must be sobering up. It's come back to me. I remember you when you were dancing at the Strand."

"Great!" she said in a harsh voice. "So, you aren't a retard. That proves that even as a teenager I can make a lasting impression on a drunk."

"You were one of the Keep Kool Cuties," he said. "You did that number with Johnny Dooley. 'A Room Adjoining a Boudoir,' if memory serves."

"Finally, you know who I am," she said, "even though I had to fuck you twice to jar that pickled brain of yours."

"I miss the Twenties back in New York," he said when she crushed out her cigarette and returned to bed for some pillow talk. "Speakeasies, dirty dances, bootleg hooch, plunging necklines, red hot jazz, flapper clothes."

"And big-dicked New York men," she chimed in. "Don't forget those."

"I didn't know too many of those," he said. "None at all, as a matter of fact."

"So you and Kenneth don't make out when that cute little Fairbanks boy isn't around?" she said.

"We're close," he said, "but only as good buddies."

"When you were taking a piss at the Cock & Bull," she said, "Kenneth told me he's had fantasies about having a three-way with you and Mary Philips."

Hump didn't say anything for a minute. "I'd better watch that one."

Since Stanwyck couldn't sleep, she decided to keep him up too. "It was Mae Clarke who taught me the joy of lesbian love, and, as you can see, I've added it to my repertoire like that thing with Kay. But, as you also know from tonight, I'm not completely weaned from men either. I don't want to deny myself any pleasure. Too much was denied me as a girl. As a woman, I'll go after what I want. If I want to get fucked by a man, you know I can go for that the way I bagged you tonight and the way I'm going to take the trousers off Dougie boy tomorrow night, or at least sometime this week. If I want a woman, I'll chase her down and get her. I've already set my sights on that blonde German bitch, Dietrich. Who knows? Miss Marlene, Mae, and me might become a threesome."

"Invite me over," Hump said. "From what I've seen of Dietrich I'd go for her in a minute. I saw Mae Clarke in *Nix on Dames*. I'd go for her too. You've got good taste, Bloody Babs. You and Mae still an item?"

"We still are," Stanwyck said. "Me and Mae saw you on Broadway in *It's a Wise Child*. She thought you were kinda cute."

"I'll take you up on that invitation for a three-way," he said. Wanting to appear more sophisticated than he actually was, he added, "I've done a quartet before with my first wife, Helen Menken, Tallulah Bankhead, and Tallu's boy friend, a rather creepy Brit. I wouldn't want to repeat that experience, but a three-way

154

with two of the hottest dames in Hollywood, that's more my style."

"You've got a date," Stanwyck said. "Now let's get some God damn sleep. You'll talk my head off and keep me up all night. I've got to look gorgeous on camera tomorrow."

***

"I heard you taught Farrell how to talk. How about teaching me how to shit? I'm constipated."

Those unlikely remarks launched a friendship that would last to the grave between Humphrey Bogart and Spencer Tracy.

Hump reached to shake the actor's hand on the Fox set of *Up the River*. "Call me Hump."

"What kind of nickname is that?" Tracy asked. "From now on and henceforth forever more you'll be known as Bogie."

Stocky, round-faced and not particularly handsome, Tracy was hardly a Hollywood hunk like Charles Farrell. A former Jesuit prep-school student who once wanted to be a priest, the Milwaukee-born actor was Bogie's age and, like Bogie, had joined the Navy in the final days of World War I.

Tracy had captured director John Ford's attention on Broadway playing Killer Mears, a convicted murderer in an all-male cast. Tracy was waiting on Death Row in the play *The Last Mile*. Ford thought that he'd be ideal in the role of a character called "St. Louis" in the 1930 prison drama, *Up the River*, opposite the Ziegfeld beauty, Claire Luce.

Bogie was cast as the fourth lead, playing Steve. He'd never met Ford but the director had seen him in a matinee performance of *The Skyrocket* and had decided Hump would be suitable for a role in *Up the River*. Ford later told Bogie in Hollywood that, "I know your wife was the star of that play. But you have the talent. Mary Philips is no actress." Hump decided to use Ford's assessment of her talent in his next big fight with his wife.

On the set, Tracy put his arm around Bogie and led him toward his dressing room. "Ford's in the front office this morning. So in the meantime, let's you and me go have some whiskey. You are a drinking man, aren't you?"

He smiled at Tracy. "I've been known to put away a few."

After the first drink, Tracy delivered the bad news. "There may be no picture. Ford is meeting right now with Winfield Sheehan. In case you're that green around here, Sheehan runs this joint."

"What's the matter?" Bogie protested. "We have contracts. They brought us out from New York."

"That doesn't matter to those fuckers," Tracy said. "Sheehan's been looking at the gross over at MGM on the *The Big House*."

"I saw it," Bogie said. "Great picture. Bob Montgomery and Wallace Beery did a fine job."

"Don't forget my old pal, Chester Morris," Tracy said. "He was in it too. Trouble is, they did too fine a job. Sheehan knows our script isn't half as good. Reviewers would unfavorably compare our picture with *The Big House*. Also, Sheehan has seen screen tests of both of us. And he doesn't want us in the picture, even if he decides to go ahead with it."

"Fuck this!" Bogie said. "I should go back to New York. I'm spinning my wheels out here in this palm pasture."

"Have another drink," Tracy said.

In spite of the bad news he reported, Bogie relaxed in Tracy's presence. The actor had a soothing effect on him. To Bogie, he seemed like a sports loving man's man, with a big head and a boar neck. It was Tracy's well-modulated voice that drew Bogie to him.

As the morning wore on and Ford still hadn't shown up, Tracy and Bogie used the opportunity to drink more whiskey and to get to know each other. Each actor seemed fascinated by the other. There was a restlessness—even a self-destructiveness—about Tracy that intrigued Bogie. He would later claim, "Spence carried around a lot of that Catholic guilt crap."

At that stage in their friendship, Bogie didn't have a clue as to what Tracy had to feel guilt about, but he was determined to find out. Surely it wasn't something as simple as cheating on your wife. All men in Hollywood did that. With all the temptation out here, how could they resist? After all, he'd hardly arrived and already Barbara Stanwyck and Joan Blondell had thrown themselves at him.

Earlier he'd learned that Tracy had been married to a minor Broadway actress, Louise Treadwell, for seven years. "It was love at first sight," Tracy said. Bogie also learned that she'd given birth to a deaf son named John. "His deafness makes me suffer a lot," Tracy said. "Somehow I blame myself. Good, healthy, Irish boy sperm isn't supposed to create a child with birth defects."

"It's not your fault," Bogie assured him as he accepted another whiskey. He feared that if they kept drinking like this, and Ford did show up, having saved the picture from Sheehan, neither of them would be sober enough to appear on camera.

"I was the terror of Milwaukee," Tracy said. "A tough Irish kid. I got into at least three fistfights a day, taking on the Sauerkrauts, the Pollack sausages, and the Dago pizza pies. I was in and out of fifteen—make that eighteen—different schools before I finished the eighth grade."

"You got me beat on that count," Bogie said. "But I was kicked out of Andover. My father wanted me to be a doctor."

"Welcome to the club," Tracy said. "My old man wanted me to be a priest. I still think about it. I used to dream of myself as Monsignor Tracy, Cardinal Tracy, Bishop Tracy. Get this: Archbishop Tracy. Every time I think of what I might have been, I get goose bumps. Of course, I could never have been celibate. Not me. If there's a whorehouse in town, I quickly become the best customer."

Ironically, although Tracy obviously never became a priest, he ended up playing one in four memorable performances—*San Francisco* in 1936 with Clark Gable;

156

Boy's Town in 1938, *Men of Boy's Town* in 1941, and a final appearance, *The Devil at Four O'clock* in 1961.

"Before I agreed to do this picture with you, I saw a rough cut of *A Devil with Women*," Tracy said. "I know you used to do some stupid juvenile roles on Broadway. But I never caught your 'Tennis, anyone?' act. Of course, that fascist, McLaglen, steals the picture from you and that cocksucker, Mona Maris. You bullshit your way through the film. One hammy disguise after another. Some clowns call that acting. I don't. If our damn flick ever gets made, watch how I do it. Don't let the camera see you running around like a chicken with its head cut off. Underplay. That's the way to do it."

As insulted as he was by Tracy's advice, Bogie listened to it. He'd never overplay a character again. "There's at least one thing I like about the script. I get the girl."

"So you do," Tracy said, pouring himself another drink. "On the screen you do. In real life, I've already got Claire. She's about to show up here any minute. The moment I introduce the two of you, I want you to get the hell out of here. I'm horny this morning, and that Ziegfeld cutie is one mighty fine piece of tail."

As if on cue, there was a knock on the door. Tracy signaled Bogie to open it.

Standing on the stoop was a stunningly attractive woman, Claire Luce. He recognized her from her photographs. "Can a lady darken these chambers? Or is it strictly a stag party?"

"Come on in. I'm Humphrey Bogart."

"Call him Bogie," Tracy chimed in. "Everybody does."

Bogie stepped back to make way for her.

"Haul that cute ass over here," Tracy said to Luce. "Give your daddy a kiss. I'm in the mood for a big, wet, sloppy one."

Excusing himself, Bogie left the dressing room, shutting the door tightly behind him. Walking toward the set, he encountered for the first time an angry John Ford, the blood vessels on his head looking as if they were about to pop.

***

"I've just got back from the front office," John Ford said to Bogie. "C'mon, let's go for a drive. I've got to clear my head."

As Bogie headed for the studio parking lot with the director, Ford didn't say a word but looked like doom and gloom had cascaded down around him. Bogie suspected that he and Tracy had been fired from the cast and had been replaced with two other actors.

"Get in," Ford commanded when they reached his car. He drove out of the studio and headed up into the hills. Back in those relatively traffic-free days, you could actually drive in Los Angeles.

As Ford floored the accelerator and took dangerous curves, almost missing them, Bogie was terrified, his eyes popping out almost as much as Joan Blondell's.

Ford kept his eyes glued on the curvy highway. Bogie wondered if Sheehan had fired him too. He even flashed on the possibility that he was playing a secondary role in a suicide run, with Ford planning to take the car, Bogie, and himself over the mountain. That would be like a real life version of *Thelma and Louise* decades before that film was eventually shot.

"For God's sake, man, look out!" Bogie shouted at him. He figured he didn't want to plunge to his death without putting up some protest.

Ford braked the car suddenly, coming to an abrupt stop at a belvedere. When Bogie got out of the car, he noticed that if Ford hadn't applied that brake in time he would indeed have destroyed the car. Ford had allowed himself only a foot of land. Bogie looked back at him. "I'd call that a close shave."

"I'm a bit of a daredevil when it comes to driving," Ford said.

"Could have fooled me," Bogie said, still shaken from the experience. He figured that it would be safer to walk back down that mountain than to get into the car again with Ford.

Ford got out of the car and stood next to a still-unnerved Bogie. "I always come up here to clear my head. It's the most beautiful view in Los Angeles."

This was the first time Bogie had looked at the view. It was indeed panoramic. The director had a keen eye for locale.

"I've got a cast and crew waiting back at Fox, but no script," Ford said.

"But I've read the script," Bogie said.

"It's been junked," Ford said, sucking in the fresh morning air. "Fox has decided that we can't compete with *The Big House*. I've been ordered to turn our film into a prison comedy."

"That's a novel idea," Bogie said.

"Get this," Ford said. "I start shooting tomorrow morning."

"Without a script?" Bogie asked, dumbfounded. Bogie was years away from facing the same experience on the set of *Casablanca*. As a Broadway stage actor, he didn't understand how a director could start shooting a film without a script.

"I'll stay up late every night and come into the studio with enough pages written to shoot for the day," Ford said. "The God damn film is only ninety minutes long. I can do it. You'll see."

"From what I've read, it's a pretty grim story to turn into a comedy," Bogie said.

"In its present shape, it's a piece of junk," Ford said, "but I can convert it into a convict comedy. Slapstick and sentiment, that's the way to go. Instead of hardened criminals, you guys can just be naughty boys. It'll be artlessly disarming."

Bogie wasn't convinced.

"Right now I'm writing a scene in my head," Ford said. "In the new version some prisoners stage a theatrical production for the chain gang. In this all-male cast, some of the prisoners can dress in drag. I'll get some discarded gowns from Mae West. Right now I can see Tracy and that actor, Warren Hymer—or is it Hymen?—dressing up like women. They'll make a break for it dressed like gals.

158

Run off to New England to thwart the evil villain's plan. When that mission is accomplished, they'll voluntarily come back to prison and turn themselves in, in time to win the annual baseball game."

"Sounds like a laugh riot," Bogie said.

"Let's go for it," Ford said. "But first I've got to ask you a question. Do you have a pair of balls on you?"

"I'd call them that," Bogie said, "although I'm sure there are a lot of guys in Hollywood with a bigger pair."

"What I mean is, do you like to fuck women?" Ford said. "Most of those Broadway sissies they send over from New York, guys like Kenneth MacKenna, had rather water the pansies in their garden than fuck women."

"I do my share of fucking," Bogie said. "Maybe more than most men."

"I'm glad to hear it," Ford said. "I'm taking you to Louise's. It's the best little whorehouse in the West. All the Hollywood stars go there. Louise has her pick of the most beautiful women in America. All the cute little milkmaids who get off the train here wanting to be stars end up as hookers, and the best of them end up with Louise."

"I could always use a good piece of ass," Bogie said.

"Get in the car," Ford said. "We're off."

Committing his life into Ford's hands once again, Bogie reluctantly got in. Ford drove even worse and more recklessly down the mountain than he did going up it. But, finally, they arrived alive at Louise's, a surprisingly elegant bordello.

Louise appeared to be over fifty but it was obvious that she'd been a beauty in her day. She kissed Ford on the mouth. "John and I go way back," she said. "He's one cowboy who sure knows how to take care of a lady." She paused. "If memory serves."

"Meet Humphrey Bogart," Ford said. "He's an actor out of New York. Who knows? He might become one of your best customers."

"I hope so," she said, looking Bogie up and down. "I'd take you on for free."

"He wants something young and cute today, dearie," Ford interjected.

"Maybe some other time," Bogie said, kissing the aging madam on the cheek.

"Okay, boys," she said. "I hope you like blondes, though. Last night I had a large group of clients from Argentina. Those horny bastards wanted only blondes. I had to order every gal in my joint to dye her hair both on top and down below."

"Blondes will be just fine," Ford said.

Within thirty minutes, Bogie found himself entering a small cubicle of a room. It was dimly lit. But there was enough illumination to accentuate the curves of a very voluptuous blonde lying nude on the bed, wearing only a pair of black stockings and emerald-green high heels. "Come on in, good looking, and lock the door."

"I think I've died and gone to heaven," Bogie said, feasting his eyes on her luscious body.

She introduced herself as Dawn Night.

"That sounds like a real good name," he said, as he unbuckled his trousers.

After he'd fucked her once, she begged him to do it again. Over some pillow talk, she became confidential. She nibbled at his ear, darting her tongue out so deep he felt that she wanted a taste of his brain. "My name is not really Dawn Night," she confessed. "I just made that one up. I'm keeping my real name a secret for screen billing. I'm going to become the biggest female star ever to set foot in Hollywood."

He'd certainly heard that line a lot from his previous encounters with chorus gals, except in New York the women always said "Broadway" instead of "Hollywood."

He kissed her as his fingers traveled south to fondle her breasts before going "deep south" to see if she was ready for his second attack. She was one beautiful, sexy girl, and he was flattered that she wanted him to fuck her again.

"The second one is on the house," she said. "I like your technique. Most men Louise sends up here don't do anything for me. I endure it—that's all."

Bogie took his mouth off her right nipple long enough to ask. "What's your real name? I won't tell. I just want to know. That way, when I see your name up on the marquee, I'll know to go in to see your picture."

"Okay." She giggled again. "If you promise not to tell."

"Trust me, I won't tell."

"Not so fast," she said. "Are you sure I can trust you? I mean, you're an actor and everything."

"Sure I know how to keep my lip zipped," Bogie said. "I sorta dig you, and I'd like to see you again."

"But not in this place. I won't be working here much longer. I've appeared on Broadway. I'm just picking up some quick cash. I'm not really a whore."

"Coming from some other gal I'd doubt that. But I believe you."

"I've already made a film for Tiffany," she said. "It was just a small part and I went unbilled. But I've got this great friend. She's an actress and she's gonna be real big. She's helping me break into Hollywood."

"What's your friend's name?" he asked. "Maybe I've heard of her."

"Joan Blondell."

He was startled but said nothing, masking his shock.

"Only the other day, Mervyn LeRoy was in here fucking me," she said. "You know, the director? He's promised to put me in a big gangster film. He said it's going to be the biggest film of the year. It's going to star Edward G. Robinson, and it's going to be called *Little Caesar*. Robinson is going to play Rico Bandello, a two-bit hoodlum. Even if he is a star, you can have Robinson. When LeRoy casts me in the movie, I'm going to chase after the co-star. That handsome hunk, Doug Fairbanks Jr., is going to play Tony Massara, Rico's best friend. Before the filming is over, I'm going to take Doug boy away from that whore, Joan Crawford."

"I think a lot of women—maybe a lot of men, too—would like to take that stud away from Crawford. Now tell me your name."

160

"Glenda Farrell," she blurted out. "Remember that name. Me and you will no doubt appear in some pictures together. You see, I'm going to become Queen of Warner Brothers."

As Bogie hardened and plowed into the future movie star Glenda Farrell, it was inconceivable to him that this would become one of his many fucks with her, a liaison that would stretch across the decade.

On that afternoon in a Los Angeles bordello, he was more interested in getting off the second time that he was in listening to a beautiful young girl's ambitions of stardom.

It was the beginning of a beautiful friendship.

If Glenda Farrell never became the actual Queen of Warner Brothers, she certainly became one of the queens. For years to come, Bogie and Farrell would laugh over their first meeting at Louise's—that is, before they headed for the sack on countless other occasions.

An hour later Bogie bid Farrell good-bye. She gave him her private telephone number. Before leaving, he'd confessed to her that he was also balling Joan Blondell.

"That's okay," Farrell said. "If a guy is real good like you are, me and Joanie often trade him with each other. A gal can't get too much of a good thing in this rotten town."

When Louise checked him out, she told him that Ford had already gone back to the studio to hole up and knock out a new script before dawn broke.

He didn't want to go back to his apartment right away, and he wandered alone on the streets of downtown Los Angeles, having some ham and eggs at a grill, but mostly booze, which seemed cheaper and easier to get here than it was in New York.

It was late when he took a taxi back to his apartment. He didn't remember the time. As he climbed the stairs, he heard a loud rapping and pounding on the door to Kenneth's apartment.

"Doug!" the woman shouted, "I know you're in there. Open the God damn door. You bastard." She pounded harder.

As he reached the top of the steps, he said, "Can I help you, lady? Kenneth's my friend. Maybe he's out."

"My husband is in there," she said, not bothering to turn around. "If he doesn't open that door, I'll divorce him."

When she finally turned around, he recognized the stunning profile. Glenda Farrell might be a cutie-pie, but this was a regal Hollywood queen.

"Hey, I know you," she said. "You're the actor that Fox brought out from New York. Humphrey Bogart."

"And you…" he said. "You're Joan Crawford."

Chapter Six

"My life was going just great, Bogart, until you brought your scarred lip, your lisp, and your faggot friend, MacKenna, to Hollywood," she said. In one gulp and with barely controlled ferocity, Joan Crawford downed the whiskey he'd poured for her once he'd invited her inside his apartment. "Haven't they heard of vodka in New York?"

"Lady, I don't touch the stuff," he said. "I invited you in because I respect you as a fellow performer—not for a cozy chitchat. I also didn't want you causing trouble for Kenneth and disturbing the neighbors."

"I've got a bone to pick with you," she said in a voice soon to become internationally famous. "Even if my husband weren't next door fucking your buddy in the ass, I was going to hunt you down."

"I made it easy for you," he said, pouring her another whiskey from his rapidly diminishing bottle.

"Did you tell Doug that I made stag movies shown at Texas Guinan's club?"

He hesitated a long moment. "So I did, a slip of the tongue perhaps. No one ever accused me of being discreet."

"For your information, I have never—get that, Bogart, *never*—made a stag movie. I don't know who you saw on the screen in Texas Guinan's club. It wasn't Lucille Fay LeSueur. Nor was it another name I've been credited as, Billie Cassin, and, above all, I assure you it wasn't Joan Crawford."

"It sure did look like you," he said. "Of course, that was before you went on that protein diet so talked about in the press and slimmed down. Texas Guinan claims it was you."

"Texas Guinan is a dyke who hit on me all the time," Crawford said. "She's also a bootlegger, a whore, and a liar. So much for citing Texas Guinan as your reliable witness."

"Then I'm truly sorry for slandering you," he said.

"Dear, gallant Doug—through lawyers—tried to buy up those blue movies in New York, but something went wrong. If anything, word that Fairbanks was trying to buy up the films only brought more attention to them. Some fart sent a copy to Louis B. Mayer. He's seen that stag film. I don't know what his reaction was, but I think I'm all but finished at Metro. I was going to become the queen of MGM."

"What can I say?" he asked. "If I contributed in any way to this, I feel really bad. Me and my big mouth."

She'd obviously been drinking heavily before arriving at his apartment building. He wanted to ease her out but she seemed determined to stay. She reached into a large purse she carried and removed a flask. "Make yourself useful. Bring me a clean glass."

He went to the kitchen and returned with a glass, which he handed to her. She held it up for inspection. "Don't you believe in washing glasses?" She got up from the sofa and headed toward the kitchen where he heard her washing the glass. That procedure seemed to go on forever.

Back in the living room, she poured a healthy dose of vodka into the glass and belted some of it down straight. "They call Doug and me the fairytale couple. Ain't that one for the history books?"

"At least you make nice photographs together," he said. "Your romance has even dimmed public interest in Garbo and John Gilbert."

"I know," she said. "It's all a sham. Doug is out there fucking every woman in Hollywood. He's a real pervert. Fucking men on the side too. I think the only reason he's fucking MacKenna is that everybody in Hollywood claims Doug and MacKenna look so much alike. I'm not Sigmund Freud, but it sure sounds like narcissism to me, at least on Doug's part."

"Even if they had let you in next door, what could you have done?"

"Maybe get some evidence I could use in my divorce," she said. "I plan to take Douglas Fairbanks Sr. and Mary Pickford for a bundle in my settlement. They think they've got the goods on me. Well, I've got plenty on Doug boy. I want him to pay and pay again even if he has to borrow the dough from Pickford herself. That drunken nympho has millions she hasn't even counted yet. What I've learned at Pickfair would fill a book. If Mayer blacklists me in Hollywood, I'll write that fucking book too. I know too much."

"You're playing with fire, woman," he warned her.

"I can handle myself. I've given up so much for my Dodo."

"Who's Dodo?" he asked. "An extinct bird?"

"Hell, no," she said. "That was my nickname for him back when me and him were in love. We made up our own language. Opi lopove yopou—crap like that. There's no more love, baby. I even gave up chewing gum for him, and my raucous laughter too. And thanks to him, I even dance the Charleston with less pizzazz. And I dress better."

"Again, I'm real sorry if things seem to be unraveling for you." he said. "in your marriage and your career. If some stupid, drunk remark I made to Fairbanks over a soggy lunch had anything to do with it, then I sincerely regret it."

"Sincerely regret," she said, mocking his words. "Even with your faggoty lisp, that's grand talk. You must have learned it in some Ivy League college in New York. I heard you came from rich parents, unlike me."

"Something like that," he said.

As she talked and drank more, a change came over her. He feared at first she was demented. Up to now, he'd never met a woman this fiercely determined and ambitious. The vodka seemed to give her a confidence she hadn't had earlier in

164

the evening when it appeared that her world was collapsing.

"Get this, Bogart," she said. "I'll survive that blue movie scandal, even the divorce. I'll end up with the big bucks. I've fallen in love too. I've already found my next husband. He's crazy about me. The guy is Clark Gable."

"I've heard of him."

"The whole world is going to hear of him," she predicted. "He's gonna become the king of Hollywood. And I, Miss Joan Crawford, is gonna become his queen." She downed more vodka and seemed entranced by the sound of her own voice. "You heard it first from me, 'the king and queen of Hollywood.'"

"I wish you luck," he said. "It's a big dream."

"A dream is a mere road map to reality," she said. "You watch and see. A hundred years from now the world will still be talking and writing about Joan Crawford and Clark Gable—note the billing—when Humphrey Bogart will be a footnote in film history, if that."

"I'm not dust yet, bitch," he said angrily. "There's a lot of life in this old New York boy."

"Prove it!" she commanded.

"What do you mean?" he asked, growing a bit jittery in her presence and feeling that she might be some kind of nut.

She stood up and yanked off her dress, slipping off her undergarments before standing nude in front of him to be inspected. "Like what you see?"

"You're a hell of a good-looking woman," he said, appraising her from head to toe. With the loss of weight, she looked far more alluring and appealing than she had in that stag movie. "You don't have all that much pubic hair, and I like that. I don't like women who have vaginal hair all the way up to their navel and half way down their legs."

"Okay, buster," she said, staring defiantly at him. "Take me into your bedroom and fuck my brains out."

***

That night would mark his only sexual encounter with Joan Crawford, although he would know her casually for years. She never married Clark Gable, yet they did become the king and a queen of Hollywood.

Regardless of what he really thought, Louis B. Mayer claimed that it was definitely not Joan Crawford in that movie shipped to him from New York. Her career at MGM would last until her pictures started losing money and Mayer pointed the way to the gate for a star labeled as "box office poison."

Joan Crawford would go on to resurrect herself many times, rising from the grave more times than Jesus Christ Superstar. Nothing could do her in except cancer, to which she succumbed on May 10, 1977 in New York. She died alone, the only silent witness in her bedroom being that of a photograph of her lady love, Barbara Stanwyck, witnessing the sad event.

Having survived the stag movie scandal, Crawford telephoned Bogart a few days later. "I'm doing just fine," she said. "You're not a bad fuck but don't get your hopes up. It was a one-night stand. However, it's payback time for that shitty story you told my husband."

"What's happening here?"

"You'll find out," she said. "No one double-crosses Joan Crawford and gets away with it."

Before the end of the week, he learned how poisonous she could be. Crawford spread the word around Hollywood that it wasn't Kenneth MacKenna sleeping with her husband, but that "other New York stage actor," Humphrey Bogart.

***

On the set of *Up the River* that morning, Bogie sat having bitter black coffee with his co-star, Claire Luce. Even though she was Tracy's temporary mistress, Bogie was plotting to see if he could take Luce away from his newly acquired friend. It was the beginning of a one-upmanship that would last until Bogie's death.

In the film, Luce played "Judy," an innocent young girl who was framed by a crooked stock salesman and sent "Up the River."

Many chroniclers of Bogie's life have confused Claire Luce with Clare Boothe Luce, (1903-87), the talented, wealthy, beautiful, and controversial New Yorker, best remembered as a congresswoman (1942-46) and playwright who penned *The Women*. She was the first female American ambassador when Dwight Eisenhower appointed her to her post in Italy in 1952. The "Luce" was added to her name when she married magazine tycoon, Henry R. Luce, of *Time-Life-Fortune*.

A much more modest achiever, Claire Luce, the actress sitting across from Bogie, launched herself as a cigarette girl in Rochester, New York, and worked her way to Broadway as a chorus girl. A Denishawn dancer, she ended up having an affair with Flo Ziegfeld who cast her in *The Follies of 1927*.

As they sat idly by, Luce told Bogie that she'd fallen madly in love with Tracy and that he had promised to divorce his wife and marry her. Even though Bogie had just launched his friendship with the actor, he suspected that Tracy had used the same line on many a chorus gal.

Earlier that morning, Bogie had eaten some ham and eggs with the handsome young co-star of the picture, Warren Hymer, the son of playwright John B. Hymer and the actress Eleanor Kent. This was already Hymer's tenth film, even though he'd been working in Hollywood only since he'd first appeared in the 1929 film, *Speakeasy*.

Ford had cast him as a supporting player in *Men Without Women*. Bogie suspected that Hymer was another one of those bisexuals. Hymer didn't admit to having had an affair with the star of the film, Bogie's close friend, Kenneth MacKenna, but Bogie felt that he could read between the lines in Hymer's talk

166

and that the young New York actor knew the exact measurements of Kenneth's dick.

"Spence is a love 'em or leave 'em type," Hymer said. "As soon as this film is wrapped, Luce won't be able to get that one on the phone. After all, *I should know.*"

Bogie paused for a moment, feeling that he didn't understand exactly what Hymer was suggesting. "Why should you know?"

"Oh, nothing," Hymer said. "All my life I've been known for blurting out stupid remarks that mean nothing. Ask your friend Kenneth if you need verification of that."

By Hollywood standards, Bogie felt that he was still naïve. Was Hymer suggesting that he'd had an affair with Tracy before Claire Luce came onto the scene. There was just a touch of jealousy when Hymer was around Luce.

"After Tracy does his philandering, it's back to mama," Hymer said.

From where he sat talking to Luce, Bogie spotted John Ford striding onto the set. Bogie would later claim that John Wayne learned his distinctive walk on screen by imitating John Ford.

Ford looked angry and hung over, as he'd been up all night trying to turn "this fucker of a prison drama into a God damn comedy."

Both Bogie and Luce were relieved to learn that they wouldn't have to face Ford's ire that day. Ford's assistant, Tom Hubbard, had told them that they weren't scheduled to go on camera. Nevertheless, Hubbard said that they had to appear at the Fox studio early every morning during the entire shoot in case Ford decided to use them.

"As long as I get paid," Bogie said.

After a brief conference with Ford, Hubbard approached Bogie and Luce with a concerned look on his face. Always the curious one, Bogie wanted to know what was the matter. Hubbard called Bogie aside, as he didn't want to speak in front of Luce.

"The first scene involves Tracy," Hubbard said, once he was out of earshot of Luce. "He hasn't shown up this morning. We don't know where he lives. The front office has a phone number for him. The phone rings off the wall. Ford said that if Tracy doesn't show up on the set by three o'clock at the latest, he's casting Jimmy Cagney in the part. It seems that Cagney is free for two weeks and can play the role."

Excusing himself from Hubbard, Bogie cornered Warren Hymer again. He knew that the actor had finished shooting *Sinners' Holiday* at Warners with Cagney and Blondell. Hymer confirmed that Cagney had told him that he wasn't set to shoot *Doorway to Hell*, co-starring Lew Ayres, for another month. "If Warners would agree to lend him out, I bet Cagney would go for it."

"God damn it," Bogie said. "This is Spence's first starring role in a feature film. If he fucks this up, he's finished in Hollywood. Word will spread like wildfire. I know he drinks a lot."

"Would you believe that if the Pacific Ocean were alcohol, Spence would have it drained dry in a weekend? I should know."

Again, Bogie felt that Hymer was suggesting that he knew Tracy's habits intimately. "Why would you know that? You hang out a lot with Spence at night?"

"Oh, nothing," Hymer said. "Me and my big mouth. Pay no attention to half of what I say."

"Where do you think he might have gone?" Bogie asked.

"He told me yesterday that he was going to check out the best whorehouse in Hollywood," Hymer said.

"That could only be Louise's," Bogie said. "Since Ford doesn't need me this morning, I'm going to look for Spence before Fox fires him."

When Luce saw him leaving the set, she ran after him, catching up with him. She was breathless. In that golden glow of a mid-Los Angeles morning, Luce looked more enticing to him than any woman he'd ever known. He wanted to run away somewhere with her instead of chasing after Tracy.

Sanity returned to him, although for years to come he would remember that young vision of her standing on the Fox set filled with anxiety. She just seemed to be reaching out for some strong man to protect her. Right on the spot, Bogie decided he wasn't going to be that man. After all, he could call Barbara Stanwyck, Joan Blondell, and maybe "Dawn Night" a.k.a. Glenda Farrell, if he needed a woman. There were just so many women a man could handle.

Bogie didn't want to get a reputation in Hollywood this early in the game as an actor who would fuck anything on the hoof that would open her legs for him. Leave that legend to John Barrymore.

He kissed Luce hard on the lips, as if tasting her breath, the freshest he'd ever known and so unlike Joan Crawford, who had a foul breath, the memory of which would linger in his mind for years.

Bogie would remember Claire Luce longer than the fickle public would. After leaving Tracy and him, she would enjoy brief acclaim as Fred Astaire's dancing partner in the stage musical, *The Gay Divorce*!

The Cole Porter number electrified audiences when Astaire and Luce danced "Night and Day," waltzing around the stage, "flying" over tables and chairs.

Luce's heart was broken when she learned that Ginger Rogers had been cast in her part in the film version, retitled *The Gay Divorcée*.

Bogie was to encounter Luce only one more time and that was when she was appearing in the 1947 play, *Portrait in Black*, a drama. Her fury at Ginger Rogers had not waned. "That God damn bleached-out tramp," she told Bogie. "I'd like to yank her hair out by its black roots—probably gray roots. Had it not been for that uptight Republican fascist slut, Miss Rogers, Astaire and I would have been one of the biggest dancing teams of all time. I hear she's fucking little Miss Goodie-Goodie, Ronald Reagan, now."

Bogie smiled and tenderly kissed her cheek for old time's sake. "All of us

have to fuck somebody. I fucked Reagan myself on the set of *Dark Victory*."
He delivered the line with such sincerity that Luce believed him, a secret in the years ahead that she chose not to keep to herself.

***

At Louise's, the madam smiled when she saw Bogie. "Back so soon," she said. "I figured you'd become one of our regulars. Dawn Night won't be here until later, but we've got three other regular gals on duty. All blonde. All hot to trot."

"I'm not here for that," Bogie said. "I'm looking for one Spencer Tracy. I'm here to save his neck."

Like the good madam she was, Louise invited Bogie into her back office where he pleaded his case. He let her know that if John Ford fired Tracy from his first feature film, he'd be washed up in Hollywood. "I've got to find him, sober him up, get him to the set."

"Spence has visited us twice since he's come to Hollywood," Louise said, "and I'm sure he's going to become one of our best paying customers." She paused as if not wanting to reveal the next disclosure. "We've also arranged a special request or two for him."

"I don't know what that means," he said.

"And I don't expect you ever will," she said. "Special requests are arrangements we make off the premises. You know, when a customer wants something other than one of our regular gals. After all, this is Hollywood, and we've got to cater to all tastes. We turn down no customer. I'll say no more."

"Over at Fox they don't even know where Spence is living. They have only a phone number for him."

"He's got a room at the Hollywood Plaza Hotel," she said.

"I know where that is," he said. "I'll get over there right away."

"Fine," she said, reaching for his hand. "I hope to see you in here a lot, Bogie boy. Dawn said you're good in bed."

"Let's call her Glenda."

She looked shocked. "She must have liked you a lot if she told you her real name. She's saving that for the marquee."

"I know." He leaned over and kissed her on the cheek. "You've been real nice, and I'll see you soon. You may have saved an actor's film career."

Back in those days of lax security, all one had to do was arrive at the hotel reception desk, ask for a patron's room number, take the elevator upstairs, and knock on the door. That is exactly what Bogie did when he arrived in the lobby of the Hollywood Plaza.

At room 401, Bogie pounded on the door. At first there was no answer. He pounded again. Finally, the door was opened just a bit as it was still bolted to a link chain.

"I'm Humphrey Bogart," he said. "I've got to get in touch with Spencer Tracy. I've come over from Fox."

Although he couldn't see too well, it sounded like a young man behind the door. "Oh," he said. "I've heard of you. You're co-starring with Spence in his movie."

"Let me in," Bogie demanded in his most forceful voice.

"I guess it's okay," the young man said.

"I'm his friend," Bogie said. "Here to help him."

The young man unfastened the latch and let Bogie into the dark room. The light switch came on. Before Bogie stood one of the most beautiful young men he'd ever seen in his life. He was definitely movie star material himself. He wore only a pair of white boxer shorts, revealing his trim athletic build. He looked like the kind of guy that Charles Farrell would chase all the way down Hollywood Boulevard. For this prize Kenneth MacKenna would dump Douglas Fairbanks Jr.

"I'm Lew Ayres," the semi-nude man said. Suddenly, Bogie realized who this boyishly handsome man was. He'd seen him on the screen in *The Kiss* with Greta Garbo. All Hollywood was talking about his success in the role of Paul Baumer in *All Quiet on the Western Front*, Lewis Milestone's World War I masterpiece based on Erich Maria Remarque's novel detailing the horrors of war and its devastating effect on fighting men.

There was talk that the part, his third appearance on camera, might win him the Academy Award for poignantly portraying a young schoolboy thrown into the frenzy of war. In the film he was supposed to be bewildered by his loss of innocence. Bogie wondered how innocent Ayres could possibly be after a night with Tracy.

Without knowing the details, the evidence against Tracy was enough to convict. His new friend was a bisexual. Like all the great "womanizers" of Hollywood that Bogie knew or would know in the future, from George Raft to Errol Flynn, these Romeos seemed to go for boys on the side. Perhaps it added the spice and variety they needed. Maybe they didn't like women that much in the first place and continued to crawl into one bed after another, never finding one woman who could satisfy them. Bogie's face blanched white, as he came to realize he might be describing himself.

Ayres headed across the suite's living room and put on his trousers and an undershirt. Barefoot, he came back over to Bogie. "Spence was doing fine last night," he said, "but as the night wore on, he drank more and more. He's in the bedroom there sprawled out totally drunk. I've been unable to get him up to go to work. I know he's due on Ford's set."

Bogie crossed the living room and looked into the small, almost alcove-like bedroom. There with the morning light streaming in, Spence lay sprawled nude near the edge of the bed, his mouth open. He was breathing heavily and his head fell over the edge of the mattress and seemed to hang in midair.

"Lew, my good man," Bogie said, turning around to confront Ayres. "Call room service for a big pot of strong black coffee. This here movie star, Mr. Spencer Tracy, and his juvenile lead are heading for the shower. I'm going to wake this drunken sod up if it kills me."

"You think you can?" a hesitant Ayres asked. "I've tried everything already."

"It won't be just the cold shower and the bitter black coffee," Bogie said. "My father's a doctor in New York. I drink a lot myself, and I've stumbled in at five o'clock in the morning when I was due somewhere at eight-thirty. Dad has these pills."

"What kind of pills?" Ayres asked.

"You know I'm not sure they have a name, and I have no idea what's in them. All I know is that when I force Spence here to swallow two of these little mother-fuckers, we're going to have him bouncing on John Ford's set with more energy than those two dancing fools, George Raft and Jimmy Cagney, combined."

When Bogie got to his dressing room, he spotted Ford's assistant walking toward him. "The front office has got another script for you," Hubbard said. "You're to start work as soon as Ford is finished with you."

"What picture?" Bogie asked.

"The thing is called *Body and Soul.*"

"Who's got the lead?" Bogie asked. "And what's my billing?"

"You'll get fourth billing," Hubbard said. "The star is Charles Farrell."

"Oh, God, no!" Bogie said. "I'll have that lovesick fool chasing after me all day long."

"You could do worse," Hubbard said, winking at him. "Charlie baby does give the best blow-jobs in Hollywood." He winked again. "I should know." He turned and walked away.

***

Long before *Vanity Fair* "outed" Spencer Tracy in the post-millennium, and years before his homosexual dalliances became privately known to the likes of such gossip mavens as Hedda Hopper and Louella Parsons, Bogie was privy to his close friend's darkest secrets.

After the first day's shoot of *Up the River*, Tracy and Ayres invited Bogie to their suite for drinks, to be followed by dinner. From the first, Bogie took an enlightened view about their relationship. He didn't exactly encourage it but he didn't condemn it either. "I say if it feels good, go for it," Bogie told both men as he downed some of their whiskey. "It's no one's God damn business but your own."

"But there's the matter of my faith, my beliefs," Ayres protested. "I don't even like to look myself in the mirror in the morning."

"That's a crock of ...." Bogie hesitated, searching for a word. He detested the use of the word "shit." "That's bull. Frankly, you guys are no different from anybody else I've met in Hollywood. Take myself, for instance. Nobody likes a broad better than I do. I've even had thoughts about taking Claire Luce from you." He smiled at Tracy to indicate he wasn't really serious. "But I've done some weird stuff on occasion. Name an actor on Broadway or in Hollywood who hasn't. The latest gossip from New York is that Milton Berle, who apparently has a foot-long hot dog, sometimes shacks up with Bob Hope."

Tracy leaned back, his face and demeanor radiating calm in spite of any inner turmoil. "Bogie, unless you were born Catholic, unless you seriously wanted to be a priest, you can't understand Catholic guilt."

"Whatever the fuck that is," Bogie said.

"I understand it," the youthful Ayres chimed in. "It's our faith that drew me to Spence. We actually met in church, not some bar."

Bogie looked at Ayres with that keen eye he used to appraise someone he was meeting for the first time. "I must say, Spence old boy, you sure know how to pick 'em. Lew here is prettier than most gals I know. Put some lipstick on him and a dress and I'd go for him myself."

"All of this seems like one big joke to you," Ayres said, confronting him.

Bogie was trying to ease the tension in the room, but was failing miserably.

There was a sudden knock on the door, and Tracy was summoned downstairs by a bellhop to sign some papers that had arrived for him in the lobby. He excused himself politely and headed down.

"I didn't mean to get your feathers ruffled," Bogie said. "But I wish you guys would lighten up. I'm just trying to be a supportive friend to the both of you."

Although Bogie's friendship with Tracy would remain steadfast, even when they were fighting over a potential screen billing in a co-starring venture that never happened, or when they were up for the same coveted role, their love for each other never wavered, jealousy or not.

On that night beginning in the Hollywood Plaza Hotel and throughout much of the Thirties, whenever he saw Ayres, Bogie never understood the man. Sometimes to friends like James Stewart, Bogie would say, "Here comes the Holy Father," whenever he saw Ayres approaching.

On the day of their first meeting, Bogie did come to realize what a deeply spiritual man Ayres was. Whenever he wasn't reading film scripts, he was studying and writing about religion. Later in his life he would produce, direct, and write a feature-length documentary on religion based on his own writings.

Bogie felt empathy for Ayres, but as time went by, he was saddened that Ayres never matched the success and acclaim he received for *All Quiet on the Western Front*. In the years ahead he became a leading man in B films, scoring great success as Dr. Kildare, an idealist young doctor with whom he'd be identified for the rest of his life. Ayres would eventually marry actress Lola Lane, one of the famous Lane sisters that included Priscilla and Rosemary. In time, in one of the ironies of Hollywood's "musical beds," Bogie himself would not only have an affair with Ayres' wife, Lola, but also her sister, Priscilla. Somehow, Rosemary would manage to elude him. To Bogie's astonishment, Ayres would even go on to take Ginger Rogers as his wife from 1934 to 1941.

Other than *All Quiet on the Western Front,* Ayre's only other real breakthrough role came in *Holiday* in 1938 where he almost stole the show from Katharine Hepburn and Cary Grant. Ayres played Hepburn's sweet-tempered but drunk brother.

Hepburn, of course, became Tracy's longtime companion, since he refused to divorce his wife. When she was starring in *Holiday*, there is no evidence that she ever knew of Tracy's long link with Ayres. Her only statement on the subject came in 2001 when the by then aging and feeble star denied the allegations in *Vanity Fair* and informed the press that "Spencer Tracy was not a homosexual," as if she were privy to all his darkest secrets, which she wasn't.

Bogie knew many of the secrets about Tracy that Hepburn didn't, but even he would admit to friends, "I love him, but I don't really know him." Bogie also always felt that whenever the probing got too deep, Tracy would merely lower the window shades and "The End" would flash on the screen, as it did in countless movies when the hero took the heroine to bed for the fadeout scene.

Over a five-dollar dinner that night in Hollywood, Tracy in front of Ayres gave Bogie more insight into the privacy of his mind than he would at any other time in his life.

The actor related in agonizing detail his life as an altar boy in Milwaukee. He claimed that after dismissing the other altar boys, Father James Donovan would take him into his back office. For a period of time lasting for more than two years, the priest would remove Tracy's penis and fellate him. Tracy told Bogie and Ayres that at no time during the months of their relationship did Donovan ever remove his own penis. "Having a priest do that to you can really fuck up the head of a young kid," Tracy said. "Donovan told me that what we were doing was a command from God. For a long time I believed him. That priest fucked up my head about sex from an early age."

At the end of the dinner, a drunken Tracy tried to end the evening on a lighter note. He said that, "If I fail in Hollywood, my Dad has offered to take me into his trucking firm in Milwaukee. He's going to call it Tracy & Sons. If you guys bomb on the screen, know that you've always got a job waiting for you driving trucks around Wisconsin."

Bogie stood on the sidewalk watching Ayres leave with Tracy, heading back to their hotel suite and "God only knows what," as he would later tell Kenneth.

Seeing the two lovers, Ayres and Tracy, walk away into the night, made Bogie feel lonelier than he'd ever felt since arriving in Hollywood. His wife, Mary, had not written once.

He went inside a restaurant and called first Barbara Stanwyck, then Joan Blondell. Neither woman was in for the evening. Since it was only ten o'clock, he called Kenneth's apartment and was surprised when Kay Francis picked up the phone. Bogie figured that Douglas Fairbanks Jr. was spending the night with Joan Crawford. Francis told him that she and Kenneth were exhausted and planned to "spend a quiet evening by the fire," even though he knew there was no fireplace in the apartment.

He was aware that his relationships with Stanwyck and Blondell had no real future but might be a "some time thing." He was ripe and ready for another woman to enter his life, someone with whom he could get involved, even for only a short time. He wasn't looking for any long-time relationships. After two unsuccessful marriages, he'd had enough commitment. He wanted someone he could have fun with and, lest he forget, fuck.

It was two weeks later on the set of his next picture for Fox, *Body and Soul*, that the director, Alfred Santell, introduced him to the film's two leading ladies, each of them gorgeous, charming, and at least in his opinion, available.

They were Elissa Landi and Myrna Loy.

***

He didn't know which woman to look at first: the screen vamp Myrna Loy or the scion of the Habsburg Empire, Elissa Landi. The problem was solved for him, when Santell, the director, called Loy to the set for a scene with the picture's star, Charles Farrell. Bogie hoped that Farrell would remember some of his speech training, but seriously doubted if he would.

Landi, in Loy's absence, wanted to discuss the characters they'd be playing, Bogie was struck by her regal bearing, cultured voice, and aristocratic beauty.

Rumor had it that Landi was the secret granddaughter of "Sissi," or the Empress Elizabeth of Austria, the beautiful but strong-willed Bavarian-born wife of Franz Josef, the final monarch of the Habsburg dynasty, who presided over the twilight of the Austro-Hungarian empire. On September 10, 1898, shortly before noon, the sixty-year-old empress was stabbed with a file carried by Luigi Lucheni, a twenty-four-year-old Italian anarchist who considered her the embodiment of a monarchic order he despised. Taken back to her hotel, she died a few minutes later.

The incident occurred on a promenade beside Lake Geneva, as she was boarding a steamship for Montreux. Because she was so tightly corseted, she was not immediately aware of how seriously she'd been wounded. Her last words, just before she fainted and died, were, "What happened to me?"

"How should you be addressed?" Bogie asked, being a little provocative with Landi because he didn't believe in aristocratic titles.

Landi took him seriously. "Countess would be fine." As he was to learn later, the actress wasn't a real countess. She'd just assumed the title from her mother's second marriage to an Italian nobleman, Count Carlo Zanardi-Landi.

Known for having made a number of British silent films, Landi came to the attention of Fox when she'd appeared on Broadway in *A Farewell to Arms*.

"Just between you and me, I think this flicker we're making is nothing but an old-fashioned hack melodrama," Landi said. In addition to being an actress, Landi was also an acute critic and would go on to write several novels. Together, they tried to make sense out of some dumb, ill-conceived plot by Jules Furthman based on an unproduced and unpublished play called *Squadron.*

After reading the script, another tiresome piece about "The Great War," Bogie told Landi, "At least I know why the play was never staged."

"As I read it, I'm thought to be this German spy named Pom-Pom, but it turns out that Myrna is the real German spy."

"It doesn't really matter," he said. "I understand that Fox is going to open it with a Mickey Mouse cartoon, a Fox Movietone, even a Hearst Metrotone newsreel, and a Mickey Mouse stage act. After all that, no one will notice what a stinker it really is."

"In the script, you're married to me for only four days before sailing, always wearing your aviator uniform, to France, where you pursue other women," Landi said. "If you were married to me in real life, you'd get such a workout you'd have no time for other women."

"Promises, promises," he said. "Since we're married—it says so right here in the script—I guess that gives me conjugal rights."

"Perhaps," she said enigmatically. "You're rather cute." Getting up, she kissed him and excused herself, heading for her dressing room.

Later, when Charles Farrell invited Bogie to lunch in the Fox commissary, Bogie accepted reluctantly and only because the actor was the star of the picture. Bogie fully anticipated more homosexual advances from Farrell. To Bogie's surprise, Farrell made no reference to that time with Bogie on the boat. He had seemingly forgotten that they had had a sexual encounter, drunken or not.

He was eager to share news of "the love of my life." He'd fallen for George O'Brien. From both directors, Raoul Walsh and John Ford, Bogie had been hearing rhapsodic melodies about what a great screen hero George O'Brien was, and Bogie himself had seen O'Brien in that epic western, *The Iron Horse*, in 1924, directed by Ford.

Fans had dubbed George O'Brien "The Chest," and he'd been heavyweight boxing champion of the Pacific Fleet during World War I. Like Farrell himself, O'Brien had been an early Hollywood male pinup. O'Brien was rumored to have had an affair with Rudolph Valentino in 1922 during the filming of *Moran of the Lady Letty*.

Farrell had first been introduced to O'Brien on the Fox lot where O'Brien was appearing in *A Rough Romance*, with Helen Chandler. Silent screen heartthrob Antonio Moreno shared third billing in that flick. When O'Brien couldn't capture the devotion of a handsome extra with a minor part, Duke Morrison (John Wayne), he'd gone for Antonio Moreno instead.

Farrell gleefully informed Bogie that he'd taken O'Brien from the clutches of that "Spanish queen," Moreno, and had captured O'Brien for himself. Or at least he thought he'd captured O'Brien's heart. Bogie was somewhat bored with another story of Hollywood musical chairs until Farrell started blasting Kenneth MacKenna and threatening to kill him.

"Fairbanks Jr. dumped him," Farrell said, "so Miss Kenneth goes for my George. I know for a fact they shacked up last night. They were seen checking into the Hollywood Plaza Hotel together. A double bed, no less."

"That's bull," Bogie said. "I happen to know that Kenneth was in the bed of Kay Francis last night."

"That's bull," Farrell said. "Francis was having a three-way last night with Mae Clarke and Stanwyck."

Bogie sighed and lit a cigarette. He felt that Farrell was a far more informed gossip columnist than Louella Parsons. "Kenneth is my friend."

"If he doesn't sign a pledge in blood that he's going to keep his pansy hands off O'Brien, I swear I'll bring in two guys from Tijuana," Farrell said. "For five-hundred dollars I can have your lover boy, MacKenna, erased from all world maps, not to mention the screen."

"You sound like you're falling in love in a big way," Bogie said. "This O'Brien must be the cat's pajamas."

"His body was created by da Vinci in drag," Farrell said.

"I'll get to Kenneth right away, and tell him to drop Georgie boy at once, and that you mean business."

"What a friend you are," Farrell said. "Now give Charlie a kiss and be on your way."

As he was leaving Farrell's dressing room, Bogie spotted Elissa Landi coming toward him. "I was told I could find you here," she said. "At 7:30 tonight, I'm giving a dinner party. Black tie. There's been a last-minute cancellation from Chaplin. Please, please fill in for him. I have to have another man to make my dinner party work. Would you pick up Myrna Loy?"

"Sure," he said, wondering where he could come up with a tuxedo on such short notice. "I didn't have anything planned for tonight."

She gave him addresses and some instructions, then hurried off. He was a bit excited to be attending his first formal dinner party in Hollywood. He would like to have invited Blondell or Stanwyck, but Loy would do. At least this would be a chance for him to get to know Miss Loy. As an actress, Loy had not impressed him with her screen work to date.

He wanted to find Kenneth and warn him about Farrell's threats. Kenneth wasn't answering the phone at his apartment.

After renting a well-worn tux for three dollars on Hollywood Boulevard, Bogie drove back to his apartment house. When he came upstairs onto the landing he shared with Kenneth, he heard loud music coming from his friend's apartment. Bogie knocked on the door.

The door opened only slightly, as the chain was kept on.

"I'm Bogart," he said. "A friend of Kenneth's. Can I come in?"

176

"It's Bogart," a man's voice said. He heard Kenneth calling in the background for his friend to unbolt the door.

The door opened quickly, and Bogie went inside. There, wearing nothing but a ten-gallon hat, stood screen idol George O'Brien. At least Bogie could see first hand why Kenneth and Farrell were fighting over O'Brien.

His fans might call him "The Chest," but as Bogie could plainly see there was much more to George O'Brien than a chest.

***

As Bogie drove to pick up Myrna Loy to take her to Landi's formal dinner, he could only hope that peace and harmony would eventually prevail among George O'Brien, Charles Farrell, and Kenneth MacKenna. Homosexual catfights were foreign to him, and he didn't want to get mixed up in any such brawl.

Instead of thinking about his date for the evening, Bogie in his ill-fitting rented tux fantasized about all the big names who'd be at the Landi home. Farrell had told him, "Elissa's soirées attract all the cream. Mostly she invites Europeans, which leaves me out. I've hinted for an invitation several times. So far, nothing. I don't think Elissa considers me couth. People at Landi's parties, or so I hear, tend to talk about something other than movie-making."

Myrna Loy was beautifully dressed and waiting out on her front porch when Bogie pulled up at her house. She scanned the sky. "I think it's going to rain tonight."

"That wasn't the forecast," he said.

Noting an ominous cloud rising in the distance, she said, "We Montana belles don't need a radio forecast to tell us when a storm is coming."

He'd followed her career on the screen, including her appearance in the silent part of *The Jazz Singer*, although Al Jolson stole that film.

In her black velvet gown, she looked lovelier than she did in the movies where she was most often cast as Asian vamps. She was dressed with a high collar, although he suspected that most of the other women at the dinner would be in plunging *décolletage*.

Noting that he was observing her high-button neckline, she said. "I have to wear this. The other night at a party, Clark Gable and his wife, Ria, offered me a ride home. Clark walked me to my door. As I was fumbling for my key, he gave me a monkey bite. His teeth marks are still on me. Our director, Santell, was furious when he saw that I had been branded like a Montana cow. Naturally, my first appearance on screen called for me to appear in a low-cut gown."

"I hear that when Clark Gable walks into a room," Bogie said, "it isn't a question of if a woman will go to bed with him. It's a question of which one he'll choose for the night."

"Something like that," she said.

As he drove toward Landi's home, he said, "I'm real honored that you're

177

going out with me. If I can believe everything that Louella Parsons writes, I'll be part of a long lineup of distinguished beaux. Let me see. Rudolph Valentino, John Barrymore, Gary Cooper."

"I know all those men, of course, but there's no romance. Rudy actually discovered me and got me a screen test for his film, *Cobra*. I flunked miserably. His wife, Natacha Rambova, took pity on me and cast me in her film, *What Price Beauty?*, but that went nowhere."

He didn't know if she were talking about the ill-fated movie which flopped at the box office, or her ill-fated affair with Rambova, which for a few months was the talk of Hollywood. He decided for once not to be provocative and drop the subject of Rambova. "I heard that you and Cooper grew up on the same street together back in Helena."

"We did indeed."

"Surely you must have played doctor," he said.

"Not that," she said. "But I did sneak off with him one late afternoon into the cellar at our house. We didn't conduct any medical examination, however. We were looking for Mother's last jar of apple jelly."

As he drove and talked to her, he found that she was a witty, intelligent, and also beautiful woman. If anything, directors hid her true beauty on the screen with gaudy makeup, usually trying to turn her into an Oriental temptress.

"You look as American as blueberry pie," he said. "Why do they always make you Chinese?"

"Beats me," she said. "I'm just a Montana cowgal. Up against Anna May Wong in that flick, *The Crimson City*, I looked about as Chinese as Raggedy Ann. I've played Burmese, Chinese, a couple of Tijuana vamps, an islander from the South Pacific, and a hot-blooded Creole. The beat goes on. Darryl Zanuck just can't believe that I can play a straight part, and I don't know why."

He was warming to this gentle, wonderful woman. She was so unlike the ambition-crazed Crawford or Stanwyck, and without the pretensions of Kay Francis and her wardrobe. "I could be wrong," he said, "and I know it's none of my business. But you seem a little sad and lonely tonight. At least that's the way I feel. I'm married to Mary Philips. She's in New York doing God knows what to whom, and I'm out here on the coast wandering around at night, getting cast in one lousy movie after another."

"Don't worry," she said, most reassuringly. "Our day will come." She rolled down the window and breathed in the air. "I am a bit sad, and I guess I can tell you about it since you sensed it. I fell in love with an actor, and I know how foolish that was. It was when we were making *The Last of the Duanes*."

"Don't tell me," he said. "Let me guess. Surely not George O'Brien?"

"That's right. George unceremoniously dumped me. I don't know what other women he's taken up with."

Having just left O'Brien in the arms of Kenneth, Bogie bit his lip. He wasn't going to be the one to fill in Loy on the nocturnal activities of her erstwhile lover.

As he pulled into the driveway of Landi's home, he was amazed at the parade of big and expensive black cars. His battered vehicle looked pathetic. Loy seemed unconcerned with such trivia. She was not a woman of pretensions like Kay Francis.

In the golden light from Landi's porch, he was awed by Loy's copper-haired beauty and her delicate, porcelain-white skin. "Once we get inside that party, we'll probably have no more chance to talk," she said in her marvelous voice, which sounded like a hoarse flute. "But if you get lonely one night and want a sympathetic ear, I'm available. Just give me a call. I don't know what will come of our getting together, but I promise to serve you tea."

"Make it whiskey, and you've got yourself a deal," he said. Her sleek, sassy nose captured his attention. He'd never seen a nose like that, and he thought it was the cutest thing. Impulsively he leaned over and kissed her on the nose.

Little could he have known that in just a few short years, hordes of women across America would be going to the offices of plastic surgeons with pictures of the star, demanding that a "Myrna Loy nose" be carved for them as well.

***

The party was in full swing when Bogie escorted Myrna Loy into the foyer where Landi was waiting to give each of them a kiss on their lips and welcome them to her home. She wore a stunning example of Parisian haute couture, an emerald-colored silk gown with a large emerald necklace, no doubt looted from the royal treasury of the Austro-Hungarian Empire.

As predicted, Loy was swept away, talking to various people she knew. The graceful hostess, Landi introduced Bogie to a circle of her friends clustered around William Randolph Hearst and his mistress, Marion Davies. In front of the other guests, Hearst chastised Marion for ordering another drink. She ignored his command.

The press tycoon returned to relating stories of his annual tour of European spas and was telling the group that while in Germany he'd attacked the Treaty of Versailles in an interview he gave to the *Frankfurter Zeitung*. "I claimed it subjected the Teutonic peoples to the domination of non-German European powers, especially France. If there is one country I loathe above all others, it's France." He looked cautiously around the room. "I hope there are no Frenchman here tonight."

As Bogie made eyes at Davies and the blonde courtesan/actress winked at him, Hearst was reporting on yet another trip he'd made. He'd just returned from St. Louis where thousands of supporters had mobbed him, all carrying *Hearst for President* signs. "They want a 100 percent American in the White House," the corpulent Hearst said. "No foreign entanglements. Independent in everything. Temperance, not Prohibition."

Finding Hearst a little too pompous for his tastes, Bogie puckered his mouth in a false kiss to Marion, but only when the media baron wasn't looking.

As he wandered the room looking for Loy, he felt Landi's fingers tighten on his arm. She gracefully directed him to where two Englishmen stood, viewing the gathering with jaded eyes. Before departing, she introduced him to W. Somerset Maugham and his handsome secretary-companion, Gerald Haxton. Haxton's neck was in a cast.

"Who roughed you up?" Bogie asked. "I should have been there to protect you."

"A little accident," Haxton said.

Maugham interrupted to give more details as if to punish Haxton for his impetuosity. "We were at this very gay party in Antibes. Gerald was certainly the life of the party. At one point he pulled off all his clothes and raced to dive into the swimming pool. It was under repair and empty. Gerald nearly killed himself. Cut his head open. Dislocated his spine. Broke a vertebrae."

Infuriated at such a revelation, Haxton excused himself and headed for the bar. "I met your first wife briefly in London when she was appearing on the stage there," Maugham said to Bogie. "Wonderful woman that Helen Menken. I talked to her again, along with Tallulah Bankhead at a party one night given by Noël Coward. That Miss Alabama is going to destroy Helen's reputation. Vulgar woman, although ideal for my prostitute, Sadie Tompson, in *Rain*."

Some members of the English colony living in Hollywood suddenly crowded around Maugham. One of them was Basil Rathbone, whom Bogie had met during his appearance with Helen Menken in the lesbian play, *The Captive*.

The two actors reflected briefly, with a tinge of bitterness, on how the New York police had shut down this play because of its strong lesbian theme. "God, if we'd been allowed to continue in that play, we would have been a *cause célèbre* all over America. Every paper in the country featured our predicament. We would have been sold out for months."

"Helen certainly did a lot for the dykes of America," Bogie said. "The last I heard, Helen was still getting letters from the Sappho crowd from everywhere. Young women still send her slave bracelets. And most ironic of all--and probably missing the point completely-- the deans of several women's colleges wrote thanking her for warning their students about 'the dangers of a reprehensible attachment.'"

"I was the one who suggested that Helen wear that ghastly white makeup," Rathbone said. "I thought it would convey the severe physical toll a woman must pay for having such 'perverse' thoughts about other women."

Both men laughed at that. "And the violets?" Bogie asked. "Throughout the play, we never saw Helen's pursuer, Madame d'Aiguines. But Helen's character was always getting nosegays of violets."

"We did some research on that," Rathbone said. "Sappho wrote about 'diadems of violets' on the Isle of Lesbos in the Seventh Century B.C."

"I hear *The Captive* and those damn violets have started a fad," Bogie said.

"It's the fashion now for women in New York and Hollywood—I'm assuming there are no lesbians in the Middle West—to send violets to each other as a sign of their love." To his dismay, Bogie suddenly spotted the approach of an English actor he'd rather avoid.

Bogie was a bit chilly when introduced a second time to Ronald Colman, remembering with bitterness how his screen test was compared unfavorably to that of the English actor's when they both competed for the male lead opposite Lillian Gish in *The White Sister.*

The talk was of the latest news about George Bernard Shaw, Cornelia Otis Skinner, Grace Moore, Irene Castle, Elsa Maxwell, and Daisy Fellowes. Knowing none of these people, except by their reputation, Bogie grew bored and wandered off.

In a city famed for grand entrances, the latest arriving guest was creating a sensation. All eyes in the room focused on the foyer. Dressed in a man's tuxedo, a blonde goddess stood under Landi's Viennese crystal chandelier, being welcomed by Landi who kissed her on the mouth.

Right then and there Bogie decided that he was going to divorce Mary and propose marriage to this sultry, alluring Venus de Milo. Her escort was some foreign-looking man, perhaps German.

Bogie's fantasy woman was heading across the room in his direction. He virtually stood in her pathway.

Coming up only two feet from him, she smelled of the most exotic perfume. The scent wasn't overpowering but had great subtlety, a sensation for the nostrils. He felt himself hardening standing close to such a sex goddess.

He was convinced that her smile was the most provocative since the dawn of time.

"I'm told that God has a talent for creating exceptional women," he said, staring into eyes bluer than any alpine lake on a summer day.

"H-e-l-l-o," she said in her German-accented voice. "You are in my way. Do I have to kiss you or fuck you to make you move?"

"For now, I'll settle for a kiss," he said, standing up to her with more bravado than he actually possessed. His knees were shaking.

"Your wish is granted," she said, leaning in to give him a quick kiss on the lips. The four wettest lips in Hollywood, male and female, exchanged body fluids. He felt the flicker of her tongue. "Since the entire room is watching, including my very jealous director, that is all for now. Catch me later." She nodded her head at some people she knew across the big room and headed in their direction.

As he passed by, Josef von Sternberg glared at Bogie. Bogie felt that he'd just blown his chance to get cast opposite the star in any of her future movies.

Before stepping down into the sunken living room, she paused and looked back at him. "Not bad," she said, her tongue darting out ever so slightly as if to taste his kiss, which still lingered on her lips. "What is your name?"

"Humphrey Bogart," he said.

"Your studio will change that," she predicted. "And, of course, you know who I am. *Marlene Dietrich*. I could be no one else but me."

He watched her go, as von Sternberg followed. Bogie's heart was beating faster, as he'd just fallen in love. He feared that he'd have to join a long line of suitors, both male and female, forming on her left and right.

After the formal dinner, Loy signaled him to take her home if they were going to face an early morning call at Fox. Bogie was cornered by the writer, Gabriel Dunkard, as the guests were enjoying their final brandy of the evening.

Without being asked, Dunkard claimed that he was writing a biography devoted solely to the lovers of Sarah Bernhardt.

Dunkard cited an impressive list: Jean Richepin, Philippe Garnier, Jean Mounée Sully, Pierre Berton, Gustave Doré, Émile Zola, Edmund Rostand, Count de Keratry, Prince de Ligne, Prince Napoleon, King Alphonso XII of Spain, King Umberto of Italy, King Christian IX of Denmark, Edward VII, Napoleon III, Emperor Franz Josef, Aristides Jacques Damala.

As Loy and Bogie tried to duck out the door, Dunkard trailed after them, "And would you believe: Oscar Wilde?"

***

The next morning, Bogie learned that Kenneth was out of harm's way. At least his friend had nothing to fear from Charles Farrell. Kenneth told Bogie that Farrell's jealous feud with him had ended in a most amicable way. All three men—Farrell, George O'Brien, and Kenneth himself—had agreed to meet for drinks in the bar of the Roosevelt Hotel. That had occurred at about the same time that Bogie was driving Myrna Loy to Landi's formal dinner party.

As Kenneth recounted later, the sexual tension of their three-way meeting in the bar was enhanced with alcohol and the high-adrenaline sex appeal of each of their respective studio images. As the three good-looking men became increasingly relaxed with one another, they decided, almost spontaneously and through what Kenneth later described as "a meeting of our eyes" to go several steps further. Rising from the booth they occupied, Farrell went to the reception desk of the hotel, rented a room, returned to the bar to pay the bar tab, and ushered his two drinking companions upstairs. Regrettably, no stag movie exists showing what that trio did that long-ago night at the Roosevelt, a great loss to gay history.

Heading for the studio and the day's shoot, Hump decided that Hollywood homosexuals played the same dating and mating games as Hollywood heterosexuals. That opinion was enforced a few hours later when a message was delivered to his dressing room at Fox from Barbara Stanwyck. Her friend from the chorus line, Mae Clarke, would be delighted to meet him. Stanwyck wanted all three of them to get together at eight o'clock Sunday night "for some fun and games."

182

Bogie viewed the upcoming tryst between Stanwyck, Clarke, and Bogart as the straight version of the Farrell/MacKenna/O'Brien orgy.

Sunday night seemed far away, and Bogie faced Friday and Saturday nights with nothing marked on his calendar. He still couldn't get that sexy hooker, Dawn Night (Glenda Farrell), off his mind. Even though Louise had been charging him by the hour, his time with her was special.

He dialed the private number she'd given him when he'd first gone to Louise's. Glenda Farrell picked up the phone. "Bogie!" she said. "I've been sitting here for days, all horny and all alone, waiting for your call."

"Flattering," he said. "I'm sure you tell that to all the guys."

"There have been no other guys," she said. "I'm not working for Louise any more. Joanie is lining up roles for me in some films. Not anything big. But it's a start."

"How about going out with me tonight?" he asked. "You made some impression on me. We sure didn't waste much time getting acquainted, did we?"

"You were the best," she said. "Better than all the others."

After they talked some more, Bogie realized that it was time report to the set. Until his next tryst with Glenda, he had another Farrell to deal with: Charles Farrell, the star of the picture. Both he and the actor were dressed in their flyer's uniforms. The "aviator" looked a little worse for wear this morning. Bogie figured that Kenneth and George O'Brien had given him one hell of a workout at the Roosevelt the night before.

Farrell made no mention of the previous evening except to tell Bogie that "the problem with MacKenna had been resolved."

At one o'clock Bogie joined Myrna Loy and Elissa Landi in the commissary for lunch. Both Loy and Bogie thanked Landi profusely for inviting them to the dinner party the previous evening.

Over a plate of bacon and eggs, Bogie learned that Landi was an avid equestrian. He told her that "second to sailing," he preferred horseback riding better than anything. After saying that, he smiled awkwardly, looking first at Landi, then at Loy, deciding they were two of the most beautiful women in Hollywood. "Of course, there *is* something I like even better than horseback riding or sailing."

Both women laughed. Loy affectionately stroked his cheek. It was just a flash, and it was quickly concealed, but Landi shot Loy a look that Bogie definitely interpreted as jealousy.

For the second time that morning, he was flattered by a female appraisal of him. Had he not already booked Glenda Farrell for the evening, he would have been strongly tempted by either Landi or Loy. In time, he reflected, he might even get lucky with both of them.

Not knowing which woman to ask out first, the issue was solved when Loy went to the powder room to take the shine off Hollywood's cutest nose. After she'd gone, Landi said, "I'm going riding in the morning. Want to drop by my house at six o'clock, and we'll head over to the stables."

"A little early," he said, smiling at her, his eyes twinkling in anticipation, "but I'll be there. Maybe a little hung over. Bleary-eyed or not, I'm ready to race you."

She got up from the table to report back to the set. "You'll find, Mr. Bogart, that your horse can easily overtake mine."

Bogie spotted Loy returning from the powder room. This woman of quick wit showed her acute sensitivity when she looked first at Landi, then at him. "I'm afraid I might have intruded on something."

***

The night Bogie escorted Glenda Farrell on his first real date with her, she was a long way (1964) from playing Elvis Presley's mama in *Kissin' Cousins*. Just years before she became known as "The Gimmie Girl" in films for Warner Brothers, this beautiful, five-foot, three-inch blonde, with the devilish blue-green eyes, was the delight he'd remembered when he'd first seduced her at Louise's bordello.

"I told Joan Blondell about our encounter at Louise's," Farrell said. "All Joanie said was, 'I hope you two had fun.'"

"And that we did," he said. "If I recall." He looked deeply into her eyes. "And I do recall."

Over dinner Bogie found the Oklahoma-born Farrell a no-nonsense dame. By coincidence her father, a horse trader of Irish and Cherokee descent, had also been named Charles Farrell, just like Bogie's co-star in *Body and Soul*.

For an actress on the dawn of a long career, Farrell had already lived a life so adventurous it would make a thick autobiography in spite of her youth. She'd made her stage debut as Little Eva in a Wichita, Kansas production of *Uncle Tom's Cabin*. "At every performance, I went to heaven on a pulley. I should have gone on from there to be a trapeze artist."

Like Spencer Tracy, she was a devout Catholic. Much of her formalized education was from the Mount Carmel Catholic Academy in Wichita.

"I always seem to get them fresh out of the convent," he said, amazed that both Farrell and Tracy could still retain such devotion to their church, in spite of the dissipated lives they'd led or were leading.

Farrell had had more experience in the theater than Bogie had realized, appearing at the age of fifteen as Meg in *Little Women*. Long before Shirley Temple stamped her oversugared lollipop kiss on the role, Farrell had appeared on a San Diego stage as *Rebecca of Sunnybrook Farm*.

She spoke with sadness over the breakup of her marriage in 1929 to a handsome, dashing sailor, Thomas Richards. They'd met as teenagers in a candy store, and Farrell claimed that it "was violent love the moment I laid eyes on him." He said that "he had to have me, and I wanted him just as much, even

184

though I was a virgin at the time." She reached into her purse and pulled out the picture of him she carried in her wallet. "Even though our marriage is over, I'm still in love with him—always will be, I guess."

Bogie didn't like looking at pictures of other beaux, especially the previous husbands of women he planned to seduce, but he politely demurred, studying the photograph of Thomas Richards.

The picture in a sailor's uniform revealed one of the handsomest and sexiest-looking men he'd ever seen, and he'd seen some male beauties recently in both New York and Hollywood.

Not until Bogie would make *Knock on Any Door* with John Derek would he ever see a man as handsome as Farrell's former husband. In fact, John Derek bore an amazing resemblance to the stunningly handsome sailor. They both had the same chiseled profile, the thick black hair, the beautiful eyes, and the gorgeous mouth. "Hell, he's so good looking I'd go for him myself. Put that picture away before I get a hard-on."

"A lot of men have chased him," she said, "and probably still do. When he was in the Navy, even his commander wanted to fuck him."

Farrell had run away with Richards and had married him spontaneously, without inviting any members of her family. Together they developed a vaudeville-style dancing act and took it on the road, working for starvation wages.

When the newlyweds discovered that she was pregnant, they were forced to move in with Glenda's parents. In her parents' house on October 7, 1921 she gave birth to her son, Tommy. "I've been involved with many men in the past, and I'm sure I'll be involved with many more in the future, but my son is the love of my life. He's a great kid. I only took that job at Louise's because I needed money for Tommy. I'm really not a whore."

"I knew that from the first moment I met you," he said.

She related to Bogie that as their financial troubles worsened, especially with the coming of the Depression, Richards began to drink more and more heavily, sometimes beating her severely after staggering back to her parents' house. "Sometimes he'd go away for weeks at a time. My cousin saw him one day coming out of a men's toilet with an older man, probably one of the many salesmen who come through Wichita. My cousin followed him, and my husband went into the Wichita Hotel with this guy and up to his room. I think he was turning tricks before I was forced into the same game. That's how he got money for liquor. I finally had to divorce him last year. I just couldn't take it any more, and he was not the right father for Tommy."

Over dinner, she told him that she'd left her son with her Alsatian mother, Wilhelmina, whom she called Minnie. "I headed for Broadway and Minnie told me not to come back to Kansas until my name was up in lights."

Fairly soon after her arrival in New York, Farrell replaced Erin O'Brien Moore in a play, *Skidding*. That silly little domestic farce was later to become the inspiration for Metro-Goldwyn-Mayer's Andy Hardy series that would bring fame

185

to Mickey Rooney and millions to the Lion.

Farrell said that one of the happiest moments in her life turned into the saddest. "I was appearing in a play, *On the Spot*, and I kept begging the Shuberts to put my name on the marquee, so I could invite Tommy and Minnie to Broadway to see it. They agreed. I wired Minnie the good news at once. She was in the hospital having an operation. Right after the curtain went down that night, I found a telegram waiting in my dressing room. Minnie had died from the operation. She never got to see my name on the marquee, and I had to put my dear Tommy in a military school while I toured around, getting work where I could find it, including that half talking, half silent movie, *Lucky Boy*, with George Jessel. What a satyr that Jessel is."

To his surprise, he learned that the director, Mervyn LeRoy, whom Glenda had entertained at Louise's, kept his promise. Bogie had suspected that LeRoy was just stringing her along. But just that afternoon, she'd been cast as the female lead in *Little Caesar* over at Warner Brothers. In it, Edward G. Robinson was slated to play Rico Bandello, with Douglas Fairbanks Jr. appearing as his best friend.

"You still plan to bed Fairbanks?" he asked.

"And why not?" she asked. "It's not like his wife, Joan Crawford, is home at night darning his socks. He's already signed to play Little Caesar's best friend in the movie. We'll have plenty of time together. I'm sure not going to go for Robinson. He's one of the ugliest men I've ever seen."

Bogie couldn't resist the temptation to put in a dig at his future rival, Fairbanks Jr. "You know, he fucks with men too," he said. "Most recently with one of my male friends."

A graduate of Louise's, Farrell didn't look surprised. "This is Hollywood. All actors out here do that. The women too: Crawford, Dietrich, Stanwyck."

"What about you?" he asked.

"No way," she said. "Joanie and I talked it over. We're strictly women for men. Kay Francis has a deal with Louise's. Of course, she doesn't show her face there. But some of the top female stars in Hollywood have some of Louise's most gorgeous gals sent over to their homes or apartments for the night. Some of the top male stars request handsome and well-hung men. Louise keeps a string of those on the side too. They're usually struggling actors desperate for money. I was once asked to go and service Francis. I don't go that route so I turned her down. Louise quickly got another gal to fill in. Even Stanwyck uses Louise's from time to time."

He smiled, wanting another drink. "Stanwyck has even used my services once or twice."

She laughed a little nervously. "Small world, this Hollywood. Humphrey Bogart and Glenda Farrell are probably the only two real heterosexuals in all of Tinseltown."

"Tonight you're going to find out just how heterosexual I really am. The

186

thing we had at Louise's was just a rehearsal. Now, the second time around, I'm going to really take my time."

"I hope you do," she said, taking his hand and kissing his inner palm with her pretty lips.

***

High in the Hollywood Hills, Bogie and Elissa Landi brought their horses to rest at a shady spot by a little stream. It was one of those idyllic places that makes a New Yorker glad that he's moved to the West Coast.

Later they were to learn from a stable hand that they'd stopped at the same spot where the Sheik, Valentino, used to take the screen vamp, Gloria Swanson, to make love to her.

On that far-away morning, as he got to know Elissa Landi, he decided then and there she was like no actress he'd ever met on Broadway, in Chicago, or in Hollywood.

Since she was illegitimate, he didn't think she wanted to talk about her relationship with Elizabeth, the Empress of Austria and the Queen of Hungary. To his surprise, he found that was about all she wanted to talk about. After all, "Sissi," as the queen was called, was one of history's most fascinating women, and Landi used her constantly as a role model.

"Sissi is something to aspire to," she said. "A fairy-tale princess and a liberated woman at the same time. Liberated I am, as you'll soon discover. Becoming a princess is not out of my reach."

"How do you plan to go about that?" he asked a little skeptically. "The Habsburg dynasty ended after World War I. There's no empire left--not even a throne."

"Oh, I won't have an empire to preside over like my grandmother, but I will become the biggest star in Hollywood. When that happens, I think many princes around the world will request my hand in marriage. It is not inconceivable for a Hollywood star to marry royalty and become a princess herself."

"A bit far-fetched," he said, "but I could see that happening."

"Sissi was always a dieting fanatic and an expert equestrian," she said. "You've seen this morning when I beat you in our race what a horsewoman I am. As far as the diet is concerned, I follow Sissi's regime, but I don't go on hunger diets like she did trying to obtain that elusive sixteen-inch waist. I eat exactly as Sissi did: a moderate portion of raw steak daily, a glass of milk, and a glass of freshly squeezed orange juice."

"I'll have to try that," he said. "Or else convert you to my diet of bacon and eggs."

"How gross," she said. "All that animal fat. Sissi also wanted to be a poet modeling herself after Heinrich Heine, whose work she adored. I too will write a great book and win many literary honors. Like Sissi, I too will become an inveterate traveler and see the world, attracting adoring crowds wherever I go. Everyone will want to see the beautiful princess, don't you agree?"

"I'm enjoying seeing the beautiful princess right now, even before she's crowned."

She obviously liked the sound of that, and her porcelain-like arms reached out for him.

"I've never been particularly intimate with royalty before," he said.

"As you seduce me," she said, "I'm going to imagine that I am the young Elizabeth hauled to the bedchamber of the emperor, Franz Josef. I am only sixteen. He is much older. He rapes me on our wedding night. I'm a virgin."

"I've played a few parts in my day," he said. "But never a rapist emperor." He hugged her closer to him. "I think it's a role I can get into."

***

In Landi, Bogie found a woman who was spectacularly satisfying, thereby inspiring thoughts that he should divorce Mary Philips and become deeply involved with Landi, despite the fact that he couldn't give her the fairy kingdom she wanted to reign over as queen. Before four o'clock came on Sunday morning, in her lavish bed, he'd promised her a different kingdom, based on the possibility of their joint reign as the King and Queen of Hollywood.

Although she'd remained tactful, responding passionately to his lovemaking, his comment provoked her first put-down. "It's in my destiny that I'm going to reign as the queen of Hollywood, I just know it. But I've heard from our director, Santell, that the future king of Hollywood won't be our star, Charlie Farrell, or even George O'Brien. I think they carry the stigma of the Twenties with them. John Gilbert is through. Santell claims it'll be one of these up-and-coming rugged he-man types like Gary Cooper or Clark Gable."

Her comments immediately diminished his erection. He turned over with his back to this empress wannabe and fell into a deep sleep.

When he awakened at eleven o'clock Sunday morning, he found her gone without a note. Her fat German maid with a Brunhilde bosom told Bogie, "Miss Landi has gone for a Sunday drive down to Laguna with a Mr. Basil Rathbone. She said I should offer you breakfast before I sent you on your way. She made it clear that she doesn't want you here when she gets back."

"Tell Princess Landi thanks for a good time," he said, storming out the door in anger although the bacon and eggs the maid was cooking smelled mighty good.

By four o'clock that afternoon he was still fuming about his dismissal by Landi. He'd almost forgotten that he had a date that night with Stanwyck and Mae Clarke, although he felt a little too battered to perform for two voracious women. The way he figured it, even if he wasn't performing at peak capacity, those two former chorus gal roomies from New York could always satisfy each other.

188

When Stanwyck called to confirm, she was directing the show once again. Mae Clarke had decided that she wanted to go dancing, which meant that they needed another man for a four-way date. That made Bogie wonder what had happened to his prospects for a three-way with Clarke and Stanwyck.

Stanwyck suggested Kenneth as a possible escort for her friend Clarke. "I know that Kay Francis has discovered the charms of the *Gnädiges Fräulein*, Miss Dietrich, so she won't be with Ken tonight."

"The last I heard, Kenneth will be spending Sunday night locked in the arms of George O'Brien."

"Lucky boy," Stanwyck said. "By the way, I've had Dougie Fairbanks Jr. Not bad. Great body and a fabulous dick. But he's a bit prissy for my taste. I don't like my men in silk drawers. I like white cotton underwear on a man—no silk and no color. You passed that test."

"Don't tell Ken," Bogie said. "Even though Fairbanks has dumped him, that boy will be jealous."

"I told Joan Crawford I'd fucked with her man, but she didn't seem unduly concerned. She claims I give better head than Dougie boy of the pink silk drawers." She paused a minute. "Hey, I've got a great idea. I ran into George Raft the other night. Seems he knows you from the Texas Guinan days. He wants you to call him. He's staying at the Mark Twain Hotel on Wilcox Avenue. Ring him up and see if he's free to join us tonight. If Mae Clarke wants a male dancing partner, George Raft is the greatest thing since sliced bread."

"My mama, Maud, didn't raise no jazz baby dancer. Raft will show all of us up."

"Don't worry about it. He may dance better than you do, but you're just as good in bed as he is. Note I said just as good and not better."

"Yeah, I heard that."

"Both Mae and I have had George." She paused again as if wondering if she should ask the next question. "You and George?"

"What do you mean by that?"

"I mean have you two guys bumped pussies in the night?"

"No," he answered sharply. "I think Mr. Valentino got there before I did."

"You should try him some night," she suggested. "He's not bad. A real blacksnake."

"Not my scene," he said. "I'll call Raft now. As for you, bigtime movie star, Barbara Stanwyck, tonight you're gonna learn just how much I'm into women."

"I've had you," she said. "You're a drunken fuck."

"Tonight I'm going to drink only club soda," he promised. "You're going to be made love to by a Humphrey Bogart with a clear head. Think you can handle it?"

"Ruby Stevens never met a man in New York or Hollywood that she couldn't handle," she said. "Pick us up at eight and make sure Blacksnake is in the car with you." She put down the phone.

***

George Raft was one Yankee dancer/actor who hadn't gone Hollywood. In black tie he was sitting in an armchair by a potted palm in the lobby of the Mark Twain Hotel, waiting for Bogie to pick him up. The beltline of his trousers seemed to come up to his armpits. He looked like he belonged, not on Wilcox Avenue, but on the corner of Broadway and 42nd Street, waiting for a blonde babe to show up.

Bogie too was in black tie, having never returned the tux he'd rented for the Landi dinner party. He figured he'd go into the shop tomorrow and buy the damn thing.

Raft jumped up from his chair and rushed to greet him. He seemed genuinely glad to see a familiar face from back East. "The prospect of a steak dinner with you guys tonight, and maybe another kind of meat later in the evening, brought joy to my heart."

"You're looking good, George," Bogie said.

"So are you, Hump, bigtime movie star."

"Out here they call me Bogie."

"So be it. Out here and back East they still call me George Raft. The one and only."

"Maybe we'd better go pick up the dames," Bogie said.

Raft glanced at his watch. "We've still got time. Let's go up to my room for a drink."

Taking the elevator to the top floor, Bogie was ushered into Raft's cluttered room, which smelled of stale cigarette butts and booze.

"Don't let these sharp clothes fool you," Raft said. "I came out here with a big bank roll. Lost all of it at the track. I ain't got but five bucks in my pocket. Can you lend me something till I get back on top again?"

"Sure thing, old pal," Bogie said. "I just got paid today. Seven-hundred and fifty bucks. I'll split it with you for old time's sake."

"Thanks, big guy," Raft said. "I'll owe you one for this. George Raft never forgets when someone does him a favor."

"If you've got no money, how are you eating?"

"An old friend of mine, Ben Lieberman, owns the Angelus Drugstore downtown. He's letting me run up a tab until my luck gets better. I'm getting fucking tired of BLTs."

"That steak you mentioned will make up for it tonight." He accepted the drink from Raft, bolting it down straight, as Raft poured him another whiskey. "So, good looking, how's your love life?"

"A lot of gorgeous dames out here, even more than in New York," Raft said. "They're throwing themselves at me every night. I had this fling with Molly O'Day. I'm trying to drop her but she's a clinging vine."

"I saw her in *The Patent Leather Kid* with Richard Barthelmess," Bogie said.

"Great looking dame."

"She was a looker," Raft said. "But she got fat and…" He paused. "Hell, I don't want to talk about Molly O'Day. Things have gone bad for her. She was balling her co-star in that flick, Richard Barthelmess until I took her away from him. Barthelmess is a pansy. But out here in California even the fags fuck women. It must be the orange juice."

Bogie laughed. When Raft offered him a third whiskey, he turned it down, remembering that he'd promised Stanwyck he was going to ball her sober for a change.

"I saw that *Patent Leather* movie ten times," Raft said. "I want to star in the talkie version of that film. I can just see myself as a cocky prizefighter who learns humility when he's crippled at the end of the picture and can't go to war like he wants. He's a real hero. That scene at the end where he forces himself to struggle out of his wheelchair and stands up to salute the American flag as the band strikes up the national anthem, that's the kind of role I want to play. I've got to get rid of this New York gangster image. Let Edward G. Robinson and James Cagney play the gangsters. From now on, George Raft is going to be playing all-American heroes."

"Hell, I'd love to play a gangster," Bogie said. "I'm tired of these juvenile roles. I'm thirty years old, for Christ's sake."

"Tennis, anyone?" Raft said, bursting into laughter at Bogie's expense, but only after he'd gotten his part of Bogie's paycheck. He looked at his watch again. "By the way, have you fucked Stanwyck yet?"

"Yeah, first as Ruby Stevens back in New York although I was too drunk to remember it."

"I haven't fucked Stanwyck as Stanwyck, but Ruby Stevens and I sure got it on. I've also had Mae Clarke. She's one hot piece. At the end of the evening, I'll ball Stanwyck and give you Clarke so you can sample some fresh meat. I owe it to you for the loan. So, we're going to be making it tonight with two of the hottest dykes in Hollywood."

"If they fuck guys, they're not lesbians," Bogie said. "Bi certainly."

"Clarke and Stanwyck will fuck anybody out here, male or female. If it's on the hoof and moving, those two broads will go for it."

"My impression is that everybody out here will fuck anybody, in any known combination," Bogie said. "Of course, New York isn't the sticks either."

"Hell, I could be a bigtime movie star right now if I'd put out," Raft said. "Take Rowland Brown, for example. He used to be this hotshot newspaper guy in Detroit. Now he's the hottest young director in Hollywood. I went to the fights the other night and was having dinner at the Brown Derby with my pal, Owney Madden, and some other cronies. I get up to go to the men's room. Brown follows me in. There are five empty urinals. He takes the one next to me as I whip out Blacksnake. He comes on real strong, and I'm about ready to belt him one. Then he tells me he's Rowland Brown, that he saw me dance at this honky-tonk in Detroit, and wants to offer me the second lead in his new film, *Quick Millions*. In New York, only the blonde belles have to be experts on the casting couch. Out here in Hollywood almost as many guys have to shuck their bloomers. I told Brown that I don't go that route."

"What about the Sheik?" Bogie asked provocatively.

"C'mom, let's not speak of the dead. Rudy was a good pal. A lovesick puppy. I felt sorry for the guy. In case you ain't heard, buddy, George Raft is a guy with heart."

He tried to get Bogie to have another drink but was turned down. "Tell me, hot shot, if you'd been as broke as I am, would you drop your trousers for this cocksucker Brown?"

"Maybe," Bogie said. "I'd certainly consider it. Getting a blowjob is no big deal. All you have to do is whip it out, close your eyes, and let some fag do all the work. While they're at it, you can be dreaming of some beautiful blonde like Molly O'Day."

"I guess you're right," Raft said. "Getting your dick sucked is no big deal. It's not like you're a fag yourself. Maybe I'd better call up Brown and reconsider his offer."

"Maybe you had," Bogie said, "because that's the last paycheck you're getting from me."

"Not even if you saw me panhandling on the street," Raft said.

"I'm a softie," Bogie said. "I'd let you move into my apartment and sleep on the sofa. I wouldn't let you starve."

"I may have to take you up on that offer the way things are going." There was a loud rap on his door, and he walked over to open it, revealing two large police officers. "You George Raft?" a tall, blond-haired cop asked.

"Yeah," Raft said cockily. "What's it to you?"

Without being invited, both of the policemen walked into the bedroom. "Who's this guy?" the red-haired and equally tall cop asked, looking Bogie up and down. "One of your New York accomplices?"

"Accomplice in what?" Raft demanded to know.

"We'll come clean with you," the blond said. "We've arrested this stickup artist. Another George like you except he claims his name is George Roberts. He's being grilled at headquarters right now and is singing like a canary. He's already admitted to a dozen robberies, and claims he had accomplices."

"I'm not a stickup guy," Raft said. "Look at me. Do I look like a guy who would stick somebody up? Look at my clothing—and the way I'm dressed."

"When Roberts was searched, your name was found sewed on to his inner pocket, and he was well dressed too," the blond said. "Real fancy tailor."

"I can explain that," Raft said. "I sold him that suit yesterday for thirty bucks to pay my rent here. I'm an actor. Temporarily out of work. I was forced to sell my suit because I was three weeks behind on my hotel bill."

"You're not fooling me," the redhead said. "The Los Angeles police department has already been alerted to your coming out here. You're a friend of Dutch Schultz."

"Not exactly a friend," Raft said. "He used to come into the club where I danced for Texas Guinan, but I never met him personally."

Bogie knew that Raft was lying, having already been introduced to Dutch Schultz by Raft.

"What about the bootlegger, Owney Madden?" the blond cop asked.

"Owney and I go way back," Raft said. "We grew up on the streets of Hell's Kitchen together. He's a good guy."

"Yeah," the redhead said. "Spent ten years in prison for being such a good guy. I think we're gonna run you in for questioning."

At this point, the manager of the hotel, Robert Parrish, came into the room since the door was wide open. "What's going on here? We run a respectable hotel—no drunks, no whores."

Raft looked desperate. "Tell them, Parrish. I sold you my ring last week. I'm having to sell my stuff from New York to raise money."

"He's telling the truth," Parrish said, holding up what looked like a ruby ring encrusted with diamonds. "I've had it appraised. It's worth five-hundred bucks. I bought it from this Broadway hoofer for fifty bucks."

"I can vouch for George here," Bogie said. "Squeaky clean, a real good guy. Just because this Roberts guy was caught in his secondhand suit doesn't make George guilty."

"Okay," the redhead said. He turned to Raft. "Let this be a warning to you. We heard about you before you even hit town. This is not New York or Chicago, but Los Angeles, a clean-living town. If you think you gangsters can come out here and take over this town, you've got another thought coming."

"I don't like the look of you," the blond said to Raft. "And I hate those pants of yours. I really hate your guts. We've had another complaint about you. At first we weren't sure about it and our sergeant wanted to drop it, but I'm going back to the station to look into the case personally. Reopen it, so to speak."

"You've got nothing on me!" Raft said. "What sort of complaint? It's a lie."

"Where will you be later tonight?" the blond asked. Raft turned to Bogie.

"We'll be dining at the Roosevelt Hotel with two of the most respectable women in town," Bogie said.

The blond looked skeptical. "Yeah, I bet. Two floozies, probably."

After some more questions and a few threats, the two policemen left the bedroom. Parrish stayed behind, shaking a finger at Raft. "You have until tomorrow to move out. We don't want your type here. I think I'm going to post a sign in the lobby, 'No New Yorkers allowed.'"

After he'd shut the door, Raft turned to Bogie. "I'd better go for that movie role and quick no matter what Brown wants me to do. It'll look good with the police if I'm a bona-fide film star. I'll do anything but take it up the ass. George Raft doesn't get fucked by anybody. I'm the fucker, not the fuckee." Raft looked at his watch again. "Hell, we're running late, and we've got the two hottest dames in Hollywood waiting for us, unless some other guys picked them up already."

In a taxi on the way to the Roosevelt, Bogie quizzed Raft again about *Quick Millions*.

Raft said that it was the story of a truck driver who'd become a ruthless gangster. "That's the star part," Raft said. "I play his bodyguard."

"What do you think Brown would say if I tried out for the role of the ruthless gangster?" Bogie asked. "I'd let him suck me off."

"Too late. The lead's already cast."

"Fuck!" Bogie said. "What meathead got the part?"

"This new guy over at Fox," Raft said. "Surely you've heard of him. Spencer Tracy."

***

Over dinner at the Roosevelt Hotel, Bogie paid less attention to Stanwyck who had once again captured Raft's devoted attention and more to the blonde beauty, Mae Clarke. She was disarmingly charming, candid, and frank, and saw Hollywood with a certain detached and wry amusement.

"I came from Philly," she said, "with the name of Violet Mary Klotz. You can see why I changed it to Mae Clarke."

Later as they danced, Bogie held her close, as he was very attracted to this delicately perfumed woman. She was full of surprises, and he secretly wanted to run away with her, minus Stanwyck and Raft.

"I'm not as pretty as Babs, and I know that," she said. "Here in Hollywood they call me 'attractive.' The studio chief told me I was 'just short of beautiful.' What every gal wants to hear."

"I think you're gorgeous," he said.

"And I think you're one good-looking man, and I hope you go on to develop your own personal style on the screen. Let Raft pick up that tired old Valentino cloak. I know that you're sometimes compared to him, but you're different. I predict that you're going to be a star like no one who was ever a star before. You're unique." At the end of their dance, when she kissed him on the lips, he'd fallen for her.

When they returned to their table, the *maître d'hôtel* explained that Stanwyck and Raft—at their own request—had been moved to a table in the palm-flanked rear where they'd have more privacy. They were obviously rekindling the romance they'd known together in New York so many years ago, when she was still known as Ruby Stevens. Bogie couldn't have written a better scenario himself. He wanted to seduce Clarke without his overtures being judged by Stanwyck and Raft, both of whom were veteran survivors of thousands of honky-tonk seductions.

In spite of her former life as a chorus girl, Mae Clarke exuded innocence, and he liked that about her. There was something about her that he found undeniably wholesome, despite what he viewed as the bad influence Stanwyck had on her. Imagining the two of them together, he asked, "You're not really a lesbian, are you?"

"Before the night is over, you'll be able to answer that one for yourself. I've been known to indulge some of the gals some of the time. I met Babs in 1924 when she helped me get a part in *The Noose*. If called upon, I can lie on my back with certain women but I don't do anything myself. And I'm not particularly oral, so I think that disqualifies me as a full-fledged, card-carrying lesbian."

He smiled and leaned over, kissing her on the nose, like he'd done with Myrna Loy.

When he looked up, and to his astonishment, he saw the same two officers from the Los Angeles police department, the blond cop and the redhead they'd encountered in Raft's hotel room, escorting Raft across the ballroom floor of the Roosevelt. Raft wasn't in handcuffs but each cop held firmly onto Raft's arms.

Stanwyck rushed over to their table. "George has been framed," she said with the same anguish she'd show in the future film, *Sorry, Wrong Number*. "He's been framed by Molly O'Day."

"Can I help?" Bogie asked, getting up.

"I've got it handled," Stanwyck said. "At least for now. I'll call you later. I'm going with him down to the jailhouse."

Standing there looking startled, Bogie watched Stanwyck in her flowing white gown disappear across the ballroom floor trailing after Raft and the two cops.

He sat back down and looked at Clarke, who at that moment appeared to him to be the most beautiful dame in Hollywood in spite of her being told that she was "just short of beautiful." "Why would Molly O'Day frame Raft?"

"I don't know what this is all about," Clarke said, "but Molly told me and Sally Eilers that Raft dumped her, and that she's going to get even."

"Sally Eilers?" he asked. "The actress who's married to Hoot Gibson?"

"One and the same," Clarke said. "Speaking of Gibson and Eilers, I once had a three-way with them. They're into three-ways. A lot of married couples out here are. It's the new thing. The current rage sweeping town."

"What combination of sexes?" he asked.

"Of course, the men—at least the predominantly heterosexual ones—want it two women to one man. Even though I was with Hoot and Sally, I learned that night they actually prefer another man in bed instead of a woman. That way, Hoot gets to share the man with his Sally. He likes to do something with the man while the guy is plugging his wife. I don't want to go into it. As I said, I'm not oral at all. Strictly missionary position for me."

"You're telling me that the rugged cowboy Hoot Gibson, more macho than Tom Mix himself, is a homosexual?"

"He takes it up the ass, Sally claims. But only after he butters himself up and only when Sally is in the same bed enjoying the fun too. That's one loving couple."

"Ah, Hollywood," Bogie said. "As you know, probably better than I do, we also have some odd couplings back in New York. I've been that route once or twice myself."

"If you were married to Helen Menken, I know you did. Helen came to see Babs and me in *The Noose.*"

"If you're going to tell a story about my Helen, I don't want to hear it," he said. "I know too much already. I still love her. In some ways, I think I love her more than I love my second wife."

"You're still married to Mary Philips?" she asked. "I thought you guys broke up when you came to test the waters in Hollywood."

"We're still legally married," he said. "I don't know for how long."

"I catch up on the Broadway gossip," Clarke said, "every time a Broadway cutie arrives at the train station out here hoping to make it big in films. The latest chorus gals keep Babs and me up to date. The word around Broadway is that your charming wife Mary has fallen in love."

His face turned into an ugly grimace. "Who the fuck?"

"I forget," she said. "Some actor. Very well known."

"An actor?" he said. "That figures."

"Do you want me to ask around and find out for you?" she said.

He slammed down his drink. "Let's forget it. I don't really want to know." Anxious to leave the dining room, he asked, "How concerned should we be about Raft?"

"In New York he was getting hauled away by the police all the time, sometimes in the same paddy wagon with Texas Guinan. He'll be okay. Babs has got a lot of clout out here. If anybody can get her Raft sprung, our gal can."

"Let's go back to my place," he said, reaching for her hand.

"You got yourself a deal," she said. "I'm tired of getting screwed by California men. Tonight I need some New York deep-dicking."

"You've found your man."

***

On his final day on the set of *Body and Soul,* Bogie received a message from Stanwyck urging him to visit her at Universal Studios, where she was starring in *The Locked Door.* Her message didn't explain why she wanted to see him, but no one turned down Barbara Stanwyck in those days. When his final scene was locked up, he drove over to Universal where Stanwyck had arranged an entrance pass for him at the gate. Even so, the security guards looked at him suspiciously before letting him drive onto the lot.

To his astonishment, the first person he encountered on the set was the picture's male star, Rod La Rocque. "The first and only actor I'll ever direct," Bogie said, embracing La Rocque warmly and not forgetting how the star had chased after him in New York. "Still got a crush on me?" he asked, teasing La Roque.

"Oh, that was so long ago, and I've gone through so many beaux since then. I gave my heart to Gary Cooper but he abandoned me for Lupe Velez. Not before I'd nicknamed him the Montana Mule."

"Sounds like you've been busy," Bogie said. "How's Miss Vilma Banky doing?"

"Talking pictures are not for her," La Rocque said. "Vilma and I make some joint appearances out here. As you might have guessed, ours is a somewhat unconventional marriage."

"I thought so," Bogie said. He noticed a handsome, blond-haired actor walking toward them.

"That's William Boyd," La Rocque said. "Even though he's got two inches less than Gary, he's all man. What a guy! He goes both ways. Barbara and I are sharing him during the filming of this stinker."

Bogie found himself shaking hands with this former favorite of the director, Cecil B. DeMille, who had cast Boyd as Simon of Cyrene in *King of Kings* in 1927. Before Bogie could become acquainted with America's future Hopalong Cassidy, a messenger came for him, summoning him to Stanwyck's dressing room.

In her dressing room, Stanwyck no longer looked distraught, so he assumed that George Raft had been released. She told Bogie that she'd posted $1,000 bail for Raft and that he'd been released. "He's been kicked out of the Mark Twain," she said, "and he's got no place to go. He said you agreed to let him move in with you until he gets back on his feet."

"I guess so," Bogie said. "That was no writ-in-blood commitment."

"He needs our help," Stanwyck pleaded, "and I've got my own private life. I can't become his mother."

"Okay, but what in hell has he been charged with?"

"O'Day claims that after he abruptly left her one night, he took $25,000 worth of jewelry."

"Tell the fucker he can move in," Bogie said. "But I'm afraid I'm going to regret this."

"It'll be just fine," Stanwyck assured him.

"I owe you one for fixing me up with Mae," Bogie said. "I went for her in a big way."

"You're too late," Stanwyck said. "I think Mae is a bit of a masochist. Ever since Cagney squashed that grapefruit in her face, she's fallen for the *Public Enemy*."

"He's already got Blondell," Bogie said. "How much more does he want?"

"He's not with her any more. He dumped her and replaced her with Mae. I don't blame him. Mae's much prettier."

"Joan was in that same movie with Cagney." Bogie said. "She didn't keep a close eye on her man, did she?"

"Joan thought Cagney was falling for this hot blonde number, Jean Harlow, who's also in the picture. But he went for Mae instead."

"I hear this Harlow is hot," he said.

She leaned in toward him and kissed him on the lips. "Who needs platinum blonde when they can have this sultry Brooklyn brunette?"

"You're still interested in me now that you've got that good-looking William Boyd?"

"What the hell!" she said, breaking from him and going over to lock the door to her dressing room. "Let La Rocque enjoy Billy boy this afternoon. He deserves his fun too." She was moving toward him. "And so do we."

***

Back at his apartment, as Bogie waited for Raft to show up broke but with expensive luggage and clothing, he received a series of phone calls. Far from being lonely and rejected as he had been when he'd first hit town, he suddenly felt like he'd been crowned King of Hollywood.

The first call was from Joan Blondell. Though still in tears at being dumped by Cagney who favored Mae Clarke, she was still upbeat and hopeful about the future. "He wouldn't be the first man who's dumped me."

Bogie asked her out for a date the following evening, and she readily accepted.

As he put down the phone, another call came in from Hobart Henley, a director at Universal. Henley told him that since Fox didn't have any immediate roles for him, he'd been loaned out to Universal where Carl Laemmle Jr. had agreed to a remake of Booth Tarkington's *The Flirt*. Henley informed Bogie that he himself had already directed a previous version of *The Flirt*--in this case as a silent film back in 1913.

"What's the name of the newest version?" Bogie asked. "Still *The Flirt?* I know you guys retitle everything in the remakes."

"*Gambling Daughters*," he said.

"Which one of the daughters do I play?" Bogie asked. "Who's going to design my gowns?"

"An actor with a sense of humor," Henley said. "Some directors like that. I don't."

Joking aside, Bogie was hoping he'd been cast in the male lead but learned that part had gone to Conrad Nagel. He couldn't help but notice that Henley was delaying telling him exactly what role he'd be playing.

"We have a great cast. Sidney Fox, ZaSu Pitts, Slim Summerville. The second female lead hasn't been cast yet but I expect to get notice from Carl tomorrow."

"And my part?" Bogie asked, fearing the answer.

"You'll play Valentine Curliss," Henley said.

"My character's called Valentine?" It sounded very dubious to him. "And the billing?"

"You get eighth billing," Henley said, "but I assure you your role of Valentine is absolutely crucial to the film. You'll walk away with the picture."

"Yeah, right," he said, feeling despondent. So much for a career in films.

After only two pictures, one of them not yet released, he felt that Hollywood stardom was fast eluding him. After assuring Henley he'd show up for work, he put down the phone.

"Valentine," he said out loud, cursing the name of his new character without even reading the script. He wondered whom Fox would cast as the other female lead. "I'll probably get to kiss Marie Dressler," he said to the empty walls of the apartment.

The phone rang again. He thought that in spite of his lack of stardom, he was getting more calls than any star.

It was "Dawn Night" (Glenda Farrell). He'd been meaning to ring her up for a date but had temporarily put her on hold. "You may—just may, I can't promise it—be getting the biggest break of your life."

"Tell me about it," he said. "Right at this moment I could sure use one."

"Mr. Edward G. Robinson—I don't know what the G stands for—has just walked out on *Little Caesar* and Mervyn LeRoy."

"You've got to be kidding," he said. "I hear that's the greatest role in town. What feather got stuck up Robinson's ass?"

"You won't believe this, but Mervyn told me that Robinson insisted on a scene in which he gets to display his legs."

"His fucking legs? Is this some kind of joke? Does Robinson think he's Marlene Dietrich?"

"The ugly mutt is proud of his legs. He's got this picture of himself in the tights he wore when he played Ottaviano in *The Firebrand*. He hangs it in his dressing room and shows it off to anybody."

"If I didn't know that you are not the joking type, I'd think you're putting me on."

"After Mervyn balled me last night, and we indulged in some pillow talk, I suggested you for the role even though he thinks Cagney would be ideal if he can get him."

"Hell, I'd love to play a gangster," he said. "A role like that would get me out of this aging juvenile crap."

"I'll tell Mervyn you're interested and if he wants me to, I'll set up a meeting," Farrell said. "You've got to strike now before they offer the role to Paul Muni. A lot of other actors will be lining up for the part. I might as well tell you. Mervyn is also thinking about that New York hoofer, George Raft."

"Raft," he said in astonishment. "The fucker is moving into my apartment. Maybe that's okay. I could drown him in the bathtub."

"Mervyn thinks Raft might be even better in the role than Robinson. After all, Raft *is* a New York gangster."

"I won't mention it to Raft tonight," he said. "Get me in to see LeRoy as soon as we can. Of course, I've got this deal with Fox but they might lend me out to First National. I'm getting eighth billing to appear in *Gambling Daughters*. A real comedown after my first two pictures."

"I'll call you first thing tomorrow," she said, blowing kisses into the phone.

After he'd gone to the kitchen and had two beers, Raft still hadn't shown up. There were many things he'd like to be doing tonight other than waiting around the apartment for Raft. The phone rang again. It was Kenneth wanting him to come over. Bogie explained that he was waiting for Raft who was going to be staying with him temporarily.

"Sorry, I'd like to see you tonight," Kenneth said. "Since you moved out, I don't see much of you."

"I thought George O'Brien, Charlie Farrell, and Kay Francis were keeping you pretty busy," Bogie said.

"They are," Kenneth said. "But all of them are busy tonight. But if you're not free to see an old pal from New York, I guess I'll accept the offer of a date from Eric Linden. Eric thinks you're real cute, and he'd be interested in a three-way with you and me. Eric has just dumped Ramon Novarro, who's a fading star anyway."

"Tell Eric there will be no three way. You sound like a busy fellow. With all these guys in your life, how do you find time for Kay?

"It's how she finds time for me!" Kenneth said. "Dietrich. Stanwyck. Right now she's fantasizing about this hot new blonde, Jean Harlow. I hear Harlow will go for someone only if they have a dick."

"Smart gal. We'll get together pal. If this Eric Linden thinks I'm so cute, why doesn't he organize a Humphrey Bogart fan club in Los Angeles? I could sure use one."

"I'll tell him."

No sooner had he put down the phone than it rang again. Bogie welcomed the now familiar voice of Spencer Tracy. But Tracy seemed despondent. Bogie soon learned that Lew Ayres had stopped putting out.

"He still sees me almost every night, but he just wants to hold my hand and talk religion," Tracy said. "I mean, I believe in The Church as much as anyone, but I like to work Lew's sweet cheeks when we're not praying together."

"Can't help you on that score, Spence," Bogie said. "Not my scene. So what are you doing?"

"I'm still going to keep seeing Lew," Tracy said. "He's got a changeable nature. He can't last long with this religion shit. He'll get real horny one night and he'll be over begging for me to plug him."

"What you doing in the meantime?" Bogie asked.

"I'll be fucking every woman in town," Tracy said. "The one I'm going after next is Loretta Young."

"I hear her tits are as cold as the Arctic."

"I'm the guy to warm them up."

"And for that other side of your nature?" Bogie asked.

"I called Louise, and did she ever fix me up. It's with this guy named Thomas Richards. He's this good-looking sailor with a dick down to his knees. You'll find this funny. He stormed over to Louise's because he'd hit Hollywood and found out from somebody that his former wife was one of Louise's funtime girls. That flesh peddler knows a stud when she sees one. She assured him that his wife no longer worked there but hired him on the spot when she got him to reveal that he's done men before, although he claims that basically he's a straight arrow. I was his first customer. I've been crazy about him ever since our first night."

"Sounds like he's filling in until Lew Ayres gets hot again," Bogie said.

"Louise told me that you're balling Tommy's former wife," Tracy said."

"And who in hell might that be?" Bogie almost didn't want to know after asking the question.

"Glenda Farrell," Tracy said.

"Small world, isn't it?"

Raft didn't show up until after midnight. Staggering drunk to his doorway in just his underwear. Bogie showed Raft in and pointed him to the sofa. "There's a fresh towel for you in the bathroom and…welcome."

"You look drunk, my friend," Raft said. "I never touch the stuff."

Raft wanted to stay up and talk but Bogie had to get some sleep. He staggered back to bed. After Raft had unpacked the two suitcases he'd brought with him, Bogie was only dimly aware that Raft was making some phone calls. He hoped that they weren't to his gangster friends back East, as he feared that Raft would skip out and leave him with a big phone bill.

Bogie was of two minds about getting some beauty sleep. He knew the role of Rico was not meant for a pretty face. He wondered if when he met Mervyn LeRoy tomorrow he should show up looking a little rough around the edges. That way, he might stand a better chance of getting the part than if he appeared looking young, handsome, and well-groomed, ready for another one of those "Tennis, anyone?" parts.

When Bogie awakened the next morning, he noticed Raft sprawled out nude on the sofa, his blacksnake in semi-erection. Bogie thought that his friend must be having a wet dream.

The phone rang, and he picked it up on the first ring, not wanting to wake Raft. It was his director, Henley, calling again from Fox. "The co-star of the picture has been cast, and she wants to meet you. She's seen you on the stage in New York and admires your work."

"That's just great," Bogie said, hung over, his head pounding from the effects of last night's booze.

"Be at the studio at nine," Henley ordered.

After hanging up, Bogie quickly called Glenda Farrell. LeRoy had left her house at six that morning, and had agreed to meet with Bogie about the *Little Caesar* role. "He's not promising anything. I happen to know he's testing George Raft for the role at nine o'clock."

"Does our friend know that?" Bogie asked.

"Of course, he does. Raft talked with Mervyn yesterday. Anyway, he'll test you at two o'clock. I'm doing the test with Raft this morning. I'll upstage him. Deliberately make him look bad so you'll get the part."

"Thanks, babe," he said. "I'll owe you a big favor for that."

"And I'm a gal who can always use a big one," said Farrell. "See you at two, lover."

After he'd hung up the phone, Bogie decided to pull a dirty trick on his new roomie. There was no way he was going to wake up Raft and get him to the studio by nine o'clock to test for the role of Rico.

"The part is mine," Bogie whispered to himself in the shower. He was quiet as could be as he hurriedly dressed, having left the key and a note for Raft on the kitchen table.

At Fox he was anxious to meet the female co-star of the picture.

Henley greeted him and asked him to be seated. "She'll be here in a minute." An assistant called Henley to the phone. Carl Laemmle Jr. himself wanted to speak to Henley.

Bogie was reading a newspaper but looked up when he heard footsteps walking across the sound stage. In a black and white polka dot dress, with wedge-heeled shoes, a blonde-haired young woman with a ridiculous hat was walking toward him. If he didn't suspect that this was the star of the picture, he would have figured her to be a librarian from a small town in New England.

As he was to recall in years to come, it was a meeting that would forever change his life, both professional and personal.

She extended her hand to him. "I know who you are, Mr. Humphrey Bogart. Nice to meet a fellow actor from back East. I'm told you're going to be one of my supporting players. I'm the star, of course. New England born and bred." She extended her hand. "I'm Bette Davis."

Chapter Seven

He took an instant dislike to Miss Bette Davis. As he was to tell Kenneth and later everybody else he knew, "This high-strung Yankee bitch needs a good fucking. Someone needs to go in there with a stick of dynamite and blast open that squeezed-tight little pussy of hers, and I'm the man to do it."

"So each of us is going to be making our first film, Mr. Bogart," Davis said.

"I've already got three pictures under my belt," he said, slightly angry that she'd obviously not seen any of them and hadn't heard of them either.

In spite of his setting Davis straight on his film career, she persisted all her life in claiming that she and Bogie made a joint film debut. That bit of misinformation also appeared in her highly unreliable memoir, *The Lonely Life*.

Before he'd finished his coffee with Davis, the first of many cups to come, Bogie sensed her fierce jealousy of other actresses. "Have you read the script yet?" she asked.

"No one's given me a copy."

"It's about two sisters—one good, one bad," she said. "A story about Midwestern provincialism. At first I thought I'd been cast in the role of the hellion. Imagine my disappointment when Hobart Henley informed me that Sidney Fox is playing the bad sister. I'm ending up in the role of the timid mouse."

"I'm sure you'll be good in the part," he said. "Sometimes you can take a role that's not so flashy and run with it." His first impression of her was that she did look a bit mousy.

But even at that early stage of her career, she was hardly timid. "Do you know how that whore Fox got the part?" She didn't wait for his answer. "Miss Foxy is sleeping with the producer, Carl Laemmle Jr. That's why. I'm quickly learning out here that it is who you sleep with that determines which role you get, not how talented you might be as an actress. The juicy parts go to sexual athletes like Joan Crawford. I heard from a very reliable source only the other day that any time Louis B. Mayer wants to be serviced, he calls in Crawford. Mayer sits in his chair, Crawford gets down on her knees and does her job. She's said to be an expert."

"I can vouch for that," he said.

"You've had the cow too?" David asked. "I'm not surprised. From what I've been told, she's screwed every male animal in Hollywood except Rin-Tin-Tin, and I'm not so sure she hasn't had that dog too. I wouldn't put it past her."

The only sympathy Bogie felt for Davis on that long-ago morning was his shared disillusionment with Hollywood. They both seemed to feel that they'd each made a serious career mistake in coming to Hollywood and that they'd eventually fail out here and return to the legitimate theater in New York.

"My first assignment was absolutely unbelievable," she said. "Talk about a casting couch. I've learned another meaning of the word. In one day alone I had fifteen men lie on top of me, pretending to play a love scene with me. They came like wooden soldiers one after the other whispering these lines, 'You gorgeous, divine darling, I adore you. I worship you. I must possess you.' Each actor's weight would then rest on my bosom as he kissed me passionately. The director would yell, 'Cut!' The next actor would then descend on me. Only Gilbert Roland had the sensitivity to see how shocked I was. Before he lowered his 170 pounds on me, he said, 'Don't be upset. This is Hollywood. All actresses have to go through it.' He was the only actor that day who made me feel like a woman and not like some mannequin."

Davis was called away, and before the day was over he'd get to meet all the co-stars of the film. From Tom Reed, one of the writers of the screenplay, he learned that the title had been changed from *Gambling Daughters* to *Bad Sisters*.

Standing before him at four feet, eleven inches tall, Sidney Fox, the film's other female star, might have captured the heart of the producer, Laemmle Jr., but she was way down the list on Bogie's chart of Hollywood *femme fatales*. Certainly she was no Stanwyck, Crawford, or Dietrich, although she looked mighty sexy when stacked up against the rather dull Bette Davis, whose cigarette smoke still lingered in the air as he shook Fox's delicate hand. He'd call her "cute" instead of beautiful.

Ever the needler, he asked her, "Why do you have a man's name?"

"Sure beats Humphrey," she said.

"*Touché.*"

She invited him to join her for lunch, and he accepted but told her he had a very important appointment in two hours. "It'll have to be a short one."

"Most men I've met out here promise me a long one but only deliver short."

Over the lunch table, he looked startled. "You're good."

He liked her brassy way of talking and quickly learned that she was not your typical *ingénue*. She'd studied law at Columbia University before deciding to become an actress.

"So tell me about this guy, Laemmle," Bogie said. "Junior, that is. Is he going to make a big star out of you?"

"Carl's okay but not all that great in the sack. The trouble with Carl is he can't decide if he likes pussy or boy-ass. During the filming of *All Quiet on the Western Front*, he was pounding that cute little butt of Lew Ayres. I took Carl away from Ayres. Now I hear cute-stuff is getting it from your buddy, Spencer Tracy."

"You're a regular Louella Parsons," Bogie said. "If this acting thing doesn't work out for you, you can replace her with a column of your own. Does Carl have big things in store for you?"

"Not really, I fear, in spite of his promises," she said. "Right now he feels that monster movies are going to take over Hollywood. He's all into this Dracula and Frankenstein crap. Mama didn't raise no monster."

He laughed but as he did he noticed the ominous approach of a messenger boy. Bogie was wanted on the phone. Excusing himself from Fox, he went to take the call.

It was Glenda Farrell. "Edward G. Robinson is back in the picture," she said. "He's made up with Mervyn. So you and Raft don't have a chance. I'm sorry. I tried."

He thanked her profusely, concealing his bitter disappointment. As he came back into the Universal commissary, he noticed that Laemmle Jr. had taken his place at Bogie's table and had one arm wrapped around Fox. Bogie decided to let them eat in peace. He was outranked.

***

With the hope of playing Rico in *Little Caesar* now a distant dream, Bogie walked up the steps to his apartment house. He'd read his minor part in *Bad Sister*. In it, he'd play the role of Valentine Corliss, a city slicker who comes to a small town to swindle local businessmen.

He was at first tempted to knock on Kenneth's door, but figured he'd better check in with his new roommate, George Raft. The prospect didn't thrill him. After the debacle of the *Little Caesar* casting this morning, Bogie wondered if he'd be competing against Raft in future film roles. Maybe he wouldn't have to worry about that dismal prospect. After the release of *Bad Sister*, he doubted that Fox would ever offer him another role.

By giving him eighth billing, the executives at Fox had already spoken. Even the prospect of having a hot affair with one of his leading ladies appeared remote. Sidney Fox was already taken by the studio's big brass; and Bette Davis had locked up her pussy and thrown away the key.

He wasn't going anywhere as a Hollywood film actor, but he was scoring with women and that was some compensation for a married man away from his New York wife. He wondered how Mary's own love life was doing. She was a good-looking woman with a charming personality, so he figured she was attracting a string of beaux, all of them actors no doubt.

As he came into his apartment, a man his own age was emerging from his bedroom. He looked startled to see Bogie but extended his hand. "Hi, I'm Rowland Brown."

"The director?" Bogie asked. "Well, tell me, old boy, did Raft get the part."

"He did indeed," Brown said, smiling. "Now I know why they call that handsome devil Blacksnake."

Disgusted with the way business was conducted in Hollywood—Bette Davis had nailed it—Bogie impulsively took Brown's hand and pressed it into his own crotch, where the director took expert measurements. "What part do you have for me?" He pushed Brown's hand away and went to get himself a drink.

"Not bad, not bad at all," Brown said, searching for his pants on the far side of the room. "*Quick Millions* is already cast, but based on what I was just feeling, you're entitled to a role in one of my future pictures."

"Glad to hear that," Bogie said. After pouring his drink, he turned to Brown. "Now get the hell out of here, you faggot. This is where I live. I'm not running a God damn male bordello."

Without saying another word, Brown hurriedly dressed and left. After he'd gone, Raft emerged from the bathroom stark naked, his blacksnake in repose.

"That Rowland boy is not a bad cocksucker," Raft said. "I needed some relief after my disappointment today. For an hour or two yesterday, I thought I had the part of Rico in *Little Caesar* until I learned that ugly, fat, stumpy-dicked lumphead, Robinson, was back in the role."

"You, play a gangster?" Bogie said mockingly. "You told me you wanted to be cast only as an American hero."

"What you want and what you get in life are two different things," Raft said. "I could play Rico in my sleep. Instead of that, I'm appearing opposite your pal, Spencer Tracy, in *Quick Millions*. Brown gave me the part. Sally Eilers is the leading lady. You've heard of her: Hoot Gibson's wife."

"Yeah, I've heard of her," Bogie said, turning from the sight of the naked Raft. "Why don't you put on some clothes? Your audition on the casting couch—or in this case, casting bed—is over."

Raft went into the bedroom and when he emerged, he was dressed as if ready to appear in the spotlight at Texas Guinan's club.

"What's all this crap about Molly O'Day?" Bogie asked. "Did you take her God damn jewelry?"

"Hell, no," he said defensively. "I've stolen a lot in my day, but I've never taken a woman's jewelry."

"Mae Clarke told me that Molly O'Day threatened to punish you for dumping her. Mae said your friend Molly made that statement in front of Sally Eilers. Try this on for size: Molly O'Day has stashed her little gems somewhere and is framing you."

"That's exactly what the bitch is doing," Raft said. "But Los Angeles is a big place. The gems could be anywhere."

"Listen, pal, you could go to jail, okay?" Bogie said. "You look like you're dressed up to go dancing. You should be working overtime to prove your innocence."

"I've got a friend, Owney Madden. He'll be arriving from back East tomorrow morning. He's got some guys out here. They'll take Miss Molly for a ride. With a knife ready to disfigure her pretty face, she'll squeal like a stuck pig and come up with those gems. She can issue a statement to the press that she misplaced them. The only thing the bitch has left is her face. Some doctor already carved up her body ”

“Fuck, man, you're crazy,” Bogie shouted at him. “That's how you guys do things back East. This is Los Angeles. You'll end up in jail for life. There's got to be another way.”

“Trust me. Owney knows how to handle dames like this.” He paused to smile at Bogie. “You've got to do me a big favor.”

“It seems I'm always doing you a favor,” Bogie replied. “Letting you live here, for example, splitting half my paycheck with you.”

“I've got this hot date with Sally Eilers tonight,” Raft said. “I was supposed to meet her at the Roosevelt at eight o'clock.”

“How romantic. Dating Hoot Gibson's wife. Real smart move, considering all the trouble you're in.”

“There's a lot you don't understand about the Eilers/Gibson marriage.”

Bogie wanted to pierce Raft's smug balloon. “Mae told me all about their domestic scene.”

“So you know,” he said. “Good. I don't have to feed you all the gory details. Anyway I want you to go to the Roosevelt and fill in for me as Sally's date for tonight.”

“If she'll fuck me, I'll keep your date.”

“With Sally Eilers, there's no question of if she'll fuck you. It's a question of if she'll fuck you before or after dinner.”

“That's one good-looking woman, better looking than anything I'm appearing with in *Bad Sister*. I think that God damn flick should be retitled, *Ugly Sister*.”

“I'll owe you one for taking Sally off my hands tonight,” Raft said, heading for the door.

“You owe me plenty already,” Bogie said. “What's so important that you're turning down a date with one of the most beautiful women in California?”

“My old fuck buddy, Mae, came through for me,” Raft said. “You know she's made this *Public Enemy* movie with Cagney. Mae wasn't the only blonde in that movie.”

“She's fixed you up with Joan Blondell? I could have done that.”

“Not Joanie, you silly thing, you. Jean Harlow, babycakes.” Raft headed out the door.

***

Across the table from him at the Roosevelt Hotel sat the actress, Sally Eilers, whom Mack Sennett had called “the most beautiful girl in movies.” Bogie wasn't sure about that but thought that Eilers was somewhere up near the top in any beauty contest. Her heart-shaped face seemed a mere prop for her flashing smile and wistful eyes.

“I'm glad Georgie couldn't make it tonight,” she said. “I'm getting a little bored with him, frankly. He might be handsomer than you, but you're cuter."

"I'll take that as some sort of backhanded compliment," he said.

"That's how it was meant."

"I thought you were a lot of fun in all those Hoot Gibson and Buster Keaton pictures," he said.

"Did you see me in *Cradle Snatchers?*" she asked.

"I didn't know you were in that," he said.

"Just a bit part, but you did so much better with it on Broadway. I heard you were terrific. Who was the star again?"

"Mary Boland. The bitch never liked me. Once, when I upstaged her, she threatened to destroy my career on Broadway."

"Here we are," she said, "both of us waiting for our big break. I think I've got mine. I don't know if you've read the novel, *Bad Girl.*"

"I've heard of it," he said, flashing a smile, "I'm appearing with Bette Davis in *Bad Sister*. Maybe I'll make my mark in *Bad Brother* or *Bad Boy*. Yeah, I like that. *Bad Boy.*"

She seemed momentarily annoyed that he was distracting her from her career revelations. "As you know, *Bad Girl* is a best-seller and it did well on Broadway."

"I know about it. My wife, Mary Philips, was up for a role in it. Sylvia Sidney got it instead."

"Frank Borzage bought the screen rights," she said. "He wanted to cast it with Janet Gaynor and Charles Farrell."

"I know Charlie boy very, very well."

"Both Gaynor and Farrell turned it down," she said. "But then Borzage cast me in the part instead. Opposite James Dunn."

Bogie allowed Eilers to babble on, as he knew it was mandatory on a first meeting to let actresses fill him in on their careers. In fact, it was all they ever really wanted to talk about.

Had he had his crystal ball that night, or at least one borrowed from Natacha Rambova, he could have foreseen that Eilers had indeed hit upon the one property that would become the surprise hit of 1931.

Cast as a brash, breezy, good-looking Irishman, James Dunn would go on with Eilers to make three more films: *Over the Hill*, also in 1931; *Dance Team* in 1932, and *Sailor's Luck* in 1933. Dunn would be almost forgotten today were it not for his pairing with Shirley Temple in a trio of 1933 hits: *Stand Up and Cheer*, *Baby Take a Bow*, and *Bright Eyes*. He eventually came back to win an Oscar for his touching performance in 1945 as the ne'er do well father in *A Tree Grows in Brooklyn*.

Eilers would never find a follow-up for *Bad Girl*, going on to appear in nondescript movies and unrewarding roles in programmers. But the night she met Bogie she felt on top of the world.

When she told him that Borzage thought she was going to become the new queen of Hollywood, it made Bogie wonder that if every gal in Hollywood was going to be the queen, who would be the princesses or the ladies-in-waiting at the court.

Since she was holding his hand, he lifted it to his lips and kissed it. "Let's not talk shop," he said. "There's something I want to ask you. First, I'll come clean myself. As you know, I'm married to Mary Philips. She won't come to Hollywood. We have an open relationship. Free to date other people. I don't get it with you and Hoot Gibson though. I mean I saw pictures of your recent marriage on his ranch. Isn't he going to storm into the Roosevelt in his ten-gallon hat with his six-shooter and mow me down?"

"No, no," she said. "He encourages me to date."

"Why?"

She snickered as if holding back some secret from him. "You'll find out." She giggled again.

He figured he'd gotten all the information from her he could, at least for the moment, so he switched to the subject of Molly O'Day. "You're her friend, right?"

"Not at all," she said. "Molly thinks I'm one of her best friends. Actually I hate her. I was up for the role of Curley Callahan in *The Patent Leather Kid*. Molly won the role and was given a contract at First National. I kissed her and congratulated her, but if I'd had a stiletto, I would have stabbed her with it."

"Do you know about the trouble Raft is in because of O'Day."

"George told me all about it."

"So, what do you think?" he asked, growing impatient with Eilers.

"I think O'Day still has all her jewelry," she said. "I think it's safely stashed away somewhere. Maybe at the home of her sister, Sally O'Neil."

"Could you arrange some little get-together? Just you, me, and O'Day? Real casual like. I'd like to meet her. Unless this is resolved in time, our boy George will be serving time. His career, everything will be wrecked."

"I guess," she said, appearing reluctant. "But if you think Molly is going to spill the beans and admit something to you, a perfect stranger, you've got another thing coming."

She looked over at him as if she were imitating Mary Pickford in the film, *Coquette*. "Maybe I'll set something up with you, me, and Molly, and maybe I won't. Let's see how the night goes."

The evening at the Roosevelt moved toward its inevitable conclusion. When she told him that her husband, Hoot Gibson, was out of town, he agreed to go back to her house.

The cowboy star's home, as he was soon to learn, looked like something in New Mexico. Tom Mix's rival seemed to have a passion for the skulls of long-horned steers.

"So this is where you and Hoot pursue your amusements?" he said, looking around the place. To a New York actor, it looked more like a Western stage set than a home where people could actually live. He could just imagine what Maud, who had objected to the Brady's "Jewish décor," would think of the home of cowboy star Hoot Gibson and his blushing bride, Sally Eilers.

After she'd poured him a drink, Eilers disappeared for fifteen minutes. When she came back into the living room, she was wearing a sheer French *négligée*. As he was to relate to Kenneth the next day, "I could see all the way to Honolulu."

By the third drink, she was sampling his wet lips. "I've been wanting to do that all night," she said when she took a break to replenish the air in her lungs. "If you fuck only one tenth as good as Georgie, I'm in for a treat."

"I'm even better," he said, pulling her close for some deep tonguing.

Within a half hour, all his clothing was off and he was walking stark naked with her to the marriage bed she shared with Gibson.

Deep into the fuck, he figured that it would take a former cowpuncher and rodeo wrangler like Gibson to handle a steer like Sally Eilers. Unlike Mae Clarke, who only lay there as she was devoured, Eilers took a more athletic approach. She was all over him. No sooner were they at the top of Gibson's gigantic bed, than they'd worked their way to the bottom, with her head hanging off the edge.

Back to center stage, he held her down for the final roundup. He was controlling the fuck now, and really enjoying himself. Eilers was one of the hottest dames he'd ever plowed. He couldn't recall when he'd had such pleasure. Unlike some of the quasi-lesbians he'd devoured, Eilers was truly a man's woman.

As his passion built, he was startled to feel hands prying open the cheeks to his ass. He jerked his head around as Eilers embraced him with more force than he'd ever known from a woman in bed. Her tongue shot into his mouth.

Then what seemed like the world's most talented tongue attacked his ass, sending him bucking in the air and wanting more. He reared up only to plunge back into Eilers. He'd never known a sexual thrill quite like this one. He was too far gone to care any longer about the stranger attacking his ass.

Tomorrow Kenneth would learn all the details of what Bogie called "the greatest fuck of my life."

It was only when he'd reluctantly pulled out of Eilers and lay flat on his back, panting for air, that he confronted the stranger who already knew one part of his anatomy intimately.

"Hi," the stranger said. "We already know each other a bit. But let me formally introduce myself, partner. I'm Hoot Gibson."

***

Hoot Gibson and Sally Eilers were Hollywood's original swinging couple. While Eilers busied herself in the bathroom, Gibson, the screen idol who had become "The World's All Around Champion Cowboy" when he was only twenty, poured a drink for Bogie.

Gibson was hardly Bogie's favorite movie star, but as he sat and talked with this doughy-faced and snub-nosed film legend, he studied himself closely. He was one of John Ford's "macho men" who appeared in some of the director's films such as *Straight Shooting* in 1917. After that experience in bed, Bogie wondered just how much of a straight shooter Gibson really was.

"So where did you get the name of Hoot?" Bogie asked, feeling awkward after the intimacy they'd so recently shared with his wife.

"For my luck in hunting owls," Gibson said. "John Ford—I call him Jack—has helped me a lot. He named me Hoot. My real name is Ed."

"Ford didn't do a God damn thing for my career," Bogie said. "Except get me laid at Louise's, and I could have done that on my own."

"Maybe you're too much of a city slicker for Ford," Gibson said. "I think he prefers men from the wide-open West."

"That I'm not," Bogie said. "I'm a city boy like James Cagney. I don't think any director will want me to play a western star." Unlike Natacha Rambova, Bogie was not a prophet, as his future film roles would reveal.

"Then I'd say me and you won't be competing for the same roles, partner," Gibson said. "But I've got my eye on a few rivals. I think this Gary Cooper is going to go over great in westerns. There's also this guy named 'Duke' that Ford is raving about all the time."

"Yeah, I've heard of him."

"It seems like you've already walked the bridge from Silents to Talkies," Bogie said. "You're so different from Buck Jones and Tom Mix. A new kind of western star favoring comedy over action."

"All well and good," Gibson said, downing his drink quickly and heading to the bar for another one. "That was then and this is now. I learned last week that I'm out the door. Universal fired me. They've stopped making Westerns. With no more horse operas, where am I?"

"You've still got a big name," Bogie said. "A lot of studios, even independent producers, are filming westerns. They'd go for you in a big way when they hear you're available."

"I'm not kidding myself," he said. "I'll find work but it's all downhill from now on."

At that point, Eilers came back into the room. In spite of her recent workout, she'd pulled herself together beautifully and looked camera-ready, living up to Mack Sennett's billing as the most beautiful girl in Hollywood.

"Baby Doll," Bogie said, looking up, "come and join us for a drink."

Gibson and Eilers had an old black man, gray haired and stoop shouldered, working for them. He came into the room, looking as if each step would be his last. "Mr. Hoot, I hate to bother you fine people, but Miss Helen is out on the terrace. She's just got out of jail."

Gibson sighed, getting up and excusing himself, as he headed for the terrace, with the old family retainer trailing him.

"That's that God damn drunk," Eilers said. "He divorced her this year to marry me. They have a kid, Lois. You may have heard of the ex-Mrs. Hoot Gibson. She starred in several silent serials as Helen Gibson. Now she's a hopeless alcoholic."

Ever the curious one, Bogie asked, "What does she want?"

"She can't let Hoot go," Eilers said. "More to the point, she can't let his money go. He was a very generous man. In their divorce settlement, he gave her half of everything. But in no time at all, she went through it all. She's already been arrested a couple of times for passing hot checks. Like a fool, he keeps bailing her out."

"I read something in the papers about them."

"When Helen got all that money from Hoot, she was conned into making this stupid investment in oil in Texas. Lost every penny within six weeks. When she was first arrested, the press came down hard on Hoot. Accused him of being a tightwad, of leaving his first wife penniless and in the lurch."

"He sounds like too generous," Bogie said. "Goes to show you, you can't believe what you read in the press."

Gibson came back into the room. He kissed Eilers. "I've got to go downtown and cover some bad checks for Helen." He walked over and shook Bogie's hand. "Nice meeting you, partner. Drop in any time."

"How about four or five nights a week," Bogie said jokingly.

Gibson's eyes lit up. "You've got yourself a deal." He turned to Eilers. "If it's okay with you, honey."

"That was some wild ride," she said. "It's okay with me."

In full western garb, Gibson headed across the living room and off into the night.

As nice and generous a man as he might be, Bogie decided then and there he'd try to avoid Hoot Gibson in the future.

Decades later, quite by accident in the 1950s in Las Vegas, Bogie ran into Gibson again, learning that this broken down former cowboy star was working as a casino greeter. In the years since Bogie had first met him, Hoot Gibson's horse operas took in less and less money. In his final pictures, the camera revealed a tired, overweight, and lethargic Gibson just going through the motions, waiting for his paycheck.

Ever the needler, Bogie in Las Vegas asked, "Still giving those lube jobs?"

Gibson looked embarrassed. "Have a nice stay here and come up a winner." Still in his familiar cowboy garb, he turned and walked away.

Bogie felt sorry that he'd made such a dig at an out-of-work fallen star. He felt even worse when the manager of the casino, Frank Tuttle, told Bogie that he'd hired Gibson as the greeter because the actor needed money to pay off enormous debts that mounted after a series of cancer operations.

Before leaving Las Vegas, Bogie left ten one-hundred dollar bills in an envelope addressed to Gibson at the reception desk. But that was a long time into the future.

The night he'd met Gibson and had had that encounter with him in bed with his wife, Bogie sat talking and drinking with Eilers. He thought that she might want to take him on again, just by herself, now that her husband wasn't overseeing the action. When she didn't seem interested in a repeat performance with him, he urged her to call Molly O'Day and get them invited over to her bungalow at the Garden of Allah.

As Bogie drove Sally Eilers along Sunset Boulevard that hot Los Angeles night, he could not have imagined that at one time he too would live, however briefly, at the Garden of Allah with three of his wives: Mary Philips, Mayo Methot, and Lauren Bacall, and that he'd enjoy several conjugal visits there from his first wife, Helen Menken.

The Wampas Baby Star of 1938, Molly O'Day, received them in her bathrobe without makeup. He found it hard to believe that this was the star he'd seen on the screen.

Over drinks she spoke candidly about her relationship with George Raft. "In New York, we were so much in love. We were seen together everywhere—at the racetrack, at boxing matches, at baseball games. George loves sports, and I went along because I wanted to make him happy. We had such gay old times with Texas Guinan and even Lillian Roth." A frowned crossed her brow. "That one drinks like a fish. And by the way, she made a play for George one night."

Noticing she'd downed her drink rather rapidly, he volunteered to get her another one, even though Eilers had warned that she tended to drink too much. "Get me the fucking drink, Bogie," she commanded and he obeyed.

"Yeah, I went along with all of Georgie boy's plans, even when it involved his old manager, Mack Gray. We were quite a threesome. George insisted that Mack go everywhere with us." She paused again. "Even to bed. I didn't like fucking Mack at all. But I did it because of George." She accepted the drink from Bogie. "A hell of a lot of good that did me."

Pretending a friendship she didn't really feel, Eilers reached for O'Day's hand to console her. "The night things started to go bad was at Texas's club," O'Day said. "One of Al Capone's henchmen, Giovanni Torello, was in from Chicago. I was wearing a beaded white dress cut real low. Real sexy looking. Texas seated us at a ringside table. Later I learned that Torello took one look at me and decided he had to have me. When he ran into George in the men's room, he demanded my services for the evening. Naturally, George refused. Being George, he went a bit overboard. 'Get out of my face, you guinea bastard,' George said."

"I've met some of those boys," Bogie said. "I can just imagine what happened next."

"Raft knows better than to mess with Capone's boys," Eilers said.

"Normally he does," O'Day said, "but he was so much in love with me he went crazy. Since George's protector, Owney Madden, was out of town, Torello ordered two of his hit men to wipe George from the map. At first George didn't take the threat seriously. I remember one night we walked into one of our favorite Broadway restaurants and the joint cleared out. The guys there figured that Torello might have George blown away right in the restaurant. Both of us were scared shitless. We locked ourselves into this dump of a hotel in Brooklyn and were afraid to open the door even for room service. We nearly starved to death." She looked over at Eilers. "And you know how I like to eat."

"So what happened?" Bogie asked, growing impatient with O'Day. What he really wanted was to ask her about the jewelry.

"When Madden came back to town, he warned Torello to lay off George. To my surprise, that protective blanket didn't cover me. I heard that Torello was still after me and planned to disfigure my face."

"Those asses will do it too," Bogie said. "Once when I was in Chicago, for some reason they went after the comedian, Joe E. Lewis. They carved him up petty bad. Somehow he escaped alive."

"While the heat was on, George told me to hide out here in California, and he'd be out to join me soon," O'Day said. "He came out to join me all right, and to take up with every other blonde in town, including that slut, Jean Harlow. He even promised to marry me."

"But did he really take your jewelry?" Bogie asked pointedly.

"Yeah, Molly," Eilers said, "aren't you just trying to get back at him for jilting you? Don't you still have those gems stashed some place?"

"Go on," Bogie urged. "Tell us where you stashed them. You could be in big trouble. You know Raft still has his gangster contacts. You don't want to get carved up like Lewis."

Suddenly, O'Day screamed and jumped up from her chair, spilling her drink. In front of Bogie and Eilers, she dropped her robe. She was nude underneath it. Both of them gasped when they saw her body. She had horrible scars on both sides of her torso.

"Don't even mention getting 'carved up' to me," she shouted at them. "See what those beauty butchers have done. They told me they could cut fat from my body. Look how they sewed me up. I could replace the monster in that Mae Clarke version of *Frankenstein*."

He got up and retrieved her robe, using it to cover her nudity.

"At least my face wasn't carved up, but my body's ruined," O'Day said. "I can never appear on the screen again in anything revealing. Maybe I can play old maids in long black dresses."

"Maybe the scars will heal," Eilers said hopefully.

"Like hell they will," O'Day said. "The studio made me do it. I eat too much. Always did love food. I was putting on weight, but my fans didn't mind." She went over and picked up a copy of *Photoplay* magazine. "Listen to this. It's from a fan of mine, Lucille Boyd of Tacoma, Washington. 'I see Molly O'Day is not allowed to be a star because she has put on a few extra pounds of weight. If the directors chose stars that had a few curves instead of girls that look like sticks, I would be better pleased. When you go to a show nowadays, all you see are girls who look like a bag of bones.'"

"When George saw me nude after the operation," O'Day said, tossing the magazine on the floor, "he pulled on his pants and within a few seconds was halfway out the door. 'I'm out of here,' he called back to me. Right in the pool area, he yelled back into my bungalow. 'I don't fuck monsters. Hook up with Boris Karloff.'"

Eilers and Bogie spent another hour with O'Day pleading with her to admit that she had hidden her jewelry and falsely blamed Raft. She adamantly refused.

After dropping Eilers off at the Gibson home, Bogie drove back to his own apartment.

Exhausted, he fell into bed and slept soundly until about three o'clock that morning when he was awakened by the persistent ringing of his telephone.

"Is this Bogart?" asked the voice on the other end. "Sally Eilers gave me your phone number. I'm another Sally. Sally O'Neil. Molly's sister. You've got to come at once. I'm in Molly's bungalow at the Garden of Allah. An ambulance has taken her away. She tried to kill herself tonight, and I've got to see you. Come at once. It's a matter of life and death."

She didn't give him much choice. As he got in his car and drove to 8150 Sunset Boulevard, it was like a scene from a future Bogie movie. Those would be fantasies. Right now he was living the real thing.

Cursing himself for getting mixed up in Raft's mess, he said out loud, "Raft is going to owe me a big favor one of these days, and I'm going to collect."

As he entered the swimming pool area and headed for O'Day's bungalow, he spotted a nude man—dripping wet—running away from the pool area. Instead of a penis between his legs, it looked like a flopping salami. He was being chased by a beautiful woman, also stark naked.

The pair disappeared into a nearby bungalow. It was only when knocking on the door to O'Day's bungalow that he realized the couple was none other than Gary Cooper and Tallulah Bankhead.

Bankhead had told everyone that she was coming to Hollywood for the stated purpose of "fucking that divine Gary Cooper." In that, she seemed to have succeeded.

The door to O'Day's bungalow was thrown open and there stood Sally O'Neil, looking even more beautiful than she appeared in her pictures.

***

The sister of Molly O'Day, herself the Wampus baby Star of 1926, Sally O'Neil had turned herself into a clone of early Joan Crawford. Sporting a tight-to-the-head Jazz Age bob and a Cupid's bow mouth painted on her sensuous lips, O'Neil was a pert, Irish beauty. For such a small young woman, she had a surprisingly deep, resonant voice, making him think she'd do well in talking pictures, building on her early success in Silents. Once again, Bogie proved that he was no prophet.

As he sat opposite her, enjoying a hefty drink of Scotch, she related with hysteria how O'Day had swallowed an entire container of sleeping capsules and had had her stomach pumped after being rushed to a hospital.

O'Neil seemed more worried about a film that they were shooting together, appropriately called *Sisters*, than she was about O'Day's condition. "It's Friday night," O'Neil said. "I'm going to drag her out of bed and onto the set Monday morning. I want to keep this out of the papers. I can't let our director, James Flood, know what Molly has done. He might fire her from the picture. He might even fire me too, for all I know."

Bogie was sharpening his needle. "If O'Day wants to stay out of the papers, maybe she'd better stop falsely accusing Raft of that jewel theft." He took a hefty swig of his scotch. "That alleged jewel theft."

"That's why I called you here," O'Neil said. "I have the gems. Molly asked me to keep them for her."

"I figured as much."

She looked disdainfully at him. "And you figured right. I tried to talk Molly out of going through with her scheme, but the bitch wouldn't listen to me. I told her Raft wasn't worth all the trouble."

"Where's the jewelry?" he asked, getting up to pour himself another drink.

She went over to a piece of expensive looking luggage and opened it. Reaching in, she removed a jewelry case. She walked over and handed it to him.

Unfastening the case, he opened it. "Mighty impressive," he said, reaching in and fondling a pearl necklace. "I wish I could present all of these to my Mary."

"There it is," she said. "Every piece of it. I won't tell you how Molly—that is, before her beauty butchers worked her over—earned those gems the hard way."

This means that my buddy Raft won't have to serve time," he said, drinking much faster than he usually did. He poured himself yet another drink. On most occasions, he could hold his liquor better than this. He felt his head was swimming yet he continued to drink. Maybe it was the early hour of the morning. Normally, he cut off drinking at two o'clock. Looking out the windows of the bungalow, he felt it would be dawn soon.

O'Neil was locking her luggage as if she were going on a trip.

"I assume you're packing that suitcase to take to Molly at the hospital."

"I really should stay and look after Molly," she said, "but Joan Crawford is insisting I go with her to Palm Springs for the weekend. And you know how SHE is. You don't say no to Joan Crawford."

"Is Constance Bennett coming with you?" he asked provocatively. He was making a reference to O'Neil's most famous silent film, *Sally, Irene and Mary* in which Constance Bennett played Sally, Crawford Irene, and O'Neil Mary.

She shot him a sarcastic glance. "No, darling Constance will not be joining us. I can't stand the bitch." The phone rang. She picked it up and told the person on the other end of the line that she was just leaving.

"Joan is already waiting for me up front in her car, and that's one gal who doesn't like to be kept waiting."

He picked up the jewelry case and headed for the door. She kissed him on the cheek. "Thanks for being such an angel, and don't forget to look in on Molly at the hospital while I'm gone. Don't tell her, though, that I'm in Palm Springs."

"You girls have fun," he said sarcastically, feeling that Crawford couldn't make up her mind whether she liked women or men. The way he figured it, she was the true Bisexual Queen of Hollywood, moving with comparative ease between the sexes.

Staggering toward his car with the gems, he got behind the wheel even though he knew he shouldn't be driving. To make matters worse, one of those quick Southern California cloudbursts came up, drenching him. Instead of waiting it out, he was impatient and started to drive. The windshield wipers weren't working too well. He'd been meaning to have them fixed.

He'd gone no more than three blocks along Sunset Boulevard when at the last moment he spotted a tall man and a little girl dashing across the boulevard right in front of his car. He braked suddenly but that action only sent his car skidding across the slippery road.

His brain dimmed by alcohol, he tried to break the skid, but lost control of his auto instead. His whole car seemed to be caving in as he felt the crunch of his vehicle pounding into a parked car.

***

It was nine o'clock in the morning, and he'd had no sleep. He was in jail in downtown Los Angeles. He'd been arrested on a charge of driving while intoxicated, having an accident, and being in possession of $25,000 in allegedly stolen gems.

A husky red-faced police lieutenant, "Lefty" James, came for him, informing him that he was being taken to the office of Police Chief Ted Taylor.

On the way to Taylor's office, Bogie cursed himself for his stupidity. What in hell possessed him to accept that jewelry from Sally O'Neil? In his drunken mind, he had some vague thought of turning the gems over to Raft, as if that would free his friend. In the cold, sober light of day, he realized that accepting the gems was the worst thing he could have done. To get out of this trap, he could tell the truth, incriminating both Sally O'Neil and Molly O'Day in a charge that could carry prison sentences for both of them.

That prospect didn't thrill him. First, he still felt like too much of a gentleman to do a thing like that. He also doubted if he'd be believed.

One of Los Angeles' most notorious police chiefs, Taylor was rumored to let movie stars off the hook if they had the backing of a powerful studio, and consequently, executives at various studios contributed big bucks to the annual "police benefit." Of all the Hollywood moguls, Louis B. Mayer was the biggest contributor as his stable of stars had more to conceal than the stars at any other studio in town.

As a contract player, and a minor one at that, Bogie felt that he was virtually unprotected.

Living up to his reputation for bluntness, Taylor immediately informed Bogie, "We've arrested your friend Raft. We should never have let him go the first time. Your apartment has been thoroughly searched. We thought we'd find the jewelry there. What a lucky break when you crashed into that parked car. You made it so easy for us."

"I can explain," Bogie blurted out, then shut up. Just what could he explain? "I want a lawyer."

"You'll get a lawyer," Taylor said, not very convincingly. He reached into his desk drawer and pulled out some papers. "Walter Winchell has sent us this confidential report from New York. He's the most reliable journalist in New York, and when he puts something on paper, it's the truth." He put on his glasses and glanced down at the document. "He says right here, and I believe him, that both you and Raft are out here in Los Angeles not to become movie actors but to front for the West Coast underworld interests of Owney Madden."

"That's a God damn lie," Bogie said. "I don't even know Madden."

"Oh, yeah," Taylor said. "The gangster happens to be George Raft's best friend, and you happen to be Raft's roommate." He looked over at his cohort with a smirk. "Lover boys, so I hear."

"You got it all wrong," Bogie protested but he feared to no avail.

"I'll admit the report we've got on Raft is ten times longer than what we have on you," Taylor said. "It seems you're just a minor cog in a very sleazy-looking wheel."

"I'm not even a screw in any damn wheel," Bogie protested again.

Taylor reached into his batch of papers and removed a glossy photograph. He handed it to Bogie. "Recognize the cast of characters?"

Bogie didn't even remember such a picture being taken. It was at Texas Guinan's club. The picture showed him and George Raft posing with Dutch Schultz. Bogie vaguely remembered some night club photographer taking such a picture before Guinan chased him away. Dutch Schultz didn't like to be photographed.

"I was at the club," Bogie said. "Schultz was there. I think I shook his hand. That was it. I don't know him. Just someone in a night club."

"I just hope, Bogart, you're more convincing as an actor on the screen than you are in this room this morning," James said.

"You said it, Lefty." Taylor turned to Bogie. "The evidence against you is overwhelming. Maybe the judge will give you only ten years. To make it lenient on yourself, you care to answer a few of my questions? Not the babble I've heard so far. Some truth for a change."

"In the presence of a lawyer," Bogie said.

"You'll get a lawyer in due time," Taylor said.

"Until I do, call me the New York clam," Bogie said.

218

Anger flashed across Taylor's face. "Throw him back in a cell," he shouted at James. "And you know the one I mean."

Leaving the chief's office, James escorted Bogie to another wing of the jail. They locked him up with ten other men, each of them arrested on the streets of downtown Los Angeles. When James and a guard had gone, with the cell's door locked behind them, a bearded, middle-aged man with a big gut came over to Bogie. He ran his fingers along Bogie's unshaven face. "Hey, guys, Chief Taylor has done it again. Sent us another pretty boy to break in."

Instinctively, Bogie drew back. "Cut it out. Get away from me."

"Playing hard to get, huh?" he said. "We'll see about that."

Two men creeping up on Bogie from behind knocked him over, sending him sprawling on the concrete floor. In a flash, Bogie realized how easily he could be overpowered by these street-toughened men.

"Just for that," the burly man said, "we're going to make it extra hard on you tonight, pretty boy. Extra hard. It's been three days since Taylor sent the last pretty boy here. From what I hear through the grapevine, that kid's still in the hospital. Still bleeding internally."

Like a frightened, cornered animal, Bogie cowered against the wall. The memory of reading about Rudolph Valentino's arrest on a bigamy charge raced through his mind. The Sheik had been thrown into a cell like this one—maybe this very same cell—where he'd been raped repeatedly.

"Tonight, pretty boy," the burly man said, "when the lights go out, we're gonna really have some fun with you. A couple of us have the clap, but you don't mind that, do you? It'll give you something to remember us by." He laughed and headed for the far corner of the cell, where he whipped out his penis and took a horse piss in a dirty toilet with no seat.

Bogie dreaded the moment when he himself would be forced to use that same toilet in front of this street trash.

Fortunately, he was spared that indignity. He was furious that Taylor had not yet allowed him to call a lawyer, although he didn't know who to ring up. He thought he might try to get in touch with Barbara Stanwyck. A smart cookie like Stanwyck, although relatively new to Hollywood, would surely know a lawyer.

When a guard came for him, he thought he'd be allowed to make that phone call. Instead he was taken into a small, nearly empty room where the film director, Rowland Brown, was waiting for him.

"What in hell are you doing here?" Bogie asked, his earlier resentment of the director flashing.

"I'm getting Raft out of jail," Brown said. "Taylor always takes some convincing. Cash helps."

"What about me?" Bogie asked, desperate at this point, needing and wanting help anywhere he could get it, even if it came from Rowland Brown.

"I'm still pissed off at you for the way you tossed me out of your apartment," Brown said. "The other actors in Hollywood show a little more respect. Frankly,

I think I should let you rot here. It would teach you some manners."

"Okay, what do I have to do to get sprung?" he asked. "You should see the creeps they've locked me up with. I couldn't make it through one night alive with that bunch."

Brown walked toward him, as Bogie backed away. The director's face reflected how offended he was. "I can be of no help to you." He headed for the door.

"Wait," Bogie shouted after him, as a panic came over him. He felt trapped. As he walked over to Brown, impulsively he reached for Brown's hand and placed it on his crotch as he'd done mockingly in his apartment. This time it was for real. Bogie just knew that nothing Brown had in store for him would match what was waiting back in that stinking hole with a cage of psychotics.

Brown's fingers seemed to be feeling everywhere. "I liked what I felt in your apartment. I like it even more now." He looked into Bogie's face as if he wanted to kiss him. Without meaning to, Bogie leaned back.

"Okay," Brown said, having been angered again. "I'm out the door."

Before Brown could turn the doorknob, Bogie approached him and spun him around, taking him in his arms. He pressed his lips hard onto Brown's mouth, feeling the director's tongue darting between his teeth.

When Brown finally broke away, he said, "Ready to be my boy?"

"Not that," Bogie said softly, having completely surrendered to Brown. "But you've got your man."

***

Out on bail posted by Rowland Brown, the two "jewel thieves" were in the same car heading east from Los Angeles to Palm Springs. Raft was driving, and the sexy blonde bombshell, Jean Harlow, was perched on his right, chatting incessantly. Sulking in the back seat, Bogie sat with his rescuer, Rowland Brown.

Harlow had albino blonde hair, the whitest blonde Bogie had ever seen, and a cute but somewhat puffy little face.

Raft drove her new red Cadillac with only his left pinkie on the steering wheel. The impressive, shiny vehicle was rumored to have been a gift to Harlow from the notorious mobster, Abner "Longy" Zwillman, with whom she was said to be having an affair.

Of all the women he'd wanted to meet in Hollywood, Jean Harlow topped the list. And George Raft had her. From that weekend in Palm Springs until her untimely death, she would always tell people that, "Bogart is a pansy—not that I have anything against the boys. They're some of my best friends." In spite of what was to transpire between them, Harlow with the stubbornness of a Missouri mule still stuck to her first impression.

Bogie was headed for one of the most memorable weekends of his life even though he'd never speak of it ever again. If he could get out of his present trouble and avoid a jail sentence, he was determined to leave Hollywood as soon as his contract with Fox ran out. It was not his kind of town.

Everybody except Bogie and Bette Davis seemed to undergo a name change in Hollywood, and Jean Harlow was no exception. "Would you believe my dad— he was a dentist in Kansas City, Missouri—named me Harlean Carpenter? When the studio agreed to change it to Jean Harlow, I feared it sounded too much like harlot."

The men laughed, all except Bogie. Of all the people in the car, he was not looking forward to this fun weekend in Palm Springs where Joan Crawford and Sally O'Neil were already installed in some house.

"I got married when I was sweet sixteen," Harlow told the men. "To a Charles McGrew. We pulled up stakes in Missouri and headed for Los Angeles."

"You mean stakes in Kansas?" Raft interjected.

"No, you dumb fool," she said. "There's also a Kansas City, Missouri. I never wanted to be a movie star. I'd settle for being a happy housewife somewhere with a bunch of kids. I was pushed into it, and I just did it for the money."

"I think you had a lot of screen presence in those Hal Roach shorts and with Laurel and Hardy," Brown said.

"I appreciate the compliment, but you can take those films and shove them where the sun don't shine," Harlow said. "The one I hated most was *Double Whoopee* with Laurel and Hardy. When I was a baby girl, Mother Jean would always say, 'Harlean has got to go make double whoopee' whenever I had to take a crap. That picture was indeed shit."

"That's behind you now," Brown said. "After Howard Hughes put you in *Hell's Angels*, the world was yours. That Howard baby can put his big shiny shoes under my bed any night."

Harlow looked back at Brown with a smirk on her face, then glanced at Raft. "From what Georgie boy tells me, you've perfected a technique that would drive Howard crazy. Where did you learn all you know?"

"You may not believe this," Brown said, "but at a whorehouse in Shanghai. I spent eighteen months in China. I actually took lessons at a bordello, practicing on sailors in port for the night. The Chinese have been having sex for centuries before we Americans got around to discovering it. They can teach us a lot."

"Sorry you're into men," Harlow said, "What a waste. I bet you could teach me a lot."

Raft leaned over and took her hand, holding it up to his lips where he kissed it tenderly. "With me as your professor, you'll have no need of Rowland back there."

Seeing an oncoming car, Bogie called out, "Eyes on the road." When he saw Harlow smiling flirtatiously at him, he said. "Sorry to yell at you, Raft. It's not your fault. With Jean Harlow to look at, what guy could keep his eyes on the road?"

"Miss Harlow appreciates the compliment," she said. This was Bogie's first knowledge that she often spoke of herself in the third person.

"I want to know more about Hughes," Brown said. "God damn it, I not only wish he'd go to bed with me but hire me to direct one of his pictures."

"Howard's okay," she said with a shrug of her beautiful shoulders, "but I've known better. I think he likes boys more than girls. Think! Hell, I know. When he took me to bed, he had three autographed photos of Randolph Scott in his bedroom. When he was fucking me, I got the impression that he kept looking at them to keep himself hard. On the set of *Hell's Angels*, Howard was more interested in chasing after the male stars, Ben Lyon and James Hall, than he was in me. Not that I blame him. I chased after Ben and James myself."

"That other James who worked on the picture with you," Brown said. "James Whale. He's becoming a bigtime director. I hear he's a homo."

"More so than William Haines," Harlow said. "Whale wanted to go to bed with Howard too. But he's too effeminate for Howard. Howard likes to seduce rugged, masculine men like Gary Cooper. That prissy--the one named after Moby Dick--will never get into Howard's pants. Whale was hired as my dialogue coach. Howard actually shot the film as a silent with Greta Nissen in my part. Then Talkies came in. Nissen speaks English with a Scandinavian accent so thick it would cut a North Sea seal in half. Howard didn't like the way I spoke either. He said my accent was so strong I could lead a mule train across the wide Missouri. That's when he called Whale in to teach me proper English."

She reached into her purse and pulled out a Fatima, offering each of the men one. Since Raft had the windows up, so much cigarette smoke filled the car that Bogie wondered how Raft could see to drive.

Before they got to the home in Palm Springs that Brown had been lent for the weekend, the men had gone through two packages of Harlow's Fatima cigarettes.

When they finally arrived at the house, Bogie found the villa palatial. There was a giant swimming pool where he planned to spend most of his time unless called away to service Brown.

For some reason Brown chose not to tell them the name of the owner of the property. Bogie figured it was another bigshot in Hollywood who was deep in the closet. He did hear later that the house where they were staying was the most notorious in Palm Springs, known for its all-male nude swim parties.

A kindly old black couple helped them unpack and then retired to the kitchen to prepare a light meal for the newly arrived guests.

Bogie put on a conservative black swimsuit and headed for a chaise longue bordering the pool with the bluest water he'd ever seen. Since the pool was painted a deep blue, he suspected that it was an optical illusion, like everything else in Hollywood.

He heard the phone ring twice. Brown took the first call. Apparently from what Bogie could hear, he was inviting some people over.

The second call was for Harlow. After listening briefly, she screamed hysterically. "God damn it!" she shouted into the phone. "He didn't have to do that." When she'd finished the phone conversation, she ran out to the patio area where Raft and Brown, still fully dressed, were chatting at the bar.

Raft went to her and put his arm around her, trying to offer some comfort. Brown tried to find out what was the matter. Since he was in earshot, Bogie remained seated.

From what he'd gathered, a Hollywood photographer, Edward Hesser, had taken nude pictures of Harlow in Griffith Park in Los Angeles when she was only seventeen. Now that she was a star, these nude photos had fallen into the hands of two blackmailers, who were demanding $50,000 under threat of destroying her career.

"I told Longy all about it," she said. "Even showed him the threatening letters. Now I find out the two guys blackmailing me were found dead somewhere along a beach in Laguna."

Those nude pictures of Harlow would eventually surface long after her death, and long after it no longer made any difference to her career.

That faraway afternoon in Palm Springs was eerily evocative of a 1950s Jean Harlow, Marilyn Monroe, who also posed for nude pictures. MM's pictures didn't destroy her career either but ended up in the men's room of every garage toilet in America.

***

Harlow spent very little time mourning the deaths of her two blackmailers and soon joined Bogie at poolside, wearing a skimpy white bathing suit that revealed more than it concealed.

"Welcome," he said, patting the chaise longue beside him. "If I didn't have Rowland Brown panting after me, I'd say I was the luckiest man in Hollywood. At least I've got the most gorgeous blonde in Hollywood."

"Thank you for that compliment," she said, easing down beside him. "I really appreciate it. When I get back to Hollywood, I'll buy you a little gift."

He thought nothing of that promise at the time. Later he was to learn that Harlow meant what she said. She had such an inferiority complex that if someone paid her a compliment, however meager, she purchased a little gift for them to show her gratitude.

Even in her bathing suit, she still wore a pair of skyscraper-high shoes, flaming scarlet-red high heels made of patent leather.

He asked if she wanted a drink, and she agreed. Without getting up, he reached for the nearby ice bucket and a bottle, pouring her a whiskey on the rocks. She propped her legs up, seemingly for his enjoyment. They hardly gave Marlene Dietrich competition, but were a fine and shapely pair of gams.

"I always look at a woman's ankles when I meet her," he said. "A woman who has shapely ankles is likely to have a shapely everything else. The other night I saw Norma Shearer come into a club. That cow will never be a bathing beauty. Certainly not a sex symbol. I heard that Mae West has such ugly legs she has to conceal them under long gowns."

"I'll show you those pictures snapped of me," Harlow said. "I brought along some to Palm Springs. When you look at those pictures, you'll realize I don't have to conceal anything." She downed some of her whiskey and raised her left leg in the air.

He noticed that she wore an ankle bracelet.

"That was given to me by Longy," she said. "That and the Cadillac. Longy's a real good guy if you need a favor done. I don't mean like doing in those blackmailers. Murder is not right! I mean things like lending Harry Cohn over at Columbia half a million big ones to get me a two-picture deal."

"Sounds like a good friend to have."

"Longy told me to always wear this ankle bracelet," she said. "Never take it off. That way, he said no harm would ever come to me."

"Longy isn't jealous?" he asked. "I mean of your dating other men like Raft?"

"Longy wants my loyalty, not fidelity," she said. "He wants me only some nights. He's got plenty of other gals. He knows I like to wake up each morning feeling a new man in the bed beside me."

"Maybe I'll get lucky," he said, reaching out to fondle her good luck charm.

She blew him a pretend kiss, before settling back to enjoy the last of the dying afternoon.

The more they talked, the more he learned about her. She wasn't the dumb blonde she appeared to be but had a certain smartness to her. He was surprised to find out that she had a photographic memory. All she had to do was read a script one time. She'd then emerge from her dressing room knowing the script letter-perfect.

"Poor Georgie," she said, looking upstairs at the bedroom window where Rowland Brown was, no doubt, seducing Raft. "He can't even read. He brought along the script to the picture he's shooting with Rowland. But I'm having to teach him the part by repeating his lines to him over and over."

"You're kidding," he said. "I've never seen Raft with a book, but I just assumed he knew how to read."

"Would you believe this?" she said. "I'm teaching him to write, 'Sincerely yours, George Raft.' He can't even do that. He knows if he becomes a bigtime movie star, he's gonna have to write his name on glossy photographs."

"You could have fooled me," he said. "I didn't do all that great in college myself, but I just assume that people I meet know how to read and write like our director." He looked up at the window again, figuring that whatever was happening to Raft in that room would soon be taking place with him. He shuddered at the prospect, although damn grateful to Brown for springing him from jail. If Brown hadn't done that, he could just imagine how many stinking dicks, many of them infected, might have been shoved up his ass in that rotten cell.

Unlike Raft, Harlow said she was a voracious reader. "I just love to read.

Detective stories are my favorite. But I also read historical novels. Some day I want to appear in a movie based on one of my favorite historical novels, *The White Witch of Rose Hall*. One of these days I'm gonna write a novel myself. It's going to be very risqué. I'm going to call it *Today Is Tonight*."

"Great title," he said, not meaning it.

To his surprise, he was to learn later that she did indeed write that novel. She even attempted to publish it but Louis B. Mayer, fearing that its risqué tone would damage her reputation, rounded up what he thought were all copies and destroyed them. That is, he rounded up all copies but one. One manuscript resurfaced and was published in 1965.

In bathing trunks, Brown suddenly appeared at the pool area. Bogie assumed his stomach was full of George Raft semen.

"I hope you guys don't mind," he said, "but I've invited Joan Crawford and Sally O'Neil over for drinks."

Harlow frowned. "You know, of course, that that bitch, Crawford, despises me," she said in a low voice to Bogie so Brown wouldn't hear her. "She's pissed off because I'm having an affair with her husband."

That made Bogie wonder if there were a woman or a man in Hollywood not having an affair with the sexy, handsome Douglas Fairbanks Jr. The actor seemed to be servicing the entire movie colony all by himself.

Harlow continued. "Doug calls Crawford's attitude toward me one of 'controlled detestation.' Don't you just love it? I didn't even know that Crawford knew how to pronounce detestation, much less what it means. She doesn't read books like I do. Whenever I come across a word that I don't know, I look it up in the dictionary. That way I can become a good writer."

At this point, Rowland, with a drink in hand, came up to where they were lying. He'd obviously heard Harlow's last remark. "The next thing I know, you'll be acting in films, writing scripts, and God forbid, taking the job of director away from me too."

"Entertaining Hollywood royalty," Harlow said mockingly. "Joan Crawford, no less. She may think she's the princess of Hollywood, but I hear Mary Pickford still treats Miss Daughter-in-Law like the former hooker she was."

"Now, now," Brown scolded her, "let's don't get too catty. Each of us has a past that's best left unexamined. I had a long talk with Joan last night. Sally told her everything about Molly O'Day's charges when they were driving down from Los Angeles. Joan claims she knows a way out of all this shit."

"If she does, then let me hear about it," Bogie said.

"There's no way that Molly is going to admit that the charges are fake," Brown said. "She could go to jail. Since they're filming *Sisters* together, Sally and Molly are going to—quote—find her missing gems stashed in Molly's dressing room."

"Sounds dumb enough to be believed," Harlow said.

At the sound of the doorbell, Brown went to greet his newly arriving guests.

Impulsively Harlow pulled off the top of her bathing suit exposing breasts that caused Bogie to harden instantly. She reached into her whiskey glass and removed an ice cube, which she smeared around each of her nipples. He didn't know exactly why she was doing that other than to make her nipples stand up and look perky.

She made no attempt to cover her semi-nudity when she saw Brown bringing Crawford and O'Neil to the patio. It was as if she deliberately wanted Crawford to confront two of the prettiest breasts in Hollywood.

"Get me a drink," Crawford called to Brown. "Vodka, not whiskey." She walked over to Bogie who did not bother to get up. She pointedly ignored Harlow as if she weren't there. "Okay, Bogart, I've come up with a way to get you out of this mess. What you boys need is a strong woman to do the thinking for you. If it weren't for me, you'd be in some shithouse of a jail getting your ass plugged."

"Mighty grateful to you, Joanie," Bogie said, actually meaning it. He couldn't believe he'd actually fucked this woman one night.

Finally, Crawford looked down at Harlow, or rather at her breasts. "Whenever alleged nude pictures of me surface, I know how to deal with it," she said. "I handle it without having blackmailers bumped off."

Harlow said nothing, only arching her back slightly to make her breasts more prominent.

When Brown approached Crawford with her drink, she forcefully took it from him and downed it in one gulp. "I could use another," she said. "I'm having a bad day."

When he went to get her a refill, she turned to Bogie again. "I hear George Raft is here. I want to meet the mobster."

"He's asleep nude in my upstairs bedroom," Brown said. "I'd tell you to go see him, but I don't think Georgie is going to be of any use to you gals for quite a while."

Crawford cast him a knowing look. "Yes, dear heart, I've heard of your technique. All of Hollywood has heard of the Rowland Brown technique learned in a Shanghai whorehouse." She headed for the stairs. "Never you mind, Lucille LeSueur has never met a man, even a flaming queen, that she couldn't get a rise out of."

So far, Sally O'Neil hadn't said much of anything. She joined Bogie and Harlow on an adjoining chaise longue. "Joanie is a little much at times," she said in way of an apology.

"I loved that movie you did with her, *Sally, Irene and Mary*," Harlow said.

"And I thought you were terrific in *Hell's Angels*," O'Neil said.

"Seems like we have a mutual admiration society here," Bogie said to Brown.

"I really want to ask you something," O'Neil said to Harlow. "Frankly, all Hollywood wants to know."

Being the smart cookie she was, Harlow said, "Yes, it takes a hairdresser, Peroxide, Ammonia, Clorox, and, get this, Lux Flakes."

"I figured it was something like that," O'Neil said. She paused, hesitating to ask what was on everybody's mind.

Again anticipating the next question, Harlow stood up on her red high heels before all three of them. "Yes, it gets the same treatment too. I like to be platinum blonde all over." Already semi-nude, with her breasts prominently revealed, she pulled down the bottom of her suit.

Only three feet from her, Bogie stared deeply into her vagina. Although he'd known many blondes, and would know more in the future, this was the only dyed platinum blonde pussy he'd ever see until John Huston fixed him up with Marilyn Monroe on the set of *The Asphalt Jungle* in 1950, when she was playing Louis Calhern's dumb blonde girlfriend and sleeping around with any influential figure in Hollywood who could advance her career.

***

The next morning found Bogie at the pool by himself at 10:30 on a Sunday morning. The rest of the household was asleep. It had been a night to remember. At last he could personally vouch for Brown's boudoir techniques learned in that Shanghai whorehouse. Brown's teachers were said to be the same ones who'd taught Wallis Warfield Simpson love-making secrets used in time to tantalize the infantile genitals of Edward VIII to get him to give up his throne and become the Duke of Windsor in exile.

The night with Brown wasn't the nightmare Bogie had expected it to be, although it had begun badly. When Brown had arranged for Bogie to take an enema, he'd protested violently. "I don't go that route," Bogie had shouted at him. "I owe you a big favor, man, but my asshole is off-limits to everybody."

"It's not what you think," Brown had said. "It's just that when I go to bed with a man, I like to work on him for hours. I don't want my special love-making ritual to be interrupted by the object of my affection having to go to the bathroom to dump a load."

"Okay, I understand, but what if I have to take a leak?" Bogie had asked.

Brown had smiled enigmatically. "That doesn't require your getting out of bed. That, in fact, I can handle myself right in bed."

"I think I get it," Bogie said. You're real kinky."

As he was to learn later, Brown was an oral gymnast. He always insisted that no man left his bed until he'd climaxed three times. Those Chinese bordello keepers had taught their pupil well.

He was especially adept at applying his skilled fingers to certain pressure points on the body, and what he could do with the feather from the tail of a white dove would drive a man into insanity. Bogie had proven to be so cooperative that by three a.m. Brown had promised that he could have Jean Harlow on Sunday night, as he planned to bring Raft back to his bed for their final evening in Palm Springs. Bogie was relieved to hear that.

Before going to sleep, Bogie had told Brown, "I'm not a faggot, and I don't plan to become one. Frankly, I don't understand you guys. Everything you did tonight was for my pleasure. I just don't see what's in it for you. All you did was jerk off after you'd done your business with me."

"I know," Brown had said, "but it's my curse. You see, I can only go to bed with straight guys. I don't have sex with homos. It's not what I do."

"If that's your curse, so be it," an exhausted Bogie had said before turning over in bed and falling asleep at once. When he'd awakened the next morning, he'd quietly dressed and had used the bathroom downstairs. He'd wanted to slip from the bedroom before Brown woke up and started to practice any more of those Shanghai techniques on him.

Bogie was into his second Bloody Mary of the morning, a terrific potion prepared by the kindly black servants, when he spotted Harlow emerging nude from Raft's bedroom. She waved only slightly at him before she jumped with her platinum hair and her platinum vagina into Brown's true blue pool.

By one o'clock even Brown and Raft had emerged from their respective bedrooms. Always the director, Brown was commanding his staff to get ready for a brunch to be staged at one-thirty that afternoon.

It seemed that all of Hollywood had descended on Palm Springs that glorious weekend. Bogie learned that the brunch was in honor of the director, George Cukor. Brown told Bogie, Raft, and Harlow that he was writing the screen treatment for *What Price Hollywood?*, which in time would become a screen classic, evocative of *A Star is Born*. The film would star Constance Bennett, part of the famous acting sisters, which included Joan Bennett.

Cukor was installed in a nearby villa. With him, he'd invited the stars of his current movie, *Virtuous Sin*: Walter Huston, Kay Francis, and Kenneth MacKenna. Bogie was both delighted and a bit jealous that his friend, Kenneth, had been given third lead in an important picture and with Cukor as his director, even though the homosexual artist was increasingly known for "handling" women better than men on the screen.

Bogie was embarrassed that Kenneth would see him in Brown's company, and he hoped that he wouldn't learn that he'd gone to bed with Brown. Bogie feared that Kenneth might write Mary Philips in New York, telling her that her husband had become Brown's new boy. In drunken moments, Kenneth still maintained his love for Mary, even though he was seriously dating Kay Francis. Kenneth himself continued his affairs with men, including George O'Brien and Charles Farrell. Bogie wondered how much realism about Tinseltown Brown planned to work into his script *What Price Hollywood?*

After greeting his newly arrived guests, Brown told them that lunch would be ready soon. Bogie stood with Cukor at the bar watching Francis move in on her prey, Harlow. Bogie had already learned that Francis had the hots for Harlow. Francis approached Harlow like a boa constrictor about to consume its next supper. The platinum blonde had certainly made herself enticing, as she had donned the bottom of her swimsuit, but not her top, and her breasts even without ice cubes were bait enough for any hungry lesbian like Francis.

Eyeing the scene between Harlow and Francis as if he were directing it, Cukor explained that Walter Huston was late. "He pulled one of his famous drunks last night and still hasn't pulled himself together."

When Kenneth was alone with Bogie at the far corner of the pool, he whispered, "Rowland has told George and me that he had you last night, and that you were terrific."

Bogie flushed with embarrassment, and he didn't embarrass easily. "Just between us, I'm not exactly happy to be taking out an announcement about it in the trade papers. You don't understand. I was in jail...."

Kenneth interrupted him. "Okay, it's okay." That was the first time that Bogie realized that Kenneth had gone Hollywood. He no longer heard what was said, even missing that remark about the jail. Back in their New York days, Kenneth would have heard every word and would have wanted to know all the facts. Not anymore. Even as he talked to Bogie, his eyes kept darting first to Francis and Harlow, who seemed to have become intimate fast, and then to the bar where Cukor and Brown stood talking. "Believe you me, an actor has to do what an actor has to do in Hollywood," Kenneth said. "Look over there at George Cukor. The ugliest man in Hollywood, and I'm sleeping with him. He likes to get fucked. Not fucked one time but fucked again and again."

"What does Kay say about this?" Bogie asked.

"She wasn't around last night to say anything," Kenneth said. "She went over to join Joan Crawford and Sally O'Neil for the night, so that George would have me for himself. George is one smart operator. Before he retires from Hollywood, he's going to fuck his way through the hottest male talent out here. He's already added Lew Ayres to his belt. They met when George was his dialogue coach on *All Quiet on the Western Front*."

"That Lew baby sure does get around," Bogie said, as memories of the Hollywood Plaza and his friend, Tracy, came to mind.

After brunch was served, Cukor donned a bathing suit. He was no male pin-up like O'Brien and Farrell. He spoke only briefly to Bogie. "I know of you, Bogart," he said. "Kenneth has told me much about you. I haven't seen any of your pictures yet."

"There's not much to see."

"Keep trying," he said. "Your big break will come."

With her eagle eye focused on a potential new director, Harlow called for Cukor to come and join her. Before heading over to talk to the platinum blonde, Cukor said to Bogie, "I bet Hollywood's sex symbol can play comedy as easily as a chicken can lay eggs." His statement proved prophetic, as he'd eventually direct her, in 1933, in the classic comedy, *Dinner at Eight*.

As Cukor hastily departed to join the bigger star, Bogie realized that his big break wouldn't come from either John Ford or George Cukor. Unlike Mary Philips, who'd turned down Kenneth for Bogie, Cukor preferred Kenneth. When Cukor had singled him out to talk to him, Bogie at first thought the increasingly notorious director was going to put the make on him. Later, he told Kenneth, "I guess I'm not his type."

"Don't worry, old boy," Kenneth said. "I took care of that already. I told George you were just rough trade. He doesn't waste his time with any guy who won't fuck him in the ass."

"That counts me out."

Cukor did encounter Bogie alone about four o'clock that afternoon. "This ditzy Kay Francis and that dear boy, Kenneth, are seriously talking about marriage. I hear you're Kenneth's best friend. Perhaps you could dissuade him."

"And why should I do that?" a drunken Bogie said with a certain controlled hostility.

"It would be a disaster, right from the beginning. First, Kenneth is seeing O'Brien and Farrell. I happen to know that Maurice Chevalier—I did a picture with him—is having a mad affair with Kay. Of course, he's cheating on her."

"Doesn't everybody in Hollywood cheat?"

"My, oh my," Cukor said. "So young and pretty, and already so cynical. Kay doesn't know this, but Chevalier is carrying on this big love affair with Marlene Dietrich. I should know. Chevalier was due on the set, and I sent for him twice, but he wouldn't come. I went to get him myself. When no one opened the door to his dressing room, I tried the knob, finding it unlocked. What I saw I wish I had on film. Marlene had her dress up and was sitting in an armchair. Maurice was down on his knees on the carpet going down on the Kraut."

"What a cozy domestic scene," Bogie said. He resented Cukor for appearing overly smug as if he had the latest word on Hollywood gossip. Before revealing his secret to Cukor, he tantalized him for a moment, deliberately holding back. Cukor seemed to sense that. "Francis may not know about the Dietrich/Chevalier romance, but she sure knows about her own affair with Dietrich."

Cukor raised an eyebrow in surprise. "That Marlene sure gets around. I don't think Chevalier is aware of that. He's very homophobic. Can't stand to be around so-called fairies and makes fun of us in every single one of his stage revues. But even though he abhors the idea of male/male sex, he regards lesbianism with wry amusement. So even if he finds out about this Dietrich/Francis dalliance, he'll handle it well. Perhaps ask to watch."

"If Kenneth wants to get mixed up in this tangled web, where everybody is doing everybody else, it's his call—not mine," Bogie said. He's really in love with my wife, Mary Philips. At least if he marries Kay Francis, he won't be able to slip back East and marry my Mary."

"Who knows?" Cukor said. "Maybe one day he will. In the meantime, if Kay is busy with her other girl friends, or boy friends, I'm perfectly capable of satisfying Kenneth's sexual desires. He throws a great fuck. Trust me on that. You should try him sometime."

"Count me out on that one."

"Kenneth has already told me how square you are. Such a pity. If you don't loosen up and start putting out, I predict your Hollywood career will belly-up."

"And what about Kenneth?" Bogie asked. "What's going to happen to his career?"

Cukor smiled. "I guess you were on the New York stage long enough to acquire a bit of sophistication. I told Kenneth that I was going to make him the biggest star in Hollywood. The replacement for John Gilbert."

"And did he believe that crap that I'm sure you've told to a hundred other actors?"

"We believe what we want to believe," Cukor said, walking away. The two men by unspoken consent seemed to agree that neither of them had a future, either socially or professionally, with each other.

Bogie went to the bar to pour himself another drink, and got there just in time for Brown to introduce him to the late-arriving Walter Huston.

This compelling personality, already the most powerful character lead in the Talkies, shook Bogie's hand.

It was the beginning of a beautiful friendship.

***

When it was time to leave Palm Springs for Los Angeles, Walter Huston invited Bogie to drive back with him "to keep me company." Cukor wanted to return with Brown so that they would have more time to discuss his script, *What Price Hollywood?* Bogie felt that Harlow's red Cadillac was getting too crowded, so he gladly accepted Huston's offer.

"We can talk man-to-man," Huston had promised him, "away from all those pansies." He'd obviously meant Kenneth MacKenna, George Cukor, and Rowland Brown, although he could have been referring to George Raft as well. Bogie was delighted that Huston didn't consider him a flower in that pansy garden.

Huston was like no other actor he'd met in Hollywood. Already in his mid-forties before his first appearance on the screen, he was no pretty boy like John Gilbert, and not handsome like Clark Gable.

The tall, angular Huston, behind the wheel of his own car, drove as if not headed back to Los Angeles but on a fast road to hell. With plenty of driving time ahead of them—or perhaps only a short time to live considering how Huston drove—Bogie tried to get to know this fascinating man who'd somehow emerged mysteriously from Canada to try his luck in America.

In Canada, he'd wanted to become an engineer but by some circuitous route had ended up going into theater and vaudeville. With his first wife, Rhea Gore, "a news hen," he'd had a son, John, six years younger than Bogie. "I'd like you to meet my son one of these days," Huston said. "I think you two guys would hit it off." Huston had never uttered truer words, as John Huston and Humphrey Bogart would become "friends until death," as they'd later pledge.

Not only did Walter Huston drive fast, he liked to drink while behind the wheel. Several times he pulled a flask from his coat pocket and downed a hefty swig, always offering Bogie some, which was refused. "It keeps the coyote dust out of my throat," Huston said.

Bogie had seen Huston only once on the screen, and he tried to relate to him on that level. "I thought you did a grand job in *The Virginian*."

Huston was not a man who could be easily flattered. "I'm good at playing bad guys. But that film was just a showcase for that pansy, Gary Cooper. Actually I got fed up with film-making and headed back to New York and the stage. But when D.W. Griffith got in touch with me and asked me to play President Lincoln, I couldn't turn down a request from the director who created motion pictures."

"I haven't seen you in that yet," Bogie said.

"Griffith wanted his first Talkie to be a masterpiece," Huston said. "But it falls short. Frankly, I think Griffith has lost his touch. He was drunk during much of the shoot. Talking pictures aren't for him. I've seen the film and some of it embarrasses me. I'm okay when I play an aged Lincoln. But I bombed when Griffith made me up to play Lincoln as a young man. He put more makeup on me than Mary Pickford and the Gish sisters combined. Lots of rouge on my cheeks and more lipstick than Barbara LaMarr at her peak. I look like a total faggot up there on that screen, real effeminate and clownish."

"Sorry to hear that," Bogie said. "They always put too much lipstick on me too."

"I've gone from playing a suave Mexican bandit in *The Bad Man*—and I was real unconvincing as a Mexican—to a Russian general for Cukor in *The Virtuous Sin*."

"How is that shaping up?" Bogie asked.

"Cukor is better at sucking cock than directing pictures," Huston said. "The script is penny-dreadful. Torrid love in frigid Russia. They pay me, but, hell, I ain't paid to make good lines sound good. I'm paid to make bad lines sound good." He reached into his coat pocket for his flask. "I'm sure I'll find more work if I stay out here. I can just imagine the roles I'll play. Corrupt judge, no doubt. Maniacal sadist for sure. For all I know, some director may come up with the bright idea I could play the devil." Again, Huston proved to be a prophet on that ride back to Los Angeles. In 1941 he was cast as the devil in the film, *The Devil and Daniel Webster*.

"After you finish with Cukor, what's your next film?" Bogie asked.

"Several things in the stew kettle," he said. "One is called *The Beast of the City*. Harlow is slated for that one, which brings up the question of the day. Did you fuck her last night?"

Since Bogie was a kiss-and-tell kind of guy, as evidenced by the tales he'd related to Bill Brady, Jr., Stuart Rose, and Kenneth MacKenna, he leaned back in the car seat and said proudly, "I did indeed. She practically swore in blood that

I'm better than George Raft."

"What was it like?" Huston asked, seeming aroused at the prospect.

"She's not as wild as Joan Crawford, who seems to have no inhibitions at all, and she's not as demanding as Barbara Stanwyck who plays the man's role even when she's with a man. Harlow, at least, doesn't go immediately into missionary position like Mae Clarke. In terms of her performance in the sack, she's somewhere between Crawford and Clarke, if you get my drift. A lady, but a little on the wild side."

"Just the way I like 'em," Huston said. "I'll make it my special mission to fuck her when I do that film with her."

Bogie smiled and couldn't resist his usual needling. "After me, she's had the best, so it's downhill for Harlow from now on."

"We'll see about that," Huston said. "Except for the women I marry, I prefer to fuck whores. Crawford's a whore. Harlow's a whore. I'll probably make a picture with Crawford one day, and I'll fuck her too." Again the prophet, Huston would one day be cast as the Reverend Davidson in *Rain*, with a heavily painted Crawford playing W. Somerset Maugham's classic whore, Sadie Thompson.

"Barbara Stanwyck, Greta Garbo, and the likes of Irene Dunne are out of my league," Huston said. "Give me a lowdown whore any day like Kay Francis."

"Please," Bogie said, pretending to be offended. "You're talking about the woman who may become the wife of my best friend."

"You mean, MacKenna?" Huston asked. "That green kid has grief waiting in the wings if he marries that trollop. I don't know if you caught it, but Francis and I made our first film together, *Gentlemen of the Press*, over at Paramount. We shot both a silent and a talkie version. She was Katherine Francis back then but by the time she appeared with the Marx Brothers, she was calling herself Kay. Francis and I met when I was starring on Broadway in *Elmer the Great*, that baseball farce by Ring Lardner. I banged her several times then. A director saw both of us and signed us to our first movie. We shot it in Astoria. After having fucked her several times, I'd still say she was a lesbian. I know she carried on this big affair with Katherine Cornell when she understudied the dyke in *The Green Hat*."

"Since every woman out here seems to be a dyke, I fuck 'em anyway," Bogie said. "Pussy from a dyke is just as good as anyone else's."

"I couldn't agree more," Huston said. "When I met Chevalier at work one day, he told me he prefers to fuck dykes like Francis and Dietrich. We were interrupted on Cukor's set before I got around to asking him why. I guess I'll always wonder."

"I think there's something exciting to straight men about the thought of two gals together," Bogie said. "I don't care which way they swing, I've set myself a goal. Since I just know Fox isn't going to renew my contract, and I'll be returning to my wife in New York soon, I'm going to have at least twelve more affairs with the beauties of Hollywood. The way I figure it, if I can't get good film roles, I might as well enjoy some of the industry's fringe benefits. Let's face it, there are more well-lubricated pussies out here on the West Coast than anywhere else in the country."

"Glad to hear that," Huston said. "When I first met you and saw you with Cukor and Brown, and learned that MacKenna is your best friend, I thought you might be a pansy too, especially with that lisp of yours. You and Kay Francis can make a film together. Call it *Lisp*."

Huston eventually arrived alive in Los Angeles, where he agreed to drive Bogie to the hospital where Molly O'Day was still convalescing in a hospital. Sally O'Neil had insisted that he get O'Day's agreement in person to drop the charges against Raft and him so that the two of them wouldn't be facing a jail term. He thanked Huston for bringing him back to town and made some vague commitment about getting together one night for a drink.

With his Irish good looks and warm demeanor, Huston, the father of John Huston and the future grandfather of Anjelica Huston, leaned out the window and said, "Son, take some advice from a man who has walked the waterfront a few times. Give 'em a good show and always travel first class."

***

In the hospital waiting room, Bogie was surprised to encounter Alfred Santell, who had directed Myrna Loy, Elissa Landi, and him in *Body and Soul*. Santell too was here to see O'Day, with whom he'd become friends when he'd directed her in *The Little Shepherd of Kingdom Come* in 1928, co-starring Richard Barthelmess.

As they talked about O'Day and film-making in general, Bogie grew more impressed with Santell. During their lackluster film together, Bogie had had very little to do with Santell. He'd listened patiently to his tiresome direction, did what he thought Santell wanted, then disappeared from the set.

His meeting and chatting with the director on a personal level had made him realize that Santell was an important figure in Hollywood. In the days of the early Talkies, film reputations were being made overnight by newly arriving directors and actors, like George Cukor and Clark Gable, as old ones like D.W. Griffith and John Gilbert faded. Bogie hoped that Santell might cast him in a future role. The director had already wrapped *Daddy Long Legs*, with Janet Gaynor and Warner Baxter. He'd also made *Sob Sister*, yet another film with Molly O'Day.

"What's your next project?" Bogie asked.

"Hearst is breathing down my neck with the script of *Polly of the Circus* to star his mistress, Marion Davies."

"I've met Marion at a party at Landi's home," Bogie said. "Has the male lead been cast? I'd really like to work with you guys."

"Would you believe that Hearst is talking of casting Clark Gable as a minister opposite his stuttering Marion?"

"Gable as a preacher boy?"

Emerging from O'Day's hospital room was Jason Robards who was co-starring in *Sisters* with her. Bogie was familiar with this famed American stage actor and tried to engage him in conversation when Santell went in to visit O'Day. Robards brushed him off and headed toward the hospital entrance lobby.

Bogie stood watching him go. "The stuck-up bastard," he said. He'd have no future link with the actor. However, Bogie's fourth wife, Lauren Bacall, would, in 1961, marry his son, Jason Robards Jr.

After Santell had left, Bogie entered O'Day's hospital room. She was propped up in bed and looked heavily made up and camera ready. "It seems I caused you boys a little trouble," she said.

"Only got us thrown in jail," he said, trying to conceal his bitterness.

"Sally was here this morning," O'Day said. "In light of the recent developments with the police, she's convinced me to drop the charges against you and Raft.."

"So all this will be but a pleasant memory for you," he said sarcastically. "I was a fucking nut to have taken the gems in the first place and gotten mixed up in all this. I was drunk out of my mind."

"I'll play along with you boys to a point," O'Day said, the muscles in her face tightening. "I might have a condition or two."

"Sally didn't say anything about any conditions," he said, fearing that the plan was about to unravel. "I mean you would be implicated too. Get into a lot of trouble. Especially if the police suspect you made up the whole thing."

"Do I look worried?" she asked.

"You look fine to me. Ready to go back to work."

"I promise to save your ass and that cocksucker Raft's butt on two conditions." She looked fiercely determined.

"Since we're still in trouble with the police," Bogie said, "I guess you're in the driver's seat."

"First, I want you to call Raft," she said. "Get his promise that he'll come to my bungalow this weekend and make love to my butchered body. I plan to keep the lights on too. Real glaring bright with the bulbs exposed. He'll see every scar left by those beauty butchers."

"To keep himself out of jail, I guess he'll go along with that," he said. "As you know, Old Blacksnake will fuck anything that's still moving."

"I know that better than you do."

"What's the second condition?" Bogie asked with apprehension.

"I want you to take me out on a date two or three times to all the clubs," she said. "Sorta get me back in circulation after this fiasco with Raft."

"I guess I can do that," he said. "If it means staying out of jail." He looked over at her and found her quite beautiful. If he hadn't seen her butchered body, he would have been pleased to go out with her. "Do I have to fuck you too?"

"Don't get your hopes up," she said. "I would never let you fuck me. I find you one of the least attractive men in Hollywood. Not sexy at all. Now why don't you return to the set of your film with that ugly little sparrow, Bette Davis?"

"Indeed," he said, getting up from his chair. "I'm late but what does it matter? I'm not needed in any of the scenes today."

"I'll let you know when I need you," she said. "But before I go to the police, I want to hear from Raft agreeing to my terms."

"A done deal," he said. As he was about to leave, she called out to him. He was heading out the door but he shut it quickly, turning to face her again.

"I've got one more condition before Sally and I deal with the police."

He dreaded to hear it.

"Here's the deal," she said. "While Raft fucks me with the lights on, I want you to watch while I humiliate him. It'll be more fun for me having his best friend watch."

As Bogie headed down the hospital corridor, he muttered under his breath. "God damn bitch. What a cow." He was going to swear off women for life.

***

On the set of *Bad Sister*, Bette Davis sharpened her nails on her *bête noir*, Sidney Fox, years before she dug into the much-abused flesh of her future rival, Joan Crawford. Even though only twenty-three years old and new to Hollywood, Davis flashed the kind of fierceness that would one day become legendary when she ruled as Queen of Warner Brothers.

Standing with Bogie to the side of the set, she said, "The director is totally insipid, the dialogue sucks. I should be playing the bad sister instead of the good one, and, to top it all, I have to wear this damn microphone in the shape of a corncob concealed in my breasts. They've got this large insulated wire attached to the wall. I virtually can't move in any direction. If I turn to face Conrad Nagel, my voice fades. I guess I'll have to speak all my lines to my stomach."

He laughed at that remark, finding that Davis both fascinated him but still annoyed him with all her whining. "You're taking home a paycheck, aren't you?"

"Christ," she said. "That's one way of looking at it if you care nothing about acting."

At the far corner of the set, Jack Pierce, head of studio makeup, along with two assistants, hovered around Sidney Fox. Barely able to control her fury, Davis said, "All Pierce did for me is to tell me that my eyelashes are far too short, my hair is nondescript, my mouth's too small, my neck's too long, and my face is as fat as a Flanders mare."

"That Pierce," Bogie said, finding his assessment of Davis right on target. "He sure knows how to build up an actor's confidence."

"Instead of offering me some help with my makeup, he hovers around Fox," Davis said. "No doubt on orders from Laemmle. If only I were screwing the boss, things would be different. She's certainly the court favorite. You weren't here for her first scene this morning. Instead of the Hoosier accent the role calls for, her voice reeks of Mayfair. I could be so deliciously wanton and impudent as Marianne, the bad sister, instead of Laura, the good little Miss Two-Shoes." She picked up a copy of *The Flirt*. "Here's how Tarkington describes my character: 'A neutral tinted figure, taken for granted, obscured, and so near being nobody at all.'" She tossed the script down in her chair. "Ain't that a pip?"

Interrupting her diatribe, Bogie abruptly asked her. "I've got to know something. Are you still a virgin?"

She flashed her pop eyes at him. "First off, that's none of your damn business. But if you must know, I am and I'm proud of it. I've never even seen a set of male genitals—not even a picture of what they're like, and I don't intend to until I'm good and ready."

Ever the needler, Bogie came up with his practical joke of the day. He'd learned that in a scene to be shot that afternoon, Davis had to change a set of diapers on a baby rented for the day by Fox.

Since Bogie was playing only a bit part and wasn't needed on the set, he got the permission of the director, Hobart Henley, to go to a local hospital to help the casting director find the right baby. "My father's a doctor," he told Henley. "I grew up with babies. I'll find one that will photograph perfectly and won't cry or take a crap when his diaper comes off."

The rather dim-witted Henley bought that. On the way to the hospital, Bogie told the casting director, Derrick Staunton, his plan. He was going to bribe a nurse to direct them to the baby with the largest genitals in the hospital.

"I thought all little boy babies have pee-pees about the same size," Staunton said.

"Not at all," Bogie said. "The dick on a baby can vary as much as the dick on a grown man. They come in all sizes."

After a fifty-dollar bribe, the nurse said there was a baby in the ward that was "truly remarkable," as she put it. "I can't wait for this kid to grow up. At his age, he's got more than my old man." He found that the blonde-haired nurse looked and acted amazingly like Joan Blondell.

Later, after obtaining the parents' written consent, and even arranging a signed contract stating the terms of the day's work with the child, Bogie drove Staunton and the mother of the baby back to the Fox lot. He hadn't actually seen the baby's genitals, preferring to take the nurse's words for it. To judge from the face of the mother, who sat in the back seat of the car, holding her child, she was right proud of her son.

That afternoon Bogie secretly assembled cast and crew for the unveiling. Henley ordered Davis onto the set and told her that she was to change the diaper of the baby. After being reassured that the diaper was clean, Davis proceeded with the scene, unfastening the safety pins and exposing the genitals of the baby.

A deep blush came over her face, but she was enough of a trouper to see the scene through to its end. Since red turns gray in a black and white film, her face came off as battleship gray when the film was later released.

As Bogie would later relate to Kenneth, "That kid had a set on him that would make some grown men envious."

After this auspicious film debut with Bette Davis, the baby would eventually mature and live up to his promise.

As a young man he called himself O.K. Freddy and worked as an extra in motion pictures. The gay comedian, Lou Costello, of the comedy team of Abbott and Costello, saw to it that Freddy got work on nearly every comedy he made. If anyone new came onto the set, male or female, Costello insisted on taking the person to his dressing room, along with Freddy, where the extra would produce an astonishing thirteen inches. If anyone needed proof, Costello would take out his tape measure for confirmation.

Freddy was paid way over the scale of an extra for these sideshow performances. After Costello spread the word that Freddy was "the Eighth Wonder of the World," many Hollywood hostesses hired him as a waiter and entertainer at their soirées. Freddy provided the entertainment for many of those evenings.

A hostess would select one of her guests as the victim, often a newly arrived and uptight personage from back East. Freddy always arrived for work with his own specially crafted salad bowl, which had a hole in it. He would insert his monster penis through a hole in the side of the bowl, which the hostess would then cover with salad, most often potato. The salad would be offered to an unsuspecting guest. She would dip wooden spoons into the salad bowl only to discover Freddy's penis. To the amusement of the other guests, the woman would scream in horror or perhaps fascination.

Freddy's greatest triumph was when Douglas Fairbanks hired him to entertain at Pickfair for a dinner party he was giving for the Prince of Wales.

The future king of England didn't scream when he discovered Freddy's mammoth organ. Quite the contrary—the prince later arranged with Fairbanks for Freddy to accompany him back to his hotel suite for the night.

At the end of the day's shoot with Baby Freddy, Davis stormed off the set where she encountered Bogie, who was laughing as if he'd pulled off the joke of the century. She immediately understood that he was behind the baby plot, and she would forever after refer to him as "that old heckler."

"If you want to see an even bigger one than that," he said to her, "try changing my diaper tonight."

"Mr. Bogart," she said, "you can keep your penis in your pants. You may have experienced the charms of every broad in Hollywood, but my name is not legs-apart Sidney Fox. Humphrey Bogart will never know Bette Davis in the Biblical sense."

"Yes, I will," he said. "Maybe not on this picture, maybe not even within the next few months. But at some time in our futures, Bette Davis is going to get intimately acquainted with Bogie Junior."

"That day will never come," Davis said before heading to her dressing room.

Great stars aren't always great fortune tellers.

Long before the release of *Casablanca,* Baby Bogie first aroused the attention of the American public when his mother, Maud, sketched this portrait of him. A leading illustrator of her day, his mother referred to this drawing as "the Maud Humphrey Baby." It, along with later derivations, became the most famous baby picture in the nation, appearing on the labels of thousands of jars of the best-selling brand, Mellins Baby Food.

The stern father, Dr. Belmont DeForest Bogart, and his successful artist wife, Maud, with her frizzy red hair and strong jaw, sat for this Victorian portrait at their summer home on Lake Canandaigua in New York State's Finger Lakes. That was the summer that young Bogie discovered that his parents had become morphine addicts. Several years later, in a drunken rage, Belmont slugged his son in the mouth during an argument, partially paralyzing his lip. Latter-day rewrites of the Bogart myth by Hollywood publicists told the American public that the injury occurred during Bogart's (virtually nonexistent) wartime action. (Reproduced with permission from the Estate of Maria Jane Haggart)

Humphrey DeForest Bogart at the age of two, "a sissy name if I ever heard one," or so his father claimed. Already there is a gleam in his baby eyes, no doubt contemplating the legendary ladies he'd eventually seduce: Louise Brooks, Marlene Dietrich, Tallulah Bankhead, Jean Harlow, Barbara Stanwyck, Joan Crawford, Bette Davis, and the beat goes on.

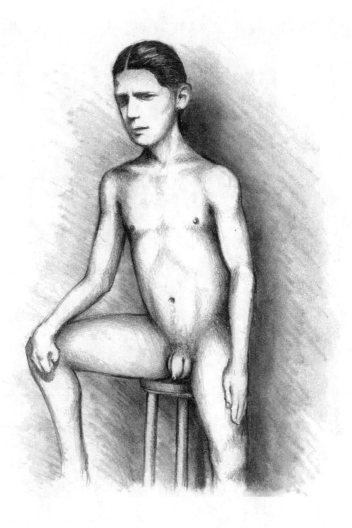

Adolescent Bogie, then nicknamed "Hump," was shocked when his mother ordered him to disrobe in front of her pupils, who were drawing nude figures from live models. Horrified at the idea, and deeply ashamed, he eventually caved in and removed his clothes. Here he is, sketched in all of his emerging manhood. The artists in the classroom were instructed to create genitalia "with modesty," regardless of actual size.

Reprinted with permission from the estate of Maria Jane Haggart.

Kicked out of Phillips Academy in Andover, Massachusetts., Bogie joined the Navy during the final months of World War I, too late to witness any fighting. His military career-
-or lack thereof--has been the subject of much speculation and, at least on the part of his
Hollywood publicists, many deliberate lies.

Good-looking confidant of Bogie during the early 1930s, Kenneth MacKenna went on to glory as the on-again, off-again husband of Kay Francis. MacKenna and Bogie share the honor of having married the same woman, Mary Philips, in 1928 and 1938, respectively.

Seven years older than Bogie, the beautiful and talented Broadway actress, Alice Brady, was one of his earliest conquests. At first, she spurned his advances "until the Navy made a man out of him."

Wearing a slave bracelet, Bogie impersonates his version of a fey dillettante as he clowns with Marie Wilson, vamping as a *femme fatale*. Jack Warner, President of Warner Brothers, was convinced that Bogie wasn't merely pretending to be a faggot, but that he actually was one.

It's not Pocohontas, but a young Tallulah Bankhead. With her pan-sexual tastes, she went after both Bogie and his first wife, Helen Menken. As Tallu said to Bogie, "Darling, I've had your wife. Now it's your turn."

A young and beautiful Tallulah Bankhead before booze and drugs took their aging toll. Bogie confided to friends that Tallu was his wife's "other boy friend." The Alabama belle vastly expanded Bogie's sexual experiences.

The toast of Broadway, Helen Menken (right) became Bogie's first wife and was the major breadwinner during their ill-fated marriage. Helen marked the beginning of Bogie's infatuation with lesbians.

A Titian-haired beauty, Helen Menken, famous Broadway star of the 1920s, didn't always look this good after Bogie blackened her eyes. When not involved with "my lady loves," such as Greta Garbo and Tallulah Bankhead, she came home to her husband.

Arrested by the New York police during a performance with Basil Rathbone in the lesbian-themed play, *The Captive,* Helen Menken is hauled off to jail, supposedly for violating codes of public decency. On her way to jail, she shared the same paddy-wagon with Mae West, who was on her way to the same jail for her appearance in *Sex.* Their unexpected rendezvous in the paddy-wagon led to the most famous and well-publicized catfight in the history of Broadway.

Brooklyn-born Mae West as she looked during her appearance in the raunchy but always-sold-out Broadway play *Sex* in 1926, which led to her arrest. Helen Menken, who was appearing at the same time in the lesbian-themed play, *The Captive,* was arrested on the same night when police officers stormed directly onto the stage during one of her performances. West was accused of writing a "profane" drama and giving a "suggestive" performance. At Texas Guinan's speakeasy, Bogie watched as she swaggered across the floor to his table. The face that launched ten thousand female impersonators greeted him in her adenoidal contralto. Regrettably, or so it seemed to Bogart at the time, only prizefighters had a chance to sample what she referred to as "the honeypot."

When Bogie first saw the three stars (Mary Boland, left, Edna May Oliver, center, and Margaret Dale) of the 1925 Broadway farce, *Cradle Snatchers,* he wisely chose to ignore them. "For once," he told a friend, "I'm not going to fuck the leading lady." Once, during a pivotal scene when Bogart forgot his lines, Boland had to frantically ad-lib. When the curtain was pulled, Boland slapped his face and threatened to destroy his career on Broadway. Boland went on to Hollywood fame playing stately scatterbrains and madcap mothers. Oliver, thanks partly to her owlish eyes and aristocratic rasp, went on to movie glory as a horse-faced character actress.

Mary Philips, Bogie's second wife, couldn't make up her mind as to which man to marry: Humphrey Bogart or his friend and confidant, Kenneth MacKenna. She solved her dilemma by marrying both of them--at different times, of course. Even though married to Bogie at the time, she insisted that she be allowed to service Kenneth and others, too. Theirs was a truly open marriage, conducted for the most part from opposite ends of the country.

At the dawn of the Roaring 20s, America was ready for a fiery sex god, and Rudolph Valentino was 'it." In *The Sheik* (1921), his imagined prowess as a lover sent tremors through audiences, and inspired sermons denouncing the new morality from church pulpits everywhere. When Bogie met the real Sheik in New York, and witnessed his off-screen behavior, he knew he'd never be "the next Valentino," despite the press speculation.

Bogie, at Texas Guinan's nightclub, encountered Rudolph Valentino shortly before the silent screen star's death. Bogie's pal, George Raft, and Valentino had been gigolos on upper Broadway, sometimes simultaneously servicing the same clients, until the future "Sheik of Araby" fell in love with Raft. Theater critics often wrote that Bogie was "as handsome as Valentino."

Here's what Bogie looked like long before his trenchcoat became a workaday uniform. In 1930, he emoted both on and off-camera with star Ruth Etting, "America's sweetheart of song."

When Helen Menken left New York, she gave her husband the telephone number of her girl friend, Louise Brooks (right). When Bogie eventually got around to opening "Pandora's Box," he was in for surprise after surprise. Her forward-gazing black eyes, her frank, direct look, her carved features, and her trademark, helmet-inspired hairdo captivated him.

Revealing a rare gay sensitivity that could have gotten him cast in *Boys in the Band,* Spencer Tracy suffered excessive guilt over his homosexual tendencies that often led to long alchoholic binges, sometimes when he was locked away in obscure hotel rooms in Manhattan and Los Angeles. Self-destructive, he would sometimes go on rampages, destroying film sets.

Bogie made his second picture at Fox, *Up the River,* with Spencer Tracy in 1930. Tracy became his lifelong friend. Stocky, round-faced, and not particularly attractive, Tracy nonetheless radiated charisma. Bogie stood by him as Tracy fell hopelessly in and out of love with one beautiful man after another.

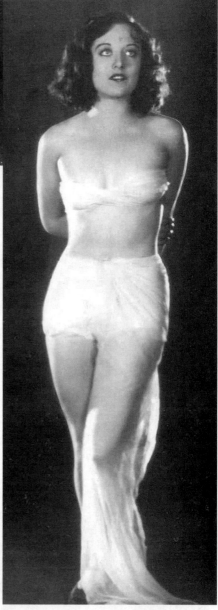

(Left). Although he had a hard time recalling their first sexual adventure in New York during The Jazz Age, Bogie knew the tough little Brooklyn showgirl Ruby Stevens long before he seduced her again after she had been re-invented as the reigning screen diva, Barbara Stanwyck.

Joan Crawford appears sweet, virginal, innocent, and stunning in her white lingerie. Before he got to sample Crawford's charms in the flesh, Bogie had seen what a sexual athlete she was, thanks to her appearance in porno flicks screened at Texas Guinan's saloon in New York.

Cowgirl Joan Blondell (right) always liked "to mow down men in my underwear," as this campy studio pose reveals. One of Bogie's most faithful and longest-enduring mistresses, Blondell was later described by Hollywood agent John Springer as "having the face of a corrupt Kewpie doll and the personality of a hip Orphan Annie."

(Left) Alhough her hairstyle in this photo is cloned directly from Jean Harlow, those "Bette Davis eyes" still shine through. During her tumultuous but long-running relationship with Bogie, she seriously, although briefly, considered becoming the third Mrs. Humphrey Bogart.

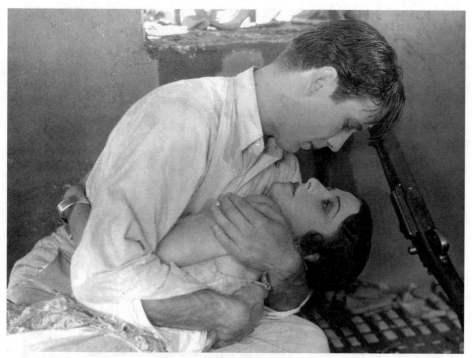

A studly Humphrey Bogart takes Mona Maris in his arms in the 1931 film, *A Devil with Women.* Before she lost the title to Nancy Davis, Mona was known as the leading fellator of Hollywood. Her sensual, perfect lips "serviced the best of crotches," in the words of her co-star Victor McLaglen.

Sidney Fox looks relatively demure in the 1931 film *Bad Sisters,* in which she co-starred with both Bogie and her nemesis, Bette Davis. Cast as the drab and mousy sister, Davis coveted Fox's meaty part, calling her "a whoring bitch" since she was sleeping with Fox producer Carl Laemmle, Jr.

Cupid with an arrow! George O'Brien was called "The Chest." But he might as well have been called "The Body." If the photographer requested it, he would toss that fabric aside for an intimate closeup with the camera focusing on his legendary endowment. He starred with Bogie in the 1931 Fox film, *A Holy Terror.*

Love in bloom! A rare picture of Spencer Tracy (right) gazing into the eyes of the sexy George O'Brien, with whom Tracy had temporarily fallen in love. Notoriously promiscuous during his pre-Katharine Hepburn days, Tracy went from bed to bed, not always confining his charms to women.

Donald Dilliway (on the left), Charles Farrell (the movie's star) and Bogie appeared together in the 1931 Fox film *Body and Soul*. Farrell, the future mayor of Palm Springs, was
one of the screen's great lovers, most often romantically teamed with perky and petite
Janet Gaynor. The ironic joke on the American movie-going public was that both Farrell
and Gaynor were gay. Farrell definitely wanted to see what lay beneath Bogie's uniform.

Looking rather butch in her silk pajamas and close-cropped hair, screen goddess Kay Francis had a lisp like Bogie's. She competed aggressively with Lilyan Tashman for the title of Hollywood's best-dressed woman. Tall and brunette, and oh, so chic, Kay eventually married Bogie's best friend, Kenneth MacKenna. But guess who enjoyed her sexual charms on the day of her wedding?

Early in his career, Kenneth MacKenna was typecast as "a second-rate Douglas Fairbanks Jr." And because he was so often compared to that charming prince of Hollywood royalty, MacKenna seduced him to see what all the excitement was about. Later, after he married Kay Francis, Kay and Kenneth looked to Joan Crawford and Fairbanks, Jr., Hollywood's most swinging couple, as their role model for marriage.

Kay Francis (left), consistently appeared as one of the most lavishly dressed women in the world. Facing pressure from her studio and her public to tie the knot, she orchestrated a "lavender marriage" to Bogie's best friend, Kenneth MacKenna. Both "Kay and Kenneth" were notorious for devouring men and women with equal fervor, often sharing the same conquests. Of her husband, Kay often said, "If a man or woman is good enough for me, then they're good enough for Kenneth."

Never noted as a fashion plate, Jean Arthur, with her cracked but distinctive and childlike voice, fell hopelessly in love with Kay Francis. She enlisted Bogie's help in a futile effort to prevent Kay from marrying his friend, Kenneth MacKenna. By 1931, both Arthur and Bogart considered themselves as Hollywood failures. Completely dejected, they traveled on the same train together back to New York, hoping to revive their careers on Broadway.

P835-151

Gary Cooper was Hollywood's most beautiful male animal. Known as "The Montana Mule" because of his sexual endowment, he gave pleasure to everybody from Lupe Velez to Howard Hughes, from Joel McCrea to Clara Bow. Bogie met "Coop" quite by chance one night in Myrna Loy's garden. It turned into an evening of sexual intrigue and revelations, ending with a stabbing that was never known to the hungry press of the time.

Mae Clarke achieved screen immortality when James Cagney crushed a grapefruit in her face in *The Public Enemy*. The writer, Anita Loos, met Clarke when she was a dancer in Broadway cabarets. Loos used Clarke as her role model for the creation of her most famous character, Lorelei Lee, the sexy, gold-digging cutie in *Gentlemen Prefer Blondes*. The character eventually brought glory to Carol Channing on the stage and to Marilyn Monroe in the movies.

Elissa Landi starred with Bogie in the 1931 Fox film *Body and Soul*, which also featured Charles Farrell and Myrna Loy. Although Elissa was momentarily infatuated with Bogie, she found the charms of Myrna more alluring. Because she was rumored to be a direct descendant of the Empress Elizabeth ("Sissi"), wife of Franz-Josef, ruler of the Austro-Hungarian Empire, Bogie teasingly referred to her as "The Empress of Austria."

A Montana-born belle who was known as "Miss Gillette Blade" because she "shaved" on both sides, the great bisexual actress Myrna Loy went on to reign as the queen of Hollywood. She was hip before hip even became a word. She was still being miscast in roles as an Oriental siren when Bogie became smitten with her. He referred to her tip-tilted nose as "one of the world's greatest treasures."

Looking like she stepped out of a convent, Glenda Farrell, the Warner Brother's star, met Bogie during her early days in Hollywood when she was moonlighting in a whorehouse. As an actress, Glenda specialized in playing gangland blondes in such pictures as *Little Caesar* with Edward G. Robinson. Of Bogart's many mistresses, she enjoyed one of the longest runs.

Lilyan Tashman strikes a vampira pose in this rare photograph where, as usual, she's overdressed. Bogie's love for her turned to hatred when she betrayed him, exposing his most private and primal acts to *le tout Holly-wood* for their voyeuristic pleasure.

Like a handsome matinee idol, Bogie looks deeply into the eyes of Claire Luce in *Up the River*, the film that starred Spencer Tracy. Tracy saw Luce first, telling Bogie that the "Ziegfeld Cutie is one mighty fine piece of tail." Although he remained a serial seducer throughout most of his adult life, Bogie--at least this time--gracefully bowed out of the romantic competition.

Matinee idol Edmund Lowe (left foreground), Bogie, and Victor McLaglen starred together in the 1931 Fox film *Women of All Nations*. During the film, McLaglen was planning future seductions of Hollywood blondes Marlene Dietrich and Mae West, with whom he would later co-star. In distinct contrast, Lowe, who was married to Lilyan Tashman, was completely turned off by women. When he first spotted Bogie on the set looking dashing in a military uniform, Lowe set out to lure the young recruit into his bed.

Blonde beauty Sally Eilers was married to fabled western star Hoot Gibson. She costarred in *A Holy Terror,* the 1931 Fox film that also featured George O'Brien and Bogie. Eilers often sought out Hollywood's handsomest hunks to bring home to share with her cowboy husband.

Bogie rather awkwardly appeared with Sally Eilers as a cowboy in the 1931 film, *A Holy Terror.* Wearing high heeled boots and padding in his shoulders, Bogie later said, "The only thing wardrobe didn't pad was my crotch." Soon after they met, Eilers invited him home, not telling him that hubbie Hoot Gibson was part of the sexual package.

Screen tough guy George Raft in an uncharacteristic pose as Little Lord Fauntleroy. This candid shot lends credence to Betty Grable's later remark, "George Raft is the biggest faggot in Hollywood, only he doesn't know it yet."

A photo of George Raft working out. His upper torso wouldn't be considered buffed by today's standards. But Raft always claimed that his best physical assets weren't exposed until his trunks came off. His lovers nicknamed his endowment "Blacksnake." He turned down the role of Rick in *Casablanca*, and the rest is film history.

PGP - 21827

This candid picture hardly reveals why, but screen vamp Lilyan Tashman was considered the best-dressed woman in Hollywood. Today a dim, though legendary, memory, this tough, worldly actress died young, the victim of a brain tumor that might have contributed to her erratic behavior in the months before her death. With her deep, insinuating voice, she lured Bogie into her bed, although she would probably have preferred an array of Hollywood female flesh instead.

At the Fat Black Pussycat in Hollywood, Bogie stood at the urinal with heartthrob Clark Gable, each of them doing the obligatory pecker checking. What Bogie then suggested as a helpful surgical alteration for the King of Hollywood caused Clark to knock Bogie out on the cold tiled floor.

Blonde bathing beauties Joan Blondell (left) and Bette Davis strike a pose for the cameras. Usually it was the other way around: Blondell was the unclothed one. If nothing else, this snapshot puts an end to the rumor that Bette Davis was well-hung.

As beautiful as any male movie star, tall and handsome Howard Hughes was desired with equal fervor by Hollywood's gays and Tinseltown's most gorgeous women. After Hughes caught Bogie fooling around with his mistress, Billie Dove, Hughes threatened to ruin Bogie if the actor didn't do his bidding. Later, he used Bogie as his pimp for some male beauties.

Known as "the most beautiful woman in the world," screen goddess Billie Dove was the captive mistress of tycoon Howard Hughes. Bogart's rather crude attempt to seduce her led to his being kidnapped and then blackmailed by Hughes. Bogie later said, "When Billie wanted you, you said yes--and to hell with the risks!"

In *Thief of Bagdad* (sic), Douglas Fairbanks Sr., always had a gleaming smile of chicklet teeth underneath a black mustache. Escorted by the police, the swashbuckler once invited Bogie out for one of his wildest nights in Los Angeles. Pathologically jealous of the rising star of his son, Douglas Jr., within Hollywood, Douglas Sr., made it a point to seduce his daughter-in-law, Joan Crawford, within the safe haven of Bogie's apartment.

Cast in little-girl roles even after she had matured into an adult woman, "America's Little Sweetheart" (Mary Pickford, right, the wife of Douglas Fairbanks Sr., above) was anything but. She liked alcohol and men in that order. Bogie's short-term role as her chauffeur gave him a rare glimpse into the bizarre private lives of Hollywood's "royalty."

En route to Tijuana to get an abortion, Jean Harlow briefly considered Bogie's offer to marry her and become the father of her baby. She eventually opted to marry the impotent and maladjusted Paul Bern, an MGM executive, instead. Just before the ceremony, in a dark garden, Bern made Bogie a very strange offer.

"The weirdest, most God-awful creature ever to set foot in Hollywood," was how Bogie later described Howard Hughes (left). To punish Bogie for moving in on his mistress, Billie Dove, the aviator/movie producer forcibly coerced Bogie on a barnstorming airplane ride that was specifically designed to terrify him. "I literally pissed in my pants," Bogie later said.

In his two-piece bathing suit, smoking a cigarette, Douglas Fairbanks Jr. poses with his bride, Joan Crawford, who's wearing high heels on a diving board. Temporarily impersonating Jean Harlow as a platinum blonde, Crawford and her hubbie Fairbanks, Jr. were called "the Prince and Princess of Hollywood," and "Hollywood's Royal Sweethearts." For the most part, their marriage was a sham, as each of them took different men and women to bed, sometimes sharing the same lovers.

With a pair of six-shooters holding up her titties, a beaming, bright-faced Joan Crawford was one of Bogie's early Hollywood seductions when he was traveling from the bed of one gorgeous diva to the next. He later told Kenneth MacKenna, "A man doesn't fuck Joan Crawford. Crawford fucks the man."

The Blue Angel of alluring bisexual sensuality, Marlene Dietrich was a sultry German-born *Fräulein,* systematically seducing the men and women who moved in and out of Bogie's life. Bogart was mesmerized by her blonde hair, which she wore like a golden halo, cheekbones that were matchless works of art, and eyebrows that arched provocatively above her blue eyes. Dietrich and Bogie often seduced the same women.

Speedtrap! A lavishly dressed Bebe Daniels was the third actress with the initials BD that Bogie succumbed to. Daniels followed in the wake of Billie Dove and Bette Davis. Bebe and her hubbie, Ben Lyons, were known as "Hollywood's Happiest Couple" despite Lyon's homosexual liaisons with Howard Hughes and other men. Hughes sent Bogie to spring Bebe from jail, where she'd been locked up after her arrest for speeding.

That loving couple, Lilyan Tashman and Edmund Lowe, were Hollywood's most typical lavender marriage. Both had designs on Bogie and both of them got their man. Some of their more notorious parties featured an orgy room with a one-way mirror, through which the shenanigans could be witnessed by other party-goers, with or without the knowledge of the primary players. Lilyan Tashman's funeral, conducted in Brooklyn, was one of the most widely-attended last rites in the history of entertainment, with a mob so unruly that one of the attendees suffered a broken leg after being pushed into Tashman's open gravesite.

Born into an impoverished Swedish family, the heavily endowed Eric Linden specialized in playing sensitive youths on the screen. Off-screen, after a momentary affair with Kenneth MacKenna, Linden fell hopelessly in love with Bogie and actually stalked him. Bogie wanted no part of the sex thing, but promised Linden that it would be the beginning of a beautiful friendship.

Chapter Eight

After receiving an urgent call from Spencer Tracy on the set of *Quick Millions*, Bogie in his rented car drove from the Universal lot where he was on loan-out back to Fox where he was under contract.

In the film Tracy was playing a truck driver who becomes a labor boss, shunting aside his faithful girlfriend, Sally Eilers, in favor of Marguerite Churchill, appearing in the role of a society beauty.

Bogie felt that his going to Fox's set of *Quick Millions* would be like homecoming week for him. After all, two of his best friends, Tracy and Raft, were starring in the film, and he'd known its director, Rowland Brown, and one of the co-stars, Sally Eilers, rather intimately.

There was a hint of desperation in Tracy's voice when he'd called. He claimed that he could not talk on the phone. Bogie had never heard Tracy sounding so flustered. Perhaps his network of romantic liaisons had backfired in some way. In direct contrast to George Raft, who attracted trouble like a blonde beauty walking nude into a construction site, Tracy tended to be very discreet, even arranging some of his more dangerous liaisons through Louise, who was known throughout Hollywood for her discretion.

When he arrived on the set, Bogie learned that Brown had summoned all the major players for a night shoot. He spotted Tracy sitting on the far side of the set in a director's chair waiting to be called for his scene. He was talking to an older man. Tracy didn't look desperate the way he'd sounded on the phone. Bogie walked up to him, and Tracy introduced him to King Baggot. To his surprise, Bogie learned that Baggot was appearing uncredited in *Quick Millions*.

Bogie was shocked to see how Hollywood could humiliate the mighty. Long before Charlie Chaplin and Douglas Fairbanks Jr., King Baggot had been "King of the Movies," "the most photographed man in the world," and "the man whose face is as familiar as the man in the moon." Six feet tall, ruggedly built, handsome, and blue-eyed, he was the first individually publicized leading man in America. Now, he was scrabbling for work as an extra.

When Baggot excused himself, Tracy looked forlornly at his departing back. "Bogie, my friend, that could be either of us twenty years from now. I love my fellow Irishmen, even though some of us, including King, have serious drinking problems. When he was co-starring with Mary Pickford, he was cock of the roost. Look at him now. Whatever money he's getting from Fox will all go to liquor."

"I'm sorry to see this guy in his decline," Bogie said. "But I don't think you brought me here for that. What's up?"

A deep frown crossed Tracy's brow. "I know you don't like the use of the word shit, so I'll say I'm in deep do-do." He reached into the breast pocket of his jacket and removed a letter, handing it to Bogie to read.

It was a blackmail letter from Thomas Richards, Glenda Farrell's former husband. He was demanding $50,000 from Tracy. If he didn't receive the money in forty-eight hours, he was going to write letters to Louella Parsons and other members of the Hollywood press. In those letters, he was going to claim that Tracy had hired him regularly as a male prostitute, giving dates, places, and the amount of each monetary payment.

Bogie sat down in the chair recently vacated by Baggot. "I see," he said, concealing his nervousness as he reached for a cigarette. "We've got a problem here," he said, knowing how ridiculous that sounded.

"You know I don't have $50,000," Tracy said. "I can't come up with the money. I'll be ruined if he carries through with this."

"Listen, pal," Bogie said, "I think I know a way out of this if you don't mind involving George Raft."

"Involve anybody," Tracy said. "Let as few people as possible know about this. But it's better a few than the whole fucking, God damn world."

"Raft ain't throwing no stones at anybody," Bogie said. With a certain sense of shame, he related his involvement—and also Raft's role—with Rowland Brown.

Tracy frowned, but not nearly as deeply as before when he'd handed Bogie the blackmail letter. After hearing the revelations, he said, "I guess I should be insulted."

"What in hell does that mean?" Bogie asked.

"Brown never asked me to drop my trousers," he said. "Okay, he's humiliated both of you. It's what women endure on the Hollywood casting couch every day. Serves us menfolk right. Maybe a few of us should learn firsthand what it's like to be a struggling actress."

"That's one way of looking at it," Bogie said. "I never thought of it quite like that."

A messenger summoned Tracy to the set. "Help me," Tracy said to Bogart, his eyes pleading his case.

"Richards gave you forty-eight hours," Bogie said. "A lot can happen in Tinseltown in forty-eight hours."

Bogie asked the messenger boy to show him to George Raft's dressing room. On the way there he encountered Sally Eilers. She called him aside for some confidential whispering. "Thank God you and George got out of that Molly O'Day mess."

"Yeah, some mess," he said.

"Now that that's over, we can party again," she said. "Hoot thought you were a great guy. We're having a big party at our place on Friday night beginning at nine o'clock. Hoot and I want you to come, so to speak. You can stay over for the weekend."

"I'm sorry," he said, "but I'm all booked up!"

"Cut the shit," she said. "I heard all about you and Raft and your weekend with Rowland in Palm Springs. Any man who plays games like that can certainly enjoy a weekend with Hoot and me."

"Who told you about Palm Springs?" Bogie asked, flashing anger.

"Rowland himself," she said smugly.

"How very cheeky of him," he said. "Anyway thanks for the good time shown by all at your house, but I've got other fish to fry." He turned and walked toward Raft's dressing room, ignoring the insulted look on Eilers' face. Even before he reached Raft's dressing room, he wished he'd handled rejecting her better. On her own, she was one beautiful woman, and he'd love to spend a weekend alone with her. But with Hoot Gibson as part of the package, it was all too much.

When he knocked on Raft's dressing room door, the actor called for him to enter. Opening the door, Bogie encountered Raft, wearing only his white shorts, and a beautiful woman adjusting her costume. She looked like she was dressed for some fancy party. In Raft's dressing room mirror, she checked her makeup.

"Bogie, meet Marguerite Churchill," Raft said. "She's Tracy's co-star. But I saw her first."

To Bogie, she was another beautiful and desirable woman, and Raft had indeed gotten to her first like he'd done so recently with Harlow. No doubt Harlow was but a weekend memory. Bogie chatted briefly with Churchill, as he was already familiar with her career. She'd been working in films for only a year but she'd already made a number of flickers, including *Girls Demand Excitement* and *Charlie Chan Carries On*.

Bogie would always remember that fleeting meeting he'd spent with Marguerite Churchill, a lovely woman who, like Harlow herself, had come to Hollywood from Kansas City, Missouri.

Within a few years, he read about her summer marriage to George O'Brien in 1933. But at the time of his initial meeting with Churchill, her future husband was turning to Charles Farrell and Kenneth MacKenna, and who knew how many others, for his sexual satisfaction.

After Churchill left the dressing room, Raft put on his trousers and shirt. "Harlow dumped me," he said. "I don't know who she's fucking now, maybe this Clark Gable guy. For sure William Powell. And at least about fifty others, too. Maybe Kay Francis for all I know. Those two pussies seemed to have a lot in common." For the first time that day he looked seriously at Bogie. "What in fuck's the matter? You've got this hangdog expression. We're off the hook with the O'Day thing, aren't we?"

"We are except for one particularly kinky request from Miss Molly. She demands that you throw her a final mercy fuck."

"Just turn out the lights," Raft said smugly. "All holes are black at night, even with her scars."

"It's not going to be quite that easy," Bogie said. "First, the lights have to be on, every bulb in the house. Second, and you'll love this, I get to watch."

Raft looked puzzled at first, then laughed. "If that's what excites the bitch, then I'm game. After all, you're talking to a professional hustler who worked with Valentino. I've had to do a lot more than that."

"I know this is embarrassing for you, and I don't want to do it any more than you do," Bogie said.

"You gotta be kidding," Raft said. "Like hell I'd be embarrassed." With a smirk on his face, he chided Bogie. "At least you'll get a first-hand lesson in how Blacksnake works his magic."

"That's tomorrow's problem," Bogie said. "There's something else, and it has to be solved today. You know I've done you a few favors, pal. You said I could call on you if I need a favor in return."

"Just ask," Raft said, putting on his black patent leather shoes.

"Spence is being blackmailed. For fifty thousand dollars. It's from a young man he's sexually involved with. Actually Glenda Farrell's former husband."

"Sit down," Raft said. "I'll get you some whiskey, and I want you to fill me in on all the details. Remember, I'm from the streets of New York. My pal, Owney Madden, will be hitting Los Angeles to take care of business tomorrow. Any time you've got a blackmailer to deal with, Owney and his boys are the men to see. They've saved my life more than once."

***

Bogie was haunted by what had happened to Harlow's blackmailers, who were each found dead on a beach. Did the same fate await Tommy Richards? He was tempted to call Glenda Farrell and tell her the whole story of what her former husband was up to, but decided against it, fearing that implicating Glenda would only make matters worse.

Later that day, Bogie phoned Raft, who immediately assured him that "Owney's in town. He got here early. I told him everything. He's gonna take care of it. He's got two of his boys on it right now."

A panic came over Bogie. He didn't want to be responsible for Richards' death. "They're just going to rough him up, right? Run him out of town, right?"

"Yeah, right," Raft said. "I understand this Richards is a real pretty boy, better looking than me, if that's possible. A pretty boy can put himself in a position to blackmail because of his good looks. Without those looks, he's history."

"What in the fuck are you talking about? Bogie asked. "You make it sound like Madden's boys are going to carve up his face."

"Something like that," Raft said nonchalantly. "Shit happens."

"Don't say shit," Bogie said. "I can't stand that word. Maybe we'd better call it off."

"Too late," Raft said. "You asked a favor. I owe you a big favor—and I'm delivering."

His nervousness rising, his fear growing, Bogie blurted out, "Call it off!"

"It's too late," Raft repeated. "Owney's boys are already out looking for this Richards dickhead. What in the fuck do you think I'm gonna do at this point? Get them on the phone?"

"You don't know where they are?" Bogie asked.

"Yeah, I know where they are," Raft said. "They're in the city of Los Angeles. I can't be more specific than that. They already broke into Richards' apartment this morning. He wasn't there."

Bogie sighed in despair, dreading how badly it might go for Richards once he met up with Maddens' boys from back East. Sometimes when a woman "misbehaved," they carved up her face instead of killing her, leaving her mutilated for life. Ironically, this would become the plot for a future Bogie movie, *Marked Woman* in 1937, starring Bette Davis.

Before ringing off to get back to the set, Raft told him, "That fuck-fest with Molly O'Day is scheduled for tomorrow night at eight. She wants both of us at her bungalow at the Garden of Allah. Be there."

"Do I need to bring my opera glasses," Bogie asked sarcastically.

"When Blacksnake puts on a show, his audience don't need a magnifying glass. You'll find that out for yourself later."

"I'll be there," Bogie said, "but I'm not a voyeur, and there are a hell of a lot of things I'd rather be doing instead."

"I've got to get this Molly O'Day shit behind me," Raft said. "I've fallen for the most beautiful gal in Hollywood. She's a dream. You've got to see her in person to believe she's real."

"That sounds like one hell of a woman," Bogie said. "Let me guess: Dietrich, Garbo? Not Harlow. She's dumped you. Surely not Sally Eilers? Dixie Lee? Marguerite Churchill? Stanwyck, maybe? Surely not Crawford."

"Billie Dove."

"Christ," Bogie said. "You must be out of your mind. That dame belongs to Howard Hughes. You fuck with Hughes, guy, and he just might chop off Blacksnake's head, and then where will you be?"

"I've got it handled," Raft said cockily. "We never go out in public. Everything happens strictly behind closed doors."

"Where is this discreet affair taking place?" Bogie asked.

"In your apartment."

"Terrific!" Bogie said with bitterness. "Every time Hughes is interested in a woman, he has her followed, and if anybody fucks, or even flirts with her during his courtship, they end up getting mugged. He's got all the billions in America. He hires only the best. So you're telling me that you think you can outfox this guy. Hell, man, he'll probably think *I'm* fucking Dove, and he'll probably cut off *my* nuts."

"Don't worry," Raft said. "I got it handled. Besides, getting to fuck Billie

Dove is worth taking a chance or two. See you at eight tomorrow night. You're gonna watch me fuck Frankenstein's daughter, stitches and all. Even in her present condition, she's better-looking than some of those broken down old broads that me and Valentino had to pump the meat into." He hung up the phone.

When he'd needed to find out where Spencer Tracy was, he'd gone to Louise's. His going there had led to Tracy. Bogie figured that if he went to Louise, she might know where Tommy Richards was. After all, he worked for her as a male prostitute. Or at least he used to work for her.

Hung over from too many drinks the night before, Louise reacted grumpily when he asked for a private conversation. "Listen, Bogart," she said. "I'm tired of you using me just as a canary. Either you come here to fuck me, which will be on the house, or you come here to fuck one of my gals, which I charge for. Do you think I'm a stool pigeon?"

When she finally agreed to speak with him privately in her office, he told her that her employee, Tommy Richards, was blackmailing Tracy for $50,000. Her hostility melted at once, and she suddenly seemed to view him as an ally. The last thing she wanted was for one of her prostitutes to blackmail one of her clients. "I've never had this happen before," she pleaded with him. "If word of this gets out, I could be ruined. No star would ever trust me ever again. Guys come here to get laid. Not to get blackmailed."

Louise told him that George Cukor had a week off from directing pictures, and that he'd become real smitten with Tommy Richards. "He's living at Cukor's house. He booked that good-looking dickhead for the entire week. Whenever I send a guy over to Cukor's, he gets a real workout."

"Yeah, yeah," Bogie said impatiently. "Spare me the gory details."

At Cukor's house an hour later, the director was chilly to Bogart. Although enthralled with Bogie's friend, Kenneth MacKenna, Cukor seemed to have ruled Bogie out as a candidate for his casting couch. The reason that Cukor had agreed to see him was because of the intervention of Louise, who'd told him, by phone, that she was sending Bogie over with an extremely urgent message. Her fear was that Tommy Richards might also attempt to blackmail Cukor, who was one of her most valued clients.

"As you know, Bogart," Cukor said, "I'm considered the grandest host in Hollywood, but forgive me if I don't offer you coffee. You see, I'm rather busy this morning."

"Could we at least talk?" Bogie asked. "I don't want anyone overhearing us, especially Richards. Is he here now?"

"Yes, as a matter of fact," Cukor said. "He's in my bedroom. As naked as the day he was born. Why Glenda Farrell let him escape from her greedy cunt I'll never know."

In the privacy of a library, with its thick oak door firmly shut, Bogie confronted Cukor. "It's about Spencer Tracy. But it might concern you too."

Cukor seemed to hear only the mention of Spencer Tracy. "That vicious queen, I detest him. If you must know, I had this thing going with that adorable boy, Lew Ayres. Tracy moved in on my turf, and I'll never forgive that alcoholic bitch."

"You and Ayres?"

"Yes, me and Ayres," Cukor said emphatically. "Are you suggesting that I'm too ugly to attract a cute trick like Ayres? He spent a lot of what I'd discreetly call 'quality time' with Tracy, and your pal Tracy is no beauty either."

"I didn't mean it like that," Bogie said.

"I invited Lew over here to talk about his movie career," Cukor said. "He told his friends that he was afraid to come, thinking I might put the make on him. He arrived nervous as hell. As he talked to me, he sat on the edge of the sofa as if ready to take flight at any minute. He expected I'd be all effeminate and swishy. Seducing an actor is easy. All you have to do is talk about what a big star you're going to make of them, and all of them, including your friend, Kenneth MacKenna, get an instant hard-on."

"Good to hear it," Bogie said.

"Just why are you here?" Cukor asked.

"Tommy Richards is trouble," Bogie said. "He's blackmailing Spence for $50,000. Louise sent me here to warn you. She said if he pulled that crap on Spence, he might try it on you. She values your business."

Cukor sat down and studied Bogie intently. "You are so God damn right, and I thank you for coming to warn me. I started using Louise's services because I don't want scandal. Two months ago William Haines and I were arrested together in downtown Los Angeles. We were trying to pick up two guys that we thought were male prostitutes. As it turned out, they were 'entrapment specialists' from the vice squad. Mayer kept the whole sordid mess out of the press not because of me, but because he knew it would ruin Haines' career. After that, I decided never to approach any man in a bar or public toilet ever again. Thus, I turned to that stupid bitch, Louise. She went on and on about how everyone on her staff was discreet and how they'd never gossip about me or make trouble in any way."

"She didn't know that Richards was such a loose wire," Bogie said.

"What can I do?" Cukor said. "I want him out of my house at once." Even before finishing his cigarette, he crushed it out and lit another one, without offering one to Bogie, who lit up his own. "Can you get rid of him for me? I mean, take him with you?"

"How do I do that?" Bogie asked.

"A thousand-dollar bill would help?" Cukor asked.

"Unless Richards is dreaming of a pot of gold at the end of the rainbow, a thousand dollars would be a heap of change."

"Go down the hall to my bedroom and get Richards into his clothes and out of my sight," Cukor said. "I don't ever want to see him again." He went over to his safe, unlocked it, and removed a thousand-dollar bill. "Queens like me and Billy Haines always have to keep cash around to buy our way out of trouble, should the need arise."

Bogie took the money and headed out the door.

"Bogart," Cukor called to him. "I believe you've done me a big favor. Some dark night before your Hollywood career ends, you're going to need some help yourself. I'm here for you."

Bogie looked at him carefully and for the first time had a begrudging respect for Cukor. He believed that the director meant what he said. Getting up from his seat in the library, and walking to the end of the apartment's corridor, he knocked on the tight-closed bedroom door.

"Come on in, Georgie baby," a male voice called out. "I've got something for you."

Bogie opened the door. In the morning light the world's most beautiful man lay in the center of the bed, playing with a towering erection.

"What the fuck?" Richards said, sitting up in bed. "Who in hell are you?"

"My name's Bogart," he said, "and I've got to get you out of this apartment right away. Louise has tipped us off. Cukor's apartment is going to be raided by the police within the hour. If they find you here, there will be a lot of questions." He paused. "Questions you won't be able to answer so easily."

Even before Bogie had finished his sentence, Richards was out of the bed, putting on his trousers.

"My car's waiting," Bogie said, stunned at Richards' beauty and physique. Bogie didn't envy many men, but right at that moment in his life he felt trapped in the body of Humphrey Bogart. He wished he could move his brain and soul into the body of Tommy Richards. If he could keep his talent but look like Richards, Bogie knew that he, not Gary Cooper or Clark Gable, would become the true king of Hollywood.

"Let's get out of here—and fast," he said to Richards, who was still buttoning his shirt as they crossed through Cukor's living room heading for the door and escape from some conjured-up police raid.

***

In his rented car, Bogie drove Tommy Richards to Pasadena for the night, after telling him that two men dispatched by the gangster, Owney Madden, were hunting him down. "If they find you, kid, they plan to carve up that pretty-boy face of yours."

"Oh, *SHIT*!" was Richards' reaction.

"Please don't use that word," Bogie said, flashing anger that quickly dissipated. He looked over at Richards, and was surprised that he felt like he wanted to protect the young man instead of chastise him or punish him in any way. "Blackmail in Hollywood is strictly for professionals. An amateur like you can never win at that game. Blackmail out here on the Coast is so well organized that it's done by a group called Black Hands. I'm not making that up. They extort money from a lot of stars, even from the studios themselves."

"Do you think I'm proud of what I did?" Richards asked.

Bogie looked over at him again. Instead of the hardened blackmailer he'd first pictured in his mind, he looked like a lost, helpless kid.

"I never expected to get $50,000 from Tracy," Richards said. "I don't know if Tracy even has $50,000. Two thousand tops—that was it."

"You're in luck," Bogie said. "I'm going to check you into a cheap hotel in Pasadena for the night. I'm also going to give you ten one-hundred dollar bills."

"Hot damn!"

"I want you on the first train out in the morning," Bogie said, "Go back to where you came from or head for Chicago, whatever. Just don't show that pretty face ever again in Los Angeles, or at least not until this thing has died down."

"I think you're really trying to help me," Richards said. "If those goons had caught me, it would have been horrible. I owe you lots and lots of favors." Richards reached for Bogie's hand and gently placed it on his crotch.

Bogie jerked his hand away. "Don't do that, kid." He was shaking as he fumbled for a cigarette.

"You know you want it," Richards said. "I could see the look in your eyes when you came into Cukor's bedroom and saw me ready and raring for action."

"I'm a heterosexual," Bogie said. "A man for the ladies. I've had quite a few broads, and I plan to have a lot more before I'm too old to get it up."

"Spencer Tracy is also a man for the ladies," Richards said. "He seduces them left and right. If he stays in Hollywood and becomes a big-time movie star, I bet he'll fuck at least a thousand actresses before the decade ends. I bet the same with you too if you're the ladies' man you say you are. But with that lisp, those wet lips, your being Tracy's friend—I just assumed you were like him. Your lips already look pre-lubricated. What a cocksucker you'd make if you aren't one already."

"I should throw you out of this fucking car for that remark," Bogie said. "Maybe run you down on the road. But I'm not going to. I've seen so much switch-hitting since coming to Hollywood that I don't know who is a bonafide heterosexual and who's a queer. Take the girls out here. When they're not sleeping with men, they seem to go after each other. Listen, I'm from the New York stage. We actors back on the East Coast are pretty liberal. But we're like a church choir when stacked up against this Hollywood gang."

"I'm sorry," Richards said. "But practically every actor I've met in Hollywood has come on to me. Tracy's not the only star I've serviced by working for Louise. William Haines and his lover, Jimmie Shields, hired me five times for a three-way. There's Cukor. I've done this director Rowland Brown. He made me climax five times before letting me up. Garbo's leading man, Nils Asther, has used me. Ramon Novarro. I visited Novarro twice and he practically fell in love with me. But he wanted me to do a couple of nasty tricks I couldn't get into. I lost my hard-on."

"Okay, okay," Bogie said. "I believe you. It's just that I don't want to hear about it. You had a nice gal in Glenda Farrell. I know her. Sweet kid. I'm sorry you two fucked it up and you got into this way of life."

"I am too," Richards said. "You're the only one who's tried to help me since I landed flat broke in Los Angeles. Everybody uses me." His voice was choked.

Bogie felt some sympathy for Richards, in spite of his sleazy blackmail attempt.

"Are you sure you won't spend the night with me?" Richards asked. "I just want a pair of strong arms around me for the night." He reached to touch Bogie's arm. "I need to be held. Told by someone that I'm loved and cared for as a human being. Not some sex tool to amuse the queers of Hollywood."

"Kid, I'll be honest with you," Bogie said. "I'm tempted. There's something about you. Something I never felt for any other man. If there's any man on the planet I'd be tempted to go to bed with, it's you. You're right. I was attracted to you when I came into Cukor's bedroom. You did see it in my eyes."

"Does that mean you'll spend the night with me?" Richards asked. "Maybe you'll like it so much, you'll hide me somewhere and keep me on as your boy. You're not like Cukor, Novarro, and the rest of those creeps pawing my body."

"What I'm saying is that Humphrey Bogart had better get a grip on himself," he said. "I'm going back to New York soon. I don't plan to live a life like Tracy, screwing half the women in Hollywood and having a cute boy like you on the side. If I've got some tendencies, I'm going to bury them deep in the closet. In fact, I'm so shaken up after my little encounter with you that I'm gonna try to put a few more notches in my belt than I had intended to. Instead of seducing another dozen broads before I ship out, I might make it two dozen."

"I'm sorry to hear that," Richards said. "I thought I might have a chance with you."

"Indeed you might have," Bogie said. "You more than anyone, and that's why I never want to see you again."

After checking Richards into a sleazy hotel for the night, Bogie walked him to his upstairs room. "There's an early train in the morning." Impulsively he took his hand and ran it across Richards' baby-smooth cheek. "What a waste it would have been to carve up a face like yours." He looked at himself in a wall mirror, then looked at the reflection of Richards. "Fuck!"

"What's the matter?" Richards asked.

"If only I had a face and a body like yours to flash across the silver screen. Christ, I'd have fan clubs around the world."

"I'll take that as a compliment," Richards said, coming over to him. He reached out to Bogie, pressed his body into his and gave him a long, lingering kiss.

Bogie did not stop him and returned the kiss. Finally, he broke away from Richards. "I've got to get the hell out of here before I do something I'll regret for the rest of my life." He turned from the sight of Richards' face where he saw a hunger that deeply disturbed him.

He reached into his jacket and pulled out a cigarette, offering one to Richards.

"There's something I heard about at Andover. I've probably got it all mixed up. It's called 'the judgment of Paris.' A man approaches a fork in the road. He can take either one road or the other, but he can't take both. The rest of his life is determined by which road he takes. Tonight, I probably reached that fork in the road because of you. But I'm going in a different direction, kid. Good luck to you." Without looking back at this incredibly handsome youth, he turned and headed for the door. Once he'd shut it behind him, he felt a kind of liberation.

In the lobby of the hotel and for some bizarre reason he didn't fully understand, he quickly dialed Glenda Farrell. He was relieved to find her home alone. She invited him over for the night.

Bogie felt that somehow if he fucked Richards' former wife all night, he'd be on the straight and narrow path once again.

Leaving the hotel, he noticed a hint of rain in the air.

Tomorrow morning he'd tell Kenneth MacKenna everything about Tommy Richards. Kenneth was his friend and would help him better understand unnatural desires.

***

On the night he drove to the Garden of Allah for his rendezvous with Molly O'Day and George Raft, Bogie was still thinking about Tommy Richards. He was confused about him and didn't understand the feelings the young man had aroused in him.

Kenneth had been a loving and sympathetic friend to him that morning. "Maybe you're becoming like the rest of us," he'd said. "You're broadening your horizons. Learning to feel more. I think being an actor does that to you. We learn to open up doors that people in other lines of work keep closed. An artist must be open to life and its many influences. Even its varied sensations."

"Sounds real pretty," Bogie had said. "But I can't see me jumping into bed with George O'Brien or Charlie Farrell." He smiled to indicate that his next statement was merely a joke. "Perhaps that good-looking Douglas Fairbanks Jr. I've had his wife. Why not him?"

"You'll never do it, my pal," Kenneth had said. "I know you too well. Unlike Stuart, unlike Bill Brady, you're too much of a square. Of all the members of our Pussy Posse, you remain the squarest of them all."

"I'm afraid so," Bogie had said. "I came close but deep down I think I'll never change. I could never see myself taking a dick in my mouth. As for getting it up the ass, I'd rather experience childbirth."

"You'll never know what you're missing," Kenneth had said. "Only the other night I got to enjoy the most delicate male flesh that was ever put on God's earth. At first he said he didn't want to go through with it. That it was against his religious convictions. But when I plugged him, he squealed like a castrated pig and begged me never to take it out."

"Don't get so graphic, God damn it," Bogie had said. "The thought of all this crap going on out here still sends shivers through me."

"Don't you want to know who it was?" Kenneth had asked.

"Some waiter?"

"The one and only Lew Ayres."

"For a guy who's so religious, and who claims he's so confused about sex, Ayres seems to know what he wants." He lit a cigarette. "And you and Kay Francis? When do you two love-birds have time to see each other?"

"We get together three times a week," Kenneth had said. "Kay still wants to marry me."

"You guys would be crazy to get married," Bogie said.

"Would you rather I go back to New York, get Mary to charge you with desertion, help her get a divorce, and then marry me? I'm still in love with Mary."

"Perhaps you are," Bogie said. "In the meantime, Farrell, O'Brien, the Fairbanks kid, and now Lew Ayres, not to mention Miss Kay Francis herself, seem to be keeping you busy. No, I don't want you to take Mary away from me. Marry Kay then. It'll be a good cover for both of you. Two of the biggest tramps in Hollywood pretending to be a loving man and wife."

"I'll marry Kay on one condition," Kenneth had said. "That you'll agree to be my best man."

Bogie crushed out his cigarette and headed for the door. "You got yourself a deal, pal. Name the time and place, and I'll show up. I own a tuxedo now."

Thoughts of both Kenneth and Tommy Richards faded from his mind as he rang the doorbell to the bungalow of Molly O'Day. Just how bizarre an evening O'Day had planned was soon to be revealed.

***

George Raft was already in his underwear when he opened the door for Bogie, inviting him in. Molly O'Day, in a sheer black *négligée*, was sitting by her fireplace nursing a whiskey.

"You're late," Raft said. "I thought you weren't gonna show."

"I knew he'd show up," O'Day said. "Bogie's a smart cookie, unlike you Raft. He knows what's good for him."

Bogie felt awkward about how Raft's exhibition in front of him would begin. He decided to relax over several whiskies and let these two New York sharpies direct the show.

An hour must have gone by, as both O'Day and Raft reminisced about the good old days in New York.

Bogie was particularly intrigued as they related tales of "Ida the Goose," a turn-of-the-century Hell's Kitchen prostitute so beautiful and so adept in bed that two rival gangs, the Trickers and the Gophers, staged a gangland slaying at New

York's Café Maryland over her favors. Every member of the Trickers, except one, was mown down in a hailstorm of bullets, scattering blood and mutilated flesh throughout the café. The only member who escaped was Ida's primary lover, who had hidden beneath her long skirt. When Ida saw most of the Trickers lying bloody on the floor, her survival-sharpened instincts were activated. Lifting her skirts, she kicked her horrified lover into the center of the floor, where he survived for only a few seconds before he, too, died in a rain of bullets.

Stepping over the dead bodies of her former lovers, Ida crossed the shattered café with its broken glass, heading for the front door with the Gopher gang, its members becoming her new lovers on the same infamous night.

Deep into his liquor, Raft claimed that he was still firm in his decision to turn down all offers to become the next Rudolph Valentino. "They had hardly carted Rudy's body off to the funeral parlor before producers started beating on my door. Of all the people in show business, I resembled the Sheik more than anyone."

"I don't know about that," Bogie said. "If I recall, several newspaper columnists have compared my looks to Valentino."

"They must have been blind," O'Day said in her drunken, sarcastic voice.

"I went along with them for a while," Raft said. "I even posed for some pictures in gaucho costume. But finally I decided that being another Valentino wasn't for me. I was determined then and I'm even more determined now to make my mark as George Raft."

Shortly after ten o'clock Raft was telling them about giving dance lessons to the Prince of Wales, (the future King Edward VIII, and after his abdication, the Duke of Windsor), stories that both Bogie and O'Day had heard before. "I remember we were in this hotel ballroom," Raft said. "When he got tired of doing the Charleston with me, His Majesty invited me to join him in the hotel steam room. Everybody in the know is aware that His Royal Highness is a homosexual, so I fully expected him to put the make on me, but he didn't. We both stripped down and went into the steam room jaybird naked. His Highness couldn't keep from staring at my blacksnake. He'd probably never seen a dick like mine. I couldn't help but stare at his prick too. He had the smallest dick I'd ever seen on any man. It resembled the cap of a little mushroom buried in a nest of pubic hair."

Interrupting a story she'd heard many times, O'Day suddenly stood up drunkenly. Before Bogie and Raft, she slipped off her *négligée*, standing nude in front of them, glaringly lit by every electric light in her bungalow.

Once again Bogie saw how the beauty butchers had carved her up. She went over to Raft and pulled down his underwear, revealing his blacksnake. In front of Bogie, she eased down on her knees, skinned back the foreskin of Raft's penis, and inserted it into her mouth.

An expert sword swallower like O'Day caused Raft to have an immediate erection. When O'Day had him fully hard, she pulled back. She took her mouth off his penis and wrapped her fingers around it, as if holding it up for Bogie's inspection. "That's why they call him Blacksnake."

She lay on her carpeted floor and commanded him, "Fuck me. Fuck me until my teeth rattle."

Such requests to this former taxi-dancer gigolo were all too familiar. Raft mounted O'Day and began to fuck her in front of Bogie who'd never seen such action before. In addition to knowing how to dance, Raft knew how to screw. By comparison, Bogie felt that he was a gross amateur. Raft had O'Day screaming and crawling all over the floor. Their performance caused Bogie to become hot and bothered. He whipped out his own penis and masturbated at the sight of the performers.

When she eventually saw what Bogie was doing, O'Day yelled for him to come over to her so that she could give him a blow-job. By the time Bogie entered O'Day's succulent mouth, he was ready to blast. As her lips closed on his dick, he heard Raft in the throes of orgasm. Bogie joined with streams of cum entering into O'Day, who was getting it at both ends.

Like a flash, Raft dismounted and headed immediately for the shower. "I've got a hot date tonight."

That left Bogie to slowly button up his trousers as O'Day headed for her dressing room. "Stick around, Bogart," she said. "You guys are good."

When Raft came out of the bathroom nude, he headed for O'Day's bedroom. In moments he had emerged fully dressed for his evening on the town.

"The night is still young," Raft said to Bogie. "I hope you picked up some valuable lessons in how to fuck a woman."

"I've got to hand it to you," Bogie said. "I might one day become a better actor than you. But I'll give you credit for two things—one your dancing. Two, your fucking. I'm no dancer. After that big show you put on, I don't think I'm much of a fucker either. Seeing you go at it has convinced me I'm a lousy lay."

"It's okay, pal," Raft said, opening the door. "All of us have our God-given talents." He opened the door, then softly shut it behind him.

***

Trying to blot out what had happened in Molly O'Day's bungalow in the Garden of Allah, Bogie headed alone into the night, planning to hit a local club. He felt like a gigolo.

At the nightclub, Bogie encountered Bette Davis on the arm of Gilbert Roland. The handsome, dashing Roland excused himself to go to the men's room, leaving Davis alone with Bogie at the table.

"You're doing very well," Bogie said. "Gilbert Roland, no less. I understand every horny woman in Hollywood—and at least half the men—are after him."

"He's mine," she said smugly, lighting up one of her interminable cigarettes. "Of all the men I auditioned that day for the kissing scene screen test, he kissed the best and was the gentlest with me."

"You've seen your first set of male genitalia," Bogie said, recalling that well-hung baby on the set of *Bad Sister*. "The question is, have you seen what a real man has hanging?"

"A real man is something you're not, Mr. Bogart," she said. "If you must know, I'm going to surrender my cherry tonight, and I've selected Mr. Gilbert Roland as the man for the job."

"Happy to hear that," he said. "You're certainly old enough to be deflowered. Personally I think a girl should be broken in well before her sixteenth birthday."

"You're such a prankster and such a juvenile, at least to judge by your antics on the set, that I would think a teenager would be just about your speed, and the perfect date for you. However, I prefer a real man, and I think you'd agree that Gilbert Roland measures up in every way."

"How would I know?" he asked jokingly. "Who knows? The night is young. I might seduce him before you do."

"So you're a switch-hitter like everybody else in Hollywood?" she said disdainfully, blowing smoke into his face. "I figured as much."

Ever the kidder, he deliberately did not correct that impression.

***

The persistent ringing of a telephone brought Bogie abruptly into his new day. His head was pounding, as he reached for the phone. It was Bette Davis. At first he thought she might be calling to report on her loss of virginity. That would come later.

"Ruthie has smashed up my car, and I need you to drive me to meet my new director, James Whale."

Later that day he'd learn that "Ruthie" was Ruth Favor Davis, the mother of Bette and a former broad-shouldered girl from Ocean Park, Maine, who'd grown up as an incorrigible tomboy insisting that her family call her "Fred."

"Forgive me," he said. "I'd love to take you. But I have a headache from hell. I've got no work, so I plan to sleep all day."

"Little wonder," she said, considering how much you had to drink last night. "Whale is casting *Waterloo Bridge*, and I'm up for the lead. It's the role of a prostitute. Before last night with Gilbert Roland, I couldn't have played the part. For Roland to get off, he likes to pretend that his girl is a Tijuana hooker. In one night I learned what it's like to be a whore."

"That's good, but I've got to beg off," he said, wanting to get her off the phone.

"The role of the Canadian soldier—the one who falls for me, not knowing I'm a prostitute—is also up for grabs. I'm asking Whale to let you test for the part. It's not that Fox has rushed to offer you another role after *Bad Sister*."

He suddenly perked up. A chance at a part—what every out-of-work actor wanted to hear. "Give me your God damn address, and I'm on my way." He jumped out of bed in search of a pencil. "Fox doesn't have a God damn thing for me. I'll be over at your place in forty minutes."

Heading for the shower, he noticed that George Raft hadn't come home last night. That Billie Dove must be some piece of enchantment.

Hoping that the cold morning shower would erase all memories of last night, he put his face up to the spout and cleansed himself. The day didn't hold out too many good prospects—Bette Davis who'd been fucked by only one man in her entire life, and only the night before, and Director James Whale who no doubt had been fucked by a thousand men, maybe more.

Davis was nearly in tears, as Bogie picked her up and drove her over to Whale's set. It wasn't the loss of virginity that seemed to be bothering her. "Laemmle Jr. has seen *Bad Sister*," she said. "I heard him tell someone that I had all the sex appeal of Slim Summerville."

"I didn't know he'd even seen the picture." Bogie said. "Do you know what he thought of my acting?"

She reached for a cigarette and eyed him sharply. "I don't think he even noticed you. He had eyes only for Sidney Fox."

"Sorry to hear that," he said, infuriated at actresses who could only talk about themselves.

"I'd be washed up if it weren't for the cameraman, Karl Freund," Davis said. "He said I had lovely eyes." Thus, the film's photographer became the first to discover "Bette Davis Eyes." "They've got me doing a stinker called *Seed*, with this adorable John Boles that I'm falling for fast."

"So soon after Gilbert Roland?" he teased her.

"Last night was the most memorable of my life," she said, puffing furiously. "Gilbert is not a man. He's descended directly from the Gods. He told me he loved me. Even that he wanted to marry me. But this morning when I called his place, a woman answered the phone. I could swear it was Constance Bennett. Gilbert wouldn't even come to the phone."

"We men are no good," he said with a slight self-mockery in his voice. "You'd better learn that sooner than later."

"Believe you me, Bogart, I knew that before I got on the train to Hollywood."

Davis quickly switched to how excited she was about the possibility of being cast as the lead in *Waterloo Bridge*, a play by Robert E. Sherwood that Bogie had heard about. Mary Philips herself had wanted to play the role of the showgirl-turned-prostitute on Broadway. It was a tragic story. The lead character feels that because she was once a whore she doesn't have the right to her lover's respect. The film ends with her suicide on Waterloo Bridge.

As Davis went to makeup, Bogie met James Whale. Since his experience with Rowland Brown and George Cukor, he was more familiar and savvy about dealing with homosexual directors. On the dawn of his own fame for his monster movies, Whale stood before him in total control.

Having grown up poor in an English mining town, he enjoyed his new success

254

and power in America. "If I survived a World War I German prison camp *and* Howard Hughes, I figure I could get across *Waterloo Bridge* without it collapsing."

"Bette told me that the role of the soldier is still open," Bogie said. "Fox doesn't have anything for me to do and they're paying me by the week. I'm sure they would be happy to lend me to you. Could I test for it?"

"Dear boy," Whale said, patting him affectionately on the arm. "The part has just been cast. You know, it calls for a handsome leading man. The type women will swoon over. I don't see you in such a part. Maybe character roles. A heavy perhaps."

"They said that about Valentino in the old days," Bogie said. "And look what happened."

"My *dear* boy," Whale said. "Trust me on this one. When it comes to casting, I'm never wrong. A natural instinct, I guess."

A fey and vapidly handsome young man emerged from Whale's office. The director introduced him to Bogie. "Meet the male lead in *Waterloo Bridge*. Humphrey Bogart, this is Kent Douglass."

"I'm thinking of changing my name to Douglass Montgomery," he said. "That's Douglass with two Ss."

"Why don't you do that?" Bogie said, giving him a limp handshake. He was resentful of the actor, suspecting that he'd been sleeping with Whale as an incentive to getting the role.

"Would you gentlemen excuse me?" Whale said. "I think Bette Davis is ready for her test." He turned back as if to seek reassurance from Bogie. "I don't know what makeup did to her. But when you brought her onto the set, she looked mousy. Definitely unconvincing as a prostitute. After all, who would pay out good money to go to bed with Bette Davis?"

"Seems to me you've already made up your mind not to cast her," Bogie said. "Why are you even bothering with the test?"

"I was ordered to," Whale said. "You do what a studio boss tells you to do. Actually I saw Mae Clarke the other night opposite Cagney in *The Public Enemy*. Clarke has prostitute written all over her." He turned and left, leaving Montgomery standing there awkwardly with Bogie.

As Bogie chatted with Montgomery, he realized that the young actor was making an assumption that he, Bogie, was also a homosexual. At the time, Montgomery was part of the growing influx of young homosexual actors arriving in Hollywood during the late Twenties and early Thirties at the birth of the Talkies. The list of hopefuls was growing by the day: Anderson Lawler, David Manners, Louis Mason, David Rollins, Richard Cromwell, Alexander Kirkland, Ross Alexander, John Darrow.

When I came out here, I thought I'd be enjoying one handsome hunk after another," Montgomery said. "It's not been like that at all. I've been sleeping with the creatures from the dark lagoon. Charles Laughton. I found him disgusting. When George Cukor's fat lips worked me over, I closed my eyes and dreamed of

God, mother, and country. William Haines and Eddie Goulding weren't so bad." He accepted a cigarette from Bogie. "I hear you're a good buddy of Kenneth MacKenna. I certainly wouldn't mind a date or two with him. How's it been with you? What ghouls have you been sleeping with, if you don't mind my asking?"

Eyeing him squarely, Bogie was eager to report this conversation to Kenneth later in the day. "I've decided on another route. For pleasure, I fuck guys. But for casting-couch advancement, I work the female circuit: Greta Garbo, Marlene Dietrich, Norma Shearer. Dietrich is perfect, but Garbo's feet and especially that pussy of hers are too big. And Shearer has fat ankles. The most disgusting broad I've ever had to fuck? Would you believe Marie Dressler?"

At that point, Montgomery realized that Bogie was putting him on. He excused himself and walked away. It would not be the beginning of a beautiful friendship between the two men.

When her screen test was over, and Bogie had delivered Davis back to Ruthie, he hadn't heard the last of her. For some reason, even though it was obvious that she held him in disdain, she'd found a kindred spirit in him and called him with frequent bulletins.

The following morning, Davis phoned him in all her rage and fury. "That God damn faggot, James Whale. Moby Dick, or so he thinks. I'm out of the lead. He's cast me in some dull part as the sister. I'm repeating the part I played in *Bad Sister*. The mouse role. He's cast your former girl friend, Mae Clarke, in the role."

"I know Mae," he said.

"Christ," Davis screeched. "She claimed you fucked her. Now she's fucking James Cagney. I guess it takes a whore to play a whore. In the film, I'm supposed to be nice to Clarke's character. How can I be nice to her when I hate the bitch's guts?"

"Because you're an actress," he said, "and a damn good one. If the part calls for it, you can do it."

That seemed to please her. The next morning she was on the phone again as if she had to give him a daily bulletin. "Whale is out of his mind," she charged. "There was a scene yesterday that called for a chamber pot to be placed under the bed. For realism, Whale insisted that the pot be half full of the real stuff. Christ, I hope they cut that scene out of the movie."

"You getting on with Mae okay?" he asked.

"I guess," she said. "I stand on the set watching her emote. I mouth her lines, saying them like they should be spoken and acted while she fucks up every scene."

"I hear this Whale is a pretty good director," he said, always wanting to take an opposing point of view.

"Whale is no director. He's a traffic cop. He handles entrances and exits— and that's it."

The next morning, Davis had changed her opinion of Whale. He was not only brilliant, but "one of the greatest directors ever to hit Hollywood."

""What brought this on?" he asked.

"He wants me for the lead in *Frankenstein*."

He laughed. "Now that's a part you can play: The Bride of Frankenstein."

"Remind me never to talk to you again, you son of a bitch." She slammed down the phone.

Forgetting her promise never to speak to him again, she called the next week. "That God damn faggot said I came off horribly in my screen test for *Frankenstein*." She seemed hysterical. "He said I'm totally wrong for the part. What a cocksucker he is. I'm off the picture."

"Who's getting the part?" he asked, genuinely curious.

"Christ, would you believe Mae Clarke? She's so bad in *Waterloo Bridge*, he's giving her *Frankenstein*. If he wasn't a queer, I'd swear he was sleeping with the bitch. Whale can't see talent if it were a roaring truck coming down the road about to run over the faggot slime. Christ, I can't stand queers."

"Now, Bette," he said, "You must learn to co-exist."

"So I do," she said. "But it's God damn hard putting up with them. I dread the day when I'll have to play a love scene with one of them and let them kiss me, considering where their mouths have been. Mae Clarke said that there are men who actually stick their tongues up men's assholes. Have you ever heard of that?"

"Can't say that I have," he said archly.

"Oh, Bogart," she said. "You're such a kidder. You probably do that yourself." For the second time in just a few days, she slammed down the phone on him.

But it wasn't the last he'd hear of Bette Davis.

***

The tough, one-eyed director, Raoul Walsh, called Bogie the next morning, telling him he'd been cast in the new Fox picture, *Women of All Nations*. Bogie was hopeful until Walsh informed him that he was playing the "seventh lead," in a film that would once again team Victor McLaglen with Edmund Lowe. They'd be reprising their roles of Flagg and Quirt which had brought them such acclaim in *What Price Glory?*, which had originally been filmed as a Silent in 1926 with Walsh himself as director,

Bogie remembered how the director of *A Devil With Women*, Irving Cummings, had hoped that the team of McLaglen/Bogart would prove so successful that they'd be cast together in several more films. No such luck. With box office revenues down because of the Depression, Fox was dipping into remakes of its past successes to sell tickets—hence, the cameras would be rolling once again on that rugged duo of McLaglen and Lowe.

"Who are the dames in the picture?" Bogie asked Walsh.

"Greta Nissen and Fifi D'Orsay," the director said abruptly before ordering Bogie to report to wardrobe tomorrow at seven o'clock in the morning.

Bogie hoped that his role might have some possibilities. As a fringe benefit, he thought he might be able to seduce that Scandinavian beauty, Nissen, and perhaps that little French cutie, Fifi D'Orsay.

That afternoon he was still hopeful when Fox sent a messenger over to deliver the script to him. He was surprised to see that the screenplay had been written by a man he knew. Barry Conners had also written the three-act comedy, *Hell's Bells*, in which Bogie had appeared on Broadway with Olive May and Shirley Booth. With the latter, he'd performed both on and off the stage as he so fondly recalled.

After reading the script—he was hardly able to find his part—Bogie was bitterly disappointed. There was virtually nothing for him to do. Any one of a thousand, even 10,000, actors—could have played the part, such as it was. Bogie felt that it was more of "a brief appearance" than a role. It was clearly a showcase for Lowe and McLaglen, but not for him.

"It's nothing but a stupid caper," Bogie told Kenneth when he went next door to have a drink with him. "My career at Fox is nose-diving by the minute. They could get some actor to do this for $25 a week instead of $750."

Bogie's only good luck that day was when he returned to his apartment to find a personal letter waiting for him from New York. At first he thought it was from his Mary. The letter was from Helen Menken instead, informing him that she was coming to Los Angeles where she'd booked a bungalow at the Garden of Allah.

Even though the lesbian play, *The Captive*, had been closed on a charge of "indecency" by the New York police, there was talk of mounting a production in Los Angeles. To Bogie's amazement, Samuel Goldwyn had expressed interest in acquiring the film rights, even though the Will Hays office had forbidden the depiction of any type of "perversion" on the screen.

The next morning after wardrobe had fitted Bogie into a crisp new marine uniform, he stared at his figure in the mirror, thinking he looked rather striking.

When he ran into the director, Walsh, he looked Bogie up and down. "You come off as queer bait—perfect for what I had in mind."

Bogie's part didn't even merit a dressing room. He was assigned a locker room with the rest of the cast, which included the grips and the assistant cameraman. Since his part was so small, Bogie didn't even know why he was needed on the set.

There weren't even any women to flirt with, as Greta Nissen and that cute little Fifi D'Orsay were nowhere to be seen. Perhaps Walsh had them lined up for his casting couch that day.

As Bogie stood idly by with nothing to do, and feeling like a jerk, one of the co-stars of the film, Bela Lugosi, came up to him and introduced himself. "I saw you and Tracy in *Up the River*," Lugosi said. "You guys did a good job."

"Count Dracula himself, I presume," Bogie said. Since neither actor had any work to do that day, Lugosi invited Bogie to the commissary for some black coffee.

Bogie relaxed with this Hungarian actor, born Be'la Ferenc Dezso Blaski in

1882 in the small town—now Romanian—of Lugosi.

When Lugosi ordered coffee from the waiter, Bogie said, "Now you've spoiled my illusion. I thought you drank only blood."

As coffee was served, Lugosi confided in Bogie after he'd promised not to tell Louella Parsons, "I really wanted a career in operettas. I have a remarkable singing voice."

"Blood curdling, I bet," Bogie said, kidding him.

"Actually before I had success as a monster," Lugosi said, "I scored well portraying Jesus Christ. Would you believe I was also a sensation playing Romeo in Budapest in 1911?"

"About you, I could believe anything," Bogie said. "You're a remarkable man. I caught you on Broadway back in '27. I don't care how many roles you've played, you're stuck with that vampire count bit. No one does it better than you."

"I know," he said. "It's both a blessing and my curse. I made up a will the other day. In my will, I left instructions that I be buried in my Count Dracula cape."

Bogie laughed. "That means you'll be back! No grave will hold you."

"Speaking of men who are vampires," Lugosi said, "here's one of the stars of the picture coming toward us. Edmund Lowe. I'll introduce you, but make sure your fly is buttoned."

"Don't you look the spiffy marine!" said the slick-haired, debonair screen star.

"Don't you look like something yourself?" Bogie said, pausing to take in the costume of a top-hatted, silk-caped magician.

"With that cape and that hat, are you trying to take over my role as Count Dracula?" Lugosi asked.

Actually, I'm doing a wardrobe test for this upcoming film, *The Spider,*" Lowe said. "I'm being considered for the lead." Lowe would win the coveted role that very year, his character in *The Spider* inspiring the look of the comic-strip character, Mandrake the Magician. "Now I've got to get to my dressing room and slip into my marine drag."

"At least you have a dressing room," Bogie said. "Walsh has demoted me to the men's locker room."

"By all means, share my dressing room," Lowe said. "C'mon," I'm going there now."

The art director on the picture, David Hall, came over to ask Lowe something. He excused himself momentarily to speak to Hall.

"If you guys are going to share a dressing room, watch yourself around that one," Lugosi warned Bogie in a whisper.

"You've got to be kidding," Bogie said. "He's married to the most beautiful woman in Hollywood."

"*Everybody* in Hollywood has to watch himself or herself around Lilyan Tashman." With that enigmatic statement, Lugosi turned and headed to his own dressing room.

When he'd finished his conversation with the art director, Lowe turned to Bogie. His fingers tightened around Bogie's arm. "Let's head for my dressing room now. I may even find some whiskey there."

"You're my kind of guy," Bogie said.

Lowe's fingers tightened even firmer around Bogie's arm. "And you're my kind of guy too. I always believe that when you need a job done, call out the marines."

***

Edmund Lowe was most solicitous.

After he'd dressed in his own marine uniform, he made a slight suggestion about how Bogie could artfully diminish the impact of his scarred lip with a clever use of makeup. "Believe me, I know more about makeup than Marlene Dietrich," he said. "We actors have to do for ourselves."

Lowe even invited Bogie to accompany him to the set. He said all the things that Bogie had been wanting to hear since leaving New York. "You are a marvelous screen presence. You could be a big star different from all others. It's the directors who are stupid."

"I guess they don't like my ugly mug," Bogie said.

"That's nonsense," Lowe said. "You are very, very handsome, and very, very sexy. I read somewhere that the New York critics considered you as handsome as Valentino."

"They must have had George Raft in mind," Bogie said modestly.

"Actually I don't think Raft looks like Valentino at all," Lowe said. "You've got sex appeal. A heavy dose." He leaned over in a confidential whisper to Bogie. "From what I hear, you're packing a powerful weapon in that tight uniform of yours."

Bogie was flattered but also a bit embarrassed. "Who in hell have you been talking to."

"I have many credible sources," Lowe said enigmatically. "You've just hit Hollywood and already some of the top stars have fallen for you."

"I wouldn't exactly call it 'fallen,'" Bogie said. "More accurately, they've bedded me and then forgotten me."

"Other than Clark Gable, who would want to go to bed with Joan Crawford more than once, if that?"

"I get your drift," Bogie said. "I called Stanwyck last night. The first time she came on strong. Now she won't even return my calls."

"Ah, Stanwyck," he said. "I don't even know why she bothers to fuck men. She doesn't even like us. With the world's most beautiful women living in Hollywood, what does our dear Babs need with a man? This may come as a surprise to you, but Babs right now is chasing after my darling Lilyan."

260

"Yeah," Bogie said, dismissive of such a coupling. "Lilyan's got you. What does she need with Stanwyck?"

"I take that as a compliment," he said reaching over and affectionately patting Bogie's hand.

"I mean you're a good-looking guy," Bogie said. "A big movie star. I read the fan magazines. You and Lilyan are called Hollywood's most glamorous couple."

Lowe laughed. "They also say that about Crawford and Fairbanks."

"Yeah," Bogie said. "They play around. But with a woman as gorgeous as Lilyan Tashman, I bet I know where you are at night."

"You are a truly adorable, darling man," Lowe said before being summoned to the set. "I'm going to try to get Walsh to make your part bigger on this picture." Before heading off, he paused. "I've got one better. I want you to be the co-star of my next movie."

"Make me your Spider Boy?" Bogie asked.

Lowe seemed amused. "No, not that. I have various roles in mind for you. I think you can be developed into one of the screen's most romantic leading men."

"You mean, the type who gets the gal in the final reel?" Bogie asked.

"Exactly," Lowe said. "Scar or not, you've got the most sensuous lips. I like the way you always keep them wet. Dietrich knows that trick too."

"With me, it's not deliberate," Bogie said. "I salivate a lot."

"It would be like dying and going to heaven to get worked over by that succulent mouth of yours." As if catching himself, he quickly added. "It would be any girl's dream, I'm sure."

"I was feeling pretty low today until I met Mr. Lowe himself," Bogie said. "I think I'll call you 'High' instead. You've made me feel real good. And thanks for letting me share your dressing room. I don't feel like a third-class citizen any more."

"I think I've made a new friend," Lowe said. "I've never met an actor in Hollywood I liked instantly like I do you. I've got a great idea. If you're not busy tomorrow night, would you come over and have dinner with Lilyan and me? I know she'll find you as fascinating as I do."

"I'd love to," Bogie said. "Sounds like my kind of evening. No red-blooded man in his right mind would turn down an evening with Lilyan Tashman. She's beautiful."

"What about me?" Lowe asked. "Am I chopped liver?"

"Not at all," Bogie said, realizing that no vain actor liked to be slighted. "Not chopped liver at all. More like a juicy T-bone steak."

"You've got that right, baby cakes," Lowe said before heading out to face Walsh's direction.

***

In his grim and bleak apartment, an angel emerged from his bedroom, clad only in a sheer Parisian *négligée*. Before Bogie stood the classic American beauty, Billie Dove herself, not just a big-time movie star but the epitome of female perfection, and widely regarded at the time as the most beautiful woman in the world.

With her large hazel eyes that seemed to drink him in, she spoke through pouty lips freshly painted a scarlet red. "Mr. Humphrey Bogart, I presume," she said in a sleepy bedroom voice that would have given even Clifton Webb an erection. "George has told me so much about you."

"If he's mentioned you at all," Bogie said, "he didn't say enough."

She moved closer to him, real close, as he took in her flawless, creamy complexion and smelled a perfume that surely was called "Seduction." At that point, Raft too emerged from the bedroom. He was totally nude, his penis at half-mast. "Billie, Bogie," he said in lieu of a formal introduction. "After that workout, I've got to take a shower. Excuse me."

As Raft showered, Bogie invited Dove to sit with him on the sofa, but only after pouring her a straight whiskey. "I could plop down in that broken down old armchair, but I prefer to sit on the sofa next to you. I hope you'll be kind. Real gentle with me. It's my first time."

"Your reputation as a kidder has already preceded you, Mr. Bogart," she said. "George has told me about the weekend in Palm Springs."

"I hope he spared you some of the details," he said, rancid with the memory of Rowland Brown and how he'd taken advantage.

"I'm sure he did," she said. "At least I know that both of you fucked Harlow. My darling Howard fucked her too."

He knew she could only be referring to her fabulously wealthy boyfriend, Howard Hughes.

"At least he tried to fuck her," Dove said. "Poor Howard can't get it up sometimes with a woman. But from what I hear, he always manages with Randolph Scott and Gary Cooper."

"Well," he said, taken aback by her bluntness. "I see you like to tell it like it is. My kind of woman."

She reached over and gently patted his hand. "Perhaps your woman in another lifetime. But in this one, my calendar is fully booked."

"Too bad," he said. "I see you made time for George."

"He and I go way back, to New York in fact. I'm only sleeping with George to get back at Howard. He thinks I don't know it, but while pledging eternal devotion to me, he's seeing Carole Lombard on the side. He even called Crawford but she turned him down."

"That sounds strange," he said. "I didn't know that Crawford turned anybody down."

"Crawford doesn't like me," she said. "She's insanely jealous. You see, in the male department, I've bested her. She got only Douglas Fairbanks Jr. I've

262

had both 'Junior' and 'Senior.'"

"I don't know about his old man, but Doug boy sure gets around." It was an observation he vaguely remembered having made several times before.

At this point, his phone rang. Thinking it was some Hollywood beauty calling him, he got up to answer it. It was Kenneth MacKenna, inviting him next door for a drink. "Eric Linden is with me," Kenneth said. "You've got to come over and meet him. He's the charter member of your fan club."

"Oh, yeah, the actor," Bogie said, hardly remembering who Eric Linden was. "I'm sure he's hot but I've got something even better on the griddle. Catch you guys later."

He returned to Dove, not only impressed by her looks but by the fact she was pulling in $100,000 a picture, and was a bigger box office attraction than Greta Garbo, Mary Pickford, or Gloria Swanson.

Flo Ziegfeld knew what he was doing when he added Dove to a bevy of beauties that at the time included Mae Murray, Louise Brooks, Marion Davies, and Dorothy Mackaill.

"I've seen you before," he said to Dove.

"Oh, I wasn't aware that we'd met," she said.

"My first wife, Helen Menken and I went to see you in that Irving Berlin thing on Broadway," he said. "I heard that Berlin wrote, 'A Pretty Girl Is Like a Melody,' just for you."

"You hear many things in the theater," she said. "I've met Helen on a number of occasions. In fact, I saw her at a party in New York. That was a while back. She was escorting around this rather shy Swedish actress. We know her today as Greta Garbo."

"My Helen knows Greta Garbo?" he said. He was aware that Helen got around. But Greta Garbo. "She never mentioned to me that she knows Garbo."

"I'm sure Helen doesn't tell you everything," she said. "Perhaps she feared that with your looks, charm, and personality, you'd take Garbo from her."

"I'll go out on a limb," he said. "I might have slept with Stanwyck, Crawford, and Harlow—note I said 'might'—but here is one thing I'll stake my life on. Humphrey Bogart will never go to bed with Greta Garbo—not that I wouldn't want to."

"Actually, Howard and I met her at a party the other night," she said. "Howard hates parties, but I forced him to take me. From the bored way she was acting, I think Garbo hates parties too. I was the only thing at that party that seemed to pique Garbo's interest. She came on strong. Even gave me her very, very private phone number."

"Are you going to melt the Swedish icicle?"

"I'm not Joan Crawford," she said. "And certainly not Howard Hughes."

"Aside from the obvious, what exactly does that mean?"

"I'm not a switch-hitter. From a very early age, I knew that Billie Dove liked dick."

"That's what I like to hear," he said. "When you get tired of Raft or that Mr. Hughes, I hope I'll be the next in line."

She leaned over and kissed him gently on the mouth. "Sometimes a seduction is best when only dreamed."

"That was the smoothest turndown I've ever had from any woman," he said.

Fully dressed, Raft came into the room. "C'mon, babe," he said to Dove. "Get back into your fancy dress. I'm taking you on the town. Wanta come with us, Bogie? I'm sure we can pick up some broad for you."

"I'll take a raincheck," Bogie said, almost sighing when he saw Dove heading into his bedroom to get dressed.

"Owney's boys never found that stupid dickhead, Thomas Richards," Raft said."

"Whatever do you mean?" Bogie blurted out a little defensively. The memory of Tommy Richards still disturbed him. "Spence hasn't heard from him again. I guess word got out that some guys were after him, and he skipped town."

"Something like that," Raft said. "Anyway, I've got good news for you. Owney's staked me for some dough. I'm getting my own apartment. I'm moving out tomorrow. Thanks for everything. I really appreciated your letting me stay here. You can still call on me if you get into trouble."

"I'll take you up on that offer," he said. "Speaking of getting into trouble, I hear that that alienated Texan, Howard Hughes, has already branded Miss Billie as his very own heifer. He's a very powerful man, as I warned you before. I hope you know what you're doing."

"I've got it handled," Raft said. "Hughes is having Billie tailed."

"Christ, man, his goons have probably followed her here," Bogie said. I bet Hughes has got a contract on *me* now. I'll end up on some lonely road one night with my nuts cut off."

"I'm not afraid of Hughes."

"I am!" Bogie said.

"I'll admit," he said, "I was afraid at first. We slipped around and saw each other on the side. But now that Hughes has been photographed with Carole Lombard, Billie wants me to take her out to a very public place and dance around the floor with her. Even get our pictures taken."

"Risky business, pal," Bogie said.

"Don't worry about it, kid," Raft said. "And thanks again for the apartment."

Billie Dove emerged in only ten minutes fully gowned and war-painted. She looked like the pinnacle of Hollywood glamour.

Bogie felt a little sad to see her go. When she kissed him good-bye, right on the lips, her aura lingered long after she'd gone.

He suspected that this was not the last time he'd see Billie Dove.

***

On the set of *Women of All Nations*, in their shared dressing room, Bogie felt uncomfortable stripping off his military uniform under the focused stares of Edmund Lowe. But after a few uncomfortable minutes, he decided "what the hell" and stripped down, as needed, anyway. Unlike Charlie Farrell and George O'Brien, he wasn't really an exhibitionist, but the actor in him appreciated the approval of an audience. Maybe all those stories about Lowe being a homosexual were true, and maybe they weren't. He was married to one of the most beautiful women in Hollywood, Lilyan Tashman.

Having gone through a marriage to Helen Menken, Bogie knew that a wedding band didn't mean a God damn thing in the theater or in Hollywood. After the dust had settled on his former marriage, Bogie was convinced that Helen preferred women. Even so, he fully expected to bed her when she reached Hollywood—no doubt at her bungalow at the Garden of Allah.

"Are you sure you don't want me to bring a date to your place tonight?" Bogie asked Lowe, as he buttoned up his fly.

"My Lilyan and I have already arranged a surprise date for you," Lowe said.

"I hope not some dog you're trying to push off on me," Bogie said, almost meaning it.

"Lilyan is a connoisseur not only of *haute couture*, but also of the world's most beautiful women," he said somewhat enigmatically. "God had a talent for creating exceptional women. Your date tonight one day will take her place alongside some of the world's most enchanting women. The likes of Cleopatra and Helen of Troy."

"You do like to tease a country boy from New York," Bogie said. "I'm sure my date is that dyke, Marie Dressler."

"Time will tell, my dear, lovely boy," Lowe said. He hovered near Bogie, who at first feared that the actor was going to kiss him. Instead Lowe took his hand and held it gently. "Until tonight, you adorable creature. Lilyan is dying to meet you. She's going to wear her sexiest outfit, a little thing she picked up in Paris."

"She's your wife," Bogie said. "Why would she wear something sexy for me? Even assuming your marriage is as open as mine, you said I already have a date."

"Listen, pet, let's don't go into morbid logistics right now," Lowe said. "The night hasn't even begun. We must go forward into that good night and welcome its surprises." With that parting comment, Lowe was out the door.

Bogie stood looking confused. He felt that he was heading for either the best or the most disastrous party of his Hollywood life. "Let the night unfold," he said before checking his appearance in the mirror.

As he would confide in Kenneth the next day, he kissed his own image in the mirror. He felt that that kind of self-enchantment qualified him as a narcissist like every other actor in Hollywood. Giving himself a final smooch, he said, "Go for it, you good-looking mother-fucker."

Even though it had been announced as just a small, intimate dinner party, Edmund Lowe greeted Bogie at the door in full evening dress.

In his dark suit, Bogie said, "I didn't know it was black tie."

"Come in, dear boy," the slick-haired actor said, taking his hand and guiding him into the foyer. "Dressed, and especially undressed, you're most welcome at the humble Tashman/Lowe abode."

It was actually a Beverly Hills mansion they called "Lilowe."

With the grace of a ballerina, Lilyan Tashman moved from her garden into the living room, crossing the parlor to greet Bogie. Her movements were so perfect that they gave the illusion of being choreographed. Even before she'd kissed him gently on the lips, he'd fallen madly in love with her.

"Welcome to our home," Tashman said. "For once Eddie didn't lie about your beauty."

"The only beauty in this room is standing before me," Bogie graciously said. "I'm a regular looking guy."

"Don't be so modest," she said, looking over at Lowe with a smirk. "I never thought I'd ever say that to an actor. I've read in the press that you've been compared to Valentino." As she seated him on the sofa next to her, he was awed by her beauty. She was dressed a little too flamboyantly for his taste, but still exquisite in a Parisian white satin gown with four diamond clasps. When she noticed him checking out her jewelry, she said, "If I happen to wear real diamonds instead of paste, who is to object?"

"Not me," Bogie said, "providing I didn't have to pay for them."

As the maid served drinks, Bogie was eager to learn anything he could about Tashman. He virtually ignored Lowe. Born in New York the same year as himself, Tashman had toiled for years in the Silents, knocking on doors of casting offices and dancing in Ziegfeld's *Follies*.

Eventually, she forged ahead in the Talkies, creating a niche playing sophisticated but sarcastic blondes. The night Bogart met her, she was an acknowledged social leader in Hollywood, consistently cited as the town's best-dressed woman.

Her home was spectacular. "Who's your decorator?" he asked. "He needs to do something—anything—to my rattrap apartment."

"You're looking at *him,*" she said. "My hobby is interior decorating."

"She also claims she decorated our Malibu Beach home," Lowe said. "But it was Jetta Goudal."

"Would you shut up?" she said abruptly to her husband before softening her features again when she turned to face Bogie. "Goudal helped, but I did most of it myself." Lowe merely rolled his eyes sarcastically, looking up at the ceiling.

"Oh, I forgot," Bogie said. He reached into the pocket of his suit and removed a small gift package wrapped with red satin ribbon.

Taking the box from him, she deftly opened it, her eyes lighting up in delight. "Miniature hands," she said, fondling the porcelain gift. "Thank you, darling." She reached over and kissed him again on the lips. "I'll add this latest pair to my collection." Reaching for his hand, she guided him into an adjoining room which was lined with glass shelves displaying what must have been the world's largest collection of miniature hands in all shapes and materials.

"I read in some column that you collected these little hands, and I wanted to add my paws to your other ones," he said.

"I will value your hands more than all the others," she said.

She was so convincing that for one brief moment he actually believed her.

As she directed him back into her sumptuous living room, he took in her figure from the rear, finding it slender and slinky. Her throaty voice evoked Garbo with a touch of Dietrich. He'd read that Eddie Cantor had called her face "fox-like."

As Tashman kept the talk bubbly, Lowe became cruder as he drank. As if jealous of his wife, his tone grew bitchy. "I've never known Lil to pay so much attention to a man. Usually it's the women at any party who have to watch out for her. No beautiful gal is safe going to the powder room with Lil at the party."

She patted Bogie's hand. "Eddie does exaggerate so."

"Whether it's a grand dame of the theater or a newly arrived teenage chorus gal from Broadway, Lil chases after them right into the powder room," Lowe said. "Often she seduces them in a private toilet stall. Her technique is amazing, I hear, and it's the talk of Hollywood."

As Bogie looked at Tashman, he found this slander hard to believe. To him, she was the epitome of elegance and taste.

"They don't call her Latrine Lil for nothing," Lowe said.

No longer able to control herself, Lilyan glared at him. "And they don't call you a cocksucking son-of-a-bitch for nothing," she said. Still, to Bogie's surprise, she didn't deny her husband's assertions. When he became too graphic describing her seduction of Louise Brooks, she said, "forgive Eddie. When he's not sucking a big dick—he's a size queen, incidentally—the true feline that lurks in his heart comes out of her cage." To change the subject, she said, "Tallulah's in town looking for movie work and fucking that divine Gary Cooper. But that Montana cowboy has given her gonorrhea, so darling Tallu is temporarily out of commission."

"She told us about you, Helen Menken, and Naps back in New York," Lowe said.

"She told you *that?*" Bogie said, infuriated at the blabbermouth.

"When I heard Naps had had you in New York, I knew you could be had in Hollywood as well," Lowe said, getting up to pour himself another drink.

"I'd rather not talk about it," Bogie said, barely concealing his simmering anger.

"It's all right with us," Tashman said. "With Eddie and me, you can let your hair down. After all, you and I have a lot in common. You've both bumped pussies with darling Tallu. I've also enjoyed the vagina of Miss Helen Menken herself."

At that point Bogie was ready to bolt from the room. What kept him glued to his seat was his utter fascination with Tashman in spite of her vile talk. She could speak freely of her seduction of women, yet he felt that she also wanted to go to bed with him. All evening, to emphasize a point, she would reach out and touch him. He found her fingers on him thrilling and wanted her to feel more of him. He regretted that Lowe had arranged the surprise date, even though he kept assuring Bogie that an enchantress was on her way.

Even as she continued to touch and feel Bogie, Tashman still spoke of women. "I've had nearly every major female star in Hollywood, but I struck out with Gloria Swanson, Norma Talmadge, and Billie Dove."

"Better luck next time," Bogie said.

"So, now that you've seen a slice of our domestic life, what do you think of our 'ideal marriage?'" Lowe asked. "That's how all the fan magazines refer to our wedded bliss."

Fortunately for Bogie, he didn't have to answer that direct question.

"Only last week I granted *Photoplay* an interview," she said. "About how a woman can hold onto her man." She flashed a look of contempt at her drunken husband. "I told the magazine that no man will tolerate a lazy woman for very long. I also told them that a woman has to look good for her man at all times. To quote *moi*, 'I never appear before Eddie looking seedy or badly groomed.'"

"That's a damnable lie," Lowe said. "I've seen my bitch here looking very disheveled after she's worked over some hot pussy and raises herself up with vagina juice dripping down her chin."

"Whenever Eddie drinks, he becomes really vulgar," she said. "You'll find out more about that later." Ideal marriage or not, she looked at him with total disdain. "I call him sewer mouth. But, as I said, you'll see what I mean as the night progresses."

That evening did move on. It was nearly ten o'clock, and Bogie's mystery date still hadn't shown up. He suspected that there was no fourth guest, and that he was here for a three-way. If they knew about the sexual dalliance that he and Helen had choreographed with Naps and Tallulah, they could justifiably conclude that he'd be game for a repeat arrangement with them. He wasn't.

Enthralled by Tashman, he wanted her alone, miles removed from her homosexual husband. He couldn't even call up his friend, Tracy, to take Lowe off his hands for the night. Lowe wasn't Tracy's type, as he seemed to prefer young, pretty boys, not ruggedly masculine actors.

The maid came in and announced that Tashman was wanted on the phone. She rose gracefully, patted Bogie on the knee, and turned to her husband. "Can I trust you alone with this darling man?"

"I've already seen him jaybird naked in my dressing room," Lowe said. "I restrained myself then, but just barely. I'll be a good boy, although I can't promise that I won't salivate a bit." When she'd gone, Lowe took Lilyan's place on the sofa beside Bogie.

Uncomfortable seated there, Bogie rose quickly to refill his own drink. Fortunately, Tashman came back into the room in only a minute or so.

She looked jubilant. "Your surprise date is also doing the cooking tonight. We are so lucky. She makes the best goulash in Hollywood. Instead of cooking in my kitchen, she preferred to cook the goulash in her own home and is bringing it over."

"Prepare yourself for a delightful evening," Lowe predicted to Bogie. "And I don't mean just the goulash."

Growing a little bored with Lowe's fabulous build-up, Bogie said, "Yeah, promises, promises."

In fifteen minutes, the doorbell rang, and the maid went to answer it.

Not knowing what to expect, Bogie was startled when his surprise date came into the living room, after handing a pot of goulash to the maid.

After kissing both Lowe and Tashman rather passionately on the mouth, she turned to him. He'd met her before, and, as before, he was overcome by her exotic allure and her beauty.

"Mr. Bogie man," she said in her seductively accented voice. "We meet again."

Not wanting to sound like some awed schoolboy, he said, "Did anyone ever tell you you're one hell of a broad?"

"So many, many times," she said, smiling at him before looking around the living room, finally focusing on Tashman. A slight smirk came onto her face. "Someone in this room is going to get lucky tonight. I don't know…." She paused as if confused about what to say. "What is the damn correct English? On whom I will bestow my charms?"

"If there is a God in heaven," Bogie said, "and at times I seriously doubt it, I am hoping that he is looking with favor on me tonight, Miss Dietrich."

Chapter Nine

Bogie woke up the next morning fully convinced that he was a sexual degenerate. After he'd invited Kenneth over for coffee and conversation, he felt better. Drawing on his experience as a former member of the New York Pussy Posse, Kenneth convinced him that what Bogie was doing in Hollywood—no different from some scenes in which he'd participated in New York—was "just the norm out here."

In vivid, graphic detail, he told Kenneth of his experiences the evening before. Long after the world's greatest tasting goulash— "that Kraut sure knows how to cook"—was served, Dietrich and Tashman had disappeared into her bedroom upstairs, leaving the door wide open and the lights on.

Lowe had directed Bogie upstairs "to see what the gals are up to." As he'd stood at the doorway to the well-lit room, he'd seen Tashman lying flat on her back, half dressed. Dietrich, still fully dressed, was going down on her. Tashman was loving it, urging Dietrich on.

As he'd witnessed the scene, Bogie had become sexually aroused in ways he'd rarely been before. He wanted to join the couple on the bed.

Ever the sexual opportunist, Lowe had stood close to him, talking dirty into his ear. "Wouldn't you like to put that big dick of yours into Lilyan's cunt? Fuck her all night? She'd love it!"

As his eyes stayed glued to the scene, he had not objected when Lowe had felt him up. At one point Lowe dropped to his knees, unbuttoned the fly to Bogie's trousers, freed his penis, and devoured it voraciously.

Tashman had reached her own climax at the moment Lowe had brought Bogie off. After that, he told Kenneth he'd been too drunk to remember exactly what happened next.

Dietrich had disappeared into the bathroom down the hall to make herself glamorous again, and Lowe had wandered off downstairs to the bar.

Still lying prone on the bed, Tashman had not been totally satisfied by the Dietrich maneuver, perhaps considering it only foreplay. She'd ordered Bogie to get undressed and join her in bed.

"My God, it was like a scene from the Arabian nights," he told Kenneth over his breakfast table. "She probably got her training in a bordello in the Sahara desert—the kind that caters to every imaginable fantasy. The woman was amazing. She might be known for seducing every actress in Hollywood—I'm sure she's already done your Kay—but she's a tigress with men. Thank God Lowe only whetted my appetite for sex. Before I crawled out of that bed around four o'clock, I did a trick or two that even I hadn't thought about before."

"Like what?" Kenneth asked. "Tell me. I might be missing out on something."

"When you marry Kay Francis, I'm sure she'll probably teach you on your honeymoon night. I'm saying no more."

Kenneth drank his coffee and seemed a little jealous. "I had a hot night too, but not as hot as yours. I spent the night with Eric Linden."

"The president of my fan club?" Bogie asked facetiously.

"One and the same," Kenneth said. "Eric is a very pretty boy, but I feel he's attracted to me only because I'm your best friend. You're all he wants to talk about, and he hasn't even met you."

"I don't want to alienate my fan," Bogie said. "Christ, I need every one I can get. But regardless of what I found myself doing in the past, I'm fully committed to the love of women. I'm pursuing them on all fronts. I'll taper off when Helen arrives."

"You mean Miss Menken herself?" Kenneth asked in surprise.

"One and the same," Bogie said. "She'll be staying at the Garden of Allah. I'm sure I'll be spending my nights there."

"Have you all but forgotten Mary back in New York?" Kenneth asked. "I'm still carrying a torch for her."

"Yeah," Bogie said. "You slept with Eric Linden last night and you're about to marry Kay Francis."

"But everybody lives like that out here," Kenneth said. "Douglas Fairbanks is married to Joan Crawford, and he fucks everything on the hoof. Crawford is carrying on with everybody from Clark Gable to Barbara Stanwyck, even Louis B. Mayer himself. Dietrich has set for herself the goal of seducing every beautiful woman and every good-looking man in Hollywood. Yet we also marry. Don't ask me why. I can't explain it. You married Mary and then left her back in New York."

"Would you have stayed in New York if Mary had married you instead of me?"

"No way," Kenneth said. "I think my future is in Hollywood. But I think I could have convinced Mary to come with me."

"In a way I'm glad she's back in New York, because I'll be returning there soon," he said. "I still want to stay married to her. We'll wipe our slates clean and start all over again."

"Does she have a clue about what you're up to out here?" Kenneth asked.

"Not unless you've written her."

"My lips are sealed."

"Cut the crap, pal," Bogie said. "Those lips aren't sealed. They're wrapped around half the dicks in Hollywood. I've done some things I'm not proud of, but cocksucking isn't one of them."

"Don't knock it until you've tried it."

"That day will never come," Bogie predicted. "In the meantime, I've got one of the most beautiful women in Hollywood, Miss Lilyan Tashman herself, begging for an encore."

"Even more than Dietrich, Tashman is the biggest dyke in Hollywood," Kenneth said in protest.

"So what?" Bogie asked. "If we guys chased after Hollywood women who never ventured off the straight and narrow path, the pickings would be rather slim. I married a dyke, and I'll soon be sleeping with her again. That is, when I'm not in bed with Tashman. Between Helen and darling Lil, I'm going to be the busiest man in Hollywood. After all, Harlow never called me again after our one-night stand."

"I think at this point in our lives, we shouldn't stop to analyze what's happening," Kenneth said. "Let's just let the good times roll."

Just as Bogie was polishing off some ham and eggs, a messenger arrived from Fox. Opening the package, Bogie learned that he'd been assigned fourth billing in his final film at Fox. Entitled *A Holy Terror*, it would be directed by Irving Cummings, who had previously guided him through *A Devil with Women*. He was startled to learn that he'd be appearing with the star of the picture, George O'Brien.

As he read the script, he was even more startled to learn that it was a western based on Max Brand's novel, *Trailin'*. In the film, Bogie was slated to play Steve Nash, foreman of the Drew ranch, who's in love with a character played by Sally Eilers.

The city boy from New York was about to play his first cowboy role.

***

Divinely adorned with jewelry and in a gown of shimmering emerald-green, Lilyan Tashman lived up to her reputation as best dressed woman in Hollywood. In a dark suit, Bogie felt underdressed. She was more dazzling than any woman he'd ever dated.

Driving her to the theater to see a Garbo movie entitled *Romance,* he couldn't resist being provocative. "While I was biding my time last night eating goulash with Bela Lugosi, who was my darling Lil dating?"

"I need keep no secrets from you," she said. "Kay Francis. We became bosom buddies—so to speak—when we appeared together in *The Marriage Playground*. I got billing over Kay in that one. I fucked both Kay and the star, Fredric March."

"You know, of course, that my pal, Kenneth MacKenna, is planning to marry Kay?"

"So what?" she said, asking for a cigarette." I'm married to Edmund Lowe. Let's face it: Ours is one of the most famous marriages in Hollywood. Given Kay's proclivities, not to mention some of the nocturnal activities of your friend, Mr. MacKenna, I'd think that marriage is a convenient cover for them."

"Would you believe this?" he asked. "Kenneth is still carrying a torch for my wife. But I can't believe he wants to be with a woman when he's always carrying on with men."

"Haven't you heard of bisexuality, my darling?" Tashman said. "I'm living proof of that. My husband, on the other hand, is strictly homosexual."

"You mean, he's never bedded you?"

"Never!" she said rather forcefully, "and I wouldn't want him to. I think that any expression of intimacy between us could destroy our perfect marriage." Puffing on her cigarette, she thought for a moment. "Actually, I think you and Mary Philips have the perfect marriage—she's in New York and you're alone in Hollywood to carry on with whomever or whatever you want. I assume in spite of that drunken episode with my cocksucking husband that you don't usually sleep with men."

"Despite my lisp, I'm not a homosexual," he said. "But it's not because I haven't had offers. I'm not a Puritan, for Christ's sake. I'm not saying that under very special circumstances I won't consent to a blow job. I'm a heterosexual, but I'm also human—and oversexed. But not like my friend Spencer Tracy. He can get involved with two women and perhaps a gentleman, sometimes all within a 24-hour period. But for me, one orgasm a day is just fine."

"Not me," she said. "I view the day as a failure if I don't have at least three."

"I'm not Louella Parsons but I'd really like to know more about you and Garbo," he said, after they'd seen *Romance*.

"And I'm the one to tell you," she said. "After dropping me, why should I keep her secrets? I'll blab but only after you've bought me a steak dinner, to be followed up by some other meat later tonight." She reached over and placed her lovely hand in his crotch where she fondled him affectionately. "C'mon, tiger," she said. "Let's hit the town. I'm hot and horny tonight."

"What about letting me take care of that horny problem for you right now?" he said. "We could drive up into the hills. Do it right in my car. It's rented anyway so it doesn't matter if we smear the upholstery."

"Don't worry about that," she said. "I've fucked both men and women in cars, toilets, wherever the opportunity arises. But tonight I want to devour you in a comfortable bed. Of course, if I knock off a couple of pieces of ass before fucking you later, so much the better for me." She looked at him provocatively before lighting a cigarette. "Let her rip, big boy."

Not thinking he was driving fast enough, she took her emerald-green shoes and bore down on his right foot, pressing the accelerator to the floor. Like speed racers, they roared into Hollywood for their night on the town.

***

Over her drink in a nightclub, Tashman told Bogie more about Garbo. "After tennis at some of John Gilbert's parties, all of us would go for a swim. Everyone wore a bathing suit except Greta. Nude, and from within the swimming pool, she

274

urged us to jump in without our suits, claiming that everyone does that in Sweden. She'd especially urge John to strip down but I think he was embarrassed by the excessive attention from Eddie's homosexual friends. Eddie has had a crush on John for years. After Greta would emerge from the pool, she'd walk around the garden nude. It certainly caused John's Japanese gardener to gawk."

"I'd love to have seen the sights," he said.

"And some sight it is," Tashman said. "Marlene, even Tallulah, are like normal sized women. Their pussies are a bit stretched out from overuse but still within the range of normalcy. Dear, dear Greta on the other hand—it's the size of the Grand Canyon. You might be trying to delicately tongue her and your whole fucking head will fall in. She's like a Venus flytrap. I've never seen anything like it. She could take the trunk of a redwood tree up there and not even feel it."

"Thank you for warning me," he said. "I'll strike her from my list of possible seductions before I leave town. I like a hole that's tight. Like yours."

"Regardless of how many times I stretch it," she said, "it always seems to snap back into position."

Most of Tashman's critics claimed she had the most obscene mouth of any woman in Hollywood, but he liked that quality in her, preferring to define it as earthy rather than obscene.

"Of course, if Garbo is ever seen wearing anything that's remotely tasteful, she owes a debt to me," Tashman said. She arched her back as her carefully encased breasts jutted forward. "When I first met Garbo, her wardrobe consisted of men's shirts, flannel pajamas, flat-heeled shoes, and stuff she bought at the Army/Navy store. I taught her how to dress."

Even in those he was about to seduce, he always liked to stick the needle in. "I saw Constance Bennett come in tonight. I read that she's now the best dressed woman in Hollywood."

"No doubt you read that crap in Louella Parsons' column," Tashman said. "That bitch hates me. She's always attacking me and building up Bennett. I'm much better dressed than Bennett. Her taste is vulgar."

"I think you're better dressed than Bennett, too."

"Of course, I am," Tashman said, finishing her drink and demanding another. There's no contest. Bennett dresses like a hooker on Tenth Avenue. And Fifi D'Orsay? That's another heifer who looks like a hooker walking the waterfront trying to pick up a sailor. But back to Greta. Just before her trip to Sweden aboard the *Kungsholm* in 1928, I went with her to select her wardrobe. I found some lovely velvet dresses, a gorgeous gray fur coat, some smartly tailored traveling suits, and three heavenly evening gowns. She surprised me by wanting some lace on them. The poor thing. She couldn't tell real lace from machine-made, and found it surprising that I could."

In those days, late-night patrons of the Cocoanut Grove, awaited the arrival of the morning newspapers, the way Broadway actors, the mornings after their opening nights, used to wait in Sardi's for the first reviews of their plays to hit the streets.

"For the past week, Louella has had it in for me," Tashman said. "I can't imagine what she's going to say tomorrow. She's already hinted at my affair with Garbo. She attacked my so-called poor taste in clothing. She criticized my acting. What else?"

A handsome waiter arrived at their table with club soda, handing the recently arrived morning paper to Tashman. Thanking him, she quickly turned to Parsons' column. After reading it, she threw it on the floor and stomped it with her high-heeled shoes. "The bitch! The *bitch*! She's never forgiven me for telling all over town about how, when Eddie and I first invited her over, she got drunk and pissed on our sofa. That cow can't hold her piss. She's left piss-stains on half the couches in Hollywood."

"What did she write?" he asked.

"She says that I'm not a beauty in the sense that Garbo and Dietrich are. With my photographic memory, I can quote the hag verbatim. 'Tashman's a bit too tall, skinny where a woman shouldn't be, and there is a definite masculinity about her features. She fancies herself a best dresser. Actually she dresses too flamboyantly and wears too much jewelry. For Fifth Avenue class and sophistication, one has to look instead at the carefully groomed Constance Bennett.' What crap!" She demanded a cigarette. "Fifth Avenue indeed. On Fifth Avenue the best stores are selling Lilyan Tashman hats, Lilyan Tashman gowns." A desperation came over her. "You think I'm pretty, don't you, Bogie?"

He assured her that she was the most beautiful of all screen goddesses, even more beautiful than Loretta Young.

Tashman didn't settle for that. Throughout the evening she kept demanding that he reassure her of her beauty.

As the night rolled on, he noted some very disturbing characteristics about her. Although still under her spell, he grew tired of telling her how beautiful she was. Finally in exasperation, he said, "I've told you ten times tonight how lovely you are. Now I want to hear from you about how handsome I am."

"Darling, you'll never understand," she said. "Even though my husband is a very handsome man, in general I don't like my male dates to be too pretty. More rugged looking, really. I feel that a man too beautiful deflects attention from me, where it belongs. Besides, if a man is too handsome, like our waiter, I secure him for my husband. He's got this thing about male beauty, demanding only the best."

"Then I should be flattered that he went down on me."

"You should indeed. I mean you're nice looking and everything. But, as you'll find out as you get to know us better, you'll learn that Eddie usually likes men who are stunners."

Tashman had gorged herself during dinner, eating the T-bone, a baked potato, a large salad with Roquefort cheese, buttery corn on the cob, and a luscious fruit tart topped with whipped cream.

"How do you pack food away like a trencherman and still keep that slim shape of yours?" he asked.

"I eat everything I want," she said. "Fattening foods. Ice creams. Cakes and butter. Mashed potatoes, my favorite. Creamy gravy. Then I go to the can and lose it all."

"You mean you take a crap?"

"Don't be indelicate, darling," she said. She took her fingers and placed them against her mouth. "Like this. I enjoy my food and then, presto, it's gone. Never digested. It's the only way a heavy eater can still look like Slim Jane on the screen. The camera adds weight, you know."

As she headed for the women's room, Bogie watched her go. Son of a doctor or not, at the time he was unfamiliar with bulimia.

As fascinating as she was, he knew that there was trouble hovering over Tashman. She was a rash, impulsive woman. He suspected that an intensity as powerful as hers would soon burn itself out. He could not imagine her ever growing old. Much later, in the Fifties, he'd have the same feeling about another actress he'd meet: Marilyn Monroe. Like Monroe, Tashman would be dead before her 36th birthday.

Tashman disappeared inside the women's powder room. To Bogie's horror, he saw Constance Bennett, unaware that her worst enemy was throwing up inside that toilet, leave her seat on the far side of the club and head for the same women's john.

If he could, Bogie would have warned Tashman or even have gotten up and told Bennett to keep control over her kidneys a little longer. As it was, he just sat there waiting for the inevitable to happen.

The Lilyan Tashman/Constance Bennett toilet encounter would later be immortalized in a scene from Jacqueline Susann's alltime best seller, *Valley of the Dolls*.

Even though he had been seated only a few yards from the women's room of the Cocoanut Grove, Bogie never fully understood what happened during the confrontation between Constance Bennett and Lilyan Tashman in what he called "the gals' crapper." Tashman never fully explained it to him.

Under advice from her lawyers, the normally outspoken Bennett had little to say the next day. Known for enjoying conflicts, she was in a constant feud with the press and enjoyed lawsuits. The next morning her lawyers filed suit against Tashman, although the case was eventually dropped, much to the disappointment of the press who relished the news and gossip potential of a courtroom cat fight between Bennett and Tashman.

All that Bogie heard on that fateful night were screaming denunciations emerging from the women's room. A battle royal seemed to have been launched, as two women attendants rushed into the toilet to see what was the matter.

A few minutes later, the fair-haired, blue-eyed Constance Bennett emerged from the toilet, her red satin dress torn, her head covered with a scarf. She hastily made her way through the club, which had grown stonily silent. It seemed that half of Hollywood, including producers, directors, and stars, watched her exit.

Far more than Tashman, Constance Bennett was a high-profile star. A recent contract with Warner Brothers had awarded her $300,000 for two films, making her the highest paid film player up to that time. Reports of her fantastic salary were so high that it caught the attention of the government, inspiring tax legislation aimed at the film industry.

Like Tashman, Bennett was a legendary clotheshorse and fashion plate. But the night Bogie saw her rushing out of the Cocoanut Grove with the scarf around her head, it seemed as if she'd dressed in secondhand rags from the Bowery.

Philippe Gramm, one of the managers of the club, came over to Bogie. "Would you please escort Miss Tashman out of here, using the back entrance? There will be no bill tonight. But please don't bring her here again."

Bogie thanked him and stood by the door to the women's room until Tashman came out. Her emerald-colored dress had been ripped, and she'd borrowed a coat from someone to conceal it. Taking her arm, he escorted the infuriated woman through the kitchen. The Mexican dishwashers stopped to stare at her.

In the car, Bogie tried to piece together the story. Tashman was incoherent, screaming in fury. From what he could gather, Bennett had entered the toilet and encountered Tashman vomiting her big dinner into the sink.

Bennett had told her how disgusting a creature she was, and as the argument escalated, Bennett had yelled at her, calling her a dyke.

"I could handle that," Tashman said. "I've been called a lot worse. But when she attacked my gown, claiming that only a hooker would wear it, I let the cunt have it. I ripped her dress as she tore at mine. When I went to pull every hair out of her head, I accidentally yanked off her wig. She'd had a bad perm and was covering her real hair."

"And then what happened?" he asked.

"That seemed to drive the bitch wild and she tore into me, trying to rip me to shreds. I let her have it."

Arriving at Tashman's home, she stormed into her parlor, followed by Bogie. In his underwear, Edmund Lowe was sitting and drinking with a very good-looking man, also tantalizingly clad only in his underwear.

Bogie immediately recognized him as the ruggedly handsome actor, Joel McCrea.

While Tashman rushed upstairs in hysterics, with Lowe trailing her, Bogie attempted as best as he could to explain to McCrea what had happened at the Cocoanut Grove that night. He felt awkward that he'd caught McCrea not only half naked but in what was obviously a compromising situation with Lowe.

In spite of the circumstances and the hysteria going on upstairs, the young man from Pasadena seemed completely natural, at ease, and even somewhat amused by the situation.

When Bogie met someone in Hollywood, he always talked shop, figuring that was the only subject that interested actors. Not so McCrea. In spite of the fact that he was becoming known on the silver screen, he didn't seem to take a film career that seriously.

The man who would go on to become one of the great stars of American Westerns claimed, "I really want to be a rancher. I fell into acting by accident, thanks to my friendship with Will Rogers, who told me to invest my money in cattle and land."

In the years to come, McCrea would take that advice seriously becoming, like Randolph Scott, a multimillionaire.

Ever the heckler, Bogie couldn't resist. "You don't seem like the other guys hanging out with Lowe."

"It's no big deal for me," McCrea said, accepting the drink Bogie offered him. "I grew up in California. As a six foot two athlete—and some say handsome—I've had guys coming on to me ever since I was fourteen. I'm used to it. If I can give them some pleasure, and if they're an important person like Eddie, I don't mind. It means nothing to me."

"That's one way of looking at it," Bogie said. "My, you young guys are sophisticated out here on the Coast. I don't think most of us back in that hicktown called New York are quite that casual about sex, especially with other men."

"I'll have many affairs," he said, "but when I get married, I'm gonna stay married. I might play around on the side—all men do—but I'll marry just one woman forever."

Even at such an early age, McCrea seemed to know what he wanted. On the set of that tepid 1933 melodrama, *The Silver Cord*, he met actress Frances Dee. He married her that year, and the union lasted until her death in 1990.

He'd met one of his earliest mistresses, Marion Davies, on the set of the silent film, *The Fair Coed*. She'd later say, "Many women would know Joel's mighty inches, but after the panting, sweating, and eruptions had ended, he always put on his pants and went home to Frances."

After Lowe had spent some time soothing his wife, he came back into the parlor. Still clad in his underwear, he told Bogie that, "Darling Lil is calling for you. Throw her a good one. She needs something to distract her."

"Glad to oblige," Bogie said. He turned to McCrea. "Good to meet you, rancher boy. See you on the sagebrush trail."

As he came into Tashman's boudoir, she was lying fully nude on the bed, smoking a cigarette and having a drink.

"I need my brains fucked out," Tashman said. "And I need to be told how beautiful I am."

An hour later, as Bogie was in the saddle, he was startled to see a nude Lowe taking a place on the same bed, and immediately feared that his coupling was about to become a three-way. He wanted to pull away, but Tashman wouldn't allow it, clutching and holding him even closer to her body.

When Bogie looked up, he knew he needn't have worried. A nude McCrea, with a big erection, was moving into position on top of Lowe.

As McCrea mounted Lowe and joined Bogie as the second top in the same bed, the handsome actor winked at him. "You've got pretty good rhythm there. Let me match it." As he penetrated Lowe, who yelled out, McCrea matched Bogie thrust for thrust.

"Ride 'em, cowboy," Bogie said.

***

He'd had a lovely evening with Joan Blondell, during which she'd served what she described as one of her favorite dishes—mashed rutabagas mixed with mashed potatoes. Fortunately, she'd also baked a ham as well. That was his favorite. As he related to Kenneth the following morning, "Sex with Joan has become what I imagine it's like between a married couple who's been together for many many years. It's comfortable and safe, but completely without fireworks."

Kenneth seemed relatively unconcerned about Bogie's sex life that morning. He was distracted by plans for his upcoming wedding to Kay Francis. Once again, he secured a promise that Bogie would be there as his best man.

Bogie agreed for a final time, then reminded him that Helen Menken would be arriving in Hollywood soon and checking into the Garden of Allah.

"I adore Helen," Kenneth said. "Bring her to the wedding."

Some of Kay's friends are throwing some parties for us this week. We'd love it if you and Helen could come to any or all of them. I'll slip the invitations under your door."

"That sounds great," Bogie said, "Helen would meet some film people. She already knows everybody on Broadway."

"Wouldn't it be ironic if Helen became a bigger film star than either of us?"

"Things like that happen," Bogie said, lighting up his seventh cigarette of the morning. "But if I make all these appearances at all these parties, people will think I'm back with Helen. Hollywood is a small town. Word will get back to Mary."

"So what?" Kenneth asked. "Mary knows you're sleeping with other gals. And don't kid yourself. Mary hasn't exactly been behaving like a nun recently. I'm sure she has a steady stream of beaux."

"That's our marriage agreement," Bogie said. "It's OK for me to fool around with other women, unless that other woman happens to be Helen. Mary won't exactly be thrilled by any of this."

"Maybe Mary will divorce you after all," Kenneth said with a wink.

Bogie clinched his fist and pretended to give Kenneth a sock in the jaw. "Still pining for Mary, huh? Here you are about to marry Kay, and you're still trying to steal my wife."

"Hey," Kenneth said, "I've got a sharp eye for a movie plot. How about writing a screenplay together about this romantic entanglement? I bet we could sell it."

280

"And maybe we couldn't," Bogie said. "About this wedding. Is it going to be a big affair?"

"No. The wedding itself will be very small. The guests include you, Helen, and one or two of Kay's friends. That's why Kay is seeing all of her friends and getting congratulations and, we hope, lots of presents before the actual marriage ceremony."

"Smart thinking," Bogie said, glancing at the clock. "I've got to go to work. Sounds like we'll have a gay old time this week with all the parties and everything."

"It's your chance to score this week," Kenneth said. "You'll be meeting some of the top broads in Hollywood. Too bad you'll be with your wife."

"My former wife," Bogie corrected him. "We're divorced, remember? And besides, even when we were married, Helen and I had an open marriage. And she's likely to be heavily booked during her time out here, spending time with some of her former girl friends, including Tallulah, who's also at the Garden of Allah."

"It's going to be interesting," Kenneth said. "I wish I could follow you around with a camera this week."

"After the marriage, are you still going to be fooling around with your men friends?"

"Sure. Kay and I both understand that our marriage will be mainly for show. I'm doing it to boost my career in Hollywood. Being married to a major movie star might help. That's why you married Helen—to advance your career on Broadway."

"Something like that," he said, as Kenneth's words evoked a sour memory.

"Kay's becoming big out here, really big. She's defined as one of the top five actresses in Hollywood, with lots of attention from the press. Her fans want to see her with a handsome and adoring husband."

"Good luck," Bogie said. "Yours will be just one of many lavender marriages out here."

"Speaking of that, how's that Lilyan Tashman/Edmund Lowe thing going?"

"This sounds ridiculous, but I'm falling in love with her. I still sleep around, but when Lilyan calls, I drop everything and come running. I'm hooked."

"C'mon, man, she's a dyke."

Bogie seemed irritated. "So what? I think on some drunken night we've covered this ground before. You're marrying a dyke. Barbara Stanwyck is a dyke but also a great piece of ass. If you and I fucked only heterosexual women, we'd be sitting home playing with ourselves."

"You're right," Kenneth said. "We've agreed on this before."

"Joan Blondell is not a dyke," Bogie said. "Glenda Farrell's not a dyke. As for all the others, I'm not so sure."

"Rumor has it that your friend, Miss Tashman, can seduce any woman, heterosexual or not," Kenneth said.

Bogie winced. "I'd rather not think about that. The one thing I know, and in spite of many offers—some of them very overt—I'm more into women than I ever was. I had a moment or two of serious doubt about my manhood since coming to Hollywood. But that confusion is over."

"I'm sorry to hear that," Kenneth said. "My friend, Eric Linden, will be disappointed. He's got a serious crush on you and I think he's about to start stalking you."

"You still carrying on with that kid?"

"Yeah, but you're fucking it up."

"How so?" Bogie asked.

"The only reason he keeps putting up with me is because I keep promising him I'll introduce him to you," Kenneth said. "I'll have to deliver the merchandise soon—or else."

"There's just no way," Bogie said. "Don't get me wrong. I'm grateful to be admired. But he's got the wrong equipment."

"Let's at least get together for a drink with him," Kenneth said. "Otherwise, I'm going to lose the best piece of boy ass in Hollywood. He's even better than Doug Fairbanks."

"Junior that is?" Bogie asked facetiously.

"You got it! You don't see me running around with grandfathers, do you?"

"Can't say that I have," Bogie said. "When it comes to men, you and Spencer Tracy fuck only from the A-list. When it comes to women, Spence fucks up and down the alphabet from hookers to extras and script gals he picks up on the set of one of his films. When it comes to women, my friend, Kenneth MacKenna, marries only big stars. The third best dressed woman in Hollywood, after Lilyan Tashman and Constance Bennett."

"You know me well," Kenneth said. "If the person I'm fucking—male or female—is famous, that's like an aphrodisiac to me. Some really big stars who are homosexual have told me that they pick up guys, get them to go to bed with them, but once in bed the young men are so awed by their partner's fame they can't get it up. Not me. The more famous my partner is, the bigger my hard-on."

"When you die, they're gonna write on your tombstone, 'Here lies Kenneth MacKenna, Hollywood's first star-fucker.'"

***

Faced with time on his hands before the arrival of Helen Menken, Bogie remembered that Myrna Loy on their first date together had asked him to give her a call. He'd liked her a lot when he'd worked with her on that Charles Farrell film, *Body and Soul*, and still thought she had the cutest nose in Hollywood.

He went to call Loy, but found that her number wasn't listed in the phone book. Even though she'd invited him to phone her, she'd never given him her number. What the hell! he thought. It was a late Sunday afternoon, and he decided he'd just drop in on her unexpectedly. In those days before it became necessary to make an appointment to see a friend, lots of casual friends did that all across America.

If he found Loy locked in the embrace of another beau, he could always slip back into his car and give Glenda Farrell a call when he got back to his apartment. He knew that Joan Blondell was probably engaged for the evening. She was making a movie called *Night Nurse* with Barbara Stanwyck and the up-and-coming Clark Gable. The last time he'd bedded Blondell, she'd told him that she'd developed a powerful crush on Gable.

"Who doesn't have a crush on him?" Bogie had asked. "He goes to bed with all his leading ladies, "Or so I hear. All except Garbo."

"Add Barbara Stanwyck to the list," Blondell had said. "That's one 'night nurse' who didn't fall for Gable."

"Then I'm sure he'll go after you," Bogie had said. "For all I know, Stanwyck will get you first.'

"You know me pretty well by now," Blondell had said. "I don't play those games, although I hardly disapprove of those who do. With her appetites and her charms, Stanwyck doesn't need either Gable or me."

"And you certainly don't need Gable when you've got me," he'd said. "After all, when I came to Hollywood, Louella Parsons wrote in her column that Fox was grooming me to be their answer to Gable. Once again, Miss Weak Kidneys got it wrong."

The people who lived in the house opposite Myrna Loy's were throwing a party, and all the parking spaces were taken. Bogie decided to drive around to the less crowded block in back and approach her house by walking through her garden in the rear.

As he strolled through her garden in the twilight, he heard a beautiful male voice singing, *Viejo Amor*. Sitting by the fountain strumming his guitar, was the second handsomest male beauty he'd ever spotted in his life, except for Glenda Farrell's ex, Tommy Richards. He was almost nude except for a thin towel draped around his slender waist. In the dim light, it took Bogie a minute to figure out that he was coming face to face with Gary Cooper.

This was not the first time he'd seen Cooper, remembering that night at the Garden of Allah when he'd spotted the actor and Tallulah Bankhead racing naked from Nazimova's pool and into her bungalow.

Looking up at Bogie, the long, lean, and lanky actor hardly acknowledged him and went on to finish his love song.

At the end of the song, Bogie said, "I know you light up the screen, but no one told me you were a singer to boot."

Without revealing that he even knew who Bogie was, Cooper said, "I've sung in pictures before. In *Wolf Song*, the one I made with Lupe Velez, I sang 'My Honey, Fare Thee Well.'"

If Bogie recalled, that film was silent. He offered Cooper a cigarette before lighting one for himself. Neither man had bothered with an introduction, each actor vain enough to assume that the other one knew perfectly well who he was.

"Forgive the way I'm dressed tonight," Cooper said. "But if you saw *Wolf Song*, you've seen more of my flesh than you're seeing right now." He motioned toward Loy's guest cottage across the garden. "A male friend and I are staying here spending the weekend with Myrna. I just took a nude swim like I did in *Wolf Song*."

"I don't remember any nude scene in that picture," Bogie said.

"That's because the director, Victor Fleming, cut it out. Too hot for the public to handle. One night he shot a nude scene with my spicy little tabasco-flavored confection, Lupe. Fleming said it was the hottest scene ever put before the cameras. Lupe got me so worked up I got a big hard-on. I think at one point my dick actually shows up in the frame." He puffed his cigarette and smiled. "Of course, they'd need a wide screen for that."

"Too bad they cut it," Bogie said. "It would have been a sensation. At least a first."

"It is, but only at private parties Fleming throws," Cooper said. "He screens it for the entertainment of his guests. That's why I've got such a big reputation in Hollywood, that and word spread about me by Clara Bow and Lupe herself."

"I always say an actor needs a good press rep," Bogie said. "I wish I had that kind of reputation. I'm about to make a movie with George O'Brien. With my crappy body, which looks like a skinned chicken when I'm nude, I'll have to leave that male pinup stuff to George, or maybe Charles Farrell. I made a flick with him too."

"If Fleming had kept in our nude scene," Cooper said, "the world would soon forget Georgie boy and Charlie boy. I know from intimate, personal, first-hand experience, I've got both of those boys beat by a Montana mile."

"You're gonna be the biggest thing in pictures," Bogie said, barely disguising the sarcasm in his voice.

If Bogart was making a dig, Cooper didn't seem to notice. "Fleming became so obsessed with getting me naked in the swimming hole that he ordered another nude scene with me and Louis Wolheim, who played my trapper buddy in that film. We're bathing at a hot spring getting ready for the big dance in the village that night. When Wolheim takes a look at my body, he says, 'A woman is going to get hold of you some day and never let go.'"

"Quite a compliment," Bogie said. "Or, if we were more sophisticated, the line might have included mention of a man getting a hold on you instead."

Cooper looked at him suspiciously. "You one of those boys I keep meeting out here, like that Edmund Goulding? When Goulding directed me in *Paramount on Parade*, I told him he'd have to let me alone from time to time so I'd have some energy left for the camera."

Both men laughed at that. "I'm not one of the boys," Bogie said. "I've had offers. Of course, they're nothing like what I'm sure you get all the time."

"More than I can shake a stick at," he said, rising from the seat by the fountain and laying his guitar down.

"Hey, I just dropped in on Myrna," Bogie said. "We're just fellow co-workers. If I knew she had a date tonight with the great Gary Cooper, I would never have shown up. I didn't have her phone number, or I would have called first."

"Myrna doesn't have a date with me," he said. "We're just good friends. She's entertaining one of her gals up in her boudoir right now."

"You mean, she doesn't have a guy for the evening?" Bogie asked.

"Not a guy exactly," Cooper said, "but I'm sure she's being entertained."

"Our dear Myrna? She walks both sides of the waterfront too? I'd never have suspected that about her."

"It's hardly a secret," he said. "When we were growing up back in Montana, Myrna was known as Miss Gillette Blade."

"You mean she cuts it on both edges?" he asked.

"You got that right."

"I'd better go," he said. "This seems like a very private party."

"Hell, no, stay," Cooper said. "The more the merrier. Myrna said she likes you a lot. I want you to say hello to my friend. He was telling me all about your scene the other night. You guys were involved in some hot, hot action. Wish I'd been invited myself."

"What in hell are you talking about?" Bogie asked. "Up to now he'd just assumed that Cooper's off-the-record friend was Anderson Lawler, as the two young actors were seen all over town together at plays and concerts. The more refined Virginian was apparently trying to expose the Montana cowboy, Cooper, to culture.

Bogie didn't plan to budge until he'd met Cooper's mysterious male friend. His mind buzzed with the possibilities. Kenneth MacKenna got around. Had Kenneth captured Cooper from Lupe Velez and Anderson Lawler? Or was it Edmund Lowe?

The timing was perfect. Emerging from the guest cottage completely nude was the second handsomest man in Hollywood, with a body even more developed than the lanky Cooper's frame.

Seeing Cooper and Bogie, he waved at both of them before plunging into the deepest end of the pool.

It was the strikingly handsome Joel McCrea.

***

After McCrea had taken his swim, showered, and dressed, he sat with Bogie at the pool waiting for Cooper to get ready. He told Bogie that they would soon be joined by Loy and her still unnamed woman friend. To Bogie's embarrassment, McCrea recalled the bed they'd shared at "Lilowe" with Edmund Lowe and Lilyan Tashman. He didn't seem in the least embarrassed.

"I thought you'd be a little shy to put on a performance like that in front of me," Bogie said. "I didn't have to be ashamed myself. At least I was with a woman even if she's a woman who likes the girls more than men."

"I like women too," McCrea said, "and one of these days sooner than later I'm gonna find me one and settle down."

The first night he'd met McCrea, the actor had expressed somewhat the same sentiment. Apparently, his involvement with Cooper had not altered his resolve. "You mean, give up playing the field?"

"That's the way it's gonna be," McCrea said. "After this weekend with Gary, I've found the man for me. I confess to hearing what you said to Gary. I overheard that remark you made about a man seeing Gary and never letting him go. After last night, Gary's my man."

"What about Anderson Lawler?"

"He's history now," McCrea said. "When Gary needs what a man has to offer, he's got me. As you saw me when I jumped in the pool, that's quite a lot. Of course, I can't measure up to Gary. No man can."

"What about Eddie Lowe?" Bogie asked.

"I guess you didn't hear me?" McCrea said. "As of last night, there will be no other man for me, nor any other man for Gary. Our days of selling ourselves to men like Eddie Goulding, Bill Haines, and Rod La Rocque are over. Eddie Lowe falls into that category too. From now on, we're bonded. Our careers are launched. We don't need to turn to influential homosexuals to advance us. We can do what we do with each other for the sheer pleasure."

Didn't you tell me last time that you're looking for a gal to settle down with? I hear that even Coop is a bit of a skirt chaser. Tallulah Bankhead, Clara Bow, now Lupe Velez."

"Those are the rules by which we're gonna play," McCrea said. "Each of us can have all the women we want, but only one man. It's like we're wed. Gary Cooper and Joel McCrea. Please note I gave him star billing, because I honestly believe he's gonna become the next king of Hollywood. Gary Cooper and Joel McCrea. Until death do us part."

"That's almost like a marriage vow," Bogie said.

"It is in a funny kind of way." McCrea said. "There was something that happened between us that was almost mystical last night. I don't want to sound like I'm a member of one of these weird cults out here. It's hard to describe. We came together in such a special way that I know I'll never desert him or he'll never desert me."

"Sounds like true love to me," Bogie said somewhat facetiously. But he could tell from the look on McCrea's face that he was perfectly serious.

"I first met Gary when I was having an affair with Doug Fairbanks," McCrea said. "Junior, that is."

"I figured," Bogie said. "That boy's name sure keeps popping up."

"That's because he makes the rounds nightly—both men and women," McCrea said. "I met Gary at a party at Pickfair thrown by Doug's father and Mary Pickford.

We found each other attractive but we only circled each other then, like Indians closing in on a group of settlers. Besides, he was carrying on something crazy with Clara Bow at the time."

"She's got Dracula now and all the football players in Southern California," Bogie said.

"It would take a football team to satisfy her after Gary," McCrea said. "I think I fell in love with Gary not in person but in that film *Wolf Song* that you guys were talking about earlier. For the first time, Victor Fleming created a screen version of man as an irresistible sex object. He had Gary slouch insolently, peering up at the camera with those sleepy bedroom eyes, his face shaded by a wide-brimmed hat tipped at a jaunty angle. I got an instant hard-on just watching it. His lush curly locks fell across his forehead. He was the strong, silent cowboy seductor type, the kind of man I've always wanted for my own. He always looked a bit sullen, just how I like it."

"As I said, sounds like love."

McCrea looked him squarely in the eye, unashamed and almost defiantly proud of his passion for Gary. "It is. After last night, it's more than that."

"I don't even have something that passionate with my wife," Bogie said, lighting a cigarette. "Especially my wife."

"That's too bad," McCrea said. "Without passion, what is life?"

"Something I plan to go on living, pal," Bogie said. "Grand passion or not. I view getting a piece of ass as a worthy day's goal. I fuck a lot. The only woman I feel any grand passion for, and you've seen that first hand, is Lilyan. She's married to Eddie, and can work me in only once or twice a week. Guess who she's dating tonight?"

"Stanwyck, Crawford, Kay Francis," McCrea said. "How long do I have to play this guessing game."

"Dietrich," Bogie said. "The Kraut herself."

"That was my first guess," McCrea said, but I rejected it. Too obvious."

"I gotta admit I'd drop almost anybody for Dietrich," Bogie said. "But I don't play in that league. I never expect to mount Dietrich and Garbo. What about you?"

"Me neither," McCrea said. "When it comes to women, a plain, simple American gal will do for me. When it comes to men, only my Montana cowpoke will do. No one hits the spot like he does."

Ever the provocateur, Bogie said, "To judge from your performance the other night with Eddie, I thought you were strictly a top man."

"I always was until last night," McCrea said. "Even when I crawled into the sack with Gary, I told him I was strictly a top. All he said to that was, 'Yeah, tell me about it.' A top around Gary Cooper doesn't remain a top for long. I feel as wide open as the Grand Canyon."

"I just don't get it," Bogie said, "Maybe this is a unique time in American history. But you guys—and the women too—seem to drift with total ease between the sexes. A man one night, a woman the next night. I think Dietrich, straight off the boat from the Weimar Republic, brought German decadence with her."

"It's not something I can explain," McCrea said, "because I don't understand it myself. George Cukor explained it best. He calls this halcyon time in Hollywood *La Belle Epoque*."

"I can buy that," Bogie said. "It's a golden time especially for the young. I know I'm drifting in and out of relationships—and having a lot of fun—but I also know I'm forming some lasting bonds. But I'm not into this drifting between the sexes."

"That's what Cukor meant by *La Belle Epoque*," McCrea said. "It's a time to test our limits, to find out what our real desires are, and in essence to discover who we are. Some of us like Gary and myself are finding out that we are many things. Many personalities live within ourselves. We've got needs and we want to fulfill those needs—not repress them."

"I don't want to pretend that I'm a total oaf from back East," Bogie said. "Once or twice I've started to open up a door to my closet. But I decided I'd better slam the door forever."

"That's your choice and I respect it," McCrea said. "What's right for you isn't right for me."

At that point a fully dressed Gary Cooper came onto the patio. As if defiantly showing off his more liberated self, McCrea got up and, in front of Bogie, kissed Cooper passionately on the mouth. Bogie felt that the two handsomest men in Hollywood would be a sensation in front of the camera. Of course, such a scene would also cause rioting in movie houses all over America. No doubt in Cooper's own state of Montana, some cowboys would actually take six-shooters and fire at the screen.

As the two men sat holding hands on the patio in front of Bogie, he felt very much a third party until Cooper made it clear that he and McCrea definitely wanted him to stay for the barbecue.

It was one of the most idyllic evenings he'd ever spent in Los Angeles in spite of his awkward feelings about intruding upon a love affair.

From that night on, Gary Cooper and Joel McCrea were the "best of friends." Like Cary Grant and Randolph Scott, their bond would extend into the twilight of their lives.

Breaking the enchantment of the evening, Myrna Loy in a sunflower yellow dress brought back the fading sunshine of the day. Bogie jumped up to give her a hug. "What a pleasant surprise," she said. "You're welcome even if you didn't call."

He kissed her cute nose. "I wanted to slip in unannounced to see who my competition was."

As if on cue, a beautiful woman came up behind Loy and wrapped her arm around her waist.

"Mr. Bogart," she said, "we meet again—and not in bed this time."

It was Elissa Landi.

"My God," Bogie said, "if it isn't the Empress of Austria herself."

***

Myrna Loy was an amusing hostess, and Joel McCrea the best short-order barbecue cook in Los Angeles. Bogie proved adept at mixing cocktails, and Gary Cooper was an articulate guest, so unlike the characters he would later portray on the screen with a "Yep" and a "Nope." Maybe before Cooper had dumped Anderson Lawler, some culture had rubbed off.

If Elissa Landi felt awkward at seeing Bogie again, she gave no indication of it. He was fast learning that in Hollywood you could have a hot, torrid affair with someone, drop her, then casually chat with her at a Hollywood party the following week, even laughing and joking with her husband as if nothing had occurred between you.

For the only time he could recall, a group of actors got together and didn't talk shop; instead, Cooper and Loy wanted to talk Montana. She recalled how "the world's most fragrant wild roses" grew along the fences of her grandfather's Crow Creek Valley cattle ranch.

"I guess we have a sky over our head out here in California," Cooper said, "but Montana has more sky than any place there is. I was growing pretty tall even when I was a boy. Sometimes I'd stand on a rock and stretch my arms as far as I could, hoping to reach up and touch that sky."

"You should have used another part of your anatomy," McCrea said, igniting good-natured laughter.

It made Bogie wonder if there was anybody left in Hollywood who didn't know the formidable weapon Cooper carried in his pants. With propagandists like Clara Bow and Tallulah Bankhead, it was Hollywood's worst kept secret. Only his current flame, Lupe Velez, found something negative to say, telling everyone who'd listen, "Garee's got the biggest cock in Hollywood but no ass to push it with."

A large black woman came from the house out to the garden and said, "You have a guest at the door, Miss Loy. Miss Lupe Velez. She's very angry."

Turning to Bogie with an affectionate smile, Loy said, "My second uninvited guest of the evening."

"She's on your trail," Landi cautioned Cooper. "Go hide out in the cottage and we'll tell her you're not here."

"Like hell I will," Cooper said defiantly. "She doesn't own me. That man-eating spitfire thinks she's branded me like I'm her pet bull or something."

"Elissa is right," McCrea said. "Better duck out of sight while Myrna gets rid of this enchilada."

Always the kidder, Bogie chimed in, "Seems that I'm the only stag here tonight. Maybe you can fix me up with Lupe."

"From what I hear," McCrea said jokingly, "she'd be too much woman for you. She leaves her Tijuana teeth marks over every inch of a man."

"And her footprints on the ceiling," Cooper said, smiling, although he glanced apprehensively toward the front of the house, perhaps wondering if Loy were getting rid of Velez. "Lupe sleeps all over Hollywood, yet she expects me to be faithful. You name them. Doug Fairbanks, Senior and Junior. Tom Mix. Chaplin. Victor Fleming. Clark Gable."

"I'll tell you who she's not had and will never have, and that's Joel McCrea," the actor said.

Cooper leaned over and kissed him gently on the lips. "You don't need a Mexican Spitfire. You already have your own Montana Spitfire."

To Bogie's surprise, Loy escorted Velez right into their barbecue area by the pool.

"*Garee*," she shouted at him, making his name sound like an accusation. "I've driven all over town trying to find you."

"I'm just here seeing an old friend," Cooper said. "Myrna and I are reminiscing about life back in Montana."

"Where is Anderson Lawler?" Lupe demanded to know. "You're hiding him somewhere. Where is that fairy? I'm going to cut his nuts out." She opened her purse as if carrying some concealed weapon there.

Ever the diplomat, Loy said, "Gary and I grew up together. Joel is here with his date. I think you know Elissa Landi."

At that pronouncement, McCrea slid his chair closer to Landi and put his arm possessively around her.

Velez looked suspiciously over at Bogie.

"Humphrey Bogart here," he said. "Ever since Myrna and I appeared in a film together, I've been chasing her."

"That leaves only Garree unaccounted for," she said. "Lawler must be hiding in that guest cottage." She stalked toward the cottage and, without an invitation, barged inside, presumably on a search. In about five minutes, she stood at the door of the cottage screeching, "Another man's clothes in here. Where's Lawler? I kill him."

"Sorry, Myrna," Cooper said. "Sorry, Joel, but I'd better go off into the night with her. Otherwise, you'll never get rid of her. She'll tear up the whole house trying to find Andie."

"You know more about women than I do," Bogie said, "but I'd keep my distance. Talk about temper. She's on the warpath."

"Bogie's right," McCrea said.

"If we call the police, all of us might end up on the front page the next morning," Landi said.

"My, oh my," Loy said. She looked flustered, the hostess who'd lost control of her party.

Ignoring advice, Cooper headed toward the cottage. In the doorway, he shoved

Velez inside as if he were going to give her hell, maybe even slap her face.

Loy and all the other guests, including Bogie, sat silently by the pool, as McCrea let the barbecued chicken burn. All eyes were glued to the doorway of that cottage, where Cooper and Velez were engaged in a fight that would not be topped in Hollywood until Bogie married his third wife, Mayo Methot, and the couple became known as the "Battling Bogarts."

Within ten minutes, the screaming denunciations reached a crescendo. The sounds of hand to hand combat could be heard. Both McCrea and Bogie rose to come to the aid of Cooper, sensing that in this case it was the man who needed the protection—not the woman.

Her dress torn, Velez ran from the cottage. As Bogie rushed in, followed by McCrea, he glanced only briefly back at Velez. She'd collapsed on the tiles around the pool, as both Loy and Landi hurried to her aid.

Inside the cottage, Cooper's white shirt was partially soaked in blood. McCrea cried out and rushed to him, ripping open the shirt.

Bogie rushed into the bathroom to emerge with a towel. Trying to imagine what his father, Belmont, might do in a situation like this, he bent over Cooper and gently wiped the blood from his chest. He saw no puncture. Then he noticed that Cooper's arm was bleeding. profusely. Velez had obviously stabbed him there. McCrea tossed him a clean shirt, and Bogie ripped it to apply a tourniquet.

"It's okay," Cooper said. "Just a flesh wound. Us Montana cowboys are used to cuts like this."

From what Bogie could tell, the cut was deep. He looked up at McCrea who appeared panic stricken. "Tell Myrna to call a doctor and be quick about it."

"I'll be okay," Cooper said. The blood was soaking through the wrapping. Before leaving the cottage, Bogie and McCrea picked up Cooper and gently placed him on his back in the double bed.

McCrea rushed outside to summon help from Loy. Bogie looked out only briefly from the cottage door. Velez was still on the tiles. "She's having a fit," he heard Landi call out to McCrea.

At first Bogie thought she was still raging and fuming over Cooper. From the bed, Cooper called out to Bogie, "She's epileptic."

At the door, Bogie yelled, "For God's sake, get a doctor, God damn it. My patient's bleeding to death and the other is having a fit."

Three hours later, Loy sat alone with Bogie in the garden. The hurricane winds had come and gone. That incredibly beautiful night had returned to its serenity. After subduing Velez and tending to Cooper's wound, the doctor, Winifred Bison, had secured Cooper's promise to visit his offices in the morning so he could re-examine the wound.

Bison left with Velez, claiming he was taking her to a clinic for the night. Even before the doctor had arrived, Landi had already fled, fearing that press photographers might show up if the police heard of this incident.

McCrea drove his car to the rear of the garden and escorted Cooper to the vehicle, claiming he would watch over him for the night.

"That leaves just the two of us," Loy said to Bogie. "No one's fighting over us."

"My ex-wife, Helen Menken, is arriving in town," he said. "Although she wasn't particularly attentive during our marriage, maybe she'll still be jealous of me."

"I'd love to meet Helen," Loy said. "I've seen her on the stage. When does she get in?"

"Tuesday afternoon," he said.

"Our party ended early," Loy said. "It's only eleven o'clock."

"I guess I'd better be going," he said.

"Don't rush off," she said. "It's a big house and I get lonely at night." As if sensing what he was thinking, she added, "Elissa fled into the night, abandoning me." She looked at him with a cute little smirk. "I'm sure Gary has told you I'm known as Miss Gillette."

"Yeah," he said. "I think he mentioned it."

"Just how sharp that shave is, you're about to find out for yourself." She leaned toward him. He didn't even need to wet his lips as they were already moist. As her mouth met his, he closed his eyes and pressed his body into hers. When he finally broke away, he kissed and nibbled at her delicate ear. "So far, it's been a fun evening."

"The fun is about to begin," she said, getting up, taking his hand, and leading him across her garden into her house.

***

It was a different Helen Menken he met at the train depot. Her immaculate clothes, even her hat, looked more Fifth Avenue than Hollywood and Vine. She had New York written all over her. He could not imagine a woman who looked less Californian.

As he rushed toward her to take her in his arms and kiss her on the mouth, he encountered a woman no longer in the spring of her life. Her face was still young but it was more mature, a bit harsher, and a bit less forgiving.

She made no effort to probe into his personal life, other than to say, "A handsome devil like you must be the sensation of half the Hollywood cuties out here—that is, the few that George Raft hasn't already subdued."

"Something like that," he said as nonchalantly as possible. He didn't want to tell her about his current involvement with Lilyan Tashman, fearing that if Helen met her again, Bogie would be the one waiting outside the locked bedroom door.

By the time they'd reached the parking lot of the Garden of Allah, Helen had brought him up to date on all the news of Broadway and several mutual acquaintances. No mention was made of his present wife, except one. "I saw Mary the other day," she said. "She's put on a few pounds, but the extra weight is agreeable to her figure. She's getting work, but neither of us is the sensation of Broadway these days, the way we imagined it would be when we were younger. In fact, with so few shows because of the Depression, Broadway is a pretty dismal place."

He wanted to ask Helen if she knew who Mary was dating or perhaps even shacked up with, but he restrained himself. "Sorry to hear about the depressed state of affairs. That's real bad news for me. I'm planning to go back to New York and try for a job on Broadway. Fox isn't going to renew me. They don't know what to do with me. In a few weeks I'm leaving Hollywood for good."

"It's a ghastly place out here," she said. "You and I are New Yorkers. We don't belong outside the civilized world."

"C'mon, let me show you to your new home." He went around to the trunk to get her luggage.

She stood looking at the façade of the Garden of Allah. "I can't believe that this was once Nazimova's private home. I still see her on and off. It's hard to imagine that she was once queen of MGM."

"Garbo seems to have filled her shoes." He looked into Helen's face for some flicker of recognition at the mention of Garbo.

She showed none. "I suppose you're right. I didn't think Garbo would survive the advent of talking pictures. I guess her audience wants whiskey pronounced *viskey*."

"You talk real pretty," he said, "and look great. I hope to take you around to a lot of parties. Maybe some director will discover you out here and make you a big star like Garbo."

"Oh, Hump," she said, heading for the reception desk as if she already knew where to go. "The Twenties are dead and gone. That was a time for day-dreaming. It's the grim Thirties now."

In the privacy of her bungalow, she told him that it was almost certain that a production of her lesbian play, *The Captive*, would be mounted on the stages of Los Angeles. "I'm out here negotiating the deal now." She paused. "That and other things."

For whatever reason, she chose not to tell him what she meant by "other things," which was a signal to him that he would be with her only on certain days, leaving the rest of her Hollywood sojourn a private affair.

"I don't get it," he said. "In New York, that play got you thrown into jail. What makes you think the Los Angeles police won't do the same thing? If anything, they're a lot more liberal in New York than out here. If what they define as perversion is depicted on the screen today, it's got to be hidden. No more Erich von Stroheim. He was the last of that era of decadence, I'm sorry to say."

"We'll see," she said enigmatically. "I have my assurances we're going forward with the project. I can't give you any details until I know more." She waved her arms theatrically. "Here I am installed in my new home in California but with yesterday's husband."

As she twirled around the room, that old sexual stirring came back to him. He still loved this woman, even though he wasn't passionate about her the way he was with Lilyan Tashman.

"I know you just got into town," he said, "and haven't even unpacked. But I've got to know something."

"Whatever do you want to know," she said, coming up to him and kissing him on both cheeks. "You divine, handsome thing you. If anything, in maturity you've grown more beautiful."

"C'mon, Helen," he said. "Even on my finest day no one ever calls me beautiful."

"Handsome then." She kissed him on the lips. "Still keeping those lips moist for me, are you?"

"Yeah," he said. "I've got to know something. When a woman divorces her husband, does said husband have to surrender his conjugal rights, or can he reclaim them at any time?"

"It doesn't matter what the legal restrictions are with me," she said. "If you're talking about that marriage contract between Helen Menken and one Humphrey Bogart, I view the bond as unbroken. Said husband can reclaim those rights whenever he wants to."

"Glad to hear that," he said, taking off his jacket and beginning a striptease in front of her.

"If you're taking off your clothes, I guess you're glad to see me."

Enroute to the bedroom, she promised him lots of loving before her eight o'clock engagement. "When she heard I was coming to California, Lilyan Tashman wrote me. She wants me to come over for dinner tomorrow night, my first night in Los Angeles. As part of your Hollywood rounds, have you met up with the Miss Tashman yet? Kitty Cornell, Nazimova, and I agree she's absolutely divine. And quite a lady for the ladies."

That did it for him. As he mounted Helen and plowed her good, he was more zealous in his efforts because his brain was flashing images of Lilyan Tashman and not the picture of the woman beneath him. From the ecstatic look on her face, Helen was none the wiser.

Later, when he was spent and she too was exhausted, she whispered in his ear. "I don't know who's been letting you fuck them in Hollywood, but your technique has improved."

***

It was after two o'clock in the morning, when he returned to his apartment after his reunion with Helen. He had to get some rest, pick up some clean clothes, and report to director Irving Cummings tomorrow morning on the set of *A Holy Terror*, in which he'd be supporting George O'Brien and Sally Eilers.

When he entered the apartment, the ringing of his telephone caused him to rush to answer it, thinking it might be Helen in distress for some reason.

"George," came the plaintive voice of a woman that could make him fall in love. That voice was vaguely familiar as if he'd spoken to her before. It was certainly a voice made for the Talkies.

"George has moved out," he said. "Maybe I could help."

"Oh, it's you, Bogie," came the silky tones of that seductive voice that in his view was meant to be heard only in the bedroom, and in no other part of the house. She giggled. "Our wet kiss still lingers on my lips."

Perhaps it was Cleopatra reincarnate, he thought, maybe Helen of Troy come back to haunt the world. Because all his kisses were wet, this mysterious woman could be any number of vamps he'd seduced. Maybe Jean Harlow. But the voice was too cultivated to be the platinum blonde's.

"Don't you know me?" that voice asked. "It's Billie. Billie Dove."

How could he fail to recognize the voice of the girl of his dreams? During those rare occasions when he was horny and forced to jack off, Billie Dove haunted his reveries. Almost more than Lilyan Tashman herself, he wanted Billie Dove and would have gone after her if Howard Hughes hadn't branded her like a Texas steer.

"May I come over?" she asked demurely.

"You can indeed," he said, his excitement mounting. In an updated equivalent, that would be like a lonely Brooklyn truck driver getting a call from Marilyn Monroe in the middle of the night inviting herself over.

As if sensing what he was thinking, she said. "It's not that. When George and I were sharing your bedroom, I lost a diamond and ruby earring, a gift from Howard. He's asking about it and wanting to see me wearing both earrings, not just one. Right now he's claiming I've hawked it and spent the money. Have you found it?"

"I don't want to brag," Bogie said, "but I haven't really made use of my bed lately. Could you hold the phone while I go and look for it?"

"You'd be a real doll if you would."

In his bedroom he tore off all the covers and shook them. His bed hadn't been made in days, as he'd had no time to wash the sheets. No earring appeared. He looked under the bed but saw nothing. He even lifted up the mattress and looked under it. Nothing.

He was about to go to the phone to tell her that he couldn't find the earring until he decided to search the room more thoroughly. He lifted the pillow from a battered old armchair beside his bed, finding nothing there.

Going to his bathroom, he searched it thoroughly for the missing gem. Suddenly he noticed the earring lying on the linoleum floor near the shower. The linoleum pattern was of cabbage roses so he hadn't seen the earring at first because it was camouflaged against the flamboyant pattern. Picking it up, it looked as if it was worth a lot of money.

Heading back to the phone, he told Dove that he'd found the earring.

"Thank God," she said. "Can I drive over right now and pick it up? I've just got to get it back. Howard's crazy. He's got all the money in the world, and he's declaring World War II over a stupid earring."

Within forty-five minutes, Dove arrived at his apartment, looking more stunningly beautiful than when he'd first met her. That had given him just enough time to shower, shave, and put on a fresh suit of clothing after his workout with Helen.

Even though it was late, he offered her a drink, which she gratefully accepted. He felt so much more at ease with her than when he'd first met her with Raft in the apartment. She was a delightful woman filled with a sense of satire and comedy. The stories she told made her vision of Hollywood sound like an episode in one of the old Mack Sennett Keystone Kops flicks.

"One day when I was in the bedroom with Howard, Ella showed up at the doorstep," Dove said.

Hughes was married at the time to Ella Rice.

"A servant came to warn us," Dove went on. "I had only minutes to make my escape. I ran out the back door stark naked, just as Ella was coming in through the front door being escorted by Noah Dietrich, Howard's assistant. To Howard's regret I'd left my mauve pelisse with a matching feather boa I'd arrived with. Howard later told me that Ella saw my clothing at once. Ella was in the house for only three minutes. She headed back to the train station and Houston where she filed for divorce. She's getting a quarter million dollars, all because of a God damn feather boa."

"That's a lot of money, more money than I ever expected to see in my whole life," he said.

"Not to Howard. It's a lot of money, for sure, but a fire sale price when you've got an estate worth $30 million."

After another drink, she asked to use his bathroom. After she disappeared inside, he was shaking all over. Sexually mesmerized by Dove, he longed to have her at any cost. After all, she'd been consistently voted "most beautiful woman in the world" in poll after poll.

The way she kept gently touching his hand or his arm as she talked to him on the sofa indicated to him that she felt sexual desire for him. He decided to make it easier for her.

When she came out of that bathroom, after prettying herself up, he was going to be ready and waiting for her.

In the bedroom, he slipped off his clothing. Standing stark nude, he concealed himself behind the closet door. When she came out of the bathroom, he planned to jump her. Once, during pillow talk, Glenda Farrell had told him that all women have fantasies of being taken by force and raped. "We pretend we don't, but we dream about such things when we're masturbating," Farrell had said to him.

He didn't think he'd have to use much force on Dove, but just in case, he was prepared to. And if she resisted at all, he thought, she wouldn't really mean it.

296

After all, she was a married woman, frequently sleeping with the likes of Raft and Howard Hughes.

Besides, he figured, he'd done her a big favor by finding that diamond earring and not pawning or selling it. From the size of it, a jeweler could take out the stones and recast them in engagement rings or wedding bands. By relinquishing the earring, he felt that he was giving Dove a lot of money. The way he saw it, she owed him something. He'd never wanted any woman more in his life, not even Lilyan Tashman.

He knew the moment was near when she opened the door to the bathroom. He heard a distinct sound of her unlocking it. Why had she locked the door? Did she think that he was going to break in on her?

He'd turned off the light in the bedroom. The only light coming in was from a single bulb over the bathroom mirror.

He was waiting for her, having worked himself up to a full erection. As she stepped deeper into the room, he jumped out from the closet.

"Surprise!"

Her scream was blood curdling.

He immediately realized what a mistake he'd made. As he'd tell Kenneth the next day, "I was probably the dumbest fool in Hollywood. It reminded me of something I did back when I was a kid and pulled off all my clothes in front of this girl I was interested in. I was an asshole."

Until she knew who had accosted her, Dove treated him like an assailant, flailing at his chest and pushing him back. He fell down on the floor, quickly losing his erection.

"Are you crazy?" she shouted at him.

"I'm sorry," he said, struggling to get to his feet. "I was playing a joke."

"Some joke!" Dove shouted at him. "You're the fucking joke."

At first, not knowing what was happening, the flashbulb of a camera went off in his face, blinding him. Dove screamed and fled from the room.

Soundlessly, it seemed that two men had entered the apartment. He hadn't heard anyone breaking in. It was as if the janitor had let them in or else they had a passkey.

These burly men restrained him. At first Bogie thought that some of Owney Madden's enemies had sent two gangsters for Raft. "I'm Bogart," he yelled at the men. "Not Raft."

From his living room, he heard noises, the sound of Dove's hysterical voice and in response, the voice of a soft-spoken man.

"Get your clothes on," one of the burly men said to Bogart. "We're going for a ride."

Having lived in New York during the Jazz Age, Bogie didn't have to be George Raft to know what "going for a ride" meant.

"Nothing happened," he yelled at the men. "I was playing a joke. Yeah, a joke."

"We're not your judge," the heretofore silent man spoke. "Put your fucking clothes on."

He heard more shouting, all coming from Dove. The mysterious man in the living room spoke in a subdued voice and was seemingly trying to be reasonable in the face of her hysteria.

He heard Dove shout, "Fuck you, you impotent bastard. You God damn faggot." The door slammed, and she was gone.

He got into his clothes as best he could. When he went for his shoes, one of the men grabbed him. "You won't be needing those."

The two men brought him into the living room where in the far and distant corner he spotted a strange and intense-looking man sitting in an armchair. The sole illumination in the room came from a dim-watted bulb on a lamp at the far corner of the room.

He couldn't immediately recognize the man's face. As Bogie was brought closer to him, he realized that the man was very tall. Compared to Bogie, a giant.

When the man raised his head, his face partially concealed under a hat, Bogie recognized him.

It was Howard Hughes.

Chapter Ten

Trapped in the back seat of a two-seater aircraft, Bogie was flying high with Howard Hughes as his co-pilot. So far, the tycoon hadn't said one word to him. Bogie had been driven to a small airfield—he didn't know where—and Hughes' two gangster-like bodyguards had strapped him in the back seat of the plane.

He'd never flown before, and he was terrified. Bogie was at the complete mercy of this madman, and Hughes seemed crazed. At first he'd thought the tall Texan was going to kill him, or at least have his boys beat him up because he'd been caught nude with Billie Dove.

It was a beautiful night that was giving way to dawn. Hughes was handling the craft expertly, and they seemed to be gliding along smoothly as if he and Bogie were on an uneventful joy ride. It didn't make sense.

Bogie felt that if Hughes planned to kill him, he wouldn't have taken him on this plane ride. That is, unless he was on a suicide mission. Since Hughes had all the money in the world, the pick of any beautiful woman (or man) he wanted, why would he want to kill himself? There was talk about how he wanted to become the most feared power broker in Hollywood. And partly because of that, Bogie couldn't understand why Hughes would sacrifice everything just to punish him for putting the make on what was only one of many girl friends ranging from Harlow to Carole Lombard.

Bogie breathed deeply, tried to keep from trembling, and settled in for the ride.

On that pinkish pre-dawn morning, he learned something about himself, as he'd later relate to Kenneth. He was completely in the power of this strange, eccentric man. He couldn't struggle or fight to save himself, so he decided to relax and let the inevitable happen. He figured that if he'd been one of the men left on the rapidly sinking Titanic, he would have gone to the bar and would have poured himself a drink. As the raging waters of the North Atlantic rose to plunge him into the murky depths of an unexplored ocean, he'd be prepared to go down, drunk or not.

Suddenly, the smooth part of the ride was over. In a flash, Bogie instinctively knew what Hughes was up to. With Bogie strapped and immobilized in the rear passenger seat, Hughes virtually had the pre-dawn sky to himself.

For Bogie's benefit and to make him shit his pants in fear, Hughes was performing the daredevil aerial feats he'd directed and filmed in *Hell's Angels*. When he saw the film, Bogie had been told that some of these aerial gymnastics had never been tried before. Bogie hoped that there were no other airplanes in the area.

He closed his eyes, anticipating his own death. At least he'd read that Hughes had been granted a pilot's license. But did he know what he was doing?

Like a demon possessed, Hughes flew the aircraft recklessly, as if recreating some of the ersatz dogfights that had been filmed in *Hell's Angels*. Hughes was propelling the plane like an air show stuntman. They seemed to be in a somersault.

Bogie opened his eyes again and looked down. To his terror, Hughes seemed to be going into a tailspin. The plane, like a dangerous missile, hurtled toward the earth. When the rooftops of some buildings came into view, Bogie knew that they were going to crash into them.

They seemed to be in a freefall. Slamming into the ground, followed by a dramatic explosion between plane and unsuspecting building, seemed a foregone conclusion. Bogie was crying, and mucus poured from his nose. He dug his fingernails into the palms of his hand. He was not a religious man, but he prayed with all his heart, and meant it.

As pilot Hughes got closer to earth, Bogie was screaming. "Don't, you God damn fool. I don't want to die!"

At the last possible moment Hughes brought the plane up from its freefall, sailing smoothly over the peaks of buildings that could have become their joint burial ground. He headed into the clear sky once again.

After that bit of insanity and aerial daring, Bogie knew that there was no reason for Hughes to perform any more stunts. A freefall like that was a tough act to follow.

When he knew he was going to live, Bogie quit screaming but he kept sobbing out of gratitude for having his life saved. His heart was still pounding furiously. He could only hope that Hughes' decision to spare his life was not just a temporary reprieve.

That death-defying moment had taught Bogie one thing: In the face of death, suicide-induced or not, Hughes was like a rock. Bogie himself felt that he was a coward, screaming out his panic like Billie Dove herself might have done when facing a similar peril.

The plane landed smoothly on the field from which they'd been so recently airborne.

Those same burly men who'd abducted Bogie and had driven him to this airfield unstrapped him from the plane.

Earth had never felt so good to his bare feet before. He looked back at the plane that could have been his deathtrap.

A long time later he learned that he'd been flying in one of the Sikorskys that Hughes had purchased and transformed into a reasonable facsimile of a German Gotha bomber seen in the footage of his recently released *Hell's Angels*.

"Hughes wants to see you in his office over there," one of the men said, pointing toward a battered old hangar, into which the death-defying pilot had just retreated.

"Gentlemen," Bogie said, "is there a toilet nearby? I've got to make some emergency repairs."

The men let him use a foul-smelling toilet in the hangar. Bogie had messed his pants. When he'd been hustled out of his apartment, he'd worn only his trousers and hadn't put on underwear. In the toilet, he washed his pants clean in cold water and put them back on wet.

As he came out of the crapper, one of the men directed him to Hughes' office. In a Stetson hat, Hughes sat behind his desk looking over some papers.

"That was a hell of a ride," Bogie said. "You sure know how to show a guy a good time early in the morning."

"I hoped that little stunt was just enough to put the fear of God in you," Hughes said, looking at him intently for the first time. "If not God, then Howard Hughes. Listen, Bogart, and listen good. I intend to marry Billie Dove. If you make any attempt to fuck her again, you'll be a footnote in Hollywood history. Definitely a soprano."

"It was all a mistake," he stammered.

"Why were you in your bedroom naked with Billie?" Hughes demanded to know.

"It was a stupid practical joke," he said. "A college prank. You know. You must have pulled a few of those in your day.

"I can't say that I have," he said. "I've got a picture of you. A candid shot with your dick hanging out."

"Yeah, about that…"

Hughes cut him off. "I'm gonna have that picture developed and maybe five-thousand prints made of it. If you fuck with me at any time in the future, copies of that photograph with your dick hanging out are going to be mailed to every influential person in Hollywood. We're talking Mayer, Thalberg, Laemmle, the works."

"No need to do that," Bogie said. "I'll be a good boy. I really mean that."

"Of course, you will." Hughes continued to study him intently. "As long as I have that picture, I can make you jump rope."

"Maybe I'm a little shaky from that plane ride, but I don't get it," Bogie said.

"Once or twice a week, I need some smooth errand boy to do a job for me," Hughes said.

"What kind of job?" Bogie asked with growing apprehension.

"No killing or stuff like that," Hughes said. "When I need to have someone's joints realigned, I've got plenty of men to do that. Like those two guys who brought you to the plane. They're good at their work. No, I'm talking something else. Some of my errands call for one of you fast-talking New York actors. A guy who can wear a tux, look presentable, and perform certain tasks for me."

"I still don't get it," Bogie said.

"Why should you?" Hughes asked. "There's nothing you need to know now. When I want you to perform a task for me, I'll get in touch with you and tell you exactly what it is I want done."

"I guess I won't learn about what you've got in mind until the time comes,"

Bogie said.

"You sound like a smart man. A wimp, but smart."

"Can I go now?" Bogie said. "I've got to report to the studio for a new picture I'm doing. It's with George O'Brien."

"I've seen his films," Hughes said. "Mr. Body Beautiful. I hear he swings both ways in the ballpark."

"I haven't personally sampled the merchandise, but I can virtually assure you that's true."

"Good to know that," Hughes said. "That bit of information might come in handy some day."

Bogie saw him scribble a note in a little book he kept in his breast pocket.

"I'm going to be late for work," Bogie said. "Can I go now?"

"Sure you can," Hughes said, "because I'm through with you, at least for the moment, and I don't want to see your ugly face again until I need you. I'll have someone else contact you." Before Bogie could leave the office, Hughes called him back. "And I want to thank you for services rendered this morning."

Bogie was puzzled. "I might owe you thanks for not killing me in a plane crash, but I hardly know what you've got to thank me for."

"Before you rush off, I've got something to tell you," Hughes said. "That ride this morning wasn't just about scaring the shit out of you. To judge from the look of your pants, I think I succeeded in that. For weeks I've been planning to put myself through a test but didn't have the courage. When I saw you as my helpless victim this morning, I decided not only to test myself, but to kill two birds with one stone. Somehow having you up there with me gave me more courage than if I'd been alone. It was also the best way I knew of warning you never to move in on my turf with Billie."

Hughes made him so nervous that he kept eyeing a package of cigarettes on the man's desk, needing one real bad. His host finally got the point and offered him one.

"When I shot *Hell's Angels*, I strapped myself into a Thomas Morse scout plane and took off into the wild blue yonder with the rest of my flying fools. I wanted to join up with the daredevil stunt pilots I'd hired for the most dangerous film footage a director has ever attempted. Up in the air I suddenly went into a spiraling tailspin. I was plunging to earth so fast I knew I was a goner."

"What did you do?" Bogie asked. "You obviously got the plane pointed upward again or you wouldn't be here this morning."

"Not at all," Hughes said. "I crashed right into this fucking macadam runway. My propeller dug in like it'd found a permanent home. My landing gear splintered. Both wings were ripped from the fuselage."

"I think I remember reading something about that in the papers," Bogie said.

"Papers lie," Hughes said. "They never print the truth. You should give up reading them. As it was reported in Los Angeles, I walked away unscathed from the wreckage. I think the exact line was, I was 'waving a lucky Stetson hat and

302

wiping off some soot and grime.'"

Hughes didn't say anything for a minute, as Bogie nervously smoked, waiting for the next revelation.

"I didn't walk away," Hughes said. "I was trapped in the Thomas Morse. Some members of my ground crew rushed to my aid. They freed me from my trap in the cockpit and yanked me out. There was no Stetson like the one I'm wearing now. When I got to Inglewood Hospital, where I'd been rushed in an ambulance, they found I had crushed my cheekbone. Not to mention all the other wounds my body had sustained. I had to have plastic surgery on my face." He held his face up to the light. "See. No more cleft in my chin."

Still barefoot, Bogie was driven away from the abandoned airfield, which still contained remnants of the planes that had been reconfigured and painted to resemble those of the British Royal Flying Corps from the set of *Hell's Angels*.

He was in the back seat of a large dark car, the make of which was unknown to him. He still didn't know where he was.

When they were about three miles from the airbase, the bodyguard in the front passenger seat turned to him. "Hughes still thinks you need to be taught a lesson. Get out."

"I've got no shoes on," Bogie said. "My wallet's back in my apartment. I don't even know where I am. You guys are gonna make me get out here with no shoes and no money?"

"I heard you New York boys were smart cookies," the man said. "You've got our message. Now get out!"

The driver said, "Count yourself lucky you got out of this thing alive. Don't fuck with Howard Hughes. Never again."

Seeing logic in that, Bogie got out of the car and stood forlornly along the dirt road looking at the strange car which left him in the dust. He didn't know which direction to head in, and saw no buildings or lights coming from anywhere.

Dawn had come. He'd try to find help where he could. Maybe a motorist would come along, although he didn't know who'd want to pick up an unshaven, barefoot man wandering around in wet, sloppy pants.

He looked back at Mines Field where Hughes' plane had landed, having no intention of heading in that direction.

In the decades to come, whenever he'd be a passenger on a commercial liner landing in Los Angeles, the memory of that long-ago night would come back to haunt him.

In time Mines Field itself would become the vastly expanded and renamed Los Angeles International Airport.

***

Bogie didn't reach the set of *A Holy Terror* until eleven o'clock that morning. After being abandoned along the road, he'd walked barefoot for a mile until he saw a little house near an orange grove. He'd stumbled toward it, where he'd startled an old farmer and his wife who were cooking up a batch of orange marmalade.

Unlike his reception with Hughes, they were kind hosts, albeit at first suspicious. When he'd related a story about how he'd been robbed and his car stolen, they had taken him in. The farmer's wife had even prepared a plate of bacon and eggs for him.

After his late breakfast, the farmer had driven him to the studio where he'd rushed to the set. Greg Brooks from wardrobe had secured a suit and some ill-fitting shoes for him. Checking his appearance in the mirror, he looked no worse for wear after a harrowing night from hell. Except for Kenneth and maybe Spencer Tracy, he didn't plan to tell anyone about his most recent ordeal.

He dreaded when Hughes would call him for future favors and hoped that the Texan was making only an idle threat. To him, Hughes was insane. Bogie wondered what that made him? Would any sane man have done what he did with Billie Dove? That bedroom farce had to rank among the most stupid pranks of his life.

Sucked up in the tangled affairs of his roller-coaster private life, Bogie had paid little attention to the script of *A Holy Terror*. But when Brooks called him for a wardrobe fitting, he began to take his role of Steve Nash more seriously. In full cowboy garb, he was to play the foreman of a ranch opposite that handsome, body beautiful stud, George O'Brien. He didn't know if O'Brien was still carrying on with his friend Kenneth or not. He suspected not.

Brooks had fitted Bogie with a beige-colored Stetson, a six-shooter, a gigantic red handkerchief, which he was to wear around his neck like a tie, a pair of black-and-white striped pants (for some reason), a black shirt, and a battered old leather jacket. Even Bogie laughed at himself when he saw his image in a full-length mirror.

After carefully studying his figure, Brooks said, "something's not right. You're just too short to be a cowboy."

"What do you suggest?" Bogie asked. "You got something to make me grow taller?"

Brooks thought for a minute before sending his wardrobe assistant to fetch a pair of shoes for Bogie. When he returned, Brooks insisted that Bogie put on a pair of elevator boots. "That way you can stand up with O'Brien eyeball to eyeball in your scenes together."

Horrified, Bogie put on the elevator shoes and walked around the dressing room. "I'm walking on God damn stilts. I feel like a fucking dummy."

"You're getting paid $750 a week, aren't you?" Brooks asked. "That's a lot more than a lot of actors at Fox are taking home every week. Why don't you just wear the shoes and quit griping?"

"Griping is what I do," Bogie said. "It's my specialty."

Flashing his antagonism, Brooks looked at him and sighed. "Then get another specialty. I've also got to dress Sally Eilers today. I've already dressed George O'Brien."

"That must have been a delight for you," Bogie said, unable to resist the impulse to be nasty.

"As a matter of fact, it was," Brooks said. "He's a real man with an incredible physique." He kept staring at Bogie's shoulders. "Unlike you, George doesn't need padding anywhere, and I mean anywhere."

"What does that mean," Bogie asked, growing increasingly irritated with the wardrobe designer. "Are you saying my dick's too small for you? How in the fuck do you know? How in the fuck will you ever know?"

"Take off your shirt," Brooks demanded.

"What?" Bogie asked, astonished. "Am I supposed to strip down for you? I've dealt with you little fairy boys from wardrobe before. With me, sweet cakes, you can dream but not touch."

"Don't flatter yourself, Bogart," Brooks snapped. "You're not my type at all. I go for he-men. Now take off your shirt. We've got a real problem here."

Increasingly infuriated, Bogie still wanted to earn that paycheck. He pulled off his shirt. Brooks went over to a drawer and pulled out two strips of white padding. "For some of our insufficiently endowed actors, we fake it. Since you don't have shoulders, I'll create some for you."

As reluctant as he was to do it, Bogie allowed Brooks to apply tape and padding to his shoulders. When Bogie put his shirt back on and stared at his image in the mirror, he was impressed. Unlike the elevator shoes, which he detested, the padding did make him look more like a fully developed man who could be the tough foreman of a ranch.

The person Bogie most dreaded encountering on the set was Sally Eilers. He still suffered from some embarrassment over that encounter he'd had with her and Hoot Gibson. He felt embarrassed at having Eilers see him impersonating a cowboy. After all, a few people in America still called her husband, Hoot Gibson, "the king of the cowboys," even though his career was waning. In an almost predictable scenario, Sally Eilers was the first person he saw on the set. She made no mention of their seduction or his refusal to repeat the process. Although he'd fucked her and she'd tongued him everywhere, she was a bit aloof and chilly.

"I'm sure he's already told you," Eilers said in a low voice. "But when I'm not hooting with Hoot, I'm seeing your friend, Mr. Spencer Tracy. He's a wild one."

That liaison had escaped Bogie. When Tracy was with him, he spent more time talking about the men he was seeing instead of the women he was seducing. "He failed to fill me in on that one."

"In the case of Spence, he's got so many women he probably loses track," Eilers said.

"That's our boy Spence," he said. "Somehow I just can't picture you, Hoot Gibson, and Spencer Tracy as part of the same act."

"We're not," she said. "I'm hot for Spence. But he's definitely not Hoot's type." She looked him over carefully. "Come to think of it, you're not Hoot's type either. But we all make exceptions to our types from time to time."

He moved closer to her. "If Hoot didn't come as part of the package, you're my type. Before this film ends, I'd like to take you on, but without your husband watching."

"Perhaps," she said. "I can't promise anything. I've got my eye on that George O'Brien. He's gorgeous. Who wouldn't want that hunk?"

"He does nothing for me," Bogie said.

"That's because you're not a fairy," she said. "George is God's gift to women and to men. I heard he put on quite a show for the little prancing boys in wardrobe this morning."

"If you've got it, flaunt it, I always say."

"Gotta go," she said, brushing his cheek lightly with a kiss before stepping back to look at him. "I think our time together in bed will be our last. Hollywood is filling up every day with more and more hunks. If I'm gonna make the rounds of most of them, I can't do a lot of repeat performances. A lot of guys I meet aren't as reluctant as you were to include Hoot."

"Sorry, but that's how I feel."

"Hoot's doing a solo act tonight, and without his Sally," Eilers said before rushing off. "Some young cowboy singer has hit town, and he thinks Hoot can help him break into pictures. As for me, I've got a date with Spence. That's one man who knows how to handle a woman. When I starred with him in *Quick Millions*, it was all that faggot, Rowland Brown, could do to get us to come out of Spence's dressing room. Guess what? I hear me and Spence are gonna make another movie together. It's called *Disorderly Conduct*. Isn't that a hoot? Get it, Hoot?"

"I got it," he said to her. She'd pissed him off. He watched her go and was glad to get rid of her. After his humiliation with Hughes, he needed some loving tonight.

He called Helen that afternoon, and she asked him to take her to the dinner at Lilowe as the guest of Edmund Lowe and Lilyan Tashman. He felt awkward about escorting Helen there. Of all the women in the world, he felt the most passionate about Tashman. The idea of sharing his beautiful doll with his ex-wife didn't excite him. He hadn't been in Hollywood long enough to become that sophisticated.

On the set O'Brien came up to Bogie and invited him for a drink. At first Bogie thought they might speak of Kenneth and their previous encounter. But O'Brien made no mention of it, so Bogie kept his mouth shut.

In his dressing room, O'Brien poured him a whiskey before filling a glass most generously for himself. "Love your shoes," he said.

"The less said about them the better. Couldn't they photograph me standing on a rock or on a staircase looking down at you?"

O'Brien pulled off his shirt. As Bogie was to learn during the shoot of *A Holy Terror*, O'Brien took every opportunity to pull off his shirt. Bogie couldn't help but admire his muscles, which reminded him of his own padded shoulders. Brooks was right. O'Brien didn't need any padding.

O'Brien was quick to detect Bogie's interest in his physique. Very bluntly he asked, "Are you a homosexual, like my best buddy, Spence?"

"Like hell!" Bogie said defensively. "I've got a lot of credentials to prove otherwise. I can summon witnesses if necessary."

"Don't get so rattled," O'Brien cautioned him. "I mean, I know you're a good buddy of Kenneth's. I just assumed."

"Time to reassume."

"Okay, okay," O'Brien said. "I wanted to know who I have to fuck on this picture. I know that Eilers is after me. I've already done Brooks in wardrobe. The director's not a fairy, or at least I don't think so. Who knows? The picture's not over yet."

"Rest assured you can keep your pants on around me."

"It's good to clear the air in the very beginning," O'Brien said. "When it comes to sex I don't like to beat around the bush. I come right out with it." He laughed at his own remark." That sounds sexually suggestive, doesn't it?"

"I'm beginning to think everything in Hollywood sounds sexually suggestive," Bogie said.

He remained long enough to finish his whiskey, but his presence in O'Brien's dressing room seemed so completely unnecessary that he quickly excused himself and left.

"Mama didn't raise no cowboy," he said to himself as he headed to his dressing room to change out of his uncomfortable Western gear.

***

Helen was still dressing when he arrived to pick her up at the Garden of Allah. He took her in his arms and kissed her with more than the usual passion. "I made a big mistake," he whispered in her ear. "We should have stayed together. I should never have married Mary."

"It was my fault," she said. "All my fault that we broke up."

His need for her—his need for any woman, but especially for her—was greater than it had been even when they'd had their reunion in Los Angeles.

Sensing that need, she said in a soft voice, "Dear, dear Lil will have to wait." She led him to her bed. "Don't worry about that one. She'll probably have Harlow's panties off before drinks are served."

It was only after some hot, passionate sex, and on the drive to Lilowe, that he picked up on the mention of Harlow. "Is the platinum goddess coming to this dinner?"

"According to Lilyan," Helen said. "It's going to be an intimate dinner for six. You, me, Eddie, Lilyan. Harlow is bringing her date for the evening. Paul Bern. I heard he's a ghoul. I don't know what Harlow sees in him."

Known only to himself, Bogie realized that he'd been the bed partner of all three of the women at the dinner. He'd even had some sexual link with Lowe himself, although he'd rather not think about that, finding the few experiences he'd had on that level distasteful. He'd be the male whore of the party, known intimately to everyone there except Paul Bern.

Bogie felt a foreboding about the evening. Tashman was a walking time bomb. In spite of his immense attraction to her, she was a blunt, vulgar woman, and might say anything to embarrass anyone. All the beautiful gowns in Paris and all the expensive jewelry she wore didn't compensate for her foul mouth. She liked to fuck and tell. To anyone interested, she blabbed about the most intimate details of her relationship with Garbo. Bogie feared that she'd get Helen in a corner and tell all about his sexual adventures with her. He prayed that even Tashman wouldn't reveal that in his drunken state, he'd let Lowe go down on him.

Even though they had arrived late, Helen and he still got to the dinner party before Bern and Harlow. In the most stunning gown he'd ever seen her wear—an haute couture number in champagne colors—Tashman rushed up to him and kissed him passionately on the lips. Standing nearby, Helen took it all in. Even though they were divorced, he was embarrassed that Helen had witnessed another woman's affection for him.

While Tashman kissed Helen with the same ardor she'd shown for Bogie, Lowe came over and tried to kiss him on the lips too. Moving his head slightly, Bogie redirected the kiss to his left cheek instead. Far more than the kiss, he wanted a drink. The household maid was only too willing to oblige.

That same maid came in three times within the next hour to ask when she could serve dinner. Lowe kept glancing at the clock. At one point Tashman went and called Harlow's house to learn that Paul Bern had just left with the white blonde. Harlow's mother told Tashman that Bern and her daughter would be there soon.

By the time they arrived, about thirty minutes later, Bogie was deliciously smashed. He didn't have that much to say to Lowe, so the two men let Helen and Tashman fill each other in on all their mutual acquaintances. Helen was a regular Walter Winchell reporting from the East, and Tashman was a Louella Parsons brimming with the latest Hollywood gossip.

At one point, and to top all their stories, he wanted to tell them about his tailspin with Howard Hughes. What he didn't want to reveal were the circumstances leading up to it, so he kept his mouth shut.

As the maid showed her in, Harlow, followed by Paul Bern, made a spectacular entrance in a white satin gown that was so sheer that it was almost see-through. With her breasts prominently on display, Bogie couldn't help but be intrigued by her prominent nipples, which he'd devoured when they'd been guests of Rowland

308

Brown in Palm Springs. He wondered if she'd put ice on her nipples before getting dressed.

Standing before him was Hollywood's premier sex symbol. She kissed him on the mouth but said nothing to call attention to the fact that they had known each other intimately. A twinkle in her mischievous eyes and a brief running of her delicate fingers across his cheek seemed to acknowledge privately that they'd been intimate with each other.

The only other acknowledgment of their intimacy came in one brief moment when they stood alone on Tashman's terrace overlooking her beautiful gardens, scented with magnolias and jasmine. "I hear you've gone on to bigger things," he said. "Raft and I are now history. Enter Clark Gable."

"Don't underrate yourself and don't underrate George," she said, again taking her porcelain hand and delicately caressing his cheek. "With Gable I've gone on to other things. Certainly not bigger, darling."

Before she could say more, Tashman, her arm linked in an intimate embrace with Helen, came out onto the patio, trailed by Lowe and Bern who seemed engaged in an argument over studio politics, specifically Irving Thalberg.

Harlow diverted herself from Bogie immediately and focused her considerable charm and attention on Helen. "I'm delighted to meet Bogie's wife, finally," she said.

"Former wife," Helen corrected her. "We're divorced. He's married to Mary Philips, the Broadway actress."

"Fuck!" Harlow said. "How embarrassing. I should read Winchell more often to keep up with all the Broadway gossip."

Helen smiled affectionately at Bogie, no doubt remembering their recent love session at the Garden of Allah. "I should never have let this man get away. We were just too young and too self-centered at the time."

"I think it's fabulous that a divorced man and wife can still be friendly," Tashman said, but it quickly became obvious that she wasn't quite ready to leave her comment at that. "And even fuck each other's brains out from time to time."

"I think that's fabulous too," Harlow said. "Before I die, I plan to marry five husbands. All my divorces will be friendly, and I'll allow all my former husbands conjugal rights."

"This is the Thirties," Bogie said. "All of us should be modern about this."

Harlow reached out for Helen's hand. "I hear you're the greatest actress on Broadway. As for me, I'd rather forget that matron, Ethel Barrymore, and that little midget mouse, Helen Hayes, or that dyke Katharine Cornell. You are the true Queen of Broadway, or so I hear. Forgive me, but I've never seen one of your plays."

"Perhaps, my dear, you'll have a chance," Helen said. "I can't discuss the details but I fully expect to be seen in a production out here."

"It's about lesbians," Tashman blurted out.

Harlow looked as if she hadn't heard right. "If you want to know anything about lesbians, ask me," Harlow said. Then, with a certain cruel jab, she looked over toward Tashman. "Or you can ask Lil here. I've had every lesbian in Hollywood chasing after me. Kay Francis fell for me in a big way. Dietrich is practically stalking me. And would you believe this? The other day I got a hand-delivered note at the studio. It was from Greta Garbo. She wants me to come over for a private dinner."

Before Harlow could make more revelations, that constantly appearing maid came out onto the terrace and announced that dinner was served. Bogie overheard her telling Tashman, "Miss Lilyan, I've had to keep it in the oven so long I fear everything is dried out."

"Don't worry about it, darling," Tashman told the maid. "This crowd is so drunk they'll never know the difference."

Apparently wanting to rearrange her guests and change partners, Tashman reached for Bern's hand to escort him into her dining room. Lowe courteously took Helen's arm. That left Bogie to escort Harlow.

Lagging a few steps behind the other guests, Harlow whispered to him, "You weren't bad in Palm Springs. I wouldn't mind a repeat."

"I don't think there is anything on God's green earth I'd like better," he said to her in a soft voice. "I'll call you."

"You still like blondes, don't you?"

"I adore them," he said looking at her hair. "The blonder the better, especially when they are blonde all over."

"You're in luck then," she said. "After my latest dye job, I'm blonder down there than ever before. Platinum all the way."

***

As the soggy night of drinking at Lilowe wore on, Bogie was able to spend some after-dinner time alone with Harlow when she asked him to escort her through the sweet-smelling gardens which were lit by pink spots.

"I tried to get in touch with you after our time together in Palm Springs," he said. "I left several messages. You never returned my calls."

"I meant to," she said, "and I really like you. But a lot of other men came between us. Most men I fuck and forget. But you and Raft intrigue me. Can I tell you a sexual fantasy I've had about you guys?"

"Spill it," he said. "We might make it happen."

"I'd like a three-way with you guys," she said, "taking it both vaginally and orally. Later, I'd like you guys to change positions. The one who's fucked me in the mouth gets his chance at the platinum honeypot."

"I think George will agree to that," he said. "We know each other rather intimately. For another chance at Jean Harlow, I'll agree to almost anything."

"Is that so?" she said, kissing him on the nose and giggling. "Like letting Howard Hughes fuck you in the ass while you fuck me."

310

"Even for another chance at you, I don't think I could go that far," he said. "The three-way with Raft is more my speed."

"I'll be in touch," she said. "Even though I'm carrying on, I'm still considering marrying Paul Bern."

"He's not the type for you," he said. "Looks a little prissy to me. A wimp, really."

"Don't go putting him down," she said. "You can't always judge a man by his appearance. Paul and I have not hit the sack yet. He wants to save that until we're married. In the meantime, I'm getting it where I find it."

"You mean, Clark Gable?"

"For openers, yes," she said. "But that didn't work out. It was a real disappointment."

"I can't say I'm sorry to hear that," he said. "I rarely admit the truth about these things, but I'm just a little bit jealous of Gable. That stud seems to have it all. Certainly all the women."

"That's his tragedy," she said. "He doesn't have it all. Yet he's got this big he-man image to live up to. Every woman who goes to bed with him expects fireworks, like on the Fourth of July. Instead of Fourth of July, Clark is more like a rainy Armistice Day."

"I wish you'd be more specific," he said. "Before I talk with my friend, Joan Blondell, I want the inside scoop on Gable."

"To put it bluntly, he's a lousy lay," she said. "For such a big man, he's got less than average equipment. There are other problems as well."

He smiled. "That gives me one up on him." He pulled her close and kissed her. "If I recall Palm Springs, I didn't hear any complaints from you about me."

"I've had bigger," she said, "so don't flatter yourself. But you're okay. More than okay really. You've got more than most men do. I don't know any woman in Hollywood who would kick you out of her bed."

"I guess I should be flattered," he said. "Except I'll keep wondering who is bigger."

"William Powell, for openers."

"I would never have guessed that," he said. "If you stood Clark Gable beside William Powell, I would have voted that Gable had the bigger dick."

"Gable has the bigger body," she said. "I'm learning that men's physical size doesn't determine their dick size. I've known some great male physiques who just didn't have it down there where it counts. On the other hand, I've also known some small men who carry a big stick. Chaplin's not a big man at all. But when he takes off those baggy pants of his, he's hung like a horse. I got to see enough of 'Charlie-horse' when I worked as an unbilled extra on his film, *City of Lights*."

"You don't have to convince me," he said. "I saw the Little Tramp in all his horny glory the night he invited Louise Brooks, her girl friend, Peggy Fears, and me back to his suite in New York after they'd seen the play I was in."

"I've crossed Charlie off my list," she said. "Actually he dumped me after three times. Maybe he doesn't like blondes."

"What list are you keeping?" he asked.

"I'm drawing up a list of all the men I'd like to seduce. Gary Cooper. Joel McCrea. Even John Gilbert."

"I hear Gilbert's a fag," he said. "At least that's the way he sounds on the screen."

"He may be," she said. "More than half the actors in Hollywood are. You can always tell a fag from a non-fag. Some of the so-called biggest womanizers in Hollywood are fags. Take Howard Hughes, for instance. But as long as they occasionally seduce women, and as long as they're not, like William Haines, exclusively into men, I keep them on my list."

"Have you put Douglas Fairbanks Jr. on your list?" he asked. "I don't know where Joan Crawford is at night, but Doug boy sure makes the rounds."

"He's definitely on my list," she said.

"He's another one who likes boys on the side," he said.

"There's nothing wrong with that," she said. "I guess I'm more liberated than most women. If I marry Paul and find out he likes boys on the side, I can live with that more comfortably than knowing he's out with another woman."

"I guess there's some logic to that," he said.

"Besides, if he's out with his boy, I'll have a night off to seduce one of those men on my rapidly growing list."

"Listen, you left me hanging with the Gable story," he said. "To all outward appearances, he looks like one lucky bastard who's got it all."

"Except he doesn't," she said. "It's sort of...medical, I guess."

"I'm the son of a doctor," he said. "You can tell me."

"I met Clark when he had a small part in this movie I was making," she said. "*The Secret Six.* Wallace Beery was the star of the flick, and he practically drooled when I walked onto the set. I wasn't interested in Gloria Swanson's rejects. John Mack Brown, or Johnny as he's calling himself now, was also in the picture. He's another one of those guys who goes both ways. He was after Clark too but I won out."

"Gable belongs in Homos of Hollywood?" he asked.

"He's not homosexual at all," she said. "He's a man for the ladies. But he fucked around with a few men, like William Haines, Ramon Novarro, and Rod La Rocque, when he was on the casting couch circuit. Sometimes he did it 'cause he needed the dough. Now that he's working steady, he doesn't have to prostitute himself as often."

"More than Paul Bern, I think Clark Gable would make the ideal husband for you," he said. "As soon as he's out of his marital entanglements, a wedding with the two of you as co-stars would be the biggest news in Hollywood."

"It'll never happen," she said. "Clark is uncircumcised, like a lot of guys. But he's got a problem with that. His foreskin's so tight it's very hard for him to draw it back over his glans."

312

"That's called phimosis," he said. "When I was a kid I had that problem myself. It can be corrected. Any doctor can do it. You don't even have to go to a rabbi."

"Since he doesn't pull it back very often, this real unpleasant odor comes from down there," she said.

"That's called smegma."

"Yeah," she said. "I learned that when he asked me to go down on him. I've smelled some rotten cheese in my day. Not only has he got that little problem, would you believe premature ejaculation?"

"Thank God you told me," he said jokingly. "Remind me to cross Gable off my list."

"I've urged Clark to consult a doctor," she said. "He refuses. He calls his dick 'my noble tool' and regards it as sacrosanct."

"Then I wish him well," he said. "But enough of Big Ears. What I want to know is how did you meet our darling Lilyan?"

"She and I did this film together, *New York Nights*," she said. "I was just an extra. Lilyan went for me in a big way, but I outran her. I ran so fast I caught up with another actor on the film, Mr. Gilbert Roland. He may be uncircumcised like Gable, but there the resemblance ends. He can go all night. He's also hung like Charlie Chaplin."

"That lucky Bette Davis," he said. "Roland took her virginity not too long ago."

"What men see in that Davis creature," she said, "I'll never know. Who would want to watch Bette Davis on the screen when they can see a Harlow flick?"

Before he could answer, Paul Bern appeared in the garden. "Jean, my love," he said coming up to her possessively and kissing her on the mouth. "Lilyan wants to show you and Helen some of her new acquisitions upstairs in her bedroom."

"See you later, Bogart," she said, smiling. Bern was rewarded with another kiss.

As Harlow headed out of the garden and into the house, Bern called to her. "Watch yourself around Lilyan. Hollywood has no greater seducer, man or woman, than that one."

***

Bogie sat in the garden with Paul Bern, each man growing more and more intoxicated. In the back of his brain, though realizing what a remote chance it was, Bogie held out the actor's hope that this powerful MGM executive, who had the ear of Louis B. Mayer and Irving Thalberg, might sign him to a contract at that much more powerful studio when and if he were ever bounced on his ass from Fox.

Through bleary eyes, Bogie carefully appraised his drinking companion as they sat in the garden. Bogie could still smell a whiff of some of Harlow's perfume, as if she'd left some of her presence behind her.

Balding and pot-bellied, with absolutely no handsome features to his face, Bern was the most unlikely candidate in Hollywood to be dating its preeminent sex symbol. Harlow was at the end of a long list of screen vamps he'd been involved with, including the "too beautiful" Barbara LaMarr before her drug-addicted death. He'd been intimate with Clara Bow, Lila Lee, Crawford, Garbo, and Norma Shearer. Bogie had heard that the executive's relationships with those women were platonic.

There was no talk of advancing Bogie's career. On that soggy night, Bern had a one-track obsession, the train running only toward Jean Harlow. "I'm trying to help Jean's career," he said. "But she doesn't always follow my advice. I tried to get her to play the amoral trapeze artist in that notorious film, *Freaks*. Her part called for her to wed a midget for his dough, then poison him. Retribution is then heaped on her by a motley crew of armless women, dwarves, hermaphrodites, and pinheads who, with her guilt-induced cooperation, magically transform her into a wicked hybrid: a half-beast, half-woman with a chicken's body and a human head."

"Sounds like a great part," Bogie said sarcastically. "I can't imagine why she'd turn down a role like that. Come to think of it, I can't imagine why she's still speaking to you." The idea of casting Harlow in *Freaks* made him doubt Bern's sanity. At first he'd thought that Bern might be teasing him, except that the film executive seemed incapable of humor.

"Bogart," Bern said, sitting up and growing even more serious. "Jean has told me about that time in Palm Springs. I know she went to bed with you and Raft." He reached out and placed his hand on Bogie's knee. "It's okay. I forgive you."

"That's good," Bogie said. "Because I think we're both too drunk to stage a duel in the morning."

"There will be no duels now or in the morning," Bern said. "I'm glad you boys went to bed with Jean. I've been thinking that I might have to ask each of you to continue to sleep with her in the future after we're married."

"Maybe Lilyan has spiked the whiskey with something," Bogie said, "but I'm not getting this. You plan to marry Harlow but it's okay if other guys sleep with her."

"What I am about to tell you is a great secret," Bern said. "If I tell you, you must swear to keep it confidential."

"My lips are sealed," Bogie said. "I've been accused of many things in my time, but no one ever said Bogart was a gossip." Even as he claimed that, he was amused at his own lie. He loved gossip and virtually told at least three men—Billy Brady Jr., Stuart Rose, and Kenneth MacKenna—every time he let go with a fart.

"I've never been to bed with Jean, and I don't plan to until we get married," Bern said. "By that time, I'm hoping that she'll love me so much and be so devoted to me that she'll be very understanding."

"You got some sort of sexual problem?" Bogie asked. "You wouldn't be the only guy in Hollywood that has one. I've already heard about Gable's."

"I know Clark very well, and I'm very familiar with his sexual inadequacies. Mine are different. You see, I'm impotent."

"You gotta see the humor in that," Bogie said. "Every man in America wants to be in your shoes. Put more bluntly, into Harlow's silk panties. And you're telling me you can't do anything about it. My advice to you is don't worry about it. I went through a brief period of impotency myself. But the situation came and went rather quickly."

"I fear mine is a lifelong condition," Bern said, looking like the saddest and most forlorn man Bogie had ever seen. "I'm not only impotent but I'm hung like a guinea pig. Even if I could get it up, I don't think I could achieve a deep enough penetration to satisfy her. I'll have to strap on a dildo."

"Then why in the fuck are you marrying Jean Harlow?" he asked.

"You don't know how happy I am when I hear the talk about me around town," he said. "Just the other day, I was passing through the commissary and I overheard one actor talking to another. 'That Bern sure has an ugly puss. But he must be something else when he takes his clothes off. I bet he's hung like a whale. Otherwise, why would he attract Harlow?' For a man with my condition, that was the greatest thing my ears could hear."

"If Jean doesn't know about your condition, and you go ahead and marry her, that's going to be one fucked-up honeymoon for her," Bogie said. "For you too."

"I know that," Bern said. "When a couple loves each other like we do, there are ways to get around our problems. Let's face it: throughout history, people in love have made accommodations in the bedroom."

"I'm sure you're right about that," Bogie said. "Just what sort of accommodation do you have in mind?"

"To be perfectly frank," Bern said, "I'm going to ask young men like you and Raft to visit Jean in her boudoir. Give her the sex she needs. Of course, I want to be there supervising. I'm really a frustrated director."

"I'm trying to get away from scenes like that," Bogie said. "As much as I'd like to fuck your wife, I'd rather do it in private. Just the two of us."

"Suit yourself," Bern said, "but I'm sure your friend George Raft will agree. You have another friend, Spencer Tracy. I talked to him about it the other night. He's agreed to participate."

"Raft and my dear friend Spence will fuck anything that's still breathing," Bogie said. "I'm much more conservative than they are."

"Then forget it!" Bern said angrily, seemingly embarrassed to have been so confidential with him. He stood up. "I want you to treat this little talk we had in the garden as something just between ourselves."

Bogie wondered if he should have agreed to go along with Bern's scheme, since Harlow was one hot piece of ass. But she'd already proposed a three-way with Raft, a combination that would be a lot more fun than a setup where a voyeuristic Bern directed his fucking. "I'm having to draw the line somewhere," Bogie said to Bern in way of an apology for his turn-down. "If I don't I'm gonna go too far, like get involved in one of Edmund Lowe's schemes for me—stuff like that. You people out here on the coast are a little much for my tastes."

"If Hollywood's not your kind of town, you can always take the train back to New York," Bern said. "I happen to know Fox is not going to renew your contract, and I also know that there is no other studio bidding for you. I certainly see no place for you in Metro's stable of stars."

"Sorry to hear that," Bogie said. "Before we had our little talk, I thought you might hire me at Metro. Let me play all those roles that Gable is going to turn down in the future. Let's face it: that's how many actors get their start. Accepting parts turned down by others."

"Mayer already has two or three Clark Gable types waiting in the wings," Bern said. "Even if he didn't, and in spite of what that newspaper columnist said about you being Fox's answer to Gable, you're no Clark Gable, Mr. Bogart." Bern turned and left.

Bogie sat in the garden feeling despondent. Two tantalizing prospects for him had been on the table tonight—America's leading female sex symbol and a career at Metro—and somehow both had eluded him, even though Harlow might resurface as a sexual option for him, with or without George Raft or Paul Bern. Not since he'd returned to New York after being released from military duty had he felt like such a failure.

He was still sitting in the garden when Lowe found him a half hour later. "C'mon, Bogie," he said. "Paul stormed out of the house with Harlow. You must have said something to insult him."

"Where's Helen?" he asked. "I'm ready to go home."

"I'm afraid she's retired with Lilyan for the night. We weren't asked to join the ladies. They have a lot of catching up to do. For old time's sake, you know." He patted Bogie's knee. "I guess that leaves just us."

"There is no us," Bogie said, standing up.

"Hey, don't be alarmed," Lowe said. "I know you're not like Joel McCrea. I've called Louise. She wants us to drive over right away. She's got a hot new import from Mexico she wants you to break in, and she's got a selection of six Gods—true hunks in every sense of the word—for me to choose from."

"You're on, pal," Bogie said. "Coop's got his Lupe Velez. A Mexican spitfire might be just the cure for my blues tonight."

*   *   *

At her bordello, Louise was delighted to see Bogie coming to her establish-

316

ment as a paying customer for a change and not as a detective seeking information about her staff or one of her customers. She kissed Lowe on the mouth, turning to Bogie. "Except for your friend, Spencer, Eddie is my best customer."

She invited both Lowe and Bogie into her private salon where one of the comely prostitutes, a girl who looked no more than sixteen, served them whiskey.

"A bit young," Bogie said to Louise after the girl had left the salon.

"I know," Louise said with a sigh. "But not young enough for some of these perverts out here. I get requests for them real young. I think a nine-year-old girl would be too old for some of my sicker clients."

"I like mine mature," Bogie said. "All grown up with everything developed. Nice ass. Respectable tits, not too big."

"Then why don't you save your money tonight and take me on for free?" Louise asked.

He smiled and kissed her gently on the lips. "I'm saving you for some big occasion like New Year's Eve."

"Yeah, right," Louise said. She went over to a coffee table and picked up two albums of photographs. The thin one she handed to Lowe, giving Bogie the thicker file.

He thumbed through the pictures, all of nude young women whose services were available tonight.

Lowe's much smaller selection consisted of six men, all of whom were photographed nude and fully erect. After scanning his album, Lowe said to Louise, "There's no contest. I want the hunky blond. I haven't seen the likes of a stud like that in three years."

"Damn!" Louise said. "I think I'm gonna remove his picture from the file. All my homosexual customers request him. Right now he's being worked over in a three-way with Ramon Novarro and Billy Haines. I don't think there will be much left of him when those two cocksuckers get through with him." She turned a page in the album. "Here's Steve. What's wrong with him? He was the captain of his football team in Pasadena. Not even eighteen yet."

"I want the blond and that's that," Lowe said with a certain petulance. "I know he'll be a bit exhausted but I've got to have him."

She shrugged her shoulders. "What about you, Bogart? When Eddie called, he said you were interested in the Mexican spitfire. She's gonna become the next Lupe Velez."

"She looks like she'll hit the spot," Bogie said, smiling. "Do you think I can handle it?"

Louise ran her fingers across his cheek. "From what Glenda Farrell told me, you can handle any woman." She sighed again. "And I'm still waiting."

After wishing Lowe good luck with her overworked stud of the night, Louise led Bogie out of the salon and up the steps to room 201. Without knocking, she opened the door and barged into the dimly lit room.

On the bed lay a young girl fully nude. Behind her garish makeup, she might have been beautiful. But she was painted to look like what she was: a cheap hooker, the kind he'd seen walking the streets of Tijuana.

"Maria," Louise said before looking over at Bogie with a smirk. "We call all our Mexican gals Maria. Our johns like that. "Maria, this is…." She paused for a moment, waiting for Bogie to give a fake name.

"Steve Nash," he said, taking the name of the cowboy he was playing in *A Holy Terror.*

Louise kissed Bogie for a final time. "My offer of a freebie still stands." She turned and left.

Before she'd gone out the door, he called back to her, "Give me a raincheck on that."

When Louise had shut the door, he turned again and stared down at the Mexican on the bed. She did look like a spitfire in some way. Amazingly, she resembled Lupe Velez, a much younger version.

When they were alone, Maria started to finger herself. After she'd done that, she placed the same finger in her mouth and sucked on it.

"Mind if I get undressed?" he asked.

She said something to him in Spanish. The only word he made out was *hombre*. Louise hadn't told him that Maria spoke no English.

"I think we can overcome the language barrier," he told her.

She said something else to him in Spanish. Again he could make out only one word. *Padre.* Maybe he was just imagining it, but he felt that she was asking him how old he was. Was she telling him that he looked like her father?

He started to remove his trousers but couldn't get the suggestion out of his mind that she was comparing him somehow to her papa. As a man in his early thirties, he probably was the age of her father. Had she been fucked by her papa back in Mexico?

He went ahead and pulled off his trousers but stood there awkwardly looking down at the girl, who continued to finger herself lasciviously and then suck her fingers. When he wasn't thinking about the possibility that he was old enough to be her *padre,* he imagined what Helen was doing in bed with Lilyan Tashman. Those two thoughts combined to make him feel ill.

Without stripping off any more of his clothes, he just knew he couldn't find it tonight. Any form of intercourse with this young girl was out of the question. He felt as if a big rock had settled permanently in his stomach, never to be digested. He put back on his trousers.

The girl rose up in bed and yanked at his sleeve. "No like Maria?" she asked, feigning more disappointment than she surely felt.

So, she did speak a word or two of English. "No, no," he said, "me like Maria." He rubbed his stomach. "Bad enchiladas." No sooner had he said that, than he realized how ridiculous it sounded. Enchiladas were the only Mexican food he could remember.

She seemed to understand and lay back on the bed, where she no longer

318

fingered herself but stared at him with a puzzled look on her face. He could just imagine that she'd never had a john like him before.

He reached into his wallet and withdrew two twenty dollar bills and handed them to her, noticing how her eyes brightened as she fingered the money.

She said something about *dinero* and seemed very pleased with her reward. For all he knew, Louise gave the young girl only five dollars for every trick she turned, and maybe not even that much.

He decided to sit in a broken down chair by the window for another thirty minutes, not wanting to go downstairs to that salon again. If he left now, he figured that Louise might be alerted that something had gone wrong. For all he knew, she might ridicule him or even say something to Lowe, perhaps mention it to those two faggots, William Haines and Ramon Novarro, after they finished with the blond hunk.

The girl just lay there on the bed staring at him. She seemed to have figured out that he wanted to be entertained just by sitting there and watching her masturbate. When she started fingering herself again, he motioned for her to stop. He didn't want that.

The room was unbearably hot, and he couldn't wait to escape from this whorehouse. He wanted to be with Helen and his darling Lilyan, but hadn't been invited to join them. He flashed on a fantasy or two, including going back to Lilowe and breaking in on them to see what they were doing.

After the longest thirty minutes of his life, he rose from the chair and looked down at the girl. "Adios, Maria," he said.

She just stared back at him, seeming to have no clue as to what had transpired in this room tonight. The way he figured it, if she were going to pursue a career as a *puta* in Los Angeles, she'd entertain far more bizarre johns than him.

Downstairs in Louise's private salon, reserved for only her star customers, he walked in to discover the madam of the bordello laughing and drinking with Haines and Novarro.

Upon seeing him, Louise rose at once, taking his hand and introducing him to these two big stars, who were fully dressed and looked none the worse for wear in spite of their supposed sexual marathon.

As introductions were made, both actors seemed to know who he was and eagerly shook his hand. Both of them also looked a little drunk, and so was Bogie.

"I bet you stretched Maria out of shape, and she'll be no good for any other man," Louise said.

He turned to Novarro and Haines. "She flatters me."

"Too bad it's wasted on a girl," Novarro said. "I think you're cute."

"He's had enough for one night," Haines said to Novarro. "We're just waiting for Eddie to finish up with that blond hunk, and we're going to this club for breakfast. If that spitfire didn't take it all from you, you can meet Ramon's cousin, Dolores Del Rio."

"That's great," Bogie said. "I'd like to hang out with you guys. I certainly would like to meet Dolores Del Rio." He turned to Novarro. "I didn't know you two were related."

"Yes, and I'm jealous." Novarro said. "She can get more men than me."

"And women?" Haines chimed in.

"Who wants women?" Novarro asked.

As the men sat drinking and talking, Bogie remembered that Del Rio had appeared as the French girl, Chairmaine, in Lowe's big silent film hit *What Price Glory?* If Del Rio showed up tonight, the two co-stars would have a reunion. Bogie was always surprised at what a small fraternity Hollywood really was.

"Cranberry told me you were great in the sack," Haines said to Bogie.

"I think that's one fruit I haven't sampled yet," he said.

"Cranberry is my nickname for Joan Crawford."

"I think I did meet up with that lady one night," he said, lighting a cigarette. "I'm glad she gave me a good mark on my report card."

While waiting endlessly for Lowe to finish off the blond upstairs, Bogie enjoyed Haines' company. Even though Novarro remained drunk and sullen, Haines was witty and filled with amusing stories, far more interesting than any Louella Parsons wrote about.

From the way Haines told his stories, there wasn't a cockroach that walked across a boudoir in Hollywood that he didn't know about.

At the time Bogie met him, Novarro was already facing a career in decline after his enormous success in *Ben Hur.* Even though his own career would soon collapse, Haines back on that long-ago night was the number one box office attraction in America, specializing in roles that called for a handsome, wisecracking romantic lead.

Haines was amusing Bogie with stories about his former affair with Novarro. "We were both young and beautiful when we met," Haines said.

"We still are," Novarro corrected him. "At least I am."

"Our affair lasted for exactly three months," Haines said. "Then we decided to become sisters instead." He looked at Novarro, then at Bogie. "In case you haven't already figured it out, I was the top in the relationship. Could you imagine Ramon being a top?"

It was at that moment that Lowe came back into the salon, adjusting his tie and putting on his jacket. He looked over at the three men and smiled as if he'd accomplished something major.

"I've paid everyone off here," he said to Louise before turning to look at the men. "It was my treat tonight. Now that our libidos have been satisfied—thanks to Louise—let's go on the town and dish the dirt. What are sisters for?"

***

The Fat Black Pussycat, run by a tall, skinny man, Jeb Broyhill from Okla-

320

homa, was a "secret address" in Hollywood that flourished briefly for only one year before its owner got homesick for the Red River Valley. Since no "fans" ever knew of the place, members of the Hollywood elite could go there without being molested by their adoring public or photographed. Most of the stars showed up for an early breakfast, often hoping to wake up before reporting to makeup at their respective studios.

Broyhill was also said to make the best coffee in Los Angeles, and his "wake-up" Bloody Mary was celebrated. Spencer Tracy always claimed that without three of those Bloody Marys, he would never be able to face the camera on most mornings.

In the Edmund Lowe party assembled that morning, Bogie felt like the odd man out. He told only a few trusted male friends, like Spencer Tracy and Kenneth MacKenna, about his affairs. These stars—Ramon Novarro, Dolores Del Rio, William Haines, and Lowe himself—kept none of their boudoir secrets to themselves. Their motto seemed to be that if you fucked around, tell the world. Of course, they also believed in telling the press nothing, giving "fantasy" interviews.

Even though Lilyan Tashman had captured his heart—and on this night of nights his former wife—Bogie was immensely attracted to Dolores Del Rio, thinking that she had a lot more sex appeal than Lupe Velez. Besides, he'd heard through the Hollywood gossip vine that Velez didn't bathe regularly, which was a turn-off to him. In contrast, Del Rio smelled like the first flower of spring. It was as if she'd just emerged from a rose-perfumed bath, like one of those that Cecil B. DeMille used to immerse Gloria Swanson in before his cameras.

Mysteriously beautiful and even more exotic than Velez, this Mexican actress, a convent-educated banker's daughter, captured all attention whenever she spoke. In person, she was just like the sultry, spirited Latin bombshell she played on the screen. When Bogie met her, she was months from being signed to play a beautiful, dewy-eyed Polynesian beauty in *Bird of Paradise*, which would become her most remembered screen appearance, that and her role of the French prostitute in *Madame DuBarry*.

"If you're going to remain a star in Hollywood, you've got to get married," Del Rio was lecturing her cousin, Novarro. "Your career is slipping because you don't find some understanding woman to marry."

"Never!" Novarro seemed adamant in his refusal. "The thought of being with a woman disgusts me."

"Oh, it's not so bad," Haines chimed in. "I once fucked Norma Shearer. I wouldn't do it again, but I got through it without fainting. Norma later told me it was one of the best fucks of her life. Far better than Irving Thalberg."

"That's because you're such a top," Lowe said affectionately to Haines. He reached for the actor's hand, lifted it off the table, and kissed its inner palm. "I should know." Lowe's face grew stern when he confronted Novarro. "Dolores is right. You wouldn't have to sleep in the same bed." As if remembering his night in the same bed with Bogie, McCrea, and his wife, Lowe added, "Of course, if I go to bed with my wife, I make God damn sure there's another man there."

"When I married Mr. Del Rio—I forgot the poor dear's first name—I was only fifteen," Dolores said. "My mistake involved marrying a man who was not understanding. When he caught me making love to my director, Edwin Carewe, Mr. Del Rio committed suicide. Can you imagine? Killing yourself because your wife fucks someone else."

"I never liked your keeping Del Rio's name," Novarro said. "I like your own name: Lolita Dolores Martinez Asunsolo Lopez Negrette."

"I think Lolita Negrette would look fantastic on a marquee," Bogie said facetiously.

Quick to take offense, Del Rio immediately shot back, "At least my name's been on a marquee."

"Touché," Bogie said before getting up to track down Broyhill to see if he could get another drink.

When Bogie got back, Del Rio was still the star of their table. "When I married my second husband, Cedric Gibbons, he was much more understanding. One morning when he walked into our garden and found me fondling Garbo's lovely tits—we'd been playing tennis—he thought nothing of it. He said something about what a beautiful day it was and then went back into the house and to bed."

"Another lesbian," Bogie thought, even as he made plans to seduce Del Rio later that morning.

When Broyhill came to the table with a drink for Bogie, he used the opportunity to order ham and eggs. Lowe suggested that the rest of the table order mango pancakes. "I've never heard of mango pancakes—cranberry maybe," Bogie said. "Sounds disgusting. No one ever topped ham and eggs."

"I once took Garbo here for breakfast," Del Rio said. "She always carries a little jar of Swedish lingonberry jam in her purse. She orders cornflakes, spoons dabs of jam over her cereal, then orders her coffee with milk, pours it into the bowl with the cornflakes and lingonberries, and eats the rotten mess."

As Del Rio chatted on, Bogie wasn't really listening to what she said, even though he generally loved Hollywood gossip. All he could think about was his upcoming seduction of her and how he was going to manage to escape with her from the clutches of Hollywood's "royalty set," as they were called.

It was obvious to him why both men and women desired Del Rio. She was an enchanting Latin beauty, and he could never imagine a wrinkle disfiguring her perfect skin. In time, Del Rio would prove his hunch true. She grew older but never seemed to age, claiming her secret was that she never went out into the sun. In 1960 when she appeared as the mother of Elvis Presley in Flaming Star, the press dubbed her "the ageless wonder."

Haines was claiming that he almost entered into a lavender marriage with Joan Crawford. "Cranberry and I seriously considered it. We'd have the respectable appearance of a happy marriage but would be free to go our separate ways sexually. We finally decided against it. We feared it would ruin our friendship."

"The only person I ever wanted to marry was Valentino," Novarro said. "He was the greatest lover I've ever known."

"I find it hard to imagine that he was a better top than me," Haines said jokingly.

"Oh, I love you Billy," Novarro said. "But you know Rudy was the man for me."

"I thought you guys were rivals," Bogie said.

"We were on the screen," Novarro said, "but not off the screen. Off the screen Rudy was the master. Around the house I was his slave."

Since it was getting late, Bogie steered Del Rio to the door after he'd finished his ham and eggs. He agreed to take her home since she lived in a different part of town from her fellow actors.

In his car driving off into the night, he was surprised at how aggressive she became. As he steered the wheel, she unzipped his fly and proceeded to give him a blow-job on the way home.

A few times he dangerously closed his eyes for too long, opening them just in time to keep from hitting another car. He fully suspected that his time with Del Rio was going to be his first and last, and he wanted to make the most of it.

Instinctively he knew that he'd be one of many in the long list of her present and future lovers that would include everybody from Orson Welles to Marlene Dietrich and Billie Holiday.

It was with sadness that in years to come he'd read that Del Rio had been denied re-entry into the United States, having been called a "commie." But it gave him pleasure to read also that she'd become the Queen of Mexican cinema and was often seen necking in Mexico City night clubs with her "love of the moment" as she called it. On more than one occasion, the love of the moment turned out to be the black chanteuse, Josephine Baker.

***

Bogie arrived on the set of *A Holy Terror* with dreams of Dolores Del Rio still dancing in his head. She might like to fondle Garbo's breasts, but she was skilled at fondling every part of a man too—in fact, she more than fondled. He wondered if Lupe Velez with Gary Cooper in her bed was the Mexican spitfire that Del Rio was.

As Del Rio readily admitted, she'd been fucking since she was fifteen. After last night, he suspected that she'd started to learn seduction techniques even younger. As he told Kenneth later, she was "one hot piece of salsa. She'd make Tabasco taste like sweet apple juice."

In the afterglow of sex, Del Rio admitted to some of her more bizarre experiences as a sexual player in Hollywood. When she'd first come to Hollywood as a young teenager, she had stalked Charlie Chaplin in the hopes that he'd notice her. When The Little Tramp finally did notice her, he brutally raped her after promising to put her in one of his movies. She also admitted that at the time, her cousin Ramon Novarro was starring in Metro's blockbuster version of *Ben-Hur*, and that she'd tried to seduce him. "I felt he'd be able to play Ben-Hur better on the screen if he'd known what it was like to go to bed with just one woman in his life." She'd sighed. "I did not succeed."

Later that morning after Bogie had filmed only one scene dressed as a cowboy, he was finished for the day. He wouldn't be needed until the following morning when he had a scene with the picture's star, George O'Brien.

O'Brien always told anyone who asked, including Bogie, that, "A man who will fuck both men and women is a lot busier than one who won't. If you'll swing both ways, it's almost assured that you've got a date every night—at least in Hollywood."

When O'Brien invited him for lunch, Bogie accepted, wondering how much O'Brien's friend, Charles Farrell, had revealed about their day at sea. When Bogie had first come to Hollywood, the image of these two male beauties, with their powerful physiques, had become one in his mind. Over lunch Bogie began to realize that O'Brien was a distinctly different personality and far more intriguing than the rather bland Farrell could ever be.

Although Bogie wanted to order his typical ham and eggs, O'Brien had insisted that he ask for *huevos rancheros* instead. "The cook in the commissary is Mexican, and they're really good."

Out of respect for his previous sexual interlude with Dolores Del Rio, Bogie agreed to order this dish of her homeland.

For himself, O'Brien asked for three raw avocados. "It's my favorite food. For breakfast, I eat an avocado sandwich on white toast. For lunch I eat them raw with just a little bit of lemon juice. At night I always make guacamole, which I eat as an appetizer before I order a very lean and very rare steak. It keeps my skin young and beautiful." He leaned over to Bogie. "Go on. Feel the skin of my face. Tell me skin like that can only be compared to a baby's ass."

"Hell, man," Bogie said, "I don't want to be seen sitting here in the commissary running my fingers across your cheek. People will think we're a couple of fags."

"Don't be such a sissy," O'Brien urged. "Go on. Rub my skin."

When he felt no one was watching them, Bogie ran his fingers across O'Brien's cheek. "That's smooth skin all right, a hell of a lot smoother than mine. I'm not aging well. Starting tomorrow, I'm gonna go on the avocado diet like you." He reached for a cigarette. "As for skin, I'd much rather feel the tits on Dolores Del Rio."

"Relax, relax," O'Brien told him. "You don't have to assert your heterosexual credentials around me. I'm not going to put the make on you. You're not my type. Either man or woman, I insist they have great bodies. You don't look like you have any physical fitness regime at all. Wardrobe told me they had to pad your shoulders. And those fucking high-heeled boots you wear—that's not my idea of a man who's tall in the saddle like I like 'em."

Blowing smoke toward him, Bogie said, "I guess that means I'm not going to get asked out by you."

Before O'Brien could respond, the waiter arrived with the food and the subject was dropped.

Since neither man was needed on the set for the rest of the day, O'Brien invited him to go swimming at Santa Monica. Bogie said that he didn't have any trunks. O'Brien told him that his house was on the way to the ocean, and they could drop off there and change.

An hour later Bogie found himself in O'Brien's home. Although the actor kept himself incredibly well groomed, he obviously didn't have a maid come in too often to clean his house. It was a pigsty. Dirty dishes piled high in the sink were growing mold, and newspapers and magazines littered the floor. Cups of coffee and platters of half-eaten, long-rotted food were seen about the living room, and the dark wood furnishings looked as if they'd barely survived the Dust Bowl.

When O'Brien emerged from his bedroom, he was stark naked, a most impressive sight. Bogie could only dream of having a physique like the star. "You're not my size," O'Brien said to him. "But your buddy, Kenneth, left these trunks here. I think you can fit into them."

"Kenneth is taller than me but we have the same waistline," Bogie said, wishing that O'Brien would put on his own trunks.

"I'll let you in on another one of my beauty secrets," O'Brien said, as Bogie stripped down to get into his swim suit.

Observing Bogie's less than perfect figure, O'Brien said, "We've got to get you on a new regime of a sensible diet and vigorous physical exercise to build up your body. You probably drink too much. I take it easy with the booze. I notice you lighting up a cigarette every minute. I confine myself to one after-dinner cigar, and I don't inhale. Your hair too is a problem. You look like a man who is going to loose his hair before he's forty. The trick is you've got to dry your hair thoroughly when you shower or go into the water. Water rots hair. If you keep your hair wet, it'll start to fall out. Since I like you, I'll give you my most closely guarded beauty secret. It's about how to care for and maintain the anus."

Almost before Bogie knew what was happening, O'Brien had turned around and bent over, spreading the cheeks of his ass.

Bogie felt himself staring directly into the man's asshole. He couldn't recall having seen a man's asshole before, and he hoped that this was the last time he'd have an intimate look at one.

"Okay, I see it, pal" Bogie said, diverting his eyes and quickly slipping on his trunks.

When O'Brien stood up and faced him, the actor asked, "Tell me the truth. Isn't my ass smooth and hairless like the skin of a baby's butt hole?"

"Frankly, I haven't inspected too many baby assholes in my day."

"Don't make fun," O'Brien cautioned him. "Most men don't take care of their assholes like I do. Be honest. After you take a shit, what do you do?"

"After I've dumped my load, I reach for some toilet paper and wipe my ass. What in hell do you think I do?"

"That's your first mistake," O'Brien said. "Toilet paper isn't enough. To keep an anus as young, fresh, and beautiful looking as mine, you've got to use soap and warm water after defecating. You've got to cleanse yourself thoroughly. Do you know that most men in Hollywood walk around with dirty assholes. I mean, Dingleberry City. You've got to assume that sex can happen anywhere and at any time. You should keep your asshole completely clean. What if somebody wants to stick their tongue up there? Do you want them to taste shit or do you want them to encounter an asshole as clean and sweet smelling as mine? From having looked at it, wouldn't you agree that my asshole is like that of a man half my age?"

"I've got no way of knowing that," Bogie said, "and it's for God damn sure that I'm not going to go out there and conduct an inspection. You should ask Ramon Novarro questions like that—not me. Let's get to the beach before the sun sets."

At the beach O'Brien the athlete attracted a lot of attention. Several of his female fans approached him asking for autographs. The actor seemed in his element, and it was obvious that he adored showing off his body. After all, he was called "The Chest."

When O'Brien went to take his final swim of the day, Bogie lingered behind, wanting to go to the toilet and have a cigarette and something cold to drink.

For the previous hour, he'd noticed a large black car with two fully dressed men parked near a refreshment stand. At first he'd paid scant attention. But as the afternoon wore on, he began to imagine that the men were spying on him. Even though he kept trying to dismiss such an idea from his mind, the suspicion lingered.

When he emerged from the toilet, one of the men got out from the passenger seat and approached him. "We were sent to see you. Mr. Hughes has a message for you. Would you get into the car for a minute, please?"

At first Bogie was tempted to run but he feared that Hughes' henchman was armed.

"Get in the car," the man ordered.

With great trepidation, Bogie got into the back seat where the man joined him. The driver in sunglasses remained at the wheel, not turning around when Bogie crawled in.

"Mr. Hughes has a very simple request," the man in the back seat said to him. "He's learned that you're making a picture with George O'Brien. Mr. Hughes is very impressed with Mr. O'Brien and has seen all his pictures. But he doesn't like the way O'Brien's career is being managed. Mismanaged, really. He wants

326

you to drive Mr. O'Brien to his home on Saturday night at eight o'clock." He reached into his vest pocket and handed Bogie an envelope. "The instructions for getting there are written out for you." If for some reason, Mr. O'Brien doesn't want to accept Mr. Hughes invitation, you're to call the number noted inside."

"If that's it, gents, I'll certainly convey the invitation to George," Bogie said. "My hunch is that he'll be happy to accept."

"Then our business is over," the man said, "and you can get out of the car. We'll contact you again when Mr. Hughes has some more business with you."

Relieved, Bogie got out of the car and walked rapidly toward the beach. He looked back only once, just in time to see the dark car disappear down the highway.

As O'Brien emerged dripping wet from the water, Bogie reached down and got a large terrycloth towel for him. Seeing that O'Brien's hair was soggy wet, he knew that the actor would want to dry his locks at once so they wouldn't rot.

"I saw you getting out of that car," O'Brien said. "What in hell's going on here?"

"George, my boy," Bogie said with a smile, "come Saturday night you've got an invitation to meet the star-maker of Hollywood."

"What are you talking about?" O'Brien said. "I'm already a star."

"All I can say is this. When Saturday night comes, you'd better use the gentlest of soaps on that cute little asshole of yours. Instead of warm water, I suggest you bathe your rosebud in warm sweet milk. I'm driving you over to the home of Howard Hughes."

***

The Broadway chorus girl turned Hollywood diva, Jeanette MacDonald, had invited Bogie and Helen Menken to her home for a party honoring Kenneth, Kay Francis, and their upcoming wedding.

Although he admired the director who'd made her a star, Ernst Lubitsch, Bogie held MacDonald in low regard. She wasn't his kind of dame. The way he figured it, all he'd have to do at the party was say hello to the diva upon entering and good-bye upon leaving. Just as he thought that Lilyan Tashman was the sexiest broad in Hollywood, in spite of her being more than a part-time lesbian, he regarded MacDonald "as the most sexless female star in pictures."

About a block from MacDonald's house at 621 North Bedford Drive in Beverly Hills, he spotted a well-dressed man standing beside an expensive, custom-made car with a flat tire. He slowed down to see if he could be of assistance. That man standing there with an impatient look on his face was William Powell.

Bogie was alone in his car, as Helen had told him that she'd be an hour late and he was to go on without her. Slowing down, he waved at Powell and pulled over to the curb. After all, he couldn't leave a big-time movie star standing forlornly along the side of the road with a flat tire.

For all he knew, Powell had been invited to MacDonald's party too. There were rumors that Powell and Kay Francis had had an affair during the recent filming of Paramount's *Street of Chance* when they'd co-starred with Jean Arthur. The film had been directed by John Cromwell, a long-ago fellow member of Bogie's Pussy Posse in New York.

"May I offer my assistance?" Bogie asked Powell as he got out of the car. When he looked Powell over more closely, he knew that the actor was too splendiferously attired to change a tire himself. Already early in his career, he was considered the best-dressed man in Hollywood. Perhaps Powell could co-star in his next film with Lilyan Tashman. Hollywood's best dressed man teams up with Tinseltown's best-dressed woman. The film could be about the fashion industry.

"Glad to meet you," Powell said. "Kay has told me you're Kenneth's best friend."

"Something like that," Bogie said. "We're also rivals."

"I know what you mean," Powell said in a stage-trained voice. "Actors are always jealous of each other. My best friend is Ronald Colman, but we'll probably be competing for the same roles one day." A potential crystal-ball gazer, Powell almost had it right. In 1947 he'd lose his chance with the Oscar for his performance in *Life With Father*, bowing to Colman for his role in *A Double Life*.

"If it weren't for that best friend of yours, the British limey, I would have been a star long ago." Bogie related the story of how he'd been screen-tested for the male lead in *The White Sister* but Lillian Gish and director Henry King had favored Colman instead.

"Ah!" Powell said, "the role that got away. All of us have bitter stories like that."

After all this chit-chat, Bogie finally addressed the issue of the flat tire. Even though he too was attired in a tuxedo, he offered to change the tire for the immaculately groomed Powell.

"Thanks my good man," Powell said, "but the garage has already been called. I'm escorting Miss Carole Lombard to the party. Since Jeanette lives only a block away, she walked ahead to call for help."

That was the first time Bogie had ever heard a man refer to his wife as "Miss" followed by her maiden name. "Mind if I wait with you until the garage man comes?" Bogie asked. "It may be the only time I have to speak with the great William Powell, and I'll need to record my impressions for my memoirs."

"I'd welcome the company," Powell said with a slight chuckle, accepting a cigarette from Bogie. What Bogie didn't tell Powell was how much he admired him and wanted to be like him. Powell was debonair, suave, sophisticated, and considered quite a ladies' man. The writer, Ben Hecht, had once told Bogie, "It's not the braggadocios who are getting all the pussy. It's those quiet types like Bill Powell. He gets laid more than any other guy in Hollywood even though married to that hot box, Carole Lombard."

Bogie was trying to impress Powell and win him over, but the perverse side of him couldn't resist a little dig. "Did you get permission from Howard Hughes to escort Lombard tonight?"

Powell raised only a right eyebrow in surprise as if he hadn't heard correctly. "I wasn't aware that I had to get permission to escort my own wife to a party. Those rumors about Howard and Carole are just that. Rumors. Billie Dove herself told me that Howard can't get it up most nights, although I hear Randolph Scott doesn't have any complaints about Howard in that department. Besides, Carole is far too free-spirited a filly to ever get corralled inside Hughes' stable. You'll see for yourself when I introduce you to her later tonight."

As Bogie studied Powell's face carefully, he realized that he was not particularly handsome, although very much in the tradition of the leading men of the 1920s, including Edmund Lowe himself but also Warner Baxter and Adolphe Menjou. Yet there was such charm and style to Powell that you forgot that he wasn't handsome.

As if detecting that Bogie was evaluating his looks, Powell said, "As you can plainly see, I don't have a John Barrymore profile. But I get by."

"You give hope to all of us regular guys who are runners-up in the looks department," Bogie said. "Reviewers have written that I was the natural replacement for Valentino or even that I was Fox's answer to Clark Gable. But I don't think producers and directors agree with that assessment."

"If Edward G. Robinson and that midget, James Cagney, can become stars, so can you. Except for that lisp and the scar on your lip, you should photograph reasonably well. My suggestion is that you try out for gangster roles. What picture does Fox have you on now?"

"*A Holy Terror,*" Bogie said. "A Western with George O'Brien. I walk around in high-heel boots and wardrobe pads my shoulders."

"All wrong for you, my boy," Powell said. "Go for the gangster parts."

At that point both men spotted the man from the garage arriving in a small truck. "I guess you're going to be rescued," Bogie said to Powell, shaking his hand. "I'll see you at the party."

As Bogie drove up the hill toward Jeanette MacDonald's house, his mind kept exploding with all the rumors he'd heard about Powell. Was he really the stud for Marion Davies, the mistress of William Randolph Hearst, the newspaper magnate turned impresario? Bogie had seen the two of them perform in *When Knighthood Was in Flower.* According to the Hollywood grapevine, Hearst's boudoir abilities were on the wane, so he discreetly allowed Davies to get serviced on the side by actors who met with the tycoon's approval. As Bogie had been told, Powell was still friendly with Hearst and Davies, but her sexual interest had shifted to Clark Gable.

Wherever Bogie went, he seemed haunted by talk of Clark Gable. For all he knew, Gable might even take Lombard away from Powell.

***

Although Bogie hadn't wanted to go to the party hosted by Hollywood's singing diva, Jeanette MacDonald, it ended up being one of the most memorable parties of his life, and one that would be gossiped about for years.

The songbird was not the type of hostess to stand in her hallway, lit by a mammoth Viennese chandelier, and greet each guest. She had her maid in the obligatory black dress and white apron escort Bogie to his hostess who sat enthroned in the garden, wearing a ruffled lace dress overly adorned. With all her frills, she looked like she was waiting for the camera to roll as she danced "The Merry Widow Waltz."

"Mr. Bogart," she said, extending her hand to him. "I'm so glad you could come." He knew none of the people around her, and she didn't bother to introduce him. But she did say, "You know everyone here, of course. Hollywood parties are nothing if not incestuous."

It was obvious he'd interrupted her in the middle of one of her stories, and she was anxious to get on with it. He whispered for the maid to bring him some whiskey. She directed him to help himself at the bar.

At the bar set up in MacDonald's garden, Bogie introduced himself to a man who appeared, like Bogie himself, aloof and removed from the party scene. Somehow he sensed in Robert George Ritchie the same outsider that he was. In those days Bob Ritchie was one of those behind-the-scenes Hollywood legends that the industry knew about, but not the general public.

He was rumored to be the husband of MacDonald, although no record of any marriage certificate ever surfaced. The list of stars that he'd seduce between 1927 and 1960 would fill a book, and indeed that was just what Ritchie was keeping at the time Bogie met him.

In Ritchie's little black book he kept detailed records of all his seductions, with the notation that Jeanette MacDonald surrendered her virginity to him at 10:19pm on April 7, 1928.

That book would grow into volumes and would include the likes of Grace Moore, another diva; both Lamarr (Hedy) and Lamour (Dorothy), along with both Gabor sisters (Eva and Zsa Zsa), plus the prim and proper Greer Garson, even Nanette Fabray. Ritchie had a particularly fondness for stars who appeared in musical comedy, although his seduction repertoire was hardly confined to "songbirds."

Ritchie's sexual prowess had already preceded his introduction to Bogie. Tall, blond, and athletically built, Ritchie had a tough demeanor, a granite-like face that looked as if it had been chiseled by a sculptor. He was not obviously handsome, but Bogie figured he had something special when he took off his clothes. Otherwise, why would half the women in Hollywood be pursuing him?

Even though MacDonald's party was just beginning, Ritchie was already drunk before half the guests had arrived. In Bogie he found someone he could talk to and relate to. It was obvious from the way he'd immediately responded to

330

Bogie that he viewed him as a kindred spirit. "Me and you are destined to spend our lives in the shadow of a female star," he said to Bogie. "You with your Helen Menken and me with my Jeanette."

"Even though I'm Helen's escort at your party tonight," Bogie said, "she and I are divorced. I'm married to Mary Philips now."

"I know of Mary Philips too, the Broadway actress." Accepting a cigarette from Bogie, he said, "There are only a few major Broadway actresses I don't know as David knew Bathsheba. I haven't worked my way around to your Mary yet because I've been held up out here on the coast."

"I wish you luck, pal," Bogie said. "Some guy must be fucking her. I'm sure not. It's a strange marriage. I live in Hollywood, she lives in New York, perhaps as strange as your marriage to Jeanette. You guys are married, aren't you?"

"Who are you?" Ritchie asked through a slurred voice. "Louella herself?"

"I mean everyone in Hollywood is asking, 'Are they married or aren't they married?' You could come right out with it and clear the air."

"I'm leaving that announcement up to Jeanette," Ritchie said. "Some people think we're married. Other people call me Jeanette's gigolo. I'm a second-class citizen, but I get ten percent of everything Jeanette makes in return for 'professional services.'"

"You mean fucking her?" Bogie asked provocatively.

"If she wants that," Ritchie said. "That is, when she's not getting it from Maurice Chevalier or Ernst Lubitsch. Lubitsch is madly in love with her. Chevalier, of course, is in love with himself. I negotiate her contracts, keep the wolves away from her, and provide an escort for her when she needs it."

"Hey, I think I could handle a smooth job like that. Fox isn't gonna renew my contract. Helen tells me that actors by the thousands are out of work in New York. I need to get a soft deal like you've got." Looking at his empty glass, Bogie said, "I like to eat. Even more than that, I like to drink. I don't think I can support myself in the coming months if I don't find some sort of a deal."

"I like you, Bogart," Ritchie said. "A lot of guys Jeanette invites over here are faggots. They put the make on me all the time. I guess these queens figure that if all the hot pussies in Hollywood want me, I must be swinging something real low in my trousers."

"I guess so," Bogie said. "I thought that myself."

"You guessed right," Ritchie said. "An even better deal for you—better than the one I've got with Jeanette—is for you to enter a lavender marriage like Edmund Lowe and Lilyan Tashman. Do you know them?"

"I think we've met," Bogie said nonchalantly. "They're a different case. Lowe is not her gigolo. He's a bigger star than she is."

"Yeah," Ritchie said. "Maybe that's not too good an example. It's the drink, you know. Take the couple we're here celebrating. Kay Francis and Kenneth MacKenna. I don't know how well you know them, but they'll have a lavender marriage. He's one of the biggest cocksuckers in Hollywood, and there are few first-class pussies in Hollywood that Kay Francis hasn't sampled. Even Dietrich herself."

"Is there anyone in Hollywood—male or female—that Dietrich hasn't gotten around to?" Bogie asked.

"I've fucked Dietrich myself," Ritchie said. "Actually, that's not quite true. She sucked me off. Dietrich likes to give blow-jobs more than she likes to get fucked. She always tries to get her guys to settle for a blow-job. If they insist on the Kraut honeypot itself, she'll go along. But she's the most oral gal in Hollywood."

"She hasn't sucked me off yet, but thanks for the tip," Bogie said. "The next time I see Dietrich, I'm gonna complain that all the women in Hollywood want to get fucked whereas I'm looking for a gal who gives great head."

Ritchie laughed and directed Bogie over to the bar for a refueling stop. "Our buddy Kenneth will be able to fuck Kay once a month or so—maybe every six weeks. The rest of his time can be spent chasing after Richard Arlen, Randolph Scott, Gary Cooper, Joel McCrea, Fairbanks Jr., and the list goes on. All those guys swing any way the wind blows. I hear even Clark Gable has swung both ways. Of course, now that he's a star he has his pick of the women and doesn't have to feed his dick to the faggots anymore, hoping those queens will advance his career. Cooper no longer has to be the male hustler either. In the beginning, he had to sell himself. Today he goes with guys like that Anderson Lawler just for the fun of it."

To Bogie, this New Jersey-born entrepreneur was a real son-of-a-bitch, just his kind of guy. Bastards like George Raft and Ritchie fascinated Bogie. In some ways he liked Ritchie because he was completely different from Bogie himself. Throughout his life, Bogie remained a gentleman. Ritchie, in contrast, liked to use anybody who crossed his path. That was a talent that Bogie never developed.

Not anxious to return to the party where he'd be viewed as "Jeanette's boy," Ritchie continued to engage Bogie in conversation at the far end of the garden away from the other guests.

"I've got it!" he said, grabbing hold of Bogie's arm. "The perfect deal for you, and she's at the party tonight. Jean Arthur. She's a friend of Kay's. They met when they filmed *Street of Chance* with Bill Powell."

"I know the film," Bogie said. "It was directed by a friend of mine, John Cromwell. He directed me in two of my first plays, *Drifting* and *Swifty*. Now he's a big-time Hollywood director. He was one of the founding members of our Pussy Posse in New York. But since I got to Hollywood, the son-of-a-bitch doesn't even return my calls."

"You're learning an important lesson out here," Ritchie said. "If you're perceived to be a nobody, you don't get your calls returned. But I think I could hook you up with Jean Arthur. She's going to become one of the biggest stars in Hollywood. We're talking five—maybe six—Oscars in her future. I mean, big. She's also a card-carrying dyke. There's gonna be tremendous pressure on her to marry some understanding guy. I saw her talking to Kay in our library. Let me introduce the two of you. I think you guys will hit it off."

If he were sober, Bogie might have rejected the suggestion of such an improbable alliance, his becoming the pretend husband of Jean Arthur in a lavender marriage. But in his soggy state, the idea held a certain appeal for him. It also had something to do with his rivalry with Kenneth. Although they remained good friends, the jealousy between them—and not just over Mary—remained strong. Bogie viewed Kenneth's star as rising in Hollywood, as his own dimmed. Not even a twinkle.

Although Kenneth would have to endure being called "Mr. Kay Francis" after his marriage, Bogie, at least on that night of the garden party, wanted to top him.

What if he hooked up with Jean Arthur, and she became a far bigger star than Francis, and maybe did win some of those Oscars that Ritchie predicted? Bogie felt that he had just as many qualifications as Kenneth—maybe a lot more—to marry from the A-list. Helen Menken and Mary Philips were well-known actresses, but not famous like Kay Francis. The way he saw it tonight, even if it was the booze talking, he figured it might not be a bad idea to lock both Helen and Mary in the closet reserved for ex-wives and dance around the bedroom with Jean Arthur, carefully avoiding hitting the sack, of course.

If she were the lesbian Ritchie had claimed, she'd make no sexual demands on him. He could help spend her money while pursuing, with a wedding band on his finger, all the beautiful women of Hollywood just like Ritchie himself did. "Yeah," he thought, he liked the sound of it. If there was no great career looming on his horizon, why not a life devoted to his own pleasure?

Jean Arthur was a beautiful woman, and he'd seen at least a dozen of her silent films. But he liked her even better when she talked.

Her voice was unlike that of any other actress in Hollywood. When Paramount's much-feared sound wizard, Roy Pomeroy, had tested Arthur's voice, he'd given up in despair. "A foghorn!" Pomeroy had shouted.

The studio czar, Adolph Zuckor, liked that foghorn quality and that distinctive, throaty "catch" in Arthur's voice, a sound that became more prominent in her later films such as *Mr. Deed Goes to Town, Mr. Smith Goes to Washington,* and *You Can't Take It With You.*

Jean Arthur had not only survived the transition between Silents and Talkies, but was fast rising on the Hollywood scene, appearing with such leading men as William Powell and Charles "Buddy" Rogers, who would go on to become the third husband of Mary Pickford.

With his arm around Bogie, Ritchie walked with him across the garden toward the library. It was a hot night and the French doors were open, as MacDonald's frilly curtains blew in the night breeze in the perfume-scented garden.

Bogie could hear Arthur's soon-to-be-famous voice talking to Kay Francis. "How can you go through with this sham of a marriage?" Arthur was saying to

Francis. "Only last week you told me you loved me."

"But Ken is understanding about such things," Francis said. "Otherwise, I would never marry him."

Arthur raised her voice. "There's going to be no marriage—and that's that. You belong to me."

***

Still in the garden, Ritchie made some drunken noise like he was singing to alert the women to their presence. As Bogie came through the French doors and into the library with Ritchie, Jean Arthur was sitting tall and serene on a satin-covered red sofa. In tears, Kay Francis was dashing toward the door and quickly disappeared.

Bogie felt that he and Ritchie could not have found a less opportune time to call on Miss Arthur, but he was too drunk to redirect the show. After all, it was practically Ritchie's house and he was in charge.

Already an accomplished actress, Arthur gave no indication that an emotional scene with Francis had just occurred in the library. "Gentlemen," she said. "If I'm going to be evaluated as a piece of flesh, I want you to sit over there. My face looks best from the right side, and I insist on being viewed only from that angle."

"I'm Humphrey Bogart," he said. "That left side of your face must be pretty bad."

"It's all scarred and disfigured," she said. "That's why I won't allow it to be photographed."

Just as he'd been taken with Myrna Loy's nose, Bogie was mesmerized by the sound of Arthur's voice, which was crisp and incisive. She gave off the aura that she was the equal of any man, maybe even better than any mere male.

Ritchie quickly excused himself and left the library, leaving Bogie sitting alone in an armchair taking in Arthur, who remained elegantly positioned on the sofa, right face only.

"You don't have to tell me what Ritchie has told you," she said. "I already know. You must be the sixth guy he's tried to set me up with. I've heard it all. He told you that I'm going to become the biggest star in Hollywood, didn't he?"

"He might have mentioned that," he said.

"That I'm going to need a manager, who might even become my husband and live off my big fat earnings," she said.

"Yeah," Bogie said, feeling uncomfortable. "I think he did suggest something along those lines." Her voice was fetchingly husky at one point, childishly querulous when it wanted to be, yet strangely reassuring when that emotion was called for.

"Let me tell you about Hollywood where I'm going to win all those fat Oscars that Ritchie predicts," she said. "I've made the slapstick shorts. Tasted all

334

the custard pies in my face. I've done my duty in B Westerns for Poverty Row companies, even appeared in *Twisted Triggers* for God's sake. And now I've recently logged time as a lackluster starlet who's a mere prop for William Powell in those Philo Vance mysteries."

"I'm sure you were great in all of them," he said, not meaning it at all.

"Bullshit!" She turned and gave him a full frontal. From his perspective, the left side of her face looked as cute as the right. "Hollywood is so impressed with me that my studio is not going to renew my contract. I'm going back to Broadway where I hope to find work."

"We're in the same boat," he said. "I just know Fox isn't going to renew me. My ex, Helen Menken, will be here later tonight. What she tells me about Broadway isn't encouraging. There are longer lines at the soup kitchens than at the theaters."

"I know that," she said. "But what am I going to do with no more offers coming in? Stay around Hollywood like every other failed actress and get a job slinging hash?"

At that point, the maid came into the library and said, "There you are, Mr. Bogart. Your wife, Miss Menken, has just arrived, and she's asking for you."

"Tell her I'm on my way," he said dutifully, turning his attention back to Arthur. The actress fascinated him, and he wanted to get to know her better.

"I'm suffocating in this room," she said. "I detest parties and I don't know why I came here in the first place. Kay tells me that you're MacKenna's best pal. Can't you persuade him not to marry Kay? I'm sure you know the whole story. The marriage will be a disaster. He's only marrying Kay to advance his stalled career."

"Why do you think she's marrying Kenneth?" he asked. "Surely not for love."

"Surely not," she said, standing up. "Kay has never loved anyone—man or woman—except that image of herself in the mirror. I was a fool to get involved in a friendship with her. I might have known it would turn out this way. Would you show me to the door?"

"I'd be honored to escort a fellow New Yorker to the door," he said. "I'd be more honored if you stayed."

"Will you promise to talk to MacKenna?"

"I'll talk to him tomorrow when I can get him alone," he said. "Is there any way I can call you to tell you what he said?"

"Of course," she said. "I'm a very private person, but I'll give you my phone number. I really want to know what he says. It's important that I know." She gently reached for his hand.

No longer serene looking, she appeared frightened to pass through the party on the way out. He felt that she needed to use him as a prop to make a graceful exit.

As they were heading to the doorway, he spotted John Cromwell coming in.

Although he'd heard that his former Broadway director and fellow Pussy Posse member frequently saw Kenneth, Bogie was now encountering him for the first time in years.

"John," he said, coming up to him and extending his hand. "It's great to see you, pal. I've called you several times."

"I've been busy, Hump," he said.

Bogie turned around and graciously presented Arthur. "Here's your star. You brilliantly directed Kay and Jean here in *Street of Chance.*"

Before he knew what was happening, she slapped Cromwell's face and ran toward the door.

Bewildered, Bogie looked on in disbelief. He confronted Cromwell. "Up to your old Pussy Posse tricks again?" he asked. "The casting couch."

"Hell, no," Cromwell said, rubbing his face. "She's a dyke anyway. I told the bitch the truth. She's a miserable actress. At the end of the shoot, I let her know that she'll never make it in Hollywood. 'Go back to New York,' I told her."

"That must have made her feel real good." Excusing himself, he rushed toward the door and along MacDonald's driveway until he caught up with Arthur who was fumbling with her keys. She was in tears.

"Are you sure you don't want me to drive you home?" he asked. "I could call a taxi to take me back to the party. It's such roaring good fun." He didn't disguise his sarcasm.

"You're a nice man," she said, brushing his cheek ever so lightly with a feathery kiss. "We'll talk soon. I can take care of myself. I've always had to do that. Good night."

As he stepped back, he was almost run down by a speeding sports car racing dangerously up the driveway.

As he waved good-bye to Arthur, he headed back to the main entrance. The driver of the vehicle came to an abrupt stop right in front of MacDonald's door.

The door was thrown open and out stepped a drunken Billie Dove.

***

"Bogart! You Yankee Jew!" There was an edge of mocking laughter to her voice as Billie Dove saw Bogie approach.

"I know you're pissed about the other night," he said apologetically. "It was just a practical joke that misfired. I'm always putting people on."

She stood back to study his figure. "My, oh my. Aren't you dressed up tonight? I'm used to seeing you jaybird naked and not in a tux. You're hung okay. I've seen bigger and I assure you I've seen a hell of a lot smaller."

Noticing that she was precariously balanced on her high heels, he asked, "May I escort you into the party?"

"If you do, do you think you can resist rape?"

"I'll be a well-behaved gentleman," he said, "and I'm truly sorry about the

336

other night."

"It's okay," she said, bending over and lightly kissing his wet lips. "I'll get over it. You probably thought I'd be amused. After all, you don't know that I still have some shreds of dignity, even though I work in Hollywood. You know me only as Howard's mistress or George Raft's slut."

Taking her arm to steady her, he said, "I know you only as the world's most beautiful and gracious lady."

"That's what I like to hear coming from you horny bastards," she said.

Once inside, he found the party going full blast with its elegantly gowned women and men looking like penguins in their formal wear. Billie demanded to see Kay Francis at once. Spotting her across the living room, she headed toward her, but was stopped and greeted along the way. After all, she was one of the town's biggest stars dating its most mysterious billionaire.

He stood forlornly watching her go, still fantasizing about taking off her clothes and raping her. Before returning to the poverty of Broadway, he definitely wanted to add Dove to his seduction belt, but didn't want any more plane rides with Howard Hughes. He was still shaking from the last flight.

He stood watching Billie Dove embrace Kay Francis. The actor standing beside them was Basil Rathbone. Bogie felt that it was like watching all three stars emote again as he'd so recently seen them in Lloyd Bacon's film, *A Notorious Affair*, for Warner Brothers.

At the sound of Helen Menken's voice, he turned around to face her kiss and a slightly accusatory question. "Where have you been all night? I've been looking everywhere for you. With all these beautiful Hollywood actresses, I guess I'm just old hat."

"You look lovely," he said, "the most beautiful I've ever seen you. No woman in this room has your New York class." He didn't say beauty because there was no way that Helen Menken could be stacked up against the stunning features of Billie Dove.

"I've just had the most delightful conversation with Basil Rathbone," she said. "We haven't seen each other since we were arrested on stage in *The Captive.*"

"An evening I remember so well," he said. "All that and Mae West too." He kissed her again. "I might have been hard to find at this party, but you've been evasive since our first night in Hollywood together. When you hit town, I thought you'd want to be with me every minute."

"Tonight, darling, after the party, I want you to go back to the Garden of Allah with me," she said. "It'll be like old times."

"That's a promise I'm going to hold you to," he said.

"Come on, dear heart," she said. "I was with Carole Lombard and her party. She's drunk but telling the most divine and indiscreet stories."

In a remote corner of the room a circle had formed around Carole Lombard. There wasn't a woman in the group, but a total of eight men, including her husband, William Powell. He looked extremely distressed as a drunken Lombard amused her fans.

Helen introduced Bogie to Lombard. She eyed him skeptically as if she'd never formed an opinion of him.

He suspected that she didn't know who he was. "I hear you are just great in *Ladies' Man,*" he said. "I can't wait to see it." Remembering that William Powell was the star, he quickly added, "And you too, Bill."

"I'm the greatest thing in that film since baby shit," Lombard said rather sulkily. The frown on her face told it all: she was forming a snap judgment of him and it wasn't favorable.

Unknown to Bogie, Kenneth MacKenna had come up behind him and had heard every word. "Don't forget to mention my intended wife-to-be," he said. "Kay was, after all, the co-star of that film." He embraced Bogie.

"When you're married," Lombard said, "maybe you'll teach Miss Kay *Fwancis* how to pronounce her r's."

"We're working on that," Kenneth said. "After all, she's marrying a New York stage actor, and we're known for our perfect speech, ideal for Talkies."

"At least you're known for something," Lombard said. "You're not known for your fucking. The men of the silent screen could fuck better than any of you smooth-talking squirts coming out from Broadway."

Powell bristled at his wife's remark. It was obvious he wanted to restrain her, but didn't know how to do so without embarrassing her and himself.

Ignoring the look of chastisement from her husband, Lombard resumed her role at center stage. Hovering around her were a group of actors who'd recently appeared in films starring Kay Francis herself. These included George Bancroft and Regis Toomey from *Scandal Sheet,* Charles Bickford and Dickie Moore from *Passion Flower,* and Jack Oakie and James Hall from *Let's Go Native.*

Before Bogie, Kenneth, and Helen had interrupted her story, Lombard was amusing these actors by revealing her involvement with Joseph P. Kennedy, "The Bootlegger."

Bogie actually liked dames who talked in the salty language of Lombard. She was said to have picked up such talk from her foul-mouthed brothers and the cowboys she'd worked with in Silents, including Ken Maynard and Buck Jones.

It was obvious that she liked gamy language for shock effect, and that she wanted to provoke Powell. She could dish out expletives in calm, conversational tones, and her closest friends were never shocked. Bogie was certain that her co-star, Clark Gable, liked such talk better than Powell, her husband.

"When I worked for Mack Sennett, I spent more time running from him than I did emoting on camera," Lombard said. "The fucker tried to hook me in with that tired old line of his that he was gonna make me the second Mabel Normand. I told him that I didn't want to be another Mabel Normand. I know Mabel. Not even Mabel wants to be Mabel Normand."

As the waiter walked by, Lombard signaled for another drink. Distracted by

338

the request of another party, Lombard was unintentionally ignored.

"You've had enough, Carole," Powell cautioned.

"Fuck that!" Lombard said, practically spitting fire at him. "The drink's on that singing sensation and tight pussy about town, Jeanette MacDonald herself, and I'm going to get her money's worth." Looking over at Bogie in his tuxedo, she said, "In that monkey suit, you look like a God damn waiter. Bring me another fucking whiskey."

In disgust, Powell walked away, but whispered to Bogie. "Don't you dare bring my wife another drink."

When he'd left, Bogie went to get that whiskey. He figured that Lombard and Powell would soon end up in the divorce court, so he'd have no more control over her.

When Bogie came back with the whiskey, she thanked him and smiled. Apparently, the Lombard story-telling was a little much for the more delicate Helen, who'd wandered off.

Lombard was still continuing with her stories in front of her enraptured audience. "After Sennett Studios folded, I got a role in *The Divine Sinner* and a contract at Pathé for 150 bucks a week. Since I was broke at the time that was big money for me. As you know, Joseph P. Kennedy, or should I call him Mr. Gloria Swanson, was head of the studio. He called me in one day. I'd heard that he likes to fuck actresses like Constance Bennett when he's not pumping his Irish dick into Swanson. When I got there, he didn't even try to seduce me. At first I thought he was going to since he was looking me up and down. Finally, he stared at me and said, 'You're too fat,' I weighed 120 pounds at the time. He really pissed me off. I turned on him even though I knew he could fire me. 'Look who's talking!' I said. 'I bet the only thing skinny about you is your uncut Irish dick.'"

She smiled at Bogie again and seemed grateful that he'd brought her the whiskey in defiance of Powell. He secretly felt that she was gaining a little more respect for him.

"I had to hold onto that $150 a week, so I went to Madame Sylvia's Studio," Lombard said. "As you slim-waisted fairies know, Sylvia is known for her reducing treatments. Would you believe it? My remark to Kennedy must have hit home. One day I encountered him in Madame Sylvia's too. He wanted to get rid of his budge as much as I did mine. Of course, within the week, he was fucking me regularly when not pumping that little meat of his to Constance or Miss Gloria. I must say this for Kennedy. As a fucker, he's all business. He pulls off his clothes, jumps on top of a gal, pumps fast and furious with what little he's got to pump with, then gets off you without a thanks, rushes to the shower, puts back on his business suit, and gets on the phone and starts barking orders. I swear he can accomplish all of this from start to finish in just fifteen fucking minutes. No one fucks like Gary Cooper, though. It takes him fifteen minutes just for the blood to rush to his big dick to get it hard. And he can go all night."

The maid tapped Bogie on the shoulder. "Miss Louella Parsons is here, and she'd like to see you in the library. For an interview."

When Lombard heard that, she called to Bogie, "Miss Piss probably wet her bloomers and wants you to help her mop up."

***

Bogie was ushered into the library where he'd so recently spoken with a distraught Jean Arthur. Seated in a large love seat beside the fireplace, the gossip queen of Hollywood, Louella Parsons, was busy emptying Jeanette MacDonald's secret stash of booze.

With his own drink in hand—he'd lost count of how many he'd had—he introduced himself to Parsons. She said nothing but motioned for him to sit down.

As unbelievable as it seemed at the time, Parsons still considered herself one of Hollywood's "glamour gals," although even then she was well on her way toward becoming the hag of Tinseltown.

She had removed a notebook from her purse into which she scribbled some information—probably misinformation—that had gotten trapped in her soggy brain. After that, she reached for her compact and smeared on an extra heavy application of blood-red lipstick, even more of a five-alarm fire tube than Clara Bow wore.

"Bogart," she said, finally staring at him with those steely eyes that had seen too much. "I've been meaning to interview you but have been too busy. With every guy on Broadway getting off the train daily, how can I possibly interview every out-of-work actor who hits town trying to make a buck in Hollywood?"

"You've got a point there, pal," he said, reaching for his drink which he'd placed on a coffee table.

"Even when I interview somebody, all I hear is their lies," she said.

"Maybe that's because the real and the illusional in Hollywood are inextricable," he said.

"God damn," she said harshly. "An intellectual. If there's one kind of actor I positively hate, it's an intellectual."

"That I'm not," he said. "You can print in your column that I was kicked out of Andover. Not only for poor grades, but for being a bad boy."

"That's it!" she said. She motioned to a whiskey bottle left on a table beside the French doors. "Pour me some of that and don't be stingy, baby. I'm misquoting a line from that Garbo flick, *Anna Christie.*"

"Yeah, I got that." He also got up to get her that whiskey and to replenish his own supply. When he gave her the drink, he asked, "What did you mean by, 'That's it!'"

"I need a peg to hang a label onto you," she said. "A college dropout. I bet that as the bad boy of Andover, you got into a lot of trouble with girls. Yeah, that's it. I'm gonna call you the bad boy of Hollywood."

"Seems like I have a lot of competition for that title," he said. "George Raft, for instance."

"Hell with him," she said. "He's nothing but a New York gangster. If he gets to play gangsters in movies, it'll be type-casting." Slugging down a hefty swig of that bootleg whiskey, she gave him her eagle eye once again. "I've got to ask you something right off the bat. That lisp of yours. It bothers me. I know you're married, but are you a fairy like William Haines? Forgive me, but I have to ask. All the butterflies from Broadway are descending on us out here. It's very hard to make fairies sound manly in my column. Just how many more times do I have to write that Ramon Novarro is still waiting for the right gal?"

They both chuckled at that, and he felt that he'd broken through to her. "I'm strictly a man for the ladies. I find myself having to keep repeating that. But I don't expect you to take my word for that. I'm here with Helen Menken tonight. Otherwise, I'd show you what a man I am."

"Yes, I've met your wife. Helen Menken. I've seen her on the stage in New York. Charming woman."

He meant to correct her and say "ex-wife," but he just assumed that the custodian of all gossip in Hollywood was well aware that he'd married Mary Philips. Considering the shaky status of his marriage to Mary, he didn't plan to mention her in the interview.

"What were you saying?" she asked. "About my not taking your word for it. If I can't take your word for it, exactly how do you plan to prove it?"

"I didn't think we'd progress this far so soon into the interview, but I do find you very attractive," he said. "If you have any doubts about my manhood, I'd like to demonstrate otherwise. What I'm saying is you can put me to the test anytime."

She smiled. "You find me attractive, do you? My God, I'm just a working newspaperwoman trying to make a living in journalism. Hearst doesn't pay me enough. I find myself having to fight off half the wolves in Hollywood."

"I didn't mean to insult you," he said. "But you are one good-looking woman. What can I say? In spite of my lisp, I like glamorous women."

"We'll see about that," she said, studying him carefully with a greatly renewed interest. "I've heard a lot of stories about you since you hit town."

"I bet at least one of them is true," he said smiling.

Her face looked puzzled. It was as if she weren't communicating on the same level with him. "I seek the truth but I'm surrounded by lies. People talk lies. They live lies, and with good reason. If the real truth were known about half the stars in Hollywood, the American public would stay away from their pictures in droves."

"When we have our interview, I'm going to give it to you straight," he said.

"I shouldn't but for some reason I believe you," she said. "I'm talking about the other people at this party. The intention of everything at this party is part of an attempt to deceive the public. We're supposed to be celebrating the upcoming marriage of Kay Francis to Kenneth MacKenna. First off, she's a dyke just breaking up after an affair with Jean Arthur. The reason I thought you might be a fairy is because you hang out with MacKenna. He's sucked off half the guys in Hollywood. I understand he even molested that dear boy, Doug Jr. If Doug Sr. finds out what MacKenna did to his son, he'll personally take his sword and challenge him to a duel."

"I'm sure those are just rumors," he said. "I've known Kenneth for a long time. We go back to New York. If I recall, when we toured the speakeasies we used to chase after the same women. He's one-hundred percent heterosexual. Take my word for it."

"Don't bullshit me," she said. "You don't look naïve. You know perfectly well what's going on. I'm tired of searching for the truth. Lilyan Tashman drapes a large blue cupid's bow around her ivory grand piano yet pretends to be the epitome of chic in Hollywood. Pola Negri tells me that Valentino was prodigiously endowed like Chaplin. Yet his leading lady, Nita Naldi, slept with him and told me that America's great lover was..." She paused. "How can I put this?" She held up her pinkie to indicate the measure of the man.

"I know you're lied to every day," he said. "That's why in my case I think a demonstration is in order." Even as he said that, he knew that he should keep his mouth shut. Still, he rambled on. "I can tell you I'm not a faggot. But how can you ever be sure? You'll write thousands of words about me in your column as my career moves along. But in the back of your brain, you'll always be asking if that lisping New York actor was just putting one over on you."

She reached for her notepad again. "Give me your private phone number in case I want to get in touch with you." As he told her the number, she wrote it down in her drunken scrawl.

He felt that he'd carried his flirtatious joking with her far enough and was eager to drop the subject. He was certain that she wouldn't remember his offer the next morning as she nursed her hangover. Even if she did, he knew that she'd never take him up on it.

"I meant to write you a note and thank you for that good review you gave Spence and me in *Up The River*. Mainly Spence, of course. I even carry it around in my wallet along with a review that Alexander Woollcott wrote of my Broadway appearance in *Swifty*. He wrote, 'The young man who embodies the aforesaid sprig is what is usually and mercifully described as inadequate.'"

"Hell with that drunken Woollcott," she said. "What did I write?"

He found her review tucked between some ten-dollar bills in his wallet. He read her own words to her. "Humphrey Bogart, talented New York juvenile, plays the part of Steve straight and does it very well."

"That was very nice of me," she said. "Actually I was very kind to you and Tracy. Frankly, I can skip prison dramas. They're too grim for my taste. America is in the middle of a Depression. We need movies with glamorous women in glamorous settings doing rich, glamorous things. Americans should be treated to a fantasy when they go to the movies. It'll take their minds off their troubles, their empty refrigerators, and all those mortgage foreclosures."

He carefully put the clipping away. "About that juvenile remark."

"What about it?" she asked imperiously, almost defying him to challenge her copy.

"It's the juvenile thing," he said. "I'm trying to get away from that. On Christmas Day, I'm gonna be thirty-one years old. I've played all those 'Tennis, anyone?' roles on Broadway. Out here I'm trying for more adult parts."

"I didn't know you were thirty-one," she said. "You don't look it on the screen. I thought you were much younger. That Helen Menken has literally robbed the cradle. She must be in her late forties or early fifties if she's a day. Women can't lie to me about their age. I can just look at a woman, no matter how much makeup she has on, and tell her exact age."

"And as for men?" he asked.

"They can fool me," she said. She gave him the look of a boa constrictor about to devour a young chicken for its supper. "Now that I know your exact age, I must say I'll have to reconsider that very romantic offer you made me. I have an absolute rule. I never go to bed with a man in his twenties. A lot of young actors proposition me because they think they'll advance their careers by sleeping with me. I've already slept with Clark Gable. With the pick of all the beauties in Hollywood, he went to bed with me. He also went to bed with that bitch, Adela Rogers St. Johns. She's my rival, you know. She thinks she knows so much about Hollywood. I've forgotten more than she'll ever know."

"I heard that Gable was born in 1901," he said. "Did he turn thirty before you guys bedded down?"

"I know I said a man has to be thirty. In Clark's case, I made an exception. In many ways, I wish I hadn't slept with Clark. Now my illusion about him is spoiled."

"I hope I don't disappoint," he said, teasing her.

"I have a feeling you can deliver," she said. "Sometimes one of us glamour gals can only laugh when these He-men take off their trousers. But I've discovered that some of you guys who look like a runt are surprisingly pleasing when you let it all hang out."

She downed the rest of her whiskey and motioned to him that she wanted a refill. "Now let's get down to this God damn interview. I know you're physically attracted to me, but that doesn't mean that I'm going to let you off easy. I don't feel like a candy-ass tonight, believe you me."

At this point Jeanette MacDonald's maid walked into the library and told Bogie that Howard Hughes wanted to speak to him on the phone.

An announcement of a new war with Germany would not have sparked such interest on the face of Parsons. The question she was obviously asking her pickled brain was why would a tycoon like Howard Hughes be phoning a failed actor like Bogie.

Before getting up to answer the phone, he looked once more into that face, the memory of which would stay with him forever.

Like a blood-thirsty hound on the trail of a helpless fox, this woman could smell news before it even happened.

Chapter Eleven

After his chat with Howard Hughes, Bogie was in a quandary. He had to excuse himself gracefully from Louella Parsons, and somehow manage to extricate Billie Dove from the party without arousing suspicion. God knows what he was going to say to Helen, who'd been planning to seduce him after the party in her bungalow at the Garden of Allah.

Hughes had instructed that Dove should be "removed" from the party at once. The tycoon had received word that the much-feared film director, Irvin Willat, Dove's former husband, was heading for MacDonald's party. Bogie was all too familiar with the legend of this tyrannical director, known for flying into fits of violent rage both on and off a movie set.

Apparently, in front of Louella Parsons and witnessed by *le tout* Hollywood, Willat planned to publicly confront Dove about her affair with Hughes and embarrass her. Hughes claimed that Willat was demanding money, and that the upcoming party confrontation was just one of several threats he was making to up the ante. Bogie agreed to escort Dove out of the house before Willat got there. As long as Hughes held the negatives of those nude pictures of Bogie, he was eager to obey.

Willat competed with Otto Preminger in out von-Stroheiming Erich von Stroheim himself as a forbidding public image. Willat was the Hollywood director you loved to hate. He also competed with Otto Preminger for the title of Hollywood's most bull-headed, thick-necked monster. Bogie had never understood why Dove had married Willat in the first place when she could have her pick of any man in Hollywood.

Bogie didn't understand why Willat was coming after Dove again. From what Bogie had heard, the details of Willat's divorce from Dove had already been settled. Amid the ruins of their marriage, Bogart wondered what was left for them to fight over.

Despite his low rank on the Hollywood pecking order, Bogie resented being anybody's errand boy. He'd already played errand boy for both Spencer Tracy and George Raft, but in those instances, he'd done so out of friendship. With Hughes, he was being forced, through blackmail, into the role of an unpaid lackey.

When Bogie went back into the library to say goodbye to Louella Parsons, she was pouring herself yet another drink. "That phone call from Howard was about Billie Dove, wasn't it?"

"I think her name might have come up," he said, hoping to avoid any revelations about Hughes.

"I don't know why Howard is being so secretive," she said. "He's divorced from Ella. Willat is divorced from Billie." Once again, with her drink in her hand, she turned her eagle eye on him. "There's something else, isn't it? Howard is not just covering up a romance with Dove. You know what I think? I think that son-of- a-bitch, Willat, has something on Hughes. I heard rumors that Hughes paid the shithead half-a-million dollars. Willat is blackmailing him for more. I can't prove it but I've got my hunches."

"I don't know anything about that," he said. "But I'll come clean with you. I've got to hustle Dove out of this party before Willat gets here. There could be an ugly scene."

She reached for his arm. "Then escort me back into the party, and tell Howard I'm writing nothing about him for the moment. That doesn't mean I won't. I've got him under close observation." Before leaving the library, she kissed him on the mouth. Her brewery breath was foul. "I'm flattered by your offer."

He had hoped that she'd forgotten it.

"We never got our interview," she said. "I'll call you next week." She looked up lovingly into his eyes. "I'm sure we'll have a fine old time when we get together again."

With Parsons on his arm, he came back into the main living room and shuddered at the prospect of facing her again, especially if they were alone.

His plan to rescue Dove before Willat arrived was too late. The angry director was already here. Lombard was still seated and encircled by her admiring actors, and Dove was standing near MacDonald's piano with William Powell.

Willat was shouting at her. "You stupid little slut!" he yelled. "You think Hughes is going to marry you. Bullshit! He's going to marry that tramp." He pointed at Lombard who remained serenely seated. Unusual for her, she said nothing.

"That's a lie!" Dove yelled at him. "You're just trying to hurt me."

"When he's not with you, he's sleeping with that horny bitch," Willat said in a voice so loud the entire room could hear him. All conversation had stopped.

"Carole is already married to Bill here," Dove said, looking Powell in the face.

Bogie was surprised that the actor had made no move against Willat, even though the director had called his wife a slut and a horny bitch.

"He's told her to divorce Powell here so they can get married," Willat said, raising his voice as if he deliberately wanted everyone to hear him, even those in the far corners of the room.

Jeanette MacDonald, accompanied by Bob Ritchie, came into the room to see what the disturbance was about.

"Get out of my house!" MacDonald shouted at Willat.

Just as Ritchie moved menacingly across the living room toward Willat, the director reached out and slapped Dove so hard she fell to the floor.

Both Powell and the actor, Charles Bickford, grabbed the drunken Willat to restrain him.

346

Bogie rushed to Dove's side to rescue her. "You okay?" he asked.

She was rubbing her face and crying.

He whispered in her ear. "I've just talked to Howard. He wants me to take you to his place at once."

With his arm protectively around Dove, he led her through the gaping party-goers. He had no idea if Helen were in the room witnessing everything. He could only imagine what she might think seeing him escorting Dove from the party.

Before reaching the foyer, his final glimpse was of Parsons. He could only imagine how this gossip maven would describe this party in her column.

Like the news-sharpened journalist she was, Parsons headlined MacDonald's party. She would write, "Instead of the peace dove, the menace of a constant beating from her former husband, Irvin Willat, hovers over the head of pretty little Billie Dove. At Jeanette MacDonald's party last night for soon-to-be married star, Kay Francis, and minor Broadway actor, Kenneth MacKenna, Willat stormed in unannounced and knocked his former wife down flat on the floor."

Bogie was grateful that Parsons hadn't written that he was seen leaving the party with Billie Dove.

But he did see his name in boldface at the bottom of her column. Parsons wrote, "At the party, I encountered that handsome juvenile actor from Broadway, Humphrey Bogart. This rising star at Fox is even better looking in person than he is on the screen. Sorry, gals. He's already taken. Also, at the party was his much older wife, Helen Menken, the Broadway actress. Speculation in Tinseltown is that Menken is here trying to crash the gates that guard the studios. There must be at least five-thousand other actresses from Broadway, and a lot younger than Menken, trying to perform the same stunt. Good luck to her in what looks like an uphill battle for movie stardom."

That column would appear in the early morning hours after the night of the party. But before that could happen, his job was to deliver Billie Dove in one piece to the Muirfield Mansion of Howard Hughes. He'd get her there but she'd be a little battered. He hadn't reached Dove in time to save her from Willat's mauling. He could only hope that Hughes was in a forgiving mood.

***

On the way to Hughes' mansion, a shaken Billie Dove let Bogie in on a closely guarded secret. "Unknown to me at the time, when Howard and I started seeing each other, Irvin hired two detectives to have me followed day and night. The only thing he uncovered about me was that I was having an affair. Through those detectives, Irvin learned some very private details about Hughes' personal life. I'm not sure what, but Howard is very worried. Irvin is making more blackmail threats. We're in deep shit."

"Please don't use that word," he cautioned her. "Wouldn't it be safer for Hughes to buy Willat off? I mean, Hughes has all the money in the world."

"You don't understand," she said. "Before Irvin granted me a divorce, Howard had to pay him $350,000 in one-hundred dollar bills. Originally he'd demanded half a million but he eventually settled for the lesser amount. We thought we had him out of our hair for good. Now he's blackmailing us again."

"It sounds like Willat will never be satisfied as long as he's got a cash cow like Hughes," he said. "Or should I have said bull in Hughes' case?"

She reached into her purse and pulled out a package of cigarettes, offering him one. It was as if she were seriously pondering his question. "In Howard's case, cash cow would be just fine."

He would always remember what an enigmatic statement that was, and he wanted to ask her more, but she remained silent and reflective, as if she'd already revealed enough.

He wondered if all the rumors about Hughes were true? Was the tall Texan and rumored seducer of half the beauties in Hollywood more like a cow than a bull? Did either Gary Cooper or Randolph Scott fuck him up the ass? Were they the bull to Hughes' cow?

Since Hughes was tormenting Bogie and forcing him to do his bidding, Bogie was relieved that this latest bit of information, vague though it was, gave him some power over the man who was emasculating him. If the delivery of George O'Brien to Hughes on Saturday came off successfully, Bogie planned to ask some serious questions when O'Brien returned to the set of *A Holy Terror* Monday morning.

At the Hughes mansion, a black male servant ushered Bogie into the palatial, antique-filled living room. Dove retreated to an upstairs bedroom to make emergency repairs to her face after the mauling by her former husband.

Seeing a telephone, he called Jeanette MacDonald's house. That same black maid informed him that Helen had left the party. "That white lady sure didn't seem too friendly when she left."

Figuring a taxi would have had time to deliver her to the Garden of Allah, he dialed her number there. He didn't know how long Hughes would keep him here, but he wanted her permission to climb into her warm bed as soon as he was released.

Helen was home all right and furious. "I've never been so humiliated in all my life. Right in front of everybody who's important in Hollywood. You were *my* escort. You walked out the door with the one actress considered not only the most beautiful woman in Hollywood, but the most beautiful woman in the world. How do you think that made me feel? Every important director and producer there was making an odious comparison between my looks and age and that of Miss Billie Dove. Thanks to you, I'll probably never get a job in Hollywood in any film. Perhaps a maid's part." She slammed down the phone.

He called back right away, but she didn't answer the phone. It was just like old times when they were married in New York. If he remembered, and he did, she slammed down the phone a lot on him in those days. He knew that she was out for the night unless he went over there and broke down her bungalow door. She'd probably call the police on him, and they'd end up not only in Parsons' column but on the front page.

As he was pouring himself a drink at the bar, Hughes came into the room, followed by three men. Having so recently been with the homosexual actor, William Haines, at The Fat Black Pussycat, Bogie recognized the actor at once. He reached out to shake his hand. "How's it hanging, pal?"

"Swinging low," Haines wisecracked. "You've got to let me top you some night."

"It's a date," Bogie said jokingly. "I'll pre-lube before coming over." He was mildly surprised that this flamboyant actor was so overtly homosexual in front of Hughes and two fellow actors.

As Hughes made the introductions to Ben Lyon and Randolph Scott, Bogie told both actors that he'd seen their movies.

Bogie congratulated Lyon on his role as one of the stars of *Hell's Angels*. In the film, Bogie had remembered Lyon as handsomer and sexier than his co-star, James Hall. "I think that moment when Harlow wearing that flimsy evening gown comes up to you and asks, 'Would you be shocked if I put on something more comfortable?' has to rank as one of the grandest scenes ever put on film."

The other actor, Randolph Scott, was called to the phone and politely excused himself. Hughes walked into an alcove where he placed a mysterious call on a second phone. Haines excused himself with a wink and went upstairs "for a serious business talk with Billie."

That left Bogie standing alone with the congenial B-list actor, Ben Lyon. Directors considered him "good-looking and reliable," but regrettably, he'd never become the star that Valentino, Cagney, or Gable would. Reviewers considered him too "boyishly cute" to be either a leading man or a gangster, and unlike Bogie, juvenile parts eluded him as well, as he was too tall, well-built, and athletic.

Bogie didn't admire Lyon's screen career as much as he did his reputation with women. Lyon was said to have seduced some of the legendary names of stage and screen, including Jeanne Eagels, Pola Negri, Gloria Swanson, and Eleanor Boardman. He was also said to have been intimate with Barbara LaMarr, Blanche Sweet, and Mary Astor. Bogie had even heard a rumor that when Claudette Colbert appeared with Lyon in her only silent film, *For the Love of Mike* in 1927, he'd seduced her too, even though she was rumored to be a dyke.

At the time Bogie met him, Lyon was married to Bebe Daniels, who'd first appeared on the stage at the age of four in *Richard III* and had been a Harold Lloyd leading lady, at the tender age of only thirteen, in the *Lonesome Luke* comedies. She'd starred in Cecil B. DeMille's *Male and Female* in 1919 and his *Why Change Your Wife?* in 1920. Ironically, at the time Bogie met Lyon, Daniels was filming *The Maltese Falcon*, which ten years later in its remake would become one of Bogie's all-time best remembered movies. Daniels is known today for her 1933 version of *42nd Street*, where she played Dorothy Brock, the tempestuous stage star whose last-minute sprained ankle gives her understudy, as played by Rudy Keeler, her big break.

"I saw your wife in *She's a Sheik* and *Feel My Pulse*," Bogie said. "She's terrific."

"Thanks," Lyon said. "Right now *Rio Rita* is revitalizing her career. I'll pass along your compliment—that is, if I ever see her again. The bitch and I are feuding. I'm staying here with Howard."

"When you guys make up, do give her my regards," Bogie said. "With her beautiful singing voice, she had no problem going from Silents to Talkies."

"No problem at all," he said. "Her second cousin, Lee De Forest, is the father of sound. He frequented the set of *Rio Rita* while she rehearsed, and gave her a lot of coaching. No one is better at improving sound quality than Lee. He could even make John Gilbert sound good. John should have gone to Lee before making an ass out of himself. Lee could even get rid of your lisp."

"Thanks, pal," Bogie said. Lyon's final comment had angered him. Yet he admired the actor at the same time.

Bogie was learning more and more Hollywood secrets. Whereas fan magazines referred to Edmund Lowe and Lilyan Tashman as Hollywood's most idyllic romance, Ben Lyon and Bebe Daniels were known as "Hollywood's Happiest Couple." But despite those associations, Kenneth MacKenna had whispered of some of Lyon's homosexual liaisons, especially with Richard Barthelmess and William Haines. Lyon had been seen once or twice at Richard Arlen's all-male and all-nude swim parties. Bogie figured that Lyon was a man about town, swinging on both sides of the fence. There were even rumors about Lyon and Billie Dove, based on their making of *The Tender Hour* together in 1927.

After they poured themselves another drink, Lyon invited Bogie out onto Hughes' terrace to sample the night air, where Bogie brought up the subject of *Hell's Angels*.

"You sure became known to the world in that *Hell's Angels*. And it sure launched Harlow as a star, too. "

"Yeah, right!" he said sarcastically. "Harlow, Gary Cooper, but mostly the aerial combat scenes got all the attention. I went virtually unnoticed. In many ways, *Hell's Angels* fucked up my life."

"I don't get it, pal," Bogie said. "A big picture like that. I would have loved to have played your part."

"I'm not talking about the picture," Lyon said. "When I started the flick, I was getting plenty of ass from Billie Dove, and from Harlow, Eleanor Boardman, and a lot of others any time I wanted it. But I really cherished my role as Howard's number one boy. That meant more to me than all the pussies in Hollywood. Let's face it: Howard's the richest man in America, and he found my dick the best. That is, until he met Gary Cooper. Howard fell for Cooper in a big way. Howard and I haven't had sex for months. He's still getting fucked by Cooper."

"How does that hot-assed Virginian, Randolph Scott, fit into the picture?"

350

"He's fucking Howard too," Lyon said. "On some nights he wants Cooper. On other nights Scott. He's already been fucked once by Scott tonight. For all I know, Howard will fuck Billie before the rooster crows. Then he might even suck off Billy Haines. One thing's for sure. Howard doesn't want me any more."

"If that's the case, why in hell are you here tonight? And why is Billie Dove at this all-male bash?"

"Howard likes to show off his power by juggling his boys and his women," Lyon said. "He makes promises to all of us. Claims he plans to rescue my career with a big role in his latest film."

"I wish he could rescue my career at Fox," Bogie said. "I'm going down the tubes faster than you."

"If Howard takes a fancy to you, he can work miracles," Lyon said. "That is, if he likes you. You're not his type, though. He goes for cowboys, garage mechanics, pilots." Lyons looked at Bogie with a sharp-eyed appraisal. "I could be wrong, but tell me, are you his latest boy?"

"I'm no one's boy," Bogie snapped at him before his anger cooled in the night air. "On second thought, I'm his errand boy."

"That means Howard has got something on you, and he's making you jump rope."

"I'll skip the details but you've got that right," Bogie said.

Lyon reached out and touched his arm, squeezing it hard. "I'm really desperate. If you've got any influence with Howard, I want you to help me."

"Believe me, I've got no influence with that Texan. I'm from New York and Texans hate New Yorkers. But, just for curiosity's sake, what do you want me to do?"

"When you're alone with him, I want you to try to set Howard straight about this Randolph Scott. Howard's fallen for him, and this Virginia cowpoke is no more than a hustler. He's got nothing but money on the brain. His eyes are like a cash register. He's just fucking Howard either to get money or to get a big break. There's no love there."

"Women in Hollywood have fucked men for years to get money or a big break. I believe in equal opportunity. Why can't a man pull the same stunt a woman does?"

"You don't understand," Lyon said. "I'm in love with Howard. I've got to break them up."

"That would still leave Cooper," Bogie said.

"I'm working on that," Lyon said. "Joel McCrea is really coming between Cooper and Howard, so I have Joel on my side."

"That still leaves the ladies," Bogie warned him. "Carole Lombard. And Miss Billie Dove upstairs in the boudoir thinks Howard is going to marry her now that they're both divorced."

"He'll never marry Dove," Lyon accurately predicted. "He's just using her. He's mostly impotent with women. He goes with them just for show. Howard was never impotent with me. Hard as a rock. Couldn't get enough. Sometimes he just likes to get fucked by a handsome, young man. But he's topped me more times than I can remember."

"Good to know that, pal," Bogie said, slightly dismissive of the lovesick Lyon. "That will come in handy if I ever get around to writing his biography."

Randolph Scott chose that moment to come out onto the terrace.

"Since Howard's taking forever on the phone, may I join you guys for some fresh air too?"

"Welcome," Bogie said.

Lyon took one look at Scott and retreated back into the living room.

***

With the night breezes intensifying, Bogie stood alone on Hughes' terrace, facing a six-foot, four-inch, strapping Virginian with a country handsomeness, definitely not a pretty boy.

"I hear you're the new Tom Mix," Bogie said. "I ride a bit myself but I'm more of an urban cowboy. I like to live in a place where, if the mood strikes, you can buy a singing canary at three o'clock in the morning." Bogie would say that line several times in his life until it fell on the ears of a future friend, Truman Capote, who not only heard it, but recorded it, making it his own.

"I'd much rather be Gary Cooper," Scott said. "Better to kiss a gal than a hoss."

"I might agree with you if I'd ever kissed a horse before."

"If it'll be your first time, you're in for a treat," Scott said. "Pucker wide, though."

As the two men sat on the terrace smoking and drinking, he found Scott relaxed, rather genuine, and seemingly sincere, not at all a conniving hustler as portrayed by Ben Lyon.

"I hear you've been working with two pals of mine, Victor McLaughlin and Myrna Loy," Scott said.

"I know both of them," Bogie said. "Victor is crazy, and Loy wouldn't be anything without that nose."

"It's pretty cute but Coop's got her beat," Scott claimed.

"Why, did you work with him too?"

"I was unbilled in *The Virginian*. That's where I met Richard Arlen. We became great friends."

Bogie wondered if Scott were one of the actors attending Arlen's all-male, all-nude swim fests. "I saw *The Virginian*," Bogie said, "But I don't remember you. I thought Walter Huston stole the picture. Great guy."

"You're wrong about that," Scott said. "When Gary Cooper's on the screen, no actor or actress steals the picture from him. What a beauty! I wish I looked like him instead of this country cowboy face I got stuck with."

"You're not so bad," Bogie said. "Don't get me wrong, pal. I'm not coming on to you."

"I was hired to teach Coop diction," Scott said. He'd been drinking heavily, or perhaps he wouldn't have made the next remark in front of a stranger. "I not only taught him how to sound his vowels but how to put those pretty red lips of his to other use."

Both men laughed, as Bogie offered him one of his interminable cigarettes.

"My mistake came when I appeared in *Dynamite* for Cecil B. DeMille," Scott said. "This really good-looking guy—and my future screen competitor—Joel McCrea, was in the film too in a featured part. One day when Coop came by the set, I foolishly introduced him to Joel. The rest is history. Out with Randolph, in with the new kid on the block, Mr. Joel McCrea. I don't blame Coop really. Joel's one of the great beauties of Hollywood."

"Billie Dove's not bad either," Bogie said, trying to steer the conversation onto a more heterosexual highway. "In fact, I've read that she's considered the most beautiful gal in the world. Hughes seems to think so."

"Bullshit!" Scott said, his speech too slurred to teach anybody proper English, much less Gary Cooper. "Howard insists on dating the most beautiful women in Hollywood. But believe me, it's all for show."

"Billie looks like she could do a lot for a man," Bogie said in her defense. "She could for me."

"She can't give Howard what he really needs," Scott said.

"And what might that be?" Bogie asked.

"Nine thick inches up the ass."

At that point, William Haines appeared on the terrace. "I thought I'd find you gals out here in *flagrante delicto*. Howard wants to see all of us drunken pussies in his library." With drink in hand, Haines performed a wiggle and shake that would challenge the skills of fan dancer, Sally Rand. "Showtime for Howard."

With some trepidation, Bogie rose from his seat. "I hope that doesn't mean we have to show it hard."

"Oh, how you city boys talk," Scott said facetiously. "Real dirty like I like it." He trailed Bogie across the terrace and into the living room, following Haines who continued to lead the chorus line, getting in a few high kicks before he finally made it to the dark, wood-paneled library where only a dim light glowed.

Hughes and Ben Lyon were already there, sitting across from each other on leather sofas. The tension in the air between them could almost be felt.

When Hughes saw the three men enter the library, he motioned rather imperially for all of them to be seated. Ignoring the rest of the men, he looked at Bogie directly. "Ben here doesn't believe in going peacefully into the good night," Hughes said. "He just can't play my game like Billy or Randy here can. They know I bore quickly. Sometimes I take off with someone—maybe one of my pilots—and it lasts only for a weekend. But I never leave a guy empty-handed. That same pilot next week might find himself with a gift of a small plane. I once took a grease monkey to Las Vegas with me. The next week he ended up owning the garage where he'd been pumping gas before."

"I don't like to get dumped," Lyon protested. He looked over at Hughes. "Haven't you ever heard of falling in love with somebody?"

"Since I've never been in love, I guess not," Hughes said. "We didn't come here tonight to talk about love. We came to talk about a film I'm going to make that will rip this town apart." He glanced over at Haines, who smiled at him and blew him a kiss. "You tell them, Billy boy."

"Right on, sugar," Haines said. "First, you gals aren't gonna believe the title of this flicker. It's called *Queer People*."

***

Since moving to Hollywood, Bogie wasn't easily shocked any more. But the scenario for *Queer People* seemed like such a searing exposé of Hollywood that Bogie doubted if it could ever be filmed. He also knew that if *Queer People*, reached the screen, it would take a maverick like Hughes to film it. Even if filmed, Bogie suspected that some theaters, especially those operated by the major studios, wouldn't play it.

He'd never read the novel but had meant to. Written by two brothers, Carroll and Garrett Graham, it was a seething indictment of Hollywood. Bogie didn't know anything about the backgrounds of the Graham duo, but he knew that they obviously had a grudge against the movie business.

Haines had been promised the lead role, that of a newspaper reporter named "Whitey." The story unfolds through his eyes. As a means of communicating the plotline of the film, Haines began to act out a tale that Hughes later referred to as "a bitter satire." Hughes told the men that Ben Hecht, whom he had hired as screenwriter, had already written five different versions of the screenplay. They would be hearing the film's latest version, although Bogie was convinced that before *Queer People* went before the cameras, other versions would follow.

Even so, Hughes' instincts—and money—were right on target. If you needed a film scenario written, Ben Hecht, screenwriter, director, playwright, and novelist, was the man to turn to. Not only was he the most prolific writer in Hollywood, he was one of the most accomplished, even though he was constantly quoted as "hating Hollywood." What better writer to indict Tinseltown than a man who hated it? Cynical about Hollywood, Hecht loudly proclaimed to anyone who listened that he wrote screen plays for one reason only, the "easy money."

When his friend and fellow writer, Herman Mankiewicz, sent him a telegram in New York, telling him that "your only competitors in Hollywood are idiots," Hecht boarded the train west. Once there, Josef von Sternberg hired him to write his classic gangster story, *Underworld*, in 1927, and Hecht went on to win the very first Academy Award presentation for a screenplay. He'd been familiar to Bogie in New York when he was collaborating with Charles MacArthur (the hus-

354

band of Helen Hayes) on the semi-autobiographical stage comedy, *The Front Page*.

In time, Hughes would use him once again to work on the script for his most controversial film, *The Outlaw*, that brought world attention to Jane Russell and "the two reasons you must see this picture."

As Haines continued acting out the scenario, Bogie realized that Hughes had ordered Hecht to create scenes and characters that never appeared in the original novel by the Graham brothers. Many of the characters were clearly rip-offs of real people in Hollywood. Even a fool would know that the movie producer depicted in the script was the actual Louis B. Mayer. The way Hecht had written it, the script was blatantly anti-Semitic.

When Haines stopped to pour himself another drink, Bogie said, "Let's face it: When us heterosexual Anglo-Saxon and WASP guys get together in private, we sometimes attack Jews and faggots. Everybody does that. But that's something to be spoken about only in private. Not splashed like political propaganda across the screen."

Hughes said nothing, but Scott endorsed the anti-Semitism of the role with vigor. "It's about time one of us stood up and revealed how the Jews are taking over Hollywood and destroying it. Right now Jews like Mayer have all of us frightened out of our underwear. If anybody has got the balls to do it, you're the guy, Howard. I'm all for you letting it rip."

This was the same Randolph Scott who one day would seek membership in The Los Angeles Country Club, which at the time banned Jews. The men who formed the club were so archly conservative that they wouldn't even let actors join, turning down membership requests from such stars as Bing Crosby and Bob Hope. The only way Scott got in was to put "oil investor" on his application papers instead of actor.

Hughes did not respond to Scott's comments. Instead he turned to Bogie. "I was thinking of asking Fox to lend me your friend, Spencer Tracy, for the part of Louis B. Mayer. I think he'd be perfect. I don't want an obvious Jew in the role."

The moment Hughes said that, the image of Tracy playing the young movie mogul flashed through Bogie's brain. "If anybody in Hollywood could play a mean Jew, it would be a good Catholic like Spence," Bogie said.

The male and female interest in the picture would center around a couple that Hughes had ordered Hecht to write into the script. To Bogie, the male/female roles seemed like a *roman à clef* based loosely on the lavender marriages of Rod La Rocque and Vilma Banky or Edmund Lowe and Lilyan Tashman.

Throughout the meeting, Hughes had continually glanced toward the staircase. Billie Dove had never come down after she'd retreated upstairs following her mauling from Irvin Willat. "I'm thinking of casting Billie in the role of the female star and getting Ramon Novarro to play her husband," Hughes said.

"An ideal duo," Bogie said. "If anyone could be convincing as a homosexual husband, it's Novarro."

"What about me, darling," Haines chimed in.

"You, too, sugar," Bogie said mockingly. "But somehow I can't see Billie Dove as a dyke."

Hughes stared very harshly at him. "Can you see Lilyan Tashman as a dyke? How about Marlene Dietrich? Garbo? Do these women come off as dykes on the screen?"

"I see your point," Bogie said, retreating from his position. "Marie Dressler. Now that's a woman who comes off as a dyke on the screen."

Hughes smiled at Haines before looking over at Ben Lyon. "And now for the role of the Hollywood agent. It'll be Ben's best role to date." He paused as if his mind were drifting back to something in the past. "I owe Ben a big favor. This role will be the greatest movie agent part in history, now and forever more."

When Haines had outlined his role, Lyon seemed pleased, his earlier hostility toward Hughes having diminished a bit.

"And now for you, Bogart," Hughes said.

"You're not thinking of casting me in this flick, are you?" Bogie asked. He was dumbfounded.

"You got any other hot properties lined up?" Hughes said mockingly.

As Haines outlined Bogie's potential part, he was mesmerized. This role was clearly based on the columnist, Walter Winchell. Bogie would play a brash, cynical, lying, manipulative, skirt-chasing, right-wing patriot, very similar to Winchell himself.

Suddenly, anti-Semitic or not, Bogie wanted the cameras to roll on *Queer People*. Instinctively he knew that this would be the part of his lifetime. He'd never been thought of for such a meaty role. No more "Tennis, anyone?" juveniles.

"I happen to have a copy of a letter that Winchell sent to the Los Angeles police chief," Hughes said. "It's about you and George Raft. He warns the chief about what gangsters you guys are. In Raft's case, that's true. I'll never forgive the son-of-a-bitch for moving in on Billie. In your case, I think Winchell smeared you. If you play this role, you'll have your chance to pay him back."

"Sign me up right away," Bogie said. "I could eat up the screen playing Winchell."

A male servant came in and summoned Hughes to the phone. The producer excused himself and left.

Ben Lyon looked over at Randolph Scott. "It seems everybody has a role in this picture except you." Lyon seemed more than a little pleased that Scott had been left out of the cast.

"Not so fast," Scott said. "One of the reasons I'm visiting Howard is to discuss a possible role for me. We've got to have some plot here. Howard and Hecht are considering making me the hero of the picture. I'll play a handsome young cowboy, a sort of Gary Cooper type. I arrive in Hollywood and become involved with the Billie Dove character. Eventually I persuade her to give up her tawdry and cynical life, divorce the Novarro creep, and ride off into the sunset with me."

"Why not a ride off into the sunset with me?" Haines piped in. "I can throw you a better fuck than Billie Dove."

"You think you'll get the gal at the end of the picture?" Lyon said sarcastically. "How romantic. But Hecht is too cynical to fall for such a cheap cop-out."

"Don't worry, old boy," Scott said to Lyon, ignoring Haines. "You'll play the agent who discovers me in the film and turns me into the biggest sensation ever seen in Hollywood. In other words, I'll become your meal ticket for life."

At that point a stern-faced Hughes came back into the library. "Ben," he called, "would you step outside? There's trouble. I've got to talk to you."

From the foyer, Bogie heard Lyon arguing with Hughes. Haines tried to divert attention from the fight by entertaining Scott, Lyon, and Bogie, with the latest scandals about Clark Gable. Bogie wasn't really interested. Ever the curious one, he wanted to know what emergency had driven Hughes and Lyon from the room.

As if in answer to his wish, Lyon came back into the library. He looked furious, as he approached Bogie. "Howard wants to see you. At once!"

"When Howard calls, I obey," Bogie said, feeling like a servant and embarrassed to be viewed as the tycoon's lackey in front of his fellow actors and potential co-stars in *Queer People*.

As Bogie headed out of the library to join Hughes in the foyer, Lyon called out to him. "Even though she's my God damn wife, you can count me out of her latest mess."

Not knowing what in the hell Lyon was talking about, Bogie walked quickly across the living room to confront Hughes.

***

Driving at night and into the wilds of Orange County, Bogie was heading for a rendezvous with his second actress of the night with the initials of BD. It was Bebe Daniels this time, not Billie Dove. Since he also knew another BD (Bette Davis) he wondered if BD was the most all-time popular combination of initials for a Hollywood actress.

Hughes had given him a thousand dollars with the instructions that he was to secretly pass the money to police chief, Fred C. Warren. The tycoon had told him that the deal had already been arranged. When Warren got the money, he was to release Bebe Daniels from a small town jail. She'd been arrested for speeding. When she'd resisted, she'd been thrown into jail.

Since he felt that Hughes still had him under his control, Bogie reluctantly agreed to rescue Daniels.

Even as he drove with the windows open to let in the night air, he bitterly resented having to perform this job for Hughes. It really wasn't for Hughes himself, since he apparently had no sexual interest in Daniels. It was for Ben Lyon. He was married to Daniels. He should be driving through Orange with the money to bail her out. But the co-partner of what the fan magazines had described as "the Happiest Hollywood Couple" had told Bogie, "Tell the bitch she can rot in jail for all I care."

This was the second incarceration of Daniels for speeding. Bogie remembered reading of her first arrest back in 1921 where she'd also been jailed in Orange County for speeding.

The event had created a media circus. It was Orange County's first celebrity courtroom drama, the conviction of a silent-film star. She'd been clocked doing 56.5 mph in her Marmon on U.S. 101 heading for San Juan Capistrano.

Daniels had turned it into the publicity break of her career. Before her trial, she'd appeared at the Yost Theater in Santa Ana in a very revealing gown for the première of her latest film, *She Couldn't Help It*. She'd sung "The Judge Cox Blues" followed by a standing ovation. Judge John Belshazzar Cox had ordered her to stand trial.

After a trial before Judge Cox, the jury had taken five minutes to find Daniels "Guilty!" as charged.

To serve her term at the jailhouse, Daniels in front of cameras had arrived with a press agent, eight suitcases, three hatboxes, and a ten-day supply of chocolates. Local merchants provided her with the furnishings for a luxurious bedroom suite for her cell, and they also agreed to cater her three hot meals a day.

Roger Wilbourne, her most ardent fan, arrived with a newly purchased phonograph and 150 records. A local Santa Ana group, the Abe Syman Orchestra, had serenaded her each night outside her jailhouse window.

Tout Hollywood had descended to call on her, including such big names as Cecil B. DeMille and Gloria Swanson. It was even rumored that the handsome matinee idol of his day, Thomas Meighan, had paid a "conjugal visit." Before she'd been released, her guest book had been signed by 792 visitors to the cell, including Judge Cox who'd sent fresh flowers every day.

After her release, her studio had rushed her into her next film, aptly titled *The Speed Girl*.

Hughes had been right about one thing. The deal with Warren had been sealed before Bogie got to the jailhouse. A man of few words, Warren had carefully counted out his money. After pocketing it, he told Bogie to wait at the rear of the jail in his car with the door open.

Within moments, a slightly giggly and intoxicated Bebe Daniels was in the seat beside him as he headed back with his prize catch toward Los Angeles, wondering if he'd fall asleep on the set of *A Holy Terror* in the morning.

If he wasn't stalking Billie Dove, with Lilyan Tashman waiting in the wings, he knew he could fall for Bebe Daniels in a big way. She was the personification of F. Scott Fitzgerald's Jazz Age flapper, even though with the Depression deepening, that image seemed dated.

In person, she looked just like she did in the movies. Although she was only slightly younger than him, she'd been making films for eleven years.

Long before anyone ever heard of Judy Garland, he'd seen her as "Dorothy" in *The Wizard of Oz*. He was ten years old at the time.

In her drunken but sexy state, she was being provocative, like Bogie himself. "You and Bette Davis sure fucked up *The Flirt*."

He knew that she was referring to the Booth Tarkington play, *The Flirt*, which she had appeared in in 1916.

"Don't you think we improved on the title?" he asked, lighting up another one of his countless cigarettes of the night. "*Bad Sister*?"

"I like the silent version better," she said, "including the title. You didn't improve on anything. First off, Bette Davis and Sidney Fox don't even know how to act. The only actress who knew what she was doing in the film was ZaSu Pitts."

"What about my part?" he asked, rather insulted.

"I don't even remember it," she said, accepting his offer of a cigarette.

Although he'd remained sullen for half an hour or so, he soon forgave her for her putdown of his film work.

"Thank God you came to my rescue," she said. "I'm shooting *The Maltese Falcon*, although the producer is considering calling it *Dangerous Female* instead. I'll go with *Dangerous Female* because it calls more attention to myself."

"I like the sound of *Maltese Falcon*," he said.

As related by her, the screenplay of *The Maltese Falcon* intrigued him, and he wished that he'd been appearing as Sam Spade in the film. It was based on a novel by Dashiell Hammett. The plot centered around the recovery of a black statuette of a falcon. The falcon held the clue to riches, and a lot of people in the film were in active pursuit of it and would stop at nothing, including murder, to get it.

As he drove her along, she appeared to him like a dewy, big-eyed child, and that was part of her allure. On the screen she possessed an extraordinarily expressive face, and that was no act. She was just like that in real life. She had huge eyes, and film critics of the day liked to write about her "Castilian beauty." She was actually Texas born, and wasn't Hispanic at all. Although she was nearly thirty years old, she still projected the quality of little girlishness that she'd so beautifully used as a foil for Harold Lloyd in all those "Lonesome Luke" films.

Before marrying Ben Lyon, she had, at least according to the fan magazines, been deeply in love with Lloyd and had wanted to marry him. Obviously something had gone wrong in the romance. Later Daniels had told the press that even though a teenager at the time, it was she who'd suggested to Lloyd that he should "carbon copy" Chaplin's Little Tramp. "Instead of baby trousers, I told Harold to dress the reverse—that is, wear too tight clothing instead of too baggy."

Hump couldn't turn down her invitation to frequent shots of liquor swigged directly from a flask, which she carried in her purse. He was holding his liquor well, but the booze was making her even more giddy than when she'd first jumped into his car.

"C'mon," she urged him. "Go faster. I'll never get to the set of *The Maltese Falcon* in the morning unless you step on it."

"Hell, I'm going fast enough," he barked at her. "You've already been arrested once tonight for speeding. Do you want me to end up in the pokey too?"

"Don't be such a sissy," she said. "If there's one thing I can't stand, it's a faggot like my husband. Howard Hughes fucks Ben in the ass, or did you know that?"

"I sometimes dream erotically about the two of them together," he said sarcastically.

"Don't tell me you're another one of those pansy boys of Howard's," she said. She turned her head sharply to look at him. "Of course, you are. I had the wrong idea about you. When I first got in your car, I thought you were all man. Now I see differently. The lisp, being Howard's errand boy. Have you replaced Ben in Howard's affections?"

That question was too provocative for him. "Listen, bitch, if you want speed, I'll show you speed," he said. "Even though everybody in Hollywood seems to think so, I'm not a God damn faggot." He floored the accelerator, zooming off into the night.

The evening had started out badly, but it was going to get worse.

Ten minutes later, he heard the sound that all speeding motorists in the middle of the night dread like a summons to Hades.

A police siren.

***

Stark naked, Bogie stood on the small balcony of his room at a motor court. Also nude, Bebe Daniels lay in a drunken sprawl on a double bed they'd rented for the night. He'd fucked her, and the act had been followed by the longest "pillow talk" in recorded history. Daniels had been silent during sex, but once it was over she'd insisted on reliving virtually every other intercourse she'd known with actors, some of them the stellar lights of Hollywood.

After being stopped by a policeman, Bogie had been booked for speeding and driving while intoxicated. A quick call to the mansion of Howard Hughes, and Bogie was promised relief by six o'clock in the morning. An attorney for Hughes would arrive with bail money. Because the arresting officer was "a great fan" of Bebe Daniels, Bogie was allowed to spend what was left of the night with her in a motor court instead of a jailhouse cell.

Still drinking heavily, Daniels seemed oblivious of the arrest and continued in her giddy mood. When she pulled off all her clothes and danced a naked Charleston in front of him, with all her plumbing bouncing, he'd become aroused. When he'd stripped down and had moved toward her, she'd welcomed his advance. Even so, it brought back unpleasant memories of his stripping in front of Billie Dove, which had led to his "enslavement" to Hughes in the first place.

In the sack, Daniels had turned out to be a world-class eroticist. She knew how to press all his buttons. If she were an expert at any sexual artifice, it was in the way she'd fondled his balls as he'd plowed into her. That act on her part had driven him wild and had led to finishing him off long before he wanted to dismount.

Before she'd finally fallen asleep in a stupor, he'd heard a lot of gossip about some of the greatest male stars of the silent screen.

Although not the best-hung actor in Hollywood, Harold Lloyd was proficient and good at the sex act, not getting off Daniels until she'd had at least two orgasms. Cecil B. DeMille had a foot fetish, and had never had intercourse with her, preferring instead to lick her dainty feet while he masturbated.

One of the matinee idols of the silent screen, Thomas Meighan, was a "stouthearted man" with a large penis who could "go all night." On the 1920 set of *Why Change Your Wife?* Swanson had pursued Meighan. But Daniels, to hear her tell it, had gotten those mighty inches instead. On the 1921 set of *The Affairs of Anatol*, Swanson "loathed" Wallace Reid, who was then considered the handsomest male star on the screen. Daniels had pursued him, but he'd been "too far gone on dope to get it up."

Her romance with Rudolph Valentino on the 1924 set of *Monsieur Beaucaire* had fizzled even though he'd stripped down for her and had gone to bed with her. He'd never penetrated her but had wanted to indulge in body worship—that is, her worshipping and paying homage to his body, which he was showing off to perfection in this fancy dress picture.

Douglas Fairbanks Sr. had been a lot of fun on the set, but in bed he was a bit lackluster. "Poor Mary," Daniels had said. "Seven and a half inches of circumcised Jewish dick but the most crooked angle I've ever seen on any man. It was downright painful the way he kept jabbing in me."

The rest of the shoot of the early 1930 talkie, *Reaching for the Moon*, had gone uneventfully as Daniels had been only too willing to give Fairbanks "back to Mary."

Daniels said that she was being talked about for a co-starring role at Universal, *Counsellor-at-Law*, with John Barrymore perhaps playing the lead. "I know the women at the matinees swoon when he comes out in those green tights. But I've heard that he pads his crotch. If we ever make that God damn film together, I guess I'll find out the truth when I pull off his tights. I'll let you know."

"Can't wait to get that report," he said facetiously. "I've spent most of my life pondering Barrymore's crotch."

In the middle of telling him "how disappointed I was" with Bing Crosby's performance in bed, she'd fallen asleep.

He, however, was as wide awake as if he'd had eighteen cups of coffee. Daylight had come and Hughes' lawyer probably wouldn't reach town for another two hours. He wanted something to read to distract himself. Finding only a Bible, he decided to search through Daniels' large leather purse. It was practically a suitcase, and he figured that she at least carried around a paperback romance. He'd even have read a comic book about Tarzan, King of the Jungle, if that were all there was.

Instead of trash, he discovered a script for a new film. Few aspiring actors could resist the sight of a freshly typed script. He figured that he could read the scenario before Daniels woke up. Who knows? There might be a part in it for him. Maybe he wasn't going to have to leave Hollywood after all.

The script was for *42nd Street*, a backstage movie musical. It was set in New York during the Depression. He'd seen MGM's backstage musical, *The Broadway Melody* in 1929, but that was all frills. As he read deeper into the script of *42nd Street*, he found it had a far more intense cutting age.

The film had been summarized on the front page. He'd read the notice of what it was about before he'd perused the actual script. Scriptwriter Tom Dirks had written, "This film is to be an unglamorized look at the tough realities of backstage life behind the footlights. The urban milieu of the film is filled with crisp slang, bitter dialogue and wisecracks, street-wise characters, topical references, desperately striving chorines, dancers, and crew, and down-and-out references to the Depression."

As Bogie read on, the role of "Julian Marsh" seemed tailor-made for him. He could "taste the part" of the ailing, but vociferous stage director. Bogie was a New Yorker born and bred and felt that he was destined to play the role. By the time he'd finished the script, he almost wanted to wake Daniels up and ask her who was going to direct the movie. He had to get to that director, regardless of who it was, and present himself as "Julian Marsh." Even if that director were the cocksucking Rowland Brown.

By the time he heard Hughes' lawyer rapping on the door to their motor court room, Bogie was elated in spite of his troubles.

The night had not been a waste. He'd saved his Hollywood career. Hughes would cast him as the tough-talking Walter Winchell in *Queer People*, and he'd follow that with the role of Julian Marsh in *42nd Street*.

The morning had gone well, as Hughes' attorney turned out to be adept at bribery and hushing up embarrassing run-ins with the police. Bogie was never officially charged, and he was allowed to drive Daniels back to Hollywood and to the set of *The Maltese Falcon*.

On the way back, she agreed to introduce him to its director, Lloyd Bacon, who was also putting together a cast for *42nd Street*. The role of Julian Marsh had not been cast.

Daniels followed through with her early morning commitment and eventually got him an interview with Lloyd Bacon.

Even though Bogie was under contract with Fox, Bacon directed him in a "secret" screen test for *42nd Street*. Bogie felt that Bacon was doing that only as a favor to Bebe Daniels, as he suspected that the director and his star were having an affair.

362

When he'd seen the results of the screen test, Bacon called to instruct Bogie to report to his office Thursday afternoon. Evocative of what was about to transpire, thunder was ripping apart the sky, and it looked as if a big storm was moving in fast.

Without any formality, Bacon said, "You flopped. You not only were miserable, but I think you would absolutely fuck up this picture if I cast you in the part."

"No one ever accused you of being subtle, pal," Bogie said. "I think you're wrong."

"Who in the fuck are you?" Bacon said. "I'm the director. I make the choices. I answer to no one."

"Not even Jack Warner?" Bogie asked.

"When I want something around this studio, I get it," Bacon boasted. "I'm going to be the biggest director in Hollywood. Six, maybe seven Oscars, for Best Picture and Best Director."

Bogie knew it was unprofessional but he ended up denouncing Bacon for refusing him the role. "You're a crappy director if you can't see that I'm right for the part. It can make me a star and it can rescue your picture."

"I don't need rescuing from a lisping little faggot like you," Bacon had shouted. "You'll never amount to anything in pictures." Bacon was still yelling at Bogie as he slammed the director's door on the way out.

In one of the ironies of Hollywood, Bacon ended up working with Bogie more than any other director. No love was lost between the two men when they made *Marked Woman* together in 1937, with Bette Davis as the co-star. Bacon's lack of admiration for Bogie continued in 1937 in *San Quentin* when Bogie appeared with Ann Sheridan and Pat O'Brien. Bogie could only sigh in 1938 when Jack Warner assigned Bacon to direct him in *Racket Busters*, in which he appeared with George Brent. Bogie would slide down in his seat when he watched the final cut of *The Oklahoma Kid* in 1939. Bacon had miscast him in a Western playing Whip McCord opposite James Cagney who looked like a mushroom in a ten-gallon hat.

If Bogie felt that Bacon was gone from his life, he was wrong. When Bogie showed up on the set of *Invisible Stripes* in 1939, he not only found Bacon but George Raft, who'd become his nemesis. It was on the set of *Invisible Stripes* that Bogie would meet a handsome young man, William Holden, who would become not only a Hollywood legend, but another nemesis of Bogie's. By 1939 Holden had long since replaced Bogie as Barbara Stanwyck's "Golden Boy."

Like a record that would never end, Bacon showed up to direct Bogie in *Brother Orchid* in 1940, with Bogie appearing opposite yet another rival for gangster roles, Edward G. Robinson. By then, Bogie had taken to calling Robinson "The liver-lipped faggot."

Right after Bogie had shot *Casablanca*, Bacon came back into his life for one final directorial effort when they shot *Action in the North Atlantic* in 1943.

Bogie would later remark, "After all those films with Lloyd Bacon, bacon and eggs remains my favorite dish, although it's a wonder he didn't turn me against pig fat for life."

The coveted male lead in *42nd Street* went to that stolid leading man, Warner Baxter, the "Cisco Kid" in the 1929 film, *In Old Arizona*, one of the first all-talking Westerns. For that role, Baxter had won the Oscar as Best Actor. With his solid build, keen eyes, and pencil-thin mustache, Baxter had become famous in the Silents, appearing in such parts as the title role in F. Scott Fitzgerald's *The Great Gatsby* in 1926 before Alan Ladd or Robert Redford got their chance at it in later adaptations.

Just as Bogie blamed Ronald Colman as the reason he never carved out a career in silent pictures, so he blamed Warner Baxter for "delaying my Hollywood stardom for a decade." Bogie always felt that he could have won the Oscar for the role of Julian Marsh and that "boring Baxter fucked up the role."

Bogie later became close friends with one of the show's other stars, Dick Powell. He'd already met Ruby Keeler, who played the chorus girl who replaces the big star of the play, as portrayed by Bebe Daniels, when Keeler was shacked up with George Raft in New York at the ripe old age of fourteen.

As Bogie was to tell his brother-in-law, Stuart Rose, when they went to see the film together, "That fucking Lloyd Bacon even knocked me out of a hot piece of ass." Bogie remained convinced that he could have seduced one of the co-stars of *42nd Street*, Ginger Rogers, appearing as "Anytime Annie" in the film.

Bogie knew that his chance for Hollywood fame was smaller than ever when he learned that Hughes had shelved *Queer People*. "Too much pressure from the big boys," Ben Lyon told him. "Mayer and those shits don't want an honest picture about Hollywood. They sell fantasies."

Losing two major parts in quick succession caused Bogie to tell Kenneth MacKenna, "The nails are being driven into my coffin out here. I'm through." He still planned to head back to New York "unless something happens and soon."

Helen Menken still wasn't taking his calls. The only possibility of intrigue for him involved a mysterious call from Bette Davis, which had come into Fox. Her message said, "It's important that we get together—and soon." It was signed "Miss D."

Since her Hollywood star didn't seem to be shining any brighter than his, he wondered what she wanted with him. He suspected that she didn't really like him, so he doubted if romance were on her mind. Maybe she'd stumbled onto a hot script that would make both of them overnight sensations.

He needed something to happen and fast.

***

Hung over, disheveled, and burnt out, Bogie arrived late on the set of *A Holy Terror* and headed for wardrobe.

364

Tapping his foot impatiently, Greg Brooks, known around the Fox lot as "the wardrobe mistress," said, "My, oh my, aren't we looking *déshabillée* today."

"Listen, you little faggot," Bogie said, "get out your fucking padding and your high heels and get it over with before I bash your skull in."

"Aren't we the ferocious tiger today?" Brooks said. "Didn't get any last night? Thank God you didn't call me." He licked his lips. "I was too preoccupied. Antonio Moreno is a real stallion."

In rage and fury, Bogie grabbed Brooks by his shirt and jerked him, wanting to smash his face.

At that moment the director, Irving Cummings, came into the department and rushed to separate the two men. Freed from Bogie's clutches, Brooks ran screaming out of the room. "Bogart tried to rape me," he shouted in front of startled workers on the set.

Anger flashed across Cummings' face as he turned to confront Bogie. "Listen, asshole, and listen good. You're not going to beat up anybody on the set of one of my pictures. I can replace you tomorrow with any of about a thousand better actors. You're totally wrong for the part, and Fox is only using you because some idiot signed a contract giving you $750 a week. Actors like you I can get for $25 a week. If I have any more trouble from you, you're fired."

"I'm sorry," Bogie said. "I guess I'm a little thin-skinned."

Cummings backed away from him. "And hung over. You smell like a brewery. I'm reporting all of this to Carl Laemmle."

"Junior or senior?" Bogie asked provocatively.

The director glared at him and seemed out of control. "After we wrap this picture, you'll never get another job in this town. I'll see to that." Cummings stormed out of the wardrobe department.

Bogie tried to get a grip on himself. He'd wanted to punch Cummings in the mouth.

Later that day, and to punish him, Cummings made him shoot a simple scene forty-five times. The director seemed to be sadistically torturing Bogie and humiliating him in front of cast members.

After Cummings finally pronounced that he'd gotten the scene right, Bogie wandered alone around the set. Badly shaken, he lit a cigarette but needed a shot of liquor instead. Bebe Daniels had it right. Carry your flask with you at all times.

Near his dressing room, he encountered Rita La Roy, a shapely, comely brunette with short hair. Without an ounce of fat on her body, she was a full-figured woman with a well-stuffed brassière, a thin waist, and hips and ass carved to sculptural perfection.

Playing Kitty Carroll in *A Holy Terror*, she had third billing to his fourth. Born in Paris in 1907, La Roy had signed to do seven pictures in 1931 alone, including *The Gay Diplomat* and *Leftover Ladies*. For some reason, British distributors never liked any of the American titles of her films and usually changed them. For example, *The Yellow Ticket* became *The Yellow Passport*, and *The Secret Witness* was retitled *Terror by Night*.

When he first met her, La Roy had just completed filming *The Yellow Ticket* directed by Raoul Walsh, who with one good eye and one black patch had also directed Bogie in *Women of All Nations*.

He liked La Roy at once, and as they smoked, chatted, and talked, waiting for one of their scenes together, he suspected that it was inevitable that the two of them would share a roll in the sack before the film wrapped.

"You didn't have to try to rape that poor little Gregie Brooks from wardrobe," she admonished him. "There are too many others in the cast only too willing to give it away. I understand that George O'Brien keeps his ass washed, perfumed, and pre-lubricated."

"Something like that," he said, not wanting to get involved in any talk about O'Brien's asshole. That reminded him that he would soon be delivering O'Brien to the mansion of Howard Hughes for God only knows what fun and games.

La Roy was filled with amusing stories about filming *The Yellow Ticket*, the story of a young Russian girl forced into a life of prostitution in Czarist Russia. "There was more prostitution going on off the screen than on," La Roy said. "You may have seen the picture."

Bogie shook his head. "That one has missed me but I'll catch it at some matinee."

"Elissa Landi was the star," she said.

"I know her," he said. He smiled to indicate he was joking. "The Empress of Austria."

"Forgive me for asking the most often asked question in Hollywood," she said. "Is that *know* in the Biblical sense?"

"I think we connected one night," he said nonchalantly. "I fear I don't have the right plumbing to please Miss Landi."

She rubbed her breast. "I certainly do. She pursued me day and night until I finally gave in. With Myrna Loy in her bed, I don't know what she needed with little ol' me. Actually, I was after the co-star of the film, Laurence Olivier."

"Yeah, I've been hearing a lot about him," he said. "The limey actor."

"He is the world's most beautiful man," she said. "I mean, I fainted when I saw him. Of course, I had to have him. But it's like with Clark Gable. They look great on the outside, but once these men take off their pants, a gal is disappointed. I couldn't get his less than adequate dick to work for me. So I had to settle for licking every inch of that gorgeous flesh of his. If I couldn't get fucked, at least I could indulge in some body worship. The male star of the film, Lionel Barrymore, had far better luck than I did. He went down on Olivier every day of the shoot. He told me that Olivier has the sweetest tasting cum of any man he's seduced, and dear Lionel has had them all."

"Sounds like you guys had one hell of a time," he said.

"I even seduced Boris Karloff who played a drunken orderly in the film," she said. "But I find him rather creepy, even off the screen."

"Personally, when I want to fuck a ghoul, it's Bela Lugosi for me."

Both of them laughed. When he offered her a cigarette, she caressingly brushed his hand. He just knew that over the lunch hour, he'd be invited to her dressing room for some body worship. He wasn't as pretty as Olivier but he figured that if La Roy had seduced Karloff, she lowered her standards every now and then.

When lunch was announced that day, La Roy predictably invited him back to her dressing room. "I have a hot plate in my room. Two friends are dropping by. You know both of them. At least one in the Biblical sense."

He was flabbergasted. Could it be? Was La Roy inviting him for a four-way, with him being the male stud to a group of beautiful, horny women, one of whom he had already seduced.

"Give us gals about twenty minutes," she said, "and then show up."

He kissed her lightly on the lips, anticipating what lay in store for him. In spite of his hangover, he was already hardening.

After taking a whore's bath in his dressing room—he wanted everything to smell fresh for these ladies—he headed for La Roy's dressing room.

On the way there, he encountered old-time actor James Kirkwood Sr., who'd been a big-time director and a leading man in silent pictures. He was another Hollywood Lothario, having seduced, or so it was said, the likes of Gloria Swanson, Mabel Normand, the Talmadges (Norma and Constance), Marion Davies, Colleen Moore, Agnes Ayres, Nita Naldi, Beverly Bayne, and Olive Thomas.

"If you're not going to be using your dressing room at lunch, mind if I borrow it?" Kirkwood asked.

"Sure thing, pal," he said. "It's yours. What's wrong with your own dressing room?"

"I'm no longer the star I was," he said. "I have to share my dressing room with two other guys."

"What's mine is yours," Bogie said.

As Bogie headed toward La Roy's dressing room, he lingered behind but concealed himself on the set. His curiosity won out. He wanted to see what actress Kirkwood was deflowering. Surely not Sally Eilers!

Within minutes, heading toward the door to his dressing room, he spotted a stagehand who was escorting a small woman in a pink satin dress. She wore a red scarf to cover her hair, and her face was concealed behind large, very black sunglasses.

After they had disappeared inside his dressing room, Bogie walked away, wondering who that mystery lady was. The image of the world's most famous woman flashed in front of him. "No, it couldn't be," he said out loud. "Not *the* Mary Pickford."

***

367

All thoughts of Mary Pickford vanished when he was received in the dressing room of Rita La Roy. The ladies assembled here had heard of his reputation for practical jokes, including presenting Bette Davis with a well-hung baby on the set of *Bad Sister*.

In honor of his visit, all the women, including La Roy herself, were sitting in her dressing room attired in the most revealing and expensive French lingerie. La Roy wore white lingerie, Elissa Landi black, and Marlene Dietrich champagne.

"Bogie man," Dietrich said, "come on in and join our sewing circle."

"The last time I was with you," Landi said, "I wasn't wearing all this much clothing."

"These are the friends I told you about," La Roy said.

He stepped in and shut the door behind him, locking it. "Ladies, I had a lot to drink last night. I just hope I'm in shape to handle all three of you."

"Don't flatter yourself," Dietrich said. "Rita invited you here for lunch. We decided to dress down to give you something to look at." She got up and went over to the hot plate where she started cracking eggs to make omelettes.

Landi rose to her feet and went over and kissed him. "Sorry, I dropped you so unceremoniously, but that Basil Rathbone is such a charmer."

"The man with two profiles," Bogie said with a certain contempt.

She kissed him lightly on the lips. "Some night when I get a cancellation on my calendar, I'll give you a call."

"I doubt if I'll be home," he said, covering his earlier rejection with bravado. "A real stud like me is too busy to wait by the phone."

La Roy came up to him. "Marlene tells me you're competing with us for many of the same women in Hollywood. Joan Crawford, Barbara Stanwyck, Lilyan Tashman. Even Myrna Loy herself."

"May the best man win," he said facetiously. He looked over at Marlene standing beside that tiny, cramped hotplate making omelettes. "If Miss Dietrich here wasn't fixing lunch, all three of you would make a tasty snack."

"We're not a snack," La Roy said. "Each of us is the main event."

Without meaning to, he found himself in a verbal sparring match with these women. "I'm sure you are. I've been doing all right for myself today. At five o'clock this morning, I was fucking Bebe Daniels. I've already had the star of this picture, Sally Eilers. For a noon-day refresher, I just left the most famous actress in the world in my dressing room. Totally satisfied, I might add." He accepted a whiskey from La Roy.

All of the women looked at him with startled expressions. Finally, Landi spoke, "Garbo is on the set today?"

"More famous than Garbo," he said. "Anybody can have her, that Stockholm barbershop girl. I go for unobtainable Hollywood royalty."

"Oh, my God," La Roy said. "He's fucking Norma Shearer."

A silence came over the room. At least he'd succeeded in getting their attention, no small feat among ego-crazed actresses. He knew their curiosity was

368

racing at fever pitch, but he would say no more. He'd tantalized them enough.

His only hope was that Kirkwood was a premature ejaculator, and that after doing his dirty deed with Pickford, he'd dress quickly and get back to the set. Surely Miss Pickford would linger behind to take a whore's bath and get her clothing and makeup readjusted before appearing in public again.

He suspected that all three women—maybe not Dietrich—would be hanging around his dressing room after lunch to see the mystery lady emerge. If all went well, and after today, Bogie knew that his reputation as a Hollywood stud would be all but secured.

Not only would Mary Pickford be seen emerging from his dressing room, but he would be spotted coming out of La Roy's dressing room, having serviced, or so it would appear, Rita La Roy herself, Elissa Landi, and the blonde goddess, Marlene Dietrich. Not bad for a morning's work. He suspected that his telephone would be ringing off the wall that night, as every horny broad in Hollywood would be calling him.

Over those Marlene Dietrich omelettes in the cramped dressing room, he told Dietrich, "I'm an egg man, my favorite food. That and ham. This is the tastiest God damn omelette I've ever had. Are you sure you don't want to give up all this stardom and come home and cook for me?"

"I'll think about your offer," Dietrich said. "I'm just a *Hausfrau* at heart."

Sitting next to Bogie, La Roy nudged his arm, as if wanting to steer the conversation to herself. "Marlene is going to get Josef von Sternberg to cast me in her next movie, *Blonde Venus*. I'm so excited."

"I'm going to wear a gorilla suit in the film," Dietrich said.

"Such a waste to cover up the world's shapeliest legs."

"Thank you for the compliment, Bogie man," Dietrich said in her most alluringly voice.

"What about me?" Landi asked, running her fingers caressingly along her lingerie-clad body. "What am I? Chopped liver?"

"You look mighty fine," he said. He knew no man would look at Landi with La Roy semi-nude in the room. And no man would look at La Roy with Dietrich in her see-through lingerie.

The lunch ended all too soon. After he'd finished his omelette, he knew there would be no playtime with these lingerie ladies. For all he knew, each of them had had each other before he even got there. As Landi dressed in street clothes, and La Roy put on her costume for the Western, Dietrich remained in her underwear. She busied herself washing the dishes but took time out to offer him a drink.

After kissing La Roy and then Landi rather passionately on the lips, Dietrich asked Bogie to remain to "talk about something very important."

After Landi and La Roy had both kissed Bogie good-bye, he stayed glued to his chair, appraising Dietrich's shapely figure. When they'd gone, and Dietrich had locked the door, he said, "So, what's on your mind, kid?"

369

Without saying a word to him, she came up to where he was sitting and dropped on her knees before him. Almost before he knew what was happening, she was unbuttoning his fly and reaching in to free his already hardening penis.

When he saw her tongue dart out to wet her celebrated, scarlet-painted mouth, he knew what fate awaited him.

***

About an hour later, Bogie encountered Kirkwood, holding a newspaper article, on the set. Kirkwood looked up at Bogie and smiled, his face indicating supreme satisfaction.

A messenger approached Kirkwood, informing him that the director, Cummings, wanted to see him. As the aging actor got up to head for the cameras, he turned to Bogie. "Thanks a lot for the use of your dressing room. Mary's still in there, resting."

Kirkwood leaned over and whispered to Bogie. "She drinks a lot and can't drive. Would you drive her back to Pickfair? She wants to leave at three o'clock. Cummings will be shooting the picture's big scene then, and the cast and crew will all be involved. That way, she's not likely to be seen leaving the set."

"I'd be honored, but what's wrong with your own driving skills?"

"Don't be ridiculous," Kirkwood said. "If I drove up in front of Pickfair with Mary, Fairbanks would either blow my head off with one of his pistols or chase me down with his sword."

"You've got a point there," Bogie said. "Sure, I'll drive her."

"Mary also needs time to rest up before three," Kirkwood said, winking at Bogie. "I got carried away a bit in there. I hope we didn't damage too much of the furniture."

"You old goat," Bogie said mockingly, softening the word with a smile. "If I'm still getting as much as you are when I'm your age, I'll count myself lucky."

"You don't know how lucky I am," Kirkwood said. "Even if I could drive Mary home, I wouldn't be able to. You see, Rita La Roy has accepted an invitation to go to a hotel with me tonight. If you ever meet up with my wife, you needn't tell her. Lila's at home with our son tonight." Kirkwood turned and walked away after thanking Bogie again.

That son, James Kirkwood Jr., became a famous homosexual playwright, winning the Pulitzer Prize for *A Chorus Line*. But movie buffs maintain that Kirkwood Junior's real claim to fame a century from now will be for his cameo role in the Joan Crawford bio film, *Mommie Dearest*.

Since Bogie wanted to give Pickford a generous amount of time to recover from her ordeal with Kirkwood Sr., he ambled around the set. He noticed several grips outside the dressing room of Sally Eilers. From the sound of things, Eilers was getting the plowing of her life. She was more vocal than she'd been with Bogie that night at Hoot Gibson's house. The grips were snickering like adolescent boys when the subject of sex came up.

"Who's putting on the sound show?" Bogie asked one of the grips. "I assume that's George O'Brien in there mounting our female star."

"Like hell it is," one of the grips said. "That's a visitor to the set. Spencer Tracy's in there."

***

Since he still had plenty of time left before driving Mary Pickford, he stood at a safe distance from the dressing room of Sally Eilers. It was obvious that Tracy had been carrying on with Hoot Gibson's wife since they made *Quick Millions* together. Eilers was the first to leave, since she was due on the set.

After she'd disappeared, Bogie walked up to her dressing room door and knocked on it. In his underwear with drink in hand, Tracy opened the door. Seeing who it was, he embraced Bogie warmly. "We're supposed to be best friends, and I never get to see you any more. Come on in."

"Aren't you afraid Hoot Gibson will show up with a six-gun?" Bogie asked.

"Not at all," Tracy said. "Sally has told me about the kind of marriage they have. Actually I learned today she plans to divorce him."

"It's probably a smart career move for her," Bogie said, accepting a drink. "Her star is rising. There's talk she's going to become big. His sagebrush cowboy is riding off into the sunset."

"Don't knock sagebrush flickers," Tracy kidded him. "You seem to be making an oater yourself."

"It's George O'Brien's flick," Bogie said with a sigh of despair.

"After I get dressed and have a drink or two with you," Tracy said, "I'm going to head over to George's dressing room. I like George a lot. He's a real loving he-man, unlike that girl, Lew Ayres."

"George and Sally on the same afternoon?" Bogie chided him. "You're more man than I am."

"We both know that," Tracy said, smiling to erase the sting from his remark. "George and Sally are both on my plate for the afternoon. Tonight I've got a date with Jean Harlow." When Bogie didn't say anything, Tracy asked him, "Did you hear that?"

"Yeah, I heard it," he said. "You and Harlow must have had one gay old time on the set of *Goldie*, a picture I think should be called *Blondie*."

Harlow's an okay kid," he said. "Mixed up in the head. A sick family life with her stepfather lusting after her, a mother who's nuts, and an even worse situation emerging with this Paul Bern creature from the dark lagoon."

"Yeah, I met Bern," Bogie said. "Not my kind of guy at all."

"He's got problems," Tracy said, "and I hear they're sexual."

"I heard that from Bern himself," Bogie said. "If Harlow goes ahead with her plan to marry Bern, you can still get in there for some platinum pussy. Since he's impotent, he asked me if I'd be one of the guys he could call on to fuck Harlow while he oversees the action like a director."

Tracy only smiled at that. "I've been in Hollywood long enough to have heard sicker requests than that."

"Spence, old pal," Bogie said, pouring another drink before facing Mary Pickford. "I like you a lot. More than I like Kenneth MacKenna. He's my pal, and I tell him everything that's going on in my life, but I have a special feeling for you."

"Are you coming on to me?" Tracy asked with just a slight touch of mockery in his voice as if to leave open the possibility he might be joking.

"Cut the crap!" Bogie said. "I have a hard time accepting that part of your life. I mean, I can see you banging Eilers while the grips outside are dreaming of being locked between your spurs. I can see you dating your co-star tonight. Let's face it: Harlow is the sex symbol of Hollywood. All the men want her. What I can't even picture—don't dare picture—is you and guys. George O'Brien, for God's sake. Mr. Avocado Sandwich. Mr. Baby-Ass."

"You know about his asshole too?" Tracy asked. "That fucker! He said it belonged to me exclusively. I guess there are no secrets in Hollywood."

"George has bent over and spread cheeks and invited me to take a preview of that special possession he's got where the sun don't shine."

"You know, I've never tasted an asshole as sweet as George's," Tracy said, "and I've had some of the sweetest. I'm an ass man myself."

Bogie allowed no expression to cross his face. He knew that Tracy was trying to gross him out, and he wasn't going to let him gloat over that triumph.

Tracy looked disappointed that he didn't even elicit a wince of horror from Bogie. "I love you, Bogie, but I feel you're very limited somehow. Many of the pleasures that God put on this earth for us to partake of, especially forbidden fruit, are not to be enjoyed by you. Your mind's closed off."

"My loss, pal," Bogie said, "and that's how I'm gonna keep it. But if you think for one minute I'm gonna picture you as a pansy like Ramon Novarro and Billy Haines, you're wrong. In spite of overwhelming evidence, I still think you're putting me on. You're too much of a man's man to lick O'Brien's asshole."

"You said it all. I'm a man's man in more ways than one."

"But I hear from people who work with you that you fuck every pretty gal on the set of one of your pictures," Bogie said. "Not just your female leads, but the secretaries, the script gal, the waitress who serves you a BLT in the commissary."

"It's true, I do," Tracy said. "I also fuck beautiful guys. By the way, I'm a top. Fucking a man in the ass is different from fucking a woman. Another kind of satisfaction. I know I'm fucked up in the head, and I have all this Catholic guilt about it, but it's the way I am. Women are too easy for me to get. All I have to do is look at them and wink and they fall all over me even though I'm no Clark Gable in the looks department. Men I view as a challenge. It does my ego proud to fuck one of them. The handsomer and more macho they are, the better I like it. I read

372

in a *Kama Sutra* book somewhere that Arab men in Arabian nights fantasies used to desire eunuchs who had been completely emasculated more than any other type—pretty boy, woman, or even a castrated male. Somehow in their brains they desire fucking a man whose sexual organs had been completely removed. It made them feel superior to the male under them. When I fuck a man like George, I feel more manly than I do with a woman. My ego craves this type of gratification."

"I know what you're saying," Bogie said "but I'll never understand it. To me, you're the least homosexual male in Hollywood."

"You'll learn as you go through life that we come in the most unlikely packages. The captains of football teams. The heads of industry. Boxers. Weightlifters. Generals. Even one of the presidents of the United States."

"What president was a fag?"

"Abraham Lincoln."

"I don't believe that," Bogie said. "You're putting me on."

"Read your history books," Tracy said. "His lover was Joshua Fry Speed. You fuck too many women at night. You should take a night off and read a history book once in a while."

"You're one to talk."

"I'm serious," Tracy said. "Read about Lincoln and Speed, a handsome young man from Kentucky who slept with Lincoln for three years in a very narrow bed. Speed later wrote that no two men were more intimate than Lincoln and him."

"Why should I doubt your word?" Bogie asked. "After these months logged in Hollywood, I've seen it all."

"If I may correct you, you've seen a bit," Tracy said. "But you haven't seen it all. After another thirty years, you'll have seen it all."

"Perhaps you're right." Bogie glanced at his watch, as an idea occurred to him. He couldn't leave the set today without outclassing Tracy in some way. Even though they had developed a friendship that would last a lifetime, Bogie would always view Tracy as a rival. "You may be dating the sex symbol of Hollywood, but I've got to gather up the queen herself in my dressing room."

"What queen?"

"The queen of Hollywood," Bogie said proudly.

"Is this another one of your gags?"

"Not at all," Bogie boasted. "When I fuck, I fuck from the top. No script gals for me."

"This I've got to see," Tracy said.

"Put on your pants," Bogie said. "You're in for a show."

Later when he'd walked Tracy to his dressing room door, he asked him to stand far enough away to conceal himself but with clear visibility. Bogie also noticed Elissa Landi and Rita La Roy standing nearby too, waiting for the unveiling. As he'd predicted, Dietrich was too grand to play a rubbernecker.

Excusing himself from Tracy, Bogie walked over and knocked on the door to his own dressing room. Within moments it was opened. Although veiled, the woman at the door was clearly Mary Pickford.

"Oh, good," she said, "Jimmy has sent a driver for me."

Bogie could only be relieved that Tracy was out of earshot and couldn't hear Miss Pickford mistaking him for a chauffeur.

Taking her arm, he guided her down three steps and onto the ground.

Very slowly in front of a small but astonished audience, Bogie and Mary Pickford made their way toward a setting sun and the parking lot.

***

Since Pickford didn't have a clue as to who Bogie was, he chose not to identify himself. Who was he anyway? An actor co-starring in a western movie with George O'Brien. He didn't think the world's most famous woman would have been all that impressed even if she knew. She was the ultimate movie star, not him. To her, he was a chauffeur, and in those days—or now—it didn't matter a hell of a lot what your driver thought. Chauffeurs were the silent witnesses to many of the dramas that were acted out in Tinseltown.

Instead of taking her to Pickfair, the star asked to be driven to a residential section of Los Angeles peopled mostly by middle class families, many of whom had a head of household earning his living at one of the studios.

She didn't tell him why a multi-million dollar movie queen, the single most recognizable female face on earth, wanted to venture into such a neighborhood where kids played ball in the front yard, men in their undershirts mowed their lawns, and housewives hung up their laundry in the backyard alongside the family barbecue pit. In this neighborhood, swimming pools were almost non-existent.

When Bogie pulled up at a rather nondescript blockhouse, he turned to her. She was adjusting her makeup in a compact mirror. Her sunglasses looked darker and more foreboding than ever. When he got out from behind the wheel and opened the door for her, she told him to wait on the front porch while she "dealt with a problem." He could not imagine what business the great Mary Pickford had with the occupants of this lackluster and rather rundown house that must have cost way under five-thousand dollars.

She knocked on the door. An older woman opened it. She was without makeup and with rather mangy salt-and-pepper hair. Seeing who it was, she stepped back to allow Pickford to enter.

Bogie sat down in the porch swing and lit a cigarette. At first the voices of the strange woman, who spoke in heavily accented French, and Pickford could be heard, but he couldn't make out what they were saying. He listened real hard. A bit of a snoop, he wanted to find out what this regal Hollywood figure wanted at this modest little abode.

After about ten minutes, the two women seemed to have entered the living room where he could distinctly hear everything said.

"Philippe was an orphan," the French woman said. "I rescued him in Belgium during the war. Since then he's been like my own flesh and blood. I can't part with him."

"How very touching," Pickford said in a halting, regal voice. "But look at the advantages I could offer him. You can give him nothing. In one year, maybe two, that childlike beauty of his will fade as he matures. Trust me. I know one can't be a child actor forever. I tried to be that long after I matured. Now I feel some of those last pictures made me grotesque."

"I don't understand," the French (or Belgian?) woman said. "You want to enjoy his youth and beauty while it lasts, but you know he'll have it such a short time."

"Then why don't you agree to give him up?" Pickford asked.

"I can't," the woman said. "It would be like selling my own son. For all the money in the world, I can't do that."

"I'll offer you one-million dollars."

Pickford's words sent electricity through the air as they traveled immediately within earshot of Bogie. He almost coughed on his own cigarette smoke.

The French woman did not respond immediately as if she were hesitating.

"One-million dollars," Pickford repeated. "I'll pay one-million dollars in cash if you allow me to adopt Philippe de Lacy."

At once Bogie knew what was happening. He'd seen De Lacy playing Greta Garbo's son, Seresha, in *Love*. Their scenes had shocked some movie-goers. It was as if De Lacy in the film was making love to Garbo, playing his mother, Anna Karenina. De Lacy was widely regarded as the most beautiful male child in the world.

Pictures of "America's little sweetheart," Pickford, posing with her newly adopted son, Philippe de Lacy, flashed through Bogie's mind. It was a stunt of such interest that the news would spread around the world, along with pictures of the pair. The human interest would be so great it might even revitalize Pickford's career.

"I need the money," the woman sobbed. "Even though he works in films, Philippe doesn't get paid very much—not like what you got paid when you were appearing as the little sweetheart. But I can't. I'll never let Philippe go."

"Then our business is concluded." Pickford said nothing else, not even a goodbye. Suddenly, she appeared at the door. The face she revealed to Bogie was an iron mask.

Since she'd been drinking heavily earlier in the day, he took her by the arm and escorted her into the back seat of the long black car. The dutiful chauffeur, he got behind the wheel. "Where to now, Miss Pickford?" he asked, figuring he was getting valuable experience if he ever were cast in the role of a driver. "Pickfair?"

"Not yet," she said in a commanding voice. "I have one final stopover before going back home." She reached into her purse and searched for an address. It was then that he noticed that she was crying behind those dark glasses. She looked at the address before handing it to him. "I can't read it," she said.

He was astonished when he saw the street and number. It was the address of the apartment building where he lived. "Are you sure this is the right address?" he asked.

"Yes, please leave soon," she said. "I can't stand being in this neighborhood another moment. I've been to the address before and can even tell you how to get there if you don't know. You must be new to Hollywood."

"No thanks, I know how to get there." He drove off, heading to another part of town.

On the way to his apartment building, he said nothing. For one brief paranoic moment, he suspected that Kirkwood had maliciously given Pickford his address for a sexual liaison with the star. Once he got her to his apartment, was he supposed to take her upstairs and fuck her?

The talk of Hollywood was that the Pickford and Fairbanks marriage was disintegrating, and that each of the stars was playing around.

Once there, he parked the big black vehicle in front of his apartment building, got out, and helped her from the car. On unsteady feet, she walked toward the entrance of his building with all the assurance of someone who'd visited this address many times before.

Once inside the hallway, she seemed to know where to go as she began a slow climb up the steps. Dumbfounded, he followed. If it were meant for him to fuck Mary Pickford, he was the man for the job. She was still blonde and beautiful, and the way he figured it, it'd make good reading in his memoirs.

At the top of the landing, right near his door, she paused and looked back at him. "That will be all for now. Would you call for me in two hours?"

"I'll be here," he said, still puzzled.

"I'll be in this apartment." She turned and walked over to Kenneth MacKenna's apartment and knocked on the door.

Kenneth opened the door immediately. Seeing that it was Pickford, he reached for her arm to guide her inside.

Spotting Bogie, Kenneth looked startled. At first he didn't link Pickford with Bogie, but perhaps figured that his friend was climbing the stairs at the same time as the star.

That belief was quickly dispelled when Pickford turned to Bogie. "Kenneth, darling, this is my driver for today. He'll be back for us in two hours."

Before shutting the door, Kenneth flashed a distress signal to Bogie, indicating for him to carry on with the show and that explanations would soon follow as to why Mary Pickford was calling on him. He quickly shut the door.

Bogie stood for a long moment at Kenneth's door. He could hear them talking but their voices were low, and he couldn't make out one word that they were saying.

Soon he could hear no more sounds. Perhaps they'd drifted into another room or were kissing on Kenneth's sofa.

376

As Bogie unlocked his own apartment door, he figured that if Kenneth had entertained Pickford's son-in-law, Douglas Fairbanks Jr., why not the big mama herself? That way, Kenneth could at least be keeping it in the family. The way Bogie felt right now about crazy Hollywood, he wouldn't even be surprised if he saw Douglas Fairbanks Sr. leaving Kenneth's apartment early one morning.

Bogie didn't get much mail. But a letter had been slipped under his door by the superintendent. It was postmarked New York. He knew at once it was from Mary Philips.

Until today, he'd almost forgotten that he was still a married man. He ripped open the letter. Even before reading it, he knew it was bad news.

***

Seated in his apartment with Mary Pickford and Kenneth MacKenna carrying on next door, Bogie slowly read Mary's letter:

Dear Hump,

It's been a long time with no word. Even between good friends, it's been too long without contact. Between a husband and wife, it really marks the end of the marriage. I was prepared to go on in this relationship, at least a little while longer. However, when I read in Parsons' column that you were back with Helen Menken, it was all too much. The bitch even referred to Helen as your wife and not ex-wife. It is as if I didn't even exist. I know that many people still think of Helen as your wife. That's because we did not have a marriage.

As you well know, during the first days of our marriage, I made love to Kenneth far more frequently than I did with you. It may be too late for us, but I realize now that I should have married Kenneth instead of you. He writes every other day, at least, and it is through him that I have had any news of you at all. Of course, Kenneth is a gentleman and leaves out all the bad stuff about you.

I'm sure you've had many affairs in Hollywood with beautiful women, actresses far more beautiful than me. There's even talk in New York about you and Barbara Stanwyck, although I find that hard to believe. Unlike you, I'm no good at playing the field. I'm no saint but I do tend to focus on one man at a time. His name is Roland Young, and I'm sure you know who he is. He's living with me, even though married to Marjorie Kummer. He married her in 1921 but I have persuaded him to get a divorce and marry me. That means, of course, that I will soon be filing for a divorce from you. Let's call it the marriage that never was.   Mary.

"Roland Young," he said out loud, carefully folding the letter. "A God damn limey." He fully intended to show this letter to Kenneth if Mary Pickford ever released his friend from sexual bondage. The way he saw it, if Mary Philips still felt that she should have married Kenneth, it might affect his imminent plan to marry that dyke, Kay Francis.

Maybe Kenneth should break off his engagement to Francis and marry his "true love" after all. After reading that letter, Bogie felt that he'd welcome the divorce, and he was ready to tell Kenneth that he didn't have to hold back any longer, and could move in on Mary if he wanted to. Right now, of course, Kenneth had another Mary to deal with. In some ways, his old jealousy of Kenneth came back again. Not only did his wife really love Kenneth, but he was next door fucking the queen of Hollywood and one of the richest women in the world.

Not aware that Mary Philips even knew Roland Young, Bogie had vaguely followed the actor's career. In the movies and in the theater, other actors kept tabs on their fellow thespians, never knowing when they would become a major competitor for a part.

Young had only recently starred in two films for Cecil B. DeMille—first *Madam Satan*, which co-starred Lillian Roth and Kay Johnson, and *The Squaw Man* with a big-name cast that included Warner Baxter, Lupe Velez, Eleanor Boardman, and Charles Bickford. During the filming of those flickers, Young had been rumored to have had affairs with both Eleanor Boardman and Lillian Roth. He'd even had an affair with Lupe Velez, although how this limey managed to compete with Gary Cooper, her other lover, remained a mystery to Bogart.

Bogie couldn't help but compare himself unfavorably with Young. He'd read in Parsons' column that Young was due back in Hollywood where a string of pictures was being lined up for him. Bogie himself, on the other hand, was facing unemployment in a Depression.

After reading the letter from Mary, and in the years ahead, Bogie would be forever jealous of Young, as he watched him score one success after another. His roles included the unctuous Uriah Heep in *David Copperfield* in 1935 and Katharine Hepburn's Uncle Willie in *The Philadelphia Story* in 1940. Young would be best remembered as Thorne Smith's befuddled banker in the 1937 *Topper*, which earned him an Oscar nomination.

Sinking deeper into a depression, Bogie had two long, stiff drinks before he heard Kenneth knocking on his door. Looking a little worse for wear, Kenneth stood in the hallway with his shirttail hanging out of his trousers and carrying his shoes. "Come on in, pal," Bogie said. "You look like you've had quite a workout from *Rebecca of Sunnybrook Farm*."

"I can explain everything," Kenneth said, coming into the apartment and sitting down on the sofa, where he proceeded to put on his shoes. "I know having Mary show up must have freaked you out, but I haven't been able to tell you what's going on. To get my job, I was sworn to secrecy."

378

"Let me fix you a whiskey," Bogie said, "and you can tell me all about it, pal."

Kenneth did just that, and Bogie was startled that all this Hollywood intrigue had been happening all around him, and he hadn't had a clue as to what Kenneth was doing, other than planning to marry Kay Francis.

While Pickford rested and refreshed herself before traveling back to Pickfair, Kenneth revealed what he'd been doing.

Mary Pickford had secretly been filming *Forever Yours*, a remake of the silent film, *Secrets*, which had been such a big hit for Norma Talmadge back in 1924. The reason Pickford chose to keep the Talkie a secret was that she planned to abandon the film after the first six weeks of shooting if she felt that it would not surpass the Talmadge blockbuster.

For the director, Kenneth said that she'd hired old-time associate, Marshall Neilan, with whom she'd scored so many past successes, including not only *Rebecca of Sunnybrook Farm* in 1917, but *A Little Princess* the same year, followed by *Stella Maris* in 1918. Neilan had also directed Pickford in two other films in 1918: *Amirilly of Clothes-Line Alley* and *M'Liss*. The duo had continued to make films together, including *Daddy Long Legs* in 1919, and *Dorothy Vernon of Haddon Hall* in 1924, in spite of the director's increasing alcoholism.

To his surprise, Bogie was invited to Pickfair that night to see the first edited reels of *Forever Yours*.

"Okay," Bogie said to Kenneth, "but you've got to tell your bitch I'm not a God damn chauffeur but a movie star, same as the two of you."

"I'll straighten that out with Mary," he promised. "She doesn't go out to see many films any more."

"I can't believe she didn't see Spence and me in *Up the River*," he said petulantly.

"I'll see that she does," Kenneth promised. "She has her own projection room at Pickfair." He stood up and tucked in his shirt. "We'd better go. We shouldn't keep Mary waiting too long."

"One thing, pal," Bogie said, restraining Kenneth's arm. "Does Fairbanks Sr. know about you and Mary? I hear he's terribly jealous. I heard that one day Valentino arrived in some fancy car at Pickfair and Fairbanks chased him away with a gun."

"He doesn't know anything," Kenneth said. "Besides, he's having his own affairs."

Not being able to restrain himself, Bogie said, "I guess you didn't tell America's Little Sweetheart that you've also been sleeping with her son-in-law."

"I think I forgot to mention that," Kenneth said jokingly, not at all offended.

"I guess I could tell sweet Mary about the night I fucked her daughter-in-law, Joan Crawford."

"Yeah, you go ahead and do that," Kenneth said facetiously.

"Pal, before you go, I've got this letter I want you to read from New York. It's from your girl friend."

"My girl friend?" Kenneth asked, looking astonished. "I no longer have a girl friend in New York."

"You do now," Bogie said, handing him the farewell letter from Mary Philips.

***

Usually as many as eight or twelve guests dined nightly at Pickfair. Tonight it was only Pickford herself along with her estranged husband, Doug Fairbanks Sr., with Bogie joining Kenneth as one of the two invited guests.

When she learned that Bogie was Kenneth's friend and not a chauffeur, Pickford treated him more cordially, although it was obvious she'd never heard of him or of the two well-known Broadway actresses he'd married. She lived in her own world of the self-enchanted. If something did not directly affect her, it did not concern her. Bogie could understand that.

Although Pickford didn't serve booze, and Fairbanks seemed to have little tolerance for alcohol, the lady of the house appeared to get drunker as the evening progressed. She made frequent exits to "powder my nose," and Bogie suspected that she had a stash of hooch hidden somewhere outside the dining room. Once celebrated as the legal union of the Sweethearts of Hollywood, the Fairbanks/Pickford marriage was all but ended, as even the most casual observer could see.

If Pickford had anything to say, she directed her comments to Kenneth. Fairbanks was clearly bored, and Bogie was intrigued only because of the grand celebrity of his hosts. He found that observing them in real life was more interesting than anything he'd seen them do on the screen. He felt that all of their movies—Fairbanks' swashbuckling roles and Pickford's little girl fantasies—were mere fluff to the drama being played out tonight. If the future playwright, Edward Albee, had been there, he would surely have found inspiration in the evening to write *Who's Afraid of Virginia Woolf?*

Pickford had been talking about *Forever Yours* all night, voicing her concern about the movie.

Finally, losing his patience, Fairbanks slammed down a glass of apple juice. "Why in hell don't you retire from the screen? You've got all the money in the world. You've had all the acclaim. Why not move aside and make way for the younger crowd?"

"God damn you!" Pickford shouted at him across the table. "In case you haven't noticed lately, I'm still young and beautiful."

"Young and beautiful describes our daughter-in-law," Fairbanks said. "Even my own son. I hate to be photographed next to him. He's like a prettier version of myself. He's so fucking gorgeous he makes me look like his grandfather instead of his father."

"What you're saying is that the great Douglas Fairbanks Sr. and his concubine, Mary Pickford, are washed up in Hollywood," she said.

"That will never happen," Bogie interjected.

"Would you shut your trap unless I ask you for something?" she barked at him, before softening that remark with a sweet smile directed at Kenneth, the same smile Bogie had seen in *Rebecca of Sunnybrook Farm*.

"What I'm saying is that romantic leading roles in films are for the young," Fairbanks said. "The future belongs to Joan Crawford, Garbo, beauties like that. Chaplin will never make it in Talkies. Swanson and Pola Negri will fail too. Look at Gilbert. He'll play at most one more role, maybe two, before he's washed up. Our day is over."

"Speak for yourself, asshole," Pickford shouted at him. Surely no words could ever have been uttered that would infuriate her more. "I *am* the queen of Hollywood, and before that, I reigned for a long time as its fairy princess. And I am STILL the queen of Hollywood. No up-and-coming, ambition-crazed bitch has even come close to replacing me." On wobbly legs, she stood up. "They call me America's sweetheart."

"They don't call you that," Fairbanks shouted at her. "They used to call you that. You were playing that little girl with the golden curls ten years after you were too old for the role."

"And what in the fuck were you doing?" Pickford shrieked at him. "Playing Don Juans when you've gotten flabby. You don't have a great body. It bulges in all the wrong places. The only place it doesn't bulge out is at your crotch. Your son has a great body. Douglas Fairbanks Sr. never had a great body, and that body has gone to seed."

"Is that so?" he said, standing up to confront her on an equal level. "Name any sex symbol of Hollywood. All I'd have to do is call her up and she'd come running." He turned to Bogie. "Put me to the test. Call any glamour gal on the phone. Fuck! Call Jean Harlow and tell her to come over here if she wants to get plowed by Douglas Fairbanks Sr. I'll fuck the dyed blonde right here on the table in front of all of you. Call Carole Lombard. It doesn't matter who you call as long as she's young and beautiful. I'm not washed up. Men like me will only be finished when they're hauled off to Forest Lawn. Aging women like you dear, sweet Mary are the true casualties of Hollywood. No wonder you hate Joan Crawford so much. She's young. She's vibrant. She's beautiful. She's sexy. All the things you've either lost or never had."

Mortified yet fascinated to be privy to such conversation between two Hollywood royals, Bogie was both mesmerized yet repulsed. It was like listening to a dog-and-cat fight between the king and queen of England.

Before priceless silver and porcelain could be broken, the dinner party was both interrupted and rescued by the arrival of Pickford's director, Marshall Neilan. Like Pickford herself, Neilan was drunk. He came up to Pickford and tried to kiss her. "Stay away from me, you old sot." She pushed him back from her.

"Isn't that like the pot calling the kettle black?" Neilan said. "Everybody on the set knows that if I don't finish a scene with you before noon, you'll be too boozed up to finish it before 2pm."

"And you're too God damn tanked by ten o'clock in the morning to even think straight, so don't you go telling me about having too much to drink!" she snarled.

To his surprise, she reached for Bogie's arm, not Kenneth's, and asked him to escort her into the projection room.

Kenneth trailed them, talking with Neilan. Before they turned the corner, Bogie heard Kenneth lecturing Neilan. "God damn it, I'm the male star of the picture. The camera has to pay some attention to me. I demand more close-ups. In case you didn't know, I'm in the picture too."

"I don't pay any attention to you because you're window dressing," Neilan told him. "It's Mary's picture. Fans will flock to theaters to see Mary Pickford. No one in the world has ever heard of Kenneth MacKenna."

With that pronouncement, the men faded from view, as Pickford led Bogie out onto the patio for a moment of fresh air while Neilan ordered the staff to set up the edited reels of *Forever Yours* in the projection room.

"Please excuse Doug's intemperate remarks," Pickford said to Bogie, showing the kindest, gentlest side of herself like he'd seen on the screen.

"It's okay by me," he said. "I think a kind of creeping waspishness comes to all marriages if a couple stays hitched long enough. With my first wife, our fighting started the day we were married."

"It wasn't like that with us," Pickford said. "Doug used to be romantic. But he's growing increasingly difficult. Aging. Failing career. It's financial too. He was very well off, one of the richest men in Hollywood, before the crash. I had warned him to stay out of the market. He wouldn't listen to the advice of a mere woman. My investments are relatively safe. I emerged from the crash unscathed. Not only that, but today Doug got a little letter from the government. It seems he owes $1,092,273 to Uncle Sam."

"That's a lot of loot," he said. "Especially to a man like me who's pulling in $750 a week at Fox."

"That's not a bad salary," Pickford said. "When some of us got started in films, the pay was three dollars a day. Sometimes even less. I've always paid for talent. When I wanted to lure my director, Sam Taylor, from Joe Schenck, I offered him $4,000 a week. Schenck was giving him $2,500. No need saying who got the services of Taylor. He turned out to be a bastard, though, but a country mile ahead of Neilan. Even before we go in to watch what's in the can, I can tell you that Neilan is finished in Hollywood. Once we wrap *Forever Yours*, I'll see that the old sot never works another day in Hollywood."

At that point, a male servant came up to Pickford and Bogie, telling them that Neilan was ready to begin screening *Forever Yours*.

In the projection room, Pickford chose to sit next to Kenneth. After the fight at table, Fairbanks had disappeared. Bogie took a back row seat, as Neilan anchored himself near the projectionist.

382

Even before the first five minutes of the film had been shown, Bogie knew that Pickford had made a disaster. It was one of the worst movies he'd ever seen. He figured that *Forever Yours* would do for Pickford what *His Glorious Night* did for the once-stellar career of John Gilbert. In other words, ruin it.

Bogie sat hunched down in his seat for the next twenty minutes. No one said anything.

Suddenly, Pickford rose from her seat in a screeching rage. With the light from the projection booth shining into the otherwise dark room, it caught her distorted face at its most agitated. It was a scene eerily evocative of the future 1950 film, *Sunset Boulevard*, when Gloria Swanson, screening one of her old films for her gigolo, William Holden, was caught in much the same light. It was also ironic that Billy Wilder would offer Pickford the role of Norma Desmond, the faded queen of silent pictures, before giving the part to Swanson. After seeing Pickford in a real life situation that night, Bogie understood Wilder's first choice years from now.

Pickford turned to confront Neilan. "You've made me grotesque! I look like an old hag. I don't look like Kenneth's lover. I look like his mother. You deliberately photographed me so much older."

Bogie knew that Kenneth was only seven years younger than Pickford, but the eagle-eyed actress did have a point. She did look as old as his mother.

"Stop showing this film," she shouted at Neilan. "I won't see another piece of footage. I'll burn the God damn film. No one will ever see it."

"God has made you old," Neilan shouted at her. "God, not me. God and a battleship of booze, you broken down old hag. Fuck you. Fire me if you want to."

Pickford screamed in rage and appeared on the verge of fainting when a servant turned on the lights. Kenneth assisted a sobbing Pickford from the room, as Neilan stormed out the other door in the direction of the pool.

Bogie sat alone in the projection room, not knowing what to do. He decided that since his hosts, and certainly Kenneth, were involved for the rest of the evening, he would remove himself from the premises. Since he didn't know where Pickford kept her booze stashed, and since he was in desperate need of a drink, he had to get out of Pickfair.

For years, he'd read how actors had eagerly sought an invitation to Pickfair. Well, he'd been invited, and now he couldn't wait to escape from the mansion.

In time he would hear Pickford deny ever having made the picture. But she didn't burn it. In 1946, an inventory of her private vaults turned up six edited reels of *Forever Yours*, or two-thirds of a completed picture. After suffering a loss of $300,000, Pickford donated the footage to the Library of Congress.

Since Bogie couldn't take Pickford's car, or didn't dare, he decided to call a taxi. As he was dialing from the foyer, he saw a police car, with dome lights flashing, pull up at the entrance to Pickfair.

A police lieutenant came to the foyer. "Where's Doug? We've come for him."

"Beats me, pal," Bogie said, putting down the phone. "What's the charge?"

At that moment, Fairbanks emerged at the top of the steps, still in athletic form, he bounded down the stairs, taking two steps at a time. "Hi, Bill, I'm ready for another fun evening on the town." Seeing that Bogie was still here, he grabbed his arm. "Come along for the ride. I assure you you'll have a grand time."

For the next four hours, Bogie sat in the back seat pursuing Fairbank's hobby. A generous contributor to local charities, especially the police retirement fund, Fairbanks was a favorite of the Los Angeles Police Department. Its members freely indulged the swashbuckling star in one of his favorite nocturnal pursuits, which involved riding around in a squad car to the scene of various dramas.

Before Bogie was finally released four hours later from the clutches of a star he viewed as demented, he was taken to a scene of domestic violence, where a black woman had stabbed her husband when she caught him in bed with her thirteen-year-old daughter and, later, where a robbery of a jewelry store was halted in progress. That had led to a shoot-out before two men were apprehended, one having been seriously wounded.

Before the evening ended, Fairbanks had given each of the two policemen a hundred dollar bill but not before they had agreed to stop by the Los Angeles morgue where the star had insisted that Bogie inspect each of the nude cadavers with him.

Back in his own car, Fairbanks offered to drive Bogie back to his apartment house. On the way there, he stopped off at a club called Flamingo Danse. "I'll be just a minute," he said before jumping out of the car and heading into the club. He emerged in a few minutes with a scantily dressed woman by his side.

When she got into the car with Bogie, he recognized her. It was the Mexican spitfire, Lupe Velez. He'd seen Fairbanks and Velez on the screen together when they'd co-starred in the 1927 film, *The Gaucho*.

Velez remembered Bogie from her dramatic appearance at Myrna Loy's home, the night she'd stabbed her other lover, Gary Cooper.

"How's Myrna?" she asked with a certain innocence. No mention was made of the stabbing.

"She's fine, I guess," Bogie said. "I haven't seen her since that night."

"You men!" Velez said. "Always wanting one-night stands. Unlike Doug here. He doesn't go for just one night and then drops you, but sticks around like a regular. It's good for women to enjoy different men all the time." She leaned over and kissed Fairbanks at the driver's wheel. "But it's even better having regular guy like Doug."

At the entrance to his apartment house, Bogie wished Velez a good night. To his surprise, Fairbanks insisted on escorting Bogie all the way to his apartment door.

For one strange moment, he feared that Fairbanks might have a lavender streak in him like his son. Bogie became a little nervous when Fairbanks insisted on entering his apartment and looking around carefully.

384

"Do you live here alone?" Fairbanks asked.

"Yeah," Bogie said. "Why? You looking for a roommate? George Raft used to room here with me."

"If you'd ever like to make a quick hundred dollars, I'd like to borrow this apartment from time to time for entertaining."

"Sure, pal," Bogie said. "I understand. It won't cost you a thing. I can't charge the great Douglas Fairbanks for having a quickie in my apartment."

Fairbanks asked for Bogie's telephone number and he wrote it down. At the door, he shook Bogie's hand and wished him a good night.

"Thanks for the entertainment," Bogie said. "I'll have nightmares, especially after that visit to the morgue. That butchered fat lady. Pretty gross."

"But eternally fascinating," Fairbanks said before disappearing down the stairs, taking two steps at a time.

As Bogie shut the door, he wondered what might happen if Fairbanks ever used his apartment for the seduction of a broad. He might encounter his wife mounting the same stairs to get laid by Kenneth. Pickford and Fairbanks, Hollywood's most famous married couple, might end up screwing other sexual partners in adjoining apartments.

He went to the phone and called Helen at the Garden of Allah. The reception desk there told him she wasn't accepting calls from him.

He stripped down and went to bed but couldn't sleep. Propped up on pillows and smoking a cigarette in the darkness, he heard his phone ring. At first he was tempted not to answer it. But the ring was persistent.

Figuring it was Helen calling him back, he got out of bed and went into the living room to answer the phone.

"Bogart?" a man's voice said on the other end.

"I answer to that," he said, wondering who in the hell would be calling him at this hour.

"It's Hughes."

"Not another fucking plane ride," he said.

"Nothing like that," Hughes said. "You don't want me to make trouble for you, do you?"

"No way, pal," Bogie said, "and I know you can."

"I have a few problems at home," Hughes said, "and I need you to get your ass over here right away."

"I'm your man," Bogie said. "Be right over."

"Good," Hughes said. "I've got Billie Dove stashed in one wing of the house, Jean Harlow in another. The shit has hit the fan!"

"I said I'll be there, but please don't say shit in front of me." He put down the phone wondering if there would ever be an end to this night.

Chapter Twelve

At Hughes' Muirfield mansion, a male servant welcomed Bogie into the foyer. "Mr. Hughes has been expecting you," the man said. "I'm to bring you to him at once."

"I'm glad someone in Hollywood has the welcome mat out for me, pal," Bogie said with an edge of bitterness in his voice.

As he was directed toward a garden-like living room, he heard angry voices. Hughes never raised his voice but spoke in a slow, deadly monotone.

The voice of a woman was extremely agitated, as if she wanted the world — not just Hughes — to hear what she was saying. Those were not the sweet, melodious tones of Billie Dove. Attacking Hughes was none other than Jean Harlow herself. No barmaid in Missouri calling for another round of drinks for a table of drunken truck drivers sounded quite as authentic as Harlow. Even though she was making Talkies, her crude, strident voice just didn't match her beautiful body. In other cases, such as that of silent screen vamp, Vilma Banky, a voice like that would have destroyed a film career. Harlow was going against the trend.

In the living room, facing the pair, Bogie looked first at Harlow with her albino face and her slightly puffy, sulky little face. In a white dress with white shoes and stockings, she was standing up confronting Hughes. He was seated serenely in a Queen Anne armchair, the wings evoking some heavenly throne. The tall Texan was clearly the man in charge tonight.

Both Harlow and Hughes only briefly acknowledged Bogie's presence, like a rich man and his wife might treat a servant bringing them another drink. Finally, Hughes motioned for Bogie to help himself to the liquor.

"Bogart," Harlow finally said, "I don't care if you hear this or not." She looked with contempt into the face of Hughes. "I was just telling this fairy here that I'm God damn tired of working for one-hundred dollars a week on a five-year contract. I want out."

"I'm forced to lend you out to other studios," Hughes said, "because I have nothing for you now. Any more movies I produce will call for a real actress. You can't act and you can't be directed. You're nothing but a one-dimensional vamp. You can wear low-cut gowns, seduce men, smoke, and drink—that's it."

"In *Hell's Angels*," she said, "I did everything you asked me to. I really suffered. Standing under those bright lights sixteen hours a day until I got Klieg eyes. I languished with burnt eyeballs for six weeks."

"During which time you were sent a weekly paycheck from my office," Hughes said. "Don't forget that."

"Who could forget your measly little check?" she shouted at him. "Not even enough to pay the grocery bill."

"It's enough for you to live on," Hughes said. "But you're supporting your crazed mother and that Wop lover of hers."

"Yeah, I've got a family to take care of—that's true," she said. "I'm also the biggest name in pictures. And the most underpaid. You found that out on that fucking train ride we took east. Big names were aboard that train. That French fairy, Maurice Chevalier. Miss Billie Dove, most beautiful woman on earth. And the richest man in America, Mr. Howard Hughes of Texas. But tell Bogart who the public turned out to see at every stop we made. Jean Harlow! I'll say it again, you deaf faggot. *Jean Harlow*. That's star power, baby, and don't you forget it."

"Okay, okay," he said, growing impatient with her. "You're a fucking star. So what? Do you think you're the only star I've known? The only star I've fucked? I can sign up any star in Hollywood I want. I can fuck them too. When Howard Hughes calls them, they come running."

"That's not because you're a great lay, baby," she said. She glanced over at Bogie again, who was already pouring himself a second drink and wondering what he was doing at this gathering.

"I've had better lays from gas jockeys I pulled into the back seat of my car while they were filling up my tank," she said. When she looked back at Hughes, Bogie had never known an actress who faced her producer with such unconcealed hostility. "Did I make you jealous?" A smirk came across her face when she looked at Bogie again. "Little baby Howie here specializes in gas jockeys. It's his favorite form of amusement. I think the smell of gasoline on their sweaty male bodies is an aphrodisiac to him."

"Shut your fucking face, you bitch," Hughes said. At first Bogie feared that he was going to slap her, but he came over to pour himself a whiskey, deliberately trying to calm his nerves.

"Because of that fucking contract," she said to Bogie, "he keeps me chained to him. All he does is loan me out."

"At least you got to fuck both John Mack Brown and Clark Gable in *The Secret Six*," Hughes said. "There were some fringe benefits to that job."

Bogie was startled. John Mack Brown was Tracy's new fuck buddy. He wondered if his pal knew that Harlow was fucking Johnny too? Or did John Mack Brown know that his boy friend, Tracy, was also fucking Harlow? Bogie figured that a heterosexual man had trouble enough keeping his affairs with women straight, but these bisexuals had an even greater task figuring their way out of the tangled webs they wove.

"Yeah," Harlow said, her shrill contempt for Hughes on the rise. "I bet you wish you had Johnny Mack Brown in your own bed. You'd kick Gable out after one night. What a disappointment. But Johnny boy is just your type. I also got to play the mistress of Wallace Beery in that film. The most contemptible scumbag who ever walked onto a Hollywood lot."

"I heard when you fucked up that shitty little boxing flick, *The Iron Man*, you

388

even seduced Lew Ayres, and most of the time, he's a pansy," Hughes said.

Bogie recalled meeting Lew Ayres himself and the actor's involvement with Tracy.

"Don't put Lew down," she said. "He might take it up the ass with men but he can also get it up for a woman." She went over and placed her face right up against Hughes, who had reseated himself in the armchair. "That's something that no mere woman can count on Howard Hughes doing for her. The tall, rich Texan and his very unreliable erection."

Impulsively he slapped her face. She backed away from him, rubbing her porcelain cheek. She walked toward Bogie at the bar. "Impotent men like to beat up on women. They figure if they can't fuck them, they can always use their strength to beat the shit out of them."

Bogie could only stare in amazement. Harlow was nothing if not a contradiction. Here she was denouncing Howard Hughes for his occasional impotence, yet talking of marriage to Paul Bern, known as the most impotent man in Hollywood.

Recovering from the slap, she poured herself a drink. The room had gone strangely silent. Bogie hoped that their fight was over and that he might learn what new errand Hughes had planned for him. Surely it didn't involve Harlow.

Bolting down a drink, Harlow stood on wobbly white high heels to look at Hughes. "I happen to know you got one-thousand big ones a week for lending me out for *The Public Enemy*."

"I also raised your salary to two-hundred a week," Hughes said defensively.

No longer able to stand the tension, Bogie blurted out to Harlow, "You certainly had tits in that film. How did you get them to hold up like that? I've been meaning to ask. So many other actresses droop on camera."

"Silly," she said, running her fingers along his cheek. "I told you in Palm Springs. I ice 'em. Actually, that's Mama Jean's job. She applies chunks of ice to my beautiful breasts before I go on camera. My nipples stand up firm for an hour. Then I go back to my dressing room and we repeat the process."

Hughes rose from his chair. From the look on his face, he'd had enough of this encounter. He still hadn't told Bogie why he'd summoned him here. Walking past Harlow, he glared at her with a steely defiance. "You certainly were type-cast when I lent you out to play a tramp opposite Tracy in *Goldie*. I think I've never heard the word tramp used on the screen before to describe a woman. Until you came along, tramp meant Chaplin's *The Little Tramp*. In your case, the word fits."

It was Harlow who slapped Hughes this time. He stood back from her but didn't strike her back.

After slapping him, she burst into tears. "Please, Howard, allow Joe Schenck to transfer my contract over to Goldwyn. You have no roles for me, no future plans. It's obvious: we're going nowhere together as a team."

As if to pay her back for that slap, he looked at her cruelly. "You haven't heard the latest. Goldwyn's not interested. He's already turned you down after our little talk. He also got a call from Darryl Zanuck over at Warner's. He told Goldwyn you're the worst actress in Hollywood. He said directors have to cut many of your scenes because you simply can't act them out." Suddenly, he grabbed Harlow by her platinum hair. He yanked a strand, as if holding it up for Bogie to inspect. "What do you think?" he asked. "A woman whose fame lies in the color of her bleached hair and some nipples on ice."

Bogie had little intention of engaging Hughes in a fight. He always ran from a brawl if he could. "Hey, pal," he said, "let's cut out the rough stuff."

Hughes released Harlow who ran to the other part of the room.

"I asked you," Hughes said to Bogie. "What do you think of this tramp?"

For want of something to answer, Bogie said, "I hear the only good coming out of all this platinum hair stuff is for the peroxide business. Sales, or so I'm told, are up thirty-five percent. All over the country—again, so I've read—women are botching the job in trying to go platinum. They don't know Jean's beauty secrets. They're ruining their hair and having to shave their heads."

Suddenly, Harlow emerged from the other side of the room. No longer the cowering damsel in distress, she was a tower of strength as she walked over to Hughes. "So, you won't give in to my demands." She placed her hand on her hip as she did in the movies. "If I'm gonna go work for Louis B. Mayer in the future, I'm gonna have to get used to dealing with a bigger shit than you. I think you'd better listen to my demands." She lifted her chin up toward Hughes' face and glared defiantly at him. "Or else…."

"What else?" he said. "You think you can blackmail me? Others have tried. When you've got money, the whole world is trying to blackmail you. What are you going to do? Call Louella Parsons and tell her we've had an affair? Parsons already knows that."

"No," she said. "I'm not calling just one columnist. Tomorrow morning I'm calling a whole God damn press conference. I'm gonna announce to the world the fact I'm pregnant. And…" She paused, looking at Hughes with a certain kind of glee. "And I'm telling all the boys who show up with their cameras that Howard Hughes is the father. On one of the few nights he could get it up for a woman, Hughes became the papa of my little bastard baby. I'm carrying around little Howard Hughes Jr. in my gut."

***

With a hysterical Jean Harlow tucked away in an upstairs bedroom, Hughes had obviously decided to deal with her pregnancy in the morning. He told Bogie he'd given her some sleeping pills to get her through the rest of the night, freeing him to deal with a more immediate problem: Billie Dove.

He ushered Bogie into her bedroom suite where she was beautifully dressed and made up, waiting impatiently for Hughes. She hardly acknowledged Bogie, but turned her most urgent attention toward Hughes. "What have you decided to do?"

"I'm going to pay the bastard," Hughes said. "Not the million dollars he's demanding, but half a million. All in cash."

"Dear Irvin will be fixed for the rest of his life, the bastard," Dove said.

Without being told, Bogie realized that they were talking about Irvin Willet, Dove's former husband. Bogie had learned that Hughes had already settled $350,000 on the director. Since Dove had now divorced him, Bogie didn't understand why this stupendous new payment was suddenly being arranged.

"Bogart will drive you over," Hughes said. "Make sure you have all the evidence before you turn over the money to him. Also, my lawyers want him to sign a document. See that Bogart here witnesses it."

"I know the bull-necked son-of-a-bitch very well," Dove said. "You think he'll keep hitting on you again and again. But I think this is it. After tonight, Irvin will have $850,000 in cash. It doesn't matter if he ever directs another film. He's a lousy director anyway."

Bogie noted the expression on Hughes' face as he stared at Dove. He didn't quite know how to characterize the look. He wouldn't call it the look of love.

"You're turning out to be a very expensive bauble," Hughes said in a voice with a sharp bite.

She picked up a hairbrush from her vanity table and tossed it toward him. "I'm not a God damn bauble. Your first payoff to Irvin was insurance money for you. Without it, Ella Rice would have taken far more than a million dollars from you in that divorce settlement. This payoff tonight has not a thing to do with me. It's your own mistake. If my boy friend, Mr. Howard Hughes, didn't have a fondness for plugging young men in the ass, he wouldn't be in the trouble he's in now."

Her words angered him. As he turned to stalk out of the suite, he looked toward Bogie. "She'll tell you what to do." From the hallway, he called to Bogie. Under the chandelier of the second floor hall, Hughes softened his features when he approached Bogie. "Is everything still on with George O'Brien? I'm expecting you to bring him over at eight tonight."

"Pal, with Dove and Harlow under the same roof, and Randolph Scott and Ben Lyon only a phone call away, it looks to me like you've got your hands full."

"That's for me to decide," Hughes said.

"You're calling the shots," Bogie said. "The last time I talked to him, O'Brien seemed only too eager to get his baby-ass over here."

Hughes gently took hold of Bogie's arm. "He's good, isn't he? I mean, surely you've had him. I know you visited him at his home and came out later in swimming trunks and that you guys went to the beach together."

"I'm sure your boys told you that much," Bogie said. "What they didn't tell you, is that I don't go that route. Call me old-fashioned, but it seems I'm the only guy left in Hollywood who believes in fucking women exclusively."

"I see." Hughes had a far and distant look in his eyes. He turned and walked away, heading back to his library.

As Bogie rounded up Dove to set out on this mysterious journey, he wondered if Hughes ever slept. Probably not. He was too busy counting his money, a good hunk of which he was planning to give away tonight.

Dove pointed to a heavily strapped suitcase on her satin-covered bed. "Bring the suitcase, would you, love?" she asked him. "The money's in there. Half a million fucking greenbacks."

He lifted the suitcase from the bed, wishing that it was his. "I hope all the highway robbers in Los Angeles have gone to bed for the night. Imagine what a haul they'd get if they robbed us."

She reached for her purse. "Remember to drive carefully. We don't want to get stopped by the police."

"What a headline that would make," he said. "The most beautiful and highest paid actress in the world, Billie Dove, arrested with half a million in cash."

"Wouldn't you fit into the headline too?" she asked.

"Yeah, right," he said. "The press would probably report, 'Driving her car was the handsome young juvenile actor at Fox, Humphrey Bogart.'"

Fifteen minutes later, with the suitcase stashed in the locked trunk, Bogie and Billie Dove set out into the still darkness of an early morning to deliver the blackmail money to Irvin Willat.

On the way there, Dove told him more about what was happening. "Howard is known for having people followed. He might have a medley of five men and women on the leash at the same time. Obviously he can't spread himself around that thin. But he wants to know what his girl friend or his boy friend is up to when he's not with them. But this detective business is a two-way street."

"I don't quite get it," Bogie said.

"With an investment of $15,000 from the money Irvin got for allowing our divorce to go through, he hired some pretty smart detectives to trail Howard. They turned up plenty of evidence about his involvement with women. But what delighted Irvin was when he saw the tremendous amount of evidence the detectives accumulated on Howard's sexual liaisons with men. Howard is too rich to be destroyed by such revelations. But he would be God damn embarrassed. Irvin has agreed to turn over all the evidence in exchange if Howard comes through with the money."

"That certainly is a risk Hughes has to take," he said. "As you and I both know, Willat might not turn over all the evidence. He might hold a lot of it back for a rainy day."

"Howard is no pussy. I'm to make it clear to Irvin tonight that if he ever tries to blackmail Howard again, he might end up as a file in the Bureau of Missing Persons."

"I think Hughes would have Willat done in a minute," he said. "Thanks to our own little embarrassing encounter at my apartment, I would never fuck with Howard Hughes. I learned my lesson that night. Since that time, I've been a good boy. Now, with me, you're safer than with any other man in Hollywood. I'll get no closer to you than seated next to you in this car."

"That's too bad," she said enigmatically. "I was hoping to reward you later." She paused to light a cigarette. "Reward myself, really. I'm sure not getting enough from Howard these days. He's too busy."

Did she mean that? Or was he walking into another trap? Before he could ponder that question, he had arrived at the darkened house of Irvin Willat.

In the moonlight, with a gentle wind rustling through the palm trees, the house looked ominous.

***

A black man in a black suit opened the door for Bogie and Billie Dove at the Willat residence. "Good evening, Mrs. Willat," he said, standing back to let them in. She barged in like a woman on a horrible mission, and didn't bother to introduce Bogie. That he could understand. At this hour of the morning, it wasn't a social call.

Standing awkwardly in the hallway, he held onto the heavy suitcase. That high-priced luggage was expensive in more ways than one. Dove told him to guard the suitcase and to wait for her in the living room. "Pour yourself a drink. I'm going to go upstairs to see Irvin in his study. I'll call you if I need you."

With that, she rushed up the steps, as the black man disappeared into the back of the house. Still carrying the suitcase, Bogie headed toward the living room, where a single light burned. He could sure use that drink. Still carrying the suitcase, he came into the dimly lit salon. To his surprise, he encountered Tommy Richards sitting on the sofa having a drink. He was shirtless and barefoot but had on a pair of tight-fitting black trousers. Once again, Bogie was almost stunned by the beauty of Glenda Farrell's former husband.

"Kid," Bogie said, "I thought I told you to stay out of town. I never expected to see you here again."

"Hi, come on in and pour yourself a drink," Richards said. "I was out of town living in Texas. I was making pretty good money. Someone introduced me to Mr. Hughes. He was the one who insisted I come back to Hollywood."

"You and Howard Hughes?" Bogie asked, astonished. "You sure get around, or maybe Howard is the one who gets around."

"Things were going fine between Howard and me," Richards said. "Then one day he got tired of me. Unlike that tightwad, Spencer Tracy, Howard was very generous in the kiss-off. He gave me ten one-thousand crisp ones."

"If you're so pleased with Howard's settlement, what are you doing here at Willat's house?" Bogie asked, lighting a cigarette.

"I would have been happy to take the money and run," Richards said, "but one day Willat came to the bungalow where Howard had stashed me. He made me an offer I couldn't refuse."

"And what was that?"

"One-hundred thousand dollars," Richards said. "I'd be set for life. He said he'd had detectives trailing Howard and that he had enough blackmail evidence on him to bury him. Irvin claims he's going to blackmail Howard into giving him one-million dollars. I could have one-tenth of it."

"That's a lot of money to be paid for getting your dick sucked," Bogie said. "A lot of money."

"Is the money in that suitcase?" Richards said. "You look damn funny carrying around that bag. Are you Howard's latest?"

"I'm not his first or his latest," Bogie snapped. "The reason I'm here this morning is a long story I'm not going into."

"Even though Howard got bored with me, I learned a lot about his type. He likes guys who fly planes and who work in garages, you know, rough-and-ready blue-collar types. He also digs cowboys. At Willat's urging, I rounded up three guys I knew Howard would go bananas for. Howard told me to arrange dates for him with each of them. In fact, he gave me a thousand dollars for my trouble."

"So, you've become a pimp?"

"Money's money," Richards said. "It doesn't matter how you get it. Just getting some—that's what it's all about."

"Go on," Bogie said, realizing he'd rapidly finished off his first drink. He went over to pour a second.

"Howard fell into Willat's trap," Richards said. "I don't know what Willat did, but he paid those guys to get Howard involved in some entrapment."

"Were pictures taken?" Bogie asked. "Stuff like that."

"I didn't ask and I still don't want to know," Richards said. "I'm staying with Willat until I get my dough, and then I'm out of here. You don't have to put me on a train this time. I'll drive out of Hollywood in the most expensive and shiny new car in town."

"Looks like you hit pay dirt, kid," Bogie said. "A dirty business."

"In case you hadn't noticed, life is a dirty business," Richards said. "I'm not the little innocent kid who married Glenda. I've changed a lot since those days."

"I believe you have," Bogie said. "Glenda's a nice gal. I couldn't imagine her wanting to marry a blackmailing hustler."

"After I get my big bucks, I'm gonna settle somewhere in Arizona," Richards said. "Buy me a ranch. Get married to some pretty little blonde with blue eyes and big tits. Raise six kids."

"And they'll never know how daddy struck it rich," Bogie said sarcastically.

"They'll never know," Richards echoed. "I'll be a pillar of the community. Maybe even sit on the school board."

Bogie raised his glass to Richards. "Good luck to you. Hughes has got me by the balls, so I'm not shedding any crocodile tears over that asshole losing any more of his money. He's got plenty more to replace whatever you and that Willat creep take him for. Frankly, I don't want any part of it."

At that moment Dove, trailed by the black servant, came into the living room. She'd been crying.

The actress ignored Richards and turned to Bogie. "Let Bill have the suitcase." She signaled to the black servant. "Irvin insists on counting every dollar. He wants to make sure that Howard didn't insert paper in any of the stacks." Finally, she faced Richards, her glowingly beautiful face distorted in anger. "As for you, scumbag," she said to him, "get your ass upstairs. Irvin wants you to help him count the money."

"To the rescue," Richards said, jumping up from the sofa. "I've been waiting all my life for a bundle like this."

As he rushed past Dove, she stepped back. "Women whores are disgusting enough. But a male whore! That must be the most despicable creature ever put on God's earth."

He stopped at the door. "You're no better than me, bitch. Male or female, it doesn't matter. You're Howard's whore just as much as I was, with one big difference. No woman can ever satisfy Howard." He groped himself. "I have something he wanted. Something you'll never be able to give him, unless you strap on a dildo for him." With that, he was gone.

Dove burst into tears and fell into Bogie's arms. He held her tightly, wanting her. He'd even give up his fantasies about Lilyan Tashman for Billie Dove. He'd never known a more desirable woman in his life. She made his first two wives look like kitchen maids.

She broke away. "Please, get me a drink."

At the bar, he poured her a whiskey straight and handed it to her.

"My stomach's turning over," she said. "Irvin gleefully showed me some of his evidence. I've never been so repulsed in my life. That male whore is right. I'll never be able to satisfy Howard. I don't think he'll ever marry me. We'll carry on for a while, and that will be that."

"Can we get out of here?" he said. "You got the evidence?"

"Everything is being arranged," she said. "Howard is sending two lawyers over in about an hour. I thought it was all settled. But Irvin is making new demands. It may take some time." She held up her glass and clanked it against his. "I feel very close to you tonight." She leaned over and kissed him gently on the lips. "It's good to know there are some real men left in the world. I sure know how to pick 'em. First, Irvin Willat. The meanest shit in Hollywood. Now, Howard Hughes. Some boy friend!" She took his hand and led him into the garden.

He followed along, desiring her more each minute, although he'd learned his lesson about making a play for her.

In the garden, as the early streaks of dawn split a pink Los Angeles sky, she turned to him. Before or since, he'd never seen a woman more beautiful. Billie

Dove, not Mona Lisa, should have posed for that portrait by Leonardo da Vinci. In spite of the tawdry circumstances, he was completely under her spell.

"I planted most of this garden myself," she said. "I'd like to say I had a lot of happy moments here, but I didn't. Being married to Irvin was a nightmare. Being the girl friend of Howard Hughes is a nightmare of a different sort. I didn't know how awful men could be until I got hooked up with the likes of those two."

Unable to resist, he held her close. He could feel her breasts against his chest. When her little pink tongue darted into his mouth, he wanted to take her right in the garden.

She broke away from him and ran forward in the yard, almost tripping in her high heels. She stopped in front of a cottage. It was idyllic, painted white and covered in roses. "This was our guest house. I'm sure the guests we put up here had a lot more fun than Irvin and me in the big house."

She stepped up to the porch and opened the door. "Let's go inside. It's going to be a long wait before all this stinking business is over with tonight."

When he came up to her, she gently kissed his lips. Her kiss made his lips tingle.

Stepping inside, she turned to him and reached for his arm, as he shut the door with his free hand.

"I need a real man to hold me tonight and love me," she said. "Not some Texas fairy. Richards is right. I can't give Howard what he wants. I'm a show-piece for him. He collects women like trophies to dangle in front of the public. To let the world know what a stud he is. Howard Hughes, the collector of the world's most beautiful women. Imagine me learning that he prefers a gas jockey with dirty fingernails to the love I could give him."

"All men aren't that way," he whispered in her ear before kissing it and nib-bling gently on it.

"I know that," she said, "but I need your reassurance."

She separated herself from him. "I need to take a shower to feel clean again after that horrible session I had with Irvin. The last time I emerged from a bath-room with you, I found you standing stark naked."

"Yeah," he said. "That's why I'm in all the trouble I'm in now."

"It's okay," she said. "So the first scene didn't work. I'm the director tonight. Hasn't a director ever demanded that you do a second take?"

"I hope you mean what I think you mean," he said.

"When I come out of that bathroom, I'm going to be gloriously nude for you. I hope to find you stripped and available."

"Lady, you've found your man."

***

As morning came over the former guest cottage of Billie Dove and Irvin Wallat, Bogie was about to launch the longest day and night he'd ever spend in Los Angeles. He had achieved what few men ever would: He'd awakened in the arms of the goddess hailed as the world's most beautiful woman.

As a sexual male, he'd never been so fulfilled. He'd had far kinkier sex with the likes of Louise Brooks, wilder sex with Joan Crawford and Barbara Stanwyck when they weren't making love to each other, and more sanitized sex with Myrna Loy. What he'd never had before was more beautiful sex. His night with Billie Dove was unlike all others. One thing he'd never understand about certain men: How could Howard Hughes be plotting a night with "the chest," George O'Brien, when he had Billie Dove at his beck and call?

Later that morning, he heard Billie Dove in the bathroom taking a shower. He was saddened because he felt that she was washing the very essence of himself off her body. In the early, pinkish light, he wandered barefoot and shirtless on the grass, smoking a cigarette.

He was glad that Mary Philips wanted a divorce. He was not in love with his wife, and feared that one of his original reasons for wanting to marry her was to spite Kenneth. Since then, however, Kenneth had become his best friend, and he found no amusement in hurting him in any way. He felt that if Kenneth loved Mary as much as he said that he did, he should call off his marriage plans with Kay Francis, return to New York, and marry Mary.

As Bogie would relate to Kenneth later in the day, the only way that plan should be abandoned was if another Mary, Pickford herself, wanted to divorce Fairbanks and take Kenneth as her third husband.

"What struggling actor in Hollywood would turn down an offer of marriage from the queen of the movies herself?" he later said to Kenneth. Bogie knew that such a sentiment reflected his most cynical side, and it echoed Bill Brady Jr.'s own admonition to him to marry Helen Menken if for no other reason than to promote his career on Broadway. The choice was Kenneth's. As far as Mary Philips was concerned, Bogie was stepping aside.

After last night in the arms of Billie Dove, he would turn down an offer of marriage from Lilyan Tashman herself. He wanted Dove for himself, and to hell with Howard Hughes. Even without seeing the evidence, he knew enough about Hughes to keep him from blackmailing him for that God damn nude photograph. He didn't think Hughes would actually use it. Besides, Hughes had enough blackmail threats based on his own activities to allow him to devote too much attention to Bogie, who had no money and no career to destroy.

From the back porch of Willat's house, he saw Tommy Richards emerge with a suitcase. Richards headed across the lawn to greet him.

"Going on a trip, pal?" Bogie asked.

"Yeah," Richards said. "Hughes' lawyers left about thirty minutes ago. Willat has concluded his business with them, and with me too. Time for me to press on."

"I trust you're richer by one-hundred-thousand big ones," Bogie said, offering the stunningly handsome man a cigarette.

As Richards accepted the cigarette, he softly caressed Bogie's hand. "Not at all. The deal with Hughes for the million dollars fell through, but I'm richer to the tune of fifty thousand. And that's more money than I ever expected to see."

"That will certainly buy a ranch in Arizona," Bogie said.

"The ranch can wait," Richards said. "All night I've been thinking. With this kind of loot, I can parlay this bundle into a fortune. Before I get through cleaning up, I'll be the owner of the biggest ranch in Arizona. Maybe the biggest ranch in Texas."

"Maybe," Bogie said. "Better be careful. Are you a gambling man?"

"How I'm gonna make money on this bundle is my own business," Richards said.

"You've got that right, pal," Bogie said, looking back at the cottage where he planned to return at once to Dove. "Good luck. See you around, kid."

"One more thing," Richards said. "I still think, and I'll always believe, that you wanted to make it with me. Have wild, hot sex with a man just once in your life. Just to see what it's all about. All your actor friends try it at least once. Some of them once a day."

"Maybe you're right," Bogie said. "It's your business what you're going to do with all that dough, and it's my business if I wanted to fuck you—and I'll never tell you the truth."

"The trouble with you is that you can't even tell the truth to yourself." With that, Richards turned and walked across the yard, carrying his suitcase, which was the same suitcase that Bogie and Dove had arrived with earlier in the morning.

It was with a heavy heart that he watched Richards go. He wanted to run after him and slug him in the mouth for that parting comment. Somehow he felt that Richards had gotten the best of him.

Kenneth MacKenna was the only person he could tell about this strange night, and he planned to do just that. Somehow unburdening himself to Kenneth was better than going to a psychiatrist.

Bogie would never see Tommy Richards again, and was saddened to read newspaper headlines in 1934, that "Ex-Husband of Glenda Farrell Arrested for Theft." For some reason, Richards had returned to Los Angeles. Desperate for money for liquor, he'd broken into a store in downtown Los Angeles after midnight but had been spotted. Someone had called the police, and he was arrested and thrown into jail.

That morning Bogie called Glenda Farrell. She sounded hysterical. "As soon as I read what had happened, I tried to help. Tommy was drunk. I know how wild he is at such times. If he were in one of his sane moments, he'd never have done such a thing."

"Can I be of help?" Bogie volunteered. "Post bail or something?"

"By some miracle, the store owner dropped charges against Tommy," she said. "It turns out that he's a big fan of mine and wanted to spare me the grief of my former husband going on trial and my name being dragged through the mud. I went to the police station this morning and found out that Tommy has been released and told to leave town. I don't know where he is. Tommy must have figured that I'd come down to the station to help him. The police gave me the note that he'd left for me on a folded scrap of paper. He'd written, 'Sorry, Tommy.' And that was it."

"Can I come over?" he asked.

"Yes, I'm feeling kinda shaky," she said. "I need you."

Tommy Richards faded that morning into the dim smog of Hollywood history and was never heard from again.

***

When Bogie went back into the cottage, a freshly showered Billie Dove was waiting for him and looking very tempting lying nude on the bed. She was posed like former screen vamp Theda Bara ("Arab Death") with a rose in her teeth. Pulling off his trousers—he hadn't bothered to put on underwear—he was soon nude with Dove in bed. As far as women went, it didn't get any better than this.

She was not only one of the most skilled seductresses he'd ever known, or would ever know in his future, she was also an actor's dream date. Here he was fucking the most beautiful woman on earth and Hollywood's highest paid actress. When they were man and wife, and making movies together, he could imagine theater marquees all across America lighting up with the names of Billie Dove and Humphrey Bogart. Bowing to her greater star status, he would gladly give her star billing.

Most dreams were only to be dreamed, as he was to learn only an hour later when he delivered her to her doorstep.

"It was great fun," she told him, kissing him lightly on his scarred lip. "I was feeling so vulnerable after seeing all that evidence against Howard. But I'm still in love with my errant Texan, so if it's okay with you, let's call this a one-night stand." She kissed him again even more lightly on the lips, as she scurried from the car.

He reached for her arm, clutching it. "It's not okay with me. I'm in love with you. I want what we had to go on and on. Hughes will never marry you. He likes dick too much. That creep, Willat, is now gone from your life. You're free."

"It cannot be," she said softly, blowing him a farewell kiss. Almost before he knew it, she'd gone like the dew of morning.

It was with a certain glee that Bogie noted that Willat directed only one final picture in 1931. In a touch of irony, the movie was called *Damaged Love*, an apt title for this B-picture romance/drama starring June Collyer and Charles Starrett. Willat's career came to a crashing halt in Hollywood, no doubt because of the behind-the-scenes manipulation of Hughes himself.

399

As a director, Willat would work again only in 1937. He directed three Westerns: *Old Louisiana, Under Strange Flags*, and *The Luck of Roaring Camp*, before becoming a footnote in Hollywood history. After that, he retired from filmmaking, living on Hughes' money until the morning he died in Santa Monica in 1976 at the age of 85, a long but hardly happy life.

In the weeks and months ahead, Bogie made several attempts to get in touch with Billie Dove, but he was never to see her again. He pursued her when he learned that her affair with Howard Hughes was over, as he could have predicted, but by then her heart lay elsewhere.

As time went by, he came to realize that he'd seduced her at the peak of her fame and popularity. The moment he drove her home that morning, her career, even with Hughes behind the scenes, headed for a downward skid. Contrary to rumors at the time, the coming of sound did not destroy her career. Her silky voice recorded beautifully.

The final blow came when William Randolph Hearst sabotaged Dove in her final film, *Blondie of the Follies*, in which she was cast as a gutsy showgirl competing with Marion Davies for the love of a playboy, as played by Robert Montgomery. Hearst didn't want Dove stealing the picture from his beloved mistress, Davies. Dove's best scenes ended up on the cutting-room floor. She also claimed that Hearst had ordered the cameramen to photograph her badly.

Billie Dove remained a pilot, a painter, and a poet, but she said goodbye to Hollywood. Long after her affair with Hughes ended, she married Bob Kenaston, a rancher and real-estate investor. She completely turned her back on Hollywood, and even said no when David Selznick offered her the role of the bordello keeper, Belle Watling, in *Gone With the Wind*.

Born at the dawn of the 20th century, she almost lived to see the millennium, dying of pneumonia on the last day of 1997 in Woodland Hills, California.

Years later, Bogie told his friend and lover, Judy Garland, "For me, Billie Dove was the woman who got away."

***

Bogie wasn't due back on the set of *A Holy Terror* until Wednesday morning, just the time he needed to drive Jean Harlow to Tijuana for an abortion. Howard Hughes had arranged it all, even giving them five-thousand dollars in cash and lending them one of his cars. As he drove along the road south, Harlow was asleep in the back seat.

"The Chest," George O'Brien, had been safely delivered to Hughes' mansion. Bogie had taken to calling his co-star "Baby Ass." He wondered how O'Brien's tender rosebud would be after the tall Texan finished working with it over the weekend.

He looked back at Harlow as they passed an orange juice stand. He was thirsty but didn't want to stop out of fear of waking her. In sleep, Harlow looked like a little girl in a convent, all pure and innocent, not the sex symbol of Hollywood with the iced nipples.

Behind the driver's wheel, he could think of nothing except his participation in the plot to abort the life of Harlow's unborn child. He was no stranger to abortion. His mother, Maud, had told him that his father had performed several illegal abortions. Maud as a suffragette had converted her doctor husband to a feminist position that was rather advanced for its time. "A woman must have her own right to choose," Maud always said. "It's a personal decision that's to be decided by her and only by her, without some man telling her what to do."

Bogie had no moral scruples against abortion, as he had more or less accepted his mother's point of view. What bothered him was the fear that Harlow would be taking the life of a person that might become the future sex goddess of 1950s Hollywood, a role that film history would eventually grant to Marilyn Monroe.

Since he assumed that the father of this unborn child wasn't Paul Bern, he figured that it must be one of the handsome actors Harlow had been dating. With a good-looking daddy and a movie star queen desired by half the male population of the world, the child would probably be gorgeous.

When Harlow woke up and he could speak to her confidentially, he was going to ask her who the daddy was. He was especially curious since Hughes and Harlow had included him in the act of aborting the baby.

Before leaving Hollywood, he had called for his messages. Since he was never at home any more, his friends got in touch with him through the switchboard at Fox. Bette Davis had phoned again, demanding that he return her call "at once." His darling Lilyan Tashman had called, inviting him to take her to a costume ball. Still no word from Helen. Before leaving Hughes' mansion, he'd called Helen at the Garden of Allah. She was still furious at him for "disgracing" her in front of *tout* Hollywood, and was refusing his calls. There was an intriguing but disturbing message from Louella Parsons. She wanted him to call her "at once," the same command issued by Davis. He could only hope that Parsons had been too drunk at Jeanette MacDonald's house to remember his offer to seduce her.

Kenneth MacKenna had also left word for him to call, along with an invitation to attend his bachelor party before they sailed to Catalina Island for his marriage to Kay Francis. Apparently, the marriage was still on, and Kenneth had decided not to return to New York and the arms of Mary Philips.

Sometime when he was in Tijuana he was going to write Mary and agree with her that their marriage had been a sham. He would explain about that link with Helen being misrepresented in Parsons' column, although he was going to agree with her that they should proceed with a divorce. The marriage was over before it had really begun.

To his amazement, he realized that he was going to be a free man. He hadn't thought much about that before. But on the ride to the Mexican border, he had to think about something. During his marriage to Mary, he had been free to seduce any woman he wanted, wedding band on his finger or not. The only difference in his status, was that he would be free to marry someone else when the divorce came through. But he wondered if he really wanted to.

Each of the women he'd seduced had known that he was married, and the wedding band on his finger had been a good excuse to end his unwanted affairs quickly. With his new freedom, he could at least think about marriage again, although from past experience, he didn't consider himself a particularly good candidate for that kind of commitment. He'd fallen in and out of love too quickly.

If Billie Dove had given him a go-ahead, he would have become her boy friend and proposed to her. If Tashman had said that she was divorcing Edmund Lowe, he would have agreed to marry her. He wouldn't have said no to Bebe Daniels if she'd been free of Ben Lyon. Once or twice he'd even thought of a possible marriage to Joan Blondell, who would surely make the most understanding wife in Hollywood.

Maybe it was something that Hughes' servant had put in the coffee that morning before they left the mansion, but a new idea was taking over his brain, even though he tried to fight it off. It was ridiculous. No, more than that. It was preposterous. It would never work. But then again it might. No, he rejected it outright. But the thought wouldn't let his brain alone. It consumed his mind like a devilish scheme to torment him. He found himself shaking nervously at the prospect.

The tantalizing prospect had its advantages. It would save his Hollywood career and make him a household word overnight. He'd be rewarded with great sex every night. They could make films together and become world famous as a screen couple, the equal of what Louis B. Mayer was plotting for Joan Crawford and Clark Gable.

He could save a sweet kid from an upcoming marriage to an impotent bastard who would ruin her life, and he might even become the father, in name, of the child who would become America's sex symbol of the 1950s when that decade eventually rolled around.

When she woke up in his back seat, he was going to ask Jean Harlow to become the third Mrs. Humphrey Bogart.

***

When Harlow woke up, Bogie asked her if she'd mind if they stopped for coffee.

"Mind?" she said, "I've got to take a piss, and soon."

"Isn't the more delicate, ladylike expression, 'I've got to go and powder my nose?'" he asked.

"Fuck that!" she said, sitting up in the car and rubbing sleep from her eyes. "I'm no lady. Even at the studio, when I've really got to take a piss, I don't care who's watching. Even Louis B. Mayer for all I care. I bet he'd like to see me take

402

a piss. Every time I'm in his office, he's always feeling my breasts. So anyway, I have to take a piss. And I'm hungry, too." In response, Bogart steered the car into a roadside burger joint.

After the bombshell had taken her horse piss, she joined him in a booth. He'd ordered a hamburger, and she decided she wanted one too, asking the waitress to put a sliced tomato and lettuce on hers.

"Lettuce and tomato on a hamburger?" he said. "You moderns. I've never heard of such a combination."

"It's called a California burger," she said. "It's all the rage out here. Try it some time. You'll like it."

"That I'll never try," he said. "The whole idea sounds barbaric."

"You New Yorkers," she said, always dismissive of anything that she felt came from "Way Back East." "As a little girl growing up in Missouri, I was told that you New Yorkers want only one thing from a woman."

"Based on your experience, did you find that to be true?" he asked.

"You got that right," she said. "You and Raft are from New York. You guys really worked me over in Palm Springs. I think it made Joan Crawford jealous. She was after me too!"

"Have you, like Barbara Stanwyck, shared your charms with Crawford?"

"I don't think I'll tell you that," she said. "I like men, preferably men with sexual stamina. That would eliminate Mr. Howard Hughes."

"Don't disparage the father of your child," he said mockingly, softening his words with a smile.

"Bullshit!" she said. "Howard has never cum inside me." She reached over and caressingly fondled his hand. "But you have. If I recall Palm Springs, and I do very well, you fucked me without a rubber."

At that point a rather surprised waitress came up to the table with their burgers. She'd obviously heard what Harlow had said. Bogie hadn't even looked at the waitress when he'd ordered. When she served his burger and coffee, he noticed with surprise that she had hair dyed as platinum blonde as Harlow herself. "You're not the *real* Jean Harlow, are you?" the waitress asked.

"No, sweetie," Harlow said. "I'm just like you, one of the million gals in America dying her hair platinum and trying to look like her."

The waitress put the burgers and coffee on the table. "But you look a hell of a lot more like her than I do. I burned my scalp something awful. I'm gonna let it grow out and become a redhead again."

"Good idea," he said, focusing on Harlow again. When the waitress was out of earshot, he leaned over the table and in a confidential whisper asked, "Confess up. Just who is the father of Junior?"

She leaned back in the booth, asking for a cigarette. She liked to smoke and eat at the same time. "Very likely it's yours. You didn't wear protection but Raft did."

"I can't believe that George and I are the only guys you've slept with," he said.

"Let's see now," she said, rolling her eyes as if she were the forgetful type. "It couldn't be Joan Crawford, could it? Maybe your friend Lilyan Tashman when we did *New York Nights* together. Would you believe Laurel & Hardy? They were a lot of fun when I worked with them on *Bacon Grabbers*."

"C'mon," he said. "Let's get serious here. I'm driving you down to Mexico for an abortion. If I'm an accomplice to a baby's butchering, I have the right to know the name of the daddy."

Her face turned deadly serious, and it was obvious his words had angered her. "How in the God damn hell do I know who the father is?" she asked, shoving her California burger plate away. "Maybe William Powell's the daddy. Spencer Tracy, most likely. For all I know, Johnny Mack Brown. Clark Gable is a possibility. If I let the kid live, it might have big ears. Both Ben Lyon and James Hall from *Hell's Angels* are candidates. Lew Ayres, definitely. I can't entirely rule out Jimmy Cagney. Maurice Chevalier seduced both me and Jeanette MacDonald when we made *The Love Parade* together. But he's a secret faggot. He always goes around attacking homosexuals because he doesn't want people to think he's one too. Since we met in '29, I still get fucked regularly by Gilbert Roland, and since I was an unbilled extra in *City Nights*, Chaplin has been fucking me about every six weeks. In some ways, I hope he's the daddy. He has more money. Those are my famous fuckers. I have a lot of other guys who work at the studio. I even spotted a guy sweeping up on the set of *The Saturday Night Kid* over at Paramount who was handsome and hunkier than any man on the screen today."

"Sounds to me like you've made the rounds," he said. "I think you're gonna be a big star, and you're gonna need to settle down with one man. You can't carry on like this unless you don't have a morals clause in your contract."

"What are morals if you're under contract to Howard Hughes?"

"I see your point." He finished his hamburger in silence. After ordering another cup of black coffee, he headed for the border with her. This time she sat up front with him.

Far from being turned off by the fact that she'd slept with countless men since hitting Hollywood, and maybe a woman or two on the side, he was turned on. Somehow he felt that if he could win her away from some of the most desirable men on the planet, like Gable and Gilbert Roland, it would be a notch in his belt.

When he got her to Tijuana and over a few tequilas, he was going to ask her the big question. If she'd hide out, probably in a house owned by Hughes somewhere, and have the baby, he'd return to New York, get his divorce, and rush back to the coast to marry her.

Maybe Louella Parsons in her column could figure out a way to explain the marriage and a fully grown baby appearing at the same time. The way he saw it, if Parsons could cover up the murder of producer Tom Ince on William Randolph Hearst's yacht, she could explain away anything.

When he got to Tijuana, and since they were spending Hughes' money, he asked for a suite at the best hotel in town. He wanted the night to be romantic.

An hour later, Harlow said she wanted to rest on their large double bed. At first he'd thought that she might object to sharing a suite with him, preferring a room of her own. But she'd seemed pleased when the bellhop showed them the bedroom with its large, satin-covered bed.

After he'd tipped the bellhop, she said she wanted to rest after the long drive down. He excused himself to take a long bubble bath to get rid of the grime of the road. He wanted to be all fresh for her that evening.

He'd been in the tub for no more than fifteen minutes when the door opened and she came into the bathroom without knocking. She was wearing a very sheer beige nightgown. Right in front of him, she pulled off the gown, letting him enjoy the sensual lines of her body and the sight of the hairs of her vagina, dyed the same platinum blonde as her famous coiffure.

She gently glided that celebrated figure into the tub with him, seemingly to fit into his strong arms as if she belonged there and nowhere else.

As his grip on her tightened, he suspected that the evening would go as he'd planned. After their first bottle of tequila over dinner, he just knew the answer to his question would be yes.

His question came when they were dancing to a Mexican band whose members were dressed in a fire-engine red color, with silver sequins. The flame-red sombreros worn by each of the ten musicians looked several sizes too big for their much smaller heads, causing Bogie and Harlow to laugh at the band even during their more serious romantic ballads.

"I want you to have the child," he said. "I'll always think of it as our love child. I want to be its daddy. More than that, I want to be your husband. When I take you upstairs to our suite, and make love to you again tonight, you'll be convinced you won't need any other man in your life."

"I want that too," she said, whispering in his ear as they danced and snuggled together. "I don't want to kill my baby like Howard is demanding. Me and you don't love each other now, but we'll learn to. We're certainly attracted to each other. That's for damn sure."

He could feel her firm breasts pressing against his chest. Her nipples were erect, and it didn't take any ice cubes to do that.

In all honesty, as he was later to relate to Kenneth, his night of lovemaking with Harlow would turn out to be one of the most memorable of his life. Nothing would ever equal his experience with Billie Dove, but sleeping with Harlow was definitely on the ladder to Paradise, if not the Paradise itself that Billie Dove represented to him.

He fell asleep that night with dreams of his upcoming marriage spinning in his head. He'd give Parsons the exclusive. Their pictures would be on the front pages of every newspaper in the country, maybe even those in Europe or around the world.

As soon as the announcement was made to the press, he expected movie offers to start rolling in. Fox would not only renew his contract, maybe at $2,500 a week, but other studios would be clamoring for his services. Maybe he'd sign with Louis B. Mayer at MGM.

A hundred years from now, or so he conjectured, audiences would be flocking to see the screen classics that Humphrey Bogart and Jean Harlow made together way back in the 1930s.

He must have been in blissful dreaming when the phone rang by his bedside. It was the hotel manager waking him up at four o'clock in the morning.

The manager's voice seemed panic stricken. "You must come at once," he said. "There's terrible trouble. Your wife…she's dying."

It was only then that Bogie noticed that Harlow wasn't in the bed.

The manager's voice hit him like a dull thud. "Come at once. I will drive you myself. Your beautiful wife. A white blonde goddess. She is bleeding to death."

As he hurriedly dressed, it became all too clear to him. Harlow had never had any intention of marrying him and defining him as the father of her unborn child. All through the night, she'd been toying with him. As soon as he was deep into his tequila-fogged sleep, she had slipped out of their bed and gone to a clinic to have the abortion, as she had always intended.

As the hotel manager rushed him dangerously into the night to her bedside, he felt like a fool. Howard Hughes had used him. Those headlines he'd dreamed about, linking him with Harlow, might become very different from those of his fantasies. Tomorrow's headlines might blare the dreadful news that Harlow was dead, and that somehow he'd be implicated in her murder.

***

Harlow lived, but without Bogie.

There would be no headlines. Howard Hughes had pulled off another of his amazing cover-ups. It didn't take great brains to cover something up. Only money, and a lot of it.

At the clinic, Bogie was allowed to see Harlow, learning that her abortion had been botched. She was bleeding severely and barely holding onto life. He excused himself and placed a call to Howard Hughes in Los Angeles. Within hours, the tycoon had rushed the best medical assistance available to his stricken star.

It began with Hughes dispensing two Mexican doctors to her aid and ended with Harlow being sent overland in a large black limousine with curtained-off windows to the best hospital in San Diego.

Bogie's role as Hughes' messenger boy had come to an end. "You really fucked this one up, asshole," Hughes had told him before slamming down the phone. Never again would the tycoon call on Bogie for an errand.

He would never know what happened to the negatives of the photographs that were taken of him that night when he was nude in his apartment with Billie Dove. Eventually, after Bogie became a big star, he heard reports that William Haines had framed ten copies of that candid snapshot and had used them to decorate the bathroom of his vacation retreat, much to the amusement of his guests.

As the years rolled on, Bogie came to realize how ridiculous he had been in his proposal of marriage to Harlow. Kenneth MacKenna would be the only friend in whom he'd confide the story of his taking Harlow to Tijuana. It wasn't something he was proud of. And although he was sorry to hear of Harlow's early death in 1937, he never wanted to speak of her again.

When he got back to Hollywood he answered Bette Davis' urgent message. She was having a cocktail party for some co-workers, and she felt it important that he attend. "I'm going to kick everybody out by seven-thirty, and I want you to stay on so we can talk privately. It's about our film future."

She'd said the right words, "film future," and he told her he'd be at her house within the hour. He took a wild guess that Davis had come up with a script that would save their fading careers, and he wanted to see what that New Englander had in mind.

As he arrived at the door to the Davis home, it was opened by her mother, Ruth. The look on her Puritanical Yankee face told him that she didn't approve of his coming to her house. To him, she was a tenacious shrew who unduly fussed over her daughter, who was also her meal ticket. He'd heard that she was the stage mother to end all stage mothers.

In a fairly low-cut dress and with no makeup except a "slash" of lipstick, Davis greeted him in her living room. It was a unique party. In her devious mind, the actress had thrown a party for "Hollywood losers," a grouping that included herself. She'd invited some male stars she'd appeared with in unsuccessful films for "tea and sympathy." The sympathy was genuine, but the "tea" was actually whiskey.

She kissed Bogie lightly on the lips. "I think we should celebrate failure this afternoon," she said, appearing a bit unbalanced and giddy. "All of us are being referred to as box-office bombs."

She introduced him to Walter Byron, Pat O'Brien, James "Junior" Durkin, and a very handsome young actor, Frank Albertson.

Bogie found himself standing on the Davis back porch talking to Albertson. He'd appeared with Davis in *Way Back Home*, which had been directed by William Seiter. Originally entitled *Other People's Business*, the film had starred Phillips Lord, who was known across the country for the Seth Parker character he played on his regular radio show for NBC.

"I have to admit it," Albertson said to Bogie, "I'm still carrying a torch for Bette. During the filming, I fell hook, line, and sinker for her. I've asked her to marry me. She's going to give me her answer this weekend."

"Good luck, pal," Bogie said, not really meaning it. For some reason, he felt jealous.

Albertson soon drifted off, his tongue wagging in hot pursuit of Davis. Bogie couldn't believe that Davis would return this young man's affection. And she didn't.

As Bette Davis' star rose in Hollywood, Albertson's twinkled out. Eventually, Bogie would see him in the character role of Walter, the brother of *Alice Adams* in the 1935 film with Katharine Hepburn. A year before Albertson died on February 29, 1964 in Santa Monica, California, he was appearing uncredited in such films as the 1963 *Bye Bye Birdie*. Hitchcock in 1960 had cast him in the small role of Tom Cassidy in *Psycho*.

The next failure Bogie tried to engage in conversation was another handsome actor, Walter Byron. He'd appeared opposite Davis in *The Menace*, directed by Roy William Neill. It had also starred old-time actor H. B. Warner and Natalie Moorhead. The picture had initially been entitled *The Feathered Serpent*, then *The Squeaker*.

"It should have been called *The Stinker*," Byron said, deep into his booze.

It seemed only months ago that Walter Byron had been hailed in the press as "Hollywood's new John Gilbert." He had landed the male role of the year when he was cast as the roistering German prince opposite Gloria Swanson's shy little Irish girl from the convent in *Queen Kelly*.

"Swanson told me I stood to be the next great male star of Hollywood," Byron said. "Imagine my disappointment when Swanson and Joseph Kennedy pulled the plug on Erich von Stroheim. That film will never be finished. If that nutbag Austrian had had his way, the movie would have been nine hours long and cost millions."

"Tell me something, pal," Bogie said. "I understand that von Stroheim filmed a scene where Swanson accidentally drops her bloomers as she curtsies to you, her prince on horseback. I was told that she wads up the panties and throws them at you. You fondle them, smell them, then tuck them in your uniform. Pretty hot stuff."

"That's pure von Stroheim," Byron said. "If the picture is ever released, I doubt that they'll let that scene stay in."

For some reason, Ruthie Davis seemed more transfixed by Byron than all the other actors at the party. Perhaps this Englishman was the only one there who was her type.

Seeing Bogie standing alone, Bette Davis came up to him to offer him another drink. "Ruthie has developed an insatiable crush on Walter, but she's welcome to him, for all I care."

"He didn't turn you on during your love scenes?" Bogie asked mockingly.

"Just the opposite," she said. "He drinks and smokes all day. There's no smell from any outhouse in Maine worse than Walter's breath. I hear only Clark Gable has worse breath. After one kissing scene, I invited Walter to my dressing room where I offered him a toothbrush, some toothpaste, and some gargle. I think that seriously pissed him off."

"He's not so mad that he didn't come to this losers' party," he said. He looked over at Ruthie and Byron on the other side of the porch. "Perhaps he'll marry

408

Miss Ruth and become your stepfather."

"That day will never come," Davis said. "Mark my words. Walter Byron is washed up in Hollywood. *Queen Kelly* did him in. He should go back to England."

"I think all these limey actors should go back to England," he said. "We can't find enough work for our own home-grown boys." He was still blaming Ronald Colman for his stalled career. "If Lillian Gish had cast me opposite her in *The White Sister*, and not that effeminate Colman guy, I'd be a big star by now."

"Sure you would," Davis said, humoring him. She looked over at Byron again, seemingly resenting her mother's fixation on the actor. "Walter is only thirty. But when we shot *The Menace*, the director, Roy William Neill, not only directed him badly, but photographed him even worse. Walter looks at least forty-five in the movie. With his drinking problem, he's going downhill and fast."

Bette Davis' crystal ball was accurate that late afternoon. It was with sadness that Bogie watched the screen career of another promising newcomer collapse. He last spotted Byron on the screen in an uncredited part as a man in a tavern in the Greer Garson film, *Mrs. Miniver*, in 1942.

After that, he lived out the rest of his life in total obscurity, dying on March 2, 1972 at Signal Hill, California.

When Pat O'Brien came over to talk to him at Davis' party, Bogie had no awareness what a key player the actor would be in his future career in the 1930s at Warner Brothers. O'Brien seemed to be a hard-drinking, witty Irishman with an insouciant charm.

Each of the Pat O'Brien/Humphrey Bogart films lay in the future: *China Clipper* in 1936, *The Great O'Malley* in 1937; *San Quentin*, also in 1937; and *Angels With Dirty Faces* in 1938.

The son of Irish immigrants from Milwaukee, O'Brien had played bit parts in the early days of Hollywood's Golden Era before graduating to starring roles, most often as a priest, warden, or gangster in all those movies with James Cagney, George Raft, and Edward G. Robinson, and, of course, Bogie himself. His most memorable film remains *Knute Rockne: All-American*, the picture that brought stardom to Ronald Reagan and made the line, "Win one for the Gipper," a popular household expression during the Reagan presidency.

As Bogie chatted amicably with O'Brien on that fading afternoon of long ago, the actor told him that he'd been very disappointed with his role in *Hell's House* with Davis and Junior Durkin. "Bette is calling it the nadir of her career," O'Brien said, "even before her career gets started."

"Sounds like a great picture, pal," Bogie said. "Remind me to save my quarter and not see it."

"Fine with me," O'Brien said. "I don't want anybody I know to see the fucker. It took only two weeks to shoot. While filming it, Bette and I formed a mutual consolation society over our career doldrums. When we saw the final cut, it looked like it'd been shot in a day and a half, if that."

"What part did Bette play?" Bogie asked.

"My gun moll, the whore with a head of platinum and a heart of gold. Jimmy Mason, as played by Junior Durkin over there, idolizes my character of Matt Kelly, a bootlegger. The public won't get it, but it's really one of the most homo-erotic films ever made. Junior falls for me in a big way."

"Is he a fag?" Bogie asked. "He sure looks it."

"Yeah, I see what you mean," O'Brien said. "But our little teenager over there gets a hard-on any time Bette Davis walks by."

"It seems like all her leading men are falling for her—except me," Bogie said.

"I'm with you, boy," O'Brien said, finishing his drink and looking around forlornly, hoping to find another one. "Bette came on to me. She told me I was sexy looking in a trashy Irish way. I was tempted once or twice, but I think my Catholic guilt took over. At the end of the day's shoot, I went home to the little wife. No one's ever going to call Pat O'Brien a womanizer. Why should I settle for chopped liver when I've got Grade A pussy at home?"

"Well, at least you can talk dirty," Bogie said. "I was beginning to think you were a hopeless cause. But you sound like a man who never puts his cock where his mouth is."

"You're a good judge of character," O'Brien said. "I talk dirty, but don't act dirty."

"I like to do both."

Later Bogie approached the teenager, Junior Durkin, and shook his hand again, congratulating him on his performance in *Tom Sawyer*. "Your director, John Cromwell, used to be a friend of mine in New York. But since he's become such a big shot on The Coast, he doesn't know me any more. In New York around the speakeasies, John, me, and some other guys were known as the Pussy Posse."

"That's one posse I'd like to join," Durkin said, looking wistfully at Davis across the yard. "I'd really like to plug Bette. Did you get in her pants when you made *Bad Sister* together?"

"I was busy with ten other broads," Bogie said. "And I'm not sure that Bette is my type."

"She's my type, especially with that platinum hair," Durkin said. "Fucking Bette would be like fucking Harlow. I hear you're a man about town. Did you ever fuck Harlow?"

He looked startled, then took a heavy draw on his cigarette. Without losing his cool, he said, "I don't know Harlow. Guess I'm missing out."

As he stood chatting with Durkin in the garden, Bogie wasn't thinking about platinum pussy but how disappointed he was in his friend, Cromwell. He felt that the director had the power to launch him into stardom, yet wasn't even returning his calls. Ironically, it was Cromwell who launched Bette Davis into stardom, as he wanted her to portray the slut, Mildred Rogers, in the film adaptation of W. Somerset Maugham's *Of Human Bondage*, opposite Leslie Howard. Cromwell managed to lure her away from the contractual clutches of Jack Warner to make

410

the film, and the rest is cinema history.

As Durkin drifted away, Davis herself emerged by Bogie's side. He was having a difficult time getting used to her. She wasn't the mousy actress he'd encountered on the set of *Bad Sister*. This was a new Davis with bleached blond hair. Somehow the new hair made her sexier and more alluring, although Jean Harlow would never have to fear competition.

She held Bogie's hand as she told him, "When I saw myself in that horrible movie you and I made, I contemplated suicide for about an hour. Makeup tried to compensate for my small mouth by exaggerating the size with lipstick. My mouth looked like a tunnel. Crawford can get away with those ridiculously exaggerated lips. I can't. Also when I'm embarrassed or insecure, and I was both of those things, I smile crookedly."

"My, oh my, aren't we a litany of complaints today," he said.

"That's not all. My outfits stunk. It was obvious I didn't have a hairdresser. Sidney Fox got all the attention. In *Way Back Home*, I looked a little better. I learned that Universal was ready to drop me until Berman—that's Pandro Berman, the producer over at RKO—wanted to borrow me for that cornspun role. A guy named J. Roy Hunt, the cinematographer, actually made me look good for the first time ever on film."

"You're a regular *femme fatale*," he said.

"Don't you put me on, Bogart," Davis said. "Actually I did look rather pretty. A lot of directors in New York called me pretty. Maybe I am a *femme fatale* and don't know it. Carl Laemmle—Junior, that is—thinks I have no sex appeal, but all my leading men fall in love with me. Douglass Montgomery—he was called Kent Douglass back then—went for me in a big way when we filmed *Waterloo Bridge* together. But I found him too delicate and effeminate. I think Douglass was more interested in sucking off the handsome grips on the set than he was in seducing me."

"Frank Albertson fell for you," he said. "And so did Junior Durkin."

"And how!" she said, breaking up. "That's the perfect lead-in for the surprise of the party." She grandly ushered the actors into her library, where she'd arranged with the director of *Hell's House*, Howard Higgin, to show her guests an outtake from the film.

Bogie sat next to Durkin to watch the clip. When the lights went out, the film went on. It was not a love scene but a clip of Davis comforting the teenage boy, as played by Durkin, who was only sixteen at the time the film was shot. The boy reacted, however, as if it had been a love scene. When Davis put her arms around him, the hard-on in his tight pants shot up so quickly it looked like Mount Rushmore.

The actors, including Bogie himself, burst into laughter. So did Miss Ruthie and Davis herself. His erection would put even George Raft to shame.

"Stop it!" Durkin shouted, rising from his chair, his arms awkwardly beating the air. In tears he ran from the library. In two minutes, Bogie heard the sound of

411

his car wheels spinning in the Davis driveway.

Davis did not seem at all concerned that she'd humiliated a sensitive, teenage boy. She and O'Brien were laughing at Durkin's reaction. "The only thing solid about *Hell's House* is Junior's hard-on," O'Brien quipped.

"It was the only good thing in the picture," Davis chimed in.

The excised footage of Durkin's hard-on would make the rounds in Hollywood, becoming a feature at stag parties.

Bogie never saw the young man again. Durkin would go on to appear in *Little Men* in 1935, playing Franz. On May 4, 1935, outside San Diego, he was riding in a car with fellow child actor, Jackie Coogan, when their vehicle crashed. Durkin was killed instantly, but the injured Coogan survived.

Coogan had appeared as a tattered, runny-nosed little waif opposite Chaplin in *The Kid* in 1921. He'd made both *Tom Sawyer* in 1930 and *Huckleberry Finn* in 1931 with Durkin.

It seemed a cruel ending for a young man who'd shown such promise on the screen. Although on a combined level, Bogie would work with Davis and O'Brien on more pictures than with any other actors, he always harbored resentment toward each of them for their rather callous treatment of young Durkin. He vowed that day if some young person ever fell for him in a big way, he'd treat the lovesick kid with a little more sensitivity.

If only he had known at the time how soon he'd be put to that test.

***

After her other guests—all losers—had left, Davis invited Bogie to remain behind for "some private conversation." He'd noticed that she'd become more self-assured and poised in the wake of having so many handsome young men, all co-stars, falling in love with her.

He too found her the most attractive and alluring he'd ever seen her, which was in direct contrast to his first impression of her. Even so, with her whitened hair and pop-eyed look, she still evoked a dime store Harlow to him.

It was as if she were still searching for a face and a look but hadn't found it yet, whereas Garbo had burst on the screen, even though very young, with a look and a poise that she'd always keep.

Both Barbara Stanwyck and Joan Crawford, after some awkward beginnings, were finding "the look" and their screen presence. Davis seemed on a desperate search, and even without a camera, her intensity to find a screen persona filled the air with electricity.

When she came out to visit with him on the back porch, she turned off the overhead light, claiming it attracted bugs. But he knew the real reason.

Thankfully, the Wrath of God, Ruthie Davis, had gone to bed early complaining of a headache. For all this stage mother knew, her daughter's guests had left. Bogie suspected that Ruth disapproved mightily of the opposite sex, viewing men as "the enemy." She seemed so fiercely protective of her daughter that it reminded him of a butch dyke, guarding her prized nymphet from the menace of preying seducers.

Once seated in the porch swing and with the warm night air blowing about them, Bogie was in the mood for romance. Still shaken over his experience in Mexico with Harlow, and the way she had rejected his marriage proposal, he seemed to take comfort sitting close to her imitation. "Merely the mock," or so he thought, "is better than nothing at all."

Regardless of the outcome of the evening, he'd have a tale to tell Kenneth in the morning. In this case, he no longer cared if Kenneth reported his seductions to Mary Philips. In some perverse part of his mind, he wanted Mary to know that many women, including stars, found him an attractive and a desirable bedmate. Even if he returned to New York, and he was most definitely headed back there, he felt that he'd take the train back East with a solid track record of having seduced some of the biggest stars of the movies, even Marlene Dietrich. Of course, that quickie blow-job wasn't a true seduction in the way that sex with Harlow, Stanwyck, and Crawford had been. Only Garbo had eluded him, and he thought she always would.

On that back porch and to his unpleasant surprise, Davis didn't want to talk about their relationship or even their future career in films, assuming they had one.

She focused her talk on one beau back East, Harmon Oscar Nelson. "I call him Ham," she said, "and he calls me Spuds."

"Ain't that cute?" he said, slightly softening the sarcasm in his voice.

"He wants to be a musician," she said. "He's equally good at playing both the piano and the trumpet. But he'll never be a star doing either. He's also talking about becoming a radio singer like Bing Crosby."

"If he doesn't knock Bing down from the mike," he said, "maybe he'll become the next Rudy Vallée," he said. "What about us? What's gonna happen to Miss Bette Davis and Mr. Humphrey Bogart? Or have you already told me what you think of me by inviting me to this party of losers?"

"Perhaps," she said. "My career seems to be collapsing. So does yours. Stanwyck and Crawford are moving up in Hollywood. You and I seem to be headed the same way of those silent-screen stars of three years ago. Did you know that Louis B. Mayer was quoted as saying that at least one-third of the stars in 1928 are washed up, and he predicts even more will fall by the wayside. I think he's right. Look around you. Vilma Banky, John Gilbert, Ramon Novarro, Bill Haines, Gloria Swanson, Pola Negri. Mayer has hated Chaplin since they got into a fistfight at the Hollywood Hotel, and he thinks Chaplin will never really make it in Talkies either."

"So, what are we going to do?" he asked. "Hunt up Natacha Rambova and have her gaze into her crystal ball?"

"Nothing like that," she said. "I think we're stage actors. Both of us should return to Broadway. Maybe we'll take the train back East together."

"Is that a proposal of marriage?" he said. "I'll soon be available. My Mary has written that she plans to divorce me. She's fallen for Roland Young."

"I know of him," she said. "From what I hear, if a woman has him in bed for three months straight, she's set a world's record."

"I'm not broken up about it," he said. "It wasn't much of a marriage. My friend, Kenneth MacKenna, is in love with her."

"The one marrying that dyke, Kay Francis?" she said.

"One and the same."

"I'll never comprehend why men out here marry dykes," she said. "Homosexuality is one perversion I'll never understand. For the life of me, I can't see how anyone could be intimate with a person of the same sex, or would even want to be. It completely baffles me."

That was a young Bette Davis speaking to Bogie that night. Her attitude and prejudices would be altered slightly over the years, although she would continue to make flippant, antigay remarks in private among her straight friends. Throughout her life she would never take a public stand supporting gay causes.

In her declining years, when she discovered that nearly all of her fans and all of her remaining friends were gay, she adopted a more tolerant attitude. She said she believed in equal rights for all, and that included sexual orientation. She applauded gays for being an appreciative artistic group, and claimed that, "They make the average male look stupid."

A lot of those words were inspired by her own overwhelming acceptance and popularity in the gay world. Gays would applaud her even when she was bad, making cult classics out of some of her worst films, especially *Beyond the Forest*, the 1949 picture that finished her career at Warner Brothers. On that back porch, Bogie lit a cigarette for her and one for himself, as they sat on that swing going up in smoke, the same way both of them would do later on the screen.

"Ham wants me to give up my career and marry him," she said. "He claims he can support the both of us, and I should be a housewife."

"And how do you feel about that?" he asked, sorry to see the conversation reverting back to Ham.

"I'm not sure what to do," she said. "I'm very confused. I met Ham at the Cushing Academy. He was one year ahead of me. He is a very shy boy, awkward, gangling. I think he brings out my maternal instinct. He's pleasant looking. He'll never be handsome. He has a large nose."

"That can be a promising sign in a man," he said.

"What in hell does that mean?" she asked.

"I'm sure it's not true in all cases, but Joan Blondell told me that a big nose on a man or big feet is a good barometer that something else is big on the man too."

"Really?" she asked skeptically. "I've never heard such nonsense. I note that you don't have a big nose. Nor do you seem to have particularly large feet."

"There are always exceptions to the rule, as I've noted," he said, smiling.

414

"You can put me to the test anytime."

"Ruthie still thinks I'm a virgin," she said. "You know better."

"Not from first-hand experience," he said, putting his arm around her. "Poor Ham. Gilbert Roland is a tough act to follow."

"Roland's taken," she said. "I'm all that Ham has in the world. Ruthie wants me to marry Ham and surrender my so-called virginity to him."

"Too late for that now," he cautioned.

"Indeed. I've already surrendered my virginity to Ham. It wasn't a successful mating."

"How so?"

"It seems that Ham has been a chronic masturbator since he was six years old. He's given to premature ejaculation and can't satisfy a woman. If I marry him, I'll have to work for months—maybe more than a year—to train him."

"I'm already trained," he said. With an arm still around her, he began to feel her right breast. She did not object or pull away.

But she did take note of it. "I'm deliberately letting you have your fun," she said. "I've been told that to be sophisticated, I've got to take up smoking and drinking which I've done. Apparently, letting a man feel your breasts is another way to be sophisticated. I went to a party the other night. No men clustered around me. I felt like the wallflower I did when I attended Newton High. Even the lesbians in the room were clustering around Kay Francis, paying me no mind. Suddenly I looked up into the face of the most beautiful young man I've ever seen. Douglas Fairbanks Jr. I knew I could fall in love with him at once. I've heard that he's breaking up with Crawford. I've also heard he's a great lover. What a headline I could make if he dumps Crawford, divorces her, and marries me. I would install myself at Pickfair with the cream of Hollywood society."

"At first I resented you talking about other men when you've got me," he said, "but I want to hear the outcome of this."

"Oh, he chatted briefly with me. Offered me a cigarette. I was wearing my most low-cut gown. Suddenly, he reached into my dress and fondled one of my breasts. I couldn't believe what was happening. Just like that he did it. The way you're feeling me right now tells me you're not disappointed. Mr. Fairbanks must have been used to bigger and better things. He withdrew his hand rather quickly. He told me I should put ice on my nipples the way Crawford does. And that was that. He just turned and walked away. I've never felt so humiliated."

"I think I can relate to that," he said. "From a man's perspective, it would be like a woman unbuttoning your fly, reaching in to measure the goodies, and then walking away after saying, 'Not enough there to mess up my mouth with.'"

They both laughed at that. "What say we forget the Fairbanks boy, Roland, Ham, and God knows who else?" he said. "You've got a man once billed as the next Valentino, even the next Clark Gable, and you're not taking advantage of the situation. You said yourself, you want to become sophisticated." He took her in his arms and kissed her deeply before reluctantly breaking away. "If you give me a chance, you'll find I don't suffer from Ham's problem. I also find your nipples divine. In fact, I wish to suck both of them."

She offered absolutely no resistance as he moved in on her. He wanted more. He pulled her as close as he could to him, as his hand traveled from one breast to the other. With his other hand, he began the glide up her leg, past her garter belt and along her creamy thigh. He was heading for homeport.

Just before he reached the honeypot itself, the porch light was switched on. In the harsh, unforgiving glare stood Ruthie Davis herself, clad in her bathrobe.

"Get out of my house!" she shouted at him. "How dare you fondle my daughter like she's some bitch in heat. The loss of virginity before marriage will ruin a woman's life."

He pulled away from Davis but hesitated to get up. His hard-on had risen like Junior Durkin's in that film footage.

Bette Davis looked down, burying her head on her chest. She began to whimper.

"Get out!" Ruth commanded.

In defiance of her, he rose from the swing with an erection tenting his trousers.

That action was not lost of Ruth Davis. "You're a slave to your genitalia, Bogart," she said. "A disgusting, perverted creature. My daughter is going to marry Ham Nelson, not you. I'm not going to let her surrender her most prized possession, her virginity, to a sexual predator. I hear you've had half the women in Hollywood. You offer nothing to my Bette but venereal disease and unwanted pregnancy. It's all over town this morning that you drove Harlow to Tijuana for an abortion and that she nearly bled to death."

He reacted in horror to that revelation, having no idea that such a story from his private life was the subject of Hollywood gossip.

"Good night, Bette," he said, adjusting his shirt in his trousers and heading to the door that Ruth Davis held open for him.

Angered and humiliated, he walked rapidly through the living room. He vowed never to see Bette Davis again. The way he figured it, a relationship between the two of them was out of the question.

How wrong he was.

Chapter Thirteen

He couldn't believe it, but here he was in the Villa Carlotta apartment of gossip columnist Louella Parsons. She'd decided that trying to interview him was too difficult at Hollywood parties because of all the distractions. When she'd invited him over, she'd promised to give him her undivided attention.

Fearing that she might remember his offer of seduction, he could only hope that her husband, Dr. Harry Martin, was home that night. But when he got there, he learned that the doctor was administering to two of his patients, Lew Ayres and Douglas Fairbanks Jr., both of whom had come down with a bad case of the clap, according to Parsons.

"Docky," as Parsons called her new husband, had launched his career as a urologist, but Bogie had heard that he was now known as "doctor of the clap" around Hollywood, having treated everybody from Gary Cooper to Tallulah Bankhead. In their case, there was an argument over which party had infected the other. Docky was also the "house doctor," or so it was said, for Lee Frances, one of the reigning madams of her day. Parsons' husband was said to have had more intimate contact with the genitals of stars, both male and female, than any other person in Hollywood.

Inspecting penises and vaginas didn't occupy all of Docky's agenda. Parsons saw to it that he was hired frequently as a technical adviser on films such as *Doctors' Wives* that required some very limited medical expertise. Parsons would then plug the film in her column, lavishing special praise on the technical direction. She'd even gotten Governor Clement C. Young to appoint Docky to the California State Boxing Commission "just for the hell of it."

At this point, a Boston bull came into the living room and immediately jumped up on Bogie's lap, practically knocking his drink from his hand.

"That's our adorable Pansy Parsons," she said, ordering the dog to get down from the sofa. The dog obeyed her but anchored itself close to Bogie's feet, eyeing him suspiciously as if he might make a tasty snack.

As Bogie sat across from Parsons, enjoying some of Docky's good whiskey, she told him of a startling new development in broadcasting that she and "my Docky" had seen in New York. They'd gone East for a gala dinner where he'd been awarded an honorary degree at the American College of Surgeons. Bogie was later to learn that Hearst and the power of his newspapers were instrumental in securing the undeserved award for Docky.

It seemed that Parsons had been asleep at her typewriter at the advent of the Talkies, and had written that, "Flickers that talk will soon shut up—a mere passing fad."

She didn't want news of such a misguided opinion to ever tarnish her reputation again, so she aggressively embraced the new technology. During their visit to New York, Docky and she had been invited to a television broadcast. "Television is sort of like radio, but with a big difference," she said. "A picture is projected."

"You've got to be kidding," he said.

"It'll be the death of the movies," she predicted. "One day people will sit in their homes watching a moving picture the way they gather today around their radio sets. It'll be like bringing a movie into your own home."

"I don't want to get into an argument with you over this, but, trust me, that day will never happen."

"It's gonna happen sooner than later," she said. "I predict that by 1935 half the homes of America will have a television set. They even told me New York that it's soon going to be possible to show films on television in color."

"Hey, you're getting carried away. The idea of sitting at home watching a movie is hard enough to take. Watching a color movie on television—that's a bit much."

"No, I mean it," she said, "and they'll do more than just present light entertainment on a home screen," she said. "Football games will one day be broadcast live. Newsreel cameras will photograph late-breaking events and flash them into your home. Presidential inaugurations will be televised. In fact, the whole presidential race will one day be decided by television."

"I don't get that," he said.

"The two candidates will square off on television. The one who photographs best and handles himself better will win the race."

"That means that an actor wanting to be president will have a better chance of becoming that than a non-actor who might be a great politician but lousy in front of a camera," he said.

"Well," she said, signaling him that she wanted a refill of her liquor. "I wouldn't go that far. No actor I've ever known could possibly become president of the United States."

At the urgent ringing of the phone in her library, she excused herself and heaved herself up from her armchair. When she returned, she told him, "It was from Docky. He went with Jack Dempsey and some other friends to Santa Barbara to see a boxing match, and later, Docky and Dempsey had a few drinks together in a tavern. Then Docky and the champ got into an argument. Before it was over, my Docky knocked Dempsey on his ass. What a man!"

Bogie would never know the true circumstances of this barroom brawl, or if Docky had indeed knocked out Dempsey.

"This will show that SOB, Benny Rubin, that low-rent vaudevillian, what a man my Docky really is."

"I guess I don't get it," Bogie said. "Why would your husband need to prove his manhood to Benny Rubin?"

"Rubin and Docky were standing next to each other in the bathroom of a hotel at a party we attended recently. He later spread the word around town about Docky. Rubin said he knows why Louella has a constant smile on her face. He claimed that thing hanging out of Docky's fly looked like a baby's arm with an apple in its hand."

"Why did that make you mad?" he asked. "Docky should be flattered."

"A baby's arm," she sputtered, practically spitting out her words. "He could have said a man's arm. I can assure you that Docky, unlike Paul Bern, is a fully grown man."

"We can assume that when your husband put on that show for Rubin, he was soft. I'm sure when hard a man's arm would be a more apt comparison."

"Don't try to pacify me," she warned him. "I'll see that Rubin is finished in this town."

Ever since the episode of Docky vs. Rubin at the hotel urinal, Parsons had been running attacks on Rubin in her column. During his filming of *Marianne* with Marion Davies, Parsons printed the untrue allegation that Rubin got drunk and broke a violin over his wife's head. On the set the next day, Hearst told Rubin that he would "call Louella and dress her down if you want me to." Gallantly, Rubin told the newspaper czar that Parsons' attacks kept his name in front of the public, and that the publicity would boost ticket sales.

Parsons tried to interview Bogie that night, but appeared far too drunk. He was explaining how helpful showman W.A. Brady Sr. had been in launching his Broadway career and how he'd been directed by John Cromwell.

"I know those people," she said, "and even wrote about them a few weeks ago. I said Helen Gahagan, the star of many a Brady play, was visiting Hollywood with her new husband, Douglas Melvyn. I also claimed that not so long ago Miss Gahagan was married to John Cromwell." She held up her drink and looked at him imploringly. "Now what was wrong with that?"

"I don't think Helen appeared in any Brady production," he said. "I know she wasn't married to John, and I think her husband's name is Melvyn Douglas, not Douglas Melvyn."

"Silly me," she said. "I refuse to look anything up. I rely on the old bean. Basically, I was right, though. If it wasn't actually Helen who appeared in Brady plays, it was someone like her. And Cromwell should have married Helen. She should never have married this Douglas or Melvyn, whatever in hell that one calls itself. He has no sex appeal whatsoever."

"Gloria Swanson must disagree," he said. "I read she's cast him in her film, *Tonight or Never*."

"Gloria also thought that that drunk, Walter Byron, was going to become some big shit in Hollywood when she cast him opposite her in *Queen Kelly*. What does she know? I also happen to know that she's trying to hide her pregnancy from the camera. She has to bind herself into elastic underwear."

As the evening and the drinking progressed, it was obvious to him that she wasn't going to write a column about him. She was all too familiar with his lackluster films, and his "Tennis, anyone?" career on Broadway clearly bored her.

Throughout the evening she seemed obsessed with the phone, which never rang again. It was as if she were waiting for some late-breaking story about to happen. Finally, he found out what it was.

"I know the Lombard and Powell marriage is on the rocks," she said, "but I'm after a bigger story that will shake up the world."

"What might this earth-shattering news be?" he asked.

"It's a double story," she said. "The break-up of two marriages, the uncrowned king and queen of Hollywood and Tinseltown's uncrowned prince and princess."

"That could only mean Pickford and Fairbanks Sr. and his son, Junior, and Crawford."

"Who else?" she said, seemingly impatient with him. "How clearly do I have to spell it out?"

As Parsons got drunker, she ranted about various brush-offs she'd received. She claimed that she'd told both Mayer and Irving Thalberg to send Garbo back to Sweden and to cast Jeanne Eagels in her roles. She'd also demanded that the studio give all Jean Harlow parts to Clara Bow, and she'd lobbied to have Blanche Sweet cast in the role of Diane in Fox's *Seventh Heaven* "instead of that dyke, Janet Gaynor." Parsons seemed infuriated that the studios were not heeding her casting advice.

She had severely lectured Howard Hughes in her column for "even considering" filming the anti-Hollywood novel, *Queer People*.

"Every time a newspaper reporter is portrayed on the screen, he's a drunk," she said, slurring her words. "But *Queer People* wanted to go so far as to make perverts out of all of us, too."

He discreetly decided not to tell her that Hughes had briefly considered him for a vital but unattractive role in *Queer People*, that of the hard-drinking newspaper columnist, Walter Winchell.

It was after midnight when Parsons on wobbly legs rose from her chair. "You've been drinking," she said to him, stating the obvious. "Since Docky won't be home tonight, after having beaten the shit out of Dempsey, I suggest you stay over here at my apartment. Otherwise, I might have to write of your arrest for drunk driving."

His worst nightmare had come true. She'd remembered his invitation to seduction at the Jeanette MacDonald party. He'd challenged her to put his manhood to the test.

Faced with the horrific possibility of having to have sex with her, he evaluated her carefully, wondering if he'd be able to get it up.

He'd read somewhere that she was claiming that she was born in 1893, which would make her only about six years older than him. He'd also heard that she'd

420

been born in 1880, maybe even in the late 1870s. That would put her in her fifties.

Figuring that an actor had to do what an actor had to do, he braced himself for the challenge.

She took his hand, leading him to her bedroom.

"I have stage fright," he whispered into her ear.

"What's the matter?" she asked. "You already told me you weren't some lisping faggot. Here's your chance to prove it to America's top newspaperwoman."

"I mean if you objected to Rubin comparing your Docky to a baby's arm— and that was when he was soft—I don't know if I'll measure up to your expectations."

"Don't worry," she said. She suddenly lunged toward him, locking him in a tight embrace. Her lipstick-slashed mouth descended on him, and her tongue darted out like a rattlesnake's. Her alcohol-tainted breath was foul, and he prayed for the strength to get through the evening.

When she finally broke away, she placed her bejeweled hand at his groin. "So, I didn't get a rise out of you yet. I'll have to revert to more drastic measures." She took his hand again, leading the march to her bedroom. "I'm sure you'll please me. Besides, you couldn't possibly be any worse than Clark Gable--no one could possibly fuck as badly as him."

***

Through Spencer Tracy, Bogie learned that Basil Rathbone had been secretly meeting with Helen Menken about reprising his stage role in *The Captive* if the film, based on the Broadway play about lesbianism, ever made it in a watered-down version onto the screen.

Still angered that Helen had refused to take his calls, he was doubly hurt that he wasn't being considered for the role of the male lead in *The Captive*. The way he figured it, it'd be a cake-walk for him to play the role of a man who falls for a lesbian. He'd had so much experience in real life that the part wouldn't be difficult for him at all. He felt that he needed a controversial film to call Hollywood's attention to him, now that Fox was about to dump him.

When Lilyan Tashman phoned him and invited him to a costume gala hosted by Basil Rathbone and his wife, Ouida, Bogie gladly accepted. He thought that he might encounter Helen there, and he'd enjoy showing up on the arm of Tashman, Hollywood's best-dressed woman and one of its most glamorous stars.

Bogie feared that he might encounter Louella Parsons there. After last night, he wasn't too eager to run into the gossip columnist, and he never intended to have a repeat performance of their sexual marathon at the Villa Carlotta. On the other hand, he didn't have to be ashamed of his performance. If he had to admit it to himself, he'd acquitted himself very well. He didn't know if he were any better than "Baby's Arm," her husband, Docky, but he felt that when he'd left her bed, Parsons was one satisfied woman. At least she would not report that he was some lisping faggot actor from New York. After giving her multiple orgasms, he'd shown her what a man he really was.

"I haven't a thing to wear," Bogie told Tashman, feigning a falsetto voice like some Hollywood matron standing in front of an overstuffed closet.

"Since every newspaper columnist claims you look like Valentino," Tashman said, "why not go as Rudy looked in *The Sheik?* I have a connection in wardrobe that will get you his actual costume. I'll come as Agnes Ayres playing Lady Diana Mayo."

"We should make a stunning couple," he said, especially when I haul you off to my tent to rape you."

"Come over around three in the afternoon tomorrow," she said. "I'm having some actors in at six for drinks.

"And where did you stash your husband?" he asked.

"Edmund's in Palm Springs," she said, "with this divine waiter. And remember, darling, you can change into your Sheik drag here. Arrive casually dressed at three. The fewer clothes you have on, the better. I hate to waste a lot of valuable time undressing a man."

"I won't even bother with underwear," he said before hanging up.

The following afternoon Tashman lived up to her promise. He quickly forgot about Helen Menken, Bebe Daniels, Jean Harlow, and even Bille Dove. After sex, when they were both winding down and gathering a second wind for the cocktail party and the costume ball, he learned some biographical details about his lady love.

Tashman was born the same year that he was, except she was two months older. She had previously been married to Al Lee, a sometimes vaudeville partner of Eddie Cantor. Her favorite restaurant for lunch in Hollywood was the Brown Derby. Her favorite dress designer was "Mr. Joyce," of Emmet-Joyce Dress Studio. When in New York, she always stayed at the Sherry-Netherland Hotel. And, finally, she was Jewish.

More startling news was on the way. He learned that Robert Florey, the director, had approached her about playing the second female lead in *Those We Love*, a film adaptation of a George Abbott play. Mary Astor was slated to play the female lead.

"Is there a part in it for me?" he eagerly asked, hoping she had some leverage with Florey.

"You would have been ideal in the role of Blake," she said. "It's the second male lead. But it's already been cast. Hale Hamilton."

"I know that fucker," he said. "John Cromwell, my fellow Pussy Posse comrade in New York who doesn't even seem to know me in Hollywood, directed Hale and me in a play called *Swifty* back in '22. But that's the second male lead. I'm star material. Has the part of the leading man been cast yet?"

"Actually Florey is enchanted with that charming buddy of yours," she said.

"He's going to offer the role of Freddie Williston to none other than Kenneth MacKenna."

Bogie leaned back in his chair and sighed. "It can't be."

"What is it, darling?" she asked.

"Kenneth is going to star opposite Mary Astor as soon as another Mary, Pickford herself, releases him from her clutches. The Gods do shine down on Kenneth."

"And you didn't even mention his upcoming marriage to that little twat, Kay Francis. What a honeypot."

"For that, I don't envy him."

"Don't knock it until you've sampled her pussy," Tashman said. "She knows what's she's doing, and I got to her before Kenneth dived in and stretched it all out of shape."

"I know you did, my little muff-diving vixen," he said, kissing the lips that had so recently brought him so much pleasure in her upstairs bedroom. "Dietrich, Garbo, you've had all of them. Even Humphrey Bogart."

"I've never deceived you," she said. "The only thing I like better than Bogie meat is a *femme fatale*."

"Thanks a lot," he said sarcastically. "I guess I'm out of *Those We Love*. Perhaps there's a script being shopped around called *The Unloved*."

He stood up and walked aimlessly around the room, heading for the garden and some fresh air. Looking back over his shoulder at Tashman on her sofa, he said, "There goes my big chance to fuck Mary Astor. In spite of her looks, I hear she's one hot broad. John Barrymore has spread the word. I guess that's one notch I won't have to carve on my much overworked belt."

Bogie spoke far too soon. His affair with Mary Astor loomed in his future when he would co-star opposite her in a remake of *The Maltese Falcon* in 1941.

When he came back from the garden after having smoked two cigarettes, he confronted Tashman. "I thought we'd be seeing a lot more of each other. After all, I'm madly in love with you, and I'd like it if you could service me two or three nights a week."

"So sorry, darling," she said. "You know me. The ladies come first. I've fallen madly in love with Claudette Colbert. We've just made a flicker together, *The Wiser Sex*. It was directed by Berthold Viertel. You know him, darling. He's the husband of Salka, that dear, dear friend of Garbo's. Claudette is the cat's pajamas. She's been keeping me so busy I haven't had time to make the usual rounds."

"Was it a film about lesbians?" he asked. "Or were there any male roles?"

"Melvyn Douglas had the lead," she said. "You know, the one that Louella calls Douglas Melvyn? This young actor from back East, Franchot Tone, came out to the coast to play the second male lead. He's educated, articulate, and a real gentleman. Finding him sexy, I dropped by his dressing room one afternoon to give him a blow-job. After that experience, I've nicknamed Tone 'The Jawbreaker.'

Wait till all those Hollywood hussies like Crawford get to work on that totem pole."

Tashman knew of which she spoke. In 1935, Joan Crawford, many months after her divorce from Douglas Fairbanks Jr., wed Franchot Tone.

"It's not just Claudette who's keeping me busy," she said. "I'm appearing in practically every film made in Hollywood. Crap like *Up Pops the Devil* with Carole Lombard and Joyce Compton. Lombard told me she hasn't had time to fuck you yet. Compton also says you're not her type. She prefers cowboys."

"Yeah, I know," he said with disdain. "We should fix Joyce up with Hoot Gibson."

"Too late for that," she said. "On the set of *Millie*, I hung out with Joan Blondell and Anita Louise. Joan says she's had you regularly but Anita told me she hasn't. Nor does she plan to. She's after Clark Gable."

"Wasn't the star of that film, Helen Twelvetrees?" he asked.

"Sorry you brought that up," she said. "Helen starred in *Millie*. She also starred in—don't you love the title?—*The Cat Creeps* with me. You'll get to meet Helen. She's coming to my party."

"Can't wait," he said. "To me, she's just a pale imitation of Lillian Gish. That tiny mouth curved downward, those eyes always brimming with tears, and those wispy eyebrows she paints so that she looks constantly surprised."

"That's our Helen."

"I hear Miss Twelvetrees is Rin-Tin-Yin's favorite actress, because he's always got a dozen places to piss on," he said.

"Oh, darling, don't pull that corny line on her. She's heard it a million times."

"Serves her right going around with a name like Twelvetrees," he said.

"I've just made *Girls About Town* with Cukor," she said. "He's coming over with the stars of the film, Kay Francis herself, and Gary Cooper's new boy friend, Joel McCrea."

"I know them both," he said.

"But have you met Anderson Lawler?" she asked.

"You mean, the one Coop dumped for Joel?"

"One and the same. Cukor was sucking off Andy so he gave him a small part in the film too. When Lawler met McCrea, those two jealous queens generated so many sparks that they almost started a forest fire."

"Is Lawler going to show up at the same little gathering with Coop and Joel?" he asked. "You're asking for trouble."

"Not only that, Andy is bringing Tallulah. Tallu herself had a brief fling with Coop until he gave her the clap. Kenneth is bringing Kay. I wanted to have them over for a good luck toast before they run off to Catalina Island to get married."

"Maybe you and Kay will toss off a quickie in the bedroom upstairs," he said. "Invite Tallulah to join you. That is, if she's over the clap."

"That's not a bad idea," she said, taking him seriously.

"Are you going to the wedding?" he asked. "I'm the best man."

424

"I'd love to," she said, "but Claudette and I are going to drive over to Palm Springs. It's just for members of the sewing circle. Marlene will be there."

"I wish I could attend or at least be a fly on the wall," he said.

"You just weren't born with the right equipment," she said. "You poor dear. A dick where a hole should have been."

At the sudden ring of the doorbell, she jumped up and checked her dress and makeup in the mirror. "With a crowd like I've invited, fireworks can be expected."

"Sounds like this party is gonna be quite a hoedown," he said. "We may never make it to Basil's ball."

"So what?" she said, heading for the door. "I hear Basil has too many balls as it is." She paused at the door. "I mean that literally. I got it on good authority. He carries around a set of three balls in his trousers. You heard me right."

"Two profiles and three balls," he said. "That should be carved on his tombstone."

Tashman threw open the door to welcome Tallulah Bankhead and Anderson Lawler.

Tallulah burst into the room. "Hump," she shouted, striding over to greet him. "I haven't seen you since I fucked you in New York." She fell down on her knees in front of him and kissed his genitals, which thankfully were hidden in his trousers.

She looked up at him as if pleading for mercy. "Get me a bourbon and branch water, darling. And go easy on the branch water. I hear Los Angeles water is polluted."

***

Tallulah introduced Bogie to Anderson Lawler, one of the most minor of players on the screen but one of the most talked about figures in Hollywood because of his romantic link to Gary Cooper, Tinseltown's prettiest and best hung man.

"This is the most divine cocksucker in Hollywood," Tallulah said in presenting Lawler. "He spent last night sucking my dick. Of course, I'm not Cooper in the meat department. My dick is more petit."

"Forgive her," Lawler said, shaking Bogie's hand. "She's absolutely stark, raving mad and I adore her."

"Glad to meet you, pal," Bogie said.

Lawler drifted off to get them drinks, as Tallulah walked alone with Bogie in the garden. He heard the doorbell ring.

"Hump, my darling, I think you and I both are getting a little long in the tooth for Hollywood," Tallulah said. "It's for kids in their twenties, not mature adults in their thirties."

"You look more beautiful than ever," he said to reassure her.

"Don't kid a kidder, darling." She brushed back her hair and symbolically looked at a fading sunset. "The bloom is off this big waxy magnolia. Somehow film doesn't capture my electrifying personality that I can convey on stage. The critics may be right. On screen I'm just a pale imitation of Garbo. My face doesn't seem to move right. My eyes don't come alive. I'm not made for the movies."

"Then let's you and me hook up, go back to New York, and become Mr. and Mrs. Broadway," he said, only partially joking.

"That's the best offer I've had all day," she said. "I might take you up on that. But I'll have to get back to you."

"What's holding you back?" he asked, bending over and kissing her lightly on her scarlet-painted lips.

"Since one of my goals—the one about fucking Coop—has been achieved, I have set two other goals for myself--and two more candidates to fuck before I leave Hollywood."

"Since you've already had me, the best," he said, "who else is there?"

"Garbo, of course. You've not plowed her yet, have you, darling?"

"No, but I got a blow-job from Marlene Dietrich."

"That's no distinction," she said. "Marlene has sucked all of our cocks. My second goal is to bed Johnny Weissmuller with his ten uncut inches."

"The Olympic swimming champ?" he asked. "I didn't think he was your type. I hear he's gonna become the new Tarzan."

"A darling Ape Man if ever there was one," she said. "I met the film's director, W. S. Van Dyke, the other night. Don't you just adore that name? Dyke? Charles Bickford wanted the part but was turned down. Too old. Spencer Tracy's latest flame, Johnny Mack Brown, lost because he's not tall enough, although he seems to satisfy Spence just fine. You won't believe this, but Clark Gable tried out for Tarzan too. Van Dyke decided that Gable wasn't muscular enough and didn't have Weissmuller's inches. Weissmuller is the Ape Man, Gable more a chimpanzee."

As Lawler returned with the drinks, Tallulah excused herself. "Keep my bourbon chilling for me, darlings. I've got to take a horse piss. Anyone care to watch?"

When she'd gone, Bogie turned to Lawler. "So you and Miss Bankhead are Hollywood's latest odd couple?"

"I'm still in mourning for Coop," he said. "Tallu's a pal, someone to hang out with. There are fringe benefits. After she has her way with Weissmuller, she's going to turn Tarzan over to me."

"Sounds like fun, pal," he said. Although a well-born Virginian, Lawler had an obscene tongue and a mocking laugh just like Tallulah, or so Bogie had heard. None of that was evident today. If anything, the tall, thin, freckled-faced young man looked like a choirboy under all that red hair. Bogie had never met too many

426

red-haired men in Hollywood before.

Since Bogie didn't want to go into the living room and meet Tashman's other guests, he stayed behind to talk to Lawler. Before meeting him, he thought the young man might be effeminate. He wasn't at all. He claimed that he shared Cooper's love of the great outdoors, and excelled in sailing, hunting, swimming, mountaineering, and even archery. But he also seemed a rather cultured man, with an interest in books, music, and art, and, in fact, had taken Cooper to many plays and concerts "hoping to broaden that Montana cowpoke's horizon."

Their conversation was interrupted when Tashman called Bogie in to meet Helen Twelvetrees. Almost instantly, he knew their chemistry wasn't compatible. "So, you're Humphrey Bogart," the actress said.

"Yeah--but you can call me Rin-Tin-Tin," he said before turning his back to her and heading for the bar.

As he was pouring himself a drink, he turned around to greet Kenneth MacKenna and Kay Francis. "My soon-to-be best man," Kenneth said, kissing him lightly on the lips. Since "going Hollywood," Kenneth had become very theatrical. No sooner had those lips left Bogie's than they were replaced with those of Kay Francis.

"Let's get this God damn wedding over with and soon," Bogie said. "These pre-wedding parties are beginning to wear me out."

"Not so soon," Kenneth said. "I'm inviting you to my bachelor party before we sail for Catalina."

"Will there be any pretty girls there?" Bogie said.

"Strictly men," Kenneth said. "It's a male lingerie party like the ones Dietrich has for the gals."

"I don't get it," Bogie said. "Lingerie?"

"All the men have to strip down to their underwear," Francis said. "It was my idea."

"I think I'd like to skip it," Bogie said.

"My best man," Kenneth said. "I wouldn't think of it. I insist you come."

As Tashman led Francis and Kenneth away to meet the other guests, Lawler rejoined Bogie, except this time he was accompanied by George Cukor who had directed him, along with Tashman, Francis, and Joel McCrea in *Girls About Town*. To Bogie, both men seemed a little drunk before the party even began.

Cukor greeted Bogie and thanked him for "disposing of Tommy Richards before he made trouble for me."

"Glad to oblige, pal," Bogie said.

"*Girls About Town*," Lawler said. "What an appropriate movie title for George to direct. I go cruising every night. I've even been arrested twice on a morals charge. Some of the tricks I pick up aren't worth it. But when I find a winner, and I often do since Hollywood is filled with so many beautiful young men dreaming of stardom, I pass them on to Georgie here."

"You might call Andy my pimp," Cukor said.

Bogie was pulled away by a tug on his sleeve from Tashman. "Dear heart, she's here. I didn't think she'd come."

He was led over to meet the French dwarf who was seated in the center of the living room in a position that might have been awarded to the guest of honor.

The Parisian, Miss Claudette Colbert, extended her hand. As she chatted with Bogie, he noted that her English was flawless. She had the most beautiful porcelain face he'd ever seen on a woman. When she spoke, her eyes lit up and her face was very animated. He found her quite beautiful and felt a bit sad that she was a dyke. She was the kind of woman he could easily fall for, had Tashman not beat him to her.

Colbert seemed very excited. She'd just met with Cecil B. DeMille. "He's offered me the chance to play the wickedest woman in the world. I jumped at it. I'm going to be Poppea in *The Sign of the Cross*. My nude scene in a bathtub full of milk will become the scandal of Hollywood."

"I hope you invite me to the set to watch it," he said.

"Like hell!" she said. "I'm demanding a closed set that day."

There was a certain earthy humor and haughty sensuality to Colbert that Hollywood had yet to see. For some reason and on an impulse, he reached for her hand and held it against his lips, kissing it gently. Her porcelain hands were just as lovely as her face.

"Why did you do that?" she asked, taking her hand back.

"Just wanted to," he said.

"When you're around a woman, do you always do what you want to?" she asked provocatively.

That made him realize that she wasn't completely dyke. Colbert could also flirt with men. "Sometimes," he said.

Just as he was moving in to get to know Colbert better, there was another tug on his arm. "They're here," Tashman said, pulling him toward the foyer.

He noticed Lawler standing only ten feet away talking with Cukor and Tallulah.

Tashman threw open the door to greet Joel McCrea and Gary Cooper. Bogie feared that his mischievous lover was going to get her fireworks when Lawler came face to face with McCrea, the usurper who had stolen his man.

Gary Cooper strode into the foyer, and the first person his eyes focused on was Lawler himself.

***

In the back seat of a taxi headed for the Rathbone costume ball, Bogie offered comfort to Tashman, putting his arm around her.

Her party had ended in disaster. The explosion she had maliciously set up

428

between Gary Cooper and Anderson Lawler had backfired. When Cooper saw his ex-, Lawler, he came up to him and shook his hand. "How are you, Andy?" Cooper had asked. He'd then turned around and headed back to the foyer, where he'd taken Joel McCrea by the arm. "Come, Joel," he'd said "there are other parties we can go to tonight."

Looking shell-shocked, Tashman had stood forlornly in her foyer, watching them go. Cooper had turned back to look at her. "Thanks, Lilyan, for inviting us. But we can't stay."

The evening had gone downhill from there. Tashman's mischief-making had ruined the party. In his hurt and humiliation, Lawler turned to the arms of Mother Tallulah and had wept against her breasts. Tallulah had become so upset by Tashman's attempt to stir up trouble that ten minutes later she'd thrown her drink in Tashman's face and had stormed out of the party with Lawler. Both had threatened never to speak to Tashman again.

Even Helen Twelvetrees had left without saying good-bye. But it had been the "dressing down" by George Cukor that had devastated Tashman. In front of Bogie, the director had attacked her insensitivity toward homosexual romances. "It may be just a silly game to you," Cukor had told her, "but we get our hearts broken too. To have tried to humiliate a fine and decent man like Andy in front of your Hollywood friends, and to go out of your way to embarrass Coop and Joel— that's unthinkable. Just for that, I'm going to cut out your best scenes from *Girls About Town*, whittle down your role to nothing, and run one scene of you where you photographed like a drunken washerwoman."

"You God damn vicious queen," she'd shouted at Cukor, slapping his face. She'd burst into tears and had run from her living room into the foyer where she'd headed up the steps, tripping once on the landing.

Bogie had gone up after her to make sure she was all right and that she wasn't going to cut her wrists or do anything stupid like that. When he'd come into her bedroom, she'd been lying in the center of her bed, sobbing. "That faggot Cukor will ruin me in Hollywood," she'd said. "I just know he will. His cruelty knows no bounds if you cross him."

He'd stayed with her for fifteen minutes, but he couldn't stop her from crying. When he'd felt she wasn't going to harm herself, he'd told her he was going back downstairs to let the guests out.

When he'd gone back into the living room, only Kenneth and his bride-to-be, Kay Francis, had remained behind. Both of them had gotten up from the sofa to embrace him and to tell him to thank Tashman for throwing the cocktail party in their honor.

Kenneth had told Bogie, "Kay and I have two other parties to attend tonight, and we have to leave at once." After promising Kenneth that he'd attend his bachelor party, Bogie had kissed both of them and had headed upstairs again to hold a still sobbing Tashman in his arms.

Although he'd urged her not to go to the costume ball, she'd insisted on dressing up as Lady Diana Mayo and going anyway. She'd demanded that he put on his Sheik costume.

In the back of the taxi, he tightened his arm around her. "It was a gag that backfired," he said. "Nothing more, nothing less."

"I feel humiliated," she said. "Word of what happened will be all over town tomorrow. I'll be a laughing stock. God knows what party Tallulah dragged Andy to and what that bitch is saying about me right now."

"Let's have the cabbie turn around and take us back to Lilowe," he said.

"No, God damn the fuckers," she said, sitting up in the seat with a fierce determination. "I'm going to show my face in Hollywood like the proud woman I am."

He settled back uncomfortably in his seat and lit a cigarette. His sharpened instincts told him that the costume ball was going to be a disaster, too.

Even before being swept into a hotel ballroom with one-hundred other guests, representing the Hollywood elite, Bogie urged Tashman not to enter. Personally he was embarrassed to show up in that dumb Sheik costume. He was no Valentino and would never be, in spite of what some newspaper columnists had written.

A fire seemed to be burning within Tashman that night, a blaze that no one—not even herself—could put out.

The Rathbone costume ball would mark the beginning of the end of the career of Lilyan Tashman.

From the night of her doomed cocktail party until Bogie too became her victim, Tashman was a raging star on fire, like one whose furnaces from hell burning most furiously and spectacularly before exploding into fragments.

***

When he arrived at the Ambassador Hotel for the costume ball hosted by Ouida and Basil Rathbone, Bogie had to take a leak. So did Tashman. He agreed to meet her near the entrance into the ballroom.

Ducking into the urinal, Bogie stood next to a man dressed as Hamlet. When he turned to look, he stared eyeball-to-eyeball at Ronald Colman. Pissing away, Bogie reminded Colman of that day in New York when the British actor had "stolen" the role of Captain Giovanni Severini in *The White Sister* opposite Lillian Gish.

"Sorry, old chap," Colman said. "We can't win them all."

"I see the readers of *Photoplay* have just voted you the handsomest man in Hollywood," Bogie said. "Congratulations." Unable to resist needling the actor, he added. "Not bad for a guy who is *at least* forty-one. Louella told me you were born in 1881—and Louella was around to know—instead of 1891."

"Louella, as always, is misinformed," he said. He was fastidious enough not to let any final drops of urine soil his drawers, so he shook himself repeatedly at the urinal. After buttoning his fly, he stood briefly in front of the mirror, checking out his suave and dashing appearance, running his fingers along his pencil-thin moustache. "Male beauty is a curse."

Bogie stood next to him at the lavatory. "Frankly, I think Doug Fairbanks Jr. has you beat in the looks department, and he's much younger."

Colman looked at him with a certain bitterness. In his smooth, well-modulated voice, he said, "Winning most handsome contests is something you'll never have to worry about, Mr. Humphrey Bogart." With that remark, he turned and left the men's room.

"Limey bastard!" Bogie said when Colman slammed the door. He couldn't help but notice that after taking a piss, this immaculate gentleman hadn't washed his hands. No doubt he was heading for the main ballroom where he'd shake the hands of the Hollywood elite.

When Bogie returned from the men's room, Tashman hurried over to take his arm. She ushered him over and introduced him to "Babyface" Nancy Carroll. "This enchantingly beautiful and talented actress will entertain you while I work the room." With that, Tashman departed.

He sat down next to this candy-faced beauty, who had starred in the Silents and had, unlike many other actresses, survived the coming of talking pictures.

Tashman and Carroll had met in 1928 when the lesbian director, Dorothy Arzner, had raced them through *Manhattan Cocktail*, with Richard Arlen as their leading man and the mysterious Edwina Booth appearing uncredited.

In a total departure from character and almost as if to mock her own saccharine sweet screen image, Carroll had come to the ball dressed as Mae West as she'd appeared on Broadway in *Sex*. Raised in New York as the daughter of Irish immigrant parents, she was only three years younger than Bogart.

Unknown to both Carroll and Bogie at the time he met her, she was at the height of her fame in the early 30s. He knew that Carroll was one of the first actresses to sing and dance on a Hollywood sound stage, although personally he didn't think she did either very well, although her voice had a trill that was pleasant enough to get her by.

"I'm furious at Lilyan," Carroll said, her flaming red hair seeming to match her hot temper. She had a cherubic baby face and sea-blue eyes. "The bitch is always trying to lure me into a lesbian experience."

"Lilyan has been known to do that," he said, lighting up. "Sometimes she services a woman before she can leave the crapper."

"You don't find that disgusting?" she asked in astonishment.

"Nothing human disgusts me," he said, lighting her a cigarette.

When he blew smoke in her face, she waved it away with her dainty, porcelain-like hand that seemed to belong more on a doll than on a real woman.

"In fact," he said, needling her, "if you change your mind and decide to get it on with Lilyan, I'd like to watch."

The gamine, red-haired darling of the Depression Era smiled her most beautiful smile at him, causing instant meltdown. "My Cupid's bow mouth was designed by Mother Nature to service men, at which I succeed admirably. In fact, all parts of my body were especially designed to provide a man—not a woman—with the greatest pleasure he's ever known on the face of God's earth."

"That is the single best build-up I've heard since coming to The Coast," he said. "I think dressing up like Mae West has given you added confidence. You're talking with all the self-enchantment of Mae herself."

"There's a big difference between Miss West and me," Carroll said. "I hear she's really a man in drag. Trust me, I'm a *real* woman."

"I would never have mistaken you for anything else, pal," he said. "And you can trust me on that."

Tashman reappeared suddenly and grabbed his arm. "Bogie was only on a brief loan-out to you," she said to Carroll. "I'll return him to you, but I've got to get on that floor—and quick—with him."

Tashman led him onto the dance floor. Deep into the dance and for some reason, she seemed to be leading, steering him toward a flamboyantly dressed pair of dancers masquerading as harlequins. Their outfits were clearly the most spectacular on the floor in stunning, electric colors of shocking pink, chartreuse, lemon yellow, imperial purple, and Picasso blue.

Tashman, still leading, was maneuvering close to the dancing harlequins. Suddenly, Tashman reached out and pinched the ass of the female Harlequin real hard. Bogie was certain it would leave a big black bruise.

The woman spun around and stared at Tashman. "You dirty bitch," she said, slapping Tashman. She took the hand of the male Harlequin and rapidly headed across the dance floor and out of the ballroom.

Since the scene was attracting attention, he grabbed Tashman and resumed dancing, steering her across the ballroom. "As God as my witness, I do believe that was the goddess herself, Greta Garbo."

"One and the same," she said, rubbing her burning cheek. "The last time I saw Garbo before she dumped me, I was going down on that Grand Canyon she calls her pussy."

"Who was her date?"

"None other than that faggot designer, Adrian," she said. "Only Adrian could get Garbo to put on that ridiculous Harlequin costume."

"I mean their faces were pretty much concealed," he said, holding her close as they danced. "How did you spot Garbo across a crowded ballroom?"

"Honeychild, I'd recognize that ass anywhere," Tashman said, "having had so many close encounters with it."

Tashman dropped him off again at the table with Carroll and faded quickly into the crowd. "Do I have to fuck you to get me a drink?" Carroll asked.

"As a matter of fact you do," he said. "First, the drink, then the fuck."

"It's a deal," she said.

At the bar he encountered William Powell whom he'd met the night of the Jeanette MacDonald party. Even though they were probably talking divorce, he'd still arrived at the ball with his wife, Carole Lombard, who sat at a nearby table.

"Carole insisted we come as Romeo and Juliet tonight," Powell said. "Surely I'm the oldest Romeo in history."

"You're looking great," Bogie assured him. "Those tights are a bit snug, though."

"I may be looking great, but I'm not feeling great," Powell said. "My doctors have discovered this lump in a place where the sun don't shine, and I'm worried it might be malignant."

"Sorry to hear that," Bogie said, offering him a cigarette as if that could cure cancer.

Powell didn't let his concern for a possible cancerous growth keep him from accepting the cigarette. As the two men smoked at the bar, Powell said, "I was just consoling Gloria Swanson who's here tonight too. She's developed a lump in her breast. We're calling ourselves The Lump Club."

When his drinks were served, Bogie said, "Good luck, pal." He turned and walked back toward Carroll's table.

From where they sat, Bogie and Carroll had a clear view of the doors leading to both the men's toilet and the ladies' room. He was startled to see Kenneth hovering outside the door to the women's toilet as if guarding it. He signaled for his old friend to come over to table. Amused at Kenneth in his green tights, Bogie said, "Robin Hood, meet Mae West. Or should I say, Kenneth MacKenna, meet Nancy Carroll."

Kenneth only half acknowledged Carroll, still keeping his eye on the door to the ladies' toilet throughout the introduction.

"Hanging out in front of the ladies crapper," Carroll chided him. "Naughty, naughty."

"It's not that," Kenneth said apologetically. "I'm here with Connie Bennett tonight. She knows Lilyan is on the ballroom floor. After that last incident when Lilyan attacked her in the women's room, she wants to make sure she can do her business in peace without Lilyan barging in to maul her."

Bogie turned to Carroll. "The last time I saw this guy tonight, he was leaving Lilyan's house to go to a round of parties with his bride-to-be, Kay Francis."

"Oh, yeah," Carroll said. "I read about Kay and you in the papers."

"Exactly where is Kay?" Bogie asked.

"Actually Kay is spending the night with Barbara Stanwyck before all of us sail to Catalina for our wedding tomorrow night," Kenneth said.

"Don't tell me you and Miss Bennett are having an affair," Carroll said.

"We've been very close friends ever since we made *Sin Takes a Holiday* together," he said.

"Well!" Carroll said, taking a hefty swig of her drink. "I learn something every day about Connie. When she's not fucking Joe Kennedy, she's balling Gilbert Roland. Otherwise, she's shacked up with either Swanson's husband, the Marquis de la Falaise de la Coudray, or Kenneth MacKenna."

"Something like that," he said, obviously embarrassed.

"Okay, pal," Bogie said. "As you know, I'm here with Lilyan tonight. So let's make an agreement to keep each of our dates on the far side of the ballroom as far away from each other as possible."

"It's a deal," Kenneth said. "No more catfights with practically every member of the Hollywood A-list looking on."

Their mutual pact was sealed none too soon. The door to the ladies room opened and out emerged one of the 20th-century's most stunning beauties. The eldest daughter of the stage matinee idol, Richard Bennett, Constance Bennett moved toward their table.

Bogie was immediately enraptured by her large, liquid, china-blue eyes and her marcelled blonde bob. As Kenneth introduced her, she spoke in a husky seductive voice. In those days, columnists wrote of her "glazed smartness." Bogie didn't have a clue as to what that meant.

Pathé's biggest star, who'd recently scored a big hit with her film, *Rich People*, joined them at table. Dressed as Maid Marian to Kenneth's Robin Hood, she immediately talked about the three-year contract she'd recently signed with Joe Kennedy, which would run until 1934.

Bogie noticed that any talk of Kennedy made Carroll appear jealous. Perhaps he was wrong. Why should she be jealous of Bennett's affair with Joe Kennedy? Perhaps it was that fat, lucrative contract that made Carroll fume.

A struggling actress could also be jealous of Bennett because of her wealth. Before returning to Hollywood, she'd been in a marriage to Philip Morgan Plant, which had led to a divorce and a million-dollar settlement on her. Bogie knew how jealous Tashman was of Bennett as they vied for best-dressed title. Tashman was furious that Bennett had so much more money to lavish on fashion than she did.

Finally, no longer able to control herself, Carroll said to Bennett, "Be careful...you may have more to fear than Lilyan Tashman tonight. Swanson's here, too. You weren't satisfied taking just one of her men. You wanted them both. Not only Joe Kennedy but her husband, Henri Marquis de la Falaise de la Coudray." Carroll seemed to delight in dragging out the somewhat mangled pronunciation of that name. "Swanson just might scratch your eyes out."

"How dare you talk to me that way, you little whore," Bennett said to Carroll, abruptly standing up and knocking over her chair. "Don't accuse me of stealing anybody's man."

"Well, you are here with Kay Francis' hubbie-to-be tonight," Carroll said angrily.

"You're fooling nobody by making me out to be some international tramp," Bennett said. "I happen to know you're trying to steal a married man yourself. I've heard it on reliable authority that you were seen in Palm Beach with Joe Kennedy, you bitch." Bennett picked up Carroll's unfinished drink and tossed it in her face.

434

***

A chastened Nancy Carroll emerged from the ladies room twenty minutes later, having made emergency repairs to her face after Constance Bennett tossed the cocktail.

"It looks like you're now on Bennett's hit list too," Bogie said. "First, Miss Lilyan Tashman, now Nancy Carroll."

"She can't believe that Joe Kennedy would prefer me over her," she said. "But I'm sure we're both convinced that ol' Joe likes either of us better than *la* Swanson."

Gloria Swanson was known for her curiosity. In her heyday it was said that a rat didn't run across Hollywood Boulevard without first getting her permission. Obviously news of the Bennett/Carroll altercation had traveled fast across the gossipy ballroom. Apparently Swanson had to see for herself what damage, if any, had been inflicted by Bennett, her arch rival, on Carroll, her newly emerging competition.

Two drunks on either side of Swanson were holding onto her arm as escorts. But it looked as if the more regal and firm-footed Swanson was actually supporting her two leading men. Bogie recognized their famous faces at once. One was the drunk, Owen Moore, an alcoholic actor who'd been the first husband to Mary Pickford before she'd dumped him for Douglas Fairbanks Sr. The other was another alcoholic actor, Lew Cody, who'd been in the news recently for having buried his wife of four years, "the female Chaplin," Mabel Normand. Cody and Moore had just co-starred with Swanson in *What a Widow!*

Swanson stopped briefly at their table. "Hello, dear heart," she said to Carroll. "I haven't seen you since the night we competed for the Oscar."

"Yeah," Carroll said. "We both lost to Norma Shearer."

"That goes to show you that it pays to be married to Irving Thalberg," Swanson said.

"Yeah," Carroll said. "I should have married Louis B. Mayer."

Swanson paused for a moment. At that point neither actress had introduced Bogie to each other. Swanson's escorts didn't appear to be in any condition for introductions. "My darling," Swanson said, warming for battle, "Louis B. Mayer is taken. Perhaps you can find some other man who's not married. Certainly not your escort here tonight, Mr. Humphrey Bogart."

So, Swanson for all her imperial air did know who he was.

"He's already married to Helen Menken," Swanson said.

Bogart didn't bother to correct her.

With steely eyes, she looked at Carroll. "Even Joe Kennedy has his Rose stashed somewhere back East."

"I've heard of the dame," Carroll said. "One ugly bitch. A midget too."

Swanson, also a midget, reared up and looked taller than she was. "All of us could do with a little more height around here." She paused again. "I hope you enjoyed your stay down in Palm Beach. My biggest problem when I heard about that trip involved a newspaper reporter in Miami who wrote that I was seen departing for Havana aboard Joe's yacht. That was a big mistake. You and I don't look alike at all. For one thing, I don't have dyed red hair. Also, my face isn't shaped like a box of Valentine candy."

"I read the article," Carroll said. "That was me and Joe on that boat all right. We sailed to Havana and met this new writer, Ernest Hemingway. While Joe was asleep one night, Ernesto fucked me. He's written this book called *A Farewell to Arms*. Over pillow talk, he told me that I'd be ideal for the female lead when they make the movie."

"I'm sure you would, my dear," Swanson said. "I really must go, but I can't resist a final warning. Has Joe given you any presents?"

"Maybe a bauble or two," Carroll said.

"He gave me a fur coat one time," Swanson said. "Later I found out he'd charged it to my account. When Sidney Howard came up with the title for my picture, *What a Widow!*, Joe promised him a Cadillac. Later I found out that had been charged to me too."

"Rest assured," Carroll said. "I'm far too smart a woman to let some John run up bills on my account. I'm also much too clever to marry a so-called nobleman for his title when all he wants from me is my dough."

"I see," Swanson said, the sharp edge of her voice surely able to cut glass. Nudging her escorts, she walked on by the table.

Swanson narrowly missed the arrival of Lilyan Tashman, who immediately commiserated with Carroll for "that venomous attack by that ragtag whore, Constance Bennett. If I'd been here, I would have beaten the bitch to a pulp for you. I'm itching to finish the fight we began in the women's crapper at the Cocoanut Grove."

Tashman sat with them for only five breezy minutes before jumping up to tablehop. He noticed that within a minute or so she landed at the table of William Powell and Carole Lombard.

When she'd gone, Carroll took his hand and looked into his eyes with a deadly seriousness. "I understand you're the best friend of George Raft."

"I wouldn't give myself such a stellar honor," he said. "George's best friend is the image that stares back at him when he looks in the mirror."

"I've got to see George tonight," she said. "He's having a big party at the Ambassador. He's invited me, and I'm going but I have some business to take up with him first. I need your help."

"Is that so?" he said. "I got a call about that party. It sounds wild. I told George I'd drop in if I could. But if things go the way I want them to, I fully expect to be occupied at Lilowe with Mrs. Edmund Lowe for the duration of the evening."

When her pleading grew more urgent, and she seemed on the verge of tears,

436

he reluctantly agreed to take her to see Raft. "That means I might be sacrificing a piece of ass from Lilyan."

"Okay, God damn it, I'll throw in my ass as part of the deal," she said. "I know you want a sample. You've been sitting here all evening drooling at me."

With that pronouncement, the deal was struck.

She began to fill him in on the details. Kennedy had dumped Swanson, but was still carrying on his older affair with Constance Bennett and his newer affair with Nancy Carroll.

"When I was vacationing with him in Palm Beach," Carroll said, "some pictures were taken. I don't know how they were taken, but they're very compromising. Those pictures could destroy his career in politics, and you can imagine what they'd do to mine in Hollywood. Joe's a real tightwad, but he's about to pay $50,000 in cash to get them back."

"That's a lot of dough," he said. "I know another tycoon—and I won't name him—who's also being blackmailed."

"It's this gang called Black Hands," she said.

"I've heard of them," he said. "They play rough."

"They're after all the big names, and they demand a lot of money," she said. "Let's face it. We can be naughty boys and girls out here in Hollywood." She reached for his hand. "I need your physical presence and your moral support. I want you to drive me to see Raft. I have the $50,000 stashed in the hotel's safe."

"I always like to come to the aid of a lady in distress," he said. "Especially when she's as pretty as you." He settled back, lighting another cigarette. "George seems mixed up in about half the trouble occurring in Hollywood. But just how does he figure into all this?"

"Joe doesn't want to pay off Black Hands directly," she said. "He wants to work it through Raft so that one of Owney Madden's boys will handle the actual payoff. The way Joe figures it, if Black Hands has to deal with Owney Madden, George Raft, and Murder, Inc., they'll probably settle for just one payoff and not come knocking on his door again."

"Yeah, I know what you mean," he said. "I've heard that many stars, those not as rich as Kennedy, have to shell out what they think is a one-time payment of $10,000, but after it's paid, the black-handed boys come calling again and again."

"Joe is smarter than your typical Hollywood star," she said. "He feels that with the threat of Owney Madden in the background, those blackmailers will take the money and run, unless some of them want to be found murdered on some lonely road in the Hollywood Hills."

On her table-hopping rounds, Tashman came back to join them again. There was an aura of desperation about her more urgent than he'd ever detected in her before, but he didn't have a clue as to why she was so agitated.

From the banquet's head table, Ouida Rathbone, the mistress of the ball, was arranging for pictures to be taken of some of her friends and guests. One of them was Swanson, who was photographed standing between Ouida and Basil Rathbone.

As Swanson posed for the shots, one of the waiters came over to Bogie's table and asked Lilyan Tashman if she would agree to be photographed with Ouida. Tashman asked Bogie to accompany her to the Rathbone table. With five photographers snapping away, Tashman suddenly realized that Ouida had arranged for her to be photographed with Constance Bennett. Obviously Ouida—along with virtually everyone else—knew about the bad blood between Bennett and Tashman. Perversely, Ouida had deliberately set up an encounter between the battling divas, this time in front of the Hollywood press corps. As Bennett's escort, Kenneth looked at Bogie in bewilderment, as both of them realized at the same time that this was a setup.

With the press watching, Tashman and Bennett didn't resume their argument but had smiles for everybody except each other. The two actresses did not even acknowledge each other but positioned themselves for the photographers, with Ouida sandwiched between them. It made quite a shot, with Ouida dressed as Marie Antoinette masquerading as a shepherdess in the Gardens of Versailles, Tashman as Lady Diana Mayo from *The Sheik*, and Bennett as Robin Hood's Maid Marian.

As soon as the photography session was over, Tashman broke away from Ouida. Having done her dirty deed, Ouida quickly excused herself to attend to her other guests. Valiantly, Kenneth tried to extract his escort, Constance Bennett, from the scene as quickly as possible.

Neither of the two divas would budge, but stood facing each other in the ballroom as if their feet were tar-heeled to the floor. "At last our little gold-digging hussy has found a dress that suits her," Tashman said with bitterness and sarcasm. "That of a milk maiden. How appropriate for the cow you are."

"What a brilliant impersonation you're doing of Agnes Ayres as Lady Diana Mayo," Bennett said. "I always thought you'd look better dressed for what you really are, a whore like Agnes herself. That one has slept with half the male stars in Hollywood. Just like you. Of course, in your case we'd have to add female stars as well."

"Don't worry, you ugly bitch," Tashman charged. "Your overripe pussy is safe from me. Gilbert Roland is telling everyone that you are prime Grade A Roquefort and that you gave him the clap."

"You dirty little Jew dyke," Bennett said, slapping her face. "That's a God damn lie. Gilbert adores me, and unlike 'Latrine Lil,' I'm clean as a hound's tooth."

Her face still stinging from that slap, Tashman pulled back from Bennett. Tashman looked dazed for a moment before deciding her next move. With all her rage and fury, she lunged toward Bennett, yanking her hair as she must have done in that women's room encounter. This time Bennett's hair must have been real—no more wigs—and Tashman's fist emerged with a hand of the genuine article. Tashman was stronger than the more delicate hothouse flower she faced, and seemed to overpower her. Bogie tried to pull Tashman away from Bennett, as

Kenneth stood by, taking in the scene but doing nothing to stop the fight.

In one sudden lunge, as Bogie was pulling her back, Tashman's right hand shot up and ripped Bennett's bodice, completely exposing her breasts in front of the stunned ballroom. All the other costumed guests had stopped dancing to form a half-moon circle around the battling women. Nothing these actresses had ever filmed equaled this real life excitement.

Bennett fell to the floor. Deep scratch marks were causing her right breast to bleed.

Kicking and screaming, Bogie hauled Tashman away toward the door as two of the hotel security guards approached. He tried to hold onto her but the guards pulled her away from his clutches.

"We'll handle this now," one of the burly guards with a thick Irish accent told him.

"We've called the police," the other guard said. "Expect assault-and-battery charges."

Seeing that two men were rushing to photograph Tashman, Bogie gave in and let the guards cart her away to the manager's office.

Stunned and not knowing what to do, Bogie stood there helplessly until Nancy Carroll came up to him. "Edmund is being called," she said. "He's being told to get their lawyer over here right away. The lawyer will have to handle this mess. There's nothing you can do. You might even make it worse for Lilyan."

"I think you're right, pal," he said, taking Carroll's arm. "Lilyan's going over the deep end. She won't listen to me."

"There's a screw loose in that gal's head, and you're not the guy to tighten it," she said.

"You said it," he said. "Get that money from the hotel safe and we're out of here. George Raft's party, here we come."

As he waited for Carroll to retrieve the money from the hotel safe, Kenneth approached him in the foyer. "I'm going with Constance to the hospital. They've called an ambulance. She's threatening all sorts of things against your buddy, Tashman."

"Your date did call Lilyan a dirty little Jew dyke, and that sounds like fighting words to me," Bogie said.

"Yeah, yeah," Kenneth said, his face flashing his impatience. "I was there. Remember?" The doorman signaled him that the ambulance had arrived.

As Kenneth departed, Bogie called to him, "See you at the bachelor party, pal." Somehow he felt that his best friend was disloyal in siding with Bennett, and was going to tell him so tomorrow morning when both of them sat down over the breakfast table to relive the night's events.

Of course, Kenneth was not only Bennett's date but was also having an affair with her. Considering everything, Bogie felt that his friend was probably behaving honorably. It still pissed him off, though.

With Carroll taking forever, Bogie knocked on the manager's door, hoping to persuade him to let him in to tell Tashman good-bye. The manager claimed that she was still refusing to see anyone, and that he'd summoned the hotel doctor since, "It appears that your friend needs sedation. You can fully expect a lawsuit from Miss Bennett. You and Tashman have thoroughly disgraced my hotel to-night." He slammed the door in Bogie's face.

At the hotel entrance, Carroll had already summoned a taxi and was holding the door open for him. As he headed for it, he felt that his life in Hollywood was reading like a movie scenario. He had to go back East if for no other reason than to restore his sanity.

As Carroll ushered him into the back seat of the taxi, he was stunned to see a beautiful blonde-haired woman sitting on its far side. Just when he thought he could handle no more excitement for one evening, Carroll piled into the cab. He found himself a "sandwich" between these two beauties who had appeared to-gether in *Manhattan Cocktail*.

Introductions were not necessary. He'd immediately recognized Metro-Goldwyn-Mayer's "white goddess" in *Trader Horn*.

It was Edwina Booth, the talk of Hollywood.

***

On the way to George Raft's party, Bogie got better acquainted with Edwina Booth. Carroll had developed an instant crush on the handsome taxi driver, who wanted to be an actor, and she was flirting with him. Apparently, she had this thing for cabbies.

Edwina Booth was the Hollywood star of the moment. It was impossible to pick up a newspaper without reading something about her exploits during the filming of *Trader Horn* in Africa.

Ironically, it was an experience eerily evocative of Bogie's own future in films when he went with Katharine Hepburn in 1950 to "The Dark Continent" to film *The African Queen*. Some of Booth's experiences on location there fore-shadowed his own.

"I don't know why Thalberg and Mayer wanted me for the role," Booth said. "Up until then, my biggest role was a small part in that piece of fluff Nancy and I appeared in, *Manhattan Cocktail*. Other than that, my resumé consisted of a brief appearance in *Our Modern Maidens*. I spent most of my time off-camera fleeing from the hot breath of Joan Crawford."

"I thought Crawford would behave herself since her husband was in the film too," he said.

"Fairbanks Jr. was having a hard enough time keeping his pants buttoned up since he was being chased by another co-star, Rod La Rocque."

"Back in New York, I directed Rod in his first picture," he said. "He developed the hots for me too but I kept him at bay."

"I kept Crawford at bay too," Booth said. "I don't do women."

Carroll interrupted her banter with the cabbie to chime in. "I wasn't so lucky. Joan and I danced together in *The Passing Show of 1924*. One night I had too much to drink, and Joan got me. I didn't reciprocate, though."

"Isn't that like smoking without inhaling?" he said to Carroll before she turned her attention back to the taxi driver.

Trader Horn was the first full-length movie ever filmed on location, and it featured exceptional wildlife footage. "At first I turned down the role even though it was the female lead," she said. "I was afraid I didn't have the stamina. All my life I've suffered from hypoglycemia, and I have low energy. The director, W. S. Van Dyke—I nicknamed him Woody—wanted me and no one else. I finally gave in, especially after I met my co-stars, Harry Carey and Duncan Renaldo, both of whom are very nice guys."

"I'd never risk my life going to Africa to make a movie," he said. "I'm more the lounge lizard type. For me, it's either the Broadway stage or a safe and cozy sound stage in Hollywood. No locations."

"Shooting the film involved one disaster after another," Booth said. "Until we got to Africa, the film was supposed to be silent, but shortly after we arrived, *The Jazz Singer* opened. On very short notice, Woody had to ship sound equipment to Africa. But when it was being offloaded from a ship, the crane broke, smashing it to pieces, and we had to wait around for weeks until new equipment arrived."

"Well, at least on location in Africa, he recorded the roar of a real lion and not that silly pussycat Metro uses," he said.

"We had only a basic plot outline, but no script," Booth said. "We had to invent the dialogue as we went along. I was pursued by every insect in Africa. Some large animal, a beast I'd never seen before, chased me through the jungle, obviously wanting me for his dinner. I developed terminal diarrhea. Woody had installed these two-seater outhouse-style toilets. I rushed in one day and plopped down. Into my explosive business, I suddenly noticed this monstrous snake coiled up on the seat next to me. I ran out of that God damn toilet with my pants down, diarrhea or no diarrhea."

"At least you came back unharmed," he said. "You look pretty good to me."

"Thanks, but actually I got malaria, and something is still wrong with me. I don't know how I got through the experience. Elephant grass cut into my flesh. The men could wear protective clothing, but Woody insisted I run around the jungle half-naked."

"This Woody seems to have held up pretty well," he said. "I heard him talking about the film on radio the other night."

"That's because he imported cases of gin for his martinis," she said. "He never drank the foul water—only gin."

"So that's why he never got sick."

"I think that's right," she said. "He was pickled all the time."

Again, the director's experience would be eerily evocative of Bogie and his own director, John Huston, during the filming in 1950 of *The African Queen*. As other crew members, especially Katharine Hepburn, came down with diarrhea from drinking the polluted water, Huston and Bogie drank only whiskey and stayed relatively healthy.

"In looking back," Booth said, "could you believe that anyone in his right mind would cast me as a mysterious white goddess ruling over a bloodthirsty tribe of natives?"

"I could imagine you playing any queen," he said. "Cleopatra presiding over the Egyptian empire. Helen of Troy. Most definitely the Queen of Sheba."

"Flattery will get you everywhere, Mr. Bogart," she said.

He turned his attention to Carroll when she stopped bantering with the handsome cabbie. Seemingly, she must have decided that he was a homosexual and had given up the pursuit.

"Have you recovered from Bennett's attack?" he asked. "Personally, I don't think Joe Kennedy is worth having all the grand divas in Hollywood fighting over that little Irish prick."

"I've called Joe several times since I got back from Florida," she said. "He's always too busy to take my call. And I know the reason why. Constance Bennett and Swanson think I'm the reason Joe isn't paying them much attention. But it's somebody else."

"Do tell us, Nancy darling," Booth said. "I promise not to get Louella on the phone."

"After fucking Louella the other night, I think I've become bitten by the gossip bug too," Bogie said.

"Old Joe Kennedy is carrying on an affair with Billie Dove," Carroll proclaimed.

The news startled him. "You can't mean it." He recalled his own memorable night with Dove in Irwin Willat's guest cottage. "Are you sure? I've been close to that scene, and I've heard no mention of Joe Kennedy and Dove linked together as an item."

"I got it straight from the Texan himself," Carroll said. "I'll tell you folks, and no one else. While Joe is romancing Miss Billie Dove, I've taken Howard as my new lover."

"Hot damn!" Booth said. "How about sloppy seconds for your girl friend over here?"

"Hell with that!" Carroll said. "With Howard, I'm lucky to get one round out of him, much less a sloppy second."

"That's what I hear too," Booth said, sighing. "Crawford told me he's called several times and tried to date her. So far, she claims she's turned Hughes down. Her good friend, Billy Haines, says he's often topped Hughes."

"I met Haines the other night," Bogart said. "He definitely looked like a

442

bottom to me."

"Crawford assured me that in spite of the silly, girlish way he acts on screen, Haines is definitely a top," Booth said.

"I'll have to ask Ramon Novarro the next time I see him," Bogie said. "That little Mexican bugger will know for sure. I mean we've got to clear up such important matters like this." He was being facetious, although the two women seemed to take him seriously.

At the Ambassador Hotel he ushered the women into the elevator and up to the penthouse suite, which had been rented by Raft for the night. The door to the suite was thrown open by Raft himself. Nattily clad in a tuxedo, he embraced Bogie warmly and kissed Carroll and Booth on the lips before inviting all of them in.

Suddenly, Bogie found himself swimming in a sea of New York gangsters and their gun molls.

"Let me make the rounds of the party with Booth and that cute little piece of candy, Nancy Carroll," Raft whispered in his ear. "Here comes your consolation prize."

Bogie was confronted with a woman who looked like the young queen of all gangster molls.

"Mr. Humphrey Bogart, of New York, meet Miss Ann Dvorak, also New York born."

***

The chorus girl standing in front of Bogie couldn't be more than nineteen years old. She had a lean, sharp face, not altogether to Bogie's liking, yet he was immediately attracted to her. In a red silk gown that clung to her body like a Harlow dress, she looked like one of the sexiest women he'd ever seen. The cleavage of that gown went virtually to her hips. With the wrong movement on her part, one of her breasts might pop out.

She took his hand and expertly guided him through a sea of gangsters assembled by Raft for the party where the liquor and champagne flowed. He looked about for Nancy Carroll and Raft but they seemed to have disappeared into his bedroom, no doubt to discuss the $50,000 payoff. He didn't spot Edwina Booth anywhere. He figured that the two actresses he took to the party could fend for themselves, allowing him to devote all his attention to this new trinket who had descended upon him.

In a corner at a small table, a waiter in a red jacket served them drinks, although Dvorak looked as if she'd consumed far more than her share for one evening. In the dimly lit room, she put one leg up over his. Her gown was split up to a creamy thigh, and he was certain she didn't have on one stitch of underwear.

He practically wanted to seduce her on the spot.

As they talked, he found her very direct and outspoken. Even though only a teenager, she didn't seem to embarrass easily. He was convinced that Dvorak had been seducing men at least since the age of fourteen.

The way she kept moving that creamy leg over his thighs was giving him an erection, a movement not lost on her.

"So how are things?" he asked rather awkwardly.

"You tell me first," she said.

"Marriage falling apart, career going nowhere," he said. "The usual. What about you?" He'd no sooner asked that question than he wished that he hadn't.

Dvorak revealed a ferocity of ambition matched only by Stanwyck herself. "I'm hot and getting hotter," she said.

At that remark, he put his hand on her thigh and began a massage. "I'm convinced of that."

"I don't mean that way, silly," she said. "I mean, my career, Stud. I owe it all to Joan Crawford. When I was one of the hoofers in *Hollywood Revue of 1929*, I met Crawford. She fell for me in a big way. Howard Hughes had been calling her for a date, and she came up with this idea. Since she didn't want Hughes, she took his call one day and agreed to go over to Hughes' mansion. But instead of Crawford, it was me who arrived on Howard Hughes' doorstep. And the rest is history or will soon be."

"Well, pal," he said, "so you fucked Hughes. What's he going to do for you?"

"He put me under contract," she said.

"He did the same with Harlow, but since then, he seems to be doing nothing for her," he said, deliberately wanting to prick her bubble.

"I know that!" she said, a slight anger flashing. "With me, it's gonna be different. He's putting together this film called *Scarface*. It's based on Al Capone, and Ben Hecht himself is writing the screenplay. Hughes wants Paul Muni to play Capone."

"An Austrian-born actor from New York's Yiddish Art Theater?" he asked in surprise. "Not Cagney, not Edward G. Robinson? What about George Raft himself?"

"Oh, George is in the film. He plays my love interest, Guino Rinaldo. I play Mini's sister, Cesca. I'm told that the scenes between Muni and me will border on incest. There's even a role for Boris Karloff in the film. Hughes wants a lot of sex and violence."

"Sounds like it's headed for trouble with the censors," he said.

"Hughes expects that," she said. "And so does the director, Howard Hawks."

"Two Howards working together," he said. "Which Howard has branded you?"

She giggled and leaned over to whisper in his ear. "I'm balling both of them. To get ahead in Hollywood, Crawford told me it's necessary to fuck both the producer and the director."

"I wish I could fuck someone to get cast in a picture," he said.

"Don't worry, sugar," she said between bouts of tonguing his ear. "When I become the biggest star in Hollywood, I'll insist that you be my leading man."

"Thanks, pal," he said, his hand starting to travel up her thigh to his target of the evening.

She slapped it down and jumped up. "Let's dance."

He didn't want to get up because of his erection but decided what the hell. The room was not well lit, and no one seemed to be paying attention to him.

In the center of the room, she moved her body into his so closely that they seemed to melt into each other. The way she was rubbing up against him, he thought he'd cream in his trousers.

Slowly, very slowly, she began to unbutton his pants. He allowed her to do that, since he wanted to feel her delicate fingers manipulating his penis. Still clinging to him, she removed his penis and began to rhythmically masturbate him as they danced.

It was getting hotter and hotter as she jerked him off while rubbing his penis against her smooth thighs. He was so carried away that he completely forgot that he was in a room filled with gangsters and their blonde-haired molls.

Too far gone at that point, he was about to erupt, and he wanted to break away but couldn't control himself. He was going to spew semen all over that slinky red silk gown.

Then two things happened at the same time. Giggling, she broke away to avoid his eruption just as a strong hand clamped hard on his shoulder. Covering himself quickly with his jacket, he dumped his load on Raft's floor.

Stuffing himself into his trousers, he turned around to stare into the face of Howard Hawks.

***

After that rather inauspicious introduction, Bogie sat in the same far corner of the room where he'd played seductive games with Ann Dvorak. Across from him sat the director, Howard Hawks, who would play such an enormous role in both his professional and personal life in the years to come.

"Keep your mangy hands off Ann," Hawks was telling him. "She's already got Howard Hughes and Howard Hawks. She doesn't need another 'H' in her life."

"We were just getting acquainted on the dance floor, pal," Bogie said. "Nothing more."

"Don't come within ten feet of her," Hawks said threateningly.

"The next time I cum, I'll be at least twelve feet away," Bogie said jokingly, not taking Hawks' anger too seriously.

I'm balling her," Hawks said. "I find that teenage girls are the only thing to guarantee my fullest erection. Don't think I'm a pedophile. I only go out with girls in their late teens. No fourteen-year-olds." He paused. "Maybe once or twice, but it's definitely not a pattern with me."

"Glad to hear that," Bogie said. "If I ever have any daughters, I'll keep them far away from Mr. Howard Hawks."

"Listen, I'm not mad at you for trying to move in on Ann," Hawks said. "You're still green in Hollywood. You don't know the ropes yet. I've issued my warning. If after you've been duly warned, you still cross Hughes and me, then I'll cut off your nuts, assuming a little lisper like you has a pair."

"Yeah, I've got a pair," Bogie said. "They're big enough, too. My problem is I haven't learned how to clank them like you're doing. Or like Hughes is doing. And don't let my lisp fool you."

"Just wanted to be sure," Hawks said. "I can't even go take a piss out here in Hollywood without some queen falling on his knees and begging to suck me off!"

"You should be flattered by such attention," he said. "That means you're a real man. Queens go just for the big studs."

"That's one way to look at it," Hawks said. "Nearly everyone I meet in Hollywood is a dirty little homosexual. There are a few bonafide heterosexuals out here, but not many."

"Name three," Bogie said, challenging him.

"I'll name three guys who've never had their dick sucked by a man," Hawks said. "In order of importance. Howard Hawks, Howard Hughes, Spencer Tracy. The rest I'm not so sure about."

"No contest there," Bogie said. "You're far more of a Hollywood insider than I am."

Hawks surveyed the party of gangsters. "I accepted George's invitation because I knew a lot of New York gangsters would be here since Owney Madden and his boys are in town. I'm soaking up atmosphere for my picture, *Scarface*, that Hughes is producing. I think the film is going to be a big success. At least three of my actors are gong to be billed above the title."

"Call me Louella," he said. "I'd really like to know who they are. It's interesting to hear that somebody's making it out here on The Coast."

"Paul Muni, George Raft, and Boris Karloff," Hawks said.

"The fourth?" Bogie asked.

"Ann Dvorak herself," Hawks said. "I've got this incredible instinct for casting. I have a feeling that a lot of movie plots in these Depression days will be about life's losers, and she's perfect for roles like that. After *Scarface*, I think she'll have cornered the market on the portrayal of doomed gangster molls with prolonged death scenes."

"Sounds like a great career," he said. "Since I'm about to be dropped by Fox, what role have you got coming up for me? I'm gonna be in need of a job pretty soon."

"*Scarface* is already cast," Hawks said. "I think my next movie is going to

446

be *The Crowd Roars*. I'm thinking of casting Ann in that movie, too, although I rarely work with the same pussy twice. She might play the second female lead. I want Joan Blondell to play the lead. The second male lead will be played by this faggot kid, Eric Linden."

"I've heard of him," Bogie said. "He's supposed to have a big crush on me."

"He's a queer, all right," Hawks said. "But he's right for the part. I'm not against casting queers in parts. Sometimes they're the only ones who can bring a certain sensitivity to a role. It's just that I keep my fly buttoned when I'm around them."

"Smart thinking, pal," Bogie said. "You said nothing about the male lead. I haven't read the script, and don't even know what the picture is about, but I think I'd be ideal."

"It's not set yet," Hawks said, "but I'm thinking of casting James Cagney."

"I knew Cagney back in my New York days," Bogie said. "He got his start appearing in drag."

"Bullshit!" Hawks said. "You're making that up. If I had to name three men in Hollywood who will never appear in drag, I'd cite Howard Hawks first, Howard Hughes second, and James Cagney third."

"Maybe I was mistaken about Cagney," Bogie said. "Too much rotgut whiskey out here in Hollywood pickles the brain."

"I don't know about you, Bogart," Hawks said. "When I was in New York, I saw you in *Cradle Snatchers*. I wasn't impressed. I guess you noticed that when I made *Cradle Snatchers* for Fox, I didn't cast you in your stage part as Jose Vallejo. I cast Joe Striker in the part and changed his character's name to Joe Valley."

"I couldn't help but notice," Bogie said. "Don't judge me by those Broadway days. I've grown a lot as an actor since then. I need one big role and I'll hit it big. A part like *Scarface,* which could make a big name for Paul Muni, as you said. He's playing Al Capone, isn't he?"

"Yeah, but that's not the official word," Hawks said. "I was visited recently by a couple of Capone goons who insisted on knowing who *Scarface* was based on. They'd heard that it was based on their boss."

"How in hell do you get out of that one?" Bogie asked. "I mean Capone has a scarface. I heard someone tried to slit his throat."

"That's right and the film is based on him," Hawks said. "But I convinced them that *Scarface* has nothing to do with Capone. I told them we're just calling it that to fool the public into thinking it might be about Capone. I said that's known as showmanship. The Chicago boys left me alone with my body intact and went away feeling like Hollywood insiders. Hughes was afraid the boys would go after him, but I assured him that I'd taken care of that too. I told the Capone goons that Hughes was 'just the sucker with the money.'"

Ann Dvorak came to table and reminded Hawks that they had another rendezvous that evening. She smiled at Bogie. "Maybe you'll be my leading man one day in a picture."

Hawks looked back at Bogie. "I don't see that ever happening." A frown crossed his brow. "On another point, I can assure you I'll never cast you in a film I'm directing."

"Sorry to hear that, pal," Bogie said. "Now you two love birds have a good night."

He watched as Dvorak parted with Hawks. That little nineteen-year-old really knew how to handle a grown man's dick, even if on the dance floor.

As it turned out, Dvorak was a better forecaster than Hawks. By 1932 Bogie would find himself playing one of the male leads in *Three on a Match,* a picture that would bring him together again with four women who would figure hugely in his life, both on the screen and in the bed: Ann Dvorak, Bette Davis, Joan Blondell, and Glenda Farrell. As he would later confide to Kenneth MacKenna, "With those four gals coming at me at once, I'm amazed I had any energy left to appear before the camera."

Hawks was not a man of his word. The year 1944 would find him casting Bogie as the lead in the film, *To Have and Have Not,* based on a 1937 novel by Ernest Hemingway with William Faulkner billed as the co-author of the screenplay. By then, Ann Dvorak was only distantly remembered by Bogie and Hawks. Both of their attentions during the making of that film focused on another nineteen-year-old actress, Lauren Bacall.

At Raft's party, Bogie wandered among the gangsters, but not for long. Edwina Booth, looking far lovelier than when she'd appeared on the screen as the white goddess in *Trader Horn,* appeared before him.

"I got word from Nancy that she'll be involved with Raft for the rest of the evening," she said. "I saw your little performance on the dance floor with Ann Dvorak. Cute. I just hope she didn't ruin you for me for the rest of the evening."

"There's a lot more spunk where that came from, pal," Bogie said.

"Then why don't you rescue me from this sea of hoodlums, and show me what little boys are made of?" Booth asked.

"You've got yourself a deal," he said, "and I ain't so little."

Taking Booth by the arm, he escorted her through the party and out the door and down the elevator. He paused briefly to suck in the night air in front of the Ambassador Hotel as the doorman summoned a taxi.

She got into the cab first. In her most seductive voice, she said, "The night is young and so are we." With her, he headed for her apartment, anticipating the unfolding adventure of the evening.

Without knowing it, he was making a big mistake.

***

Bogie floored the accelerator of his car, heading for the Malibu retreat of Spencer Tracy and his newly acquired friend, the matinee idol, Johnny Mack

Brown.

It had been a night he didn't want to remember. Smoking incessantly and badly hung over, he found himself shaking uncontrollably. He felt that he was coming apart. He rarely thought about his wives (former and current), as he was caught up in a whirlpool of his own making, with a cast of characters, most of whom he was meeting for the first time.

Taking Edwina Booth home the night before had turned into a nightmare. She'd virtually invited him to seduce her. But it was not to be the night of passion he'd anticipated.

As he'd seduced her, he'd never known a woman to sweat with such ferocity. She'd also moaned, and he'd interpreted that as passion, feeling he was really getting to her.

Suddenly, her sweat had no longer seemed hot but cold. She'd trembled all over and had called out to him. As he'd tried to kiss her, he'd found her biting her own tongue. It was bleeding.

One of his proudest erections had deflated within moments. He'd pulled out of her and raised up over her to discover her writhing on the sheets, biting into the pillowcase. "Help me!" she'd screamed. "Help me."

In panic he'd placed his hand on her vagina, feeling that his penetration had caused her to bleed. Turning on the light, he'd seen no evidence of blood. Booth's color had changed. She had turned a sickly shade of yellow-green.

Help me!" she'd called out again. Her whole body had been drenched in sweat. "I'm dying."

Getting a towel, he'd wet it under the sink's faucet and had placed it on her forehead. She'd immediately thrown the towel aside.

Fearing there was nothing he could do, he'd gone immediately to the living room and dialed for an ambulance. After that, he'd dressed quickly and had returned to the bedroom. Booth had passed out. He'd tried to awaken her but couldn't. The ambulance must have come down from San Francisco, but finally it had arrived. Its attendants had rushed Booth to the nearest hospital.

As the night had worn on, the medical staff had been particularly brusque with him and had finally asked him to leave "since you're not immediate kin." He was only told "Miss Booth is resting comfortably and has been heavily sedated." He'd been assured that her nearest relative had been summoned. A call had even gone out for Louis B. Mayer, who'd dispatched someone from MGM to investigate the matter.

Fearing unwanted publicity, especially the front-page kind, Bogie had left the hospital through a back entrance. The day before he'd gladly accepted Tracy's invitation to be his weekend guest at Malibu. He'd wanted to get away and leave Hollywood behind. No one there, it seemed, led an uncomplicated life, and he was always allowing himself to get sucked up into other people's troubles.

It would be months before Bogie learned more details about Booth's attack. Malaria had not been all that the actress had suffered while filming *Trader Horn* on location in Africa. She'd succumbed to some strange disease that the doctors had called "jungle fever," since they were unable to diagnose it otherwise.

After having been hailed as Hollywood's grandest new star, she'd appear in only three more films, each of them a serial: *The Vanishing Legion* in 1931, *Trapped in Tijuana* in 1932, and *The Last of the Mohicans* in 1932.

After that, her health deteriorated so rapidly that she was forced to live in darkened rooms for the next six years, because her delicate eyes could not withstand the sharpness of daylight.

As compensation for her physical problems, she sued MGM for $1 million, but Mayer finally settled the case out of court for $35,000, providing that Booth would seek medical help at tropical disease centers in Europe. She traveled to London, Vienna, Berlin, and ultimately Paris but no doctor could cure her. She was said to live in constant pain.

In Hollywood her legend grew. Since she'd faded from the scene, it was widely reported that she'd died. In 1990, when Katharine Hepburn wrote her book, *The Making of the African Queen: How I Went to Africa with Bogart, Bacall, and Huston and Almost Lost My Mind*, she reported that Booth had died "some years ago."

It was later revealed that Booth was alive at the time. She died on the morning of May 18, 1991 in an obscure California nursing home. The people who'd surrounded her in the final decades never knew that she was the once-famous co-star of that grand epic, *Trader Horn*. The picture that immortalized her also destroyed her life.

But on that morning driving to Tracy's rented cottage, Bogie had no idea of what lay ahead for Booth, not even what was the matter with her.

All he did was light another cigarette and say out loud, "Brother, do I know how to pick my broads."

At Tracy's cottage, he pulled into the driveway. Emerging from the beach in a skimpy, form-fitting bathing suit was one of the handsomest men he'd ever encountered. He figured it could only be Johnny Mack Brown.

***

After Johnny Mack Brown had shown Bogie to his bedroom overlooking the ocean, and after he'd showered, Bogie joined the actor for a walk on the beach. Tracy was in the bedroom across the hallway recovering from a massive drunk.

Plopping down right on the sands, Bogie accepted a drink from the flask Mack Brown carried in his beach bag. "Spence told me that you and he have become asshole buddies and that I could tell you anything," Mack Brown said in the same, slow Southern drawl he'd been learning since he was born one frosty Dixie morn on September 1, 1904 in Dothan, Alabama.

"I love the man," Bogie said, "but asshole buddies is a bit much. We're more into the handshaking stage."

"Asshole buddies is just a Southern expression," Mack Brown said. "It refers to two guys who can let it all hang out together. It doesn't mean sodomy—that's something else again."

"Yeah, I guess so," Bogie said. "I am a few things and there are many things I'm not. No one ever said I was one of the world's great sodomites."

"Don't knock it till you've tried it," Mack Brown said. "But let's drop that subject and talk of loftier matters. Like what ol' Spence did yesterday."

"If this is gonna be about what you guys do in bed, pal, I think I'll skip it," Bogie said.

"Nothing like that," Mack Brown said, reaching for that flask again. "It was at the studio. As you know, Spence is battling Fox about the roles he's been assigned. I mean, a dreadful piece of shit like *Six Cylinder Love* co-starring that queen, Edward Everett Horton. What a turkey! Yesterday, on the set, Spence had had his fill of the studio and probably the entire film industry as well."

"I don't think I want to hear the rest of this story," Bogie said. He closed his eyes and lay back to get sun. To his surprise, Mack Brown lit a cigarette for him and placed it in his mouth. "Thanks," Bogie said. "I don't usually let men light my cigarettes, though."

"You'll get used to it," Mack Brown said enigmatically. "Anyway, Spence showed up on the set of *She Wanted a Millionaire* in evening clothes. He'd been out drinking all night. He was taking out his frustrations with Fox by acting like a rebellious child. He didn't know his lines and he'd have been too drunk to say them even if he had. He went around making lascivious remarks to all the gals on the set, pretty or otherwise. He even went up to the fluttery Una Merkel and asked her if he could play with her pussy. Later he came up to the star of the picture, Joan Bennett, and bluntly asked her, 'Do you want to fuck?'"

"That's understandable," Bogie said. "I'd like a piece of Miss Joan myself. She's even younger and prettier than her older sister, Constance."

"It's more complicated than that," Mack Brown said. "The plot thickens. First, Spence was already furious that Joan got all the best lines in the flick. He told the press he's Bennett's prop, with dialogue best reserved for a wooden Indian. To make matters worse, the director, John Blystone, is in love with Bennett himself."

"God damn it," Bogie said, sitting up and inhaling deeply on his cigarette. "This sounds like a more interesting plot than any of his movies."

"That's not all," Mack Brown said. "Bennett slapped his face. When Blystone rushed over, Spence said to him, 'The script is dishonest.' Then he passed out."

"No wonder our boy is part of The Irishmen's Club in Hollywood," Bogie said. "Those boys sure know how to drink. I drink all the time but I moderate it. Spence, I've noticed, either drinks or doesn't touch the stuff. But when he drinks, he empties the equivalent of Lake Michigan. My father's a doctor. He calls men like Spence a spasmodic alcoholic."

"Well, he's in one of those spasms this weekend," Mack Brown said, "so be duly warned. I don't know what Fox is going to do with him. When the crew revived Spence about an hour later, he immediately barged onto the set again, took out his dick, and pissed on an expensive sofa they were using in a scene. The same sofa where Bennett was supposed to sit." Mack Brown leaned back and eyed Bogie carefully. "There's more. Then he went on a rampage. He turned over lamps, sending them crashing to the floor. There was this bookcase with glass doors. He picked up an ashtray and broke its windows. Finally he stood on an armchair and lunged for the crystal chandelier. He was swinging on the chandelier when he fell off, hitting his head against something. That caused him to bleed profusely. The big man himself, Winfield Sheehan, had been called to the set. He saw it all."

"Sheehan's gonna can Spence," Bogie predicted. "I just know it. Spence is gonna be on that train back to New York with me. We'll start a club. Two former Fox stars pounding the pavements of Broadway looking for work."

"I agree with you," Mack Brown said. "Spence is a great actor, probably the greatest in Hollywood. But he's been assigned a series of stupid potboilers, each with really bad scripts. His pictures are bombing at the box office. Let's face it? His behavior is outrageous. He'll come right up to a woman and fondle her breast. Or he'll reach up her dress. I mean, Spence is not a thigh man, he goes right for the honeypot at the end of the rainbow."

"Maybe Sheehan will tolerate that kind of behavior in a big star cleaning up at the box office," Bogie said. "Someone up there in the Garbo league. But you can't make potboilers that lose money and pull such crap."

"I don't know why Fox hasn't kicked him out on his ass by now," Mack Brown said. "If I acted like Spence, I would have been canned long ago. To make matters worse, Spence will disappear for weeks at a time. He'll lock himself up in a hotel suite and stage a big drunk."

"I hate to see the guy suffer," Bogie said. "He's a real pal of mine but he seems possessed by some hidden devil that's got his soul. Do you understand it?"

"Part of it," Mack Brown said. "It's his love of this." He took both hands and stretched the fabric of his bathing suit real tight, making an already prominent bulge look even bigger. "Hollywood's biggest and most outrageous womanizer can't stand the fact that he loves this too."

"Hell, man," Bogie said, looking away. "What have you stuffed in there. Two socks?"

For the rest of the afternoon, Bogie was content to lie on the beach, drink, and smoke, and listen to the sound of Mack Brown's Southern drawl, which he'd come to find rather soothing. He needed this rest after his troublesome experiences of the past few days.

The more Mack Brown talked, the more intrigued Bogie became with him. He still couldn't picture Mack Brown in bed with Tracy, and didn't want to, although he'd heard of stranger couplings since reaching Hollywood.

Bogie had read all the interviews Mack Brown had given the press, and he'd seen all his pictures, but here he was hearing autobiography from what the Alabamian called "the hoss's mouth."

Unlike Bogie, Mack Brown had made an impressive number of A-list pictures with some of the biggest names in Hollywood. *Slide, Kelly, Slide* with William Haines; *The Bugle Call* with Jackie Coogan; *The Fair Co-Ed* with Marion Davies; *The Divine Woman* with Greta Garbo; *Our Dancing Daughters* with Joan Crawford; *A Lady of Chance* with Norma Shearer; *A Woman of Affairs*, also with Garbo; *Coquette* with Mary Pickford; and *Montana Moon*, also with Crawford. But ever since King Vidor cast him in his lavish wide-screen Western as *Billy the Kid*, Mack Brown's fate had been sealed. His days as a romantic leading man at MGM had come to an end.

With some exceptions, for the rest of his life he'd make sagebrush "oaters" for Poverty Row studios. He did appear in a gangster film, *The Secret Six*, with Jean Harlow, and in 1934 he'd star opposite Mae West in *Belle of the Nineties*. Before getting that part, he'd be summoned into West's apartment, where he'd be told "to drop drawers for a little inspection, and it had better not be little."

Bogie had fallen asleep in the sun. When he was awakened as two shouting kids ran by, Mack Brown was still talking. "Everyone says I fucked Garbo on the set of *A Woman of Affairs*," he said. "As usual the rumors got it wrong. I was fucking my two other male co-stars: Douglas Fairbanks Jr. and John Gilbert. Gilbert likes to take it up the ass. The Fairbanks lad is a top. As for me, I'm versatile."

His memory of Mary Pickford and Kenneth coming back, Bogie asked the big question. "Did you make it with Pickford when you did *Coquette*? I mean, she was playing a flirtatious flapper."

"Everyone seemed to think so," Mack Brown said. "Actually I was balling Matt Moore. When Mary was married to Owen Moore, Matt was her brother-in-law."

"Yeah, I've heard of the brothers," Bogie said.

"Now I hear Matt is having an affair with Kenneth MacKenna," Mack Brown said. "The guy who's marrying that dyke, Kay Francis. Have you heard of him?"

"Yeah, I've seen him around," Bogie said.

"Don't think I go just for men," Mack Brown. "I balled Shearer when we were filming *A Lady of Chance*. Crawford and I carried on something wild when she was a dancing daughter. The way I figured it, if I had the groom, why not the bride? When I appeared with Harlow in *The Secret Six*, she suggested to me the film should be retitled *The Secret Nine*."

"You sound like quite a big man," Bogie said. "I'm beginning to believe you don't stuff your crotch." "Clark Gable was in the same movie," Mack Brown said. "Billy Haines was the first actor I'd seduced in Hollywood, and he's always talking about this big affair he had with Gable. I figured I could follow in Billy's footsteps. But when I went to Gable's dressing room and made a pass at him, he punched me in the mouth. I couldn't appear on camera for two days."

"Tough luck, pal," Bogie said, "but from what I hear, you didn't miss all that much."

"Yeah, I heard that later too," Mack Brown said. "Even if a guy doesn't pack the meat, you can always fuck them."

"If you say so," Bogie said. "So you just hop from bed to bed, male or female?"

"You said it. That way, you have a far better chance of getting laid. Lose Gable. Gain Harlow. Or in the most heavenly of situations, get both the man and the wife like Crawford/Fairbanks Inc. I want to sample them all. Occasionally someone falls in love with me like Davies when we filmed *The Fair Co-Ed*. After all, she's not getting that much from the great William Randolph Hearst these days. Davies made all sorts of promises about what she was gonna do for my career. But she tired of me real soon and dropped me. I hear she's fucking Gable these days."

"I wish I could fuck an actress who'd advance my career," Bogie said, "especially if she's gorgeous. I even married a big-shot actress on Broadway, Helen Menken, but she didn't do much for my career."

"Try Norma Shearer," he said. "She can't get enough."

"She's got Irving Thalberg," Bogie said.

"She does and she doesn't," Mack said. "Shearer told me all about what sex with Thalberg is like. Shearer likes rough sex, but Thalberg has got a bad heart. She has to give him a very gentle blow job until he gets hard. Then she eases herself up and down on him—still very gently—until he experiences a very timid climax."

"Sounds like great fun," Bogie said facetiously. "I'll have to try it some time."

When a kid's volleyball hit Mack Brown, he showed his athletic prowess by tossing it back. He leaned back and lay down on the sands facing the dying sun. "MGM has kicked me out on my ass. They don't like the way my Southern accent comes across on the sound track. Do you know anyone I could fuck who hands out movie contracts?"

Bogie thought for a minute. "As a matter of fact I do. And you're just his type. Howard Hughes."

"Does that tall rich Texan like boys?" Mack Brown asked, looking astonished. "If you could fix me up with Hughes, I'd give you ten percent of all my earnings."

"You've got yourself a deal, cowboy," Bogie said. "Since I can't make it as an actor I'd better take up pimping."

Later that day, Bogie went to his bedroom to sleep off his own drunk. But first he called George O'Brien. He hadn't checked in with him since he'd delivered him into the clutches of Hughes.

O'Brien was bubbling over with excitement. "Howard and I had a great time. Real kinky sex. Not only that, but he gave me ten-thousand dollars, and I need the money."

"For that kind of money, I'd sleep with Hughes myself," Bogie said.

"You're not his type," O'Brien said.

"Yeah, I keep hearing that," Bogie said. "Just so I get this straight, exactly what is his type again? Gary Cooper? Johnny Mack Brown?"

"Howard can have Coop any time he wants to," O'Brien said. "Now Johnny Mack Brown, that's his type. Come to think of it, that handsome Alabama football player is also my type. Want to fix me up with him? I hear he's a good buddy of your good buddy, Spencer Tracy."

"I think Mr. Johnny Mack Brown is fully booked," Bogie said. "But I'll keep you in mind."

"I learned one deep, dark secret about Howard," O'Brien said.

"Call me Louella," Bogie said, an expression he'd keep using until he returned to New York.

"Howard is a drag queen.

The revelation stunned Bogie. "I can't believe that. I can't even picture it. Hughes in a dress? He's pretty tall to be wearing gowns."

"He spent our first evening together dressed in drag," O'Brien confided. "That is, until he demanded that I tear off his dress and rape him."

"Sounds like you guys had a real swell time," Bogie said. "But tell Hughes to stay away from polka dots. He's too tall for them. We'll stay in touch, pal."

"And thanks again for doing me a big favor," O'Brien said. "Hughes is a very generous man."

"Not with Jean Harlow," Bogie chimed in.

"Harlow has tits," O'Brien said. "I've got something Howard likes even better."

"Protect those jewels," Bogie said, before ringing off. There was a knock on his door.

After hanging up, he went to open it. Mack Brown said that Tracy had awakened and wanted to see him.

He found Tracy sitting on a narrow balcony overlooking the ocean. He looked sad and depressed.

"Good to see you again, pal," Bogie said, giving him a warm handshake. "I hear you pulled a big one last night."

"I'm glad you could come out," Tracy said. "With all the assholes out here in Hollywood I've been dealing with, you're the only pal that seems real."

"I'm real all right, and fucked up too, but not quite as fucked up as you are," Bogie said, sitting down beside the actor and lighting up another one of his cigarettes.

"You'll get no argument with me about that," Tracy said. He looked at the evening waves washing up on the beach. "I don't think I'll ever be at peace with myself until I go to my grave."

"That's a pretty gloomy forecast," Bogie said.

"There's this thing inside me that's like a demon tearing my guts apart," Tracy said. "I can't get rid of it. The only way I can keep it under control is to drink so much I temporarily drown it. But it always come back. I think this beast within me will live there until my body dies, and then the God damn thing will move into someone else's body."

"If you don't start taking better care of yourself, pal, the morticians will get you sooner than later."

"Sometimes I wish that was true, but it's not going to work out that way," Tracy said. "I paid one-thousand dollars to bring the three best fortune-tellers in Los Angeles together to predict the date of my death. I'm going to live until the morning of May 27, 1967 when I die of a heart attack in Beverly Hills."

Amazingly, although Bogie wouldn't be around to see it, Spencer Bonaventure Tracy eventually died in Beverly Hills on June 10, 1967.

***

The following night when he'd driven back to his apartment and had visited with Kenneth for an hour, relating all the events of the weekend, Bogie felt tired and retreated to his apartment. He planned to cook himself some bacon and eggs, but was too short on energy.

No sooner had he stripped off his clothes and piled into bed than the telephone rang. Wearily getting up to answer it, he knew he wasn't interested in accepting any invitations, even if Dietrich herself called wanting to give him another blow-job. Perhaps it was his crazed friend, Lilyan Tashman, inviting him over for a night of passion at Lilowe, perhaps a three-way with her newly acquired friend, Claudette Colbert.

It was Helen Menken filled with remorse about her refusal to take his calls. "I was humiliated at Jeanette's party," she said. "The most glamorous women in Hollywood were there, and I felt old and ugly. I felt you didn't love me or need me any more in your life and that you could have your pick of some of the most beautiful women in the world. When you left the party with, indeed, the most beautiful woman in the world, I went into a rage."

"Billie Dove wasn't on my plate that night," he said. "I was an errand boy hauling her over to the house of Howard Hughes."

"I learned that only recently and my behavior is inexcusable," she said. "I'm truly sorry. Please forgive me."

"We've done worse things to each other," he said.

"Please come right over," she said, a sudden urgency in her voice. "But before we can taste the forbidden fruits together, I want you to drive me somewhere."

"At this hour?" he asked. Even for Helen and a reconciliation, he wasn't that interested.

It's only ten o'clock, dear heart," she said. "Early for Hollywood."

"You're on the west coast now, not New York," he said. "Stars have to go to bed early so that we can look gorgeous on camera."

"Please," she said. "Tonight is so important to my career. Mercedes de Acosta has invited me over to her home to discuss writing the screenplay for *The Captive*. Her lover, Garbo, wants to play the part of Madame d'Aiguines."

"What kind of role would that be for Garbo?" he asked. "In the play the character doesn't even appear on stage but is just referred to."

"That was Broadway," she said. "This is Hollywood. Mercedes is going to rewrite the play for Garbo and actually bring the stunning Madame d'Aiguines onto the screen. I'll keep my same role. Starring Helen Menken and Greta Garbo, the film will become a classic."

"Okay, toots," he said, "but I don't think Louis B. Mayer is gonna go for that billing. It'll be Greta Garbo starring in *The Captive* with your name running under the title."

"Please, dear one, it's gauche to talk about billing now. We'll work out the petty details later, perhaps a co-billing above the title. Do come over. I'm due there at eleven."

"Will Garbo be there?" he asked.

"Regrettably not," she said. "Perhaps we'll meet her later."

At that moment he wanted her to clarify what relationship she had, if any, with the great Garbo but decided against it. All these actresses who slept with other women in both New York and Hollywood seemed to have formed quite a network, or "Sewing Circle," as they called it.

"Okay," he finally said, agreeing to drive over and pick her up. "I'm getting dressed and on my way. But I too have a demand. You must fire Basil Rathbone and cast me in the male lead."

"Not a bad idea," she said in her most tantalizing manner, as if to suggest that she would consider such a possibility.

Later at the Garden of Allah after a passionate embrace from Helen, he drove toward the home of the mysterious Mercedes de Acosta.

The affair of Garbo and this enigmatic Spanish beauty was the talk of Hollywood. He'd heard all the rumors. This child of a wealthy family was celebrated in lesbian circles as the seducer of some of the world's most important women, including Dietrich, Alla Nazimova, Eve Le Gallienne, Eleonora Duse, Isadora Duncan...and now Garbo herself. She was Hollywood's most famous star chaser, or "star fucker" as Lilyan Tashman always put it.

De Acosta also had accomplishments other than being a world-class seducer who bedded only the A-list. She was a poet, playwright, set and costume designer, and an accomplished scriptwriter.

Within thirty minutes of leaving the Garden of Allah, Bogie and Helen arrived at the doorstep of the tasteful but modest home of Mercedes de Acosta.

"Oh, Helen, my darling woman," de Acosta said as she opened the door. "I haven't seen you since that dinner party I gave in New York."

"I remember it well," Helen said, kissing de Acosta on the lips.

"I wanted to bring together the most marvelous women in New York to shine and glitter for me," de Acosta said. "What a cast! Elsie Ferguson. Constance Collier. Laurette Taylor. Helen Hayes. That dear, Katharine Cornell, with whom I was in love at the time. Helen Hayes who didn't have a clue as to what was going on. And, to put icing on the cake, the great Helen Menken herself."

"You flatter me so," Helen said, kissing her again. "I love it." She seemed suddenly aware of his presence. "Oh, this is Humphrey Bogart."

As a woman who grew up in a house of servants, de Acosta eyed him with a certain disdain reserved for the hired help. "You can wait in the kitchen until it's time to drive Miss Menken back."

"Darling, you don't understand," Helen said. "Hump is my husband."

Did he hear right? She called him her husband and not former husband?

"Oh, I see," de Acosta said, stepping aside to let them in. "Perhaps you'll join us then."

He noted she'd said "perhaps," as if she were none too pleased at this extra male garbage Helen was lugging around in the middle of this Hollywood night.

As de Acosta led them into her living room and prepared drinks for them, she said, "Greta is absolutely broken hearted that she can't join you tonight. She was so looking forward to seeing you again."

Helen looked around the living room as if she might discover Garbo hiding in some dark corner.

"John Gilbert is threatening suicide tonight," de Acosta said, "and Greta had to rush to his aid."

As she handed Bogie a drink, de Acosta said, "I have a husband too. Abram Poole. I keep him conveniently stashed in New York. I make a point of seeing him as little as possible."

"Helen and I have that same kind of relationship," he said. Ever the provocateur, he couldn't resist adding, "During the first two years of our marriage, Helen spent more time with Tallulah Bankhead than with me."

"Oh, dear," de Acosta said. "Too much time with Tallulah will retard one's spiritual growth. We drove out to Hartford one time, and after a weekend with Tallulah I had to return to New York for a month's rest."

"Tallulah's a marvelous girl," Helen said, "but she should be taken in small doses like cocaine. You don't consume a bushel of a powerful drug like that in one night."

On her coffee table de Acosta had spread an array of glamorous photographs of herself. Hoping to offset her chill, he said, "You should be in front of the camera instead of writing behind the scenes." He picked up one glossy photograph. "This one is very alluring."

She thanked him without smiling. "I'm supposed to select a photograph I admire of myself to run in a picture book of glamorous Hollywood women. I'm also supposed to provide a quote to run with my picture." She walked over to a desk in an alcove and picked up a piece of mauve-colored paper, no doubt perfumed. Here's what I wrote:

'Never shall I be subdued nor the real secret of me understood; passionately and violently my body may be possessed, but my spirit, always virgin, will wander on, forever unpossessed.'"

"That's a mighty powerful quote," he said.

"Mighty powerful!" Helen proclaimed in her most theatrical way, as if mocking Bogie's earlier phraseology. "What an understatement. The quote is divine. It's brilliant. It will bring you immortality. Years from now, when you're writing your autobiography, you should entitle it, *Forever Unpossessed."*

"My autobiography, based on the rich life I've already lived, will be one long book," de Acosta said. "I've crossed paths and have had delirious relationships with so many great minds and talents of the 20th century: Jean Cocteau, Vaslav Nijinsky, Igor Stravinsky, Jean Cocteau, Pablo Picasso, Henri Matisee, Miguel de Unamuno, Edna St. Vincent Millay, Enrico Caruso, Ezra Pound, Dorothy Parker, Robert Frost, Rodin, Edith Wharton, Sarah Bernhardt, Arturo Toscanini, my beloved Ivor Novello, Pavlova, Noël Coward, Natacha Rambova, John Barrymore, D'Annunzio, my spiritual guru Krishnamúrti, and, of course, Gertrude and Alice. Regrettably I've known all the lesser lights as well like Elsa Maxwell and Cecil Beaton who thrive like vampires on the blood of celebrities."

For once Bogie kept his mouth shut, although he felt that de Acosta had sucked more celebrity blood than any other figure in the history of the world.

"Such charming guests you are," de Acosta said, a frown crossing her brow. "It's getting late. Let's get down to business."

She sat down on her sofa, a very large couch for such a small woman. Her features, figure, and manner of dress were that of a European woman. On the streets of Kansas, she would look exotically out of place. A kind of radiant but decadent beauty shone through, like that seen in 19th-century portraits hanging in provincial museums of France.

"If we must be blunt and business like," Helen said, "will you agree to write the screenplay of *The Captive?*"

"I might divert my very valuable time from current projects to work on *The Captive,*" she said. "As it is, I'm committed to two scripts. One a special project for Greta, the other a screenplay for Pola Negri who is fighting like her arch rival, Swanson, to become the reigning screen vamp of the Thirties as she was in the Twenties. Pola has also fallen hopelessly in love with me. I fear it's a fatal attraction."

"Negri is hopelessly inept as an actress," Helen said, "but if I wouldn't be too intrusive I'd like to inquire what special project you're preparing for Greta."

"The story of St. Francis of Assisi," de Acosta said.

"I don't quite see what role Garbo would play in that flick," Bogart said.

"The saint's wife?"

"Don't be foolish, dear," de Acosta said, avoiding eye contact. "The part of St. Francis himself."

Rebuffed, he said, "You gotta be kidding. "Replete with beard?"

For the rest of the evening, no more words were exchanged between de Acosta and him. It was obvious that his name would not be added to her ever-growing list of celebrated friends around the world.

"It is with regret, Helen, that I must tell you that the screen version of *The Captive* will focus entirely around the character of Madame d'Aiguines," de Acosta said. "Your part, the former lead, will be reduced to supporting actress."

"I'm very sorry to hear that," Helen said, not masking her disappointment as she usually did.

"In the play it was suggested that Madame d'Aiguines is an ethereal beauty, one of such refinement and grace that no mere mortal stage actress could be brought on without the audience experiencing disappointment. That's understandable. No actress on Broadway could pull off such a feat. But we're in Hollywood now where fantasy reigns supreme. Greta Garbo is that great ethereal beauty. She can bring magic to *The Captive,* something that it lacked on Broadway. I envision Greta making her first appearance on the screen in an elegant, flowing white gown. She'll be in a garden with the world's most beautiful flowers. But her own face will out-dazzle the most stunning rose. Perhaps she should be bathed in pink spots. Greta will never have looked as lovely on screen as she will in *The Captive.* Women all over the world—and not just those inclined to lesbianism—will be enraptured by her beauty. *The Captive* will mark the beginning of Greta Garbo as divinity."

He couldn't help but notice that Helen's fragile ego seemed more and more deflated as de Acosta rhapsodized about Garbo's beauty and her major role in the film. After all, Helen was the actress who had arrived in Hollywood to star in the film.

"If I treat it right, and I always treat a script right, this film will enter the history books as Greta's greatest," de Acosta predicted. "Maybe it will become her most memorable portrait in a string of films known only for memorable cinematic portraits by her."

At the top of the stairs, a familiar voice called down. "Did I hear someone mention my name in vain?"

De Acosta sharply turned her head toward the steps. "Come on down. That dear Helen Menken is here."

Bogie noted that there was no mention of himself.

Slowly and theatrically, this mysterious figure descended the steps as if the cameras were rolling. She was dressed like a teenage boy and wore no makeup.

But it was unmistakably Greta Garbo in the flesh.

Chapter Fourteen

Garbo called it "the bus," but it was an old black Packard, and Bogie was in the passenger seat being driven to the coast at a point called Casa del Mare. He'd been walking in the garden with her as Helen and de Acosta mulled over *The Captive*, when Garbo had been seized with an impulse. "He wants to go for a drive, and he wants you to go with him."

Her voice was commanding, and he felt he had to obey her. He also wanted to go with her into whatever unknown adventure she was propelling him into. He'd finally figured out that when Garbo said "he," what she really meant was "me" or "I." He'd never known anyone who used pronouns like Garbo.

Their initial meeting had gone brilliantly, beginning when Helen had presented Garbo with an autographed copy of Eduardo Bourdet's *La Prisonnière*, on which the lesbian play, *The Captive,* had been based. Helen also had carried along a nosegay of violets, symbol of lesbian love. When Helen had presented the violets to Garbo, de Acosta had hardly masked her jealousy. Bogie suspected that Helen had had some involvement with Garbo when she was in New York. He'd been almost certain that Helen had "bumped pussies," as he called it, with de Acosta.

Garbo had enthralled them with stories of her discomfort "playing a bad woman" in the film, *Susan Lenox: Her Fall and Rise,* in which Clark Gable was her co-star. "He always has bad breath," Garbo had said. "More than that, there is no poetry in the man. He seems to feel women are like cows in the field longing to be mounted by the bull. He could only be a man of America. There is nothing of the European male's *savoir-faire* in Gable. Work on the picture is hell, a nightmare that this boy must live through before he can return to Sweden with a little money to buy himself a cottage on some lake surrounded by a mysterious forest."

Impulsively after that gloomy report on her career, Garbo and de Acosta had folded up an Oriental carpet and placed a record on the phonograph, "Daisy, You're Driving Me Crazy." De Acosta had danced with Helen, and Bogie had danced with Garbo. One dance had not been enough. They'd played the same record four times before Garbo had invited him to walk with her in de Acosta's garden "while the ladies discuss the dreary business of film scenarios."

At the coast, Garbo braked her Packard and got out. He joined her and attempted to light her cigarette but she preferred to do that herself. She invited him to climb a little mountain with her, and he followed, learning that she was a much more experienced climber than he was. At the top of the mountain she stood with him looking out at the vastness of the Pacific Ocean, which that night had seemed almost artificially lit by moonlight.

"This is his favorite place," she said. "He always comes here when he feels he is going crazy in America."

Bogie was having a hard time adjusting to Garbo talking of herself as "he." At any minute he felt that this mysterious "he" would emerge in the moonlight.

On the mountain was a little tree that looked dead. "This is his favorite tree in all of California. Sometimes he comes here at night and ties a little red ribbon on it."

He did see several ribbons tied to the leafless branches of the tree.

"The tree is actually dead," she said. "It decided it could survive no more on this lonely mountain and chose to leave the earth, as he himself will do one day. He shares the pain of the tree. The tree and him are soul-mates. The tree also reminds him of Sweden. Many of our tress look like this in the autumn. The cold winds come and blow all the leaves from the trees. They look barren and all alone. But then the snows of winter come and give all these branches a wonderful white coat, just like those wonderful white furs many of the womens of Stockholm wear. Sometimes the womens is all covered in fur except for a bright, rosy-cheeked face peering out into the cold."

She pulled out another cigarette but he made no attempt to light it for her. Instead he took out his own cigarette and lit it, inhaling deeply even though he knew it might be healthier breathing the fresh breezes coming in from the ocean.

He was aware that Garbo had absolutely no interest in him and didn't even appreciate a response from him. She seemed completely self-enchanted and wanted to share her moods with the ocean, the night breezes, and the moonlight, and especially that tree, more than she cared to relate to him.

He didn't mind that. He was in awe of her and welcomed any moment he could spend in her presence, knowing how precious that time would be. He suspected that he'd relive this night many times in his memory.

Inhaling deeply on her own cigarette, she spoke in a rather mournful way. "He has been smoking these horrible cigarettes since he was but a small boy growing up in the slums of Stockholm, the daughter of a butcher."

"Yeah, I got hooked early too," he said.

She looked up at the moon. "It must be beyond the tock-dock of midnight, and he is still awake, like the vampires. It is not his usual custom. By nine o'clock on most nights, except special nights such as this, he retires early to be alone with his dreams. Dreams are better companions than folks-people, especially when those folks-people inhabit a horrible, unformed country like America."

The provocative side of his nature was rising, even though he tried to suppress it. "I've been wanting to ask a question all evening. How do you guys think you can get Louis B. Mayer to produce a film about lesbianism? It was even too much for the Broadway stage."

"That will be no problem for Mercedes and the star," she said. "Film is about suggestion. There will be no need for dreary pornography. On the screen he will evoke his love for woman without graphic details. The audience will know it's

462

about lesbian love. They do not need to be told in banal words."

"Good luck if you get away with it," he said.

"It will be just one of many innovations he will bring to the screen," she said. "He was eavesdropping when he heard Mercedes tell you and Helen about his desire to play St. Francis. St. Francis is just one of the characters that he will make live again on the screen. He also plans to bring Oscar Wilde's *Dorian Gray* to the screen." She paused for dramatic effect. "And Shakespeare's *Hamlet*. It goes without saying who will play Hamlet."

"These are all ambitious projects, and I wish you well with them," he said. "If there's any role in them for me, give me a ring. I'm gonna be out of work soon, and I'm a damn good actor."

In the moonlight she looked startled at his blatant solicitation of work.

"He does not belong with you on the screen," she said. "The types are too different. From the very first time he met you tonight, he knew that you could play one role and brilliant—that of a detective. You should seek out authors who will write detective stories for you. A good actor must find his own writer. No studio will do it for you. He found Mercedes. But even she is wrong for the St. Francis scenario. He has not told her yet, but he plans to invite Aldous Huxley over and ask him to write the role of St. Francis."

"I'd shelf all those male parts," he advised her, "and play Joan of Arc."

"That too has been suggested many times," she said. "Mercedes has already written her scenario based on her own play, *Jehanne d'Arc.* Eva Le Gallienne played the title role at the Odéon in Paris in 1925."

"You'd make the greatest Joan of Arc ever," he said.

"He lets them talk and talk about Joan of Arc," she said, "but he has no intention of appearing as Joan of Arc. If I ever play a female saint on screen, it will be St. Teresa of Avila."

"Now that's more like it," he said.

"Everyone tells him what he must do, what roles he must play," she said. "Only today it was suggested to him that he revive *Queen Kelly*. Rescue the film made bad by Gloria Swanson and Joseph Kennedy."

"Without Erich von Stroheim this time?" he asked.

"No, with!" she said. "I understand him. A pure genius. He too is European. He knows how to portray decadence on screen. Our artists' hearts beat as one."

Suddenly, the figure of a beautiful woman in a black cape was climbing to the top of the mountain. The sight in the moonlight was eerie. He was startled and a little bit alarmed, fearing for some odd reason it might be an assassin. Was some demented, jealous female trying to kill Garbo?

Seemingly unafraid, Garbo stood her ground and faced the strange woman.

"I thought I'd find you here," the woman said. "I've been looking everywhere for you. When I can't find you, I know you'll be standing on this mountain."

"Bogart," Garbo said, turning to him, "this is the woman Mayer brought to

Hollywood to replace *him*. Here is the so-called 'second Garbo.' Eva von Berne."

***

As he sat in the small kitchen of Eva von Berne, Bogie found it amazing that the real Garbo was having an apparently deep involvement with her pale imitation. Before excusing herself to shower, von Berne had just prepared for him the best plate of ham and eggs he could ever remember being served.

Maybe von Berne had won Garbo's heart by her cooking alone, although she was one hell of a sexy woman.

Having his third cup of coffee, even though it was only four o'clock in the morning, he sighed, realizing that once again he'd deserted Helen and hadn't called. The first time he'd left her was at Jeanette MacDonald's home, as he'd escorted Billie Dove, the world's most beautiful woman, away into the night. The second time he'd departed with Dove's rival for the title of the world's most beautiful woman, Garbo herself. Garbo too had dumped her lover Mercedes, as unceremoniously as Bogie had abandoned Helen.

Instead of ending up in bed with Garbo, as he'd anticipated, he'd found merely the mock in von Berne.

After arranging for von Berne to drive Bogie home, Garbo headed down the mountain and back to her car alone. Before doing so, she'd told Bogie the bad news. "You must deliver the *coup de grâce* to your wife. He plans to go ahead with *The Captive*. Mercedes will do the screenplay, but Helen will not be his costar."

"But she's counting on it with all her heart," Bogie had said. "She invested more agony in that play—including years of toil and sweat—than any other person alive. She's even been thrown into jail for it. And besides, I think she's got the property under option."

"We'll deal with that later," Garbo had said. "He has decided he wants Barbara Stanwyck to play Helen's part. She's very butch, don't you think?"

"I think she's one hell of a butch broad," Bogie had said. "But..."

Garbo had interrupted him with a passionate kiss on the lips. "There, now, are you satisfied? Years from now, you can tell your grandchildren you kissed Garbo on the lips." Without saying anything else to von Berne, she'd turned and had headed down that mountain. He was never to see her again.

From what he'd learned this morning, he figured he knew as much about von Berne as anybody else in Hollywood, except Garbo herself. First, her name wasn't Eva von Berne. It was Eva von Plentzner. She wasn't from Vienna as reported in all the newspapers, but was actually born in 1910 in Sarajevo, the site of the assassination of the Archduke Ferdinand, heir to the Austrian throne. The assassination had launched World War I. Von Plentzner had fled to Vienna when war was declared.

When she was sixteen, she'd met Irving Thalberg. The weak-hearted producer for Metro had fallen in love with her and had given her a film contract.

Once at Metro, Thalberg had turned her career management over to Paul Bern, MGM executive and Jean Harlow's intended groom. He'd changed her name to his own, calling her Eva von Berne but adding an "e" at the end.

Bern decided to retain the "von" in her name as it sounded aristocratic, and Americans were impressed with European royalty, or what was left of titled personages after World War I.

Bogie had read of von Berne's arrival in New York. At that stage, Hubert Voight, MGM publicity man, had tried to launch her as "the greatest thing since sliced bread." Voight eventually succeeded in getting von Berne's beautiful face splashed over all the New York newspapers

Until then, Voight's record as a publicist had been dubious: Earlier, on July 6, 1925, he'd failed to interest the press in a frizzy-haired, plump Swedish girl from Stockholm, Greta Garbo. The blundering free-lance photographer he'd hired, James Sileo, had inadvertently arrived at the session with only three plates in his camera. During that preliminary photo shoot in New York, he shot most of Garbo's poses without film, much to the chagrin of latter-day Garbo fans.

Apparently, Voight's only suggestion to MGM was that Garbo's name be changed. "Her name sounds like garbage." Voight's suggestion was that Garbo be renamed Greta Valencia. "He no flamenco dancer named Valencia," Garbo had angrily told Voight. "Garbo remains his name, or else I sail back to Stockholm."

Although Bogart had never expected to meet her, he found von Berne's saga fascinating. After she arrived on the West Coast, Paul Berne had thrown a series of lavish parties for her, introducing her to the cream of Hollywood. For a few brief months, von Berne had been the toast of the town.

Thalberg had ordered her to be cast in the 1928 silent film, *The Masks of the Devil*, starring John Gilbert, Garbo's sometime lover and the reigning matinee idol of the Silents.

The director was to be Victor Seastrom fresh from his triumph of directing Lillian Gish in the acclaimed *The Wind*. "I go from Gish to von Berne," Seastrom complained to both Thalberg and Mayer. "Any high-school drama department in America has better actresses than von Berne." Thalberg ordered him to keep her on the film, although several scenes involving her character were cut because she couldn't play them. The role of the actress, Alma Rubens, playing Countess Zellner, was enhanced to compensate for von Berne's ineptness.

"A wooden Indian could play the part better," Mayer had said upon seeing von Berne emote on the screen opposite Gilbert. He'd told Thalberg that MGM would make no more films with von Berne. Mayer had called her into his office and told her to return to Vienna where she was "to study acting and lose twenty pounds. Once that is done, we'll relaunch you in Hollywood more spectacularly than we did before," he'd promised, having no intention of keeping such a commitment. It'd been a mere ploy to get her out of town. On October 28, 1928, she'd been given a check for three-hundred dollars and had been bid *adieu*.

Since that day, no one among the Hollywood press had ever heard of her again, and it had been reported in one newspaper that she'd been killed in a car crash somewhere in Europe.

Bogie's sighting was the only evidence that von Berne was still in town, living modestly in a bungalow in the Hollywood Hills, some of her bills being paid by Garbo.

In *The Masks of the Devil*, Gilbert's role received some of his greatest critical acclaim, his acting hailed as "worthy of John Barrymore." Von Berne was universally panned, but no one can judge her acting today because all prints of the film have vanished.

Fresh from her shower and clad only in a see-through nightgown, von Berne came into the kitchen and invited Bogie to go with her into her little garden. "Since I have nothing else to do in my life these days, I always sit here and watch the sun come up. At first the sky is pink, then it becomes a rosy red. Suddenly, there's this magnificent yellow-red flash and the sun rises from the east. After that, I go to bed and sleep all day. Perhaps Greta will come at night. Often she doesn't. I know no one. I'm very lonely."

In the garden waiting for the sun to rise, von Berne spilled out her bitterness to him. She was seething with hostility at the way MGM had treated her.

"All the MGM executives have small pricks," she claimed, sitting with him on a wooden bench watching the early morning sky. "Thalberg seduced me when I was only sixteen. I wouldn't call it a seduction. He lay on his back while I blew him. He'd warned me not to get him too excited because of his heart. His prick reminds me of a good-sized finger."

"Surely that's not why they call him 'the Boy Wonder,'" he said facetiously. "I heard when Norma Shearer first met him, she mistook him for an office boy."

"Mayer also had me go down on him," she said. "A short, stubby dick. It had no cap on it. I'd never seen a man's dick without a cap. It looked disgusting. To me, a man must have a cap, or else it's nothing for me."

"The idea of anyone going down on Louis B. Mayer is more than my feeble mind can conjure," he said.

"Paul Bern was the worst," she claimed. "I've seen five-year-old boys with bigger pricks. I can't believe Jean Harlow is actually going to marry him. She's obviously not gone to bed with him. When he failed to get an erection, he beat me so severely I had to go to the hospital. He paid me five-hundred dollars to keep quiet."

"Those are big spenders over at MGM," he said sarcastically.

"It was through Gilbert that I met Garbo," she said. "We had a three-way. She does not love him, and actually feels sorry for him, so she occasionally allows him to make love to her. She says that Gilbert can't satisfy her sexually. Considering that cavity Greta has, even the biggest, blackest buck in Harlem couldn't satisfy her. Gilbert is built just like an average man. Whether it's a man or woman, Greta is just too demanding."

466

After she'd finished talking, he turned to her and looked into her eyes. "Do you like men or women?"

"I like men providing they have larger pricks than Thalberg, Mayer, and Bern," she said. "I actually like a man who's got more to him than John Gilbert. He may be billed as the screen's great lover but he really isn't." She sighed. "The women are always after me. Mercedes de Acosta, Louise Brooks. I even got a call from Joan Crawford, but I never returned it. Greta makes love to me and I cooperate with her, but I don't love her. She's taking care of me. I return her love for food and this cottage. What I need is a real man to take care of me."

"I think I'm that man," he said.

"Are you a full man or have they cut away part of you?" she asked.

"I think you'll find everything to your liking," he said, leaning over and kissing her passionately just as that sun that had already awakened the people in New York rose with a bright red vengeance over Hollywood.

***

Bogie didn't leave von Berne's cottage until nine o'clock that evening, at which time he drove back to his apartment, showered, and changed into new clothing. If he called Helen at the Garden of Allah, he figured that once again she would not speak to him. He decided to drive over to see her in the flesh, figuring that he might come up with some explanation as to why he'd abandoned her and had disappeared into the night with Garbo, evocative of the way he'd dumped her for Billie Dove at Jeanette MacDonald's party.

At the Garden of Allah, a young man at the reception desk told him that, "Miss Menken checked out this afternoon to return to New York." Bogie asked if she'd left a message for him, but was told there was none.

Just as he was about to leave, he heard the sound of loud, raucous laughter in the foyer. He spotted those two madcap Alabamians, Tallulah Bankhead and Anderson Lawler, asking the doorman to call them a taxi. Both of them had more in common than a birth state, having just survived separate affairs with Gary Cooper.

Tallulah seemed delighted to see him. "Hump, darling," she called to him. "We're going to Jimmy's Backyard tonight. If you'll go with us, I'll fuck you later and let Andy suck you off."

"An invitation like that sounds irresistible," he said, shaking Lawler's hand and kissing Tallulah on the mouth, feeling the serpentine darting of her tongue. He volunteered to drive them to the notorious club he'd heard spoken of only in whispers.

A few hours later, Tallulah and Lawler piled into the front seat of his car, with Lawler in the middle. On the way to the club, Lawler rested his hand on Bogie's knee.

"Before she checked out," Tallulah said, "I ran into your adorable wife. Helen was furious. She told me about the double-cross from Mercedes and Garbo. Those two dykes want Barbara Stanwyck to costar in *The Captive*. The two pussies should have asked me." She laughed hilariously at something she was about to say. "Of course, I understand why they didn't consider me. No one would believe me in the role of a dyke."

"You are the true epitome of ladylike refinement," Lawler said.

"You bet your cocksucking lips I am," she said. She leaned her head over to get a better view of Bogie. "We must get together soon and catch up on the latest Hollywood gossip. I'll tell you my tales. You can tell me your tales. Later, I'll show you my tail, and you can show me your tail. Not that I haven't seen it before, darling."

"Don't clean up your stories for Tallulah," Lawler cautioned. "The dirtier the better."

"Andy's right," she said. "If your tales are too colorless, you can exaggerate the truth a bit to amuse me. It's a Southern tradition, especially in Alabama."

"I'm from the New York theater and I live and work in Hollywood," Bogie said. "I don't know about the sleepy, cotton-pickin' South, but out here and on Broadway there's no need to embellish any tale. If anything, we need to tone down our true-to-life adventures to make them more believable."

"A point well taken, my good man," Lawler said, his grip on Bogie's knee tightening. For the rest of the way to Jimmy's Backyard, Lawler took turns with Tallulah, trying to top each other with their wickedly funny and indiscreet stories about the man who'd jilted both of them, Gary Cooper. From Bankhead, Bogie learned, as if he didn't already know, that Cooper had "the greatest dick in Hollywood but no ass to push it with."

Lawler told him that Cooper's dick was so long it could penetrate half way down his throat. "When they cast the Montana cowpoke in *The Virginian*, the director hired me to pound some good ole nigger talk into Gary's head so he'd sound like a Southerner on the screen."

On the night Bogie arrived at the doorstep of Jimmy's Backyard, on Ivar Street, it was the height of the "pansy craze" in Hollywood. It had become fashionable for even the biggest stars in Hollywood to attend clubs frequented by homosexuals with oh-so-gay entertainment that included female impersonation. As one club was raided, another would open the next week, often in private apartments. That still didn't prevent the police from beating in the door. The mostly male patrons at these clubs were not referred to as homosexuals, but as "temperamental."

Even such top stars as John Gilbert and Greta Garbo had shown up at these clubs. One night at Freddy's, Gilbert had escorted Garbo to witness a female impersonator do a wicked and deadly accurate impression of her.

The most successful and the best attended of the clubs was Jimmy's Backyard, opened by Thomas Gannon, who must have been paying off somebody on the Los Angeles Police Department because his club defiantly stayed open as

468

competitors were systematically shut down.

Gannon in theory could serve no booze, but Tallulah assured Bogie that there were enough bootleggers and cocaine dealers on site to keep all the patrons high.

Lawler and all the other male patrons in the club wore tails, even though Bogie was dressed only in a black suit. He was the most underdressed man in the club. After Gannon had kissed Lawler and Tallulah on the lips, they were ushered to a ringside table. Tallulah was obviously Gannon's favorite.

As Bogie made his way through the "backyard," he noticed that the best table in the house was presided over by Billy Haines and attended by Ramon Novarro, Joan Crawford and her husband, Douglas Fairbanks Jr., and the dearly beloved character actress, Polly Moran. At another table, Bogie spotted fading screen vamp Pola Negri on the arm of the notorious homosexual tennis star, "Big" Bill Tilden. He was known to have this thing for teenage boys, the younger the better, and was said to have seduced Fairbanks Jr. when he was only thirteen years old.

Before sitting down, Bogie stood surveying the patrons having an elegantly gay time even though a grim Depression was casting deeper and deeper shadows over the American landscape. He didn't know what it was, perhaps a whiff in the air, but as he was to tell Kenneth later, he feared all of this mad gaiety was about to come to an end, like the last days of the Roman Empire.

As the Depression would take hold, the times would allow for little frivolity, and there would be no compassion for nonconformity. So far, Bogie himself had escaped the reality of the Great Depression with his $750-a-week paycheck for doing almost nothing, but he feared that in the months ahead he'd not be insulated from economic hardships.

When Bogie finally sat down, Lawler informed him that the whitewashed walls of the club, in the words of its owner, "are to suggest the moral purity of my clients." On the other hand, the carpeting was done in what Gannon called "virgin's blood red."

At an adjoining table Bogie nodded briefly to Constance Talmadge who was being escorted by the actor, Lowell Sherman, who had been a villain in the 1920 *Way Down East* with Lillian Gish but had more recently been seen on the screen opposite Garbo in *The Divine Woman*. Catching a glimpse of Talmadge, Tallulah whispered to Bogie. "A fag hag." He'd never heard the term before.

When Tallulah almost immediately excused herself to table hop, she darted over to have a few jokes and some amusement with the Billy Haines party. When out of her presence, Lawler's gay mood grew slightly bitter as he spoke of his disappointment in Hollywood.

"I was canned by Paramount," he said. "I was being touted for a role opposite Nancy Carroll in the *Devil's Holiday* but I lost it. I can see the writing on the wall. My dream of fame and fortune in the movies is fading if it hasn't already blanked out completely."

"Welcome to the club, pal," Bogie said. "My screen career, if you'd call it that, is a dud too."

"The fucking high point in my career was in *Half-Marriage* in 1929," Lawler said. "What crap! I jumped to my death from an upper floor when I learned I was losing Olive Borden in the film. Who writes such crap, and for me no less? My mother was convinced, though. She took a train all the way from Alabama to Hollywood to see if I had survived the fall."

Impulsively, Lawler invited Bogie to go to the men's room with him. At first Bogie thought he was going to be the recipient of a blow-job from Lawler. Bogie admitted to himself that he was curious about the sexual techniques of sword-swallowing Lawler, who had already enraptured Gary Cooper.

Once in the men's room, Lawler introduced Bogie to a pusher who sold them cocaine. Right in the men's room, the two men snorted the coke, which Bogie hadn't sampled since his New York days when Tallulah had invited Helen and him for a night on the town.

Feeling high as they walked back to the table, Bogie had no way of knowing that Lawler would soon launch himself into his next career by doing exactly what they were doing that night: walking. Lawler would be the founding father of all "walkers," an escort to famous women. The parade of A-list Hollywood grand dames would seem endless: Zoë Akins, Ilka Chase, Ina Claire, Ruth Chatterton, Hedda Hopper, Paulette Goddard, Constance Bennett, and inevitably Dietrich herself. In the years ahead, he'd show up frequently on the arm of Virginia Zanuck, wife of Darryl Zanuck. Surprisingly, after his true love, Cooper, dumped the older Countess di Frasso, Lawler appeared with this dowager on his arm at major Hollywood functions.

He would later recount to Bogie that in 1934 he was offered $10,000 to escort Kay Francis to Europe. "One night Kay, smashed out of her head and stark naked, appeared suddenly in my room." He did a brilliant impersonation of her lisp. "I may be a big movie star but I am also a woman of flesh and blood. Tonight I demand that you fuck me. Somehow I got through the evening but it was the hardest $10,000 I ever earned."

Bogie looked up at the entrance of a trio of late-arriving quests creating a sensation. It was Marlene Dietrich herself with her husband, Rudolph Sieber, on one arm, and her director and lover, Josef von Sternberg, on the other. All three of them were attired in carefully tailored white flannel suits.

Tallulah chose that moment to rejoin Lawler and Bogie at table. "I've had that German housewife many, many times," Tallulah said in a voice loud enough to be heard ten tables away. She looked with amusement at Haines' table. "Naturally, I've fucked both Joan Crawford and her husband, but not at the same time. Both Andy and I have fucked that divine Gary Cooper as all the civilized world now knows." She noticed Constance Talmadge looking with a certain disdain at her boisterous show. "But unlike the rest of Hollywood, I haven't fucked the great Constance Talmadge yet." A gasp could be heard coming from Talmadge. That act of delicacy seemed only to goad Tallulah into more action. Raising her voice, she called out to the next table, "Constance, darling, I heard when you aren't fucking Irving Thalberg, you and Billy Haines go cruising for sailors. I also heard the police arrested the both of you and booked you on a morals charge. Thanks to Louis B. Mayer, the charges were dropped."

"How dare you!" Constance said in a voice whose harshness eventually triggered the end of her career with the advent of talking pictures. She reached for Lowell Sherman's hand as he guided her to the door.

Before Tallulah sat down, she held up her glass and directed a toast at three nearby ringside tables.

"Here's to my conquest," she said. "Miss Tallulah Bankhead, First Lady of Alabama, is setting out from this day forth to bed a peasant girl from Sweden, Miss Greta Garbo herself."

The tables of gay young men applauded loudly.

Although it had already been born in New York, and later transplanted to London, the Tallulah legend became airborne that night in Hollywood.

***

Fueled by cocaine and bourbon, Tallulah was on a roll, having apparently decided to be the sensation of the "backyard" despite the fact that she was surrounded by far bigger names in the film world. No longer speaking in whispers, she didn't give a damn any more about being overheard.

Still Garbo-obsessed, Tallulah told Bogie, "I've met Garbo twice. Once at the home of that dyke and her mentor, Salka Viertel. Once again on the tennis court at Clifton Webb's house. That queen sat there holding his mother's hand watching Garbo beat the shit out of me." She turned directly into Bogie's face, blowing smoke. "I can say shit, darling, because I'm a lady."

"Tallu and I heard that Garbo takes long walks, alone, along this particular part of the coastline," Lawler said.

"I know those hills very well," Bogie said, recalling his encounter not only with Garbo but with the exotic Eva von Berne.

"We're roughly aware of the time of day Garbo goes for her walks," Lawler said. "Tallu demanded that I accompany her up into those hills. She wanted to 'accidentally' encounter Garbo."

"Those God damn walks left me gasping for breath," Tallulah said, coughing in Bogie's face in remembrance. "Once we actually spotted *La Belle* but she was out with that little rat, pussy-licking Mercedes de Acosta." She burst into a kind of hysterical laughter. "God knows, we've all had Mercedes, darling."

"One day Tallu and I armed ourselves with a telescope to spy into Garbo's garden," Lawler said. "We hoped to catch her sunbathing in the nude."

"Miss Tallulah Bankhead actually climbed a tree for the first time in her life," she said. "I had to. There was no way I could see over those fucking high hedges around Garbo's garden. I got up in this God damn tree and skinned my knee so bad I'm probably disfigured. Suddenly, just as I trained my telescope on Garbo's backyard, I look down to see myself surrounded by three of the most ferocious man-eating dogs since the days prehistoric monsters roamed the world. With their fangs bared, they started barking at me. Garbo, I later learned, keeps these beasts to prevent Mata Haris like me from spying on her."

"You obviously weren't dinner for them, so how did you get down?" Bogie asked.

"Clever Alabama gal that he is, Andy rushed to a little market nearby and bought ten of the world's juiciest steaks," she said. "I mean as blood red as my painted scarlet lips. While the bulldogs were devouring those steaks, with blood running out of their mouths, I climbed down from that tree. We made our get-away."

"I keep telling Tallu that in spite of several botched attempts, she'll get Garbo yet," Lawler said.

"Of course, I will, darling," she said. "I always get my prey. Greta Garbo and Tallulah Bankhead are going to have an *affaire*." She slammed down her bourbon. "Of course, when I seduce her, I understand that she's so big down there, I'll have to wear swamp boots to keep from drowning."

Suddenly, two waiters arrived and added another table to theirs, covering both of them with a large white cloth. "You inviting more company?" Bogie asked.

"Wait until you see the guest list Tallu has assembled tonight!" Lawler said.

"I've invited your girl friend, Lilyan Tashman, and that dashing gay blade husband of hers, Edmund Lowe himself." She leaned over and placed her hand on Bogie's. "You and I will have to make it again some time. It's been too long since that night in New York. We'll let Andy here join in our fun, naturally." In a voice growing louder, she said, "Hump and I fuck the same pussies any way. So much so he and I are practically kissin' cousins. In fact, during all the time his wife, Helen, was at the Garden of Allah, I fucked her more than her husband did."

"Helen and I are no longer married," he said, a bit too defensively.

She ignored his remark. "At the Algonquin in New York I had this fling with Lilyan who seems to fascinate you so, and last night, just to keep it in the family, I seduced the intended bride of your best friend. Yes, Miss Kay Francis herself, whose lisp is even more adorable than yours." She paused. "I forget the name of that damn actor she's marrying." She looked across the room where Dietrich sat engrossed in a conversation with von Sternberg, as she pointedly ignored her husband. "I've had Marlene. You know, darling Kay was one of Marlene's first loves in Hollywood. Last night after we'd lapped up pussy juices, Kay confessed to me that she based her role in Zoe Akins' *Girls About Town* on me, the divine one. Isn't that adorable?"

Bogie spotted Tashman arriving with Lowe, as Tallulah called across the room for them to come over. Lowering her voice for the first time, Tallulah turned to Bogie. "The reason Lilyan isn't always available to you is that she's fucking Douglas Fairbanks Jr. It all started, darling, on the set of *Scarlet Dawn*."

472

Tashman sat next to Bogie after giving him a long, hard kiss on the lips. He hadn't seen her since the night of that ill-fated ball when she'd ended up in police custody. Lawler kissed everyone but Tashman on the lips before departing hastily to join the fun at Billy Haines' table. Apparently, Lawler had not forgiven Tashman for inviting Gary Cooper and Joel McCrea to her home the same night she'd invited him.

The entertainment of the evening was Rae Bourbon, all in feathers, boas, and wigs, and one of the leading female impersonators in America. Swishy, campy, flamboyant, Bourbon gave no clue that he was born to dour cattle raisers in western Texas. Opening his show with a rousing number, "I'm a Link in a Daisy Chain," he ended the song to loud applause. He obviously spotted—or else heard—Tallulah and grandly invited her to join him for a duo. Staggering to the stage, Tallulah performed a giddy reprise of the number, which drew even louder applause.

At the end of the act, and after several curtain calls, the band played dance music.

Tashman invited Bogie to the floor for "a mean rumba with lots of hot cha-cha-cha."

After everyone had exhausted themselves on the dance floor, Bourbon returned to the stage to do a series of impressions, leading off with a scathingly accurate, take-no-prisoners impersonation of Joan Crawford doing an aggressive Charleston in *Our Dancing Daughters*.

The biggest laughter throughout that act was coming from Crawford herself.

When Tallulah's table had reassembled, she said, "Darlings, I have a grand surprise for all of you. Wait until you see who's going to fill those two empty chairs at our table. Howard Hughes and a date I arranged for him. When Howard is not sucking cock in private, he likes to be seen in public with only name pussies. I called him and told him that one of the biggest stars on Broadway was visiting Hollywood to see her brother. I claimed that this mysterious woman was legendary. Bigger than any name he'd ever dated before. Not only that, but her grace, charm, and beauty would make a puppy dog of a Tyrannosaurus rex. Howard agreed to pick up this divine creature and bring her to Jimmy's to join us tonight."

No sooner had Tallulah made this pronouncement than her guests of honor were seen making their way across the room. All heads turned to look at these newcomers.

It was Howard Hughes all right. Bogie would know him anywhere except perhaps in drag.

The mystery woman?

Bogie was shocked to see Hughes escorting Ethel Barrymore.

***

In the backyard of Jimmy's Backyard, Bogie stood snorting cocaine with

Howard Hughes. "I've been rough on you, Bogart, and I know it, but we'll call a truce. I just wanted to teach you a lesson. You won't be the first man—or the last—I need to teach a lesson to."

"So, I'm off the hook, pal?" Bogie asked.

"Absolutely," Hughes said. "I'll destroy those pictures of you." After delivering George O'Brien to me, I owe you a favor."

"Not to mention the Harlow thing," Bogie said.

"Sorry you messed that up, and I'm sorry you brought up the subject," Hughes said, snorting more cocaine. "Some accounting is in order. I gave you five-thousand bucks, with the instructions that you were supposed to pay Harlow's medical expenses. But the way things worked out, I paid most of the bills myself directly from L.A."

"I still have more than four-thousand of what you gave me," Bogie said. "But I was hoping since you have so much money, and I have so little, you might let me keep it."

Hughes seemed to think a minute. "Considering that George O'Brien treat you brought to my door, I'll call it even."

"Hot damn!" Bogie said. "I'm gonna need the money. Fox is not gonna renew me. Perhaps you'll put me under personal contract."

"You're not my type," Hughes said. "The only way you could get any more money out of me at this point is to come up with something better than George O'Brien."

"If I could top myself," Bogie said. "I mean, come up with the handsomest stud in Hollywood, do you think you could spare another five thousand? You see I'm goin' back to New York, and I hear ninety percent of the actors along Broadway are waiting in line at the soup kitchen."

"I don't think you could do it," Hughes said. "O'Brien would be a tough act to follow."

"What about Garbo's leading man?" Bogie asked.

"I wouldn't hire most of Garbo's leading men as my butler," Hughes said.

"Not even Johnny Mack Brown," Bogie asked.

Hughes looked stunned. "You're bullshitting me. That handsome cowboy is available?"

"I even took the liberty of discussing you with him," Bogie said. "He's ready, willing, and able. Just waiting for your call."

"You have Johnny Mack Brown delivered and tied with a red ribbon at my house on Saturday night at eight o'clock, and I can guarantee you that the five-thousand bucks are yours."

"You got yourself a deal, pal," Bogie said, shaking Hughes hand.

"One good thing about having money is that it allows you to obtain the unobtainable," Hughes said.

"Maybe we'd better be getting back to the party," Bogie said. "Tallulah might send a posse out looking for us. Or, knowing her, spread rumors that the two of us

474

have sneaked off together to have sex."

"You wish," Hughes said. "Where I'm concerned, you can only dream dreams that will never be. As a consolation prize, I'm offering you an evening on the town with me and Ethel Barrymore."

"That's not so bad," Bogie said. "I'd love to get to know Ethel Barrymore. Maybe when she returns to New York, she'll cast me in a play opposite her. I need the work."

"Ethel it is for us tonight," Hughes said, taking one final snort of cocaine before facing the crowd inside. "But the deal is, if Ethel demands that one of us fuck her tonight, you've got to do the honors."

***

Lingerie parties were all the rage in Hollywood during the early 1930s, although Bogie had never attended one. The "gals" threw parties, as did straight couples. But no one had ever invited him, especially to an all-male version.

The bachelor party being given in honor of Kenneth MacKenna's upcoming marriage to Kay Francis was at the home of Richard Arlen, who was known throughout Hollywood for his all-nude, all-male swim bashes, many of which had been staged in Palm Springs and on Catalina Island.

It was only out of respect for Kenneth that Bogie was going at all. The idea of parading around in his skivvies in front of a group of men didn't enthrall him. Yet there was a certain morbid curiosity.

Bogie's only hope was that George Cukor wouldn't be there. The sight of the director attired only in underwear might be a little much.

Kenneth and Richard Arlen were good friends, and, Bogie assumed, lovers as well. An actor from Virginia, Arlen was exactly Bogie's age. No reader of fan magazines or movie devotees was unfamiliar with this ruggedly handsome silent-screen idol whose 1927 film, *Wings*, was still playing all over the world.

Bogie had only recently seen both Arlen and Gary Cooper starring together in *The Virginian*, with Cooper using Southern speech patterns taught to him by Anderson Lawler, among other stunts that Alabama boy had imparted to Coop. The word in Hollywood was that Arlen's star was falling from the sky and that his glory days were behind him. Dozens of grade-B action films lay ahead of him, often with fat sidekick Andy Devine. Arlen's final appearance occurred in 1976 in the undeniably silly *Won Ton Ton, the Dog Who Saved Hollywood*.

When a servant ushered Bogie into the living room to meet Arlen, the star was already stripped to his boxer shorts. He had a rugged physique and was quite muscular, as if he worked out a lot in the gym. Maybe it was because Bogie had seen Arlen in *Wings*, but the actor still evoked a fighter ace, which was what he was during World War I when he'd served in the Royal Canadian Flying Corps.

"Glad to meet you, Bogie," Arlen said, shaking his hand firmly.

Bogie decided then and there that he could no longer spot a faggot. He was quickly learning that the more masculine a man was, the more likely he was to prefer men. All his past misconceptions were challenged.

Bogie greeted Arlen warmly, telling him how much he admired his acting in *Wings* before a servant ushered him upstairs to one of the bedrooms. Arlen had suggested that he strip down to his underwear before joining Kenneth and the other guests by the swimming pool.

Bogie had gone out and purchased a new pair of blue underwear just for the occasion, something not too revealing in the crotch. As he stripped down, he looked at himself in a full-length mirror, and was none too pleased. He felt that he made a far sexier appearance when fully dressed. When stacked up against some of Hollywood's greatest male physiques, he didn't measure up. His chest wasn't very developed, and he didn't have a pair of legs to make women swoon. He figured he was okay in the cock department, but he didn't plan to be showing that tonight.

Summoning his courage from some hidden reservoir, he self-consciously made his way down the stairs and out to the large palm tree-lined patio around the pool. Arlen had lit it with pink spots, creating a seductive atmosphere with mood music playing in the background.

Before Bogie's eyes was a sea of some of the world's handsomest men, laughing, talking, flirting, and drinking illegal booze. Kenneth spotted him at once and walked over to kiss him on the mouth. Bogie broke away quickly but he hoped not too quickly. He didn't want to make Kenneth feel that he was being rejected. After all, this party was in Kenneth's honor.

As Bogie surveyed the "meat rack" by the pool, he felt that he had the worst body here. Kenneth and Arlen knew all of Tinseltown's best specimens.

Within ten minutes Bogie found himself shaking hands with Douglas Fairbanks Jr., who was wearing red silk drawers that had no doubt been purchased by Joan Crawford herself.

Reunited with Gary Cooper and Joel McCrea, Bogie took refuge in their company. If prizes were being given out tonight for male beauty, those two lovers, Cooper and McCrea, would surface near the top.

At a tap on his shoulder, Bogie turned around to see Kenneth again. This time his best friend was accompanied by Ramon Novarro and Billy Haines, whom Bogie had already met.

Haines chatted with them only briefly before saying, "You girls will have to excuse me. Jimmy Shields will be here in an hour, and he keeps me on a tight leash. Before he gets here, though, I've got to check out all the baskets. Darling Richard has given me permission to reach inside the fly of every one of his guest's underwear." He paused before heading off. "That is, the few I haven't already sampled."

Novarro invited Bogie to sit down on a chaise longue by the pool. It was obvious that he'd been drinking heavily before he'd arrived at the party. Surveying all these semi-naked men, the star of *Ben-Hur* ran his hand up and down his perfect physique. "With a body like I have, I've never had the slightest shyness about stripping in front of anyone, especially the camera. When I was struggling to break into movies, I posed nude for art classes. Most producers I've worked with order the writers of the screenplays to see that at some point I strip on cue. I've always been exquisitely beautiful."

"I saw those nude stills of you that MGM released for *Ben-Hur*," Bogie said. "Was that real pubic hair showing?"

"It was!" Novarro said proudly. "When I saw the stills showing a tantalizing glimpse of my silky pubic hair, I thought they'd never release such pictures to exhibitors. But they were sent out all across the country. I heard that fans, often male, stole every print."

"You're pretty daring," Bogie said. "My God, pal, you were practically naked in *Where the Pavement Ends*."

"Hell, I'd do a full frontal if you want me to," Novarro said, standing up.

"That won't be necessary for me, pal," Bogie said. "Although it looks like some of the guys here wouldn't mind at all."

Right in front of Bogie, Novarro dropped his drawers, revealing his uncut Mexican cock. In the pink spots, he walked to the diving board. Knowing that all eyes were on him, he jumped up and down on the board, his cock and balls bouncing rhythmically.

The moment he dived into the pool, at least two dozen young men dropped their underwear and jumped in with him.

Feeling out of place at the party, Bogie wandered back toward the living room, the source of the music.

On the way there, Bogie spotted Arlen sitting on a flowery sofa in his plant-filled California room entertaining a group of ten young men, each clad in his underwear. They were passing some object around for each man to examine.

"I can't believe the size of this thing," one of the men said. "It must be at least ten inches long. I think Rudy's sculptor exaggerated a bit."

"Not at all," Arlen said. "Rudy and I became lovers when I was twenty years old and a bit-player on the set of *The Sheik*. We were both boxers. Rudy and I used to spar with each other at the Los Angeles Athletic Club, then go shower together and do other things. If he had an electrifying charisma on screen, it was nothing like what he had first-hand, in bed. I still say that Rudolph Valentino was the world's most beautiful man. What a physique! What a lover!"

"I've seen Valentino photographed in very revealing swimwear," another man said. He looked well hung, but not ten inches."

"Starting from a rather solid base, he just grew and grew until he was fully extended," Arlen claimed. "God damn it, he could practically write his full name on that dago prick when it was erect. As all of you guys know, yours truly is one of the best hung men in Hollywood, and I'm not bashful about parading my wares at any nude party. But even on my finest night, I can't manage more than eight and a half inches."

"Since Rudy is dead," one of the men said, "we'll have to take your word for it. But I've seen dicks like the ones you described. Others are the exact opposite. I had sex once with Joel McCrea. He's a different type altogether. Big prick. But it hangs down five inches soft and extends only to a good eight. It's almost as big as yours, Dick."

At that point, Arlen raised his head from the sofa and spotted Bogie. "C'mon in and join the fellows," his host called to him.

When Bogie stepped with caution down the steps into the California room, Arlen handed him a ten-inch Art Deco dildo. All in black, it was initialed "R.V."

"Mighty impressive," Bogie said, "but not quite in the same department as this foot-long piece of sausage I'm carrying around."

"You wish!" one of the queens called out mockingly.

"Rudy had an artist fashion twelve of these from real life," Arlen said. "I got one. George O'Brien another. Ramon Novarro and Paul Ivano each got one, and Norman Kerry has one. I'm not sure who owns the others."

Handing the dildo back to Arlen, Bogie excused himself, feeling out of place at this penis party.

He continued his retreat into the safety of the living room, which was occupied by Arlen's co-star in *Wings*, "America's boy friend," Charles Rogers, whom everybody called "Buddy." A band leader and musician himself, Rogers was scanning Arlen's selection of records. Arlen's taste definitely centered on Rudy Vallee and Bing Crosby. Upon seeing Bogie, Rogers turned around to introduce himself.

Once again, like he'd done when he'd met Arlen, Bogie flashed on a scene in *Wings*. To his knowledge, that picture had contained the first scene in a major film where a man was depicted kissing another man on the mouth. It occurred during the death scene of the film's hero, a fighter pilot ace played by Richard Arlen. The kiss was planted by his aviator pal, Charles Rogers, who tearfully delivered it as part of a final rite after accidentally shooting down Arlen's aircraft.

Six feet tall, slim, and with trusting brown eyes and black hair, Rogers made a striking appearance. Bogie figured that if he looked like Rogers, he wouldn't be getting the boot from Fox.

On the screen Rogers played pilots, college boys, lawyers, and salesmen, a real All-American boy. "Paramount cleaned up with that *Wings* flicker," Rogers said. "I got only sixty-five dollars a week and a parting gift of three suits of clothes."

"Well, I'm making $750 a week at Fox," Bogie said, "but it's all coming to an end. I didn't catch on in pictures, and I'm not getting my contract renewed. I don't think they'll give me even one suit of clothing as a parting gift, though."

As they sat drinking and talking, listening to the shouts coming from the pool area, Rogers told him that he really wanted to make films like the one in which he'd appeared with Mary Pickford, that whimsical 1927 *My Best Girl*. "But those parts are few and far between. I'm in love with Mary." He said that in a confiden-

478

tial tone. "When she breaks up with Fairbanks, I'm moving in on her. I've always loved her. She's the only gal for me, even though Clark Gable is trying to break up our romance. That stinker is trying to move in on Mary too. But he just wants her money. I could offer her real love."

Bogie looked up to see who'd just come into the living room. It was the dashing son of a dashing father, Fairbanks Jr.

Bogie wondered if Fairbanks had overheard Rogers declaring his love for his stepmother, Pickford. Bogie also wondered if either Fairbanks Jr. or Rogers knew that Kenneth, the guest of honor, was having an affair with Pickford as well.

If Fairbanks Jr. overheard them, he was very discreet and made no mention of it. Bogie was surprised that when Fairbanks sat with Rogers on the sofa, he reached for his hand and held it up to his lips, kissing the inner palm. "I adore this man," Fairbanks said. "They call me handsome. But Buddy here is pretty, prettier than any gal I've ever bedded."

"And I hear you've bedded them all," Bogie said provocatively.

"A few from time to time," Fairbanks countered. He reached for Rogers, putting his arms around him and holding him close. Bogie saw Fairbanks' tongue shooting out as his lips enclosed over Rogers' mouth. Rogers took one of his delicate hands and slowly eased it into the fly of Fairbanks' underwear.

Figuring it was time for him to go, Bogie walked back to the pool where he immediately encountered Kenneth.

"He's here!" Kenneth said, a touch of glee in his voice, but also with a sense of mischief on his face.

"Who's here?" Bogie demanded to know. "You make it sound like God herself has just arrived."

"The one man in all of Hollywood who has been begging me to bring you two together," Kenneth said, deliberately delaying telling Bogie who it was. "The young beauty who says he dreams of you day and tonight. The one star who has pictures of you plastered all over his bedroom."

"Rin Tin Tin?" Bogie asked.

"No, you fool. It's that divinely beautiful, sweet-lipped, rosy-cheeked, and hot, hot, hot…"

"C'mon already," Bogie said. "I've already met Buddy Rogers, and he's engaged." He glanced back toward the living room.

"Don't be a silly twat," Kenneth said. "I'm talking about Eric Linden."

***

The young man who sat across from Bogie in almost bikini-like sheer underwear had been recruited for films right out of Columbia University. On the dawn of meteoric career, Eric Linden had just made his auspicious movie debut in *Are These Our Children?* for RKO.

Even on their first meeting, Bogie sensed that the fire raging within this flamboyant young man had such incandescence that it would burn out quickly as it shot across the Hollywood night sky.

In the early 1930s, Linden was on the dawn of cornering the Tinseltown market in portraying artistic, sensitive, smart but weak-willed juvenile males, those who hovered somewhere in space between boyhood and manhood.

Linden's face looked so young that Bogie imagined that it would never age. A good ten years younger than Bogie, Linden had been born of Swedish parents in New York City in 1909.

He seemed to practically drool in the presence of Bogie. Kenneth had been right. Linden had a crush that seemed almost obsessional. In a way, Linden was like a cute little puppy dog licking the hand of its master.

Bogie had to admit to himself that he was flattered. With the handsomest and most well-built men in Hollywood at this party, and with many of them stark naked out by the pool area, Linden had chosen him as the object of his affection. Bogie found this a bit amusing but also realized that he had to put a stop to it at once. He was going to explain to Linden that even though he was Kenneth's best friend and was attending this all-male party, and in spite of his lisp, that he was not a homosexual. An affair between the two of them was out of the question.

Before he could utter those words, Linden startled him by saying, "The first time I saw you with Spencer Tracy in *Up the River*, I was totally captivated by you. You remind me of my father."

Bogie lit a cigarette and used the moment to collect his thoughts. Maybe this wasn't a sexual obsession after all. "I guess I must be getting old, kid, and I've been told a lot of things in Hollywood, but never that I reminded someone of their father."

"His name is Philip, but I don't know where he is today," Linden said. "He was born in New York but at one point he went back to his native Sweden where he got a job as a pianist and an actor in the Theater Royal in Stockholm. It was there he met my mother, Elvira Lundborg. She'd been born on a remote little island in the Baltic Sea. Until she was thirteen years old, she'd never seen any other human beings except her parents. A real pretty little girl, she was shipped off to Stockholm to work as a maid at the Grand Hotel. It was there she met and fell in love with my father and married him when she was only fifteen."

"That's an intriguing story," Bogie said, "especially about not having seen any other people except her parents. I don't think I've ever heard a story like that."

"My parents came to New York after they were married," Linden said. "They had five children, and I was the youngest. One was run over by a car. But when I was six, my father deserted us, leaving my mother stranded. I've hated him ever since."

"Wait a minute here," Bogie said. "I remind you of someone you hate. This is making me a bit uncomfortable."

"It's not hate exactly," Linden said. "It's very complicated. I mean it *is* hate.

480

But it's overwhelming love too. I'll never forgive him for the suffering he brought to my mother and the rest of my brothers and sisters. There were many times we went to bed hungry. We were forced to live over a choir loft at the Trinity Church on 126th Street in Harlem. All of us kids had to work to put food on the table. At the age of seven I was the loudest newsie on Tenth Avenue shouting the headlines of the day."

"This is interesting biography and all," Bogie said, "but I don't get the tie-in between me and your old man."

"I don't understand it either," Linden said. "It's not that you resemble him that much. When I saw you on the screen, I felt that you moved like my father, you talked like him, and you walked like him. You seem to hiss out your words like he did, and you have the same facial expressions. Now that I meet you in the flesh, I feel that more than ever."

"It's just a passing fancy," Bogie said, looking for a quick exit. He was feeling great unease at the intense scrutiny he was getting from this young man.

"I saw your film eighteen times," Linden said. "I began to fantasize about you. I know it doesn't make sense, but I suspect that since my relationship with my father was cut off abruptly like that, I might continue it with you."

"I'm not an adoption agency, kid," Bogie said, shifting uncomfortably. As he did, he felt his left nut pop out. He quickly adjusted his underwear in front of Linden's intense gaze. "I'm not going to become your father. I'm going back to New York. There can be no relationship between us."

Linden looked mortally wounded. "I'd do anything for you just for your friendship," Linden pleaded. "Anything." He reached for Bogie's hand.

Linden's face seemed to tremor, and Bogie didn't immediately withdraw his hand out of fear of rejecting him so suddenly. Clark Gable at this point might have punched Linden in the mouth. But when Bogie looked into his intensely deep brown eyes resting under a head of unruly light brown hair, he decided to proceed cautiously with the boy, although fearing he was some sort of mental case. The way Bogie figured it, Linden needed a psychiatrist more than he needed a substitute father.

"When Kenneth was fucking me next door, I imagined you only a wall away," Linden said. "Suddenly, it wasn't Kenneth fucking me, but you."

"There will be none of that," Bogie said, slowly withdrawing his hand. "That's not my scene and you've got to get it through your head."

"I know that already," Linden said. "I'm no fool. Even though I want it desperately, I realize I'm not going to share that part of your life."

"Then what do you want?" Bogie asked.

"Your friendship," Linden said. "Just to be in your presence if only for an hour a day would make all the difference in my life. If I'm not allowed to have that, I'll kill myself."

"No need for that, kid," Bogie said, patting his hand for a gentle reassurance. "I guess many of us have these urges and obsessions. I've had one or two myself." He took a final draw on his cigarette before crushing it out. "With women," he quickly added. "but I find I get over it in a day or two."

"I'll never get over you," Linden said, gazing deeply into his eyes.

"You've just met me for Christ's sake," Bogie said. "I'm not that character up there on the screen, the one in *Up the River*. That's not me at all. I bet if you got to know me, you wouldn't be able to stand me. I've got a lot of bad habits."

"Such as?" Linden asked.

"I smoke too much," Bogie said. "Drink too much. I fart in bed. I leave skid marks in my underwear." He lit another cigarette. "And I'm a skirt-chaser."

"With all your faults," Linden said, "I want us to become very close friends. You'll learn to like me a lot. I'm a good person. I would never force myself on you or do anything that would be more than you could deal with. That's a promise."

"The way I see it, friendship is something that just grows naturally," Bogie said. "If it happens, it happens. It's not something you ask for."

"I know that," Linden said. "On the other hand, if I didn't throw myself at you, you'd walk out of this party tonight and forget I ever existed. I'm having to do something to make an impression on you so that you'll not forget me. I want to count for something in your life."

"Listen, I don't see how this is going to work out," Bogie said. "Since sex has been ruled out, just what could you do for me?"

"If our friendship has to be based on barter, I can deal with that," Linden said. "The guys over at RKO said I'm going to become one of the biggest stars in Hollywood. I've been following every step of your career. I know Fox isn't going to renew you. I'm becoming a big star, considering the reviews I'm getting for *Are These Our Children*? I'll insist that you have a co-starring role in all my movies."

"I can't see that happening," Bogie said. Even as he issued a bleak forecast for such an eventuality, he had a strange foreboding that what Linden was saying might come true. After all, this was Hollywood. What Bogie was sensing that night was his intuition that he might indeed appear on the screen with Linden one day.

Even as they talked that night at Arlen's party, Ward Morehouse and Lillie Howard were working on the screenplay for *Big City Blues*, based on Morehouse's own play, *New York Town*. Unknown to either star at the time, the leads would be played by Eric Linden and Joan Blondell. Bogie would appear as one of the co-stars.

"Can I go home with you tonight?" Linden impulsively asked. "With Kenneth marrying Kay Francis, I'm going to have a lot of free nights."

"Sorry, pal," Bogie said. "It's not possible. My bed gets quite a workout. Sometimes I don't even have time to change the sheets."

"Let me come and stay with you," Linden said. "If I lived with you, I'd see that you had crisp, clean sheets all the time. I'd iron them myself. When you entertain your lady friends, I'd go for a walk. I'm a good cook. I'd prepare all your favorite foods."

"I'm sort of a picky eater," Bogie said. "Mainly bacon and eggs, or ham and eggs. I sure like eggs."

"Wait until you try my omelettes," Linden said. "I make even better omelettes than Marlene Dietrich."

"You sure know the way to a man's heart," Bogie said. "As tempting as that sounds, I still have to say no. It won't work out. There's no future in my being your father. You're a good-looking kid, and you'll meet some man your own age. Maybe at this party tonight."

"Arlen has already arranged that," Linden said.

"What do you mean?" Bogie asked.

"I'm the party favorite tonight," Linden said. "In an hour or so, I'm to go upstairs to one of the bedrooms and pull off my underwear. I'm to lie flat on my stomach. Any man at the party who wants to use me can come upstairs and have his way with me."

"Don't do it, kid," he said, feeling strangely protective of Linden. "Don't let these guys use you like that."

"I won't if you'll let me go away with you tonight," Linden said.

"I can't, kid, I just can't," Bogie said. "It's not in me." The room was closing in on him, and he excused himself, telling Linden good-bye, although some part of him told him that they would meet again.

Once upstairs, Bogie was breathing better. In spite of his concern for Linden, he felt a sense of great relief to be removed from his presence. The boy's desperation suffocated him. Looking for the bedroom where he'd left his clothes, he entered the dark chamber.

The sound of love-making on the king-sized bed assaulted his ears. He made a quick decision. He was going to turn on the light quickly, grab his clothes, turn off the lamp, and retreat into the night.

He turned on the lamp. Even though he didn't mean to, he couldn't resist looking at the nude male couple fucking on Arlen's bed.

The two men hardly acknowledged his presence, as both of them seemed to be reaching the throes of a powerful double climax.

Spotting his suit, he grabbed it and reached for his shoes. Turning off the lamp quickly, he darted into the hallway.

The image of Douglas Fairbanks Jr. plowing Buddy Rogers would be forever ingrained in his brain.

Fully dressed, he made his way out the door, fleeing from Kenneth's bachelor party and not bothering to thank Arlen for inviting him

In the years ahead, Bogie would always wonder what Mary Pickford might think of that scene of her son-in-law fucking her future husband, or "America's boyfriend" as he was called.

On Catalina Island Bogie sat on an embankment with Jean Arthur overlooking the ocean. "Why do we always fall for the wrong people?" she asked him, a forlorn expression on her beautiful face.

"That's no question to ask a man with two failed marriages," he said. "Come to think of it, I don't think I loved either of my wives. Helen Menken or Mary Philips. Mary and I are heading for the divorce courts."

"My first marriage wasn't anything to get a divorce over," she said, a bemused expression coming onto her face. "In 1928 I married this Jewish photographer, Julian Ancker, more or less to spite my mother and all her Christian Science fervor."

"How'd it go?" he asked.

"A disaster from the beginning," she said. "First, mother threatened suicide when she heard the news that we'd eloped to Santa Barbara. After the wedding, when we returned to the cheap motel where we were staying—both of us were poor as church mice—I took a good hard look at Ancker. Right then and there I decided the marriage would never be consummated. I should call it my one-day marriage."

"Talk about short marriages," he said, lighting another one of his interminable cigarettes. "Did you guys get a quickie divorce?"

"We had our marriage annulled," she said. "Actually I need not have bothered. It wasn't long before Ancker went fishing, suffered a sunstroke, and keeled over dead."

"I always knew the outdoors was bad for a man," he said. "A man should sit in a dark room smoking and drinking all the booze he can steal. That's the only way to stay healthy."

She laughed in her distinctive, husky voice. "Why are we sitting here avoiding the subject and not saying what's on our minds?"

"Okay, kid, I'll let you have it straight," he said. "I spent two hours last night in Kenneth's hotel room trying to persuade him not to marry Kay, just like you asked me to. I lost my argument. He admits he's marrying Kay for career advancement—I mean, let's face it, she's a big star. He's perfectly aware of all her girl friends, including you, and he tells her about all his boy friends. It's going to be a marriage of convenience, like Edmund Lowe and Lilyan Tashman. Kenneth doesn't even like to sleep with Kay. They hit the sack a few times, but it did nothing for either of them."

A little sound not quite like a gurgle escaped from her throat. "I'm so very sorry to hear that," she said. "Ever since we met that night at Jeanette MacDonald's party, I was counting on you as my last hope. Kay has told me how close you are to Kenneth. I'm told you guys share each other's secrets and everything."

"Yes, we're very close," he said, "I appreciate telling him about some of the crazy adventures I'm having in Hollywood."

484

"Kay thinks her groom is actually in love with you, even though he's been sleeping lately with a lot of other guys.

"Kenneth gets around," he said. "He also beds women, maybe not his wife-to-be, but Grade A Hollywood pussy like Mary Pickford."

"But why marry Kay?" she asked. "I don't understand why a marriage has to be a pretend marriage. Better no marriage at all than what those two are trying to pull off to deceive the public."

"Don't tell me you're against lavender marriages," he said. "What would Hollywood be without them? Hell, the whole town would fall apart."

"I suppose you're right," she said.

"You were locked up for a long time in Kay's room this morning," he said. "Couldn't you persuade her not to go through with the marriage?"

"I tried, but she wouldn't listen," she said. "I'm still dreaming of living with Kay in a rose-covered cottage overlooking the ocean. Long walks on the beach with two big dogs running before us. Cozy meals by a fire of blazing logs we gathered ourselves. A life of contemplation and solitude and of devotion to each other."

"Now come on, Jean," he said. "We're talking about party-going, clothes-horse Kay Francis here. The woman was destined to lead the life of a movie star—glamour, excitement, and endless devotion from her screaming fans."

"We're talking Kay Francis, international tramp," she said bitterly. "How could I have been so stupid as to think I could reform Kay? The list of women she's seduced in Hollywood reads like a *Who's Who* of American entertainment, beginning with Marlene Dietrich." She leaned back on the grass and sighed as she ran down the list. "Then, obviously, there was Lilyan Tashman. Also, believe it or not, Clara Bow. Then there was Ruth Chatterton, Joan Crawford, Barbara Stanwyck, Tallulah Bankhead, Katharine Cornell, and Dolores del Rio. And probably Mercedes de Acosta, too. And failed attempts with Nancy Carroll, Billie Dove and Carole Lombard."

"I get the point, pal," he said. "I've fucked from the A-list too."

"Kay even succeeded in doing what Valentino couldn't," she said. "She seduced both of his former wives, Jean Acker and Natacha Rambova."

"So, why don't you face the music?" he asked. "Take the next boat back to the mainland and forget her. Get on with your life. I know your career is going badly right now, just like mine. But a lot of people out here who know talent think you've got it, kid, and that you can go places."

"I'm going places all right," she said, "right back to Broadway where I belong. I'll find stage work there. You'll see." She rose from the ground.

"I'm going to be leaving in a few days myself," he said. "I've got a great idea. Let's take the same train back East."

"I like you," she said, as if considering the possibility. A frown crossed her face. "Don't get the wrong idea. I could only give my heart to a woman—never a man."

"I'm an equal opportunity fucker," he said.

She looked down at him where he still lay on the ground. "Exactly what does that mean?"

"I fuck both straight women and lesbians," he said. "In fact, I've scored better with lesbians out here than I have with straight women. Lesbians sometimes tell me that I have the soul of a sensitive woman." He smiled at the absurdity of such an idea.

She laughed at that and reached down for his hand, and he took it, rising to stand beside her, looking out at the sea for a final time before heading back to their hotel. She was going to pack to return to the mainland, and he was going to get ready to stand in as Kenneth's best man at his wedding to Francis that afternoon.

"I would like some companionship on that train ride back to New York," she said. "Let's buy our tickets together."

"It's a deal," he said. "Mind if I seal it with a kiss?"

"I don't mind at all," she said. "Just so you don't get the wrong idea. But you wouldn't be the first man I've kissed."

"I know that," he said. "The story of you and David Selznick is all over town."

"Oh, David," she said with a sense of despair reflected on her face. "My burly, bespectacled pursuer. Not so long ago, he was completely smitten with me. And he got me work. But I fear he has other ladies in his life now."

"Are you completely off his list?" he asked.

"We did make a good-bye commitment," she said. "David claimed that he's going to become a bigtime producer. He said one day one of the greatest roles in Hollywood history would emerge, and that he'd cast me in the lead. My one chance for screen immortality."

"That's one God damn big promise," he said. "Pillow talk?"

"More than that," she said. "He had such sincerity in his eyes that I actually believed him. Who knows? It might happen one day. This is Hollywood."

"About that kiss?" he said.

"I guess I owe it to you," she said. "After all, you did intervene on my behalf with Kay." She fell into his arms, bestowing on him one of the most memorable kisses of his young life, complete with tongue. Lesbian or not, she was a skilled kisser. He was tremendously attracted to her but felt that any sudden and aggressive move would backfire at this point. On that long eastbound train ride, there would be plenty of time for his maneuvers.

As Bogie and Jean Arthur made their way along the dunes back to their hotel, it was with a certain irony that both of them would be caught up in David Selznick's casting call for *Gone With the Wind*.

Perhaps remembering his early promise to her, Selznick seriously considered casting Arthur as the charming, beguiling, and resourceful Scarlett O'Hara during his casting search for *Gone with the Wind*.

Amazingly, in one of the worst casting possibilities of all time, an idea so ludicrous it brought laughter from Hollywood insiders, the producer also briefly considered testing Humphrey Bogart for the role of Rhett Butler.

***

After he'd seen Jean Arthur off on the boat returning to the mainland, Bogie walked back to his hotel. It was still four hours before the wedding, and he felt at loose ends. He'd made a pact to return with Arthur on the train to the east coast, but the life that awaited him in New York filled him with dread.

He'd married two women he didn't love, and seemed to fall for a different woman every week. In Hollywood, all he had to do was stand still and the women came to him. He definitely felt that he could play romantic leads. Trouble was, no Hollywood director, including his former friend John Cromwell, felt the same way.

In the lobby as he was asking for his key, the young man at the reception desk handed him a note. It was from Kay Francis who asked him to visit her in her bedroom suite the moment he returned. She was not sharing a room with Kenneth, who had sailed to Catalina with his newly acquired friend, Anderson Lawler. The way Bogie figured it, Kenneth was helping Lawler get over the loss of Gary Cooper.

In the best suite at the hotel, the one with the wide terrace overlooking the ocean, Kay Francis was in a sheer silk nightgown. Inviting him in, she kissed him on the lips but seemed very distraught. He knew that Jean Arthur had left her suite only an hour ago, and that her departure had left Francis in this highly emotional state. She looked like one of the characters she played in one of her "Warner weepers."

"Jean wanted to possess me," Francis told Bogie as she seated him on her terrace and offered him some illegal booze. "I can't let that happen. Kay Francis belongs to the world. Her public. Not locked away in some little vine-covered cottage in northern California."

"You've got a point there, pal," Bogie said. "If you don't want to be tied down, though, why are you marrying Kenneth today?"

"We photograph well together," she said. "What more reason is needed?"

"That makes sense," he said. "I should have taken two brides that I take a good picture with. There are some photographs of Mary Philips and me that make me look like a Broadway faggot and Mary like a hook-nosed spinster who definitely won't get the beau in the third act."

"In our business, illusion is everything," Francis said. "I think Kenneth is handsome. A sort of dime-store Douglas Fairbanks Jr. Frankly, I could generate a hell of a lot more headlines if I married the real thing, providing Joan will let go of him. Their marriage, incidentally, is practically over."

"You don't need to be a Hollywood detective to know that," he said. "I think the Fairbanks kid and Crawford are the two most active stars in Hollywood. Both of them seem to be sexual athletes."

"I've had them both," Francis boasted. "Joan's much better in bed than Doug. At least Joan reciprocates. Doug is after his own pleasure too much to truly satisfy a woman."

"Thanks for telling me," he said. "I'll definitely cross him off my list."

"Don't do that because of what I said." She lit her own cigarette and sat down next to him on a chaise longue. "Kenneth has told me all about Doug. He's different with men than with women. Kenneth claimed Doug threw him the greatest fuck of his life. As for me, I found William Powell and Fredric March better. Your friend, John Cromwell, isn't bad either. He's already directed me in four of my movies. I even fucked two of the Marx brothers, Groucho and Harpo, when I made *The Cocoanuts* with them over at Paramount."

"Groucho sort of turns me on," he said facetiously, still somehow amazed at how Hollywood women talked so openly about their affairs.

"He isn't very good in bed," Francis said. "There's a lot of talk about what he's going to do with you and no action. He doesn't have all that much to work with, either. Harpo is much better."

"How was the great Maurice Chevalier that you and Dietrich seemed to be competing for?" he asked.

"A French fop," she said. "He's not all that good. He's more in love with himself. Marlene can have him. Actually he goes around denouncing homosexuals. But he's nothing but a faggot himself. Marlene told me he takes it up the ass, especially from this very handsome male companion he hires as a sort of secretary-valet."

"Well," he said, leaning back and looking out at the ocean, which seemed strangely turbulent today, as if a storm were about to descend from some mysterious place in the Pacific. "If you want an understanding husband, you'll find one in Kenneth. I confide all my secrets to him. He's wonderful."

"I adore Kenneth," she said. "When we're married, we'll both sit over the breakfast table the next morning and tell each other who we fucked the night before, leaving out none of the juicy details."

"A marriage made in heaven." He sighed, closing his eyes and enjoying the last of the sun's rays. The sun looked as if it were about to disappear for the day, leaving Catalina in a cloudy mist. He opened his eyes and looked over at Francis, as he was beginning to find her sexy. His mother, Maud, would view her as a loose woman, but he found her alluring in her debauchery. "You've been married before? Right?"

She merely nodded her head.

"Kenneth said you and I were born in the same year: 1899. That makes us two children of the 19th century."

Francis sat up, her anger flaring. "Dear Kenneth has got it all wrong. Before any wedding takes place today, I've got to straighten him out on that issue. I was born July 13, 1910 in Oklahoma City. The story of my birth traveled all over town. On the night I was born, my daddy got drunk and rode on horseback into our hotel. He rode the horse right through the hotel lobby and up this big staircase right to the door of our room."

"The hotel manager must have loved that," he said.

"My dad was such a drunk that my mother eventually divorced him," she said. "Before her marriage, my mother was a well-known actress, Katharine Clinton. After she left my daddy, her career never took off again. She took what roles she could. We made our way from one filthy, roach-infested theatrical boarding house to another. Sometimes all we had to eat for supper was overly salted popcorn and water from the tap."

As the noon sun faded, Francis claimed that she'd been educated at the Holy Angels convent in Fort Lee, New Jersey, and later at the Notre Dame School in Roxbury, Massachusetts. She would make those claims for the rest of her life. No records exist to prove that she attended either school.

"What made you take up acting?" he asked. "Following in your mother's footsteps?"

"Something like that," she said. "Actually I wanted to be a trapeze artist."

"That's funny," he said. "I saw you in *Dangerous Curves* with Clara Bow and Richard Arlen. Of all things you got to play a trapeze artist."

"I was great in the part," she claimed. "But I never planned to be an actress. My first role was as a man. My classmate, Katty Stewart, had written this play, *You Never Can Tell*. Since I was at an all-girl school, I was chosen to play the male lead."

"You're a great actress," he said, "but I could never mistake you for a man."

"Thanks," she said. "I later modeled for Leo Mielziner and had this mad affair with him."

"I've heard all about that one," he said. "Leo Mielziner, the father of your groom, Mr. Kenneth MacKenna. What the hell! You knew the father as David knew Bathsheba. Why not his son? That way, you're keeping all the fucking in the family."

"You asked me if I'd been married before," she said, "and I sort of avoided answering you. I was married in 1922 to James Dwight Francis. He was very handsome. His family from Pittsfield, Massachusetts, were rather wealthy. He was a playboy and drank like a fish. He used to beat me. That marriage lasted for about a year before I fled."

"Sorry it didn't work out," he said. "Don't worry about Kenneth. He's no wife-beater."

"I came to New York. Had this hot, hot affair with a handsome devil named Bill Gaston. He got me pregnant, or so I thought. I married him in secret. When I discovered I wasn't pregnant after all, we got a divorce. It was then that I rented an apartment with a newly acquired friend, Lois Long. It as through Lois that I learned I liked a woman's love a hell of a lot better than getting painfully jabbed by some man."

"I like women too," he said, reaching over to the coffee table and pouring himself another drink.

"In spite of this dreadful lisp I have," she said, "even worse than yours, I took to the stage. My first job was as an understudy to Katharine Cornell in *The Green Hat*. We had a torrid affair. Fortunately, she never missed a performance. Could you imagine me going on instead of the great Cornell?"

"Stranger things have happened on Broadway," he said.

"When I first came to Hollywood, the director, Millard Webb, cast me as the female lead opposite Walter Huston in *Gentlemen of the Press*. Somehow Millard was taken with me. The role originally called for a blonde menace but he ordered that it be changed to a brunette menace. He was worried about my lisp so he hired a dialogue coach, John Meehan, to teach me how to speak. After the first voice lesson, we were fucking and we married soon after that. But I quickly found out that John was interested in other things. That marriage ended so abruptly that I didn't even have time to tell my friends."

"Three marriages under your belt, and you're ready to do it again," he said. "You're a brave woman."

"Fools rush in where angels fear to tread," she said. "But I'm being very careful this time. You may have wondered why my note to you sounded so urgent," she said. "A bride-to-be inviting her groom's best man to her boudoir before the marriage."

"I thought you'd get around to telling me when the time came," he said.

"I talked to my lawyers in Los Angeles," she said. "Since Kenneth doesn't have a lot of money, they suspect he might be marrying me for mine. After all the starvation and poverty I've known in my day, I plan to hold onto what money I already have and what I make in the future. They've drawn up this prenuptial agreement. I want you to take it to Kenneth's room, have him sign it, and bring it back to me."

"I'll be your messenger boy," he said.

"There will be something in it for you if you do," she said enigmatically, getting up suddenly, presumably to retrieve the document.

She was gone about fifteen minutes as he stood drinking, smoking, and just looking at the ocean. When he got money, and if he ever returned to Hollywood, he wanted to buy a boat and sail over to Catalina every weekend. He could think of no better way to live than that.

"I've got the document ready and it's waiting on a table by the door," she said.

He turned around finding Francis standing nude in the doorway, assuming her most seductive pose. "Even before you deliver the papers, I want you to have your tip."

"Lady, you're giving me an instant hard-on," he said. "No wonder Jean Arthur fell so hard for you."

490

"Why don't you come over and heat up this cool, serene beauty and turn her into a raging wildcat of lust and desire?"

"That sounds like a line from one of your movies," he said. "Even so, it's an invitation I can't turn down. What's a best man for, if not to break in the bride for the groom?"

At three o'clock the wedding took place as scheduled in a little chapel at Avalon. After a lot of balking at first, Kenneth had signed the prenuptial agreement.

To the caretakers of the church, it was a fairly routine marriage performed in front of only a few friends. The only oddity about it was that Francis decided, for reasons known only to herself, to appear in the chapel as Greta Garbo and had proceeded to do a wicked imitation of the mysterious Swede during the entire ceremony.

That night as Bogie wandered slightly drunk and alone on the hotel grounds, he looked up several times at the bridal suite of Kenneth and Francis. Having so recently known what an accomplished trapeze artist Francis was in bed, he could only envy Kenneth the wedded bliss he was surely enjoying up in the suite Bogie had so recently vacated.

He wondered if Kenneth would ever fall in love with his own wife the way he had with Bogie's wife, Mary Philips. Thoughts of Mary crossed his mind. He imagined that at this very late hour in New York, his Mary was in the arms of "that God damn actor," Roland Young.

Bogie looked up one more time at the Francis/MacKenna wedding suite and headed off by himself into the night air.

He could not have even imagined that within a year Roland Young would be at Warner Brothers appearing opposite Kay Francis in *Street of Women*, and that Young and Francis would be engaged in a torrid romance.

***

In Joan Blondell's dressing room at Warner Brothers, Bogie had just finished showering after he'd bedded her on the carpet in front of her vanity table. She was his kind of broad. He liked her tremendously, although he wasn't in love with her. She was loyal, dependable, and always there for him when he needed a woman's company. She was warm, loving, and forgiving, and he felt that he could confide anything to her and she'd protect his secrets or else overlook his weaknesses.

He suspected that this former clerk at Macy's Department Store would never make it as a big star, but as an actress she'd always show up for Warner Brothers, taking any part offered, never complaining, never going on suspension, even if they worked her into dizziness, making four films at once.

She brought the same vitality to sex that she did to the gold-diggers she played on screen. She was brazen and fun to be with, and she didn't take herself too seriously. After bedding Blondell, he felt ten feet tall. He couldn't understand why James Cagney had dumped her.

After they'd dressed, he drove her over to the first screening of *Night Nurse*, the movie she'd recently made with Barbara Stanwyck and Clark Gable. The showing of the film was to be followed by a small private party at The Fat Black Pussycat.

On the way to the screening, he asked Blondell, "After we've each gone through two or three more spouses, do you think we'll get married and settle down somewhere in Ohio, growing old and gray together sitting out in our rockers on the front porch, watching people go to Sunday morning services?"

"I can see it now," she said. "Right before noon, I'll rise from my chair if my rheumatism will allow it, and head back into our little kitchen with its wood-burning stove. Bacon and eggs for you, and rutabagas mixed with mashed potatoes for me. That's my favorite dish."

In the lobby of the small theater, Bogie and Blondell encountered Ben Lyon and Bebe Daniels. Considering his brief past with both stars, he found conversation with them in such a public place stilted and awkward. Their marriage still seemed to be holding strong in spite of Lyon's romance with Howard Hughes and Daniels' own recent (or so it was rumored) affair with Douglas Fairbanks Jr., with whom she'd co-starred in *Reaching for the Moon*. Bogie wondered if there were any man or woman in Hollywood that Fairbanks Jr. wasn't having an affair with, or at least a one-night stand. These sexual dalliances must be one-night stands. Otherwise the poor, overworked actor wouldn't have the sperm count to make the rounds of so many bedrooms.

As a quartet, the team of Bogie/Blondell and Daniels/Lyon had little in common. After making polite excuses "to see you later at the party," Lyon disappeared with his beautiful Texas rose inside the theater.

After they'd gone, Blondell turned and looked up at him with her pop eyes. "I fear their greatest films are behind them." It was not meant as an unkind remark. She seemed to be stating a sad truth.

"C'mon, toots," he said. "If Daniels is fading, the star of Blondell is rising across the Hollywood sky. I bet I'm going to see a performance tonight that will make you next year's Oscar winner."

"Yeah, right," Blondell said, taking his arm as he escorted her into the theater. "With Stanwyck emoting all over the place and eating up the scenery, I'm gonna win the Oscar?"

As Bogie sat in the theater holding Blondell's hand, he'd seen only fifteen minutes of the 72-minute film when he realized that *Night Nurse*, in spite of its stellar cast, was not going to win Oscars for anybody. Playing a tough, scheming chauffeur, a character called Nick, Gable manhandles the cast, including Stanwyck, but the female members of the audience seemed to like this testosterone-driven violence. He wondered if most women secretly wanted a man to beat them up.

Unlike her usual screen portraits, and in spite of Blondell's appraisal, Stanwyck played her typical dancehall gal on one note throughout. Blondell had exaggerated. Stanwyck not only didn't eat up the scenery, she seemed strangely subdued in her role of Lora Hart, a young woman hired by a rich, drunken widow to act as a private nurse to her children. Not because he was holding her hand, but Bogie felt that Blondell brought the only life and humanity to the film. Ben Lyon's role of a breezy bootlegger could have been played by almost any actor in Hollywood, especially Bogie himself.

Bogie was startled to see Mildred Harris in the film in a part so small she practically wasn't even billed. Once she'd been the jailbait bride of Charlie Chaplin. How the big names of Hollywood's yesteryears had fallen, he thought. The era of the Talkies had hardly begun, yet the heyday of silent pictures seemed like something from an antediluvian past.

There was only polite applause at the end of the film. As the manager of the theater slipped the stars of *Night Nurse* out of the rear door, Bogie felt that that was an unnecessary precaution. He thought that Stanwyck, Lyon, Blondell, and Gable could have walked out the front door without being overpowered with any screaming fans demanding autographs.

As they made their way to their cars down an alleyway, two clever fans had figured out their escape route. To everyone's surprise, these two female autograph seekers cornered Mildred Harris demanding her autograph. The teenagers completely ignored Stanwyck, Blondell, Gable, and Lyon.

As Bogie walked along the alleyway with Blondell, he heard one of the fans demanding to know from Harris, "What is Charlie Chaplin really like?"

At The Fat Black Pussycat, the party was already in full swing when the cast of *Night Nurse* arrived. As they walked in, the crowd—mostly employees of Warner Brothers—loudly applauded their entrances. Bogie felt as if he—not Gable—had been one of the stars himself.

So far, Gable had only shaken his hand and had not seemed at all enthusiastic about meeting him. Maybe he didn't like the competition. After all, Bogie had come to Hollywood with the press billing of "Fox's answer to Clark Gable." Gable had seemed to size him up and dismiss him as no challenge in the way that Gary Cooper was.

On Gable's arm was the stunning blonde beauty, Madge Evans, with whom he'd co-starred in a film about horseracing, *Sporting Blood*. Evans didn't have large breasts, but what tits she did have she seemed to want to expose in a gown whose décolletage almost plunged to her navel.

The actors, including Blondell, were quickly sucked up by well-wishers. Bogie found himself standing alone with Gable's date. He asked Madge Evans if she wanted a glass of bootleg hooch, and she gladly accepted. She seemed miffed that she'd been so unceremoniously abandoned by her escort. Bogie wondered if Gable would even bother to take her home that night. Looking over on the far side of the room, Bogie saw Gable surrounded by three young actresses who looked far more gorgeous than Evans herself, and that was saying a lot.

He really didn't know what to make of Evans, nor, or so it seemed, did Holly-wood itself. He'd first heard about Evans from his friend, Alice Brady, who had worked with her in 1914 when Evans was a child star, appearing with other well-established actresses such as Marguerite Clark and Pauline Frederick. Bogie wondered if Evans was aware of Gable's affair with the older actress, Frederick. From silent screen diva Pauline Frederick to ingénue Evans, that Gable sure made the rounds. Perhaps he wasn't as active as Douglas Fairbanks Jr., but Gable seemed to attract women the way prize money lures people into contests. Bogie wondered if Harlow had lied. Surely the dick on such a lady-killer as Gable couldn't be all that inadequate, much less medically challenged.

With her drink in hand, Evans shared fond memories of Alice Brady with Bogie. Since both of them had been well-known child models, they also related on that level, laughing at how silly they must have seemed to the American pub-lic. Bogie claimed that friends still kidded him about his early fame as "the Maud Humphrey baby."

Evans herself had appeared as a child model who sat on a Fairy Soap bar and asked, "Have you a little fairy in your home?"

Suddenly Blondell was back at his side, kissing him on the lips and rescuing him from Evans, who wandered alone into the crush of the party, obviously hop-ing to reclaim Gable.

At the bar Blondell excused herself to go to the women's room. Bogie found himself standing next to Mildred Harris. "Glad to see you escaped those auto-graph hounds," he said.

"They were very kind," Harris said. "It's good to be remembered, even though my parts have become ridiculously small."

A little drunk and feeling his provocative self, he asked her, "So, did you tell those gals what Chaplin was really like?"

She frowned as she looked at him, as if Chaplin were a painful memory to her and she didn't want to be reminded of The Little Tramp. "Charlie Chaplin?" She made the name sound like a question. "Who in hell is that?" As her drink was served, she bolted it down in one gulp and demanded another. "What the fuck? If you must know, all dick—no man."

Getting into the swing of it, he leaned over and whispered in her ear, "Is it true that you also took the virginity of both Lillian and Dorothy Gish?"

As her second drink was served, she took it and held it tentatively. For one moment, he felt that she was going to toss its contents in his face. Instead she slapped him real hard and walked on.

Almost within the second, Blondell came back to the bar with Stanwyck on her arm. "She turn you down, Bogart?" Stanwyck asked. "I had her on the set of *Night Nurse*. Perhaps I'm more demanding as a lover than Lillian Gish, but I didn't find Harris all that great a lay."

Stanwyck too was drunk. Caught between two of the most provocative actors in Hollywood, Barbara Stanwyck and her future co-star, Humphrey Bogart,

494

Blondell excused herself and headed over to chat with the director of *Night Nurse*, William Wellman. Maybe she was seeking a role in his next picture.

That left Bogie standing alone at the bar with Stanwyck. "I hope you don't speak that way about all your former lovers," he said. "With my career in decline, it wouldn't do me any good if you spread the word that I'm a lousy lay, too."

"You're okay, Bogart," she said, downing a large shot of whiskey. "I've had bigger and I've had better. I sure as hell have had a lot smaller and a lot worse. I think men are just so much talk anyway. Joan Crawford knows how to make love better than that rotten whore of a husband of hers. The great screen lover, Rod La Rocque, would rather suck off William Boyd than me. That asshole actor, Philip Strange—did you catch me in my only silent, *Broadway Nights*—is aptly named. Lowell Sherman—*Ladies of Leisure*, remember? As for Sherman, Garbo can have him but I don't think she really wants him." She leaned over to him as if to whisper a deadly secret. "Get me another drink."

When he ordered it, he turned to Stanwyck again. "I don't know why but I'm going to tell you something I've told nobody," she said. "When Sherman took me to his home to fuck me, he insisted on strapping on this big black dildo. He likes to insert large objects into vaginas." She lowered her voice and looked around. "Don't tell anybody this but I have this theory. Sherman accompanied Fatty Arbuckle to San Francisco on that famous trip when fatboy inserted some blunt object into that hooker, Virginia Rappé, and ruptured her bladder. Based on my one encounter with Sherman, I would almost testify in court that it was Sherman—not Arbuckle—who inserted that blunt instrument himself."

"It was a milk bottle, or so I've heard," he said. "Your theory may be right. At least I've never heard it before."

"I know I'm right!" she said, almost angered as if challenged. "When it comes to murder, I'm never wrong."

"You know from having bedded me that I use the real thing," he said. "No dildo. As long as I can get junior to rise to the occasion, I don't need a fucking dildo."

Both were getting sloppy drunk and enjoying it. Stanwyck ignored his remarks about his own sexual prowess as if she weren't impressed. "I've also got this theory about who murdered William Desmond Taylor."

"You've solved Hollywood's most famous murder?" he said, practically mocking her boast. "Let's get Louella on the phone."

"Fuck, Louella," she said. She looked up at him, as a bemused expression came across her face. "Speaking of fucking Louella, don't tell me that you actually committed that dastardly deed. There's a rumor going around that you bedded the old bag."

"It's a God damn lie!" he said. "I never fucked Louella."

Stanwyck looked across the room at Gable, still surrounded by beautiful, aspirant actresses. "If Gable can get it up for Louella, so can you. You actors would fuck anything for a lousy part." Downing another drink, she said, "Now, listen, God damn it! I'm about to solve for you the most famous murder case in the world, and you don't even seem interested."

The director of *Night Nurse*, Willman, came over, pointedly ignoring Bogie. He asked Stanwyck to step over and pose with Blondell and him for a picture to run in *Variety*.

Without excusing herself, Stanwyck tottered off to be photographed, although Bogie felt that she looked disheveled.

He stood alone at the bar until Blondell arrived with the newspapers, each containing a review of *Night Nurse*.

Blondell grabbed his arm and retreated with him to a secluded table far removed from the crowd. "Read them," she said, shaking all over. She put her hand on his wrist, tightening her grip. "Don't read anything bad. I can't stand anything bad."

He quickly skimmed the reviews looking for some favorable comment about her. "Listen to this in *Film Daily*. 'Joan Blondell, in the role of a sister nurse to Miss Stanwyck, walks off with a big slice of the honors as a result of her wise-cracking and comedy antics.' Here's what the *Hollywood Reporter* said. 'The best things about *Night Nurse* are its title and cast names plus the Misses Stanwyck and Blondell stripping two or three times during the picture.'"

At that point several acquaintances of Blondell suddenly joined them at table, ending their private moment.

It was past two o'clock when he found himself standing at a urinal in the rear of The Fat Black Pussycat, emptying an overworked and booze-soggy bladder. A tall man came up to the urinal beside him and unbuttoned his fly. Like a pecker-checker, Bogie appraised the man's dick, figuring him to be a lightweight contender, no competition for him. It was only after checking out the man's small, uncut penis that he looked up into the face of his fellow pisser.

It was Clark Gable himself glaring back at Bogie.

"Listen, pal," Bogie said, "Harlow has told me all about the problem you have in not getting the skin to pull back. My father, Belmont Bogart, is a doctor. I can have him take the train out to Hollywood. He can nip off that elongated piece of skin, which you don't need anyway. Within four days, and I guarantee this, your little dickie will be up again raring for action. By the way, pal, with a little piece of okra like you've got, how did you become the stud of Hollywood?"

All Bogie remembered next was waking up on the tiled floor of the latrine. He'd been punched out cold.

***

"How in hell did you get into my apartment?" Bogie demanded of Eric Linden when he turned the key at eight o'clock the following night.

"Bogie!" Linden exclaimed, his face lighting up with happiness. He rushed to embrace him. "I've missed you something terribly."

Bogie barely responded to the hug. "Pal, you didn't answer my question. How in hell did you break into my apartment?"

"I didn't," Linden said. "I used a key. It was lying on a table next door in Kenneth's apartment. The key had your name on it. I'm looking after Kenneth's apartment while he's on his honeymoon with Kay. I figured instead of wasting my time sitting over there, I might as well come over here and make this place more homelike."

Bogie surveyed his apartment and didn't recognize the place under its transformation. For the first time since he'd moved in, it actually looked like someone could inhabit the joint comfortably. Every single item had been put away, fresh flowers filled the room, the floor was swept, and the furniture polished. From the kitchen came the aroma of a baking ham, one of his all-time favorite dishes. He wondered how Linden had found that out. Or was the ham baking in the oven a coincidence?

"Listen, kid, you're one good-looking mother fucker," Bogie said. "But if you think I'm gonna take you for my next wife, you can wipe that idea right out of your head. I may be the lone holdout in Hollywood, but I still like girls. I'm not Kenneth who can jump from bed to bed regardless of which sex is occupying it." He came over and gripped Linden's arm, tightening his hold. "Are you getting that through your lovesick skull?"

"I know all that," Linden said, breaking away. "It would have been great to fall in love with someone who would reciprocate, someone to love me back. I may be just a kid but I know that life doesn't quite work in that orderly manner. You're the object of my affections, my desire, really. And you don't give a shit about me."

"Don't use the word shit around me," Bogie cautioned him. "I can't stand that word."

"It will never cross my lips again," Linden promised.

"I'm grimy," he said. "I'm going into my bedroom to take a shower. When I come out, I want you gone. Thank you for cleaning up the apartment. I appreciate that. Thanks also for the fresh flowers, the dinner cooking in the oven. But I'm eating alone tonight. If I get horny later on, and I just might, the trusty fingers on my right hand will get lucky tonight. And that's the way it's gonna be until I find the right woman who will do for this place what you've done for me."

Linden looked crestfallen as if he didn't know what to say. "Have I done something wrong?" He seemed bewildered. "I mean, I just wanted to have everything perfect for you."

"It is," Bogie said, scanning the room again. "You're quite a homemaker. But me and you don't make it."

"I'll settle for friendship," Linden said. "Anything to be around you, even if you use me as your doormat."

"You should have more self-respect than that," Bogie said.

"I know what I want." Linden seemed adamant.

"And I know what I don't want." Bogie turned from the young man's intensity and headed for his bedroom where he shut the door, pulled off his clothes, and walked toward the bathroom. He was going to stand for a long time under that shower tonight, running the water as hot as he could stand it, turning his small bathroom into a steam room.

After the cleansing of his life, he finally emerged into the steam-filled room searching for a large towel he'd lifted from a hotel. He was suddenly confronted with Linden who not only had the towel but unfolded it and proceeded to dry his back.

Linden didn't say a word, and neither did Bogie. The way Bogie figured it, attendants in the few Turkish baths he'd attended had performed the same service for him that Linden was doing right now. The kid was doing a real good job of drying him off. Bogie had never been dried off with love before. If Linden got his kicks performing this task for him, Bogie felt comfortable with it. However, he issued a word of caution. "Just the back part. I'll dry myself in front. I don't want you to get the wrong idea."

After he was fully dried off, Bogie stalked nude into his bedroom and opened the top drawer to his chest of drawers. He was confronted with a dozen new pairs of fancy underwear, far more expensive looking than any he'd ever owned.

He turned to confront Linden, who still stood at the door to his bathroom, taking in the sight of his nude body. "What happened to my own underwear? I'd grown kind of fond of it?"

"I replaced them," Linden said. "Even the dirty pairs you kept in that clothes hamper over there."

"That so?" Bogie said. "Even the ones with the skid marks on them?"

"Even those." Linden said. "I'll treasure them always."

"Whatever turns you on, kid," Bogie said, slipping into his new underwear. He had to admit these new drawers felt a hell of a lot better on his skin than his old ones.

"Do I really have to go?" Linden asked. "I've worked for three hours on dinner. Can't I even be allowed to serve it?"

"Come to think of it," Bogie said, "I'm starved and that ham smells awful good."

"I'm hungry too," Linden said. "Just as hungry as I used to be when I was taking every job I could get to help support my mother after my father abandoned her and my brothers and sisters."

Somehow that did it for Bogie. He felt a compassion for Linden he'd never felt for anyone. He put his arm around him. "Thanks for cooking dinner. I'll get dressed and be in the kitchen in a minute or so. I'd consider it a privilege if you'd eat with me. After all, you cooked it."

Linden's face brightened. "Thanks," he said, before leaving the bedroom and heading for the kitchen.

Fifteen minutes later Bogie found himself enjoying his best home-cooked meal since he'd arrived on The Coast. None of his friends knew how to cook. Linden had even baked a loaf of fresh bread. It turned out to be a Swedish rye made with a beer batter. "Alcoholic bread," Bogie said, smiling at Linden for the first time. The young man got him to taste a big helping of creamed broccoli, a first for Bogie. He loved that dish as well as the Swedish pancakes with lingonberries Linden had served. "Never had that kind of berry before. This is God damn good. You sure know how to cook. Your mama must have taught you."

"I taught myself," Linden said. "My poor mother never had much to put on the table. Sometimes all we had was a little bit of food I bought with what I'd earned that day hawking newspapers on the streets."

As the dinner progressed, Bogie's respect for the young actor increased enormously. Bogie himself had been a fairly privileged kid born to a comparatively rich family. Because of his own cushioned background, he was always in awe of kids such as Linden who'd been thrown out on the streets of New York at too early an age and told they had to survive in any way they could.

Later, as they sat in the living room drinking, Linden told him his whole sad story of growing up. By the time he was thirteen, he was selling himself to older men in exchange for a dollar. "I didn't have to do anything to them," the young man claimed. "Just go with them somewhere in a dark alley and drop my pants. Sometimes I had to endure no more than two or three minutes of stabbing pain before it was all over. That's what most guys wanted to do—fuck me. A few wanted to give me blow-jobs, and that was the easiest money of all. One old man gave me five dollars one day, and that was the most money I'd ever had in my pocket at one time. For the first time in a year, I was able to buy a slab of beef to cook for mother and my family. I was real proud of myself that day. It was easy for me to forget how I'd earned it."

"You're amazing," Bogie said. "I don't think I know anyone who came up like you. When I first came in the door, I never thought I'd be saying this. But I like you. Don't misunderstand me. Personally I have nothing against homosexuals. As you know, Kenneth is my best friend. I confide everything in him. I knew a lot of homosexuals on Broadway. Clifton Webb is a special friend of mine. Many of my best friends out here are homosexuals."

"You mean, Spencer Tracy?" Linden asked.

"Spence is not a homosexual. He fucks anything. Call him pansexual."

Linden laughed and somehow Bogie found that endearing. Sitting on the sofa, he reached over and put his arm around Linden. For some reason he felt protective of him, the way a father feels for a son.

"Don't be afraid to touch me," Linden said. "I understand where I stand with you. I'll make no moves on you. I want more but I'll be content to settle for a warm friendship."

Bogie withdrew his arm. "Just so long as you understand what the score is." He got up to walk across the room to pour himself another stiff drink. He felt like pulling a big drunk tonight. He offered Linden some more booze but he said he didn't want another drink.

Bogie studied Linden carefully. As he was to tell Kenneth later, for the first time in his life he felt a nascent desire to be the father of a son "Sometimes I think I'm missing out on a lot of fun by not being a bisexual," he said. "Everybody I know, especially Kenneth and Spence, are having the time of their life out here. They're experiencing far more thrills than I'll ever know. But making love to a man is just not in my heart. I've tried to fake it a time or two, but I think I was dreaming of a woman while I did it."

"It's okay," Linden said reassuringly. "Maybe in time you'll change your mind. If you do, I'll be here for you."

"I'll be old and gray by then," Bogie predicted.

"Never too old for me" Linden said. "I don't care how decrepit you become, you'll always be welcome to put your shoes under my bed any time."

"That sounds like love," Bogie said.

"It is!" Linden said that with the same intensity he'd display before the cameras in his upcoming juvenile films.

"Don't get me wrong, and don't feel that there's anything wrong with you," Bogie said. "There's no doubt about one thing: you are the prettiest young boy in Hollywood. If you were a gal, I'd be right in that bedroom next door fucking your brains out."

"Just hearing you say that is music to my ears," Linden said.

The phone rang. Bogie wondered if this were another invitation for a late night rendezvous.

He was surprised to hear Douglas Fairbanks Sr. on the other end of the phone. "Hi, Bogie," he said. "I'm sure you remember our night on the town and you taking me to your apartment."

"How can I ever forget a night like that?" Bogie asked.

"It's your apartment I'm calling about," Fairbanks said. "I really got lucky tonight. I'm in desperate need of an apartment, and I don't want to be seen going to a hotel with this lovely lady, whose face is becoming almost as famous in Hollywood as my own."

"Listen, if you want the bedroom, you're welcome to it. I'm here..." He paused, almost as if he were going to say "alone." "I'm here entertaining a male friend."

"If it's a male friend, that's okay," Fairbanks said. "The lady isn't shy around men, but she wouldn't want another woman to see her with me. After all, men can keep secrets. For a woman, that's biologically impossible."

"Come on over," Bogie said, "and have a drink with us. My friend Eric and I will fade into the night after the first drink. The night is yours. Or hers."

"You're a real pal," Fairbanks said. "I won't forget this when the next film role comes up, one that would be ideal for you."

"That sounds intriguing," Bogie said. "At last I've found out how to get cast

500

in something."

"I'll also leave five-hundred bucks on your coffee table before departing."

"That's a lot of money but it won't be necessary."

"Time is precious," Fairbanks said, "and the lady might change her mind."

Bogie could hear the sound of a woman's voice in the background.

Fairbanks came back onto the phone. "What in hell am I being so secretive about my lady friend here? She just confessed that she's visited your apartment before. See you in fifteen minutes."

After Bogie put the phone back on its receiver, the tantalizing words of Fairbanks seemed to ring in his ear. Who was this mysterious date? Surely not Billie Dove? He turned to Linden. "A Hollywood legend is about to mount those stairs out there. If I know this character, he'll take the steps three at a time." He paused. "Incidentally, he'll be accompanied by his lady love. She'll probably be some famous movie star herself. Let's get out our autograph books."

"Too bad," Linden said, looking disappointed. "I was hoping we could be alone."

"There will be other nights for that," Bogie said.

Linden's face lit up. "Do you really mean that?"

"Of course, I do," Bogie said. "But it's a friendship, not a love affair. There's no reason we can't keep company with each other."

"That will be fine," Linden said, "so long as you don't expect me to go on the town with you looking for dames."

Bogie smiled and walked over to Linden. He ran his hand affectionately across Linden's smooth cheek. "You're okay, kid." He surveyed his apartment once more. "Considering the distinguished company about to descend on us, thank God you made my joint look livable."

"You may not believe this," Linden said. "But this is the happiest night in a life that's not had too much to be happy about before now."

It was the beginning of a beautiful friendship.

***

The bell rang, and Bogie went to open the door.

The great Douglas Fairbanks Sr. was expected. Although Bogie felt that nothing in Hollywood could ever shock him again, he was startled to see the date of the swashbuckling actor. She had indeed visited Bogie's apartment before.

Fairbanks' daughter-in-law came right up to him and kissed him on the lips.

"Good to see you again, Bogart," she said. "Thanks for inviting us over."

It was Joan Crawford in a rather dazzling white gown cut low.

As superstars, Fairbanks and Crawford were gracious and charming to Bogie, since he was, after all, their host and was doing them a favor. Both stars hardly acknowledged Linden, and seemed a bit put off that this relatively obscure actor was in a position to be privy to their darkest secret.

As Crawford sat across from Linden and Bogie, holding Fairbanks' hand and gazing affectionately into his eyes, she looked like everything Mary Pickford wasn't. Instead of the delicate, sensitive "America's Sweetheart" roles that Pickford had played in Silents, Crawford was the exact opposite. She was brash, energetic, a dancing chorine who had emerged into the public's eyes as a flapper. She was still identified as one of *Our Dancing Daughters* before she'd go on to reinvent herself several times before her twilight years.

As Louella Parsons had loudly proclaimed at parties, "Joan Crawford has snatched the boy with the famous name from the cradle. Little Baby Doug even had to lie about his age to get a marriage license. He claimed he was nineteen. This marriage is just making Doug Sr. look far older than he is."

That time, Parsons got it right.

What Parsons didn't know was the story unfolding on the sofa in front of Bogie. Douglas Fairbanks had the hots for Joan Crawford, daughter-in-law or not. Parsons' famous weak kidneys would surely fail her on the most expensive Hollywood sofa if she got wind of this.

"I think I first fell in love with Doug," she said, pausing awkwardly. "Senior, that is, on the night of this fancy dress ball. Everybody who is anybody in Hollywood was there."

"Eric and I weren't," Bogie said facetiously.

A sudden silence came over the room. Obviously Crawford didn't like one of her stories interrupted. "I wore this beautiful baby blue formal gown with a train that could stretch to New York. That idiot, Robert Montgomery, stepped on it. I think he did it on purpose. Uncle Douglas, as I called him then, saved the day. He swung my train over his arm and we kept right on going. With the grace of a true Prince Charming, he guided me through the long line of VIPs, and no one was the wiser. It was then and there I decided that Doug was my kind of man."

"I've asked Joan to marry me," Fairbanks said.

Surely he was joking, Bogie thought.

"As soon as I get Mary to agree to divorce me," Fairbanks added.

"That would be needed, of course," Bogie said. For once, he tried to conceal the sarcasm in his voice.

"And, of course, as soon as Joan's divorce from your son comes through," Linden said.

Crawford glared at him, but didn't say anything. There was no expression on Fairbanks' face at all, although he pointedly ignored Linden.

Years from that day, Bogie would try to understand why Douglas Fairbanks Sr. seemed to go temporarily insane for about six weeks in his life. As his own career faded and his looks dissipated, his resentment of his good-looking and photogenic son grew more pronounced. Bogie had heard that there had been many arguments at Pickfair when Jesse Lasky, a partner of Adolph Zukor, had offered the thirteen-year-old, Fairbanks Jr., a movie contract. Fairbanks Sr. had been bitterly opposed to that, claiming that Lasky was "just trying to capitalize off my fame," and that Lasky was promoting his son, the handsome new star-in-the-making, as a way of "getting even with me, the king of silent pictures, for past grievances."

With Crawford as his trophy, Fairbanks Sr. seemed locked in a bitter contest for male supremacy with his own son. By seducing his daughter-in-law, Fairbanks Sr. asserted that he was the more virile of the father-son pair. That his son had practically set his wife adrift did not seem to have occurred to the older Fairbanks. His son was out every night with another woman or another man, and seemed to have lost all interest in his legal spouse.

Crawford's motivation in pursuing the older Fairbanks seemed all too career motivated. By wedding the "king of Hollywood," would that not make her the queen of Hollywood? Certainly the marriage would be the scandal of the world, knocking Garbo and all other stars off the front pages for at least a year.

Bogie felt that they were making a dangerous and impulsive move with all the wrong motivations. If Fairbanks Sr. divorced Mary Pickford, and Joan Crawford divorced her husband, and Fairbanks Sr. and Crawford married each other, it would destroy all their careers. The movie-going public in 1931 could not tolerate such a marital rearrangement. The way Bogie saw it, Fairbanks Jr. would emerge relatively unscathed and could go on with his career, as he was sure to gain the sympathy vote.

Momentarily flattered by the attentions of Joan Crawford, the elder Fairbanks would in short time regain his senses. Even so, he'd go on to marry a woman twenty years his junior, Lady Sylvia Ashley, whose husband publicly accused her of adultery.

"Uncle Douglas" would die in 1939, and Lady Ashley would in time marry Clark Gable. During that marriage, Crawford continued her lifelong affair with Gable. Gable's attempt to turn Mary Pickford into his mistress failed. When he couldn't get Pickford to have an affair, he proposed marriage. She turned him down to marry that cute Buddy Rogers instead, "American's Boyfriend" wedding "America's Sweetheart."

The last time Bogie had seen Pickford's husband-to-be, he was lying flat on his back getting plugged by Douglas Fairbanks Jr. As Bogie was to confide in Eric Linden later that night, "Hollywood at bedtime is a very incestuous place."

When Bogie had talked to William Haines about his best friend, Joan Crawford, whom he called "Cranberry," Haines had told him that "to win her hand a man must be both a bull and a butler."

As Fairbanks Sr. and Crawford sat across from him, Bogie felt that Haines had nailed it. Fairbanks was still holding onto his career, still the king of Holly-wood although about to be replaced by Clark Gable, Crawford's other lover. But Bogie noticed that he had entered the apartment a few paces behind her, letting her make a star's solo entrance if only into a dingy apartment.

He also carried her lapdog and a knitting bag, since Crawford was always knitting. As he sat with her on the sofa, he was very solicitous of his new mistress, lighting her cigarettes or refreshing her drink. Unlike everybody else in the room, Fairbanks did not drink.

Somehow "Don Juan," as Bogie privately referred to Fairbanks Sr., could perform all these tasks for Crawford without losing his masculinity.

A silence came over the room. Maybe everybody was thinking the same thing. There was a certain irony here. Fairbanks Sr. had gone to great measures to prevent his son from marrying Crawford, the very thing he was now contemplating for himself. Bogie had heard that Fairbanks Sr. had even purchased the famous blue movie that Crawford had made in New York, the one Bogie had seen with Texas Guinan. Suddenly Crawford slammed her drink down on the table. She looked over at Bogie. "Gentlemen," she said, "I bet you two love-birds have an appointment somewhere. Los Angeles is a big town. Surely you're due somewhere else tonight."

"I see your point," Bogie said, getting up. He motioned to the bedroom. "Everything's spic and span," he said, "thanks to Eric here."

"Thank God," Crawford said. "The last time I was here I had to clean Bogart's bathroom. It was one filthy mess." She smiled at Linden, the first time she'd acknowledged him all night.

After saying good night to Crawford and Fairbanks Sr., Bogie stood outside his apartment complex. Linden had reluctantly trailed along, although he'd urged Bogie to retreat with him to Kenneth's apartment "so we can be alone."

Bogie didn't think that was such a good idea. Instead he walked for several blocks with Linden until he tired of that and suggested that they retreat to The Fat Black Pussycat where he was always welcomed.

Later that night at the after hours club, three starlets, one of them a buxom blonde, approached Bogie's table, trying to pick up these two handsome young men. Linden ignored them completely, but Bogie spoke to each of them, turning down their offers. The buxom blonde said, "Oh, well, the two of you have each other. What do you need a woman for? Silly me. It's obvious that neither one of you would know what to do with a woman anyway." With that, she'd stormed off.

While sitting and talking with Linden for a few hours at The Fat Black Pussycat, Bogie cemented his bond with the beautiful young man. Far from being turned off by Linden as he was at first, he was beginning to like the total adoration he was getting, providing it wasn't linked to performing sexually with Linden. Bogie had never known anyone who completely worshipped him.

He knew that Linden could have any man he wanted in Hollywood. Howard Hughes, Spencer Tracy, even Douglas Fairbanks Jr. Certainly Kenneth MacKenna would leave the bed of his bride, Kay Francis, to service Linden. Considering the competition, Bogie was flattered.

As Bogie's thoughts drifted from the conversation, Linden suddenly said something that arrested his attention again. "You know, I will eventually get you."

"I don't know that at all," Bogie countered.

504

"Not tonight or even tomorrow or even next month," Linden said. "In time I'll have you, and I'll be so good that you'll like it and want me to repeat it again and again."

"I don't deny that it's possible to get any man in the whole world if you try long and hard enough, and he's had enough to drink. It seems to me to be a waste of time, though. The way I see it, you're pretty enough to have any man in Hollywood you want, even the straight ones. Why not go for Clark Gable himself?"

"His dick is too small," Linden said.

"You've got a point there," Bogie said, remembering that ill-fated encounter with Gable at the latrine.

"I'm more into what you've got hanging between your legs," Linden said. His tongue darted out between pink, succulent lips.

Bogie turned away. The sight looked too enticing, as he was later to relate to Kenneth when he returned from his honeymoon.

In a way, by having Linden fall in love with him, Bogie was scoring a point over his best pal, Kenneth. Even though Linden had seduced Kenneth several times already, it was to Bogie that the boy was expressing his love.

It was 5am when Bogie left The Fat Black Pussycat. Linden had urged Bogie to let him return to the apartment, if only to hold him in his arms that night, but Bogie turned him down. "I need to be by myself to think over some things," he told Linden. "I figure that even a swordsman like Don Juan must have satisfied himself with our darling Joan by now, and I'll have the place to myself."

After Bogie had promised to meet Linden for lunch tomorrow, the young man reluctantly faded away into the early dawn.

Back at his apartment, Bogie was mildly perturbed that Crawford and Fairbanks hadn't even locked his front door. To his surprise, he spotted Crawford's gown and lingerie on the sofa. Figuring that Fairbanks had gone to sleep in his bedroom with Crawford, Bogie turned off the light.

As he was retreating out the door, he heard movement in the bedroom. "Is that you, Bogart?" Crawford called out.

"It's me," he said. "You guys carry on. I'll sleep next door in Kenneth's apartment."

"Like hell you will!" Crawford said.

He looked over to his bedroom door where Joan Crawford stood completely nude, the memory evoking Kay Francis' same appearance in her hotel suite on Catalina Island.

Crawford positioned herself, especially her legs, in her most alluring and seductive fashion, as if she were camera ready for another porno flick.

"Tonight it's sloppy seconds for you," she said.

He moved toward her to claim his prize.

***

505

Knowing it was going to be his last day on the Fox lot, Bogie arrived three hours before his scheduled meeting with Winfield Sheehan, head of production. He was sure going to miss his paycheck of $750 a week. Although he'd meant to save most of it, he never got around to doing that, seemingly thinking the money would last forever.

He did have a stash from Howard Hughes based on that tycoon's payment for such favors as escorting Jean Harlow to Mexico or delivering a freshly showered and all dressed-up Alabama cowboy, Johnny Mack Brown, to Hughes' doorstep.

If he counted all his stash, Bogie figured that he'd be getting on that train to New York with Jean Arthur with about $10,000, the most money he'd ever had at one time in his whole life. He could only hope that it would tide him over in Depression-riddled New York until he found a job in the theater.

Maybe once again the Brady family might come to his rescue, as they had when he returned from his term of duty in the Navy. Bill Brady Jr. had been his best friend for many years, and before he left for Hollywood, Bogart had sincerely intended to write to him frequently. But in Hollywood Bogie had turned to Kenneth MacKenna as his confidant instead. Those letters to family and friends back in New York were meant to be written but never were.

Bogie was uncertain where he would even stay in New York. It seemed hardly likely that Mary Philips, as she prepared to divorce him, would want him living with her and that actor, Roland Young, her new love.

Bogie was sitting outside a sound stage on the edge of a curb, his face buried in his hands. He must have looked a pathetic sight when Herb Gallagher approached him. He'd seen the elderly man puttering about the studios, but had never spoken to him.

"Everybody knows Winnie is going to fire you this morning," Gallagher said. "But you're a young man. You'll find work at other studios. Maybe Warners. I'd say Paramount but the smart money is that they're about to go belly-up."

Bogie looked up at the man, squinting his eyes to blot out the morning sun. "You're the janitor, right? I mean everybody here, even the janitor, is in on the details of my getting the boot?"

"I don't mean to get you riled up," Gallagher said, "but your pictures have bombed. You've bombed. Frankly, you were lucky to get that $750 a week. I don't know how you conned them into that."

"Hell, you even know what salary I was drawing," Bogie said. "Are there no secrets in Hollywood?"

"You know the answer to that," Gallagher said, spitting out some tobacco juice only three feet from Bogie. "I was fired myself by Winnie."

"Then why are you still here?" Bogie asked, standing up in hope of avoiding getting hit with the next launch of tobacco juice.

"I was the chief script reader back in 1924," Gallagher said. "When I turned down three scripts that later became hits at other studios, I was canned."

"As I said, why are you still here?" Bogie asked.

506

"I know too much about Winnie to get the final boot like you're about to get this morning," Gallagher said. "Winnie let me stay on. Instead of reading scripts, I get to sweep up the sound stages. It's a living."

"I once thought Sheehan was going to be my big white hope," Bogie said. "In spite of all the trouble he causes, Spencer Tracy still has a contract, and I don't."

"Maybe Winnie's judgment about you is all wrong," Gallagher said. "From the looks of you, I don't see it, but you could go on to become a big star in spite of your ugly mug, puny body, your lisp, and that scar on your mouth."

"You sure know how to make a guy feel good on the day he's about to be kicked out in the midst of a Depression."

"What the hell!" Gallagher said. "That's how the game is played out here. Look at Pola Negri and Gloria Swanson. The two biggest screen vamps of the Twenties. Now they can't get arrested. Look at John Gilbert. The biggest screen idol of the Silents."

"I know, I know," Bogie said impatiently. "I've read all the screen biographies in the fan magazines."

"In two, maybe three years, Winnie himself will be out the door when a better, more aggressive, and more talented producer comes along. Winnie doesn't know that much about film-making any way. William Fox gave him the job because Winnie blackmailed him."

"What sort of blackmail?" Bogie asked. "Sexual?"

"Nothing like that," Gallagher said. "At one time Winnie was the secretary to the police commissioner in New York. Fox routinely violated the bylaws of the Motion Picture Patents Company. Somehow, and I don't know how he did it, Winnie covered for Fox and kept him two feet in front of the law during all Fox's time in New York. When Fox pulled up stakes and headed west, his boy Winnie was in too."

"So that's how you became head of production at a major studio," Bogie said.

"Winnie didn't know a fucking thing about movies when he got to Hollywood," Gallagher said. "He was just a teenager when he joined the Army to fight in the Spanish-American War. After he came back to New York, he was a cub reporter and then a police reporter. He gave that up to work for the police commissioner. Now he's making and breaking stars. In with Spencer Tracy, out with Humphrey Bogart."

Gallagher was called back to duty, and Bogie wandered alone into the Fox commissary where only three tables were full. He decided that he'd order ten cups of black coffee before facing Sheehan.

In time, Bogie would learn that the janitor knew exactly what he was talking about. By 1935, when Fox emerged with Twentieth Century, Sheehan was out, having been replaced by a far more talented and brilliant producer, Darryl Zanuck, who had managed to get rid of Sheehan for $360,000 in severance pay.

As he sat drinking those endless cups of coffee, Bogie came to realize that his whole attempt to become a movie star was a bit ridiculous. At that very moment, he felt that he was the least likely candidate in Hollywood to become a movie actor.

When he'd made *Up the River* with Tracy, Bogie had had such high hopes of stardom, but it'd been a downward spiral ever since. He felt that he was better looking than Tracy but his friend could act, and Bogie wondered if he even knew what acting was all about. Bogie could snarl and hiss, or even look vapid but he couldn't be as natural or as convincing on screen as Tracy was. As the director, Raoul Walsh, had once barked at Bogie on the set of *Women of All Nations*, "Footage of actors like you end up on the cutting-room floor."

At eleven o'clock that morning, Bogie, jittery from too much coffee, was ushered into the office of Winnie Sheehan. The studio chief was known for his gregarious style and a certain charm, but Bogie found his dapper boss with his "black Irish features" and his legendary "ol' baby blues" rather dour today. At that time, Sheehan was known for chasing skirts and throwing the best parties more than he was celebrated for making great movies. Without looking up at Bogie, he sat at his desk going over some papers, not bothering to greet the actor or shake his hand. Sheehan routinely fired stars, directors, and studio executives every day.

"Bogart," he said in a sharp voice, looking up at him for the first time as he signaled for him to take a stiff armchair in front of his desk. "You're not only untalented, but you're in violation of your contract's morals clause."

"I've bedded a few dames since coming out to the West Coast," Bogie said. "Any law against that?"

"Not against that," Sheehan said. "If there was, I'd be locked away in the dankest cell. No one fucks higher on the list than Winnie Sheehan. Only A-list pussy. When I want a piece of ass, I go only for stars: Jean Harlow, Sally Eilers, Joan Crawford, Elissa Landi, Joan Bennett, Ann Dvorak, Myrna Loy, Sidney Fox. Even Helen Twelvetrees."

"*Even her?*" Bogie said, rather mockingly.

If Sheehan knew he was being ridiculed, he gave no indication of it. "It's this *panz* stuff I'm concerned about." He reached into his top drawer and removed a candid eight-by-ten snapshot which he handed to Bogie.

Bogie studied the picture carefully. He was drunk at the time, and hardly remembered the photograph being taken. It was either at The Fat Black Pussycat or Jimmy's Backyard. In the picture Bogie sat between Edmund Lowe and Lilyan Tashman, with his arm around each of them. Also in the picture was Billy Haines, with his arm around Anderson Lawler. At the far left of the picture Charles Farrell was paying more romantic attention to Kenneth MacKenna than he was to the actor's new bride, Kay Francis.

"You not only go to *panz* clubs," Sheehan charged, "but I heard you attended an all-male lingerie party Richard Arlen threw for Kenneth MacKenna."

"That's true," Bogie said with candor. "I was seen there running around in my Skivvies." He handed the glossy photograph back to Sheehan. "For your bathroom wall," he said, a bite of sarcasm in his voice.

"That overseer of Hollywood morals, Will Hays, has been warning me about using dual-sex boys and lesbos in Fox films," Sheehan said. "If directors like George Cukor had their way, all men in film would be effeminate, flaunting their perversions on screen. I've had a study made of all Fox pictures by my assistant, Sidney Kent. His conclusion is that the sooner we get away from fairies and degenerates in our scripts, and the more family-oriented we become, the bigger the profits for Fox." He picked up a letter on his desk. "Here's what Kent wrote. 'The fairies must be sent packing back to New York where they belong.'"

"Unless I misread the scripts, I wasn't aware that I'd been playing flaming pansies on the screen," Bogie said.

"It's implied in your performances," Sheehan said. "Up against real he-men on the screen, guys like Victor McLaglen or Spencer Tracy, you come across like a lisping queen. I know you played all those faggot juvenile roles on Broadway, coming out in fancy sports dress with a tennis racket and cruising all the handsome men on stage, inviting them for a game of tennis. What the smart people in the audience knew was that you really wanted one of them to join you in the showers after the game."

Bogie chuckled at that preposterous summation of his stage career. "Hey, let's don't get carried away here. I never played any such part. Ask the directors like John Cromwell. And playwrights like Maxwell Anderson."

"It was a subtle thing and you could get away with it on the New York stage," Sheehan said. "But the camera picks up the slightest nuance. For example, *Variety* a few months ago ran an article about all the pansy dancers and chorus boys used in musicals. It demanded that from now on every studio cast real he-men as chorus boys. If a boy is just too dainty and pretty, he's going to be out on his ass in the musicals of the Thirties. And fussy, over-marcelled hair is out too. Film-goers, especially male film-goers, resent seeing effeminate men on the screen. I've seen all the footage you've shot for Fox at the ridiculously overinflated salary of $750 a week. There must have been a typo in your contract. It should have read $75 a week, and even then you would have been overpaid. Let's face the truth: You've got some effeminate mannerisms, and they're even more intolerable because of your lisp."

"So, you're saying that I'm getting kicked out on my ass because I act like a pansy on the screen?" Bogie asked, not concealing his anger which had flared suddenly.

"You amaze me with your perception," Sheehan said sarcastically. "I think my point is obvious. My recommendation is that you give up acting. You and that co-star of yours in *Bad Sister*, Bette Davis, have no talent. Neither of you have presence on the screen. She looks like a little lost wren, and you look like a sneaky rat. You're not ugly enough to play a villain like Edward G. Robinson, nor handsome enough to be a leading man like Joel McCrea. You've made your last picture for Fox."

"I think I figured that out even before I came into your office today," Bogie said.

"The camera, my boy, is an amazing thing," Sheehan said in worshipful tones. "It creates an illusion of reality so great that it can surpass reality. All studios, not just Fox, have got to show a greater respect for the camera and not parade freaks of nature before it. Guys like John Gilbert, Billy Haines, Ramon Novarro."

"And you're adding the name of Humphrey Bogart to that list of queens?" Bogie asked in astonishment.

"If the shoe fits, wear it," Sheehan said harshly. "Tomorrow's screen belongs to the Clark Gables or the Gary Coopers. You won't find those two out sucking dick or taking it up the ass any more. We've also got to have real he-men directors like Raoul Walsh, not fancy-pantsy George Cukor, directing real men like my latest discovery, Marion Morrison. For *The Big Trail*, I had him get rid of that pansy name and call himself John Wayne. To get ahead in the Twenties, Wayne occasionally let one or two of the stars of his films suck his dick, hoping for a big break. And Clark Gable did the same thing. So had Gary Cooper. Wayne confided to me the names of guys who had gone down on him: Billy Haines in *Brown of Harvard*, John Gilbert in *Bardelays the Magnificent*, Richard Barthelmess in *The Drop Kick*, George O'Brien in *Salute* and again in *A Rough Romance*, and your faggot buddy, Kenneth MacKenna in *Men Without Women*. And now, like Cooper and Gable, Wayne is a star. He won't have to drop his pants ever again for a Hollywood cocksucker."

"When history books are written years from now, I'm sure they'll credit Winfield Sheehan with bringing masculinity to the movies," Bogie said bitterly.

Sheehan took him seriously. "And they'll be right. I did pretty well with George O'Brien in *The Iron Horse*. George is one he-man. I nicknamed him The Chest. In fact, I did all the publicity for *The Iron Horse* in 1924. I came up with the line, 'George O'Brien is not a sheik or a caveman or a lounge lizard. He's a man's man and the idol of women.' Not bad, huh?"

"That sure would have lured me into a movie house," Bogie said, still amazed that Sheehan was taking his sarcastic remarks seriously.

"Just between you and me, Fox is on the verge of bankruptcy, and I've got to save the studio," Sheehan said. "Lisping fairies on the screen won't do the job for us."

"You're telling me that in the new Hollywood big-dicked studs will direct only big-dicked studs. Balls will be clanking so loudly technicians will have to tone down the sound track. John Wayne will come across like a giant phallus spewing semen into the audience."

"Don't disgrace yourself in front of me by getting carried away with too many of your sexual fantasies," Sheehan cautioned.

"Okay," Bogie said, wondering why Sheehan was prolonging this firing. "I'm out the door. Who's next on your list? After you kick out the pansies on their ass?"

510

"I met with Joseph Breen yesterday," Sheehan said. "As you well know, he works hand-in-glove with Will Hays to safeguard the industry from perversion. Breen is not only against sexual perverts on the screen but lousy Jews like Louis B. Mayer. Breen calls Jews the scum of the earth. A Jew will do anything for money. They'll agree to any sexual taboo on the screen if they feel it'll turn a fast buck. These money-grubbers will depict the vilest of scenes. Breen thinks the ultimate aim of the Hollywood Jew is to undermine Catholic morality."

Bogie stood up abruptly. "I've heard enough. I'll be off the Fox lot in fifteen minutes. Watch me go. I'm not going to sit here any longer listening to your shit." He actually used the word "shit," which he detested when other people said it. But no word other than shit seemed to describe the garbage pouring out of Sheehan's mouth.

"I'm one cocksucking pansy faggot queer lisping queen, one slimy sissy—a bumbling fluttery butterfly, lipstick-wearing, take-it-in-the-ass, dithery, unmas-culine fruit."

"That's how I'd describe you," Sheehan said. "And let me congratulate you on the honesty of your self-portrait. The most accurate I've ever heard."

Bogie walked rapidly toward the door, opened it, then slammed it in Sheehan's face as he headed down the corridor and off the Fox lot, never to return.

Amazingly, when Bogie appeared to accept the Oscar as best actor for his role of Charlie Allnut in 1951 *The African Queen*, he singled out Winfield Sheehan specifically for a special thank you for launching him into motion pictures.

***

In bathing suits, Bogie lay on a chaise longue at Lilowe, while his hosts, Edmund Lowe and Lilyan Tashman, received their guests in front of the house. Tashman and Lowe were throwing him a farewell-to-Hollywood party. At first Bogie had been reluctant to attend, thinking that his failure at Fox wasn't some-thing he wanted to announce to the world.

The ever-erratic Tashman had finally convinced him that some bigtime direc-tor at her bash would probably discover him and sign him to a contract before the end of the evening. Out-of-work actors like to believe in fables like that.

On a chaise longue opposite him lay the silent screen star, Eleanor Boardman, who'd been famously married to director King Vidor, who'd immortalized her by casting her in the 1927 *The Crowd*. Helen Carlisle of *Movie Magazine* had chris-tened Boardman "The Most Outspoken Girl in Hollywood," and she was living up to her reputation in her talk with Bogie.

Bogie had taken an instant liking to this fascinating creature who spoke her mind. "Is it true that you and Vidor, Garbo, and John Gilbert were supposed to have had a double wedding?"

"Indeed," she said. "We waited and waited for Garbo to show. Mayer at some point took Gilbert aside and asked him why he needed to marry Garbo.

'Why not just sleep with her?' Mayer asked. Angered beyond belief, Gilbert punched Mayer. After that, Gilbert was virtually finished in Hollywood."

"Like me, you mean?" Bogie asked.

Boardman had sympathized with his demise at Fox earlier in the day. "You might as well include me in the unemployed, too. My contract with MGM will be up in 1933, and I'm getting out of town. When I was a teenager, I was the Eastman Kodak Girl in print ads. Before that, I was a star in some of the WAMPAS Baby ads. But the handwriting's on the wall. I suspect that that God damn third remake of *The Squaw Man* that I did for DeMille will be my last major picture."

"What does somebody do when he or she leaves Hollywood, especially after they've been a star?"

"I expect to begin the best part of my life," Boardman said. "I'm free of King Vidor, still white, still beautiful, and with enough money to live on. I'm going to Europe. I'm sure many dashing men over there would like to fall in love with the celebrated Eleanor Boardman."

Now that he was free of any commitment to Mary Philips and without a career, Bogie began to eye Boardman in a different light.

He knew that Jean Arthur was just as broke and out of work as he was, and that train ride back to New York with her might not be fruitful. He also felt that Arthur was too dyke-oriented to team herself with a man for very long.

Unlike Arthur, Boardman was still on the Hollywood A-list, a frequent guest of Hearst and Davies at San Simeon and of Fairbanks Sr. and Pickford at Pickfair. Her friends included Joan Crawford, John Barrymore, Lillian Gish, Gloria Swanson, and Zelda and F. Scott Fitzgerald.

He wondered if Boardman preferred girls like Tashman and Jean Arthur, or if she were strictly a lady for the menfolk. Before he made a sudden move toward her, he decided to find out. "Since you're so outspoken, I've always wanted to ask you something. I've heard a lot of talk about you and Garbo."

Boardman laughed outrageously at the suggestion of a romantic link between the Swede and her. "Rumors. All rumors. The last rumor I heard was that I'd fallen madly in love with Marion Davies, and she with me. Garbo and I were just shopping friends."

"Shopping for what?" Bogie asked.

"Things," Boardman said. "Garbo always admired my taste, and wanted me to go shopping with her. I remember one day I took her to this divine shoe store in Beverly Hills. Garbo must have tried on a thousand pair of shoes. She finally purchased this brown leather pair. She wanted to wear them out on the street. Before we'd gone one block, she complained that the shoes hurt her feet. She demanded that I go with her to the store and return them. I protested the store wouldn't take them back after she'd walked on the sidewalk with them. Believe it or not, the manager agreed to take back the used shoes. 'Just tell the customer that Greta Garbo wore these shoes, and demand twice the price for them,' Garbo told the salesman, who, as it turned out, was her biggest fan."

"So, she never made a play for you?" Bogie asked.

"She made many a play for me," Boardman said. "I go shopping with women. I go to bed with men. Even if I were a lesbian like Lilyan, I wouldn't go for Garbo. She's too selfish. I used to spend hours of my time doing favors for her. She never thanked me once. She just assumes that because she's Greta Garbo, she's entitled to be on the receiving end of favors. She takes and takes, demanding more and more. Nothing is ever enough for her."

"Why did you put up with it?" Bogie asked.

"Because she's the most fascinating woman I've ever met." Boardman squinted her eyes as she looked up at the fading afternoon sun. "Or will ever meet again."

Since Boardman had been so candid about her relationship with Garbo, he decided to press her for more information. "In that Squaw picture, I noticed you appeared with Roland Young. That bastard is currently shacked up with my wife in New York, Mary Philips. Perhaps you've heard of her."

"Certainly I've heard of Mary Philips," Boardman said. "I've even seen her on the stage in New York." She finished the rest of her drink and looked in need of another one. He'd get it for her but first he wanted to hear her pronouncement about Roland Young.

"He's a serial seducer," Boardman said. "No affair he has lasts more than eight months. I don't know how long he's been with your Mary, but believe me, eight months is his absolute limit. He'll drop her." She sighed. "I should know."

"You and Young?" Bogie asked. The expression on her face answered his question for him. "I guess any man who learns his wife is shacked up with another man wants to ask *the* question."

"It's okay to ask it," Boardman said, smiling at him. "The most outspoken woman in Hollywood will tell all. He's a great lover and has the equipment to do it with."

"So I have reason to be jealous," Bogie asked.

"Not unless you stuffed a sock in your bathing suit," she said. "You look more than adequately endowed if that's for real."

"It's for real," he said, leaning over to get intimate.

Before that mission was accomplished, she whispered to him. "Here comes a very handsome young man in a very tight trunks who looks as if he needs to stuff a sock or something in there. A perfect concave."

Suddenly, standing before him were Laurence Olivier and Elissa Landi, fresh from having completed a film together, *The Yellow Ticket*.

"The Empress of Austria," Bogie said facetiously, getting up to kiss his former costar with whom he'd had a one-night stand. Bogie sized up Olivier, shaking his hand and being impressed by his male beauty. He seemed on his way to becoming the next big star of Hollywood. If only he could act, those looks were incomparable. Except for that unfortunate concave in the bathing suit, Olivier had a magnetic charm about him. Bogie turned to Landi. "What an improvement over Basil Rathbone."

Before any of them could talk, Tashman appeared, clutching Bogie's arm. "Time to dress for the party," she said. "Fun at the pool is over. The sun is setting."

After excusing himself and shaking Olivier's hand again, Bogie abandoned his future conquest plans for Boardman and headed upstairs to change his clothes in the same bedroom with Tashman and Lowe. There was nothing wrong with that, he figured. He had no secrets to keep from that swinging duo, the poster couple for a lavender marriage.

He'd put on a terrycloth robe as he made his way down the hallway, and was glad he had some clothes on. Before they'd reached the stairwell, Tashman had already greeted Paul Bern, who ignored Bogie, and Jean Harlow, who looked stunning in a low-cut white gown. Bogie hadn't seen Harlow since her abortion in Mexico and their pillow talk that final evening. She'd kissed him on the lips like a long-lost friend. No mention would ever be made of Mexico.

Later in her bedroom, Tashman slipped off her swimsuit and stood nude before him, and Edmund Lowe also pulled off his bathing trunks. Faced with the nude couple, Bogie retreated to the bathroom to change into his tuxedo, which he'd brought over earlier that evening before the pool party, which was now turning formal.

When he came out, Lowe too was attired in his tuxedo. The actor came over and kissed Bogie gently on the lips. "What a hunk!" he said. "I'd love to taste you right now."

"Get down to welcome our guests," Tashman said, shooing him away.

When he'd left the room, she gave Bogie a long, lingering kiss. "Please understand about tonight, darling. I won't be able to pay you much attention. In front of A-list Hollywood, I'll have to make goo-goo eyes at Eddie all night. To complicate matters, the love of my life will be here."

"Is it still the French dwarf?" Bogie asked.

"Still Claudette Colbert," Tashman said. "She's divine, and her pussy, unlike Garbo's, isn't as big as a football field."

"I'm glad to hear that," he said.

She grabbed his crotch and stroked it aggressively. "But don't think I'm going to leave this thing dangling all night. Even though I can't attend to it personally, I've arranged a date for you. She finds you alluring. She's going to provide you with your farewell fuck to Hollywood. I know the two of you will hit it off."

"Who is this damsel who's going to get lucky tonight with me?" he asked.

"The one and the only Lili Damita, in person."

***

At the far end of Lilowe's dinner table, Bogie sat staring into the eyes of the beautiful French actress, Lili Damita, touted in all the fan magazines as "the new

514

Garbo." His dinner companion and arranged "date" for the night had launched herself into films as a star in the final days of silent pictures. Although her heavy French accent did not record well on sound tracks, she was still finding occasional work in talking pictures.

The movie mogul, Samuel Goldwyn, had lured her to Hollywood to appear opposite Ronald Colman, Bogie's nemesis, in the film *The Rescue*, where Damita had interpreted the role of Lady Edith Travers, replacing Vilma Banky who had originally been up for the role.

From there Damita had gone on to play the fiery dancer, La Pericho, in the 1929 film, *The Bridge of San Luis Rey* starring opposite Ernest Torrence.

Damita had come into Lilyan Tashman's orbit when she'd appeared in 1929 with Edmund Lowe and Victor McLaglen as Mariana Elenita in *The Cock-Eyed World*.

Damita had just finished making a talkie, *Fighting Caravans*, with the young Gary Cooper, with whom she had reportedly had an affair.

Over Tashman's squab, she was telling Bogie of her latest project. She had just read the script that day for a new film, *This Is the Night*. One of her co-stars was to be an English actor, Cary Grant, who had just arrived in Hollywood. For another male lead, Roland Young had been suggested. "Do you know of him?" Damita asked Bogie.

"Even as we speak, it is midnight in New York," Bogie said. "The bastard is in my bed there fucking my wife, Mary Philips."

Damita's face brightened. "I don't find that objectionable. I think if a man has a wife, many other men should fuck her."

"Maybe that's how you guys do it in Paris, but in America, we're more provincial," Bogie said. "Some Americans—no one in Hollywood, of course—believe in being faithful to one's mate."

Her lovely face looked disappointed. "If you're one of those faithful husbands, it's going to be a sad night for the Little Lady."

"Who in hell is Little Lady?" he asked.

"That's me," she said. "Damita means Little Lady in Spanish."

"I see," he said.

"What was your real name before you changed it to Humphrey Bogart?" she asked.

"Believe it or not, I was born with it," he said.

"I can believe that," she said. "No one would deliberately choose the name of Humphrey Bogart." Both of them laughed at that observation.

Later, over an after dinner cognac, Damita talked more about her upcoming film. "They tell me Cary Grant is a homosexual, so I guess I'll have to turn to Young to get fucked. At least I'll find out what's so alluring to your wife, Mary Philips."

"Yeah," he said sarcastically, "give me a full report." Conversations about Young pissed him off, even though he planned to file for divorce as soon as he returned to New York.

"Eleanor Boardman claims Young is quite a lady's man," Damita said.

Concealing his bitterness, he said, "Eleanor more or less conveyed the same report to me too out by the pool."

As he talked to Damita, sitting on a love seat in the far corner of the Lowe/ Tashman living room, he studied her carefully. Tashman knew how to pick her women. Before the night was over, he fully expected he'd seduce Damita. He thought that she no doubt would be his last fuck in Hollywood, and he wanted it to be good. With Mary no longer waiting on ice for him in New York he felt that the sexual pickings on Broadway might be slim for an unemployed actor.

He'd read about Damita in fan magazines. What he hadn't read, he'd heard by rumor. The daughter of a French actress, she'd trained for the stage at the Paris Opera. At the age of sixteen, she'd become a leading dancer with the Folies-Bergère in Paris and later had replaced the legendary Mistinguette as the star of Casino de Paris.

Damita had made her first silent picture, *La Voyante*, in 1923, and before coming to Hollywood had appeared in a number of films in France, England, and Germany. Some of them had been released in America under the titles of *A Woman of the Night* in 1924, *Red Heels* in 1925, *The Road to Happiness* in 1926, and *The Golden Butterfly* in 1926. Bogie had caught only one of her films, *The Queen Was in the Parlour*, and he'd not been impressed. Damita off-screen was far more alluring than Damita on screen.

She was a sensual, beautiful woman with a fiery, dynamic personality, though rather petite in stature. Although still young, there was a world weary cosmopolitan air about her.

Earlier when he'd complimented her on her extremely tight-fitting midnight blue gown, she laughed, "If monkeys can have blue assess, I can have blue tits!" That line was to become one of her favorites. In those days she wore only white during the day and only blue at night.

Even though reared in convents in Portugal and Spain, she chose not to become a nun but went on to quick success as a music hall performer and as an entertainer of Allied troops in World War I.

Three of her films made in the Twenties had been directed by the Hungarian, Michael Curtiz. The tempestuous director would in time direct Bogie in the film, *Casablanca*.

Even before arriving in Hollywood, Lili Damita's love affairs were already notorious. She'd been the mistress of King Alfonso XIII of Spain, the lover of both those "switch-hitters," Mistinguette and Maurice Chevalier in Paris, and the lesbian *protégée* of Marlene Dietrich in Berlin.

As the night wore on, the talk between Damita and Bogie became more personal and more provocative, and he liked that, especially when such talk came from a woman.

By three o'clock only the most "hard core" guests remained at Lilowe. Colbert had departed, leaving Tashman to wander alone around her living room. It was obvious that Edmund Lowe had staked out the handsome bartender for the rest of the night.

Coming out of nowhere, Damita said, "I may marry one day but it will be to a man who dislikes women as much as I dislike men."

"Hey," he cautioned, "give me about an hour to figure that one out. I hope you like men sometimes. If you haven't, I've struck out tonight."

"On occasion I like to go to bed with men," she said. But I don't like to socialize with them. Straight men are too boring. I prefer to run around to the clubs with the fey set. For entertainment, I like my male companions to be very, very gay."

"Well, I may not be very, very gay, and I'm probably a dull talker, but I hope to at least entertain you in bed."

"We'll see," she said. "It depends on how you go about it. When I make love to a man, I believe in fierce, almost theatrical foreplay, the use of props if necessary. I view sex as an elaborate ritual. The stage must be set. I see love-making as a mating dance. Two wild beasts stalking each other in the darkest jungles of Africa."

He seemed consumed by her and mesmerized by her talk. The image of a female tiger came to his mind. He'd be the first to nickname Damita "Tiger Lil."

Earlier in the evening, Tashman had told him that Damita was considered "the greatest lay in the world." She had a streak of obvious exhibitionism in her. One night, or so he'd heard, she'd been fucked by a waiter in full view of at least twenty spectators at Jimmy's Backyard.

Bogie wondered if he were man enough to tame this wild goddess of the jungle.

"I must confess before I go to bed with you that I fuck better than any woman in Hollywood," she said. "But I need more than that. I have this mad desire for cunnilingus. That's not something I get from most American men here, especially Gary Cooper who finds the act a bit revolting." She seemed to think for a moment. No doubt remembering Ronald Colman, she said, "British men, unlike Frenchmen, don't seem to take to it either. Since I love to have cunnilingus performed on me, I often turn to women. Dietrich is very skilled at it. So is darling Lilyan over there. I hear she drives Colbert crazy like she occasionally can do to me."

"Speak of the devil," he said, "here comes 'Latrine Lil' now and she's heading right toward us."

"I saw her whispering to all of the other guests in the room." Damita said. "She's ushered them away, into other areas of the house. That leaves only the two of us sitting here in this big living room."

"Now what fun and games do you think Lilyan is going to propose for the two of us?" Bogie asked.

Damita stood up to kiss Tashman on the mouth. "Give me some of that

517

talented tongue," Damita said to Tashman.

"Dear hearts," Tashman said, leaning over to kiss Bogie with her succulent mouth that contained not only her own lipstick, but a generous glob of Damita's as well. "Before the rooster crows, there will be nothing about each other's bodies that we won't know intimately."

***

Bogie walked on the rooftop of his apartment building, watching the dawn break across the Los Angeles skyline. As he smoked his tenth cigarette since coming up to the roof, he pondered the madness that had driven him here where he'd actually considered, however briefly, taking a jump off that roof.

It'd been the most humiliating night of his life. He'd never forgive Lilyan Tashman for the trick she'd played on him.

Only two hours earlier, he'd left Lilowe never to return. Tashman, he feared, was completely out of control. She seemed to have taken leave of all her senses as her behavior grew more and more erratic.

He actually hated her for what she'd done to him, and he cursed the day he'd ever entered her insane world. She'd shamelessly used him for the entertainment of her other guests, and he swore that morning he'd never let another woman do that to him for as long as he lived.

Kenneth was due back at his apartment that morning after his short honeymoon with Kay Francis. He too was moving out of the building to live with his new bride under whatever marital arrangements they'd worked out together. Before leaving on the train to New York with Jean Arthur, Bogie had to tell Kenneth what had happened to him the night before.

In lieu of Kenneth, he thought he'd call Spencer Tracy and unburden himself but decided against that. He didn't want Tracy to know how vulnerable he was and preferred for his newly acquired actor friend to maintain the illusion that Humphrey Bogart was one tough old bird like Tracy himself.

The shank of the evening at Lilowe had held out such promise when Tashman had approached Damita and him. An invitation to seduce two of Hollywood's most beautiful and glamorous women, Lilyan Tashman and Lili Damita, had been such a tantalizing prospect that no horny young man would have turned it down.

To his surprise, Tashman had not invited them to her bedroom but to a small cottage in the garden. He'd seen the cottage many times but had had no reason to go inside, figuring it was reserved just for special guests. When he'd once asked Tashman about it, she'd laughingly dismissed his interest. "Darling, you're strictly a guest for the main bedroom at Lilowe. The cottage is for guests I don't want to run into too frequently—much less sleep with." Once inside the rather brightly lit cottage, he'd found it gaily decorated in shades of pink, green, and white, with both a mirrored wall and a mirrored ceiling.

"You believe in a hell of a lot of mirrors," he'd said to Tashman. "It looks like these mirrors can capture the action on that bed from any angle."

"It's how I figured out I could be both a participant in love-making and a voyeur at the same time," she'd said.

She'd put on some soft Bing Crosby music in the background, as both Damita and Tashman had performed a striptease duet, the most enticing he'd ever seen. He'd felt that if both of their movie careers failed, they could take their act on the road, playing to packed audiences of eager-eyed men.

Bogie had sat in a well-padded armchair sipping a bottled beer that Tashman had thoughtfully provided. The beer had been cold and very satisfying. But he'd been thirsty for far more than beer. A dry heat had seemed to flow through his body, scorching him as it began in his throat and traveled sensually to his groin.

"*Olé!*" he'd shouted as Damita and Tashman had slipped off their lingerie and had stood before him for inspection.

"See anything you want, big boy?" Damita had asked him.

On shaky legs, he'd risen from the chair and had kneeled in front of them, his tongue darting out to taste each of them, treating them as his prizes of the evening. He'd never recalled being so turned on sexually. Rising to his feet, he'd smiled. "That's just a lick and a promise."

He'd taken Tashman in his arms to give her his first deep kiss of the evening, and then had pulled Damita into his orbit, wondering if the taste of Tashman was still in his mouth as Damita had sucked his tongue with even more vigor than Tashman.

As Crosby sang of love, both women had moved to undress him. As they had done that, he'd reached out to fondle whatever pair of breasts was near at hand. Both women had breasts that rivaled those of Venus de Milo, and slim, smooth waists.

It was Damita who had knelt on the floor, unbuttoning his trousers. When his pants had fallen down, she had reached for his penis and had swallowed it to the root in one gulp. Although Tashman had done that for him countless times, Damita had proven that she was the expert sword-swallower of the trio.

As Damita's head had bobbed up and down on him, Tashman had attacked him from the rear, parting his cheeks, her pink tongue darting in where almost no one had ever been before. He'd cried out in pleasure, no longer able to control himself. Tashman had reached around and had fondled his pendulous balls as Damita had continued her attack. He'd found himself rapidly approaching climax but wanting to hold back. It'd been too soon, too fast. He had to figure out a way of pulling back and making the evening's love-making last longer.

As if sensing that, both Damita and Tashman had pulled away from him, leaving him in a state of unfulfilled agony. Damita had steered him to the king-size bed, as Tashman had picked up his unfinished bottle of beer and had trailed them.

Damita had bounced up and down on the soft bed, as he'd descended on her to kiss her and to feel her breasts. To his absolute amazement and shock, Tashman had taken the bottle of beer and had thrust it deep into Damita's gaping hole. As the suds had run out of Damita, Tashman had attacked her vagina with her tongue, capturing its liquid juices. Raising herself up, her mouth oozing with white froth, she'd reached out and placed her delicate hand on the back of his neck, inviting him to sample Damita, too.

Smacking his lips like a connoisseur of good wine, not beer, he too had followed Tashman's lead, his lips and tongue moving over Damita, causing the French actress to squeal in delight until Tashman had covered her mouth with her own. It had all been too much for him. He'd greedily tongued Damita until she'd experienced a shattering orgasm, crying out with the sheer pleasure of it all.

The next hour—or was it two hours?—had been the most glorious and sexually fulfilling of his life. The wet kisses and caresses from two flaming tongues had brought pleasure to secret areas of his body, which heretofore had been explored by no other. When Damita had been licking at his balls, her tongue darting in and out of his hole, Tashman had attacked his armpits, a sensation he'd never experienced before.

His body had been switched on like an electric light brightening a darkened room. His sexual energy had vibrated through every atom of his being. He'd lunged for both of them, deciding to enter Damita first. As he'd fucked Damita, Tashman had straddled him, biting his neck and nibbling at his ears until it was her turn to be mounted.

When he'd finally entered Tashman, her legs had grasped his hips like a vise, as if she never wanted him to go. As she'd thrust her pelvis against his, her entire body twitching in ecstasy, Damita had found his lips to give him an added thrill.

Three thrashing bodies were caught in upheaval on that bed, their nerves rippling with pleasure. His first climax had come inside Damita. It had been utter rapture. The sheer physical intensity of his explosion had been something to relish, like an event that he'd wanted to continue forever.

When he'd been worked up a second time, an hour later, his body stiffening once again, Tashman had mounted him while he lay on his back and had ridden up and down on his penis, as he'd given her a knifing penetration, plunging deeper and deeper. Damita had crawled on top of the bed to feed him her breasts one at a time. Tashman had continued her rising waves of frenzy, going up, and then down on him. Each of her plunges had caused his volcano to move rapidly toward its eruption, which came violently.

When their love-making had finally come to an end it seemed that a lifetime had passed with these women. All three of them had lain on the king-sized bed, not wanting to get off it, not wanting to surrender so quickly the pleasure that had been theirs. It had been as if each of them had wanted this to be their eternity. Neither had seemed to desire any life other than that which they'd discovered on the bed.

One hour later, when all three of them had showered in the small cubicle in the bathroom, he'd emerged from the cottage fully dressed. He'd kissed both

Damita and Tashman good-bye, leaving them lying nude together on that king-sized bed. In the early dawn, he made his way through the garden and to the main house, where he'd left his wallet and his swimming trunks in Tashman's bedroom when he'd changed into his tuxedo.

Lowe had stood at the door to the bedroom on the opposite side of the hall. Attired only in his underwear, he'd given Bogie a warm embrace. Bogie had thanked Lowe for throwing the party for him, claiming, "it was the greatest night of my life."

"Trust me," Lowe had said. "It is Lil and I who should be grateful to you for coming." Lowe had smiled mischievously when he'd said "coming," and Bogie had felt that there was something he wasn't getting.

"Eddie," a man's voice called out. Bogie looked inside Lowe's bedroom to discover the bartender lying nude on the actor's bed, playing with himself and obviously wanting more action.

Bogie had hurried down the steps, eager to be gone now that his farewell-to-Hollywood party had ended.

In the foyer of Lilowe, he'd discovered a slightly drunken Eleanor Boardman, his poolside companion of that afternoon.

"What a show!" she had said to him, smiling and kissing him lightly on the lips. "What a *stallion*, I should say." She'd reached into her purse and had handed him her card. "I've written my private number on the back of my card. I want you to come over tomorrow night. Daddy, I want some of that action."

"Thanks for the invitation, and I'll certainly call you," he'd said. "What man would turn down an invitation from the beautiful Eleanor Boardman?" He paused, taking out a cigarette and lighting one for himself after she'd turned down a smoke.

"Exactly what did you mean about my putting on a show?" he'd asked. "You mean, I made a fool of myself and got too drunk?"

"No, darling," Boardman had said. "I mean that show you put on for Lil's guests in the cottage. Lil's chosen few, including Eddie, were on the other side of that mirror, watching the three of you perform. Frankly, my dear, I think now that you're not at Fox, you should hire out for stag parties."

"You saw it all?" he'd asked, dumbfounded.

"Of course, she'd said. "All of us were seated comfortably in chairs watching you go through the motions with Lil and Lili. As I said, some show! Surely you knew."

"I didn't know," he'd said, totally bewildered.

"Don't kid a kidder," Boardman had said. "Lil and Eddie stage performances like that for their guests all the time. That's what makes their parties the talk of Hollywood."

Turning from Boardman, he'd hurried out the door, slamming it behind him. Searching desperately for his car, he'd had to escape from Lilowe at once.

***

Back in his own apartment, and safe after his lonely walk on the roof, he received a phone call from Bette Davis, who was demanding to see him. She'd been fired from Universal. Her party for losers had been completely accurate as a harbinger of events to come.

Although within the recent past, he had vowed never to see her again, he invited her over anyway, hoping that two actors, kicked out of Hollywood, might be able to console each other.

The pain associated with his having been fired from Fox was enormous. But he carried an even greater pain for having performed sexually before those Hollywood voyeurs. No doubt news of his performance with Lili Damita and Lilyan Tashman would be spread across town by now.

He never wanted to see either woman ever again, and he was also determined never to call Eleanor Boardman, as tempting as the offer had been at first until he'd learned the truth of the evening. He felt that his ultimate privacy had been invaded.

Fate would decide otherwise in the case of Damita, whom he'd encounter frequently in the Hollywood of the future. She would go on to marry one of his future best friends, Errol Flynn, in June of 1935, following a much publicized romance. In Flynn's autobiography, *My Wicked, Wicked Ways*, he'd single Damita out for special loathing, following their divorce and his final settlement on her for one-million dollars, money he couldn't afford. Together they'd have a beautiful son, Sean Flynn, who would disappear in Cambodia after running into a Vietcong roadblock on April 6, 1970. Captured, he'd be taken off into the jungle never to be seen again.

After that nightmarish experience at Lilowe, he'd never see Tashman again. He'd been saddened to learn of her death on March 21, 1934 in New York. No more would she grace the movie world as the sarcastic, sophisticated, well-dressed blonde. She'd just completed her last film, *Frankie and Johnnie*, which would not be released until 1936 because of censorship problems.

The tumor in her brain had advanced slowly but inexorably, perhaps explaining her erratic behavior during her last days in Hollywood when she seemed to be a woman out of control, inflicting damage and upsetting lives with gleeful abandon.

In New York she'd submitted to an operation, but at Doctors' Hospital in Manhattan surgeons had told Lowe that, "It's hopeless. The tumor is too far advanced."

Although the operation had provided her with some momentary relief, the pain had returned with great violence at a lonely house in Connecticut to which she'd retreated with Lowe in hopes that she might recuperate.

On March 16, she'd been rushed back to Doctors' Hospital for an emergency operation. She would not rally.

In memory of the good times, not that final evening at Lilowe, Bogie had ventured over to Brooklyn to attend funeral services for her at the Washington Cemetery. She'd launched herself from Brooklyn, and it'd seemed fitting that her body would be returned there for her final rest.

Once in Brooklyn, Bogie encountered a mob of some 10,000 fans, mostly women. Such a mad frenzy had not been known at a funeral in New York since the death of Rudolph Valentino in 1926.

Even before the rabbi could finish with his words, pandemonium broke out. Fans screeched and fought each other for souvenirs, including floral wreaths. Three women were pushed into Tashman's gravesite. Florence Margolis, a Brooklyn housewife with three children, suffered a broken leg. Eddie Cantor called Tashman's burial, "The most disgraceful thing I've ever witnessed." Bogie had remained behind with the chief mourners. Embracing him and kissing him on the mouth, Lowe invited him into a small anteroom to join the elite of the other mourners, including Sophie Tucker, Mae Murray, Mrs. William Randolph Hearst, Fannie Brice, and Jack Benny.

Although widely celebrated at the time of her death with legions of fans all over the world, Lilyan Tashman would soon become one of the "forgotten stars" of Hollywood, a city that seemed eager to forget her and her scandalous ways once she was in the ground.

All thoughts of Lilyan Tashman and Lili Damita ended with a knock on the door of his apartment. Crushing out his cigarette, he got up to answer it.

Opening the door, he took in the vision of a very distraught Bette Davis who had been crying. She immediately fell into his arms, sobbing more intensely and violently than she ever would on the screen.

***

Davis sat on the sofa across from him, as both of them enjoyed booze and cigarettes, two narcotics that would become lifelong addictions for each of them. Since storming into his apartment, Davis had talked incessantly about her career, offering only minor condolences about his own dismissal from Fox.

"When I came to Hollywood," she said, "America was in a great depression. It still is. Garbo had learned to talk, and the first thing she said was '*Gimme a viskey.*'" Her imitation of Garbo was right on the mark. "Garbo is still talking. Dietrich had arrived to appear in high heels and expensive gowns running around in the sands of *Morocco*. She's still dressing up, still running around. Norma Shearer had won the Oscar. Norma Shearer is still getting Oscar-winning roles. Hollywood is virtually intact. And it certainly won't miss Bette Davis." She looked over at him. "I'm not movie star material. Like you, Bogie, our faces weren't meant to grace the silver screen."

"If only we'd gotten the right parts," he said defensively. He didn't like admitting failure.

"As far as I'm concerned, both Carl Laemmles, Senior and Junior, can take their so-called 230-acre film factory and give it back to the mustard farmers from whom they took the land in 1915."

"Considering the films those two creeps turn out," he said, "maybe mustard greens would be easier to swallow."

She seemed not to have heard his remark. "'Bette from Boston,' they called me. All the good parts went to that whoring bitch, Sidney Fox. She spent more time fucking Laemmle Jr. than she did on camera. *Frumpy* they called me. Odd-looking. Sexless. Somewhat ugly. Christ. *Somewhat!*" She virtually spat out the word.

"Look at all the guys who've fallen for you," he said. "You're hardly sexless. Why, all the losers at your party had the hots for you. Even me."

She smiled at the remark. "Laemmle Jr. goes around saying I have all the sex appeal of Slim Summerville."

As he got up to pour her another drink, she too rose to her feet and pranced around the apartment, with the same kind of stalking movement she'd demonstrate in several films. She was a woman with a violent temper, and filled with turbulent emotions. "I've failed miserably in films. I can't even stand to see myself on the screen. I'm that bad."

"You came close to getting roles here or there that could have launched you," he said, reminding her.

"Close," she said with a certain contempt. "But miles from the goal. My one hope was that William Wyler would cast me in *A House Divided*. It was my last chance for success at Universal. Even though the women in wardrobe objected, I found this dark plaid cotton dress. The bodice fit real low, and I definitely showed cleavage. After all, let's face it: My breasts are my most alluring physical asset. I'm sure you'll discover that for yourself later tonight."

This was his first indication that he was going to get lucky.

"When I came onto the set showing my major assets pre-packaged in that dress," Davis said, "Wyler took one look at me and dismissed me. I heard him tell his assistant, 'Who in hell do these *ingénues* think they are? They think that if they show off a big pair of tits, they've got the part. Fuck! Hollywood is just one big tit." She sighed before taking a deep drag on her cigarette. "I was so upset by him that I was tongue-tied during the screen test."

Ironically, Wyler would become not only "the love of my life" for Bette Davis, but her best and most favored director, guiding her through her classics, such as *Jezebel*, her consolation prize for not getting cast as Scarlett O'Hara in *Gone With the Wind*, and in Lillian Hellman's *The Little Foxes*, a role that had been created on the stage for her arch rival, Tallulah Bankhead.

"Laemmle Jr. called me into his office to fire me in person," she said. "I think he enjoyed humiliating me, telling me that I had no future in films. After seeing us together in *Bad Sister*, he predicted the same fate for you."

"I know that," he snapped at her. "We've been over all that before."

"I don't know about you," Davis said, "but I'm going to return to Broadway and become the next Lynn Fontanne."

"Can I be your Alfred Lunt?" he asked. Although he'd meant his remark to be facetious, by the time he came to the question mark, it had become serious.

She looked over at him as if sizing him up. "You're not homosexual enough to replace Lunt."

"I'll take that as a compliment," he said. "Maybe we'll be the next Alfred Lunt and Lynn Fontanne, but we'll be more virile. Not as fey."

"Maybe that's not such a bad idea," she said, her pop eyes widening as if the revelation just might be possible. "I could see the names of Bette Davis and Humphrey Bogart in lights."

"We could become the new king and queen of Broadway," he said, daring to hope that such a dream might actually happen.

"You and I are not film people," she said. "We belong on the stage. The theater is in our blood. We'll get the right properties. Get Maxwell Anderson to write a play tailor-made for us. Maybe even Ben Hecht. He'd be great. We'll become the next legendary acting team in Broadway history."

He held his glass up to hers, and she toasted him back. "Of course, your talent will never be as great as mine. But I think you can develop a real stage presence. Sometimes having a distinct personality is more important than acting talent. In my case, I was blessed with both talent and a personality."

He listened patiently, though rather disdainful of her proclamations of her own greatness.

By ten o'clock that night, she'd agreed to go onto the roof with him for his final look at Los Angeles at night.

A wind was blowing in from the ocean, and the night had turned suddenly cold. Wearing only a thin cotton dress, she was shivering. "Hold me!" she commanded. There was desperation in her voice. Without her bravado, she appeared strangely weak and vulnerable, in need of a man's protection.

"I'm here for you," he said, moving toward her. He took her in his arms and kissed her passionately, feeling her quivering response. So great was her need for him that she was moaning softly. She knew that he knew that she was his for the taking, at least for the night.

"I need to feel like a woman again," she whispered seductively in his ear. "Take me downstairs and make me feel like that woman I long to be, but never was."

"You've got yourself a date, lady," he said, kissing her once more. With one arm around her waist, he guided her toward the lone door on the roof, leading down the iron steps to his apartment.

Once inside the apartment, she appeared talked out. There would be no more need for words.

By four o'clock that morning, he'd made more passionate love to her than he had any other woman in his life. He'd made Bette Davis his woman. She hugged him with the kind of desperation a couple faces when they stagger blindly but bravely into a new but uncertain future. Throughout the night they'd clung to each other like two people who, when dawn came, would face the gallows together.

Both of them had convinced the other that their future careers were entwined. Together they could make it as a team, or so they'd told themselves.

Before the night ended, she had begged him to marry her as soon as his divorce from Mary Philips came through. "I didn't know what love-making was until I went to bed with you. I thought sex was something that men did to please themselves with women. Hop on, hop off. You taught me what a thrill it can be for a woman. You've taken me to another dimension, a place I didn't think I could find with any man. You've awakened a desire in parts of my body that I thought were incapable of a sexual response."

She had obviously regained her articulation. He buried the sound of her voice when he'd moved over her again, giving her a deep, impassioned kiss. Even though he thought his entire body had been fulfilled as never before, he found himself hardening again.

After he'd finished both of them off for the last call of the evening, he urgently pleaded with her, "Get on the train in the morning with me," he said. "Let's go back to New York." Somehow he'd forgotten that he had already extended that offer to another actress, Jean Arthur, who would soon be waiting for him at the station. Kenneth had agreed to drive him to the depot for a final good-bye to Hollywood.

Like a good New England housewife, Davis rose from his bed and began packing his luggage. But she turned down his invitation to leave with him that morning because, "It's impossible—that's why."

She did commit to him, though, claiming that when, "Ruthie and I shut down our house in Hollywood Hills, I'll be on the next train east. It'll take about six weeks, but you can count on me to be there. In the meantime, you've got to search for a suitable apartment for us. In New York, we'll pound those sidewalks of Broadway together."

"I'll be in New York keeping the sheets warm," he said, "until your train pulls into Grand Central station." He kissed her on her nose as he headed for the bathroom. She packed his clothes, some of which had been gifts from his new friend, Eric Linden, who had sent him a present virtually every day since they'd met.

Over breakfast, which included bacon and eggs, Davis proved herself to be a capable cook. "You've liberated me as a woman," she claimed to him, her wide eyes popping with a new kind of joy and a dawning reality. "I'll be a better actress because of this night we spent together."

"The first of many such nights," he assured her.

She stood up to pour him some more coffee. "Miss Bette Davis, formerly of Universal Studios and now a Broadway star, will become the third Mrs. Humphrey Bogart. It is her first marriage. For Bogart, it is his third. He was previously married to Broadway actresses Helen Menken and Mary Philips."

She had seemed so sexually fulfilled that morning in his apartment that her later remembrances of him appeared needlessly cruel.

When he'd rejected her for the role of Rose Sayer in the 1951 film, *The African Queen*, favoring Katharine Hepburn for the part, Davis had turned on him. From that day forth, she'd spread the word in Hollywood that, "Bogart is a lousy lay."

That had not been the pronouncement of the woman he'd left standing in the doorway of that deserted Los Angeles apartment.

"This past night in bed with you will have to last me for several weeks until we're together again in New York," she said. "There can be no other man for me but Humphrey Bogart."

He kissed her one final time, holding her long and close. He made a parting remark before rushing down those stairs where an impatient Kenneth MacKenna was waiting to drive him to the station.

He turned back and looked with a nostalgic regret at the apartment house where he'd lived during his brief, ill-fated Hollywood career. All he could think about was Davis up there in his bathroom, applying lipstick to her face before she too left the building forever to return to her own home.

Each day for him would be a long one until she was with him in New York and cuddling him in that ample bosom that William Wyler had rejected.

On the way to the train station, Bogie tried to blot out of his mind how he was going to deal with Jean Arthur once he got on that train with her and headed East. He would think about Arthur in an hour or two. Not now.

All the way to the station, he wasn't really in the car with Kenneth, but remained still back in that apartment with Davis. His good-bye to her would stab at his memory forever.

Years later, on the sound stage at Warner Brothers in 1942, during the filming of *Casablanca,* he would summon up that memory for another departure scene, the most famous such scene in movie history, when his character of Rick bids a final *adieu* to Ingrid Bergman's Ilsa.

He'd argued bitterly with the director, Michael Curtiz, about how that film should end. Finally, the tempestuous Hungarian relented, allowing him to say the same words, on film, that he'd said to Bette Davis on that chilly, long-ago morning when he'd left Los Angeles, convinced that he was washed up as a film actor.

"Here's looking at you, kid."

The End

Illustration of Bogie that hung in the men's room
of Tony Soma's speakeasy in New York for
three years during Prohibition.

INDEX

F

Fairbanks, Douglas Jr.
*132, 135, 138, 149, 160, 163, 186,
189, 225, 312, 332, 415, 417, 420,
453, 483, 492*

Fairbanks, Douglas Sr.
*164, 342, 361, 370, 379, 380, 381, 382, 384,
385, 420, 500, 503*

Falkenstein, Medora *36, 37*

Farewell to Arms, A 174

Farrar, John *70*

Farrell, Charles
*130, 131, 132, 133, 135, 137, 138, 171,
175, 176, 182, 208, 324, 508*

Farrell, Glenda
161, 183, 184, 186, 199, 240, 242, 394, 398

Farrell, Wilhelmina *186*

Farren, George *62*

Fay, Larry *82, 83, 84*

Fears, Peggy *75, 88*

Feel My Pulse 350

Ferguson, Beth *3*

Fielding, Mary *9*

Fields, W.C. *26*

Fighting Caravans 515

Firebrand, The 199

Fitzgerald, Scott *56, 57, 58, 59, 60, 79*

Fitzgerald, Zelda
56, 57, 58, 59, 60, 79, 112

Flaming Star *323*

Flappers and Philosophers 58

Fleming, Victor *284, 287*

Flirt, The 198, 237, 359

Florey, Robert *422*

Flynn, Errol *522*

Flynn, Sean *522*

Follies of 1927, The 166

Fontanne, Lynn *116*

For the Love of Mike 349

Ford, John
130, 155, 157, 158, 159, 167, 169, 175, 211

Forever Yours 380, 382, 383

Forrest, Sam *87*

Four Horsemen of the Apocalypse 77

Four Marx Brothers *94*

Fox, Sidney
198, 203, 204, 205, 236, 411, 524

Frances, Lee (Madam) *417*

Francis, James Dwight *490*

Francis, Kay *150-
152, 173, 176, 178, 186, 228, 233, 241, 250, 273,
328, 333-337, 342, 347, 378, 415,
423, 424, 429, 433, 434, 470, 472,
485, 489, 518*

Frankenstein 257

Frankie and Johnnie 522

Franz Josef, Emperor of Austria *174*

Freaks 314

Freddy, O.K. *238*

Frederick, Pauline *494*

French, Bert *69*

Freund, Karl *254*

Front Page, The *114, 355*

Furlow, Floyd *31, 36*

Furnall, Betty *46*

Furthman, Jules *175*

G

Gable, Clark
*165, 177, 186, 309, 311, 312, 332, 357, 388, 404,
408, 426, 453, 454, 492, 493, 494, 496, 505*

Gahagan, Helen *419*

Gallagher, Herb *506*

*Gambling Daughters/Bad Sisters
198, 204*

Gannon, Thomas *468*

Garbo, Greta
*28, 256, 263, 274, 275, 293, 314, 322, 375, 420,
426, 432, 457, 459, 460, 461, 462, 465, 466,
468, 471, 511, 512, 523*

Garden of Alla/Allah, The *28, 213*

Gaston, Bill *490*

Gay Divorce/ Gay Divorcee, The 168

Gay Musician, The 82

Gaynor, Janet
133, 134, 136, 137, 208, 420

Gentlemen of the Press 233, 490

George, Grace *25, 33, 34, 62*

Gershwin, Ira *21, 25*

Gibson, Helen *211, 212*

Gibson, Hoot
195, 206, 209, 210, 211, 212, 240

Gilbert, John
134, 136, 383, 453, 458, 465, 466, 510, 511

P

Q

R